Dorset Journey

Alan R Bennett

Dorset Journey

Alan R. Bennett

Foreword by
Paul Atterbury

RED POST

Published by:
Alan R. Bennett
BH21 2NW

Set in Minion
Printed and bound by Cromwell Press Group

ISBN 978-1-90153-301-9

Acknowledgements

I owe a huge debt to so many individuals for making this book possible. Most I have already mentioned in the text but not all and I would like to thank the following by mentioning their names here.

There are two gentlemen, in particular, without whom the book would never have appeared in print, Crispin Goodall, my designer, and Russell Beeson, whose technical skills and patience saw me through many crises. I am so grateful to both of them. I would thank my friend Roger Guttridge for his advice at a critical moment. I must express my enduring appreciation of the contribution of my principal photographer, Geoff Hill, with whom I travelled many miles across the county. My old chum, Roger Holman, responded with typical generosity to my requests. The splendid Clive Hannay could not have been more kind.

Next I must thank my long-suffering wife, Elaine, for enduring the clutter of boxes and files about the house for so long and my daughter, Fleur, for her constant encouragement.

The following list is printed in no particular order of importance.

Charles and Myra Seely of Bradpole, Paul Bennett of Beaminster NFU, Sue Chadney, Woodroffe School, Petrina Hughes of Eype, Rosemary Niven of Marshwood, Bill Taylor of Wootton Fitzpaine, Valerie Todd and Susan Woodford of Sherborne TC, Linda Woods and Peter House of Sherborne Abbey, Annette Brown, Gryphon School, Barry Welch of the DWT, Jill Cox and Liz Butler of Bridport TC, Becky Ford, Dorset Police HQ, Winfrith, Carrie Horlock of Dorchester, Angela Hapgood and Graham Sharp of Christchurch, Ronna Taylor of Shaftesbury, Ron Butler, Jan Hale and Pam Bowyer-Davis of Wareham, Emma Cawte of Upton House, Pam Naylor, Christine Willis and Sharon Collier of Sturminster Newton, Insp, Peter Meteau and PC Kevin Eames, Weymouth Police, David Harrison of Bournemouth Council, Peter Hayton of Towngate Publications, Poole, Mick Cunningham, media manager, AFC Bournemouth, Shelley Fletcher and Sarah Lambert of Monkey World, Kevin and Gillian Coetzee of Bere Regis, Devina Symes of West Lulworth, Michelle Luther and Nina Henderson, *Bournemouth Echo*.

I thank each and every individual for your contribution, be it great or small. I also apologise to those I have inadvertently omitted. Remind me when next we meet and I will buy you a drink!

Contents

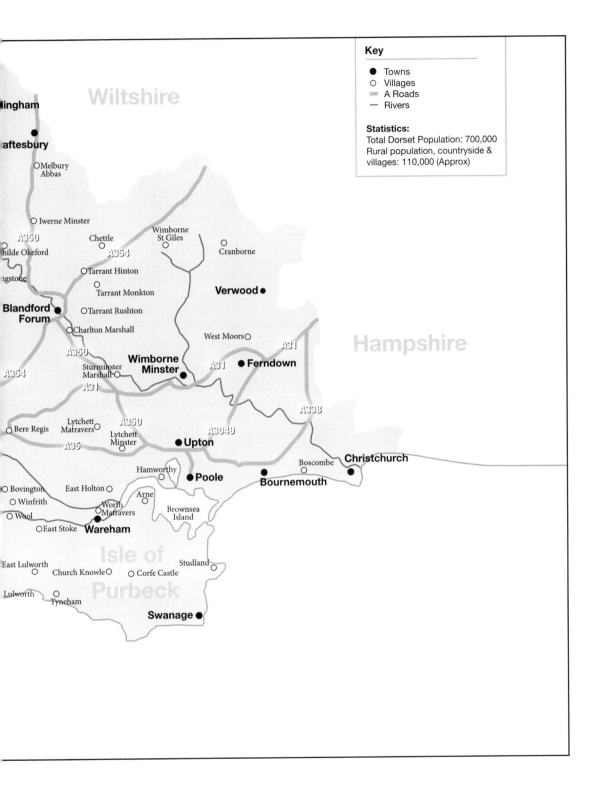

A few words from the author

Everywhere I have travelled in the county I have been received with the most amazing warmth and kindness by so many good people. Not content with merely welcoming me into their homes and their lives, innumerable individuals have gone way beyond extending the hand of friendship and co-operation. They have positively sought to assist me in a hundred different ways. I feel it is entirely appropriate, therefore, to give something back to the community in order to express my immense gratitude. For that reason I have decided that for every copy of Dorset Journey sold the sum of £2.00 will be divided between two admirable Dorset charities dear to my heart. I have invited Julian Fellowes to write a few words about the work of the Weldmar Trust in Dorchester and Peter and Linda Thornton to write of the John Thornton Young Achiever's Foundation in Ferndown.

The Weldmar Trust

As part of his delightful *Dorset Journey*, Alan Bennett has decided to benefit the county he celebrates in his book by donating a percentage of the profits to two local charities. One of these, I'm happy to say, is the Weldmar Trust in Dorchester, an organisation of which I am proud to be a Vice President. The Weldmar is dedicated to caring for the terminally ill, enabling the patients to live to the full, both in-house and in their own homes, and helping them to plan for the end with a maximum of dignity and choice. To me, the work of the hospice is about living, quite as much as dying, and every penny received will go towards making many lives as rich and rewarding as they can be. I am a complete believer and I thank every one of you who buy the book for contributing to this wonderful cause.

Julian Fellowes. September, 2009

The John Thornton Young Achiever's Foundation

The John Thornton Young Achievers Foundation was set up in memory of our son Lt 'JT' Thornton RM who was tragically killed in Afghanistan on 30th March, 2008. He was commanding the Fire Support Group of Charlie Company, 40 Commando Royal Marines, when his vehicle was involved in an IED explosion. John was 22 years old and died doing the job he loved. The Foundation has been an extremely positive focus for the whole family and has definitely helped us all through an enormously difficult time. We are comforted by the fact that we know John would be incredibly proud of his legacy which is helping young people to achieve their dreams, just as he did.

Peter and Linda Thornton. October, 2009

Foreword by Paul Atterbury

During a rather varied life, I have come to know England quite well, a knowledge based both on the practical experience of domesticity and travel and the pleasure of maps and books. The latter, of which there is an endless variety, offer a timeless vision of landscape, architecture and the other structures that make England so distinctive.

My Dorset life began in 1987 when I bought my house in Eype, then a rather primitive weekend cottage. Prior to that I had few Dorset connections and little knowledge of the county, though distant cousins, the Streatfeilds, had lived in West Dorset for centuries. As is common with many incomers I quickly became interested in the history of my adopted county and, in particular, the area that had, by chance, become my home. This led, among other things, to the exploration of local history via old postcards and the walking of long-lost railway lines. Meanwhile, the Dorset shelf in my library seemed to grow steadily with that characteristic mixture of the classic, the familiar and the obscure.

Books about Dorset, in common with most books about the topography of England, concentrate on places and buildings and references to people are generally historical. Only a few authors, such as J.B. Priestley, have based their England vision upon the people met along the way.

Alan Bennett has chosen to take this route and, in travelling round Dorset for a year, he met many people and then wrote about their conversations. The result is a very different vision of a familiar county, and one that is constantly interesting. A journey is about both places and people and Alan merges both elements together in a way that brings Dorset to life. It also offers the future a particular view of life in an English county in the first decade of the 21st century, and that may be its ultimate and enduring value.

Departure

Wimborne, New Year's Eve 2007
The suitcase is in the car. For once, it's not raining.

How do I feel on the eve of my journey across the county in which I have lived for the greater part of my life? Exhilarated? Yes, for the project has been taking shape in my head for many months and I would be dull of spirit if I was not excited by the challenge before me. Apprehensive? Of course, for I know I shall be utterly dependent upon the goodwill and co-operation of hundreds of individuals in countless walks of life. Without their generous support there will, very simply, be no book. As of this moment I know not a soul in most of the towns and villages I intend to visit. At best, I am acquainted with a very few. The notebook is full of blank pages. I shall travel with few pre-conceptions and, I trust, with still fewer prejudices. I must judge people and situations only as I find them. Nor do I wish to duplicate what other writers have written. There are already many fine books on the county - its topography and history, its country houses and churches, its famous sons and daughters, its sinners and its saints. Sometimes I shall point my readers in the direction of those writers who have gone before me, some celebrated, some unfamiliar, that their observations and wisdom may illuminate my own text.

In 1902 the celebrated novelist H. Rider Haggard, author of such titles as *King Solomon's Mines* and *She*, published *Rural England*, a detailed survey of life in the English countryside. It had proved a monumental exercise even for such an experienced writer, eventually appearing in two volumes of densely packed prose. Haggard wrote these reflections on the qualities required to complete such an undertaking.

'He (the writer) *must be physically strong, never fall ill, every night prepared, at the end of a long day, to plunge into unknown society, to make acquaintance with many new faces and listen to many fresh views or arguments, without showing signs of an exhaustion which his host or their guests might, not unnaturally, attribute to a lack of interest and proper gratitude. Never for one instant must he allow his attention to flag, his powers of observation to become dull, or his sight and hearing to miss anything that is of importance to his cause.*

His mind should be that of a trained lawyer, able to weigh and sift evidence, discriminating between the true and false, the weighty and the trivial. Vexations, disappointments, even occasional impertinences and rebuffs, should not disturb him; with a smile he must try again elsewhere.'

Haggard's meticulous research was, above all, designed to inform and educate the public as to the state of the English countryside. I doubt he felt any need to entertain. But I know a dry recitation of facts would make for turgid reading. A hundred years ago the written word remained King. There was no competition from television, cinema or the Internet. I must persuade those who pick up this volume to keep turning the pages with an eager curiosity to discover what comes next. From time to time I hope my readers will look up from the page with a smile on their face, even laughing out loud on occasion at some amusing tale or absurdity. And, above all else, I will have ignominiously failed if my readers do not empathise with many of the individuals whose names appear in this story. They will come in all shapes and sizes, of all ages and colours and creeds. Of course, there are certain to be longeurs, passages where my readers may find their concentration or interest waning. But not too often, I trust, though I do wonder quite how I shall make certain topics compulsive reading. However, that is for me to worry about tomorrow. It's time to begin my journey.

I turn the key in the ignition.

West Dorset

Lyme Regis

The Marine Parade: A few minutes before midnight.
No easterly tonight to chill the bones. An easterly is the most disagreeable wind in Lyme Bay, wrote John Fowles. Happily, Atlantic influences prevail. It's a still, mild evening, comfortable even for the scantily-clad, fancy-dressed revellers mingling cheerfully outside the Harbour Inn on the Marine Parade. Friends and strangers alike are greeted with warmth and an almost exaggerated courtesy. Within the Harbour Inn a Roman centurion proudly displays bulging biceps to admiring eyes. Waitresses scurry between tables and diners consult their watches. Are all glasses charged?

Outside there are no church bells, nor the chimes or hands of a town clock to confirm the precise moment. But, suddenly, exuberant laughter and raised, jubilant voices fill the night air. A colourful carnival of youth entwined in scores of embraces beneath a starless sky. Through the milling throng Mark Oldfield, proprietor of the Harbour Inn and old friend Maxwell Parker, thread a path towards the sands. For six years past it has been the same. When does an event repeated many times become a tradition? Two thousand wretched, disappointed souls may be waiting in vain fifty miles to the east on Bournemouth prom, but not we who gather on the Marine parade. The sky lights up in a brief, exhilarating display of pyrotechnic brilliance. No charge though upon overburdened taxpayers. Mark foots the bill. It's a fitting beginning to another year.

The behaviour is beyond reproach. The young of Lyme and district do themselves proud. Parents and teachers would be gladdened, if they knew. We wend our way back through Lister Gardens to the Kersbrook. A convivial evening in friends' good company.

January 1: New Year's Day
Despite the late night I feel surprisingly fresh as I set out to find a newsagent – and a *Racing Post*. I've always found it a particular source of pleasure to be up and about early in a town new to me before the general population stirs. The eye and the ear are not distracted by triviality or movement. It's possible to see a place for what it really is – its buildings, the care or absence of care its citizens lavish upon it, the state of the pavements, the smells of a town before the streets are full of people and cars, the delight of finding a bakery where they are actually baking bread, meeting the 'early birds' and discovering whether they speak to strangers – a thousand and one details that can tell you so much of the nature of a town or village. Several years ago in Sorrento, at just such an hour soon after dawn, I would walk the same stretch of deserted road from the hotel and meet three mongrel dogs – obviously great friends – trotting down the hill from their small village the mile and a half into the town. At dusk they would wend their unaccompanied way back to the village, their bellies presumably filled by the scraps given by tourists. It was an image of Italian country life that has never left me. This morning I see no stray dogs in Lyme, just a couple of docile beasts padding along behind their owners. Though barely past 8am, the first visitors of a brand new year are already

rolling into town. Thankfully I find a newsagent – and a copy of the *Racing Post*.

We stroll together briefly along the Marine Parade. I would judge him to be eighty or so, though still spry and mentally sharp.

"I was born in Lyme and I hope to die in Lyme. My first job was here on the sands – '41 or '42 it would be. We used to collect up the deck chairs in late afternoon, then roll the barbed wire down on to the beach to deter Jerry. As long as I can make my way down here every morning, then go back home and sit in my chair with my paper, I'm a contented man."

I understand my companion's sentiments perfectly. There can be few more magnificent locations on earth than Lyme Bay on a fine morning – on any morning, for that matter. A wild Channel gale presents a no less spectacular scene .We approach Langmoor Gardens. I express my admiration of the designer's handiwork. The old fellow's tone is guarded – wistful even.

"It used to be a lot more overgrown when I was a lad. More private. It was where half of Lyme's youngsters learned the facts of life."

He laughs. "Me included!"

I ask his name. He shakes his head.

"I don't want my name in no book. When I was in the army I learned to keep my head down. Don't volunteer for nothing. That's the way I prefer it."

We shake hands and wish one another a Happy New Year.

Back at the Kersbrook it's a late breakfast for most guests. The national dailies scarcely make for

New Year's Day, 2008, Lyme Regis. *Picture: Geoff Hill*

'I'm going to have to organise a mouse jihad'. Mark Anthony Cannon and didgeridoo. *Picture: Geoff Hill*

'Oyez! Oyez!' Philip Street, Town Crier. *Picture: Geoff Hill*

cheerful reading. Benazir Bhutto's assassination and the burning down of a church in Kenya with the deaths of thirty villagers lead to gloomy Editorial speculation. There are more uplifting thoughts locally. In the *Lyme Regis News* Chris Carson writes that the 'Seafront shelters are to get the go-ahead', while in his *View from Lyme*, Philip Evans announces that the Town Museum is set to raise £5 million for a major extension. Compelling evidence, if it is needed, that the local press does lend a sense of perspective to the world about us.

I miss the annual swim on the front but arrive at Woodmead Road just as the stragglers in the duck race are reaching the finishing point. RNLI volunteers are retrieving hundreds of yellow plastic ducks in a large net. I suppose it makes a change for our brave friends from plucking to safety those in peril on the sea.

"We usually lose a dozen or so each year," I hear one of them explain to a bystander. Has it been a planned escape, I wonder? Like racing pigeons deciding not to return to their lofts but to forge exciting new lives on the cliff-tops, did our yellow plastic ducks decide a life on the ocean's waves offered more adventure? The Town Crier, Philip Street, presents the victor, Mrs. Wilson – I fail to catch her first name – with her prize. A special cheer is reserved for Cara Fachau, who receives her consolation prize for the last duck to finish. We British do love our valiant losers, especially when they smile as sweetly as Cara.

Outside the Bell Cliff restaurant Mark Anthony Cannon BA (Fine Arts) is in philosophical mood.

"My New Year's resolution? To smoke less baccy, to drink less red wine, but what I do drink for it to be of better quality – and to write and illustrate my children's book."

Where is Mark living this mid-winter?

"I'm in a tent in the middle of a wood at Uplyme, not far from where the bones of my ancestors lie in the cemetery. When I woke this morning I found a mouse had decided to join me. It's after my food, I fear. I'm going to have to organise a mouse jihad!"

No earnest interviews today. It's a public holiday, after all, though I do call in at the Harbour Inn to compliment Mark on the quality of his cuisine and the firework display.

"My wish for 2008? Plenty of sunshine and not too much rain."

When you employ 30 or so staff in winter and more than 50 in summer Mark values fine weather more than most.

In mid-afternoon we idly watch the swarm of figures beneath us on the beach and the Cobb from the heights of Lister Gardens. If this is January how many will be here in August – with their cars of course? And that is a major headache for the town. Even with park-and-ride it's a bit like trying to squeeze a quart into a pint pot. But there can be few complaints from the owners of the pubs and cafes and shops today. They'll be smiling at their bank managers in the morning.

Just days ago Marjorie Waters from the Dorset Wildlife Trust told me of the purple sandpipers at the end of the Cobb. Though a bird-watcher since childhood I've never seen one. Max Gallop at the Marine Aquarium confirms these winter visitors from Iceland and Spitsbergen are still about. Frequenting rocky shores, it's a perfect habitat for them round the Cobb. Half a dozen rock pipits flit cheerily along beside me. Momentarily I wonder if they might just be laughing at me, but I'm not sure that birds possess a sense of humour. I've just about given up on the purple sandpipers when I spot my quarry. Three of them, difficult to distinguish in the fading light, their plumage so closely matches the grey rocks. I am delighted. I must thank Marjorie.

So it's off to the Pilot Boat, weary but exultant. Fish and chips come highly recommended. Or shall it be the steak and kidney pie? Sometimes life presents us with such agonising choices.

A few pages of Jane Austen's *Persuasion* before I close my eyes. Napoleon has just been packed off to Elba while an English frigate patrols the waters nearby. His escape, the Battle of Waterloo and his final, humiliating exile on St. Helena lie in the future. Thousands of discharged soldiers and sailors are roaming the land in search of work in an England victorious in war but, for many unfortunates, hungry in peace. Not that Miss Austen ever mentions Master Boney, the unemployed or the war-maimed veterans of Wellington's Peninsular Army. Her sea captains and admirals are mostly wealthy from their share of the prize money garnered in two decades of war with France. In Bath and Lyme they are seeking suitable brides or husbands for their daughters, buying fine estates or renting handsome properties. Captain Wentworth is worth a reputed £25,000 – in 1814! But it is an infinitely more trivial matter that concerns me. Why do none of Miss Austen's characters complain about Lyme's hills? I know the impetuous Louisa Musgrove suffered a near fatal tumble on the Cobb but Granny's Teeth are not located on Pound Street or Silver Street. Everyone in the town knows that unless you live your entire life on the Marine Parade, you have only to step outside your door and you are confronted by a hill. If you begin your journey going down a hill, you will conclude it by returning up the hill. Or vice versa. Could it be that Miss Austen invariably descended into the town or departed by carriage? Was the dear creature never obliged to carry a heavy bag of shopping up Broad Street? I fall asleep wondering.

It's more serious themes this morning.

'A man who is Lyme through and through' and 'A political maverick with a big heart' are but two of the milder epithets applied to the man sitting in his armchair before me. Stan Williams, former Mayor and long-serving councillor, joined the council forty years ago, though one or two of his fellow councillors have joked that it seems more like two hundred years ago. Stan is in jocular mood. He's off to India tomorrow morning providing his daughter can locate his insurance in time.

"Going to warm old bones," he laughs. "When I return, spring will nearly have arrived."

Spring must look particularly magical through the large lounge window with its view of two counties and rolling green meadows and woodland. I remark upon Stan's good fortune in finding such a location – even if it is in the wrong county.

"We are the lucky ones. It's so difficult now for Lyme's young families. With about a fifth of our housing stock either holiday lets or second homes, property prices have rocketed beyond the reach of our local youngsters. They must either move inland or leave Lyme altogether."

Stan was chairman of the Building Committee thirty or so years ago when the building trade was the most important form of local employment. Is there any building land left now to develop?

"Just three fields remain where houses could potentially be built."

I mention the exhibition that has just opened at the Town Museum devoted to 'Lyme's disappearing farmland' which has been assembled by Ken Gollop and Graham Davies.

"You've hit the nail on the head. No one concerned with the environment wants to see development where it can be avoided. Such green spaces are precious to the community. The exhibition perfectly highlights the dilemma that confronts us in Lyme."

"Personally, I would raise the council tax on second homes to punitive levels."

The topic is still housing as it is so often in Lyme. But this time I am sitting in Cliff Cottage, off Cobb Road, with Merry Bolton and Carl Salter. I suggest to Merry that those with second homes would probably shrug their shoulders and dip a little deeper into their pockets. We agree there is no easy solution.

There may be comparable views across Lyme Bay from other properties but there can be none better than that from Cliff Cottage. Gazing seawards Merry introduces me to the phenomena known as the Charmouth Dragon and St. Wite's Lines, both clearly visible in different weather conditions. Actually Merry and Carl have not long returned to their home after a two-year long exile. The last major landslip necessitated a major engineering and design project in the surrounding area.

"It's hoped it will last fifty years."

Merry is chairman of the Environment Committee.

"Actually I did initially have a few anxieties about the replanting in Lister Gardens. But thanks to the influence and wise advice of Professor Ghillean Prance, the former Director of Kew Gardens, and others like Alan Kennard, David West and Barry Trott, the outcome is, I believe, rather splendid.

Merry is absolutely right. Notwithstanding the reservations of my ancient companion on the Marine Parade, the Lister and Langmoor Gardens are a triumph which will delight visitors and locals for decades to come, always providing the fifty years estimate is right. I suspect Lyme's young people will contrive to find alternative locations for learning the facts of life. With experience of running an adjacent tea garden and fish restaurant Merry and Carl are typical members of the town's social and business life. At different times Carl has organised boat trips and ghost and historical tours. Only recently he was to be seen garbed in the costume of a mature Captain Wentworth at a Jane Austen festival at the Marine Theatre. Knowing that when I have left Cliff Cottage I must face a steep climb up Cobb Road I ask Carl about Lyme's hills. He smiles wryly.

"Lyme demonstrates Charles Darwin's 'survival of the fittest' theory perfectly. Our hills cull the unfit and the weak. The estate agents lick their lips when the obese and those with heart conditions step inside their offices. They know the properties will soon be up for sale again!"

Unlike one of Darwin's Galapagos finches I fear I have yet to adapt to my new environment arriving breathless back at the Kersbrook. But, then again, it probably took the finches hundreds of years, if not thousands, to evolve. I've been in Lyme barely forty-eight hours! I ask Margaret Davies who, with husband Kenneth, runs the hotel about the hills that surround their property.

"I do recall about twenty years ago being with the boys, Charles and Alex, at the top of Broad

Street. Alex was in the pushchair when they started bickering. Momentarily I took my hand off the chair and it began to roll downhill at a rapidly increasing speed. Of all things I was in high heels and there was no way I could possibly catch up. I was screaming at the top of my voice for someone to stop the pushchair. I had visions of Alex disappearing over the sea-wall. Fortunately someone stopped it before disaster struck!"

Alex, now a church organist and talented all-round musician much in demand around the town, recalls an incident from the previous summer.

"I heard a loud knocking at the door. Confronting me was a very substantial young woman with her equally substantial family in tow. She couldn't have been more than twenty-five. Her face was bright red and beads of perspiration were rolling down her cheeks. She was clearly very irate. She clutched in her hand our hotel prospectus. Gasping for breath she croaked: 'It says in here....'Pause. 'That your hotel is....'Pause. 'Five minutes walk from the sea!'. I told her that I could certainly walk to the sea in five minutes, but I'm afraid she was distinctly unimpressed. She tore up the prospectus and stormed off!"

Though Lyme has only three and a half thousand residents out of season and has never been that populous, its history has been of no small consequence. Here it was the Duke of Monmouth began his misguided attempt to seize the crown from James II. Even today the spot where he landed in 1685 is known as Monmouth beach. Lyme is well-known too for its landslips with the Blue Lias clay regularly tumbling over the sandstone cliffs. It was here too that a remarkable 11 year-old called Mary Anning lived for it was she who discovered the first complete specimen of an Ichthyosaurus, a marine reptile that lived 50 million years ago. Later Mary found a number of other fossilised remains that led to the area between Lyme and Charmouth being regarded as one of the most exciting and productive sites for scientific investigation of this kind. Today, of course, it is designated as a 'gateway town' to the Jurassic Coast World Heritage Site and an Area of Outstanding Natural Beauty. Then there are Lyme's literary and artistic associations, Jane Austen and John Fowles being the most celebrated authors to have set some of their literature in the town and surrounding locality. However, in 2008 there does live in Lyme still another literary figure of some significance and it is to her home that I am bound this morning.

Many summers ago I accompanied a party of children to Farnham Rep to see a play called The Knack. Adapted to the silver screen and starring the fine young actress Rita Tushingham, it was a highly entertaining and illuminating exploration of young people in the Sixties. For me it is quite extraordinary that so many years later I am sitting in Colway Manor with its author and long-time resident, Ann Jellicoe.

"We've got workmen in and I'm counting the hours to their departure!"

Her husband, the internationally acclaimed photographer, Roger Mayne, brings in the coffee as we discuss Ann's remarkable life.

"I first fell in love with Dorset during holiday visits to Monkton Wyld and Maiden Newton. To tell you the truth, there came a time when I found myself less and less keen to return to London even though my theatrical life was there. We'd enjoyed great success at the Royal Court – it was simply the most exciting place for actors and writers to work."

It was a theatre I knew well myself where I first became acquainted with Arnold Wesker, Harold Pinter and John Osborne.

"But, in the end, we found this spot and this has been my home ever since. And, do you know, I think in some ways my greatest personal satisfaction has actually derived from the community plays I have directed here in Dorset – in Dorchester and, not least, here in Lyme itself. Organising a hundred plus actors, as well as writing the story of the women of Lyme and their heroic role in the defence of the town during the Roundhead siege, that was wonderful!"

At one time Ann shared responsibility with John Fowles as a curator of the Town Museum. Today she is a patron of the Town Mill. At eighty she remains a doughty lady.

"Though I'm afraid it now takes me much longer to do the things I like to do."

And are there any remaining ambitions?

"I like to follow where my instincts lead me." She laughs. "Who can tell?"

The offices of View From Publishing Ltd *Broad Street*

One of Lyme's most industrious gentlemen is journalist and newspaper proprietor, Philip Evans, who has no fewer than 12 titles under the umbrella of *'View From Publishing Ltd'* which are published in 3 counties.

"I am quite prepared to be controversial. I will raise issues that need to be confronted here in the town. What is, I feel, a particular weakness of local government is the lack of young blood. Young people are simply not coming into politics at the local level."

As Philip was Mayor at the age of just 34 it is understandable that he feels impatient. Is it, I ask, that most of the energetic young people now leave Lyme at 18 to go off to university and seldom return because there is no suitable employment and they cannot afford to buy their own homes? He agrees that is probably a part of the explanation but also believes that young people are largely alienated from the whole political process. But there is one exception to almost every rule.

Philip laughs. "Lucy Campbell! She is a remarkable young woman. Will she beat my record as Lyme's youngest ever Mayor? Quite possibly."

The Red Lion

What could be more appropriate than that I am I am now in the company of Lucy Campbell, Lyme's youngest councillor? A Londoner by birth she came to live in the town at the age of eleven, attended Woodroffe before returning to the capital to secure a degree in silver-smithing and metalwork at Camberwell College of Art. With Philip Evans bemoaning the lack of young blood on the council why is Lucy the exception?

"My parents discussed politics not in a partisan way but rather they encouraged me to take an interest. When the Youth Worker, Geoffrey Mann, and Marcus Dixon set up the Insparation Youth Club where young people could meet socially I became involved. As a result, much to my surprise, I was selected as West Dorset Community Champion in 2005. When a seat became vacant on the council I stood and was elected. I was just 22 at the time."

At the most recent elections Lucy was third out of 23 candidates, a considerable tribute to her personality and energy. Her personal ambition is to make a living in jewellery-making and, with her boyfriend, Jason Turner a carpenter and maker of bespoke furniture, to buy a house locally. She is, however, like so many of her age, alarmed by the property prices and the number of second homes in the town.

"What's my immediate goal as a councillor? For ages, we've been talking about a skate park – let's get it sorted and built as soon as possible!"

Barely have I left the Red Lion than I am back – truly a great hardship – this time in the company of Adrianne Maslen, the local reporter for the *Bridport & Lyme News*. The personable young journalist from Caerphilly finds Lyme politics frustrating at times.

"Everyone on the council undoubtedly wants what is best for the town but, unfortunately, there's no common vision. There's a struggle between the traditionalists who want to see Lyme remain very much as it is and those who want to pull it into the twenty-first century. Personal history and relationships often seem to determine how people will vote. I feel I can, with reasonable accuracy, predict how people will vote on any given issue on the basis of their friendships."

We discuss the contrast in content between the West and East Dorset regional newspapers. I mention the two murders in the same street in Bournemouth in a single weekend, the jailing of a rapist and drugs raids on a number of properties as recorded under banner headlines in the Bournemouth edition of the *Daily Echo*. Adrianne smiles wryly.

"Shall I tell you the precise content of my last police report here in Lyme? A broken wing mirror, a stolen handbag and a missing statue!"

And the headline above her latest story in the local paper – I know because I happened to read it.

"Dog fouling! Yes, it's perfectly true. You must appreciate that dog mess is a real problem in a town dependent upon tourism. But isn't it lovely that Lyme doesn't have the same kind of social problems as Bournemouth – at least, not on the same scale."

Adrianne and boyfriend Anthony have just bought a house in the town.

"I love it here. It's a town, I think, that has a quite separate identity from the rest of Dorset. I like to think of it as 'the town that time forgot'."

As we're leaving I overhear the conversation between the young barman and a customer. The barman, pale and looking distinctly under the weather, is complaining loudly that he is suffering from a terrible hang-over. The customer grins unsympathetically.

"We've all been there at sometime, mate. I'm fifty-nine and I still suffer the occasional hang-over."

The other barman present, whose name I happen to know is Patnan Iswan, laughs.

"Fifty-nine! That's very young for Lyme!"

Patnan's quip makes us all smile but the reality is that, at the last count, 49% of Lyme's population is over sixty compared with a county average of 29% and, in the past twenty years or so, Lyme has recorded a significant inward migration of older, retired people. In the longer term, of course, such a trend is likely to present several potentially serious problems, not least in the provision of health and nursing care. And one man charged with preparing for such an eventuality is by my side this morning as we set out from his office at St. Michael's Business Centre in Church Street for a stroll along the sea-front. The name of Marcus Dixon has already been mentioned in uniformly approving tones by several of my previous interviewees.

"My rather grandiose title is that of chief executive of Lyme Regis Development Trust. Put very simply, my main function is to assist in the implementation of the Town's *Community Plan 2007-2027*. In consultation with a broad cross-section of the people we completed a comprehensive profile of the town – its economy, environment, the health and well-being and safety of the community, housing, sports, culture and life-long learning facilities, traffic and transport, young people – the lot, and then we set ourselves targets to achieve during the next 25 year period."

We pause in our walk and conversation in the churchyard at the grave of Lyme's most famous citizen, a mere stone's throw from where her house once stood.

"That's Mary Anning's final resting-place. But for that lady I doubt Lyme would be the place it is today, nor would I be talking to you about a Development Plan."

Having thumbed my way through the pages of the most worthy document – not that I relished some of the mind-numbing jargon so characteristic of almost every official publication these days – I ask Marcus to summarise its conclusions.

"To tackle the problem of providing affordable housing for local people, the displacement of the town's young people which is in part related to the first point, the general dearth of well-paid jobs,

'The world's their oyster', sixth form with head of year, James Thomas. Woodroffe School. *Picture: Geoff Hill*

the closing of many shops that sell basic amenities, hotels being converted into apartments, housing being converted into holiday homes and lets, the demographic imbalance and so on."

I can only wish Marcus well. I understand why he is so well regarded. He's sincere, dynamic, a visionary and possessed of the priceless quality of being able to relate to people and carry them along on a tide of enthusiasm. We've reached the Lister Gardens. I mention the comments of my ancient gentleman on the Marine Parade.

"Yes, I understand perfectly. I'm sure young people will be glad to see everything grow so there is some cover for their nocturnal activities. On the other hand, it was designed to deter vandalism."

No Adrian Gray, stone balancer, on the sands today. It's too early in the year for him, I imagine. He's a bizarre and rare talent certainly. We stroll on to the Boat Building Academy where Marcus introduces me to boat-builder Gail McGarva who is supervising the construction of a gig.

"The launch date is set for June 28 and there's a competition to name it. What do you think?"

(I learn later from Diane Attenborough that the name chosen is Rebel after the Monmouth Rebellion and a second gig is now under construction with a launch date set for July 2009)

Where else then in Lyme before I take my leave?

Up the hill first to Woodroffe School to meet members of the Sixth and the Head of Sixth, James Thomas. I invite the students to express their thoughts on the theme of growing up in the far west of the county. One or two, I discover, actually live over the border in Devon but it would be unworthy of me to hold that misfortune against them! Natasha Wiscombe, James Morrow, Simon Long, Lucy

Hare and Eliane Stenning all write affectionately of their childhood though most anticipate exile to distant parts as they pursue university and career ambitions. The most eloquent is Abi Bennett (no relative !) who says she appreciates the solitude and tranquillity of the coast 'when I need to be alone, but also those small events that draw a community together, when people emerge from their houses to a place of good vibes, laughs, smiles and happy times to store away in their memories forever.'

The Woodroffe students, incidentally, should also take immense pride in their own 'in-house' author, Gilly Warr, the Administration Manager, who has written an excellent and exhaustive history of 'The School on the Hill'.

Back down now on the Cobb, recently voted one of the top ten most romantic places to propose marriage, I discuss with the amiable Max Gallop at the Marine Aquarium, where they've just celebrated their 50th anniversary, the vexed question of scallops dredging on the seabed of Lyme Bay. The decision is promised in early summer. We talk too of some of the legendary figures of Lyme, Harry May the boatman, the Gallop and Wason fishing families, Dave Smith, a man who plays many roles but recently suffered the misfortune of having a leg amputated. Philip Evans in his column *View From Lyme* reports that Dave told him his replacement leg was 'far more shapely than the original'. It's further rumoured that John Stamp, Chairman of the Lyme Regis Skittles League, is organising a collection for 'Smithy' to buy him a parrot!

And so along the Marine Parade for the last time, up the steps, across the road into Broad Street, the commercial heart of the town. A pleasing proportion of shops are still in independent, local hands though, sadly and extraordinarily, no butcher survives. Inevitably, many shops cater for the tourist and, fortunately, Lyme's visitors are now all the year round. Someone whispers in my ear that I absolutely must poke my head round the door of Hilary Highet's – the lady has two retail outlets. Ladies' wear isn't really my scene but, notwithstanding, it is evident Hilary has fashioned a niche role for herself – high-class garments with a close attention to her clientele's needs. As she puts it herself: "The HH look is a bit arty, intelligent, very relaxed and it somehow fits equally well in Lyme Regis, around the country and even London." Incidentally, Hilary doesn't stop extolling Lyme's wider virtues. Was I aware that Lyme has no fewer then 64 different societies and clubs? I do now, Hilary. Unsurprisingly there are a number of shops specialising in fossils, art in its various guises and a couple of excellent bookshops. However, I do discover one startling omission – no betting shop! I understand some individuals have tried and failed to make a living. Does that make the locals the shrewdest punters in the kingdom, or is a Nonconformist, anti-gambling heritage still alive? And just how do the good people of Lyme contrive to have a 'flutter' on the Grand National when half the nation enjoys a fun bet? In Coombe Street I'm impressed by Richard Austin's photography. As for the Town Mill Bakery, where Clive Cobb practises his craft, the aroma of freshly baked bread and ground coffee is well-nigh irresistible. Back down to Bridge Street then, past the excellent Town Museum where Ken Gallop and his merry band of volunteers do sterling service, and on to my last port of call – the Marine Theatre. As I enter I am disconcerted to discover dozens of individuals swathed in bandages or with arms in slings. Has there been some dreadful accident? Are they rehearsing a new play set in a hospital? The ever helpful Nicola Tee hastens to reassure me. It's a volunteer's training day. New recruits are being trained in first-aid. I breathe a sigh of relief. Meanwhile, Nicola introduces me to a number of the regulars and John Bartholomew relates something of the theatre's chequered past.

"It has enjoyed several incarnations – as drill hall and village hall – and periods of disuse. People will tell you that 'You dirty rat' James Cagney appeared here during WW2 when American troops were stationed nearby. The Town Council handed it over to a Trust in 2003 and the Trustees have a clear mandate from them to make it a success, despite inherent financial difficulties like shoring up an old building. Most of the core funding does come from the Council though it's never enough and

The cast of *Hickory Dickory Dock,* Marine Theatre, 2008. *Picture: Geoff Hill*

the Trustees are constantly trying to find new sources of revenue. Without volunteer support the theatre simply wouldn't exist, but I do believe the theatre has established a reputation for excellence in the arts community."

The theatre does clearly play an invaluable role in the life of the Lyme community being regularly used by a number of local societies – panto, operatic, youth, dramatic among others – besides providing a varied programme of live entertainment. Two families, in particular, have long been associated with the theatre, the Streets and the Rattenburys. Andy Rattenbury, the TV screen-writer, is a patron. Every theatre is precious and Lyme's Marine is more precious than most, the town's isolated geographical location meaning any comparable venue is many miles distant. All credit then to all those citizens who give so generously of their time and energy to support such an irreplaceable community asset.

So I emerge into the fading evening light. A wild westerly is beginning to blow and the first spots of rain are falling. I cast one last, lingering look across to the Cobb and the lights of the harbour. It's time, at last, to take my leave of most hospitable Lyme – and its hills. I dared not have asked for a better start to my journey.

Charmouth
Twinned with Asnelles (France)

A grey, winter's morning with a stiff southerly and I feel distinctly chilly on Evan's Cliff even in an overcoat.

"Its fine up there," say Martyn Howe with a grin and a glance skywards. "We're well wrapped up in our thermally insulated clothing."

I'm prepared to give him the benefit of the doubt. Martyn and Christine Squibb, together with several companions from the Devon and Somerset paragliding/hang-gliding club are packing away their gear after a morning spent a couple of thousand feet above the Charmouth cliffs and shoreline.

"I went down as far as West Bay over Golden Cap."

At 617 feet Golden Cap is the highest point on the southern coast. West Bay lies five miles or so to the east.

"You have to watch what's happening at sea – for any likely squalls and so on. And you need to keep a permanent eye on the weather and the way the birds are flying. How they are holding their wings, for example. They are all clues you need to take on board to be safe. There was a peregrine up there with me this morning. Last year a buzzard actually attacked me. I guess I was invading its territory during the breeding season."

I've always felt that if the gods intended me to fly they would have equipped me with wings. I also entertain no great desire to be savaged by a rampaging bird of prey. Further, I do remember the dreadful fate that befell the Member of Parliament for Malmesbury, Walter Powell, in 1881 at a point not far from where Martyn and I are chatting. The ill-fated W. Powell MP had set off on 10 December from Bath in a War Office, gas-filled balloon named the Saladin with two crew members to record information for the Meteorological Society. Clearly ignorant of the admirable advice of such as Martyn Howe , the crew carelessly allowed the balloon to collide with ' a coastal pasture at Eype', at which point our two crew members fortuitously exited, before the wretched MP for Malmesbury continued his journey, now a solo affair, out into the Channel. Quite what awful speculation must have gone on in Mr.Howe's mind as he saw the cliffs of West Dorset disappear from view we can only hazard a guess at. Suffice to say, it was some weeks later that what was thought to be the wreckage of the Saladin was discovered in the mountainous region of Sierra del Piedroza. Of Mr. Powell MP there was, alas, no sign.

With such thoughts in my head, I wish Martyn a cheery goodbye but mentally resolve I will not be applying to join his club. Besides which, the prospect of lunch at The George or The Royal Oak seems a much safer prospect – and infinitely warmer!

Having spun a coin I settle for The George. Dean and Maria Herbert have run the inn for the past five years since taking over from Dean's father-in-law, Ray Capewell and wife Christine, who were resident for the previous sixteen years.

"We've built a steady trade, trying to provide excellent food and a warm welcome for our locals. We're all hoping for a fine summer and lots of visitors."

Dean recommends the steak and kidney.

"It comes from Sean of Axminster Meats. I actually advised Sean on the contents and the texture of the pastry. He won a Gold Award at Westpoint!"

It sounds like a wise choice. And so it proves.

The Abbott's House

Across The Street I meet Paul Crosby, busily engaged on behalf of Nick and Sheila Gilbey in the renovation of the Abbott's House, formerly the Queen's Armes. It's clearly a superbly executed piece of craftsmanship. Paul has a fine reputation in the locality, having been recently responsible for a major restoration of The Bull Hotel at Bridport. I also make the exciting discovery that Nick Gilbey, a freelance photographer by profession, is the nephew of the legendary 'Quinny', Anthony Gilbey, author of *Fun Was My living*, one of the classics of horse-racing literature. With such an illustrious pedigree Nick is clearly a fine fellow. Sheila, a civil servant and passionate chef, gives me a quick guided tour.

"We're naming the rooms after local personalities – Mary Anning, Thomas Chard the last Abbott, Thomas Hardy and our friend James Crowden, the author. We intend to concentrate on providing weekend breaks with fine food and lovely accommodation together with a restaurant service for the local community."

The Elms, The Pavey Room – Later in the week

I have wandered up from the beach through the village and met scarcely a soul. True, it's a wild winter's morning when most of the world, save those already at their places of work, prefer to be snug indoors. Yet within the Pavey Room I discover a hive of bustling activity as a steady stream of callers arrive bearing ancient family photographs, crumpled maps or collections of village reminiscences for the Pavey Society's archives. Named after Reginald Pavey, a native of Charmouth who returned after retirement to devote his energies to chronicling the history of the locality, the society is dedicated to

(left to right) Keith Grinter, Jeff Prosser, Brian Bowditch, Peter Press. *Picture: Geoff Hill*

continuing the research he pioneered. Its chairman is the avuncular figure of Peter Press, a former history teacher, and the inspirational dynamo at the heart of the group's activities. Another stalwart is Pat Stapleton, former parish councillor and a leading light in the women's branch of the British Legion. Pat arrived in the village in 1969 with her husband Kenneth to run the Court Hotel.

"Actually as a council we all get along very well together. We are a consensual body unlike, from what I have heard, the Lyme Regis Council which appears to be very argumentative."

Mention of their larger neighbour brings a smile to the face of John Whatemore who moved to the village as a six year-old in 1932. He vividly recalls distant rivalries.

"Before the war there were often suspicions that the Lyme fishermen were in the habit of raiding our lobster pots. And the football matches between the two sides were very physical affairs, to say the least!"

Keith Grinter, a former fisherman and for many years the local butcher, confirms that the suspicions of the Charmouth fishing community were well founded.

"I actually saw one of my lobster pots in the bottom of one of their boats in Lyme harbour. It even had my initials on it! And there was often real fun and games when the mackerel arrived each year!"

John Whatemore chuckles. "And, of course, Mary Anning's discoveries were mostly made nearer Charmouth than Lyme but, since she took her finds back with her, it's Lyme that tends to get the glory! It's understandable because it is a bigger place but some folk do get a little peeved."

Richard Stirk, who was born in the servants' quarters of the manor house at nearby Wootton Fitzpaine, mischievously adds: "For years we village lads knew it as Slime Regis!"

Keith Grinter remembers Ken Gallop, a former Charmouth man now at the Town Museum in Lyme, commenting: "It's a good job there's a big hill between us!"

Everyone acknowledges the village has been transformed in the past half-century. Pat Stapleton recalls that when she first arrived there were many more hotels and pubs.

"It was still the case that most holiday- makers stayed a week or two in the same hotel or b&b. Now we have fewer hotels and just two pubs and visitors are staying in caravans or holiday apartments."

The subject of caravans has long been a contentious issue across the county and Charmouth is particularly well endowed. Brian Bowditch, a born and bred Charmuthian now resident at nearby Catherston, takes up the story.

"The first caravans began to arrive in the Fifties. There were some right old legal battles between their owners and the Dorset County Council in the early days but, in the end, compromises were reached. I understand there are now 5,000 beds in the village, mostly in caravans."

With an electoral roll of about 1,400 it is apparent that the population of Charmouth is swollen nearly four-fold in high summer. I ask Pat about the visibility of the caravans.

"To tell you the truth, we don't notice them very much because most are well screened by trees."

What Pat says is quite true. At ground level they are not conspicuous. It's not until you walk up on the surrounding hills that the number of caravans becomes apparent. They are undeniably an eyesore en masse and anyone who loves the English countryside would prefer that they were not there. Yet it is impossible to overstate the significance of the holiday-makers who stay in the caravans from spring to autumn each year to the local economy.

"It's because of the visitors spending their money here that we are able to maintain a good range of shops. We have a post office, a chemist, our own butcher – which even Lyme no longer possesses – a couple of general stores, besides other businesses providing a range of services. It's only because of their takings in summer that their owners are able to survive. We all benefit from their continued existence as a consequence."

Pat is absolutely correct in her analysis. It's all very well for purists to sneer. The simple truth is that tourism is of vital importance to the health of the local economy and, if caravans are a large part of the equation, their presence needs to be accepted. However, there are downsides to the new pattern of holiday-making. Jeff Prosser, the landlord of the Royal Oak, and his wife Carol are strongly committed to the local community but recognise the expansion of caravan sites has adversely affected their business.

"Several of the bigger sites now have their own bars and recreational facilities which mean that parents, especially those with small children, often prefer to stay on site in the evenings. At one time, when the whole caravan business was in its infancy, holiday-makers would stroll into the village and drop in for a drink. That's something they no longer do on the same scale. I fear we have enjoyed the best of the pub business. With the introduction of the smoking ban it's increasingly difficult to make a living."

Aside from the arrival of the caravans, the most significant recent event in Charmouth's history has been the building of the by-pass. John Whatmore is adamant it was for the best.

"Until 1991 Charmouth was The Street. It was the through route for traffic on its way to the West – and on its way back. It was awful! Even now we do have problems with the parking. Lots of people prefer to park for free and walk to the beach."

There is little doubt that 'the final straw', the ultimate catalyst for change, was an event that occurred on an otherwise inconsequential afternoon on 16 March, 1987. At this point I will allow Brian Peach, the former proprietor of the stores in The Street, to recount the events of the day in his own words.

"It was 2.30pm. Anne and I were at home and wondered why the traffic outside had suddenly ground to a standstill. Anne rang our daughter Margaret at the shop to ask what had happened and Margaret explained that a lorry had crashed into the shop bringing down the wall and a part of the roof of the single storey building. The only customer, Mrs. Ingrid Richardson, was tipped into the deep freeze which was pushed across the shop. The poor lady was covered in what was first thought to be blood but, on closer inspection, proved to be tomato sauce. However, she was naturally very shocked – as anybody would be if they went in to do a little shopping and suddenly found themselves inside a freezer cabinet! Happily, she was otherwise unhurt. On hurrying the 200 yards or so to the shop we found the emergency services quickly on the scene. Many customers and friends rushed to our aid moving undamaged stock – the off-licence section was untouched – into the adjacent house store. The lorry driver, Albert Tench from Verwood, and his mate were also unhurt. Happily, within a few days, after lots of phone calls to our insurers, we were able to resume trading in restricted circumstances until our new shop was built."

And the by-pass?

"The by-pass 2.7 miles long, built at a cost of £10.7million, was opened by Sir James Spicer in July, 1990."

So it was that a new era began in Charmouth life – and certainly a more civilised and much safer one. Not least for customers at Brian and Anne Peach's village stores!

The Pavey Room – Another day

I glance at my watch. It's twelve minutes past.

"Don't worry. Mallory's always late!"

At that moment loud laughter erupts in the doorway. I am aware of a big grin, a firm handshake and more laughter. The man exudes good nature and fellowship. He sits down beside me at the table.

Mallory Hayter, the chairman of Charmouth Parish Council, glances about him as if to ensure no enemy spies can overhear what he is about to divulge. When he speaks it is of 'dark, wintry nights' and 'clandestine meetings with estate agents so no one could see what we were doing.'

"We used to meet in the old school-house but it was cramped and unsuitable – especially for us bigger fellows. I could hardly get my legs under the table!"

I cast a swift, casual glance at Mallory's legs. I've seen few finer specimens among front-row forwards at Twickenham. All the subterfuge clearly paid dividends when Mallory and his fellow council conspirators secured The Elms on behalf of the local community for 'a very reasonable figure'.

"We now have a comfortable council chamber, office space for the lovely ladies Lisa (Tuck) and Pamela (Berry), the Pavey Room and there's a doctor's surgery below paying rent."

And, happily, our hero can now squeeze those legs under the table without undue discomfort. Mallory was actually born on the wrong side of the A35 at Monkton Wyld, though I refrain from taxing him on the point, and educated at the village school where Miss Head was his headmistress.

"She was a real terror! Like everyone else, I lived in fear of her. When I left school I joined the Royal Navy at the age of fifteen. Later I married Pauline, left the RN and joined the Fire Service."

As chairman of the Parish Council, what are his ambitions?

"My aim is to make sure Charmouth is heard at the highest possible level. If I had one wish it would be to make sure that local youngsters are not driven out of the village by property prices. It's a free society, I know, and I do not deny the right of people to buy freely but it's the law of unintended consequences. Unless something is done, we will become a village of geriatrics with great demands upon services for the aged. The existing regulations are as much value as a chocolate fireguard. At the moment a developer will acquire a site, submit a plan to build town houses that are of no value to the young people. If we object, he will appeal and then appeal again. It's Sod's law he will win in the end. Somehow we have to be able to create exception sites with the District Council to guarantee affordable housing – and then frame the law so that the houses cannot later be sold on at a profit. To put it simply, I cannot accept that it's morally right for someone from Croydon to have a house at the expense of a local."

On the subject of incomers to the village Pat Stapleton believes age is a critical factor.

"If they are over 70 and coming merely to retire they tend to keep themselves to themselves. However, if they are in their fifties or sixties, it's quite likely they will become involved in community activities."

Keith Grinter has his personal regrets. "Nearly all the people living between West Cliff and Five Acres are incomers. I can walk through and not know a soul. The old Charmouth is disappearing into the history books. On the other hand, of course, there are positive aspects. People do get about a lot more compared with the old days. It used to be said that almost every young man in the village would marry a girl from the village because there was simply no transport. If he did marry someone from outside, it was only because he had a horse!"

Pat also laments the loss of Dorset words and expressions.

"For instance, I love the word 'backalong' to signify anything that happened in the past but such words are fast disappearing. Education and TV are gradually killing off the old Dorset dialect and that's a shame."

On Evan's Cliff – The following week

This time the warning is unequivocal. Actually there are two notices, one clearly post-dates the other. The first reads: 'This landslide started in the winter of 2005-6 but has not finished.' The second reads: 'The landslide has won and the coast path is now closed.' Reluctantly I retrace my steps to the beach.

Even in mid-winter, on a fine day, family parties with small children clasping their buckets and old ladies exercising their dogs are everywhere. I realise immediately I am wearing the wrong footwear.

The experienced and sensible investigating the rock pools are in wellington boots. Everyone else is wearing stout shoes.

The tapping is insistent. Were I in woodland I'd assume a woodpecker was exploring an old tree for beetles. In fact, it's human activity. The man is moving systematically among the rocks and grey clay which has spilled down in the most recent landslip. I tread warily. It's slippery underfoot.

"As soon as there's a fresh fall the professionals are out – even at night with their torches, if need be. There'd be seven or eight in the locality. More than once the lifeboat has been needlessly sent to sea because the lights from their torches have been misinterpreted. But that isn't my scene. I'm not a fanatic. Besides, it can be a hazardous business – many a time I've tumbled over on my backside!"

Mike Jeffries from Mike's Minerals of Lyme resumes the tapping with his geological hammer.

"Actually it's been a passion of mine since I was a small boy. I find the whole study of fossils and evolution absolutely engrossing."

He points to the scene twenty yards away, his finger discreetly placed to his lips. A boy of about six is watching, with rapt concentration, as a man, presumably his father, taps earnestly upon a large black rock. Mike whispers.

"He'll never find anything in there." He smiles wryly. "You do need to know the sort of rock to investigate."

For an instant I'm tempted to relay Mike's advice but I dismiss the thought as quickly as it arrives. You don't embarrass dads in front of admiring sons. Has Mike ever found anything valuable?

"A few nice ammonites but nothing of great worth."

And the Ichthyosaurus that was found nearby a couple of years ago by Dr .Paul Davis and now resides in the Natural History Museum in South Kensington? Where exactly was it found? Mike shrugs his shoulders.

"Nobody's telling. No one does in these circumstances."

It's a reflection of my naivety that I am mildly shocked. I'd assumed the exact spot would be marked with a flag or something. I didn't realise the jealousies and commercial implications that existed. Anyway, surely that particular location was no more likely to reveal another similar find than any other?

"Who can tell?"

Mike gazes along the foreshore.

"You know, even if I find nothing, and that's common enough, I've still enjoyed myself. I love the solitude and the scenery."

The solitude – is Mike trying most politely to tell me something? But it is obviously time to leave him in peace. I hope he finds an Ichthyosaurus of his own one day. It couldn't happen to a more polite and patient fellow.

Charmouth Primary School – A couple of days later

"Yes, we do try to take advantage of our location whenever we can. If there's a valid reason we'll be on the beach. Of course, certain subjects do lend themselves more easily to shoreline activities."

The school is situated just a few yards from the foreshore. There's nothing comparable in the county. The contrast with many London inner-city schools, set in the midst of mean streets and tower-blocks with no tree or Cockney sparrow to be glimpsed, could be no greater. Chris Vincent, Headmaster of Charmouth School, is one of those individuals you immediately warm to. He also appears refreshingly free of the educational gobbledygook and cant I have grown to loathe in recent years.

"At the moment we have 193 on the roll and we employ 25 staff. Marshwood Primary covers the

Art lessons on the beach with headmaster, Chris Vincent, Charmouth Primary School. *Picture: Geoff Hill*

Vale. What would I hope for when pupils leave us? That they are all literate, numerate and possess practical skills in ICT but, above all, I would wish them to be good people. If we can build a firm foundation so they take full advantage of the opportunities for them in secondary education then we will have been successful."

And I know Chris is fond of one of Archbishop William Temple's dictums that sums up his teaching philosophy?

"Education should develop all those qualities that distinguish people from, on the one hand, the animal kingdom and, on the other, from machines."

Amen to that!

Charmouth Heritage Coast Centre
It's just a few paces from the school to one of Charmouth's prime assets. Founded in 1985 the Centre attracts large numbers of visitors throughout the year, including many enthusiastic school parties. To escape from the confines of a classroom is always a bonus, to be mucking about on a beach

fossil-hunting or rock-pooling, or just splashing your mates when the teacher isn't looking is joy unconfined. Open for much of the year there are film shows, inter-active displays, a museum area and a shop. Whenever I call by, there's always someone to answer questions. If it's not the Senior Warden herself, Meiral Thwaites, then it might be one of the two other wardens.

Newlands

I decide to make a call on by far the largest of the holiday accommodation sites in Charmouth. Newlands is run by Rex and Jackie Ireland and it's an impressive establishment with the most up-to-date facilities for all the family.

"We have 200 units with 80 statics, a number of pine lodges, apartments and rooms, together with the space for touring caravans and campers."

Jackie clearly takes great pride in Newlands being a family run business with that extra degree of personal involvement that follows.

"My husband Rex has been in the holiday business all his life. This summer our daughter Natalie will be organising fossil hunts, while our other daughter Michelle will be working with us in some capacity during her summer vacation. Our head gardener is also arranging bug hunts. Actually we're probably the biggest employer in the Charmouth area, aside from the school. We have 10-15 full-time staff, plus summer employment for students and we also make a point of using local craftsmen and cleaners so we feel we are contributing significantly to the local economy."

Cummins Farm

"The entrance to the farm is opposite the Fernhill Hotel."

I find a house positively swarming with children – a happy house full of happy children to judge by the laughter and chatter.

"They're not all mine, I assure you!"

Nicky Coleman laughs. She tells me she is a nurse facilitator. I am none the wiser.

"It means I teach nursing skills in institutions like nursing homes to those who are progressing towards NVQ qualifications. Since the Government brought in mandatory training schemes to raise the standard of patient care staff need to gain the appropriate qualifications. That's where I come in."

Nicky still nurses when required as well as bringing up a young family.

"I love my job but I do sometimes despair at what is happening in the NHS. Matrons have too little power and spend too much time at meetings."

I've actually come to talk farming with Nicky's partner Brian Lugg. As it happens I'd cheerfully talk longer with Nicky about the NHS but she's already half-way out the door and on her way to 'facilitate'. Brian's on his third slice of toast and marmalade and his second cup of tea. He was out early checking the stock and that is guaranteed to give any man an appetite.

"The family has farmed here since at least the 1830s. For a long time the family were the tenants of Lord Bridport. It wasn't until 1948 that my grandfather bought the land outright. I believe he paid a little over £2,000 for the 70 acres which works out at about £30 per acre. To tell you the truth, it was little better than hand-to-mouth, subsistence farming. When I took it on it was a mixed farm with a few caravans in one field. We asked for planning permission and, after a bit of a battle with the Council, we were granted a licence for thirty touring caravans. It's a different scene from the bigger caravan parks. The caravans are grouped around the perimeter of a five acre field with a designated recreational area in the middle for families and children. It's aimed at those who prefer an inexpensive, informal holiday set-up. The caravans are screened, we provide good on-site facilities and we get on famously today with the county officials who recognise we are providing a well-run facility. The reality is about half our income derives from the site and our two phone masts for Vodafone and Orange."

What about the farming side?

"We have 220 breeding ewes and I raise turkeys for the Christmas market. In recent years prices haven't been good for lambs. It's been a buyer's market, I'm afraid. I wish we had a strong regional co-operative which would act on our behalf in our dealings with the supermarkets. As it is, I spend about 80% of my time with the sheep but earn barely half my income from them. And, of course, Nicky's contribution is essential to our well-being. The farm economics don't really add up. It's something you'll find with most farming families. I also wish we could return to more traditional rotational methods of farming with less emphasis on fertilisers. The old farmers knew what they were doing."

As I bump up the track from Cummins Farm and prepare for my departure from Charmouth, I find myself reflecting on the splendid host of characters I have met in the village. One mischievous thought recurs. What a pity Charmouth doesn't have its own boat-building yard where the natives might construct a gig to compete against their friends 'over the big hill' in Lyme. With Keith Grinter as the coxswain of the Charmouth boat and Stan Williams occupying the same position in the Lyme boat, now that would be a spectacle in Lyme Bay worth travelling a long way to see.

The Marshwood Vale

'A somewhat sullen hollow, shunned by man.'
Sir Frederick Treves, *Highways & Byways in Dorset, 1906.*
'Cold, vapourish and miry.'
William Crowe.1745-1829 Rector of Stoke Abbott
'Hardly passable by travellers but in a dry summer.'
John Hutchins (1698-1773)

It's time then to leave the A35, where the traffic is fast and furious, and enter a different world – a world that is the Marshwood Vale.

Just days before my projected stay at Sue Johnson's converted barn at Cairdsmill Farm, Whitchurch Canonicorum, she warned me that access to the village was all but cut off by heavy rains and the flooding of one of the tributaries of the River Char. Now, at least the floods have receded, the water levels are returned to normal and the sun is actually shining from a clear blue sky. Even today the Marshwood Vale is scarcely known by many who have lived their entire lives in the county. Dorset born and bred they may be, they will freely acknowledge their ignorance of such evocatively named villages as Whitchurch Canonicorum, Wootton Fitzpaine and Fishpond Bottom. As for the tens of thousands who hurry along the A35 to or from Devon and Cornwall, the village names are just words on signposts.

And what of this traveller? To my shame, I am no less ignorant than so many of my fellows. As I turn left out of Morecombelake towards Ryall, I am journeying into the unknown. What, I wonder, shall I find?

The Five Bells Whitchurch Canonicorum – The same evening
"If ever the pub closed there'd be nothing left for us."

It's a common sentiment among the drinkers at the Five Bells this winter's evening. Friday is

Darts night, Five Bells, Whitchurch Canonicorum. Michael 'Millsy' Reeve (chief cheesemaker at Denhay) takes aim.
Picture: Geoff Hill

darts night and an opportunity for the regulars to relax at the end of a busy working week. Not that everyone seated at the bar lives in the village. Suzanne and Chris Miller have just travelled down from Oxford.

"We discovered the area a few years ago." They look relaxed and comfortable among old friends.

"It's lovely to escape from the pressures of modern life. It's like stepping back in time."

Brothers Richard and Tom Legg farm at nearby Berne Manor. Their father was born at neighbouring Ryall so their roots go deep in the locality. They agree with the assessment of Suzanne and Chris Miller.

"It is hard work and we certainly don't make much money but we both realise we are privileged to live here."

Paul White, a builder, grew up just down the road in Wootton Fitzpaine. He's also a bell-ringer at the 'Cathedral of the Vale', the nearby church of St. Candida and the Holy Cross.

"Sometimes, at the end of the day, we'll just stand chatting for twenty minutes or more – about nothing in particular. It's all part of the way of life here. The great thing is there's no rush and tear."

Paul Newberry's also from Wootton Fitzpaine. However, his motivation for living in the village is more earthy.

"It's my passion for this lovely village girl here."

Claire Richards laughs. The feeling is obviously mutual.

Among his country skills Michael 'Thistle' Smith is a part-time gamekeeper rearing pheasants and ducks.

"It's a community thing. We all contribute financially and organise the shoots. Everyone participates and we enjoy a good day out together."

Although it's Saturday tomorrow Michael 'Millsy' Reeve will not be having a lie-in. He's the chief cheese-maker at Denhay and proud of his position. 'Millsy' took over this important role from prize-winning Bill Parsons who retired a couple of years ago.

"It's a 4am start in the morning but I'm used to it. It's good to be a part of a successful company."

"Don't let him sell you a Flymo!"

It's a cry I hear several times. 'Millsy', it seems, has another string to his bow besides the cheese-making. He laughs good-naturedly at the banter. I tell him my mower is in good working order anyway.

Stacey Barrett is the daughter of Pat the landlady.

"When Dad died a few months ago everyone rallied round to help. The lovely thing about all these people here is that if I asked anyone for help they would do everything in their power to assist."

Dave Green is a relative newcomer. Heartbreakingly, after choosing the country life, Dave's wife died only a couple of years after their arrival.

"Why did I leave London? Have you been there recently?"

There's more teasing.

"Dave's one of those who's pushed the locals out."

Everyone laughs, including Dave.

Richard and Tom Legg are debating the rights and wrongs of the recent TV series featuring Hugh Fearnley-Whittingstall. Hugh's River Cottage was originally not far removed but he's not long crossed the Devon border into Axminster. He's not an unknown face at the Five Bells.

"Don't get me wrong. I'm all against factory-farming myself but we do get irritated by the 'celebrity bit'. It's not doing much for ordinary farmers, is it?"

Julie Eaton lives near the village hall.

"I've visited most of the big, glamorous cities around the world but it's always a joy to return to Whitchurch and my friends. I've come home."

The Five Bells – One morning later in the week

There's still some clearing up to be done in the bar but Pat Hawkins is pouring the coffee and we're seated at a table reflecting on the vagaries of life. Having the time to sit and chat is something that's been in short supply in Pat's life in recent months. It was, after all, only a few short weeks ago that her husband Laurence died suddenly leaving Pat to run the pub with the help of her daughter Tracey. As I have already discovered Pat is a much loved and respected figure in the village. It's not only that everyone recognises how hard she works. More importantly, she possesses the qualities of warmth and kindness which we all appreciate in any individual. It's hardly surprising then that Pat's loss inspired villagers to rally round and help at a moment of crisis.

"When my husband and I first drove down to Whitchurch to look at the pub it was a bright, sunny day and, as we came through the trees at Ryall, a scene opened up before us of the Marshwood Vale – the blue of the flax, the yellow of the rape and all the shades of green making up this wonderful patchwork quilt. To me, it's like reading *The Lion, The Witch and The Wardrobe*. You go into the wardrobe and, when you come out the other side, it's a magical kingdom. I said to Laurence, 'I feel I've come home' and he felt exactly the same."

It's not in any sense a grand pub, The Five Bells. The brewery hasn't spent thousands in making it into something that doesn't belong. It's a simple, unpretentious pub with inexpensive tables and chairs and fittings. But it's comfortable, a pub the locals can relate to. It's an integral part of a not especially affluent location. There may be some expensive properties about but a number of those are second homes. Most of the villagers have ordinary jobs. They're not high-flying executives with cash to burn.

"I could tell you which day of the week it was just by walking into the bar and looking at the customers. On Sundays there's a pool team tournament, Tuesdays we have the bell-ringers and pool practice, Wednesdays it's Supper Club night, Thursdays the Smith family come in – they're all friends and we have a new member since Katherine gave birth to Jessica only last week – and Fridays it's a dart's match. That's the one night we're always full in the winters. Obviously in the summer months we do get the visitors and people sitting out in the garden."

With many pubs across the country closing, it must be a struggle?

"We keep our heads above water – just. To make big profits a pub needs to sell lots of food. We don't. I charge just £7.50 on Supper Club nights. That's for a two course meal, a glass of wine and coffee. It's not a great money-spinner but it's a pleasant social occasion and a chance for everyone to have a good natter."

Are there problems with drunkenness?

"Drink and drive is taken very seriously here in the village. Fortunately most of our regulars are within walking distance. Binge drinking doesn't happen in village pubs. I believe that if cheap supermarket promotions were banned, it would go a long way towards solving the problem in the towns and cities."

Running a country pub like The Five Bells must make big demands?

"In the winter I estimate it's fifty plus hours a week with another ten for the paperwork. In the summer it would be nearer sixty, plus the paperwork, and another ten in the garden."

And the future – what does it hold?

"I'm looking forward to the Olympics in 2012. That should mean lots of visitors and extra campers."

It's time for me to leave and let Pat get on with her labours.

"You know, I love all my locals. They've been my backbone since Laurence died. They were here for me when he died and they've been kindness itself ever since."

Pat has recently acquired a new title 'The Duchess of Dreadnought' which she will hold for a year. She did try to explain the significance of the title on darts night but, in the hubbub of chatter and laughter, I lost the thread. It was something to do with her customers buying the right to the title for her at a charity night as a mark of their esteem. Does it matter that I don't quite understand the details? Not really. But it's no surprise that her loyal customers regard her with such affection. We give one another a hug as I leave. The lovely lady deserves a good year and many more besides.

Crabbs Bluntshay Farm, Broadoak

Before I began my exploration of the Marshwood Vale I was fortunate enough to chance upon Sylvia Creed's admirable *Dorset's Western Vale* (Dorset Publishing Co. 1987). This morning I am seated opposite the good lady herself in the kitchen of the 65 acres farm which Sylvia runs with her husband Malcolm Castle. If ever someone was equipped to write about the Vale it is the unassuming Sylvia. Born at nearby Peace Living Farm of farming parents, there were no fewer than seven branches of the family in the vicinity before the Great War. Her great grand-father actually bought Crabbs Bluntshay in 1914.

"Sadly, however, the Creeds in modern times have all been girls so the Creeds will soon die out in the Vale as a farming name."

Sylvia, after various adventures and journeying across several continents, returned to Dorset as a teacher, for some years at the Colfox in Bridport. Naturally, when Sylvia turned her inquisitive mind to the history of the Vale, education was one area she investigated with particular interest.

"It's hard to believe that the village school at Whitchurch had 140 pupils at the end of the nineteenth century, Numbers declined steadily until the school was closed in 1970."

Sylvia has witnessed many other changes – and some crises too – in her lifetime. In the past decade the foot and mouth hit the Vale hard causing acute financial loss and emotional anguish. The disgraceful returns to dairy farmers may be coming to an end but the improvement has come too late for many. The all too familiar absence of available housing is driving young people out of the locality. Sylvia regrets the disappearance of 'characters' and the local dialect. How does she view the coming years?

"I do fear for the future of the Vale. I fear particularly for the future of the small dairy farmer. When a small farm comes up for sale today more often than not the agent advertises in Sherborne – the thinking being that it is more likely to catch the eye of a wealthy prospective buyer there. The farm is then fragmented into saleable parts which are sold off to individuals who like the idea of a property in the country. Farm buildings too are sold off to be converted into holiday let properties. Given the passage of time such buildings will then receive planning permission to be expanded."

Even as I record Sylvia's words there are media reports of rapidly escalating land prices. Less than a couple of years ago the land was about £3,000 an acre. In some areas it has nearly doubled as city investors hedge their bets by buying land. Such a trend is going to make it even more difficult for the genuine farming community.

We stroll outside in Sylvia's orchard and garden.

"Some of our cider apple trees are probably 100 years old or more. Malcolm is the chief cider-maker. I keep a few geese and we have about 20 beef cattle. We let 30 acres as grass keep."

Sylvia's days are still full. She does a little teaching, is a Char Valley councillor and acts as a liaison officer for Ancient Monuments. She and Malcolm also offer holiday accommodation.So I take my leave, wish Sylvia all good fortune and set off to a very different farming enterprise.

Fivepenny Farm, Wootton Fitzpaine

The Tamworth sow, surrounded by her piglets, eyes me curiously and begins to chew hungrily at my shoe. I am dressed neither for ankle deep mud nor the attentions of inquisitive pigs. Thankfully the sow decides my shoe is insufficiently appetising and trots off across the quagmire followed by her family. Jyoti Fernandes laughs. It's all very well for her. She's suitably attired in thick jacket and stout boots.

"If you look over there you can see we have already planted four acres of fruit trees and half an acre of soft fruit. We're also carrying out small-scale woodland planting, hedge-laying, hedge planting and grassland management. One project is to convert the fields to wildflower meadows. We're also replanting woodland for its commercial and amenity value. Naturally we grow our own vegetables. In addition we have 3 breeding Tamworth sows, 100 Black-Rock free-range hens and 20 Jacob's ewes with their lambs. And, of course, everything is organic."

Jyoti might also add that she's the mother of 4 girls aged eleven, eight, six and four, and her husband David is a highly skilled woodworker making hand-made chairs and furniture. They share responsibility for running Fivepenny Farm with another couple and their 2 children.

How is it that a Louisiana born young woman, descended from Indian parents, should be farming in Wootton Fitzpaine?

"David and I were living in a bender in woodland near Glastonbury – a bender is a hazel structure with a tarpaulin draped over it. We were members of a 'tinker's bubble', a community of a dozen like-minded individuals. In such a community members construct their own dwellings, use no fossil fuels – just woodland timber in wood-burning stoves – employ only herbal medicines and earn a living from land-based activities. We wanted to find a piece of land where we could farm but, of course, a conventional farm would have been out of our financial reach so we went to the Triodos Bank in Bristol. This is an ethically based bank where the investors are more interested in financing ethically approved projects than simply money making for its own sake. We persuaded them that we had a good case so we bought this land – 43 acres in all spread over 7 fields."

And it was then, so I understand, that the problems began?

"When first we arrived we lived in a tent but it was obviously unsuitable for a family. So David built the shack with timber he'd already prepared in Somerset. And, yes, it did lead to a sustained battle with the local planning authorities. We didn't have planning permission for the shack and the enforcement officer from West Dorset District Council turned down our retrospective application and our appeal. It caused a lot of controversy in the local community. Many people supported us but there was also some hostility. Our opponents suspected we were simply New Age travellers setting up an illegal encampment and deliberately flouting planning rules. They didn't realise we are serious young people who want to farm this land responsibly and enjoy good relations with the wider community. We went to a higher court in Bristol which found in our favour and granted us permission to live here – four years temporary personal planning permission tied to a management plan for the land. We're currently in the third year and hope to be able to prove the viability of the farm and reapply for permanent permission."

There is no doubt in my mind that the court in Bristol made the correct decision in granting Jyoti and her partners permission to remain. All around me is the evidence of their absolute commitment to their project. On the other hand, I also understand the initial scepticism of planners and some locals. Clearly, it is not acceptable for 'travellers', be they New Age or any age, to occupy a site anywhere and defy regulations designed to protect the law-abiding majority. Equally, it should not be difficult, I suggest, for any intelligent planning officer to distinguish between the Jyotis of this world and the phoneys and the undesirables.

Assuming permission for permanent residence on the farm is granted what further plans are afoot?

"In fact, we're presently collaborating in an informal network with 46 other small producers. As you can see, we are building a barn – Nick Bloors from Lyme Regis is responsible for its construction – which will be the base for other like-minded producers to prepare meats, preserves, jams and chutneys and so on under one roof. We have existing outlets in Bridport market and several shops and are constantly looking for others. And over there you can see our 2 turbines – the smaller provides electricity for the house, the larger one for the store."

Jyoti passes me a publication headed *Low Impact Policies for Sustainable Development in Dorset* and a copy of *The Land*, a journal devoted to the theoretical ideas that lie behind small producers like her. Jyoti is a member of the editorial board of the publication. Browsing through its pages I recognise ideas drawn from a variety of radical and idealistic traditions of the last 200 years. But what actually impresses me most about Fivepenny Farm is that the vision of Jyoti and her colleagues is actually being put into practice with visibly successful results. What is crucial for the long-term success of this experiment is that the producers succeed in capturing a sufficiently large share of what is a niche market – no matter the general economic climate. They deserve to succeed.

Marshwood Primary School
"At present we have 58 children on our register of whom I would estimate at least 30 come from

farming stock."

The Head-teacher of Marshwood Primary, Rosemary Giles, looks up from her desk.

"For the most part their parents are not wealthy farmers. Rather they are small survivors who have negotiated all the recent difficulties in agriculture. Farming is still very much in the blood of these children. Many of them hope to follow their fathers on to the land when they leave school. You should see them in the summer playing with their tractors making silage."

Rosemary is justly proud of her village school. It recently won warm praise from the Ofsted inspectorate and, wherever I have travelled in the locality, Rosemary and her colleagues are spoken of with respect and affection.

"We are the second smallest primary in the county, the smallest being Powerstock and because of our location we actually draw children from the neighbouring counties of Devon and Somerset."

The school began life in 1842 and sits alongside St. Mary's church at the top of a windswept hill above the village on the road to Broadwindsor. The school enjoys an unusually close association with St. Mary's using the building as a classroom for a number of its lessons. As Paula Griffiths, Head of the Church of England's Cathedral and Church Building Division, commented, "St. Mary's, Marshwood, is a wonderful example of mutual co-operation. The school needed a hall, the church could provide it. The whole community has benefited from the link."

Though there is a strong Christian ethos in the school Rosemary and her colleagues believe it is very important in the contemporary world to acquaint their pupils with other faiths.

"We also seek to widen their horizons, to familiarise them with the world outside Marshwood, to raise their expectations. Every other year we take our children on a residential trip to London. We have also forged a close association with Uganda, in particular with a school in Mishenyi."

In truth, Rosemary, her staff, the children and their parents, all deserve the warmest praise because they raised no less than £2,000 to provide a new roof and other repairs to the school. As a member of the Association of Christian Teachers attending a conference in neighbouring Zambia,

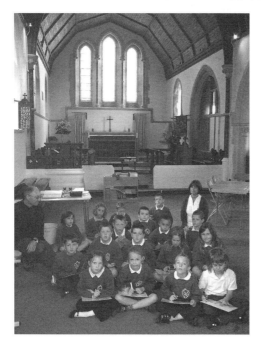

Marshwood Primary; what fine young scholars!
A lesson in St. Mary's. *Picture: Geoff Hill*

Rosemary was able to visit Mishenyi herself.

"I must confess I was reduced to tears when I saw how little the teachers and children had and we will, of course, continue our efforts to provide what we can for them. One of their teachers was able to come to Marshwood to thank everyone. I believe it was a wonderful lesson for the children."

Outside, the pupils of Marshwood are creating a wildlife garden and developing a wind turbine project. I suspect the latter will prove a great success for, on both occasions I call by, what feels like a Force Nine is blowing on this exposed hill. I ask Rosemary to sum up her feelings about her school.

"Though we may be a very small school, I believe we do have a very big heart."

As I leave I meet an old gentleman in the churchyard walking his dog. He lives just yards away down the lane. His name is Jack Bartlett and the dog's name is Jesse. Both Jack and Jesse are well known to the children.

"Marshwood is a wonderful school with lovely children and a fine staff. And, as for Rosie Giles, that lady has done so much good over the years!"

(Since the number of teachers at Marshwood is so small I shall mention all their names. They merit nothing less. Besides Rosemary Giles, there's Tracey Scott, Anna Cope and John Davis).

Pilsdon Manor

How to describe Pilsdon to those for whom the word signifies nothing?

It was in 1958 that the Revd. Percy Smith and his wife Gaynor purchased at auction Pilsdon Manor, its walled garden, an orchard, a large grassy courtyard, two farm cottages and an adjacent field for £5,000. Even in yesterday's money it sounds an absurdly low figure. Percy and Gaynor were two remarkable individuals, both deeply committed to their Christian principles and determined to help others and acquiring Pilsdon was but the first step to the fulfilment of a vision. Both were inspired by the example of a young man, Nicholas Ferrar, who in 1625 bought a manor house at Little Gidding in Huntingdonshire for £6,000. Nicholas wanted to live and work and worship in a small community and serve all who came to it. It was the first Anglican community after Henry VIII's dissolution of the monasteries. The reader may now deduce at least a part of the story of

Pilsdon Community. *Picture: Geoff Hill*

Pilsdon Manor 'There's always work to be done'. Revd. Jonathan Herbert (left), Tobias Jones (right), author of *Utopian Dreams. Picture: Geoff Hill*

Pilsdon since that momentous day in October, 1958, when the hammer fell at the auction at the George Hotel, Axminster. At this point I can do no better than quote directly the words of Gaynor Smith in her book *Pilsdon Morning*. She writes of those who, during the next twenty or so years, came to stay at the manor house.

'Most, but by no means all, of the 'guests' were weighed down by an almost insupportable burden. Men and women, boys and girls, they came with problems of every kind – some labelled as psychotic and some tarred with the brush of social disgrace; some haunted by guilt, real or imaginary, and all of them unsure of themselves and their place in life. Where else, and in what other circumstances, could men and women off the streets, from mental hospitals and prison cells, from schools and factories, universities and offices, teachers and tramps, bishops and knife-grinders, have all lived together?'

For those who may wish to follow the events from 1958 onward at Pilsdon, I do most warmly recommend Gaynor Smith's utterly absorbing and frequently moving account. Since Gaynor and Percy left there have been three other wardens, the Revd. Stuart Affleck, the Revd. Peter Barnett and the Revd. Jonathan Herbert.

My own Pilsdon Morning

Having lost my way, a not infrequent occurrence in the Marshwood Vale for most travellers, I arrive later than intended. I am greeted most warmly at the door by Jonathan who promptly places me in the care of Sheila. With a quick glance at her watch, Sheila decides we have just enough time for a quick tour of the farm buildings where I meet the three cows that supply all the milk for the manor, two donkeys named Peter and Paul, innumerable hens and the Pilsdon cat Jaimee. We have barely returned inside before it's time for lunch and Sheila escorts me to my seat in the big hall of the manor

A quiet refuge for residents, Pilsdon Church.
Picture: Geoff Hill

house. Already most of the twenty-five or so diners are taking their seats at the trestle tables. Lunch is preceded by a prayer and a personal greeting from Jonathan for myself and another visitor. The menu, most appropriately for such a dank, cheerless day, is good hot soup and excellent home-made crusty bread, followed by fresh fruit. The main meal of the day is eaten in the evening. Amongst my companions are two or three volunteers who have come in for the day to give a hand, together with a couple of paid staff. We are of all ages and I have no way of identifying staff from residents. Everyone seems to have a healthy appetite which is scarcely surprising since many have been engaged in some kind of physical work during the morning. The feeling is cordial and businesslike. An afternoon's labour lies ahead. Lunch is a break for re-victualling, not relaxation. Most people are chatting though two or three seem locked in their own worlds. Jonathan stands to say a few words about the afternoon's arrangements. He's taking a party out log-sawing. Jonathan, I discover, works as hard, if not harder, than anyone. It's something I quickly realise about Pilsdon. Everyone contributes. It's expected. It's a part of the deal. You may be at Pilsdon for just a day, a week, months, years even, but each person plays his or her role in the life of a busy community. It's a part of the therapy, if therapy is the right word – binding a very disparate group of individuals into a family with a sense of common purpose. After lunch Sheila introduces me to some of her friends and I arrange with Jonathan to call again another day. As I drive away I am strangely moved. Though I have been at Pilsdon barely three hours, I feel I have experienced something of the unique quality that exists in this unlikely and remote corner of the Dorset countryside.

In mid-summer, I return to Pilsdon where I am made welcome by the lovely Lis Leigh and meet the young writer, Tobias Jones, author of the highly acclaimed study of similar communities entitled *Utopian Dreams*, a book that receives the ultimate accolade of a serialisation on BBC radio. I will quote just a few lines from the book that reflects Tobias's own experience of living for a time at Pilsdon.

'We felt amazingly happy here because it was never pious or impious; it was just a bunch of people surviving together. One chap who lived here years ago and still comes back regularly, said he had never felt so at home anywhere else. And that, after only a month, was what it felt like to us.'

Later in the year, in his Christmas Newsletter, Jonathan describes the celebrations on October 19 marking Pilsdon's fiftieth birthday. Three hundred guests were in attendance, including Gaynor Smith who read from *'Little Gidding'*, while the band Thinker and pianist John Hall provided musical entertainment. Jonathan also reported on the progress of the appeal to raise funds for the building of extra accommodation. 'The figure of £980,000 has now been reached which includes a grant from the Government as part of its Places of Change programme aimed at getting rough sleepers off the streets and back into work.' Jonathan also writes that the former Shell Oil executive, Charles Handy, has offered advice on how Pilsdon might augment its income and reduce its 'carbon footprint'.

In concluding this piece I ask Jonathan about his thoughts for the future of the Pilsdon community. 'I'm convinced more than ever that there is a great need for places like Pilsdon. Places of radical hospitality and real inclusion in a fragmenting and often alienating world. In itself Pilsdon is a small thing, but it represents something much bigger. Our struggle to live out the values of God's kingdom on our small patch of land, day in and day out, inevitably attracts and inspires others to do the same, if not here then in their daily lives.'

The Denhay Farms, Broadoak

'Marooned three years agone and lived on goats since then, and berries, and oysters. Wherever a man is, says I, a man can do for himself. But, mate, my heart is sore for Christian diet. You mightn't happen to have a piece of cheese about you, now? No? Well, many's the long night I've dreamed of cheese – toasted, mostly – and woke up again, and here I were.'

So Ben Gunn addressed Jim Hawkins after three years marooned on Robert Louis Stevenson's *Treasure Island*.

Somehow, after saying my goodbyes at Pilsdon Manor and, with Jonathan's precise instructions ringing in my ears, I contrive to locate George Streatfeild, Managing Director of Denhay, in his office at the end of a farm track in the middle of nowhere, having negotiated a series of disconcertingly narrow, twisting lanes that I feared were never coming to an end. Next door the company secretary is at her computer and, in an adjoining office, George's wife Amanda is also sitting in front of a screen.

"Everyone knew him as The Commander. He came here in 1952 after being invalided out of the Royal Navy. At that time Denhay comprised 2 mixed farms employing just 4 men. Today we have 4 farms with 1,000 Friesian Holstein dairy cows in 5 herds. Actually it was in 1959 that my father began cheese-making."

Beside my chair is a cabinet displaying an impressive array of certificates bearing the details of innumerable awards won by Denhay in recent years. Last year the company produced no less than 720 tons of traditional Farmhouse Cheddar. Denhay has clearly travelled a long way in the past 50 years from such modest beginnings in the middle of the Marshwood Vale. It's a success story that reflects huge credit upon the whole Denhay team, not least director Simon Hill who plays an invaluable role alongside George and Amanda. When 'The Commander' died in 1977 George, armed with a degree in agriculture and management experience garnered elsewhere, was prepared for the challenge though it is doubtful if even he would have dared to imagine the scale of Denhay's commercial growth in recent times. I mention that I made the acquaintance of 'Millsy' in The Five Bells a few nights earlier.

"Millsy's a character," George smiles wryly. "And he's a first-rate cheese-maker."

'Is there anything in the west of the county?' 'The Master of Denhay' – George Streatfeild. *Picture: Geoff Hill*

But it's not only cheese for which Denhay is justly acclaimed. There's also the dry cured bacon and the air dried ham, all sourced from British outdoor pigs which enjoy, George assures me, the highest standards of animal welfare with a diet free of antibiotics and growth promoters.

That very day a leading daily newspaper has, in the light of the widespread pollution by plastics of even distant oceans, initiated a campaign to reduce the amount of plastic packaging. What is George's response?

"I absolutely agree in principle and we do try to keep packaging to a minimum, but it's essential that we employ the most hygienic, safe method of transferring our products from the farms to the consumer. I believe it's up to the scientists to come up with a viable, recyclable alternative."

It's the answer I might have expected – logical, concise and irrefutable. What of the relationship between Denhay and the supermarkets? After all, it's a highly contentious issue for many in the farming industry, though Denhay has managed to build up highly successful contracts with not only Waitrose and M&S, but other giants of the High Street. "No problem," says George with another smile that almost certainly cloaks some interesting bargaining over the years. And what plans are there for the future?

"We hope to go on being successful. Currently our exports represent 15% of our output but there's always scope for growth here and abroad."

As I prepare to leave, I ask George about the relative isolation in which he lives at Broadoak. Does he ever feel cut off from the mainstream of life?

"There's nothing in the east of the county, is there?"

What about all those motorists speeding past on the A35 who know nothing of the Vale?

"Good! Let them continue to speed past."

I haven't counted the number of wry smiles that afternoon on George's face but there's another as I leave.

P.S Denhay would be Ben Gunn's idea of paradise on earth – but he'd need a good compass to find it!

Dunster Farm Broadoak – Another morning

"I did once take eight for twenty – those were my best ever figures."

John Hutchins still likes to turn his arm over on a summer's afternoon even if his glory days as a club cricketer are but a fond memory. Once he donned whites for Bridport, now it's Melplash CC. As a man who often puts in a 70 or 80 hour week I reckon John deserves his few hours of recreation. We're in the farm drive looking on as his son Adrian and young trainee, Chris Dare, clear out a ditch with a digger and replace an old drainage pipe. There's definitely something therapeutic about watching other people at work.

"Grandfather became a tenant here back in 1930. My father Henry, or 'Harry' as everyone knew him, bought the farm outright in 1967. It was the finest day's work he ever did."

When John assumed the mantle of responsibility the farm covered 72 acres, now it's 150 acres with a dairy herd of 120 cows and 300 beef cattle. John's milk finishes up on Tesco's London shelves. I ask him how he'd kept going when milk returns were less than the cost of production?

"We simply couldn't have carried on if we'd been paying rent. And we were working all the hours God sends, certainly an hourly rate below the minimum wage. And, of course, my wife Linda was doing a brilliant job with the b & b which was an absolute life-saver for us."

With the surrounding hills of Pilsdon Pen and Lewesdon in the distance, it's a splendid location in which to live and bring up a family. However, it's not difficult to imagine the frustration and quiet rage of men like John and Adrian and their fellow farmers when the returns on their labour were so poor. Fortunately, the corner may just have been turned.

"Because so many have got out of milk the price for a litre has risen in the past couple of years from seventeen pence to twenty-seven pence. With demand rising and supply falling, the supermarkets are guaranteeing their future production by paying us more. Beef has also picked up so we feel more optimistic than for some years."

Across the road is one of the Denhay farms. John's daughter Caroline is married to Alan House, one of the Denhay team. I mention that I visited the prize-winning cheese-maker just a few days before.

"George (Streatfeild) is a fine fellow. He does a lot for the local community."

It's a warm tribute to a fellow farmer and clearly sincerely felt. John's neighbour until recently was Hugh Fearnley-Whittingstall.

"A lot of Linda's b & b came down to attend his cooking classes."

I walk down the drive lined by daffodils and narcissi to the white-washed, thatched farmhouse. Soon the cows will be out again enjoying the first spring grass and the swallows will be returning to the barns from South Africa.

"We've got a decent swallow population but, do you know, I didn't hear a single cuckoo last summer."

John is but the latest to report the same depressing statistic. What is an English spring without a cuckoo to herald its arrival? And what will the letter writers to *The Times* do if the cuckoos cease to come? I wish John a good farming year and some respectable bowling returns. Melplash CC expects!

The Church of St. Candida and the Holy Cross, Whitchurch Canonicorum

After the hoar frost of early morning the day is becoming England at its most benign, wintry best, with a cloudless sky and sufficient warmth in the sun to remind us that spring is not too far distant.

"That's Georgi Markov's final resting-place."

We're standing in the churchyard gazing at the inscription on the headstone. Don Newman and his wife Judith live just up the road at Peal House. Don is our invaluable guide for the day.

Left: The church of St. Candida and the Holy Cross, Whitchurch Canonicorum. *Picture: Geoff Hill*
Above: 'The Grand Inquisitor', Sir Robin Day's last resting place. *Picture: Geoff Hill*

'In Memory of Georgi Ivanov Markov, novelist and playwright. Most dearly loved by his wife Annabel and daughter Sasha, his family and friends. Born Sofia 1.3.1929. Died London 11.9.1978. In the Cause of Freedom.'

Was it really thirty years ago we first heard Markov's name? Read the details of his mysterious death in the newspapers? Several months elapsed before the story unfolded in its grisly detail. It became known as 'The Umbrella Murder'. It was a story that appeared to leap from the pages of an Ian Fleming or John Le Carre spy novel. What did happen on that fateful September day on Waterloo Bridge? First of all, we must remember that this was the era still of the Cold War when vile Communist dictatorships still exercised their tyrannical grip on most of the countries of Eastern Europe. Markov was in exile from his native Bulgaria, a vocal critic who made regular broadcasts to his fellow countrymen on the BBC World Service and on Radio Free Europe. The KGB wanted him dead and one of their agents using a high powered pellet gun shot him at close range in the thigh. The pellet, it later transpired, contained the deadly poison ricin. Markov believed initially he had been merely poked in the leg by an umbrella. He died three days later in hospital aged just 49 – his assailant was never traced. But why is Markov buried here in Whitchurch Canonicorum? The answer is very simple. His wife Annabel, who also worked for BBC World Service, came from the village and her mother still lives in the vicinity. Don Newman tells me that every year there's a steady stream of Bulgarian visitors making the pilgrimage here to honour a brave man dedicated to the cause of freedom and democracy.

There is another name just yards away in the churchyard that we recognise. The inscription is simple – *The Grand Inquisitor* – Sir Robin Day, who politely but clinically dissected politicians for so many years, also rests here. Sir Robin's widow lives in the locality.

One of the finest views in the county. *Picture: Geoff Hill*

We clamber into Don's Landrover Freelander, an eminently practical vehicle for the Vale's often muddy, watery lanes and set off on our guided tour – first to Coney's Castle, the vast earthworks which rises to 800 feet.

"This spot is much favoured by all who love bluebells. They are absolutely stunning in springtime."

Beneath us the ground falls away dramatically to Fishpond Bottom and a tributary of the Char. It's where we are bound next. Don points the building out to us.

"It's known locally as Three Gipsies End. It seems three gipsies took shelter in the lee of the building which was then a chapel on a night of extreme cold. They were subsequently found dead from exposure. I am told by his grandson Alan Knight that Charles Knight, who was then the village tailor and Parish Clerk, was summoned to confirm their deaths."

We move on to another ancient earthworks, Lambert's Castle, which lies on the edge of the B3165, from which we gaze across to Hardown Hill, Golden Cap and Stonebarrow. We are blessed by a day of perfect visibility. Is there a more glorious view in the entire county, we ask ourselves? And so on to Pilsdon Pen, at 909 feet believed by some to be the highest point in Dorset. Others argue for Bullbarrow. Even Lewesdon has its supporters. But what are a few feet one way or the other between friends, I ask, especially on such a day? Alas, we have exhausted our time. Don has done us proud. It's a fitting conclusion to my travels in the Vale.

I began my days in Marshwood with blank pages. I find it extraordinary that I leave with so much written. There have been moments, I confess, when I have experienced a feeling akin to claustrophobia. The narrow lanes, the high hedges, the miles when I have seen not a soul – each in its turn has contributed to this uneasy sensation. Living in the east of the county, I am not used to the nature of the countryside that is characteristic of the Vale. And, though the sun has shone, I have also known many days of rain and gloom which seem to compound the sense of secretiveness and isolation pervading parts of the Vale. But when the clouds break and the sun appears, the Vale becomes a place of rare beauty. Before the invention of the internal combustion engine, before the days of electricity, wireless and television, I suspect I would have shared the sentiments expressed by Treves and Crowe and Hutchins with which I began this chapter. Happily, we live in the twenty-first century, the world has changed and the motor car has revolutionised travel and I have found a wealth of material of interest to me in the Vale. I have experienced an extraordinary range and intensity of emotions in this one small location. I have also met innumerable splendid individuals and, once more, I have been the grateful recipient of unfailing kindness and support. I leave the Marshwood Vale a richer man than I entered.

Morcombelake & Chideock

Leaving the Marshwood Vale as I entered, through Ryall and back on to the A35, I have travelled but a mile or two before I am pausing briefly where tens of thousands have stopped ever since the motor car and the coach began to bring holiday-makers to its doors. The Moores family have baked in the vicinity for 150 years and the bake-house on the old turnpike Exeter-London road at Morcombelake was acquired in 1879. Through various vicissitudes, including the two World Wars, the business survived but its turning point came in 1967 when it was sold to Keith and Gill Moores who subsequently opened a shop to cater for the increasing number of visitors. Gill, by the way, is a very gifted painter. Eager to buy authentic West Country gifts for their family and friends, this passing trade focused particularly on the curiously named Dorset 'knobs' which were originally 'dunked' in tea by local farm-workers. In recent years the knobs have been supplemented by a range of sweet biscuits and cakes. Calling by at the shop I discover the actual production has been transferred to Bridport.

Moores' Bakery, St. Andrew's Road, Bridport – Another day
"If we were going to increase production space, we had no choice but to move here. Unfortunately, at Morcombelake, we had a split-level working area which created all sorts of problems."

The most appropriately named Joanne Cake is the Technical Manager of the unit where the production of Moore's celebrated 'knobs' and biscuits is continued.

"Keith and Gill have retired and their step-son, David Winship, now runs the business so the family tradition is maintained. And no, the recipe for the 'knobs' has scarcely changed except that we do use vegetable oils rather than butter. Fortunately the shop remains as popular as ever and everything looks set fair for the future."

I understand a gentleman named Nigel Collins plans, as a part of the Frome Valley Food Festival at Cattistock, a brand new event 'Dorset knob throwing'. Could it become an Olympic event? Would Moores be able to keep pace with demand?

At Chideock I call by on John McMorrow who acquaints me with the backcloth to the village's major headache – the volume of traffic passing through.

"There were, at one time, moves to build a by-pass. The land was actually compulsorily purchased but later sold back. The issue did split the village in a regrettable way. Unfortunately the proposal didn't find favour with the residents of North Chideock for reasons I entirely understand. Now it simply isn't discussed. It's not on the agenda. So we have to make the best of the existing situation."

It is a genuine dilemma. While the speed of the traffic may be restricted, the emissions from the engines are scarcely welcome. If the traffic actually comes to a standstill, the problems are exacerbated. While many in Chideock do rely for their incomes on the holiday trade, the village enjoys a distinctly ambivalent relationship with the motor-car. Down the road at Seatown, it's a similar story. At the wonderfully located Anchor Inn its very success has created acute traffic difficulties at peak times. Palmer's Brewery quite understandably wishes to capitalise upon the inn's popularity by extending the premises. On the other hand, Chideock Parish Council, the owners of the beach the Wraxall family, and Charles Wild, the District Councillor, all have grave reservations about the desirability of Palmer's plans. I am relieved I do not have to adjudicate.

Eype

Downe House Farm
"That's the original farmhouse where he lived."

Dean Exton points to the substantial property lying a hundred yards or so inland from Downe House Farm.

For the moment I forget the primary purpose of my call. Little did I suspect negotiating the narrow twisting lane down to the farm that one of England's finest twentieth-century playwrights and screen-writers had once lived nearby. It was as a student in London that I first saw R C Sherriff's deeply moving play of life in the trenches of the Western Front. Yet the script for *Journey's End* was initially rejected for being too depressing for a generation grown weary of war – he submitted the play in 1929. It also lacked a leading lady, a serious deficiency in the judgement of West End producers. Only after innumerable difficulties and setbacks did the play finally open – to rave reviews from the sternest of critics. It has seldom been out of production somewhere in the UK ever since. Reading Sherriff's ironically titled autobiography *No Leading Lady* I was intrigued to discover that the role of the central character Stanhope was originally played for two trial performances by a then unknown 21 year-old – his name was Laurence Olivier!And here it was then in Eype that Sherriff subsequently enjoyed many happy years, a far cry from his life in the trenches of the Western Front.

But to return to Dean and life at Downe House Farm, what were the circumstances of his arrival?

"I first saw an ad in the *Farmer's Weekly*. It was for a 140 acres dairy farm that had lain empty for twelve months. There were 110 applicants but, after attending various interviews and presenting a farm plan, I was offered the tenancy. We farm the long, narrow strip between the A35 and Golden Cap. Since I arrived the farm has expanded to 500 acres. It's National Trust property and this farm was the beginning of their Enterprise Neptune project when the Trust began buying up coastal land. In fact, the Trust has now acquired nearly all the land they wanted here except for one small pocket. The total holding now runs to 2,400 acres. When I arrived I brought with me 450 ewes and a dozen beef cows from Wales. But, as time went on, I decided to go organic. The Soil Association carried out the necessary inspections and we've been fully organic now for eight years. The livestock goes to an organic abattoir in Devon, a retired butcher quarters the carcasses and then the meat's hung for three weeks. We sell our meat through the farm shop and the West Dorset County Market at Bridport and also supply the Golden Cap Caravan Park and Martin Cox at Highland's End. I do, of course, also sell some of the stock on to other farmers."

Inside the bungalow it's the turn of former Special Needs assistant Nikki to explain her role. Like so many farmers' wives she's clearly possessed of considerable reserves of energy and initiative.

"Our farm shop is open 6 days a week and we've built up an incredibly loyal clientele. In addition, from March to October, we open a garden cafe providing cream teas and refreshments. A surprising number of walkers do find their way to us. At the busiest times we'll have a couple of hundred customers a day. The cafe gives us a cash flow when the income from the livestock is more irregular. Happily, we've built up a wonderful staff of girls, some still at school and others back from university."

Are there any particular problems being a NT tenant in such a location? Dean shakes his head.

"Not really. The Trust is responsible for the coastal paths and stiles but with public access we do have to be especially vigilant with the livestock. Cows are generally peaceable but, if approached when they are with new-born calves, they're understandably protective. Walkers must behave sensibly."

Nikki recalls an anxious lady bringing a lamb to her door. "She'd carried it in her arms for some distance thinking the mother had deserted it. I explained that it was most unlikely and it would have been better if she had left it where it was. Dean had the job of finding the ewe and re-uniting it with the lamb. We often get reports of cows being in terrible pain and making the most awful noises when they are simply giving birth."

Dean smiles ruefully.

"One member of the public assured us she'd seen a cow with her insides falling out. In fact it was just the afterbirth. Obviously I am constantly monitoring the livestock but we do get the occasional death and you can be absolutely sure it will happen in the most conspicuous public place."

Nikki is clearly well practised in the art of diplomacy.

"When the public report things to us we always say 'Thank you very much' because we know they mean well, but you do get the occasional individual who can be very rude and aggressive"

Something's that often puzzled me on coastal paths is the extraordinary proximity of animal dung to cliff edges. Dean offers me an explanation.

"What happens is that in warm weather the up-draught keeps the flies away so the livestock like to take advantage and get as close as possible to the edge of a cliff. We won't fence because it's not NT policy for insurance reasons. It then only takes one animal to nudge another for it to go over. It's clearly distressing but it's one of those unfortunate accidents."

Are there problems with predators?

"We've had a fox eating a ewe's udder just as she was giving birth and other similar incidents and ravens can and do attack vulnerable livestock. But our general philosophy is if the foxes and the ravens leave us alone, we're happy to live side by side with them."

Back out in the yard, as Dean prepares to go round the farm, I meet two of the most endearing, bright-eyed dogs I have ever encountered.

"This is Dougie and the other's Tess. Dougie's so sharp he constantly anticipates me. He'll be waiting for me in the next field even before I've left the one I'm in."

Dean points out Thorncombe Beacon with its views to Chesil in the east. It is the most glorious location though I suspect Downe House Farm must sometimes be seriously buffeted by gales tearing up the Channel. I notice there's a good clump of gorse cover on the Beacon where one peckish scribbler could take shelter from the south-westerly, enjoy the scenery and eat his beef sandwiches.I might even spare a thought or two for all the poor wretches stuck behind their desks or haring up and down the motorways. I set out at a pace to Thorncombe Beacon.

(Robert Cedric Sherriff, 1896-1975, generously gave 176 acres, including the 508 feet Thorncombe beacon, to the National Trust in 1966)

Paul Atterbury: *Picture Chrissie Atterbury*

Whin Bridge

"The striped jackets? It all happened by accident really. But people seemed to like them and it all went on from there. Now if I don't wear one people actually complain – it's expected of me!"

And does he pay large sums to bespoke tailors in Savile Row for them? Paul Atterbury, BBC's Antiques Roadshow's ceramics and pottery expert, laughs.

"Generally I find them in charity shops. I've got eleven in the wardrobe at the moment."

Chrissie, Paul's second wife, arrives bearing a tray of coffee cups and sets them on the table before us in the garden of what was known for many years as Railway Cottage. It's an idyllic spot and wonderfully eccentric in a very English way.

"The original GWR railway carriage made in 1903 was brought here in 1921. I actually saw it some years before it became available. I bought the place in 1987 with its three quarters of an acre of land. The memorabilia you see around you, like the signal at the bottom of the garden, I've picked up over the years. Actually, it was initially a weekend retreat for myself and my daughters, Zoe and Polly. The facilities were very primitive. I think my children were possibly the last not to have a lavatory in the county. When I met Chrissie she was adamant, quite understandably, that she wasn't going to live in an ancient railway carriage. So we've had the extensions built on."

Chrissie shows me round the garden which terminates in a magnificent wilderness of wild flowers and trees. She's a local girl (maiden name Aldous), I discover. Chrissie has, like Paul, two children by her previous marriage, Laura and Anne.

"The Portland – Weymouth area. My grandfather tended the gardens at Fortuneswell and I organised classes in the prison for a while."

Though Paul leads a hectic life – he broadcasts, lectures and writes extensively – he's also thoroughly embedded in the life of the local community. As chairman of the Eype Arts Trust he explains the dilemma that faced the village.

"As with so many small country churches, St. Peter's had reached a crisis point. Built in1863 for a congregation of 200 it was getting barely a dozen worshippers. Where we were to go? It was either the redundancy route or conversion. The vicar persuaded a local charity, the Wallbridge Trust, to let us have £200,000 on condition it was put to local use. As a result we were able to install modern facilities in the building but it remains a place of worship. Chrissie and I actually had our marriage blessed there. As a community we wanted to create a large space for festivals and musical events. The church has fine acoustics so we removed the pews but the pulpit stayed. Historically the nave has been a public place. Today the Eype Arts Trust pays a rent to use the building. It's a blueprint. Any community can do the same. We are maintaining the church as a focal point of village life and it is justifying its existence with great success. So, although we have a tiny population, with our Director Mark Culme-Seymour at the helm, we are able to provide an amenity for a wider Dorset public."

What has happened here in Eype accords perfectly with the views of Sir Roy Strong, the former Director of the National Portrait Gallery and the V&A, who argues in his book *The English Country Church* that people 'must use them (our churches) or lose them'. Sir Roy reminds us that historically the functions of the country churches extended far beyond Sundays, that they were at the hub of village life and some even possessed their own breweries to raise money for their maintenance.

Paul leads a hectic life. Best known, of course, are his regular TV Roadshow appearances.

"Michael Aspel was quite the nicest man imaginable to work with – absolutely without ego. We were all very sorry to see him go."

Paul is also a prolific writer. He has recently written a series of sumptuously produced railway books. Having bought one myself, I can warmly recommend them.

"I am especially fascinated by the social history of railways."

In addition, he is passionately interested in the Battle of the Somme in which he lost a great uncle.

"I walk the battlefield every year, most recently the German front line in July, 1916."

We talk of craftsmanship in the modern age.

"It's still very much alive. I have no concerns on that score. Styles change but there are many superb craftsmen."

I spend two hours in the company of Paul and Chrissie. It's been a brilliant morning. Paul remarked that Michael Aspel was a man 'quite without ego'. Were I to express similar sentiments of Paul I know they would be echoed by his friends and neighbours in Eype and, no doubt, on The Roadshow. It is refreshing to find a man as talented, as unassuming and as affectionately regarded.

The New Inn

Chris Deacon from the West Bay Tavern and Vicki Morency from Durbeyfield House have just tramped over from West Bay. I cannot resist asking them the 'burning question' of the day. What do they think of Quay West?

"We actually quite like it as a building but whether it's right for West Bay is something else."

Behind the bar I meet Donal Falvey and his partner Jackie Gough. I know Donal, Jackie and their chef Kelly Stoodley have created an excellent impression since their recent arrival in the village. "When we came it was a blank canvas. Now we feel we're gaining acceptance in the community. We're looking forward to the next raft race in Bridport which is raising funds for the RNLI. It's a cause dear to Jackie's heart because her Cornish uncle is a life-boatman."

Bridport
Twinned with St Vaast-La-Hougue (France)

'Why Bridport is the new St. Ives.'
David Dawson. *News From Bridport – In And Around West Dorset.* 2008.
'Is Bridport Notting Hill-on-Sea?' *The Dorset County Magazine* 2007
'Bridport is a wholesome, homely, county town with an air of substantial simplicity. It has no more pretence or assurance than has an honest yeoman's wife in homespun.'
Sir Frederick Treves, *Highways & Byways in Dorset,* 1906

Mountfield, The Council Chamber
"Bridport – Notting Hill-on-Sea? That's just plain silly!"

Geoffrey Ackerman, Mayor of Bridport for five separate terms of office, is one of those transparently decent, no nonsense, warm-hearted individuals who are the very backbone of rural English local government. A Bridport man through and through, the former engineer speaks with a gentle Dorset lilt and describes Bridport as 'a brilliant town where there is always so much to do'.

"Not for one moment did it cross my mind when I decided ten years ago to stand for the council that I might one day be Mayor. But there, it's happened, and I'm very proud of the honour bestowed upon me. Charles Wild was appointed the leader of the Town Council and he co-ordinates the work of the local committees. I'm more of a ceremonial figure representing the town at various events through the year. Although there are party divisions – there is a large Lib-Dem majority-we do actually get on very well together."

Of course, sharing a common foe unites even the most disparate of interests and there is little doubt the West Dorset District Council , based at Stratton House, Dorchester, is not regarded with any great affection by many on Bridport's Town Council. I decide I may as well take the bull by the horns and raise the subject of the latest development at West Bay.

For one dreadful moment I fear the mild-mannered Geoffrey may be about to explode.

"Quay West is absolutely horrible! It's totally out of character with the town. It's something I feel very strongly about. The developer got his way and the feelings of the Town Council were completely disregarded."

However, Geoffrey does recognise there have been instances when Bridport, working on its own, would have been unable to finance important projects.

"That's true. I must give credit where credit is due. Without outside funding we would never have been able to carry through the coastal-defences scheme. Previously boats entering had to negotiate a very narrow space between the two piers. Now we've got the Jurassic Pier. There do remain problems relating to the sand and silting and it looks as if the jetty we'd hoped for is not going to happen. It would have been far better if that had been built earlier but now the cost has risen. What exasperates a lot of folk is that we don't have the income we might have had if we'd been able to keep control of the car-parks. West Dorset District Council pockets that revenue. And, in more general terms, it was in my opinion a very bad day when Poole and Bournemouth became autonomous at the time of reorganisation. They've got an awful lot of chimneys and the rest of Dorset has suffered as a consequence ever since."

Geoffrey sits back in his chair and reflects.

"If I were summing it up, I would say that Bridport is a wonderful town to live in but we are not wholly in charge of our own destiny and that's very frustrating."

Bridport Mayor Geoff Ackerman with other civic leaders at Civic Night held in Bridport Art Centre.
Picture: John Guard Dorset Echo

Descending the stairs I decide that Geoffrey would have cheerfully fitted into the Bridport of 1906 – or any age. Quite without pretensions he is a man of whom Sir Frederick Treves would have thoroughly approved – so much for Notting Hill- on-Sea and St .Ives! And yet?

The Greenyard Cafe, East Street

"When I first arrived in Bridport as a small child in 1952 the only organisations of any consequence – for young people at least- were the Brownies, the Scouts and the Young Farmers. Life was generally very staid and ordinary – and not only for those who were young. Now I see one of the county magazines suggests Bridport is being spoken of as Notting Hill-on- Sea. Make of that what you will."

This time my companion has raised the subject first but Sandra Brown, long-time resident, at different times a county, district and town councillor and former Mayor prefers to look beyond the superficial image to the fundamental realities of Bridport and its citizens.

"It's quite true that in the past few years the town has become a centre of artistic activity – and that is exciting – but I fear there also exist serious underlying problems, not dissimilar to other areas of the county. Our current population is between 7-8,000 and an increasingly ageing one. People have retired here, they're living longer and there is a growing demand for age-related care provision. As a councillor I am increasingly confronted by quite invidious decisions such as – do we support the closing down of certain day centres, which often provide invaluable services, simply because we lack the finance to support them? We are the second lowest funded county in the country. Central Government seems to imagine Dorset is much richer than really it is. Yet there is real social deprivation in some localities but we cannot raise council tax to support necessary services. Apart from the sheer unpopularity of such a policy we would immediately be capped. Our hands are tied. It's very unsatisfactory and frustrating."

Even as we are sitting at our table a lady, overhearing our conversation, leans across. Her name, she tells me, is Joan Hart from Berkeley Terrace and she is in her eighties.

"The lovely thing about Bridport is that it's got everything I actually need. I can do all my shopping here and there's somewhere for me to go every day of the week. This afternoon it's the WI."

The significance of Joan's final observation is considerable. For the elderly, especially those living on their own, loneliness can be a dreadful companion but having meaningful activities near at hand is a priceless asset. Joan's life is thankfully full and satisfying. However, when Sandra speaks of invaluable day centres being shut down through cash shortages the dangers are obvious. Almost inevitably the most vulnerable are likely to be the hardest hit. Carers will lose precious respite time from their daily responsibilities. Surely when cash is scarce the most vulnerable of our citizens should receive first priority.

Of other matters, I ask Sandra more about the town and its people.

"It's such a shame you weren't able to meet two wonderful characters, both of whom passed away in the last couple of years. Both were absolute legends. One was Bernard Gale, or 'Bern' as he was always known, of the Lyric School of Dance. The other was Rex Trevett, otherwise known as 'Mr. Music'. There's a figure of him in stone with his saxophone by Karl Dixon in the Town Hall. Both 'Bern' and Rex were much loved characters who added so much joy and happiness to the Bridport community."

It gives me great pleasure, Sandra, to honour their names in these pages.

The Offices of the 'Bridport & Lyme Regis News'

Upstairs Chris Carson, Chief Reporter, is ploughing a lonely furrow, if such imagery is appropriate for a man at his computer. Helen Dommett, i/c Advertising and Sales, is snatching a quick bite at her sandwiches between answering the telephone and attending to the desk. Helen is a Burton Bradstock girl.

"It was a great place to grow up even though the 'townies' called us a load of 'carrot crunchers'. I feel it's lost a lot of its charm today – but maybe that's just me getting older!" Now Helen lives on a smallholding at Broadwindsor with husband Bill, daughter Jennifer and 'various animals'.

"Living where we do there aren't the facilities for youngsters but it does have its advantages. Jennifer belongs to the Marshwood Young Farmers which is a marvellous organisation. As parents we get invited along to events and the youngsters are so well-mannered and lovely. They organise speaking competitions and suppers – they manage to do so much."

We are joined by a new arrival. Helen performs the introductions.

"Welcome to one of Bridport's – and England's – national treasures!"

Mark Grinter, for twenty years a local hairdresser, has brought his sandwiches -and his opinions.

"If there's one thing Bridport people don't like it's plastic people," he declares."They also don't like being taken advantage of!"

Who exactly has Mark got in mind, I ask myself? He's looking straight at me as he speaks. But it seems Mark is not at all happy about 'dysfunctional families being bussed down to the area by nameless officials from Manchester and London to take up housing that rightly belongs to locals.'

"If you wish to qualify for housing it seems you either have to be 'Sharon up the duff', or 'Kevin with an ASBO'. And it's a disgrace and so unfair on all the decent people in our community."

Helen feels equally strongly that badly behaved school-children often appear to benefit from their ill-discipline at the expense of the well-behaved.

"Quite often the louts finish up with one-to-one tuition while the other children have to muddle along as best they can."

Both Helen and Mark are expressing views that I have found commonplace on my travels. 'As a nation we have become too soft', 'The lazy, feckless and lawless are laughing at the rest of us', and 'The country's leaders and politicians in general are out of step with the feelings of most ordinary hard-working, law-abiding people'.

And for Helen – what then of Bridport ?

"In some ways I fear the town has become a victim of its own success. It does have an image that attracts people to it. We have such a regular influx of numbers in the summer months that there are the most acute parking problems. And, at weekends, it's become impossible. I'd never come into the town after 10am on a Saturday. It's chaos on the streets. And it has become two towns – Bridport by day and Bridport by night."

Mountfield, the Council Offices

I never cease to wonder at the helpfulness and courtesy of our council staff in Dorset. There's not been an office yet where I have not been welcomed. Linda Bullock is not only no exception – she's positively brilliant! She grew up in Puncknowle, taught at Powerstock and Symondsbury primaries, lived for a time at Burton Bradstock and now resides in the centre of Bridport itself. She's a walking

Ron Coatsworth, left from Bridport, Chairman of WDDC and the Mayor of Dorchester, David Barrett join the Mayor of Bridport, Geoff Ackerman, right, in admiring the work of one of Bridport's famous sons, the artist Fra Newberry. The painting of the Lady Chapel altar piece was at the Town Hall – on loan from St Hilda's Church, West Jesmond, Newcastle-upon Tyne. *Picture: Jim Tampin, Dorset Echo.*

encyclopaedia and treasure house of local knowledge and personalities. Where I am ignorant she informs me, where I am wrong she corrects me, where I am uncertain she advises me.

"You absolutely must visit the Fra Newberry exhibition at the Town Hall and the Arts Centre. And if you want to find your way around later, here's a copy of the artist, Jim Coplestone's Friendly Map."

I have to confess my ignorance of Fra Newberry but how can I possibly ignore Linda's recommendation? And Jim's map is both fun and useful. And before I leave the office I must give a mention to Jill Cox and Liz Butler who have been every bit as obliging and courteous.

The Town Hall

'Born in Devon in 1855 Fra Newberry arrived in the town aged just five, attended the General School, progressed to the Bridport School of Art, which was situated on the first floor of the Literary and Scientific Institute, and qualified as a teacher. Setting off to London he continued to teach and paint before returning with his wife to Corfe Castle where he died in 1940 at the age of 91.' So much I glean from the leaflet given me by Bernard Paull who, with his wife Christine, is ensuring no unscrupulous art-lover walks off with one of Newberry's canvasses under his coat. In conversation with Bernard and Christine they kindly invite me to look them up should I visit Loders. I resolve on the spot to visit Loders, As for the paintings, they are both readily accessible and pleasing. My favourites are scenes of boat-building at West Bay and a classroom full of children at Corfe Castle. An enterprising lady named Crystal Johnson has most imaginatively designed a Fra Newberry Trail incorporating half a dozen venues across the county during the coming month. Certainly the exhibition fits snugly into Bridport's contemporary image as a town of the creative arts, and the existence of a School of Art and a Literary and Scientific Institute in the town as early as 1834 is proof of both a significant intellectual and artistic tradition. Reading David Dawson in *View From Bridport* under the heading 'Why Bridport is the new St. Ives', it is apparent there exists a sizeable colony of painters, sculptors, furniture makers, photographers and other artists working in and around the town, centred on the St. Michael's Trading Estate, once renowned as the home of the rope-making industry. As David Ross comments, 'You can see why artists flock to Bridport – land and seascape, lots of places to drink and eat and to relax and a genuinely welcoming community.'

So it's along West Street and left into St. Michael's Lane. St. Michael's Studios is the largest complex of the Estate. It's been established, I understand, for nearly a decade and has sixteen artists in residence. Certainly it's an impressive location with the work of many artists on display. Is this the definitive proof that Bridport is the new St. Ives or Notting Hill-on-Sea? Not quite, I suggest, but let's cross the road to Gundry Lane and meet a man with his feet very firmly on the ground.

Bridport Youth Club, Gundry Lane

"I was teaching at a primary known as the 'rat pit'. It consisted of poor whites, Biafrans, gipsies and Turkish Cypriots among others. My particular contribution lay in language development, drama and remedial learning. After a time the Youth Service offered me a job on the Downham Estate, the biggest of its kind at the time in Europe – overwhelmingly white with lots of criminal elements – Kray types and supporters of Tindall's National Front. You could say it was a challenge but I did enjoy it. "

A perfect preparation, I suggest, for his arrival in Bridport as the local Youth Officer. Arthur Woodgate, now Senior Youth Worker for West Dorset, laughs. Within minutes of meeting we are discovering common threads in our lives. Before heading west to Dorset Arthur worked in Lewisham where his three children were born, as was this writer. Arthur worked locally as a librarian and

Youth work in Bridport – young people taking over! *Picture: Dean Brooke*

teacher, as has this writer. At Brixton and Lambeth public libraries my abiding memories are of locating and reserving the romantic novels of Barbara Cartland for that first generation of West Indian mums who never stopped smiling at me, and waking the tramps asleep in the Reading Rooms when their snoring disturbed the concentration of the more earnest readers. Arthur's experiences were, we decide, more demanding than mine.

"To tell the truth, when I arrived here I found the premises run down and drab, the facilities, such as they were, scarcely used and the staff demoralised. After a few days I felt very depressed and wondered if I'd done the right thing. But it's vital to go out into the community and get things moving. A couple of months later I had calls from a butcher and a baker – no candle-stick maker in Bridport, as far as I know – with offers to help. You do get the most wonderful support from many of the traders in Bridport. One I must mention is Mike Fowler, a local builder and the owner of two and a half trading estates. He came to me one day and said 'I've done well in this community. Now I'd like to put something back'. Mike is now the Chairman of the Youth Club Committee. He also funded our motor project called 'Bandits'. Some lads actually got jobs out of it. Ryan Bennett was

'Take off'. *Picture: Geoff Hill*

nominated Vauxhall Young Mechanic of the Year and he's now Vice-Chairman. Someone else who was brilliant was Humph Dibdin, a teacher and Labour councillor and a volunteer youth worker."

At this point Arthur escorts me to an adjacent room and shows me a plaque on the wall. It reads: *'Humph Dibdin – A Tireless Advocate for Young People.'*

"Sadly Humph died 6 years ago but he worked every Friday night for many years and helped so many of our young people."

Back in the office, busy at her computer, Arthur introduces me to someone he describes as 'The Rock'.

"This is Maggie Chivers – and she's absolutely brilliant."

I also meet another of Arthur's team, Justine David.

"My particular responsibility is the young parents who come in for advice and support. They were mostly with us in the Youth Club so they feel they can trust us and relate to us. We try to encourage good parenting skills – not just among the mothers but the young dads as well."

I know Justine's making an impact. I've already met a number of the young mums and dads, with their prams, on the way into the building. Arthur picks up the thread.

"We also have a basketball group called Evolution working with Tom Glover, the youngest qualified coach in the UK. There's a sound studio and our project Zest promoting local music, the Youth Bank providing grants for projects chosen by the members, a library partnership scheme encouraging young people to read, a mentoring programme aimed at helping children to transfer happily from junior to secondary education – altogether a dozen different projects involving more individuals than ever."

It's clear Arthur's infectious enthusiasm has transformed youth facilities in the 16 years he has lived in the town. But he's very anxious to share the credit with his team of paid workers and volunteers. He's also grateful for the support of the Town Council and West Dorset District Council.

And so to the inevitable issue of drugs and crime for while Bridport may be a healthier, saner society than many, nowhere in modern Britain is entirely free from the scourge of drug abuse.

"Of course, we do have drugs in the town. There are pushers and they have their customers but we do our best to keep them out. As for criminal and anti-social behaviour we do attend case conferences with agencies like the police, the schools and social services. It's a delicate balancing act. My role, as I see it, is to find ways to divert offenders away from the wrong path, to look for reasons for their behaviour in the first instance and then to find positive solutions, especially with employment and developing job skills. Councillor Phil Lathey heads the Outreach team and does a fine job. Magna Housing has actually provided funds to prevent anti-social behaviour. It benefits them as well as the wider community."

Leaving the club premises we stroll across the town to a recreational area where Arthur introduces me to several young members displaying their cycling prowess.

"You see the hut with the murals – those were painted by the lads. What is noteworthy is that it hasn't been defaced in any way though the painting was done some months ago. It's an interesting point that when they're given the responsibility of looking after their own property, more often than not they'll rise to the challenge in a positive way."

It's an impressive set-up at Bridport Youth Club. Using imagination, psychology, considerable reserves of energy and enthusiasm, allied to the organisational skills of Arthur and his team, some outstanding work is being done. Everyone involved is deserving of the highest praise.

Of food and people

To be in Bridport and not to write of food would, in the eyes of many, be tantamount to a 'hanging offence'. As David Ross observes the town has many fine restaurants and eating places, though it would be invidious on my part to select any particular establishment. However, I can without prejudice draw attention to the Bridport Food Festival and the Bridport Local Food Group with its particular emphasis upon local producers who are much in evidence on the twice weekly market days – Wednesdays and Saturdays. Descended as I am from at least three generations of bakers and confectioners, I am especially interested in the quality of the bread and cakes in any place that I visit. On that score Bridport is certainly well served with the award winning Caroline Parkins at Leakers and Peter and Katrina Benn at George's Bakery, their shops being separated only by the breadth of the road in East Street. I know F.G.Pitcher was recently voted the finest fishmonger in the county where Ricky Pitcher and his team of Jackie Loveless and Barbara Jacques are very popular with their customers. While I am on the subject of fish the name of Clive Samways has been several times mentioned to me as most deserving of praise. I understand it was his father Clifford who actually began the business, cycling to fish off the pier at West Bay before he was able to afford a boat! Tim Crabtree of Bridport Food has been providing hot meals for schools and the elderly which seems a most commendable enterprise. Another well-regarded figure is Simon Holland of Washingpool Farm, while at the newly refurbished Bull Hotel, Nikki and Richard Cooper and chef Matthew Cook have clearly created a good impression with the Sunday Times Travel writer who described their hotel as 'one of the finest places in England at which to stay.'

Although Bridport's traditional rope and netting industry may no longer be a visible presence on the streets of the town as once it was, many of the old specialist skills remain. What was Bridport Gundry is now Amsafe and recognised internationally as a leader in textile cargo restraint, manufacturing cargo nets and the like. Robert McIlwraith is the Managing Director of the company in its new form.

Two places to visit that come highly commended are the Town Museum, where the Curator

Alice Martin has staged a series of widely praised exhibitions, and the Electric Palace where Peter Hitchin deserves great credit for his work over several years in restoring the theatre. Peter, who lives at Symondsbury Manor, has recently passed over the day-to-day running to his daughter Gabby. Gabby has several years experience working in theatre management both locally and in London and relishes her new challenge. Peter tells me the theatre is drawing full houses to a wide range of entertainments and has added, he feels, greatly to Bridport's appeal as a cultural centre. A particular thrill was being able to stage the World Premiere of Julian Fellowes's *The Young Victoria* in aid of the Weldmar Hospice

Palmer's Brewery West Bay Road

"The only thatched brewery in the UK? It was a question on someone's chosen specialist subject on Mastermind – and they got it right!"

John Palmer, the amiable Managing Director of Palmer's Brewery, chuckles.

"It was most recently thatched by Guy Gale from Solwayash. Guy is a superb craftsman. In fact, we think so highly of him we actually named a pub in Taunton after him calling it The Master Thatcher. And curiously enough, his wife Elizabeth coached me in Maths as a private pupil when she was a young woman."

With the media full of reports of the almost daily closing of pubs across the country, I've come to discuss with John the state of the brewing industry and the licensed trade in general. John produces a file of papers.

"These are some statistics prepared years ago by my father. They make for fascinating reading. In 1880 there were 16,798 brewing companies in the UK. By 1939 the number was down to 885. In 1964 the figure stood at 304. Today there are fewer than 50 and Dorset has just two, Hall and Woodhouse and us."

Most of us will readily recall the demise of Eldridge Pope in Dorchester and Devenish in Weymouth. To what then does John attribute Palmer's survival in an age of vigorous restructuring and rationalisation?

"It's absolutely essential to be responsive to the operation of market forces. It's like turning the rudder of a great ship. There has been a social revolution. Once every village had its own pub but, when trade became insufficient to support it, there was no option but closure. I know some people have suggested we have closed many pubs but the reality is that we've also opened several. A few years ago we had 70 pubs. We still have 57 and they are almost invariably located in attractive rural locations providing not only food and accommodation but able to cater for special occasions like weddings and parties. What we have seen is a decline in the traditional 'wet only' pubs. In many villages, especially on the main roads, the cars go speeding through and with the drink drive laws motorists simply do not stop. Some locals will remember the Traveller's Rest on the Dorchester Road, the London Inn at Symondsbury and The Ship at Morecombelake. They were all casualties of this major change in social habits and, of course, discriminating customers demand much more than the scampi or chicken in the basket which was all the rage twenty years ago."

With all the difficulties confronting the licensed trade, not least the recent smoking ban, is there a future for the ambitious young man or woman who wants to run a pub?

"Absolutely. Being the tenant of a pub is still a great opportunity for anyone with energy and determination. It is possible for not a great capital outlay to take over a tenancy and make a good living. We do exercise a great deal of social responsibility in selecting our tenants to ensure they are well suited and taking on a viable business. Aside from paying rent and selling our drinks, tenants enjoy complete freedom to choose their own menus and create their own distinctive ambience in their pubs. In fact, let me give you an example right here in this locality. A young lady, Laura King, who's just approaching her 18th birthday, recently successfully completed the training course and received her 'certificate of competence' to become the licensee of the King's Head, Bradpole, where her mother has been the landlord. I know Tim Woodrow, our tenanted trade director, was absolutely delighted. We believe Laura must be the youngest licensee in the country – and a very personable young lady into the bargain."

It was a decade ago that the brewery celebrated its bi-centenary. Originally founded by the renowned Gundry family the Palmers acquired the business in 1896. John's right-hand man is his brother Cleeves, formally the sales and marketing manager. It will be fascinating to follow developments in the brewery trade in the coming years. Is further rationalisation probable? Will there be a growth in the very small breweries supplying 'niche' markets? John Palmer remains quietly optimistic of his own company's future but takes nothing for granted. As I leave I suggest to John a question which could possibly figure in another Mastermind series.

"Which is the only brewery to employ as its assistant retail manager an anthropology graduate able to discourse at length on the life style of the Nuer tribe in Africa, while promoting the qualities of the company's wines and spirits?"

John Palmer laughs. "I suspect the answer lies downstairs."

John is quite correct. Luke Machin is the young man's name and on the afternoon of my call, is sharing responsibilities in the wine store with colleague Ronnie Mace. I ask Luke if his knowledge of anthropology and human behaviour has proved useful in his job?

"I would say it's probably the most appropriate subject in the world to have studied when you're dealing all day with customers, wouldn't you?"

(I learned recently that Guy Gale, the husband of teacher and writer Elizabeth and a greatly admired craftsman and much liked man, the 'Master Thatcher' himself, passed away early in the New Year, 2009. Having had the pleasure of making the acquaintance of Guy and Elizabeth on my travels at their farm at Solwayash I was much saddened to learn of Guy's passing.)

West Bay

'West Bay, the harbour of Bridport, is probably the queerest seaport in any part of the British Isles........ The essential hamlet is made up of disorderly old houses of the humbler type, which are arranged with no more method than if they had been emptied out of a dice box. Among the more seaward of these are picturesque thatched cottages which have stumbled on to the very beach, and are standing there, knee-deep in shingle with their backs turned to the ocean, and with a suggestion that they were wondering how they had ever managed to get there..... A block of dwellings has been dumped down in the unoffending hamlet, where a 'terrace' – although in itself architecturally admirable – looks as out of place as an iron girder in a flower garden.'
Sir Frederick Treves, *Highways & Byways in Dorset* 1906

"Yes, it's quite true. It is rather like the contents of a child's box that has been emptied out."

Cecil Amor, Chairman of Bridport Historical Society and long-standing resident, chuckles. We're sitting in a cafe analysing from west to east the scene before us and discussing West Bay's distinctly mixed architectural heritage.

Away to our left stand various blocks of modern apartments and holiday lets, functional buildings at best. Then it's Splish Splash Aquafun and Arcadezone – Family Fun and Games, two E.S.Prior (1852-1932) 'Arts & Crafts' movement houses facing one another, a line of brightly painted kiosks selling every form of fast food, The George Inn c1800, the Old Custom's House, a listed thatched cottage formerly a C18 Seamen's Mission, St. John's Church, the West Bay Hotel, a 1930s newsagent and a closed Wesleyan chapel. And a few others I've missed out. I am indebted to Cecil for providing the approximate dates and uses of certain buildings. Architecturally, it's chaotic. It is coherent only in is sheer incoherence. And yet, extraordinarily, it works. Of course, it's not Weymouth's old harbour, or Cerne Abbas or Milton Abbey. But, then again, West Bay does not pretend to be anything other than what it is. It has no airs and graces. It is fun – pure, unadulterated exuberance – and definitely not for the strait-laced aesthete.

Leaving the cafe Cecil guides me away from the harbour beyond Quay West in the direction of the new apartments.

"It's difficult to believe that 150 years ago this area was a hive of shipbuilding activity. A clipper 'The Speedy' was built here in 1853. The last vessel the 'Lilian' was completed in 1877. Of course, they often had acute problems launching from the old harbour. The entrance was so small and there was the constant problem with the mud and the silting up. All kinds of nets were made here too even down to nets for billiard tables and snaring rabbits."

What about the railway – it did enjoy a period of prosperity?

"That's on the other side of the harbour, of course. There's still a carriage or two over there. And, yes, it was initially successful. The line was built in 1884 and over 5,000 people travelled on the first day on March 31. But, sadly, the passenger line was closed in the 1930s and the goods line in the 1960s."

Pier Terrace – A couple of days later

"It's a monstrosity! Its sole virtue is that it hides what lies behind it. I believe a man from Birmingham said he approved of it. Perhaps in the centre of Birmingham it might actually look attractive!"

We're seated in the comfortable lounge of Number 9, Pier Terrace, gazing across at Quay West, the latest addition to West Bay's varied architectural heritage. Peggy Chapman-Andrews chuckles mischievously.

"Actually, I've never been to Birmingham. Do you think I might offend someone by my remark?"

But what of Pier Terrace itself? What did the locals say back in 1884 when that was built? Were they complimentary? Certainly Sir Frederick Treves entertained considerable doubts about its precise location some 20 years later.

"I take your point, of course. In truth, we don't really know but I do feel it wasn't out of keeping with the buildings around it – not like that terrible thing!"

Designed by E.S.Prior, he initially intended that it should face the sea but moved it 90 degrees away from the waves. Originally it was built as a terrace of ten houses but in 1928 a fire engulfed Numbers 9 and 10 which were subsequently restored as four flats – Numbers 9, 10, 11 and 12.

"Over the years all the others have also been converted into separate flats except Number 5 which remains as the sole surviving house. Actually, at one time it was co-owned by the broadcaster Mary Stocks and her brother. Mary was a very sweet lady."

Now there's a name which brings back echoes of my childhood. Eight o'clock on Friday evenings was Any Questions with Freddie Grisewood in the chair and a panel which included politicians and guests such as A.G.Street, Jack Longland, Ralph Wightman from Piddletrenthide and a certain Mary Stocks.

"Few people remember her now when I mention the name." Further proof, I fear, of the advancing years!

"My late brother bought Number 8 some years ago after he retired from the diplomatic service – he had been the British ambassador in the Lebanon. After his death when we were sorting through his papers, we found a letter from Louis Mountbatten in which he described a holiday he'd greatly enjoyed at West Bay when he was at Osborne Naval College IOW during WW1. It appeared he stayed at the pink house nearby which is called The Bunker."

There are so many memories for Peggy at Pier Terrace. It was to Number 7 that she originally came with her late teacher husband Wilfred, better known as 'Andy', in early 1946. After 15 years the couple moved to Jessopp House in Bridport before returning to Pier Terrace, this time at Number 9 in 1987. During those years she raised a family and made such a distinguished contribution to the Bridport community that the title of Honorary Townswoman was conferred on her in 1985. Yet Peggy remains disarmingly modest about her achievements, founding the League of Friends of Bridport hospital, filling the role of secretary of the Music Club and playing a pivotal role in securing the former Wesleyan chapel as the Town's Art Centre for just £8,000. In more recent times she initiated the Bridport Literary Prize which annually attracts in the order of 10,000 entries and adds to the town's status as a cultural centre. Unfortunately, selfless work on behalf of others offers no guarantees of immunity from the pain of personal sadness. My earlier visit to Peggy was postponed when she had to fly at short notice to Barbados after the death of her much loved son Paul.

As I rise to leave our eyes are inevitably drawn again to Quay West. I ask her what her other son Peter thinks of it.

"He maintains what I can best describe as a discreet silence. However, I do tell him that should my grandson, Thomas, who is an architect, ever design such an appalling thing I will instantly disown him!"

Despite the twinkle in Peggy's eyes I fear she will not soon be reconciled to Quay West.

Quay West – From the inside looking out

I decide I must gain legitimate entrance and see for myself exactly what I would be getting for my money, were I sufficiently astute to back at ante-post prices the winners of all next year's English classics, linked in an each-way accumulator with the Grand National winner, and decided to splash my winnings on an apartment at Quay West.

Goadsby are handling the properties for Wyatt Homes and the lovely Lorraine is my guide. The apartment I like best is on the Third Floor – with sea views. The price is a trifling £435,000. One of the things that's just a little bit disappointing about its 'sea views', however, is that these days there's actually little to look at in the Channel apart from the sea. What I mean is that there are precious few actual boats passing by. It's not that I want to see the Spanish Armada sailing up the Channel again, though that would certainly be a spectacular sight, but I do think I prefer the countryside to look at given a straight choice. I'd rather have goldfinches and chaffinches than herring- gulls outside my window, if you see what I mean. Having said that, the apartment is fine but I'm not convinced I will be buying, not this year anyway.

I thank the lovely Lorraine for her time and courtesy. I don't have the nerve to tell her my visit has been all part of my research, though I don't think she'd have minded terribly anyway. Perhaps it's just as well I've decided not to buy. Whatever would I have said to Peggy when she found out that I'd moved in?

On the quayside, The Mound – A couple of days later

"That's the Dawn Mist over there. She belongs, I believe, to Hugh Fearnley-Whittingstall and Nick Fisher of 'Catch & Cook' fame"

We're seated on a bench below the area known by the locals as The Mound on the most perfect

Pier Terrace. *Picture: William Holden*

spring morning England could fashion. A score of small craft are resting quietly before us in the harbour. The plaintive cries of the herring gulls wheeling above our heads are the only sounds to punctuate the silence, aside from the quiet buzz of conversation from the customers at the tables in front of JB's kiosk. It's a scene far removed from London where Tony Bunyan and his brother Peter grew up and worked for many years. "I was a retail manager with a big company. When changes came I felt I was just a number on the payroll. It was time to forge a different life style. We took over in 2000."

Tony lives at Bradpole, Peter at Puncknowle.

Why is it that on this particular morning I feel less irritated by Quay West? Is it the mood of quiet contentment induced by the warmth of the sun after the long winter, the excellence of the mug of hot tea Peter has put in my hand, the sight of the brightly painted craft in the harbour, the relative absence of cars and crowd? I'm not sure, though perhaps it's because I can only see the offending building out of the corner of my eye. Whatever the explanation, I do know is that I am falling under the spell of West Bay.

"A few years ago the *Sunday Telegraph* said West Bay was in the Top Ten of popular holiday destinations. Then *Which?* magazine came along and said that we were 'just concrete and cars!'"

Thankfully, from where I am sitting, I can see few cars and even less concrete.

"When we took over we knew we must listen to our customers. Ask them what they liked and wanted. Of course, you make mistakes but, if you listen, you're more likely to get it right."

Tony would like permission to have a canopy over the area in front of the kiosk.

"We'd like to make it an all the year round attraction. There's a lady here who sells clothes but it's a limited season for her. We do put up flags and bunting to create a continental atmosphere but it would be better still if there was protection from the elements. No, you wouldn't get a tan as you eat, that's true...."

"But that's what we have two award winning beaches for."

Peter laughs. The brothers make a good team, the Mike and Bernie Winters of West Bay – for those who remember them – perhaps Ant and Dec for the modern generation.

What about Quay West which has caused such a furore?

Peter again. "The critics have got to get real. We're living in the 21st century. There are dinosaurs out there in the rocks. There are also dinosaurs living here today in the town of Bridport!"

Are the brothers optimistic about the future? Tony picks up my query.

"Yes and no. There is the parking, of course. Sometimes even we cannot find somewhere to put our cars. Then there are problems for the angling community with the rock armour and the dithering over a new jetty. Are disabled anglers going to be able to fish from their wheel-chairs? On the other hand, the diving fraternity are making a bee line for us with any number of wrecks lying only a mile or so offshore. Then there are the Olympics which should bring publicity, visitors and money into the economy. On the other hand, British holidays are so expensive. Hotels and restaurant prices are often exorbitant. I'm afraid there are some very greedy people about. For families a British holiday can be far more costly than going abroad with no guaranteed sun. But West Bay does have a lot going for it. Celebs like the place because they can walk about unmolested and we do get quite a few. I absolutely love the place. So does my son David who works with me and Tracey Howard who makes up the team. There are so many very nice people here – like Dave Sayles, for example, who's the chairman of the small boat owners and the youngest harbour-master in the country. And do you know we even have half a dozen regulars who come here every morning for their breakfasts? We call them our 'breakfast club'. And, if someone fails to show, we'll even give them a call to make sure they're OK. What we need, above all, is a good summer weather-wise. In recent years we've suffered the effects of foot and mouth, the pier building, then the flats going up and some lousy weather. We keep saying 'This will be the year'. Maybe 2008 really will be just that!"

It's almost time then to leave Bridport and West Bay, but I take one last stroll past the kiosks that line the waterfront – The Ship's Galley, The Tea Caddy, The Moulin Rouge and several others. The critics will doubtless label the names pretentious, but to me they simply confirm the sense of fun and joie de vivre that pervades the place.

At the Moulin Rouge I meet Alain Toudic, once of Toulon, who married an English girl named Patricia, at which moment his fate was sealed.

"My son David painted the sign for me when he was just fourteen. Today he is a professional artist. Do you like it?"

It's a splendid splash of French colour, incongruous but absolutely right for West Bay. We chat idly over an excellent cup of tea. Whoever said the French can't make tea? We talk of Toulouse-Lautrec and Montmartre and his early life in la belle France. Alain is considering selling the Moulin Rouge.

"I have been here a long time. It's almost the moment for me to retire."

Even as we talk we are joined by Mark Wormleighton who is thinking of changing his life style. He's a social worker. He asks Alain the price he is seeking. I leave them to their deliberations.

I began with questions. Notting Hill-on-Sea? St Ives? 'A town of substantial simplicity, wholesome and homely?' In truth, Bridport is something of each and, as I have discovered, much else besides. But why do so many people feel a need to attach labels? I suppose it's the fashion – the search for a quick journalistic headline. Bridport is Bridport. A splendid town with lots of individuality, character, a resourceful and talented populace and a bright future – and that's enough surely.

Burton Bradstock

It's a moment that never fails to thrill. Five thousand miles it has flown from its winter quarters in South Africa. Across the Sahara and the Mediterranean, up through Spain and France, safely negotiating the hazards of predators and storms, and I am privileged to be its first witness as it makes safe landfall on an English shore. No companions. How many, I wonder, set out with this particular bird? Was it faster than the others, or simply the luckiest? Where will it rest its weary frame this evening? On a ledge in a barn where first it saw the light of day a year or two earlier?

Mike Hancock spots it too but Tess, to her chagrin, misses our first swallow of 2008. No matter – she's enjoying the novelty of the day.

"These are the first weeks of Mike's retirement and it's wonderful to be able to sit here on a day like this."

Mike and Tess were quietly picnicking in the sunshine on the Burton cliffs – until my arrival. But they don't seem to mind too much that I have intruded upon their peace. Mike, I discover taught at Kingston Maurward Agricultural College and he and Tess live in Tincleton near Puddletown. We speculate on the future of the Burton Cliff Hotel. It was only that morning I read in the Bridport News of plans by business partners, Mary-Lou Sturridge and Anthony Mackintosh, to redesign the 27 bedroom hotel.

As Ms.Sturridge says: "The setting is fantastic and we want to do something fabulous for Burton Bradstock and for Dorset."

Perched on the cliff-top overlooking the Channel, it is indeed a magnificent location with amazing views in every direction, with a Socialist singer-songwriter as a neighbour.

St. Marys Church

I hear them as I stand in the porch reading the notices. Powerful lungs, but the melody defies recognition. I doubt the vicar would welcome them into his choir. Do they look just a little embarrassed and sheepish when they see me enter?

"Our radio has broken and we've got to make our own entertainment today."

Robert Stephenson laughs. "Yes, I can actually claim a distant relationship to the great man."

His distinguished namesake, son of George, was born in the north-east and a brilliant engineer. Robert is an electrician and lives in Bradpole. His workmate is Daniel Rowe is from Bridport. They're carrying out a contract for Simon Scott Electricals.

"We're renewing everything. Some of the wiring must be fifty years old."

Have they encountered any particular problems?

"We've found it's definitely a good idea to remember all your tools before you climb to the top of the tower. It's a long way down!"

I leave Robert and Daniel to their rewiring. They haven't resumed their singing.

Beside St Marys Church and Burton Bradstock Primary School

I hear their animated chatter before I see them. Like the junior regiment of Giuseppe Garibaldi's redshirts they are advancing at a lively pace along the narrow pathway. Eighteen inches to my right the mill race (of the Bride) pursues its meandering course beneath the overhanging branches. Will one of the bolder spirits among the foot-soldiers extend a crafty leg and send me tumbling into the water? My fears prove groundless. In the vanguard and to their rear, the teachers of Burton Bradstock Primary oversee their charges with watchful eyes as they continue their cheerful, exuberant but eminently courteous progress along the footpath to the playing-fields for Friday afternoon games.

In the garden of The Rookery a yellow-helmeted scarecrow stands patient guard. In my childhood scarecrows stood in every other village garden and in many a farmer's field. In recent times I fear they have become an endangered species but this fine fellow is clearly a labour of love.

Local resident Alison Davies seems mildly surprised by my query. I'd heard, I explain, that there are some who grew up in the village years ago who believe it has changed for the worst in recent times.

"I think they may be referring to some of the building on the fringes but here in the heart of the village it's no less lovely than ever it was "

Her companion on her afternoon stroll, Sue from Bothenhampton agrees.

And a similar point of view is shared by Lynne Taylor at nearby Garden Cottage who has lived in Burton since she was four.

"You only have to look around – it's still quite unspoilt here."

Certainly, where now I stand, just yards from the church and the school, the scene is without discernible flaw. As Alison and Sue continue their afternoon ramble so I explore the silent byways. In several cottage windows neat posters advertise a range of village activities. On Wednesday afternoons I could learn to tango if I so chose. It would be a waste of time for all concerned, I fear. I always was a useless dancer. Am I tempted instead to purchase some 'Newly hatched tadpoles'? Not today, I think. I still wonder, in idle moments, what happened to that jar of tadpoles taken from the River Lea that I left behind in Luton when I was eight. I remembered them just as the removal van pulled away from Norton Road. Ever since that moment I have never been able to look a tadpole squarely in the eye. And, on the subject of Luton, I heard on the radio the other day the town now has a population of 30,000 Muslims and 14 mosques. I wonder if any little Muslim boys now collect tadpoles from the River Lea as I and my friends once did?

I have been looking and listening for the evidence of contentedly grunting pigs in the locality but, to date, without success. I understand there's something called the Burton Bradstock Pig Project organised by residents David Dixon and Tim Farrell. They've set up a commune involving a number of good-natured Saddlebacks acquired from Tim and Julie at Modbury Farm. The theory is, I believe, that our porkers live the life of Reilly before a journey to the Bridport butcher, Richard Balson, after which rendez-vous they duly return in altered form to be consumed with eggs and fried bread, apple sauce, or some similar culinary accompaniment by the good folk of the village. I must confess an invitation to breakfast, lunch or dinner would not be dismissed out of hand, but no one has yet approached me.

In the Post Office and Village Stores the manager Jerry Bown is stock-taking, when he's not selling stamps or accepting packages for posting. Unfortunately Jerry's wife underwent a major operation in mid-winter and is still unable to work so Margaret Harding, from just across the road, has thoughtfully organised a rota of 'volunteers' to attend the store's other till. The Parish Council bought the PO Stores for £80,000 when it was under threat believing its survival was essential to the well-being of the village. The money was provided by a generous benefactor, I understand. Besides the essential, everyday items on sale, there's a surprisingly good stock of local books on display, including Elizabeth Gale's splendid *Two Days In Summer* which recounts the sale of a large part of the village in July 1958.

Graham Rees, the most affable and courteous of English gentlemen, is this afternoon's 'volunteer'. A constant stream of shoppers come and go with lots of small purchases that ensure a lively till. I am delighted the Parish Council's bold purchase appears to be a success. The banter seldom stops.

"I came third. Twenty-three points on the first nine, not so many on the second nine."

David Smith plays with the Veteran's Section of Bridport and West Dorset Golf Club. Graham commiserates but he does so with a smile.

"I live in Shipton Gorge though there is no gorge," David tells me. "It's named after a Frenchman, I believe. A de Gorge, of some description."

It's true that one learns something every day though some things are more useful than others. Jim Reeves passes through the shop.

"A pillar of the British Legion," whispers Graham.

"Do you sing," I ask.

Jim smiles at me tolerantly on his way to the door. How many times has he heard the same sad witticism?

Basil Dent, a refugee from the North, bell-ringer, churchwarden, and one-time manager of Burton Bradstock FC, confesses that he supports Stockport County. I've never met a Stockport County supporter before. I doubt there are many so privileged. I observe Basil closely. He seems sane enough but one can never be sure after such an admission.

Basil and I fall in with Janet Guppy as we ascend the hill. Janet was born in the village, a farmer's daughter.

"I deliver 38 parish magazines. Twenty of them go through the letter-boxes of holiday cottages. In the village I would estimate there are 60 cottages in all occupied only for short periods."

"I'm afraid their occupants do not put roots down in the village," reflects Basil. "Very few contribute much to the life or economy of the village."

We're back at the church. It's almost time for the end of afternoon school. Janet points at the nearby cottage.

"This is where I grew up. I well remember there were 8 children in those cottages alone. Now there are none."

All around us in the narrow lanes cars are drawing up, their drivers trying to squeeze into a space where they might wait for the exodus through the school gate.

"I know the school now has about 100 pupils but they come from all over the area. Few actually live here – perhaps a half? Their parents are waiting to take them away from the village."

Perhaps this is what they are referring to, those who regret what is happening to their village of happy memory. Unoccupied cottages, scarcely a property a young, impecunious couple could afford, the sound of children's laughter and chatter seldom heard in the streets when the school is closed – and vehicles, some as large and intimidating as Sherman tanks – occupying every square yard of space each morning and afternoon.

(In *Two Days In Summer* Elizabeth Gale refers to a 2005 survey of the village which reports that of 580 dwellings about 13.3 were second or holiday homes which does confirm Janet's estimate of 60 or so homes. The figure of 106 pupils on the school roll in 2005, of whom perhaps a half according to the school secretary actually live in the village, contrasts with 174 children in the village school in 1846.)

Loders

There's something about railways. Not Clapham Junction perhaps. Nor the overcrowded commuter trains, and certainly not stations littered with the rubbish of our throw-away society but the idea of railways – above all, those small branch lines which were once such an integral part of our lives as a nation. Even those tracks now closed and silent but for birdsong, thanks to Dr.Richard Beeching (later Baron Beeching).

It requires but a small leap of the imagination for us to join those travellers of the past setting off on journeys to every part of the kingdom and Empire, or returning from distant wars and adventures to their loved ones. And what of all those small boys for whom the romance of the railways inspired

St Mary Magdalene Church, Loders. Picture: *Clive Hannay*

an ambition to be an engine driver and removed them, at one bold stroke, from a narrow rural routine that would, in all likelihood, have bound their lives within a 20 mile radius?

Bernard and Christine Paull live in Highacre overlooking the old Maiden Newton to Bridport line. It's an enviable location. We met, the 3 of us, at the Fra Newberry exhibition in Bridport Town Hall. Now we're sitting in the garden reminiscing about the Golden Days of Steam.

Bernard grew up in Loders, attended the village school, became in the fullness of time Bridport's town surveyor. Now he walks his grand-daughter Abigail to the same village school.

"Mike Kite's the headmaster. The school enjoys an excellent reputation."

Bernard's daughter, Julia, lives in his mother's old house in the village. It's all come full circle.

Bernard and I discover a mutual hobby – deltiology. What's that, I can almost hear the curious reader ask? Look it up, I politely whisper. We all learn something totally useless every day of our lives. Bernard urges me to take a stroll through the village and seek out a young lady named Jessie Barrett. "You won't be disappointed," he assures me. "She lives at Wellplot, "he adds.

It's blissfully warm, one of the few days this spring that has not felt more like winter. Loders is a picture, as people say. It's full of flowers, olde worlde cottages and the Askers brook flows lazily through the village. Why have I never visited before, I ask myself? It's a question I've posed already several times on my journey.

I long ago learned the truth of the old adage that 'faint heart never wins fair lady', so I knock the door in Wellplot, explain my business and the most hospitable Jessie bids me enter.

Jessie Barrett's been at the heart of Loders life for as long as anyone in the village can remember.

She too attended the village school before going off to the local grammar school. She's chairman of the village hall committee, helps with the flowers at St. Mary Magdalene Church, has organised the fete according to one unnamed acquaintance since the coronation of Queen Victoria and she delivers the morning papers to half the village.

"A boy used to do it but he gave up. No other boy or girl wanted to do it, nor any OAP. I was upset to think we would lose the service so I agreed to do it – temporarily. That was seven years ago!"

The newspapers are delivered to Jessie's doorstep by Derek from East Bridge News at 6.15am each morning. What's so remarkable about doing a paper round, you might ask? In itself, nothing in particular, but when the delivery girl is fast approaching her eightieth birthday then it does become something rather exceptional!

"Saturday's the problem with all those supplements and the small letter-boxes. If I need a day off then my friend Pam Crabb steps into the breach though how much longer I'll carry on, I just don' t know."

Like Bernard at Highacre, Jessie walks to the school every morning with her great- niece Jordan. Then she begins her paper deliveries.

"One Christmas a couple of years ago when I came home I found 9 bottles of port on my doorstep – my Christmas presents from my customers. It seems a couple of the local supermarkets were selling port at reduced prices. Everyone must think I'm an alcoholic!"

Jessie's father was the head gardener at Loders Court, the home of the Hood family.

"My father planted 1,000 daffodils one spring, I remember. There's always the most wonderful show even today. It was Lord Hood who gave us the land for the village hall. It was very much a community effort – securing the hall. Maurice and Pam Crabb and Arthur and Barbara Crabb contributed greatly. Our greatest inspiration though was John Hyde. He never stopped encouraging me. We made five applications to the Lottery and, at last, we came up trumps. Someone else who has done a lot for our village is John Hughes, a retired naval officer with his Young Players Theatre group. Then there's Bill and Vera Budden. Bill was in the RAF and flew Churchill in and out of Potsdam at the end of the war. We've some wonderful characters here in Loders."

Thanking Jessie for her hospitality, I decide to walk back through the village to the church. Barely have I arrived, sat down on a bench in the churchyard and unwrapped my sandwiches, than I discover that I have left my mobile at Jessie's. Even as I make the discovery I hear a voice calling out to me.

"I've just had a phone call from my sister. She's bringing your phone down as quick as she can!"

Jessie's brother, David Crabb, I learn, lives almost opposite the church. Within moments Jessie is with us – on her bicycle – having pedalled furiously through the village to catch me. What wonderful people I am meeting at every step of the way on my travels! Jessie decides it would be an opportune moment to show me the church of St. Mary Magdalene and to point out Loders Court that stands hard by.

"It's here at Loders Court where we always hold the fete. Very sadly Lady Hood passed away just a few weeks ago. You must have heard of her brother, Humphrey Lyttleton, the jazz trumpeter and broadcaster. He's often about the village and such a nice man. I hope we'll be seeing Lord Henry down here at Loders Court more often in the future. They are a very well-liked family."

(It was only days after my visit that Humphrey Lyttleton himself died suddenly. One of the giants of the traditional jazz music scene for half a century and a very amusing broadcaster 'Humph', as everyone knew him, will be much missed.)

The Loders Arms
Millie the Rottweiler regards me enigmatically.

"She may be just a bit hot. We've just had a walk."

I cautiously withdraw the hand I'd begun to extend. An accident involving my typing fingers at this point in my life would be more than a minor nuisance. Clive Legg was for 6 years the landlord of the Loders Arms. His name may no longer be above the door but he enjoys his lunchtime tipple. Louise and Graham Rowe are the landlords now.

"It's quiet today but we've got the Weymouth Wanderers cycling club coming out tomorrow lunchtime – 30 or so usually."

"Anyone who cycles up Eggardon Hill has earned himself a pint or two, if not three, I reckon!"

Clive's days of cycling up Eggardon Hill are clearly long past. I notice the glass case on a shelf near my elbow bearing the caption 'The Ashes of Old Knobbly'.

"It's a skittles tournament. Old Knobbly was an unusable ball we burned. Each year there's a contest between Dorset and the Rest of the World. It's the major sporting event in the calendar here."

"Sometime between Christmas and the New Year," adds Louise.

For Henley it's the Regatta, for Wimbledon it's tennis, for Ascot it's racing, for Loders it's skittles!

As I am about to leave I hear Clive's voice calling after me.

"If ever you get to the Half Moon at Askerswell, look out for Fido May. He's an old Harrovian and the finest shot in Dorset. He'll tell you that for himself!"

Askerswell

More than forty years ago in her meticulously researched Inside Dorset, the redoubtable Monica Hutchings wrote these words : 'If I had to show a visitor what Dorset country was really like in a limited time, I should bring him up here.... the views from the top of Eggardun itself are more than memorable. On a clear day one can have a better idea of the extent and range of West Dorset scenery than anywhere – better even than from Lambert's Castle in the Marshwood Vale.'

Unfortunately, today the skies are grey and the visibility restricted but I can readily appreciate Miss Hutching's enthusiasm. The views are spectacular. Today I am sharing those views with my companions, Ian and Mary Russell of Redway House, Askerswell, and a considerable number of grazing ewes and their lambs. The latter are scrutinising us with the bold and curious eyes of the young. Vowing to return another day when the sun is shining, I follow Ian and Mary along the road to the Spyway Inn where we are warmly greeted by Vivien and Kevin Wilkes. From browsing the columns of the Parish News it is apparent the couple have already established a warm rapport with their customers and the wider community. Their wholehearted involvement in social and charitable activities has deservedly earned them respect and affection. They've also clearly impressed the AA inspectors having just been awarded the accolade of a 4 star rating.

However, my primary purpose in visiting Askerswell is to talk with Mary who edits the *Eggardon and Colmer's View* monthly parish magazine. Ever since Jessie Barrett in Loders pressed a copy into my hand I was resolved to meet its Editor and compliment her on the standard of both the writing and the presentation.

"For many years Gill Evans was its Editor and it did win an award during her stewardship so Gill does deserve much of the credit."

Although the role of Editor must make considerable demands upon her time Mary, like the contributors, is unpaid for her services.

"Our correspondents are the lifeblood of the magazine. Though it's invidious to pick out any individual I suspect Sylvia Johnston, our contributor from Dottery, is probably the one most of our readers turn to first. Although she has the occasional rant at the Government, she's an absolutely charming lady – and she's nearly 80!"

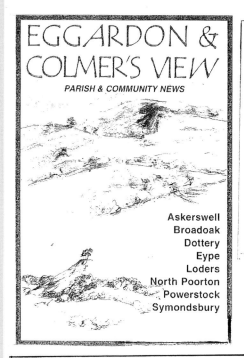

EGGARDON & COLMER'S VIEW

PARISH & COMMUNITY NEWS

Askerswell
Broadoak
Dottery
Eype
Loders
North Poorton
Powerstock
Symondsbury

ASKERSWELL NOTES

Correspondent: **Chris Roberts,**

St Michael & All Angels

No problem in picking the headline news this month. Gill Evans has been awarded the MBE in the Queen's birthday honours. Gill's award is for her services to the community over many years. These services have included her work for Riding for the Disabled (RDA), for the W.I. and for her long stint as editor and Askerswell correspondent for this august publication. Many, many congratulations for her richly deserved award, which brings the village's tally of MBEs to two, Tina Cornish having been so honoured a year or so ago. How many comparatively sized villages could make that claim?

FARMING

Correspondent: **Mark Roberts**

GETTING STARTED

For those who are determined enough, and in many people's opinion, foolhardy enough! to go farming there are a limited number of options.

It used to be said that the only way it was possible to be a farmer was to either be a farmer's son – or 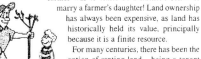 marry a farmer's daughter! Land ownership has always been expensive, as land has historically held its value, principally because it is a finite resource.

For many centuries, there has been the option of renting land – being a tenant farmer. Many of the great estates in Dorset have a portfolio of tenanted farms, and have usually welcomed a succession from father to son on the tenancy agreement, as they know and trust each other. So, if you are a farmer's son, there is a chance of either being set up on your own farm, or succeeding on the tenancy.

What if you are not a farmer's son, with limited capital, or not the eldest son (or daughter of course)? What are the options? This problem was recognised around the turn of the 20th century, and the local authorities started to become landowners, in order to have an estate of small farms to let to those starting off in farming.

Dorset County Council purchased its first farm, at Marnhull, in 1911. In 1974, the holding consisted of 32 estates, comprising 121 farms. Originally known as the County Council Smallholdings, they provided a place to live, some buildings and adequate land to provide a living. The average herd size in the 1960s was around 30 cows, and this was quite sufficient to live off. Times change, and the farms have been amalgamated and rationalised.

Dorset still has a large portfolio of farms, now numbering 75, totalling 2888 hectares (or 7,136 acres), an average size of 38.5ha or 95 acres. Many county councils have sold off their farms as some councillors see the farms as assets to be realised, without appreciating the great benefits of maintaining an estate. There are now 50 local authorities in England and Wales with agricultural estates, comprising 96,000 hectares, farmed by 2,836 tenants, an average of 56 tenants with 33 hectares each per local authority. Sadly, a drop of 43% in land and 58% of tenants nationally since 1984.

Dorset, one of the smaller shire counties, has an above average estate, which is only right in such an agriculturally important area. The estate enables DCC to be involved in, and understand, agriculture. Perhaps just as importantly, the council also has practical involvement with conservation and environmental schemes, countryside management and countryside access.

With considered and carefully planned management, the assets of the estate (so attractive to new councillors), can be maintained whilst still contributing to the income of the council. There is obviously the rent, which is at market rates. Additionally, DCC has been able to amalgamate adjoining farms, often releasing a substantial farmhouse, which with some traditional buildings and an acre or two can be sold off for a considerable sum to boost council income, and to enable modernisation and repairs to existing farms.

LODERS & UPLODERS NOTES
Correspondent: Mrs Janet Robson,

St.Mary Magdalene

Message in a Bottle - a delightful story from Bill Budden: "Walking along the bank of the Asker in my field a few days ago, I found a plastic bottle lodged in some undergrowth. Inside it was a letter typed by Thomas Richards, aged 7, of Hembury House, Askerswell. It was dated 17th March but no year, but had his address and telephone number. On the lower half of the message was a coloured painting of a large house in a background of green hills. Thomas wrote that he was at prep school, and attended seven lessons each day, and hated geography but loved science! I toyed briefly with the idea of sending it on to my friend in New York, asking him to write to this enterprising young boy with some details of life and happenings there - but that would have been cheating! So I phoned the young writer, and, surprise, surprise - he is now 15 years old! The letter has been floating down the Asker for eight years -less than 400 metres a year - *or - 2000 metres in a day, then shipwrecked for eight years!* Good luck Thomas, and thank you for letting us print this saga."

EYPE NOTES

St. Peter's   *Correspondent:* **Mrs. Bev Chisnall,**

Forget the Olympics – it was hot competition in Eype all this month! We started with a rather wet competition in West Bay when teams representing Eype House Caravan Park and The New Inn took to the waters for the RNLI Raft Race. Graham Dannan press-ganged Eric and James (of the RNLI committee) and friend Steve from Bothenhampton to man 'No Problem' in a laid back sort of a way. They looked really cool in their rasta outfits and lifejackets but were so unconcerned about their success that their photographer was allowed to go back to Australia with their photos! 'No Problem' finished in 5th or 6th place from 29 entrants, but a source close to their training camp tells me that their only ambition was to beat the New Inn!

'Cirrhosis of the River' was the New Inn entry, but their dignity faltered a little when Jackie fell in the river whilst still on the slipway! They would have been unmanned anyway as they had fielded an all-female crew of Jackie Gough, Amy Dannan, Julie and Pippy Brook but they came a creditable 7th, which wasn't bad considering the general mayhem!

SYMONDSBURY NOTES

Correspondent of the month: **Mrs. Rosa Lidington,**

St. John the Baptist

Just recently I have been wondering and inquiring about what changes have taken place in this very small and peaceful village during the past few years. It seems that up to about 1960, most people living here would have been employed on the land in one way or another, and as late as 1987 there was a village shop and post office serving the community. Only about 25 years ago, recreational activities included the Church choir, bell ringers, WI meetings, occasional jumble sales in the school, village cricket and football, entertainment by the Mummers and also the Symondsbury Players (who performed in the school, which in those days boasted a stage).

Now, in 2008, life is very different and most people are not employed locally. With the rapid growth of TV and computers, plus the increase in car ownership, there is not the same need for D.I.Y entertainment and some of the groups have discontinued.

However, the Symondsbury Players (who now perform elsewhere locally), the Mummers and the sporting activities continue, and the pub and the school flourish. It appears that community life is moving in a different direction and new growth is gradually taking place, as Phil Davies (our regular correspondent) has pointed out in recent editions of these notes.

In 2004, with great regret, the Symondsbury WI closed after 84 years. Some of the members had been friends for 40 or more years and were loath to lose touch. They decided that they would continue to meet regularly for tea, or an occasional local trip, and so, four years on, a handful of veteran members continue to congregate at Rectory Cottage on the 2nd Tuesday in each month.

Eype book club has started the year with two novels from the emerging genre of fictional historical biography:

Conceived perhaps as a literary salon, the book club is primarily a pretext for a good old get-together and chat. As one member recently commented, "It's a funny sort of book club really. We hardly talk about the book at all. In fact most people don't even read it."

Correspondent of the month: **Lu Orza,**

One of the most delightful aspects of the magazine, having now read several issues, is that although I am personally unacquainted with the individuals who figure in its pages, yet I am being drawn into the narrative of their lives and that has to be a mark of good writing.

"We distribute 1,300 copies every month. Some are even posted overseas. Of course, we owe a big debt to our wonderful band of volunteers who deliver around the villages – people like Bill Budden in Loders, for example. And do you know we actually have a waiting list of advertisers?"

I can believe it, Mary. Your magazine is unreservedly splendid and all your correspondents deserve the warmest praise. Its role in maintaining a sense of community in the various parishes is absolutely invaluable. It is for that reason that, I reproduce just a few of the pieces that caught my eye.

Beaminster

Twinned with St James (France)

> 'Sweet Be'mi'ster, that bist a-bound
> By green an'woody hills all round
> Wi'hedges reachen up between
> A thousan' vields O'zummer green.
> Where elems' loft heads do drow
> Their sheades vor hay-meakers below,
> An ' wild hedge-flow'rs do charm the souls
> O'maidens in their evenen strolls.'
> William Barnes

Beaminster, pronounced 'Bemminster', appears upon first impressions a most contented town. Barely a town indeed, by modern standards, more like a large village. Comfortable, at ease with itself, possessed of an unassuming dignity and with little to divide one man from another. Or might it be a hotbed of intrigue and dispute that renders my early judgement hopelessly misguided?

I call first at the public hall where I make the acquaintance of two charming and helpful ladies, Corinne Regan and Christine Bright, who most lucidly proceed to illuminate the local scene for me.

The Town Council, I learn, is presently conducting a public opinion survey on the subject of what Sir Frederick Treves described as Beaminster's 'queer little Square'. That was a hundred years ago and today it's a very busy little Square. What then are the issues to be considered in this survey?

In an adjacent room I examine a display of the various options for change. How should the parking bays be arranged? Would a one-way flow of traffic be of benefit? Does part pedestrianisation have any supporters? A tree, or even two, might they be planted to advantage?

Poring over the diagrams and maps, interpreting arrows this way and that, Caroline and Roger Lake appear uncertain. Roger's a bell-ringer at St. Mary's.

"I'm not sure about The Square but we do have the finest bells in the county! And the best fruit and veg shop in the county. The couple who run it are Kevin and Angie Denmen. They have their own market garden out at Merriott so much of the produce they sell in the shop is their own."

I pick up a copy of a View From Beaminster at the Co-op and settle down with a drink at a table near the window in The Red Lion. It's all about the public consultation in the paper. Margery Hockings writes that the artist Ann Day and her husband Robin Samways, who own the nearby Gallery cafe, propose a fountain as they have in Bridport. It would attract visitors, they believe. Marjorie Broadhead would welcome more plant baskets and displays to brighten up the neighbourhood and put a smile on faces. Whatever decision is made, there must be no reduction in the number of parking spaces, insist the traders, understandably fearful for their livelihood. Indeed, County Cllr. Peter Gregson, whose son Charles is a butcher in the town, has already expressed his anxieties at a higher level. Notwithstanding allreservations, Cllr. Rebecca Knox, who is leading the review, hopes for an informative response

At the bar I overhear a conversation. Two elderly gentlemen. No names, no pack-drill.

"You know, whether 'tis ladies reversing into traffic, or into space, 'tis all the same. The poor souls they have enough of a problem going out frontwards. Sometimes I just can't bear to watch!"

Of course, what concerns the Town Council and Beaminster Society much more than the fine tuning of the movement and parking of locals is the general topic of traffic passing through The Square. Through the window of The Red Lion I watch a steady convoy of HGVs and other vehicles squeezing through the narrow A3066 which carries traffic between Bridport and Yeovil. There's already been one collision in recent months when a HGV knocked off part of the porch of Daniel's House in Hogshead Street, one of the town's historic buildings, besides innumerable near-misses.

It's said that 'they', at some lofty level of decision-making, are considering the future of 'vehicular movements'. I understand the new 'sat-navs', supposedly a device for resolving and reducing problems, are being held responsible for creating fresh problems, as drivers religiously obey the instructions and converge single-mindedly upon new 'hotspots'. How ever did we negotiate our way about the kingdom before their invention? Didn't we once use road-maps – and common sense? How did they manage during WW2 when there were no headlights after dusk and most signposts had been removed?

Whatleys

This morning I'm bound to meet Sir James (Jim) Spicer and Lady Winifred (Winfy) Spicer who, first at Higher Meerhay Farm and, most recently at Whatleys have for thirty years been an integral part of the Beaminster scene. Jim, of course, has led an adventurous life, first as a soldier, then a farmer and businessman and, above all, as a distinguished politician. Elected as the Conservative MP for West Dorset in 1974 Jim held many important offices – Vice-Chairman of the national party, Chairman of the International Office, Chief Whip in the European parliament, the first Chairman of the Westminster Foundation for Democracy , to mention but a few. He counts Lady Thatcher as a friend – both she and Denis stayed with Jim and Winfy at Whatleys – and he's met many of the world leaders of modern times, not all of whom, I suspect, were greatly to his taste. One, in particular, who springs to mind is a certain Saddam Hussein.

Jim recalls a very different Beaminster when he first arrived in 1958.

"For 20 years after the war the West Country was for most people Devon and Cornwall. Few people came to Dorset by road. People travelled down by train, of course, to Weymouth and Swanage. In those days Bournemouth was still in Hampshire. Certainly Dorset in general and Beaminster, in particular, saw virtually no holiday-makers. I had never been to Dorset myself until I came down to Higher Meerhay. Beaminster was mostly dairy farms. In 1908 there were an estimated 118 in the Beaminster Rural District alone. There was the milk factory, of course, a small plastics factory and Bugler's, the firm of agricultural engineers in the town centre. Now most of the farms have disappeared, or been amalgamated. The milk factory has gone, replaced by Danisco's, a Danish company that manufactures an enzyme that stops cheese fermenting. The plastics factory has long since closed and Bugler's are moving to the outskirts of the town. Further afield, Parnham House was for many years the home of the Makepeace School, where young Linley learnt his craft. That is now in private hands though the new owners do want to play an active part in local life, I understand. So what is Beaminster today, you ask? Predominantly it's retired and elderly with few young married couples with children. Like a number of other Dorset towns there is a serious imbalance in our population. We badly need an infusion of young blood which is, in turn, dependent upon local jobs and housing. On the subject of youth, I am personally much involved at present in raising funds for the Memorial Playing Fields. We're aiming for £500,000. I'd love to see the fields a hive of activity again – as they were years ago."

Bugler's Engineering

I'm just able to squeeze my car between two enormous tractors in Bugler's yard. Ralph, now eighty-four and one of the elder statesmen of Beaminster, has offered me a guided tour of his beloved town.

"My great grand-father founded this business in 1851, the year of the Great Exhibition. It was a blacksmith's and wagon builders then. My father Francis later took it on before it was my turn. Now I'm passing it on to my son John and we're moving lock, stock and barrel out to a new site on the Broadwindsor Road. These old premises, as you can see for yourself, are just too small and cramped. This site will be developed with a variety of houses and shops."

Ralph drives out on to the Broadwindsor Road where construction of the new Bugler empire is already well under way. He points.

"You can see my house up there on the hill. June and I will be able to look down here from our window – and vice versa. I'll just come down from time to time and try to avoid being a nuisance to John."

We're off again around the town. Everywhere holds fond memories for it's the story of Ralph's life, his wife and family and friends. There's an anecdote every few yards. We drive out on to the Crewkerne Road, through the tunnel and turn right to ascend the rise to Buckham Downs.

"See, this is a lovely spot."

I recall the lines of William Barnes. Though, alas, the elms are no longer evident and the number of houses will have grown, yet it is a scene he would still recognise. And, for Ralph Bugler, it is still very much 'Sweet Be'mi'ster'.

"You know, I think I love best coming back on the Dorchester Road and dropping down into the town. It's always a welcoming sight. I've been a very fortunate man to live in such a beautiful place and to be a part of such a wonderful community."

As we wish one another goodbye, I ask Ralph about the survey on The Square. He smiles indulgently, like a father patiently excusing the child who asks the same question over and over again.

"The Square. It's a topic that comes round with the seasons. But you mustn't expect anything to change, leastways, not dramatically. That wouldn't be Beaminster's way."

(Shortly after our conversation Ralph Bugler was rewarded with the title of Honorary Townsman for all his efforts on behalf of the community he loves so dearly. He joins two other Honorary Townsmen, Fred Paulley and Warren Riglar and Townswoman, Janet Page, each one of whom has given sterling service to Beaminster life over many years.)

Clipper Teas – Broadwindsor Road

The name is brilliantly and perfectly chosen, evoking in a single word an age of graceful sailing ships with raking bows and masts full of sail hastening across oceans from distant worlds, India, Sri Lanka (Ceylon), Kenya, South Africa, their holds full of precious leaf for Western caddies and tables, of merchants in finely coloured silks and hard-headed dealers from Europe haggling over quality and price.

There is a wonderful aroma even now in my nostrils.

"I absolutely never tire of it," laughs marketing manager Julie Rideout as she guides me through the tea-blending workroom of Clipper Teas.

Michael Brehme founded the business in 1984 and actually began by blending teas in his own kitchen. The old saying that great oaks from little acorns grow is certainly true of Clipper Teas, for today it is the largest employer in Beaminster with 90 employees. However, Michael Brehme sold the business a couple of years ago and Tony Revill-Johnson is the new chief executive officer.

"We are very proud of the image of Clipper Teas. We were the first company in the UK to produce a tea bearing the Fairtrade symbol and the first to launch a range of organic teas and coffees and the first organic Fairtrade hot chocolate. We feel a particular responsibility to the growers in the poorer countries and we pay an extra premium on our tea and coffee which is passed on to the growers."

It is an image of principled trading with which many readers will be sympathetic and Julie is a persuasive advocate. Certainly it is a remarkable success story, supplying as it now does not only natural food shops and independent food retailers, but a number of the High Street supermarkets. It is a company deserving of wide public support – and it's here in quiet little Beaminster.

Having been strongly recommended to call by at Kevin and Angie's 'the best fruit and veg shop in the county' in The Square I do just that and understand why they are so highly regarded. A couple of years ago my friend, Keith Bird, as 'fine a painter and decorator as any in the county', introduced me to a variety of potato I'd not previously heard of or tasted. The variety was Picasso and it fully justified Keith's high praise. I'd never seen it in a shop until this morning in Beaminster – fresh from the market garden of Kevin and Angie at Merriott. I am delighted. I'd cheerfully take half a hundredweight but I can carry no more than a few pounds. I also peer in at Roy Barrett's excellent and idiosyncratic collection of paintings, mostly of cars and motor-cycles. I also bump into the actor, Martin Clunes and his wife in Frampton's 'deli'. Martin is a popular man in the locality, opening fetes and supporting various charitable causes.

The Old Vicarage

From Murray Rose's book-lined study we gaze across the rooftops of the nearby houses towards the 100 feet, fifteenth-century tower of the church of St. Mary's.

"In Hardy's time it was glebe land between the vicarage and the church. More recently the land was sold off and the houses built."

I fear Tess would now find it difficult to locate the Old Vicarage where once she came seeking her estranged husband Angel Clare.

"Every year we get lots of tourists, especially American and Japanese, who come to stand and stare."

It's a curious thing, isn't it, that thousands of admirers travel half-way round the world to follow the Hardy Trail when so few of the natives have even read a Hardy novel. Of course, Hardy's philosophy of the stoical acceptance of fate is hardly compatible with contemporary Western values, but that is only a part of the explanation. As a nation do we really value writers? When many 'celebrity' figures boast that they have never read a book, is it surprising that so many young people follow their lead?

Murray acquired the Old Vicarage, which was built 35 years before Hardy's 'Tess of the Durbervilles ' was published in 1891, on his return from Switzerland and ran his engineering software business here before his retirement. Today I am here to discuss, in particular, Murray's role at the Town Museum and his chairmanship of the impressive Annual Festival of Music and the Visual Arts here in the town.

"A number of us felt that while visitors would spend a couple of hours looking around St.

Mary's and the town itself, there wasn't really enough for them to spend longer here. So a Trust was established and we managed to secure the former eighteenth century Congregational Chapel for just £5,000, on condition that we allowed the church to continue to function. Actually, when we took it over there were 8 regular members of the congregation, now just one remains. We have, of course, spent a lot of time, energy and money on renovating the building. In fact, the Museum has proved a great success. We stage a variety of displays and attract many visitors and school parties. Happily, we have many retired professional people in Beaminster who provide the solid backbone of our volunteer staff. Apart from myself, Warren Riglar is the sole surviving member of the early days of the Museum, but we owe a lot to so many good people for making the venture a success."

And the Festival, customarily staged across a fortnight in June and July?

"It has become a major cultural event in the county attracting top-class performers and excellent audiences. St. Mary's is, of courser, the focus for our classical concerts and we stage a number of fringe events at The Red Lion, The Bridge House Hotel and the Ann Day Gallery cafe. We also stage a family theatre production in the Memorial Gardens and a jazz concert at Mapperton. In fact, if you look at the programme, it is a very varied blend of music, drama, pottery, painting, photography, sculpture, textiles, talks, poetry and so on. This year will be the fifteenth Beaminster Festival. Our director is Tanya Bruce-Lockhart and the president is Ron Emett who has been such a key figure in so many Beaminster activities over the years. Indeed, Ron was awarded the MBE last year for his services to he community."

Flax Mill House

"You know when I moved here I discovered Beaminster and Sherborne were both referred to as 'God's waiting-room.'"

Though born in India, June Cull returned to England as a child where she was educated at Talbot Heath in Bournemouth. She spent her working life in London becoming Head of Industrial Design at the Design Centre. Her husband was a lecturer in Architectural Design at Middlesex Poly.

"After retirement we were looking for somewhere to live and we discovered Beaminster which, I was told, was 'very friendly, very wet and where the roads never meet.'"

With her background it was a logical step for June to become involved in the Beaminster Society. June is now the editor of their seasonal Newsletter.

"Formally our objectives are to encourage high standards of town and country architecture, to stimulate an interest in and care for the history, natural history and environment and, generally, to secure the preservation of places of historic interest and so on. Often it's in the smallest detail that change can make such a difference. To get rid of an eyesore can dramatically improve a location – graffiti, litter, untidy hedges or verges, overhanging trees, holes in the road, street lights not working properly. If we report such matters to Mr. Morfitt, the Town Clerk, he will try to do something about it. I work very closely in the Beaminster Society with a number of colleagues – Peter Body, Bob Lake, Brenda Cooper, David Gardner, John Willis and John Spooner. Tony Cooper was very active but he's on the point of moving away to be nearer his young family. I feel we're a good team and we all do our bit to try to make Beaminster a better and more aesthetically pleasing town in which to live."

I am intrigued by the house in which June and her husband live.

"Flax Mill House is one of the oldest surviving properties in the town having survived several fires that did so much damage to the town. If you'd looked out of the window 200 years ago you would have seen a sea of blue which was the flax that was grown locally. Though this was initially built as a house it became a flax mill until around 1850."

As I take my leave of June and her fascinating house, I find myself reflecting upon the changing colours of the English farming landscape. Like so many of the older generation I grew up in what I remember as an essentially green England. Of course, as the summer wore on, we saw the various shades of yellow and ochre as the corn fields ripened and harvest-time drew near. But the planting of thousands of acres of oil seed rape, in particular, in recent years has seemed to many of us like the introduction of an alien colour to our countryside, as if nothing comparable had ever happened before. And that's not to forget the blue of the linseed, nor the latest addition, the lilac of the opium fields of Dorset. Yet, as June Cull aptly reminds us, vast tracts of the Dorset countryside, especially in the far west, were once 'a sea of blue'. Plus ca change, plus c'est la meme chose.

St. Mary's Church

I have an appointment with Dr. Colin Smith but I've arrived twenty minutes early for our appointment at St. Mary's. It's an opportunity to explore within. But I'm not the first arrival.

"Do come through. We're called First Steps. It's an activity for the under fives. The children sing a few songs, we have a bible story while the mums enjoy a cup of tea and a sit-down. It's all very nice."

It clearly is – very nice. Everyone looks happy, the four elderly ladies, half a dozen young mums and a similar number of children. I'm introduced to the helpers, one by one.

"Hazel Lincoln, Ruth Dunford, Judy Livingstone and Jan Godfrey, the leader. We love so much to see the children and it's a welcome break in a busy day for their mothers."

Two more young women clasping small hands arrive. It's time for me to leave them in peace. Besides, I notice a gentleman has followed them in. It must be Dr. Colin Smith. A retired GP and one of the 'incomers' to the town, Colin actually found his property in Beaminster through West Country Homes Search, run by Robert Hayman in Lyme Regis. Colin must always have been an active man and retirement has clearly not changed him. He's a churchwarden, sings in the choir and, I later discover, has written a number of the booklets for sale in the church shop. But, first of all, we discuss the magnificent new organ, the pride and joy of St. Mary's.

"We commissioned Anton Skrabl in Slovenia to manufacture it for us. First of all, they sent a delegation but, thereafter, we communicated electronically by computer. He was able to incorporate a third of the pipes from the old organ. Interestingly, the removal of the previous organ revealed a Tudor chapel we didn't know existed. In fact, the Church has really been improved by the changes. To date we've raised £140,000 for it so another £10,000 is needed. English Heritage helped us considerably and the Friends of St. Mary's have raised large sums. Some are not religious but simply love St. Mary's."

Colin also shows me the altar recently made by the very talented furniture maker and a major figure in the Beaminster Festival, Ron Emett.

"And a John Makepeace student made the ten bells for us."

I notice on a wall plaque that the church has been highly commended for its Living Churchyard project and Colin, I have been informed by several of his friends, has been largely instrumental in much of the initial 'donkey work'.

"The Dorset Wildlife Trust has a set of precepts for such a project. Two retired school-mistresses, Joan Holland and Elizabeth Bousfield were the original inspirational figures behind it all. But if you'd like to step outside, I'll show you what we have accomplished to date. The grass simply used to be mown and that was that. It was, at the beginning, an uphill struggle against the coarse grasses. It is still mown in spring and autumn but, in the meanwhile, we do allow a variety of wild flowers and plants to flourish. We've also created a flowery mead and a herb garden and planted a Millennium yew, cultured from a tree 1,000 years old. We managed to cadge a palette from Travis Perkins to make our own compost, so we are making progress and all our volunteers deserve a pat on the back."

There are few churches in the county so pleasingly surrounded by buildings that so perfectly complement it as St. Mary's. The seventeenth century almshouses and the cottages are unreservedly splendid. I always like to peep over the wall at the gardens beyond. Though many churches have their resident jackdaws, few seem more vocal and cheerful than those at St. Mary's high up, in the words of Monica Hutchings, 'among the soaring, golden pinnacles of its tower.'

Fleet Street – Some weeks later
This Sunday morning I have, at last, caught up with the genial Doug Beazer, for the past two years the chairman of the Town Council.

"I was born and bred in Beaminster."

Do I detect a certain hesitation in Doug's use of the word 'born'? I decide that, though I am in his house and drinking his coffee – actually it was his lovely wife Lynda who brought it in – I cannot, as a man in pursuit of the truth, the whole truth and nothing but the truth, possibly let the matter pass.

"To be absolutely accurate, my mother brought me into the world at Horn Ash, Broadwindsor, which I would describe as the 'hinterland' of Beaminster. But I was brought here to Beaminster when I was just so big."

Doug arranges his hands into the shape of a small infant. However, it is an admission I find shockingly reminiscent of my old friend and colleague at Poole Grammar School, Tony Farquhar. The proudest Scotsman I have ever met this side of Hadrian's Wall, Tony wriggled like an embarrassed eel when colleague Simon Powell and I discovered his official birthplace on the all important certificate was Paignton! 'An ersatz Scotsman, of the MacDevon clan' was Simon's withering description, as I recall. Will those born within the sound of the bells of St. Mary's still accept Doug as a true man of Beaminster after this revelation?

"How about this then to establish my credentials? When Beaminster Comprehensive opened in January, 1963, I was actually the first pupil to be let in through the door. I was waiting there at 8am for the caretaker to admit me. It was, of course, the terrible winter of 1962-63 and lots of the children from the outlying areas couldn't get in, so they shut the school later in the day and those of us who had struggled in were sent home. When they reopened on the Wednesday I was again the first boy to go in through the school door."

Doug is certainly trying hard to convince me and I must give credit where credit is due. He's also lived a life since without obvious blemish. Twenty-five years army service in the REME, before returning to Civvy Street and a new post at Yeovil College as a technical support engineer, Doug was co-opted on to the Council in 1989 and has served ever since.

"For the past two years I've been chairman of the Town Council – an honour of which I am immensely proud. I always say that Beaminster gave me a wonderful education and start in life and I am so happy to be able to put something back into the community I love."

I ask Doug about Beaminster's size and the fact that it does to me have the feeling of a large village rather than a town.

"I know exactly what you mean. Actually there was a defining moment a few years back when someone – we never discovered who – pointed out that Beaminster had a population of 2,500 and something and we were, therefore, no longer eligible to play in the Haig Village Cricket competition. The rules were that a village had to have fewer than 2,500 inhabitants to be eligible. At that point we thought we might as well call ourselves a town. Today the population is a little over the 3,000 mark."

And Beaminster today? What does its present proud Chairman have to say?

"I suppose we are what might be called parochial. The pace of change is slow but there's wisdom in that slowness. It's very easy to rush at things and make mistakes. We like to take each issue as it

Beaminster town council Civic day, Thursday 17 April 2008. Centre left, Mrs Lynder Beazer, centre right Councillor Douglas Beazer with various guests attending the day. Picture: *Douglas Beazer*

comes and try to find the best route forward without lots of argument but through quiet discussion and co-operation, if possible."

I ask Doug about the outcome of the Council survey on The Square and, in passing, mention Ralph Bugler's observation.

"We're going to have a feasibility study," says Doug with a smile.

Mapperton

"My father, Lord Hinchingbrooke, bought Mapperton in 1956 after the death of its previous owner, Ethel Labouchere."

How extraordinary. Not that my companion, sitting just across the table, could possibly appreciate the significance to me of such an innocent statement of fact. Fifty-odd years ago I was a miserably puny, gauche teenager living in the South Dorset constituency represented in the House of Commons by Lord Hinchingbrooke. At election time the windows of innumerable houses about Upton and Lytchett Minster were filled with posters exhorting voters to place their crosses against the name of Lord Hinchingbrooke. Sometimes a loudspeaker-van would tour the lanes and a tall, lean figure would address those same voters. In 1956, the same year Lord Hinchingbrooke was completing

Glorious Mapperton. Picture: *Roger Holman*

his purchase of Mapperton, that puny, gauche teenager was posting angry letters to his Member of Parliament protesting against the Conservative Government's decision to invade Suez along with its French and Israeli allies. Little did I guess that half a century later I would be sitting at a table in agreeable conversation with his most courteous and amiable son, John Montague, Earl of Sandwich. I find myself shaking my head and smiling ruefully at the twists and turns of fate.

I know that Country Life has described Mapperton as 'the nation's finest Manor House' and The Independent placed Mapperton 'in the top ten gardens in Britain.' The constraints of time and space preclude me from going into detail about either fulsome tribute. Besides, Mapperton speaks for itself. It is magnificent. It is everything other writers have described so eloquently elsewhere. It will delight everyone who visits. Rather I would prefer, on this occasion, to draw attention to those who deserve the credit for restoring Mapperton to its contemporary glory.

"Ethel Labouchere created the formal Italianate garden in the 1920s. When my father bought the estate after her death he rescued the gardens from their decayed state and restored them to their original splendour, planting a variety of shrubs and trees and bulbs and converting a field into an arboretum. In more recent times my wife Caroline and our splendid team of gardeners have devoted innumerable hours to further enhancing the gardens, adding to the variety of rare plants and perennials especially. A new Spring Garden extension has also been planted. Caroline deserves particular praise for contributing so imaginatively to all the additions of recent years."

So it is then to Caroline, the Countess of Sandwich and her team of gardeners, that we are all indebted for the pleasure Mapperton provides today. But, before I take my leave, I will add a line or two about the present Earl, John Montague, who sits as a Crossbencher in the House of Lords. Most admirably, John has engaged himself energetically in the campaign to abolish slavery wherever it still exists in the world today and he has given great support to the work of Christian Aid and Save the Children projects which seek to ease the suffering of the poor and vulnerable.

Lord Hinchingbrooke, as well I remember, was a man of independent and forthright opinions. The puny, gauche teenager of the 1950s is delighted to make acquaintance, albeit briefly, with his son and heir, John Montague, Earl of Sandwich, so many years later. I am also pleased to encourage those, as yet unfamiliar with Mapperton, to pay a visit at the earliest opportunity. You will not be disappointed.

Kingcombe

Kingcombe Meadow Farm, Toller Porcorum
"I really like the word."

Ian Smart laughs. Three minutes into our conversation and he's already used the word half a dozen times. I tell him that although I've seen the word on the printed page I've never, insofar as I can recall, heard the word spoken aloud before. Yet I am beginning to understand why the word is such an important part of his responsibilities.

'Sward.' (Shorter Oxford Dictionary definition) 'The surface or upper layer of soil usually covered with grass or other herbage.' And, of course, in Ian's world, the composition of the sward is of critical importance in determining a number of his policy decisions.

"If x becomes predominant, for instance, and it's an annual we'll graze the sward the following year which will have the effect of considerably reducing its presence."

We're standing in the middle of one of Kingcombe's ancient meadows. Though it's warm enough, it's raining steadily as it has for much of the day. I could not possibly do justice in words to the range and subtleties of the colours about us. Were Claude Monet here with his easel and brushes – and a large umbrella – he could not fail to paint a masterpiece.

"These meadows have always been traditionally farmed. No chemicals have ever been used. It's been described as 'the farm that time forgot.' When the Wallbridge brothers sold up 20 years ago the Dorset Wildlife trust bought lots totalling 200 acres. Subsequently the DWF has purchased a number of the remaining lots. What's fascinating is that the colours of the meadows vary on a weekly basis as certain species of wild flowers become dominant. The field we're standing in now provides a perfect example of what I was referring to a few moments ago. You can see the Yellow Rattle which is semi-parasitic on grasses and, therefore, a very desirable species to have present when establishing a hay meadow because it allows wild flowers to gain a competitive edge over the grasses. This, in turn, increases the diversity of plants within the sward over a shorter period of time. Yellow Rattle can become quite dominant within the sward. When this occurs, it gradually reduces the yield of hay to a point where it is not cost effective to take a hay crop on that field. However, it is an annual plant and easy to control. You graze the field for a season instead of laying it to hay and the Yellow Rattle is then reduced in dominance and the hay crop in subsequent years noticeably increases."

It is a fascinating example of just one aspect of Ian's work.

"Most of the meadows on Kingcombe are species rich, by which I mean there are fifteen or more species of plant per square metre. Besides a wide range of plants, we also have a similar variety of fungi, particularly many wax cap species. Lichens are abundant. Our birds include barn owl, tawny owl, yellow-hammer, willow warbler, chiffchaff, linnet and siskin. Butterflies include marsh-fritillary, silver-washed fritillary, ringlet, gatekeeper and small copper. The ancient trees found in the miles of hedgerows are abundant with dormice and many remnant woodland species and reflect an almost forgotten woodland past."

Ian studied Environmental Science at Greenwich. Today he's the area manager here and speaks with a passion about his work. Ian's 'remit', which he shares with assistant wardens, Neil Croton and Dutchman Mauritz Pontein, embraces Kingcombe, Powerstock Common and South Porton – 1,000 acres in all.

"At the end of June we'll begin cutting. We turn by hand. We'll make about 2,000 small bales of hay and about 700-800 bales of haylage. Haylage is meadow grass dried for just 2 or 3 days, then wrapped in plastic and stored outside. Hay, of course, is dried for 5 or 6 days. On the livestock side we have a suckler herd of 70-80 cows, about 30 steers for grazing and a small flock of sheep. Though I'm fortunate in that I don't have to make a profit I do try to balance the books. We derive our income through the sale of livestock, using native breeds, and the Government sponsored Countryside Stewardship scheme for planting hedges, scrub control and generally maintaining the countryside. We are, of course, also funded by membership, legacies and grant."

For a young man who so manifestly loves the English countryside, its botanical richness and diversity – and its sward – it seems wonderfully appropriate that he is married to a young lady named Amaryllis and recently became the proud father of a second daughter named Flora and a sister for Peggy.

The Kingcombe Centre, Toller Porcorum
The Centre, originally set up by Nigel Spring, was opened in 1988 and is owned and run by the Kingcombe Trust. It describes its role as 'specialising in holidays and courses that celebrate the beauty and diversity of Dorset.' Thumbing through the prospectus for the year, it provides an enormous variety of activities and courses for all ages – everything from Botanical Painting, Birdsong in Nature and Human Culture, Herbal Medicine, Exploring Dorset Churches, Thomas Hardy's Wessex, Nature Photography, The Wildlife of the Lulworth Ranges and so on. Set amidst the 430 acres of the Kingcombe Meadows Nature Reserve, it's an idyllic place to escape from the cares and responsibilities of the modern world.

Evershot

"There's no doubt many people have been influenced by the likes of Jamie Oliver and Lesley Waters. You see a new generation not satisfied with what so often passes for bread in the supermarkets today. Then there's the older generation who can remember what bread tasted like years ago when it was made from top quality ingredients and baked properly."

It's my first ever visit to Evershot and I've descended without warning upon Steven Crayte and his wife Jackie at their bakery. Most hospitably, they've invited me to look around and now we're sitting in Steve's office drinking coffee and reflecting on the state of the baking industry.

"I actually began working here in 1978. Then the opportunity arose 10 years ago to buy the business and Peter Knott, my partner, and I took the plunge. It's generally a 3 am start – then we have just 4 hours to get everything ready for our 3 van drivers who leave at 7.30 to make deliveries across the area. We supply 40 village and farm shops across a 25 mile radius. Then we have our customers calling at the door. It's a busy life but we usually manage to shut the door by 4pm, have a cup of tea and put our feet up."

A 13 hour day? What would the EEC Commissioners say? Remembering that my father, like my companions a small independent baker and confectioner, didn't take one day off in 10 years – not even a Sunday and never knew the meaning of a holiday – I ask Steve when he gets a break?

"Having a partner in the business means both Peter and I can get away for a holiday every year which helps us to keep sane. And we've got a great team around us. You've met Emma Bristol in the shop at Beaminster who is a 'part of the furniture' and our assistant here, Heather Melpas. We all work together to keep our customers satisfied."

It's a great set-up, Steve, in an unlikely location. Where so many similar bakeries have disappeared in the past 50 years, it's a delight to see you prospering in such a competitive market place. You set yourself high standards and I congratulate you all. I know my father would have been so pleased to see family businesses like your own and the Oxfords at Alweston flying the flag for the small man.

Before I leave the village I stroll up the road to take a look at the source of the Frome. It's always a source of wonder that rivers can begin their lives so humbly and inconsequentially, but then that's true of so many things in life, isn't it?

Melbury

Melbury Manor, The Ilchester Estate

"I believe it's possible to recognise very easily those areas of the countryside which remain in the hands of the large estates. You will see a consistency in the buildings and a balance in the landscape itself with woodland, well-maintained hedges and wildlife habitats. You only have to look at Minterne Magna, Cerne Abbas, Abbotsbury, Evershot or, further afield, Longleat. In fact, I would defy anyone to walk around Abbotsbury and identify the new houses the Estate has built, not least the affordable properties."

Marcus Scrace, personable and affable, is the General Manager of the Ilchester Estate which he administers from his office in Melbury Manor in the company of his secretary, Pat Molyneux, and the rest of his administrative team. A Cirencester College trained chartered surveyor, specialising in Rural Practice, Marcus cares passionately about his responsibilities.

"Whatever decision I make on capital expenditure projects, let's say, I ask myself 'Would I be doing this if it were my own money?' Only if I am wholly convinced do I proceed."

The owner of the 14,000 acres estate is the Honourable Charlotte Townsend, the grand-daughter of the Seventh Earl of Ilchester. She is also the owner of a considerable area of land and property in the Holland Park area of West London, just a few minutes walk from Kensington High Street. Holland House, once the Ilchester family seat, was seriously damaged by German bombs during WW2 and now serves as a Youth Hostel. The park, a personal favourite of this writer, is well worth a visit to anyone unfamiliar with it and, in the grounds, a splendid modern mural of an Edwardian garden party depicts 'society life 'as it was at its grandest in the years before the Great War.

"The family regards itself as the custodian of the estate with an obligation to pass it on to the next generation intact and in good order. Everything we do is thoroughly discussed and great care is taken to protect the well-being of the staff – we employ 150 people in various capacities – and that of tenant farmers and residents. Administering such a vast estate and 300 properties is no mean task and we must continually invest what we receive in rents into maintaining the quality of our holdings. With regard to our residential portfolio we endeavour to ensure there are no absentee tenants and we vet very closely any applicants wanting to buy or let. We give priority to those born or employed locally. We also take very seriously our responsibilities to retired employees and their spouses. We aim to repaint all our houses every five years. We use all our own craftsmen to guarantee the quality of the workmanship."

Like the neighbouring Digby estates in Sherborne, the Ilchester Estate administers a large 'in hand' portfolio of farms with no fewer than 3 managers.

"A number of our former tenants, especially those who ran the dairy farms found it difficult, if not impossible, to make a living. The upshot was that, in a number of instances, their sons had no ambition to make a career in farming. 'Why should we work long hours for so little return?' they asked. And who can blame them? The consequence is that we now farm a little over one third of the agricultural land ourselves. We play to our strengths. Much of the local terrain is best suited to grass. We are presently seeking to develop a bio-gas project which the Germans have pioneered with considerable success. Cattle, as you will appreciate, produce vast quantities of manure. We plan to convert this into gas. It goes into a digester, silage is mixed in until it resembles a gurgling pot of wine though it's not quite so drinkable! The gas drives a turbine which feeds into the grid. We estimate we could produce enough energy annually to provide the power for 500 homes."

And the residue – can it still be used on the land?

"It is still an effective fertiliser – with the addition of small quantities of nitrogen. And it's much less smelly. We're hopeful we'll get the go-ahead from the West Dorset District Council. We estimate ten years would see the costs recovered and, thereafter, it would be profitable. It really is a win/win situation."

It's impossible not to be favourably impressed by Marcus and his team. There is an atmosphere of calm, happy efficiency about the Ilchester Estate.

"You know, the days of the big, bad landowner are largely gone. Estates like this one have a very important and constructive part to play in the future of the English countryside. Being efficient as producers, guarding the landscape and wildlife and ensuringthe local people are well cared for – that's the ethos of Ilchester."

North Dorset (1)

Yetminster

The White Hart

"But it's not really a free society, is it? Politically, yes, but not economically. How can it be with the disparity in salaries between London and the south-east and here in Dorset? I do actually feel a degree of vulnerability in my position here in the village, you know. I'm one of the incomers from the south-east who's made it more difficult for locals to find a home of their own."

John Maslen's frank, rather touching admission that his escape from Hitchin to Yetminster causes him feelings of guilt is appreciated by his listeners.

"But, John, you do actually live here. You are not a second-homer."

Catherine 'Cat' Foster, the manageress of the White Hart and the great, great grand-daughter of Benjamin Jesty, the man who discovered the cure for smallpox even before Jenner and once lived in the village, has just been explaining how she and her brother Tom – and Tom's girl-friend – still share the family bungalow because none can afford local house prices.

"And because there are so few young people here, numbers at the local primary have fallen. The two youngest classes of just 15 and 13 have been amalgamated."

For Joanne Rivers, the daughter of the landlord Jim and Carol Bayfield, and husband Barry and the mother of 2 small children, such a trend is disturbing. Though the school is viable today, what will be the situation 5 years hence if numbers continue to decline?

"When I was in the same school the class numbered 40," confirms Cat.

It's a familiar story across the county – the remedy, infinitely complex.

I wander down the road to the railway station. I see from a plaque on the wall they celebrated the 150th anniversary of the station's grand opening last year. But the old Railway Tavern in which travellers once quenched their thirst has long since closed its doors. In the old station yard small businesses flourish – Thornford Transmission, Yetminster Motor Co and the Buccaneer Motor Co. Shiny motors occupy the spaces once filled by horse-drawn wagons.

I peruse the timetable. Yetminster to Weymouth, change here for the train to Waterloo? Or to Yeovil and change there? Probably the latter. You can be in the capital in 4 hours. Let the train take the strain. But what about the strain on the pocket? We'd all like to use the trains more but the fares are so expensive. Prohibitive for many. Whatever would those who optimistically climbed aboard the first steam passenger train out of Yetminster on 20 January, 1857, have made of the fares today? But then, inflation over the past 150 years has eroded any meaning from the actual figures and, at least, there's still a functioning station here even if no staff are visible.

The odd incongruous bungalow has somehow been allowed to insinuate itself between 'olde worlde' thatched cottages. In Chapel Meadow, near the Methodist Church, stand several handsome newly erected properties. Joanne at the White Hart said one recently changed hands for a fraction under half a million. What would our earnest Wesleyans have made of it all? The main street testifies to the farms that once proliferated – Lower Farm Cottages, Petties Farm House, Cross Farm House, Manor Farm, Holm Farm. Cheerful jackdaws abound. But, of course, jackdaws don't wake in the middle of the night worrying about their mortgages. And we delude ourselves we are superior beings.

At the Village Stores Guy Cupper is painting the exterior woodwork. Guy arrived with his wife Jackie from Philadelphia four years ago.

"We looked around, liked what we saw and here we are. Yetminster has about 1,300 inhabitants, I suppose, but the satellite villages like Leigh, Thornford and Chetnole bring in lots of passing trade. And it's surprising how many small businesses can be successfully run from home today, thanks to Broadband and the like. There's an international stock dealer not a million miles from where we're standing right this moment."

For our rail traveller of 1857, for the farm labourer trudging to the fields from his humble cottage, for the ragged children attending the village school until they were ten or eleven, Yetminster, 2008, would be an unfathomable mystery. Only for our merry jackdaw friends does life remain in all its essentials unchanged. In fact, for them life is infinitely improved. There are no longer small boys with catapults about the village.

Manor Farm House

"The village was very different when I married Jack 51 years ago. He was a farmer and I had no experience of country life, or being a part of a close-knit community. My mother was running a pub in Sherborne at the time but I had grown up in Hitchin. The land locally was very fragmented with lots of small, independent farmers with 50 acres and 20-25 cows. That's how it had been for many years – dairy cows, butter, Blue Vinny, the whey and barley-meal fed to the pigs for bacon. Our milk was collected by Unigate and sent off to London. The population of the village then was about 600. The big events in the calendar were the annual Flower Show, which was intensely competitive, and the Church Christmas Bazaar. We had one bus a week into Yeovil or it was the train. Of course, my 4 children also kept my hands full!"

Ann Partridge recognised the need for radical change.

"As the years passed I became a parish councillor and it was evident we needed a structure plan for the village. We needed mains drainage, improved transport, a proper doctor's surgery, a new school and so on. Alan Swindell, the chief planning officer, was very sympathetic and supportive. We also found incomers arriving in the village. Mrs.Smith from the WI was determined it shouldn't become 'Them and Us 'and we succeeded in integrating our new arrivals into the community. The new blood helped to revitalise and energise the village. At the same time we farmers' wives began to get together to form Dorset Farms and Country Holidays and I set up the Dorset Tourist Information. We would be on Waterloo station handing out leaflets encouraging tourists to come to the county."

And, of course, the vision of Ann and her friends has paid off. She recognised that diversification was absolutely crucial for the farming community and local tourism was a part of the answer. Offering holiday accommodation in the countryside for city dwellers is now a vital part of the rural economy. Today Ann and Jack are still very much a part of that picture providing in their 17th century farmhouse, 'Traditional cooking with local produce and the hostess is happy to offer her expert knowledge of Dorset to her guests.' But what of farming today in the locality?

"Practically all of the farms have been amalgamated. Economics and the consequences of inheritance have both played their part, so that we now have one large local West Hill Farm run by

Ian 'Bo' Buckland. What I do find a great shame is that the cows and pigs have practically disappeared from so much of our countryside. As for the properties in Yetminster, they are mostly in good order. Historically many were owned by the second or third sons of the local gentry. You've seen some of the more recent developments in the village which are also of very good quality. Obviously what we do need are properties that the young locals can actually afford to buy or rent."

And so I arrive at what, in the eyes and to the ears of many, must rank as Ann's greatest claim to fame and an assured place in the annals of musical history. Too many summers ago to count, Ann and her friend Barbara Brooker ran the Yetminster & Ryme Intrinsica Junior Folk Dance Display Team, transporting a mixed team of 10 children around the local countryside to fetes and garden parties. Among the boys were 3 very youthful scouts, Malcolm 'Mac' McCulloch, Maurice John 'Bonny' Sartin, and Peter 'Pete' Shutler, who also loved to sing around the campfires at night. In the fullness of time the boys grew into young men who became known to the wider world as The Yetties, one of the country's most popular folk music groups. It is a remarkable and endearing story for, on both sides, those affectionate bonds forged so many years ago remain as strong as ever. Ann is very proud that her 'little boys' have remained so close to their roots and still perform in the village where it all began.

Though I might have included the following piece in the Sherborne chapter I have decided it belongs here in Yetminster where the story of our heroes began nearly half a century ago.

The Weaver's Club, Sherborne – One morning a couple of weeks later

'Dorset is beautiful wherever you go
And the rain in the summer time
Makes the wurzel bush grow.
And 'tis pleasant to sit in the thunder and the hail
With your girl-friend on a termite clamp
To hear the sweet nightingale.'

"Groupies? They do tend to be knocking on a bit these days!"

"We might get the odd pair of very large bloomers thrown at us!"

"Or false teeth!"

We're sitting in The Weaver's Club, coffee cups and a large and splendid plate of assorted biscuits before us, 'Bonny' Sartin, 'Mac' McCulloch and Pete Shutler, collectively known far and wide as The Yetties. The responses and quips come thick and fast.

"'Mac' and myself come from Ryme Intrinsica. We were in the same class at school."

"And I'm a Thornford boy and got to know Pete and Mac when I joined the scouts."

It's been a remarkable journey that began with the innocence of sing-songs round the camp fire and dancing at fetes under the watchful and motherly gaze of Ann Partridge and Barbara Brooker. 'Mac' remembers the time with affection.

"Of course, the best bit of all was the singing and snogging with the girls in the coach on the way back! We graduated the three of us and Bob Common, the drummer in the early days, to local folk clubs. 'Bonny' did most of the vocals and banged anything that needed to be banged and we played accordions and guitar and whatever else was needed."

It was in October, 1967, that our three young heroes, by now formally known as The Yetties, decided to turn professional.

"We thought we'd give it a try for three months. And here we are still at it forty years later."

'Dorset is beautiful!' Yetties in concert at Witchampton. *Picture: Mike Rose*

They acquired a manager, Jim Lloyd, sold millions of records and the World Council sent them on a world tour. Pete picks up the story.

"When I heard we were due to play in Kathmandu on April 1 I thought it was an April fool's joke. Actually we played on April 2 and we went on to tour 7 countries in 7 weeks. And our music went down wonderfully well wherever we travelled."

Did they ever, I wonder, see my old pal, Wimborne's 'Mr.Laughter' and comedy actor, Billy Burden? 'Bonny' remembers clearly.

"We were in Eastbourne when he was topping the bill so we all went along to see him. We all thought he was absolutely brilliant."

There has been so much fun and pleasure along the way. One of their fondest memories was their association with another of this writer's favourite people, the unmistakeable voice of an English summer, the Basingstoke born former police constable who became cricket's greatest ever commentator, John Arlott. 'Mac' explains the sequence of events.

"We recorded a series with him called 'The Sound of Cricket' and we were lucky enough to be invited to stay with him on his island home at Alderney. We also enjoyed a memorable visit to his other home at Alresford when Laurence Whistler was there. What a cellar of wines the great man had!"

I remind them of a story I'd heard only that morning from someone who was an amused observer of the scene. 'Bonny' describes the incident.

"Will we ever forget it? We were entertaining on a cruise boat between Lymington and the Isle of Wight. We went ashore, the passengers and ourselves, and the captain said he'd give a blast on the horn as our cue to get back on board. We'd been counted on and off but what happened was that

2 other people got on thinking mistakenly that it was the ordinary ferry going over to Lymington. 'Mac' had already got back on when the captain, thinking everyone was safely on board set off without giving a blast on his horn. Pete and I were still sitting on the quayside when we saw the boat moving off. We couldn't believe our eyes! When 'Mac' told the skipper what had happened he said there was no way he was turning round so 'Mac' had to entertain solo on the crossing home. He wasn't best pleased!"

For 'Mac' and Wendy, Pete and Marian, 'Bonny 'and Cynthia and Richard Helson, 'who's played fiddle and mandolin with us when he's not been off fire-fighting', it has proved a very happy musical journey these past forty years. 'Mac' sums up the collective feeling.

"You know, if we'd stayed in our everyday jobs and not taken that chance, our lives would no doubt have been pleasant enough, but we would have missed so much. We've met so many wonderful people and visited so many places."

Pete nods his agreement. "Sometimes when we've been driving back on a wet winter's night and we've been tired and not got home until 3am, we've always been able to say to ourselves, 'Well, we've given people pleasure and put a smile on their faces.'And that makes everything worthwhile."

I'd heard the boys' music, of course, and like tens of thousands of others tapped my toes and sung along to the lyrics of 'Dorset is beautiful ' and other songs from their vast repertoire, but I'd never met them before, not until this memorable morning in The Weaver's Club. And I can confirm, without reservation, that the fellers are as much a delight off stage as on – funny, kind and thoughtful. Thanks, 'Bonny', 'Mac' and Pete for all the pleasure you have given so many people over the years. May you long continue to entertain us.

P.S You may choose the definition you prefer, boys.

'Yetti' – 'A creature said to resemble a large ape, whose tracks have supposedly been found in snow on the Himalayan mountains'. (Shorter Oxford Dictionary.)

'Yettie' – 'A ruggedly handsome creature, whose footprints have indisputably been identified in various taverns in Yetminster, Sherborne and the wider Dorset countryside. Known to sing most harmoniously for its supper. Once even spotted in Kathmandu!'

Bradford Abbas

"Like most Dorset villages Bradford Abbas has no particular claim to fame. No one of national significance has emerged from the village and nothing of great importance has ever happened here."

We're standing in North Street, Tony White, secretary of the 70 strong Bradford Abbas Historical Society, and my old 5A classmate at QEGS, David Park, now a local resident.Tony's a Londoner by birth, a builder by trade and formerly the West Dorset Clerk of Works.He has lived in the village for more than 30 years at nearby Wisteria Cottage, a former medieval 'open hall' built around 1450 and 'modernised' in 1550!

Notwithstanding Tony's modest description of Bradford Abbas history, the reality is that such villages have been the backbone of every county in the land. The people have gone their quiet, undemonstrative, uncomplaining way about growing the food that has sustained the nation through wars and blockades and provided the men for the same conflicts in which we have been involved. Though little of national note may ever have occurred to disturb the tranquillity of life, one tragic episode is still talked about. A local taxi driver, Samuel Blackmore, was murdered on 2 August, 1963, and found several days later in a ditch near Yetminster. Tony points out the cottage where the unfortunate Mr.Blackmore once lived.

"Unfortunately it remains an unsolved case on the police files and, 40 years on, I doubt the mystery will ever be solved."

All around us stand picturesque cottages of the kind so beloved by chocolate box manufacturers.

"It may seem odd today that the previous tenants of most of these cottages were delighted to move out half a century ago when the opportunity arose. But the truth was these dwellings were full of damp with leaking thatch roofs and lacking the modern amenities of the newly built council houses in Queen's Road. Coincidentally, it was of benefit to the village that the locals actually continued to live here so ensuring we remained a thriving community."

Moving around the village my attention is drawn to a major restoration project being undertaken.

"This terrace of mid-17th century cottages was ravaged by fire 3 years ago. The restoration has to match the vernacular of the area – all of the building materials, the timber windows and so on must be in harmony architecturally. Such conditions are attached to all such restoration work today. It's a shame such laws didn't apply 50 years ago."

Lunch is at David and Lorna's where David and I decide that though we both dearly love the game of cricket, the latest Twenty 20 craze is not for us. Cricketing dinosaurs we may be, but the subtle skills of the longer form of the game are what we prefer with Test Matches the ultimate challenge between bat and ball. In fact, the name of Park is synonymous with cricketing prowess in Dorset. David himself was a fine player in his day and currently two Park brothers, Chris and Nicholas, the sons of his nephew Barry, both play for the Dorset Minor Counties XI. And there are others lurking in the wings, notably a young fellow named James, whose perky young countenance was often spotted over the desktops by this writer not so long ago.

The Village Post Office & Stores

"He's called a Field Change Advisor. If I don't get a call from him then I may presume I'm safe."

Ever since 'rat-catchers' were transformed overnight into 'rodent operatives', I've never ceased to marvel at the ingenuity of officialdom to pervert the English language at every opportunity. A Field Change Advisor? Surely he must be advising farmers, leaning over a gate discussing crop rotation or leather-jacket infestation, following in the honourable footsteps of 'Turnip' Townsend and Thomas Coke of Holkham?

"Then there's a six week gap."

A forty-two day interval between a telephone call that may or may not happen and what – an actual call? Or another non-existent call? How does one distinguish?

"At that point those that are not going to close will receive a letter of confirmation."

Of course. What a duffer I am. It is so obvious.

"But there is a further period of a month for appeals and consultation when changes to original decisions could yet be made."

Neil and Sue Pierson own Bradford Abbas Post Office Stores.

"Like so many others we are waiting and wondering. Our futures are in their hands."

So our friendly Field Change Advisors are employees of the Royal Mail and have nothing to do with agriculture.

"The PO salary represents a third of our income. Could we survive on our general sales alone? It's impossible to know at this stage how much of the income might disappear without the existence of the PO."

I wonder if our Field Change Advisors and their masters and the politicians, especially those representing urban constituencies, really appreciate the enormous importance of their decisions? The accountants sitting in front of their computer screens may know the sums, but do they truly understand the implications of closures for the scattered communities in our English countryside?

(Bradford Abbas Post Office survives and Neil and Sue Pierson breathe a sigh of relief. Not everyone in the county is so fortunate.)

Silverlake Farm

"Organic isn't going to feed the world, is it?"

Brian Lock was just 22 when his father died. Inheriting the family's seed merchant's business founded in 1888, he decided to put the farm his father rented into the care of a manager while he travelled extensively for the next 25 years as a seedsman both in the UK and overseas. With a degree from Cambridge in Agriculture the fortunes of Silverlake Farm were, however, never far from his thoughts and he subsequently expanded his agricultural interests by buying a 200 acres dairy farm at Charminster near Dorchester.

In 2004 Brian made a major decision.

"I decided to participate in a Government funded GM (Genetically Modified) Trial of spring sown forage maize, oilseed rape, fodder beet and sugar beet. I saw Lord Melchet in a white suit ripping up maize and I felt I must participate. His approach was entirely unscientific. It was purely an emotional response. So I planted a 33 acre site. Initially there were no problems – not until details of the trials were published on a web site with the location given a grid reference. My phone didn't stop ringing. I said nothing because I knew that whatever I said was certain to be misconstrued. In August hundreds turned up to demonstrate. We were surrounded by protesters. The police even sent a helicopter. A party of eco-warriors destroyed a part of the field."

Brian Lock was not the only Dorset farmer involved in the GM trials. Michael Cox from Lower farm in Hilton, near Blandford, also had a section of his GM rape destroyed. Joe Coleman from Clyffe Farm in Tincleton, near Dorchester, pulled out of the trials after pressure from campaigners. Joe recently said he still feels GM offers the way ahead for farming and Owen Yeatman, who farms at Belchalwell near Blandford, believes the debate on GM should be renewed. These are far from isolated opinions.

It is impossible for most of us, with a limited understanding of the science, to judge objectively the evidence. I do recall one study which revealed that in 2 out of 3 GM crop trials in 2003 a significant fall in insect and plant numbers was confirmed which would have a serious effect on the availability of food for birds. On the other hand, Brian is a serious, principled farmer who believes the science of GM is proven. I understand from other farming friends that virtually all imported soya, for example, which no doubt many eco-warriors devour with gusto is GM soya. For the moment, however, protagonists on both sides are quiet. The issue lies dormant. The sincerity of both camps is manifest, the science to the layman contradictory and confusing. It wasn't so long ago it was fashionable to dismiss out of hand any expansion of the nuclear industry. Now we seem to be preparing for a new generation of nuclear power stations. GM hasn't gone away. As Brian Lock comments, 'Organic, however desirable, will not feed the world.' Will 'conventional' agriculture, whatever that is, feed the world? What would the 18th century pioneers who revolutionised farming for us all and enormously increased the output of food be saying today? What would Arthur Young, the Farmer's Friend, be advising? Would he stand alongside Brian Lock and Owen Yeatman, or Prince Charles and Lord Melchet? One thing is certain. This writer has absolutely no idea.

(I will mention one interesting fact which has nothing whatever to do with GM or farming in general with which Brian acquainted me. The redoubtable Monica Hutchings, from whose splendid *Inside Dorset* I have several times taken extracts, lived just across the road from Silverlake at Romany Cottage. Brian tells me he often saw the lady on her bicycle, no doubt pedalling off to explore yet another village or two for her book.)

SHERBORNE
Twinned with Granville (France) and San Gimignano (Italy)

The Vicarage

The Revd. Canon Eric Woods, Vicar of Sherborne, Rector of Lillington and Acting Priest of Longburton, beckons me to a handsome chair in his study while he disappears to the kitchen to make coffee.

What does the Canon read in his spare moments, I wonder? The shelves are overflowing – and there are a lot of shelves – mostly with titles on theological matters, which is hardly surprising in the circumstances. At a guess I reckon it would take several lifetimes to read all the titles on display. I do spot three collections of John Betjeman's verse in a separate pile and there are lots of classical CDs. No Elvis, Stones or Beatles but perhaps he keeps those hidden.

Canon Eric returns bearing my coffee. He's a big man with the most amiable of grins. I mention he is uniformly spoken of as 'a character'.

"That definitely means I'm getting old," he laughs. "People only refer to you as a 'character' when you're getting old!"

I tell him I have been reflecting for some days on the subject of Sherborne's schools. It's not a topic I would place at the top of my list in any Dorset town other than Sherborne, but it strikes an immediate chord with Canon Eric.

"I am actually vice-chairman of the Governors at the Gryphon, an ex-officio Governor at Sherborne School and Honorary Anglican Priest at the Roman Catholic Lewesdon, which is an independent girls' school 3 miles outside the town."

He begins a quick tally of the students at the various educational institutions around the town.

"The Gryphon, Sherborne's comprehensive, 1,400; Sherborne School, the boys' public school, 600; Sherborne Girls, the girls' public school, 400; the International College, a prep school attached to Sherborne School providing education for pupils whose first language is not English,200; Lewesdon, 300; the Abbey and County primaries together with the prep school, 800 between them."

The total is a staggering 3,700.

"To that figure you must add the teachers, classroom assistants, office staff, cleaners, canteen and ground-staff, the local craftsmen and towns-people associated in some way with one or other of the schools"

At the most conservative estimate, the total is 4,500 and it's highly probable the figure is nearer 5,000. It is very evident that education is Sherborne's 'industry', for out of a population of 12,000 more than a third are in some way engaged in the business of education. In the light of its enormous importance to the economy and life of the town it is a subject to which I will return later in the chapter. But for most visitors to the town of Sherborne itself, it is the magnificent Abbey and the surrounding buildings that draw them in their thousands each year.

"The Abbey is, I believe, without fear of contradiction, the finest building in the county," says Canon Eric." It daily gives me so much pleasure to be closely associated with it and the spiritual life that surrounds it."

Oxford educated and a young graduate with a social conscience, Eric joined 'Shelter', the campaigning group for the homeless led by Des Wilson and, like his wife Sandra, taught for a time before reading Theology at Cambridge where he encountered John 'Honest to God' Robinson and was duly ordained. Arriving in Sherborne in 1993 he soon became deeply involved in the life of the community believing that to be an essential function of his role as a churchman.

"I am passionate about the Gospels but I would not describe myself as desperately 'churchy'. I do

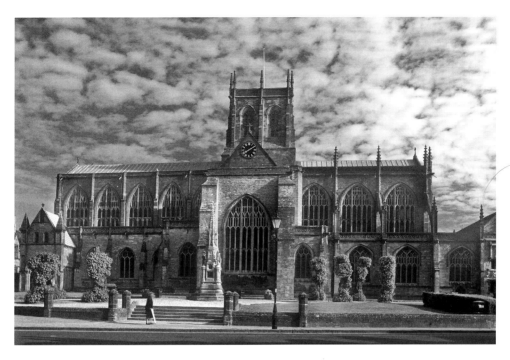

'The Abbey is, I believe, without fear of contradiction, the finest building in the county.' Canon Eric Woods.
Picture: Roger Holman.

particularly admire men like Capt. Peter Love, the former Master of the *Oriana*. On his retirement he became the chairman of the Yeovil Night Shelter, something very practical, putting his beliefs into practice on behalf of others. When my time comes to retire, I'd like to find something equally useful to do with my life. But I am not one for grand gestures. There are two ways to make a fire burn. You can poke it vigorously or blow on it gently. I am a gentle blower. Quite what I shall do at this stage, I simply do not know."

Canon Eric pauses for a moment.

"Someone you absolutely must meet is Canon Tim Biles. Tim is a true radical and a prophet. How would I define a prophet in this context? Someone who can discern, speak the truth and not count the cost to himself. Tim has huge integrity with no self-seeking."

Hound Street, A couple of days later

After such a recommendation, there is only one place I can be this morning though it wasn't just the words of Canon Eric that prompted me to seek out the man. I had heard his name several times before, most notably in Beaminster and the villages of the Benefice. And so here I am this morning in the home of Canon Tim Biles and his wife Joan, together with a number of items of football memorabilia. To be more precise, the items all appear to relate to one particular football club, Southampton FC. Though I am an AFC Bournemouth supporter, all South Coast football people do follow the fortunes of our neighbouring sides with interest. Discovering another man's sporting loyalties, or indeed their absence, invariably adds to an understanding of the individual in the round, I feel. I view Canon Tim with renewed curiosity. Though retired from full-time ministry Tim remains active within the local church community. We begin by discussing a number of the issues that have confronted the Church of England in recent times.

"It would probably be useful to give you the background to many of the changes in the past 50 years. After the war the country parishes were full of ageing priests, declining congregations and many churches, especially the Victorian ones, were suffering from serious structural problems. A church roof has, on average, a life span of 150 years and many were reaching the end. In years gone by the old-established families would send a craftsman or two along to their local churches and get the little jobs done. The manor house and the village church were inextricably linked. After the war the old order began to change. Many of the family estates were sold up, people were leaving the countryside and congregations in an increasingly secular age were declining. It was a double whammy. Suddenly village communities had to wake up to their responsibilities. Previously no one had done anything because it had been done for them. Now, if they wanted to preserve their local churches, they had to act. In most instances, they did."

Tim and Joan met when they were both teaching at St. Francis, Hooke Court, an institution for the maladjusted. After Tim's ordination he became Vicar of Toller Porcorum and Hooke, before Melplash and Mapperton were added to his responsibilities. Joan recalls their wedding day as a perfect illustration of the state of many village churches thirty years ago.

"We married in Hooke. There was damp everywhere. The grass had to be scythed so I could actually get into the church."

Tim adds to the picture.

"On another occasion when the Archdeacon preached in a nearby church, he carried an umbrella because of the leaking roof. The half a dozen worshippers were used to it. But there were, of course, wider issues than the physical state of the church buildings. George Reindorp was the Bishop of Salisbury between 1972 and 1982. It was part of his brief to implement a Church of England enquiry known as the Sheffield Report which called for a fairer distribution of clergy. Very simply, the clergy were over-represented in the countryside and under-represented in the cities. In theory the idea was to have one vicar for every 2,500 people. Dorset was just about the most protected with the least change. Of course, some of the smaller livings were perfect for ageing clergy who may have been in physical decline but could still draw a salary and retire from some of their more onerous duties with dignity. But the expense of providing every parish with its own vicar was costing the church a vast sum. It was clear there was need for a radical upheaval. There had to be amalgamations. The Bishop faced two very different approaches. He could ask but he could not instruct. He needed the co-operation of the local clergy and, for my part, I gave him that support. By this time I was the Vicar at St. Mary's, Beaminster, and, in fact, Beaminster was the first to act upon it. I know many in the parish interpreted such changes as the church 'withdrawing'. I saw it rather as the church 'regrouping' for a new age. Another inevitable consequence was the sale of vicarages. There was quite a furore about it. Parishioners regarded the vicarage as a place they could go to see the vicar, have a cup of tea and discuss their problems. At St. Mary's I might have lived in the old vicarage. As it happens, I preferred the new one because it was not damp but I do remember looking round the old one. It had a paddock, a croquet lawn, stables, a walled garden and the upstairs was given over to staff accommodation. Along with the Manor, it was one of the two finest buildings in the parish. In a sense, the two vicarages represented the changing face of Anglicanism. We were living in a false age. Reality had to dawn. The sale of the vicarages proceeded. We sold Toller Porcorum, Netherbury, South Perrott, Melplash and Broadwindsor though the latter was rebuilt. We also had to decide what to do with the buildings themselves. Melplash was a classic example of a church that was far too big for the parish. It was built by a benefactor in 1846 who believed the flax industry would spread across the county and the population would grow accordingly. As we know, it didn't so we had a church with a capacity of 300 with an active congregation of just 6 who couldn't hear the sermons and regularly froze to death! When I proposed at the Parochial Church Council that we cut the church in half, erect screens and put in a badminton court poor Nell Stevens actually fainted, she was so horrified. We even had some difficulty reviving her!"

Canon Tim can afford to laugh at the recollection today.

"But there was a lot of criticism. I was accused of vandalism – and that was the least of it."

But Joan Biles remembers the support for her husband's proposal.

"A farmer from Toller Porcorum, Peter Billen, stood up and said: 'We farmers have had to make changes over the years – why not the church?"

Tim nods his head.

"The case was unanswerable. Change was essential. Even dear Nell eventually became a supporter. After we put in the screens we reduced the capacity to 50, but the congregation can now hear properly and the building is warmer. And, when the need arises, on big occasions, we can remove the screens and accommodate the bigger congregation."

And today – how does Tim regard the future?

"Today I am not a pessimist about rural churches. Forty years have passed and I see only progress. Something had to be done. Yes, a few churches have gone but the majority remain and there is now a much higher standard of maintenance. Enormous improvements have occurred almost everywhere."

What about the 'team ministries' that evolved out of the changes?

"When the team here began a lot of people were against it. They feared the smaller villages would be swallowed up by the larger – in this instance, Beaminster. So we made sure every parish had 3 votes so they could outvote the bigger. The first Sunday South Perrott joined I said to some of the 'team': 'Let's go over and augment their congregation.' So we did. One, Mark Budden, went over on his motor-cycle wearing his leathers. He arrived early and went into the church. The local churchwarden saw him and rang the police to report 'Someone has gone into our church and I don't recognise him!' When you consider the message of the Gospels and the instruction to welcome strangers....."

But it's not simply been a matter of rationalisation and restructuring that has concerned Tim over the years. He's also given much thought to the very changed society we have in Britain today.

"In 1987 for the 6 weeks of Lent we decided to invite speakers to St. Mary's from the great world religions – a Muslim, a Hindu, a Christian, a Jew and a Buddhist, together with a Humanist. I thought it was a perfectly laudable idea, a way of getting different religions together. But all hell broke loose. We had anti-Muslim demonstrations outside the church and we were obliged to summon the police. Sadly there were many Anglicans among the protesters. Yet we had a full church on each occasion, the Bishop supported us and so did Archbishop Runcie of Canterbury. But we'd clearly touched a raw nerve. Look how far we've come since that time!"

Joan Biles smiles ruefully. "You can understand now why Tim has sometimes been regarded as a bit of a rebel!"

I've noticed in exploring many of the churches in West Dorset that they share close ties with African countries, especially the Sudan. What was the origin of these?

"How did it happen? Well, it was in 1973 that the Bishop of Salisbury was drawn into involvement by the Bishop of Jerusalem. I regard it as one of 'God's little jokes' that he should have linked Salisbury and the Sudan. The diocese of Salisbury is everything the Sudan isn't. It enjoys stability, security and prosperity and is very much a part of the 'establishment'. The Sudan, in contrast, is a seething cauldron of problems – civil and religious conflict, poverty and famine – total insecurity. We do try to assist. Two of the principals have been Rear-Admiral Robin Musson, who is the secretary of the Partnership with Sudan, and Mrs. Mary Treacher. Both have done stalwart work for the beleaguered country."

Sherborne and Beaminster have both received many 'incomers' in the past twenty years or so. How does Tim see their arrival?

"We hear much of the negative impact of 'incomers' but the reality is often quite the opposite. They have rejuvenated many village communities. Many arrive with 5, 10, even 20 useful years of life remaining. They have an enormous resource of wealth and skill and vision. This has been a blessing and perceptive clergy have had the wit to use this new energy. Dr. Colin Smith in Beaminster is an excellent example. The 'living churchyard' was his project and he did much of the hard graft. It is doubtful any local would have undertaken it."

From time to time on my travels I have met someone who has illuminated a major theme with great clarity and insight and Canon Tim Biles has done just that. I must add that Tim is no mean author himself with several titles to his credit and one, in particular, 'In Every Corner Sing', the diary of a country vicar, I have found both fascinating and highly entertaining and I do warmly recommend it.

As I leave I ask Tim about the pile of footballs outside his window and the Southampton FC memorabilia. For the first time he seems distinctly coy.

"People don't want to hear about that," he smiles.

On the contrary, Tim, we all commiserate with you. What is happening at the club is desperately sad, when we remember the glory days of Lawrie Mac and Ted Bates, Mick Channon, Matt Le Tissier and all the other brave lads of Soton FC. Alas, those triumphs are fast fading memories, most unlikely to be repeated in our lifetime. Never have the South Coast teams collectively found themselves in such dire straits. And everywhere it's the same story – excessive ambition without the finances to match.

At the Abbey – Another day

'Never volunteer for nothing.' The old fellow I met on the Marine Parade at Lyme Regis reminded me of the old soldier's maxim. In certain contexts, it's an entirely understandable strategy.

"But what would we do, I ask, if people didn't volunteer? Or what if we all went on strike? How would society manage?"

Commander Kenneth Harding chuckles. Kenneth's a volunteer at the Abbey. Meeting visitors, answering questions, pointing the uncertain in the right direction, Kenneth is just one of the Abbey team without which the place simply wouldn't function as smoothly as clearly it does. Andrew Cross, the verger, is doing a great job but he can't be everywhere at the same time.

"My son calls me a 'Sherborne stodger'. We're the perfect stereotypes of a large section of Sherborne society – retired professionals who spend their time doing community work of some description."

Kenneth's wife Ethnee also helps at the Abbey with the cleaning, besides voluntary work at the Yeatman hospital. Another Abbey volunteer I meet is Hilma Snowden.

"One of my little jobs is to look after the 'votive' candles."

To my shame I must confess to my ignorance of the precise nature of 'votive' candles and Hilma's work.

"A 'votive' candle stands before the altar of a saint. And it's my job to scrape off the old candle wax. It's not exactly glamorous work, but it all helps to keep the Abbey going and enable our visitors to enjoy their experience here."

The Bishop of Sherborne, the Rt. Revd Tim Thornton

It would be remiss of me not to pay my own tribute to Tim who leaves Sherborne to take up a fresh challenge as the Bishop of Truro. Long before I began this journey a number of friends urged me to make acquaintance with Bishop Tim. The unanimous opinion was that ' Tim is a splendid fellow', both at a personal level and as a forward-thinking, compassionate cleric. With our diaries never quite in harmony a face to face meeting has proved impossible but we have spoken on the telephone. Certainly on a whole range of issues from homosexuality, the role of women in the Church to relations with the Muslim community, Tim's views are constructive and imbued with a spirit of tolerance and love. Let me take this opportunity to wish Tim and his wife Sarah great happiness and fulfilment in their new lives in Truro. Everyone within the Christian community and outside it will, I know, share my sentiments.

The Three Wishes, *Cheap Street – Later that morning*

He's deep in conversation with an elderly lady as I approach from the direction of the *Half Moon*. I would guess from his demeanour he is offering words of comfort. The lady departs with a grateful smile even as I arrive. Someone else bids him 'Good Morning' as we shake hands and make our introductions. Seated at our table in *The Three Wishes* another lady exchanges a few words with him on her way to the door. He may not be wearing his chain of office but it is obvious Keith Batten is a familiar figure to the people of Sherborne.

"I'm a local boy born and bred. I sang in the Abbey as a choirboy and, in my later years, I was the full-timer verger there. You could say I'm 'steeped in it'."

A softly spoken man Keith cuts a very different figure from the stereotypical former shop steward the media delighted in lambasting in days gone by. That he's also the only Labour councillor on an otherwise overwhelmingly Conservative council speaks volumes for the quality of the man sitting across the table from me. It is no exaggeration to say that everyone I have spoken to in the town holds Keith Batten in the very highest regard.

"I feel so privileged to be Mayor. It's a wonderful town, you know. We have some excellent councillors, we try hard to debate sensibly and work together to represent the people of Sherborne as a whole."

Yet Keith's background was not an easy one. Growing up on a council estate his father died when he was a child.

"It wasn't easy for my mother bringing up three boys."

Twenty-four years at the local fibre-glass factory taught him the worth of quiet diplomacy with management. Finding a way through the complexities of industrial relationships to sensible outcomes was a perfect preparation for council office.

"The town's changed, of course. There were two dairies and two large glove factories. They're all gone. Even the fibre-glass factory has fewer employees. I do remember the days when they sent out buses to pick up labour from the villages and offered bonuses if you could recruit someone."

We discuss the Barton Farm development on the Marston Road.

"The plan is for 280 houses, one third affordable. Mind, what is affordable? There is anxiety over the development and, obviously, there must be the infra-structure in place. What is important is that our young people do have somewhere to live and local employment in the form of light industry on the site."

Keith has always closely identified with the needs of young people but he firmly believes that rights come with responsibilities.

"It's a difficult balancing act. Some young people in Sherborne argue too much attention is paid to the older generation and too little to them. I've spent time talking with them at the Gryphon, for example, and pointed out that they do have a youth club and access to a sports centre at the girl's school, though I know they have to pay to use it. Some of them want an unsupervised place where they can just 'hang out'. But, at some stage, there has to be organisation. Unfortunately, just 'hanging out' without supervision in the Pageant Gardens led to serious vandalism and the shelter had to be demolished at some expense to the community."

If I describe Keith Batten as an unaffected man of old-fashioned values it is meant as a sincere compliment. He and his wife Sonia have known great pain and heartbreak in losing two children in tragic circumstances.In spite of everything, Keith remains the gentle personification of decency and goodness that the towns-people of Sherborne recognise with warmth and affection. Sherborne is fortunate to have a man of such calibre at the heart of their community.

Marjorie Snowden arrived in Sherborne in 1997 from Sutton.

"Why did we choose Sherborne?Very simply, it has just about everything we were looking for. It's possible to walk everywhere, safe for children, possesses a wide variety of shops, enjoys good transport links east and west and, of course, it's a very beautiful town.My brother also lives not too far away in Broadstone. Someone did say it has only one disadvantage – it's just six miles from Yeovil, but that was rather mischievous!"

Marjorie was a 'political animal' long before she came to Dorset having been a councillor in London. Like Keith she is watching very closely the happenings at Barton's Farm.

"We do want to ensure the affordable housing is indistinguishable from the rest and we are looking at the experiences of Poundbury. It's terribly important that it is 'pepper-potted' about the estate. Persimmon claims such a policy makes it all the more expensive and that's the reason they've been pushing for four-storey buildings but we will resist that strongly."

Like everyone else I have spoken to Marjorie regards the 'Digby influence' in the town as a benign one.

"We built the Digby Hall, our public hall, from money from the Simon Wingfield Digby Trust."

One of Marjorie's close friends and council colleagues is Drusilla Gurzynski.

"I became a councillor at the same time as my partner, Malcolm Boustead, who will be Dominic Elliott's Deputy this year."

Drusilla was Mayor herself in 2006 when Keith Batten was her Deputy. She is presently responsible for supervising the work of Sherborne's 18 Council employees. Like Marjorie, she is concerned to ensure that all the housing development within the town is compatible with its architectural heritage.

"We are a historic town. Future generations will not forgive us if we detract from the beauty of the town with building eyesoresI am also worried about where Barton's Farm people are going to shop. Yeovil is just half a dozen miles down the road. To come into Sherborne they will have to negotiate 4 sets of traffic lights. Will they bother to do so? And how much control will we exercise over who is put in charge of the affordable housing?There might be difficulties and a clash of interests between us and West Dorset District Council. That is why it is so vital that we thrash out these matters before they become serious problems."

Drusilla shares Keith Batten's views on the responsibilities of the younger generation.

"Yes, we want to provide the best facilities possible for them but it was very sad that the beautiful old shelter had to be demolished after vandalism. I know it is a small minority that is responsible but I feel the majority should try to exercise a degree of moral authority over the trouble-makers. It does make me despair sometimes."

But, like her fellow councillors, Drusilla is optimistic about the future.

"Of course there are always issues – that's life. But Sherborne remains a wonderful place in which to live within a splendid community network."

Marston Road – An hour later

Whenever possible on my travels I try to see for myself the 'problem spots' and so it is that I set out on foot along the main Sherborne to Yeovil A30 road – the Marston Road – alongside the Barton Farm development. It's easy to see what the locals fear. If buildings of several storeys are built they will effectively block out the historic views of the town for the residents. In a driveway I spy a figure moving and decide to approach. The man eyes me warily.

"You haven't come to sell me anything, have you, because I'm not buying."

I hasten to assure the gentleman my business is merely the pursuit of truth and opinion.

"Then you must come in and meet my wife."

Now, there's a recommendation in itself. With extraordinary courtesy and hospitality Eddie and Sally Westlotorn invite me on to their patio, bid me pull up a chair and proceed to ply me with cake and tea. I never cease to delight in the kindness of people and my singular good fortune. Or is it that I merely look in need of nourishment? I suppose one day my luck is bound to change and I will encounter a rabid dog or, far scarier, Cherie Blair.

"How people feel about the Barton Farm development depends to some extent upon which side of the road they live. If like us they live on the north side with unbroken countryside stretching into the distance that is unlikely ever to be built upon, they are inclined to feel less strongly than if they live on the other side of the road with views that are threatened. But, of course, we do understand the concerns and it is important they get it right."

I learn that Sally is the secretary of the Sherborne Chamber of Trade with 115 paid-up members who are much troubled by the scale of the town's car-parking charges.

"They are deterring shoppers and damaging business."

I'm sure Sally is right and, if ever she came to Poole and Bournemouth and saw the charges there, she would be even more right.

I discover that Eddie and Sally are also racing enthusiasts and friends of the Tizzard and Dimond families just up the road towards Milborne Port. At moments my good fortune is truly astonishing. To think I might have approached some crotchety old crone, or blimpish retired colonel, instead of which I happen upon the most hospitable couple imaginable and racing people into the bargain! Eddie and Sally promise to arrange introductions to both the Tizzards and the Dimonds.

Toll Cottage, Oborne Road – A couple of days later

"When I was two weeks old I caught pneumonia and Mother summoned the vicar. He looked me over and said he feared I wouldn't last the night so Mother said: 'We'd better give him a name. We'll call him Jack after his grandfather before him.' That was in 1925 and, as you can see, I did get through the night and later they officially gave me the name William John but everyone's always called me Jack."

True to their word Sally and Eddie have fixed it for me. Wherever I've travelled in Sherborne and district and whoever I've met, the advice has been the same, 'You must meet Jack Dimond. The man is a legend in his own lifetime'. And here I am at Toll Cottage on the Oborne Road, with the great man himself. We're sitting outside in the yard watching the swallows flitting about the barns.

"Swallow numbers, I reckon, are about the usual but I haven't heard a cuckoo."

How many times have I hear the same lament, even from farmers who spend their lives in the great outdoors.Personally, I've heard just two, both in the Wimborne area. Twenty years ago I'd long ago have given up counting although friends tell me there are more in the north and Wales and Southern France is full of cuckoos, or is that just anecdotal?

Jack Dimond has spent a lifetime in farming like his grandfather before him.

"When we were young if Dad could feed the family and pay the rent we were happy. I grew up catching rabbits with my ten ferrets and selling them in the market."

Today Jack's son Ian runs the adjacent mixed farm and specialises in breeding high-class Friesians.

"His cabinet is overflowing with cups."

Another son Robert lives across the border near Wincanton where he has created two large commercial coarse fishery lakes. Another son Richard lives across the road and runs a riding stable. He also has a daughter Peggy who lives at Henstridge. For Jack his family has always been at the centre of his life, not least his wife Mary.

"I've been blessed with the most wonderful wife any man could ever wish for. I'll give you an example of the sort of woman she's been. She was hand-milking at five-thirty in the afternoon. One hour later she was giving birth in Yeatman hospital. She's always worked so hard with never a word of complaint and, of course, she's given me four lovely children and now we have eleven grand-children. Everything really begins in the home, doesn't it? Good manners. Politeness. Please and thank you. I can't stand bad language. When I hear it on the TV I just turn it off!"

Jack's son Richard from across the road joins us. For the Dimonds horses are in the blood. Many years ago Jack held a permit to train under NH rules so it was hardly surprising that Richard as a boy was often riding around the family farm. Leaving home at sixteen Richard joined the legendary Capt. Tim Forster at Letcombe Bassett where he trained many fine horses including the Grand National winner Well To Do.

"When I arrived at Letcombe I was greeted by the stable's amateur, Brough Scott. Do you know Brough?"

For many years a member of the Channel 4 racing team and later Sports Journalist of the Year, Brough kindly wrote the Foreword to my first book 'The Extraordinary Mrs.D', the biography of the racehorse trainer, Mrs. Louie Dingwall.

Following a number of crashing falls Richard was obliged to abandon his dream of becoming a successful jockey and took out a licence to train. He'd scarcely settled into his new profession before a terrible accident nearly cost him his life.

"I thought I'd lost him," Jack recounts."Richard was in a box when he was kicked in the head. He was in a terrible state. There was blood everywhere. For six months his jaw was wired and he lost his memory for a whole year. And, of course, he had to give up his career as a trainer."

At least the riding stables Richard runs today with his wife Ruth have kept him close to his beloved horses.

"Besides our regulars we get students from the local Sixth Forms and the International College so we're kept busy. We also offer b & b accommodation."

The next part of Richard's story was, in part, already known to me before I arrived that morning at Jack's. It was about a year ago that a young gelding called Joe Lively won a modest race at Newton Abbot for the Milborne Port trainer, Colin Tizzard, ridden by his son Joe Tizzard. Joe Lively proceeded to win a further six victories during the season netting a six figure sum in prize money for his very proud owner – a certain Richard Dimond.

"We've known the Tizzards for years. Our two families are great friends," adds Jack. "And young Joe Tizzard is Richard's godson."

At this point in our conversation Richard goes off to the kitchen to make a pot of tea and Jack whispers to me.

"I'm so thrilled for Richard. If ever anyone deserved a really good horse he did – after all his accidents. It's wonderful and especially so because our two families have always been so close."

(The threads of this particular story are resumed later in the book.)

Racehorse trainer, Bill Turner, aboard Zebedee. The Cheltenham Gold Cup, Bill? *Picture: Racing Post.*

When Jack retired from farming a number of friends and acquaintances encouraged him to put pen to paper and record his experiences. The resulting books have both proved local best-sellers – *Dimond Gems* and *More Dimond Gems*. I will quote the words of Richard Wood, Group Secretary of Sherborne NFU in his Foreword. *'To call Jack Dimond a character is an insult, the term has been devalued. Jack, who I have known for many years, is a true prince of Dorset farming, a man admired for his ability to farm and his love of the countryside, long before the term 'environmentally friendly' was coined.'*

I count meeting Jack Dimond one of the highlights of my journey to date. He's wonderful company and represents so much that is good in the life of the English countryside. He is one of nature's gentlemen

Just up the road at Sigwells Farm, Corton Denham, Bill Turner, the racehorse trainer recently celebrated another Brocklesby winner at Doncaster with Sally's Dilemma, the first significant two-year old race of the turf season. Bill's also recently acquired a 14 month year-old zebra from Belgium which he has taken to riding around his 300 acre farm. Bill even rides the zebra named Zebedee to his local.

"I ride him with a saddle and I take him into the village. The first time I did it a few people outside ran back in thinking their beer was a bit strong!"

Oborne Road, with the Mayor Incumbent – Later that morning
"I remember young Dominic as a lad out flying his kite."

So said Jack Dimond when I told him I was calling by on the Mayor incumbent. I recall the remark as I settle into the armchair in Dominic Elliott's lounge which looks out upon the old railway line and a tributary of the River Yeo. But I trust there'll be no mischievous 'kite-flying' when Dominic assumes the robes of office as Sherborne's first citizen with his friend Malcolm Boustead as his Deputy. Besides, Dominic has been out of short trousers for some years now and this former RAF man and five years a councillor, is keen to do his bit for the town.

"It's a great honour and I see it as my duty to work hard on behalf of the towns-people in the coming year."

Dominic is particularly concerned by Government plans for an extra 11,000 houses to be built in West Dorset.

"Yeovil's getting closer every year. It's coming right up to the edge of the county boundary. With the greatest respect to Yeovil what we don't want is a long line of ribbon development that practically joins the two towns together, Yeovil does have its difficulties. Only this morning I heard on the radio that the number of Polish children in one of their primary schools is so great the teachers are having to learn Polish. At the moment the proposed development at Barton's farm will slot into the

Sherborne Castle. *Picture: Roger Holman*

north-west quadrant. But it's imperative that the infra-structure is in place together with some light industry. In the longer term we must preserve Sherborne's integrity. If you look at the town aerially you will see it is surrounded by a landscape of considerable natural importance and conservation land."

Dominic is an impressive advocate for his town and I am quite sure he will give an excellent account of himself during his term of office, though it is not going to be an easy ride for any of our elected representatives in the coming period. With ever increasing population pressure points it's clear there are going to some tough battles with Whitehall and Central Government, whatever the political complexion of the party in office.

Robin Legg and 'Good Old Farmyard Smells'

Robin Legg, County Councillor and journalist, writing in his column *In My View*, says of the proposed Marston Road development: *'I shall miss the farmyard smells which waft across Newell and Marston Road on a winter's evening from Barton Farm. There can't be many towns in England which still have a working farm within their bounds. The farm's location is a link to a bygone era when the seasons and the farming year of planting and harvest dominated the lives of our forefathers. So it will be a shame when Mr. Amor and his cows are finally displaced by bricks and mortar and the motor car, as will surely happen before long.'*

But Robin's piece is no mere elegy for a passing era. He is deeply uneasy about the Government's Regional Spatial Strategy which states that a further 19,700 new houses will be needed in the Yeovil area by 2026. Robin continues, *'The Report adds ominously that Yeovil's growth options will need to be explored in West Dorset, notably in Sherborne.'*

Add together the figures being mooted for West Dorset in general by Dominic and those proposed to meet Yeovil's needs quoted by Robin and the Barton Farm development begins to sound distinctly small fry.

The Digby Estate Offices, Cheap Street

"Number 1 is actually in Castleton Terrace, Sherborne. Up to the 200s the houses are likewise in the town. The 300s are in Haydon, Goathill and Alweston. The 400s are in Thornford. The 500s are in Bishop's Caundle and Caundle Marsh. The 600s are in Charlton Hawthorn and the 700s in the hamlet of North Wootton. The last house is Number 775. The Digby estate houses are numbered concentrically."

So, both concentric and eccentric. It all began when I noticed the houses in Bishop's Caundle were numbered in the 500s, yet there were just 163 recorded households with green fields at each end of the village. How wonderfully endearing that in the eminently rational, meticulously organised world of the Digby estate there exists this trifling, delightful idiosyncrasy. Do the local postmen drive their vans or pedal their cycles round and round in ever decreasing circles – or vice versa, of course – until their heads are spinning and their deliveries become ever more erratic? Does the householder at Number One ever receive the mail for Number 775? At least, there would be good excuse. Then there's the family crest to be seen on the door plates of many of the houses – an ostrich with an upturned horseshoe. I cannot begin to speculate upon its precise significance.

William Beveridge, Somerset born, London School of Economics educated, is the affable public face of the Digby estate who greets me in the office in Cheap Street beneath a portrait of George Wingfield Digby, who inherited the estate in 1856 and died in 1863. Most curiously, William is the namesake of the former Director of the LSE, who produced his famous report at the end of WW2 which laid the foundations of the Welfare State. However, William assures me he is not related to the great man. But his responsibilities are considerable and demanding.

"We have 13,000 acres in all, 267 properties, 800 roofs and innumerable farm buildings, together with a 17 strong workforce of builders and maintenance staff."

I've never heard of an estate being quantified in terms of its roofs but I do understand their significance. They need an awful lot of maintenance and loving care.

The backcloth to the Digby family is a complex one. Suffice to explain that in 1856 the title emigrated to a branch of the family in Ireland though Lord and Lady Digby do live today at Minterne Magna. However, the bulk of the land remained with the present branch of the family at Sherborne. The present owner is John Digby who resides at Bishop's Caundle. John's father was Simon Wingfield Digby who, in his time was MP for West Dorset and the owner of the former National Stud at Sandley near Gillingham. John Digby inherited the estate and its responsibilities in 1998.

"We farm 'in hand' about 2,500 acres under a farm manager, Paul Carter. I am actually the Assets Manager with the responsibility of ensuring the estate is economically viable.Not all of our property earns an income, some is a public amenity but we still have to maintain fencing and look after the trees."

I know, because of the complimentary remarks I have heard about the locality, that the Digby family is well-regarded for its quiet generosity and social responsibility.

"The Digby ethos is one of long-term commercial sustainability tempered by a certain sense of philanthropy. The family has always preferred a no-fuss, understated approach. Nothing ostentatious, no trumpet blowing. I know that is the way Mr.Digby prefers that it should be."

Having spent many hours in the Sherborne community and talked with a wide cross-section of its citizens, including a number of tenants of the estate, I know that William Beveridge is regarded with great respect and an excellent ambassador for the family. He kindly arranges for me to see John Digby himself.

The Digby Estate Offices, Cheap Street – Another afternoon
"No man could wish for a better landlord."

The words were spoken to me just a day or two before by one of John Wingfield Digby's long-standing tenant farmers.

"But he does appreciate it if you ask him first – if there's anything you're thinking of doing – but that's the way it should be, isn't it?"

Now I'm sipping Earl Grey in the Estate Office while the owner of 13,000 acres of Dorset countryside observes me thoughtfully and I reflect on two predictions. 'When John's had enough of you, he'll look at his watch and start fidgeting. Likely he'll stand up and that will be your cue to leave. I give you ten minutes.' 'Remember he's a busy man. He will be very polite but I give you no more than fifteen minutes.'

With a distinguished MP for a father and a Canadian mother, John Digby tells me he was educated at Harrow, Cambridge and Cirencester. As one of the four largest landowners in the county he does indeed have great responsibilities. We discuss in general the theme of the great landed estates in contemporary society and the implications of inheritance taxes and the trusts set up to protect the integrity of those estates. We talk of the Digby tradition of benevolence by stealth. He tells me about the Simon Wingfield Digby Trust set up after his father's death to channel charitable gifts discreetly to local good causes and projects. The family motto is 'Deo Non Fortuna' – 'By God not Fortune' (Luck). He asks me if my book will be biased? Momentarily, I am thrown. No one has asked me that question yet on my journey. Does he suspect my LSE credentials? I did earlier in our conversation confide them. Many still remember the student demonstrations of 40 years ago though, even at their height, the LSE Conservative Society was always larger than the Labour Society. Besides, the admirable William Beveridge, his estate manager, was educated at the identical establishment. But if 'biased' means will I unequivocally condemn the drugs scene, foul public language, the coarsening of TV by unfunny oafs, the 'celeb' culture and the absurdities of political correctness, then Yes, I must confess my book will be 'biased'. But, in general terms, I hope I will remain an objective and dispassionate judge of all I see and hear. John Digby nods his approval.

I notice two surreptitious glances at his watch though it seems a mannerism more than anything else. Our conversation remains stimulating and, at moments, positively jocular. But I know I must not take advantage. I must spare my host the awkwardness of getting rid of a guest who has stayed too long. I begin to thank him for his time and his courtesy.

"Do you know about our wine?" he asks and slips away into another room. It must be three minutes before he returns with a list of wines from the Sherborne Castle Estate vineyard. I note that 10,000 bottles are produced each year from a number of grape varieties – Pinot Noir, Brut, Special Reserve, Bacchus-Reichensteiner, Schonburger and Wine Brandy. Alas, John doesn't actually bring a complimentary bottle, but I vow to buy a bottle from the list at the first opportunity. We shake hands and wish one another well. The Digby family has long been highly respected, even affectionately regarded in the locality. I understand why. I glance at my watch as I leave. Thirty-five minutes have passed since I was introduced.

Sherborne School

Not to write about Sherborne's schools and their importance in the life of the town would be absurd. Unlike Canford and Bryanston, the county's other large public schools, which are physically detached from the towns of Wimborne and Blandford, Sherborne School, in particular, is situated at the geographical heart of the town. In my earlier conversation with Canon Eric Woods we established that between 4,500-5,000 men, women, boys and girls are engaged in some capacity in the 'industry' of education in Sherborne. Not that education as an 'industry' has quite such a long history in the town as is sometimes imagined. Of course, there always have been schools in the town but as Huw Ridgeway, the present Head of History at Sherborne School points out, it was the arrival of the railways and the vision of the dynamic Headmaster H.D. Harper in 1860 that led to the establishment of Sherborne School as we know it today. The consolidation continued through Victorian times into the 20th century, both in terms of the numbers of students and buildings. However, though acknowledging the enormous importance of the schools to the life and prosperity of the town, how exactly I should approach the subject has caused me no little unease for education, as we all know, is a hugely complex and sensitive topic. Readers will look in vain in other books on the county for any reference to the controversial issues underlying the theme. Sir Frederick Treves describes the buildings of Sherborne School as *exceedingly picturesque, made up of rambling halls and houses of all ages, scattered about the Abbey grounds, as well as secluded courtyards and lawns, of unexpected entries and passages and half-subterranean cloisters.* Monica Hutchings writes of *'the golden stone of the buildings, all in harmony.'* But of the teachers, pupils and the character of the education itself there is nothing. However, these are the very areas where I must tread, albeit with sensitivity and measured step, not least because of the divide between the independent, fee-paying schools – and there are four dealing with pupils of secondary age – and the state provision of the comprehensive Gryphon School.

By nature I am a builder of bridges, not an architect of division. But I must ask the questions, even if they are awkward ones. Does there reside still a feeling in the town of 'Them and Us'? After all, the parents of the boys and the girls at the Sherborne independents are paying in the order of £20,000 pa for the privilege of boarding their sons and daughters at the schools, a figure which will exceed the annual income of a number of parents with children at the Gryphon. There were undoubted tensions in the past. There was a time, of course, when the boys of Sherborne School were conspicuous in their straw boaters and distinctive uniforms. Many would have had more money to spend in the shops than the boys from ordinary local families. A certain resentment would have been perfectly understandable.

There is no doubt that education and class have been inextricably intertwined in Britain. Is it right that a 'better' education can be bought by those parents with sufficient means, assuming it is indeed a 'better' education? To what extent is a public school education with all that it implies a route to a more privileged life-style? Does the existence of private education constantly reinforce the existing class structure? These are matters altogether too complex for this book and, as such, are best left to sociologists and philosophers. Besides, this is a book about the world as it exists today, a world often riddled with contradictions and inconsistencies, but one that never ceases to fascinate and enthral.

Let me return to Canon Eric Woods for one moment. These are his words on the subject of Sherborne's schools.

"The Gryphon was a school on three sites at one time. A lot of credit for its early success is down to the former Headmaster, Chris Sheppard, and Steve Hillier is continuing the good work. At the same time many of the parents who send their children to be privately educated often do 'scrimp and save' and make sacrifices, not least grandparents. Certainly their motives are entirely honourable. They want to see their children, or their grandchildren, enjoy the best possible start. I respect all parents, from whatever background, who give great priority to their children's education, be it at the Gryphon or any of the other schools in the town."

Sherborne School, The headmaster's study

This morning I count myself doubly privileged for I am in the company of not one headmaster but two, Simon Eliot of Sherborne School and Steve Hillier of the Gryphon School, who have most kindly agreed to see me together.I ask Simon first about the general background to Sherborne's schools.

"Very simply, we – the different schools – are serving different sections of the community. However, Steve and I and the other Heads share the common ideal of providing every one of our students with the best education possible."

Steve nods his head.

"I absolutely agree with Simon. And regarding the issue of 'Them and Us', I see little evidence of such sentiments. Of course, there are always a few idiots but, no, I believe the staffs and students of both our schools get on very well."

Simon is keen to make a further point.

"It is actually the collective will of the town that we all get on. Sherborne is, by and large, a happy and unified society and everyone has a vested interest in making it work. As you point out, education is Sherborne's principal 'industry' and so many people work at the various schools that it is in the interests of the whole community that we function harmoniously."

What about inter-school co-operation? There was little years ago. Have things changed? Simon picks up the point.

"Let's take, first of all, the Joint Schools Symphony Orchestra. There is an open audition every September and the finest instrumentalists from the schools are chosen to rehearse and perform

Romeo and Juliet. A joint production by Sherborne School and the Gryphon School. *Picture: Glen Coombs.*

together. And they are very good."

Steve points to another example.

"We recently enjoyed a joint school production of Romeo and Juliet directed by Vicky Clayton which was a great success. We hope very much to build upon that sort of venture in the future."

Back to Simon and the sporting links.

"Sherborne is very much a rugby town and our fixtures are, as you may imagine, very competitively but sportingly contested. Many of the boys will later graduate to Sherborne Rugby Club XVs and play together."

Steve refers to a recent staff get-together.

"At a staff level we meet each term – Simon and I – to discuss matters as they arise. We have also organised very successful joint staff training sessions with the object of learning from one another, looking at different teaching approaches and resources. In some instances we've found that one school appears to be ahead in certain respects and vice versa."

Simon mentions the sharing of staff expertise.

"One of our teachers William Duggan, the head of Classics, is providing a crash course in Latin at the Gryphon."

"For which there is a class of twenty-five," adds Steve. "And both our schools have chaplains, Jonathan Triffit at the Gryphon and Stephen Gray at Sherborne and they meet to discuss any problems that may occur."

I ask Simon to sum up the existing relationship between the schools.

"I would say that we are co-operating wherever we feel it is of mutual benefit. But it's something that cannot be forced. It must an organic process but you can be absolutely sure that Steve and I will

Main picture: *Daily Mail* under XV cup, Gryphon School 48 Sherborne School 0. **Insert:** action shot of the game
Pictures: Glen Coombs.

continue to do everything we can to foster an excellentworking relationship between our schools."

So, have my original anxieties been allayed?Certainly in part they have. What people may say in the privacy of their homes, their common-rooms, even their dormitories or bedrooms, who knows?

But as Canon Eric Woods stresses, "It is the will of the people of Sherborne that we make a success of ALL our schools."

And he is absolutely correct. Sherborne's schools undoubtedly bring a prosperity and stability to the town, not least in employment.That in itself is definitely a major factor in ensuring that Sherborne will weather the economic storms better than many towns. It is also very apparent that we have two Headmasters who are on the very best of terms, even if one of them is a Queen's man and the other from King's!

As I prepare to take my leave of the town I realise I have included nothing of Sherborne Castle, the old castle and little enough of the Abbey. Yet Sherborne's glorious architectural heritage is well described elsewhere by many other writers. Alas, there is no time or space either for the fine variety of shops and restaurants and pubs. But, then again, that never was my primary intention. Sherborne is a town of great beauty. To sit in the Abbey grounds and watch the world pass slowly by for even a few minutes is to experience a sense of peace and serenity that is beyond measure and price in our ever more frenetic world. The good people of Sherborne know they are singularly fortunate to live where they do without being reminded by a passing stranger.

Milborne Port

Venn Stables

"You can't miss it. You'll see the hurdles and fences in the field opposite."

Jack Dimond's precise instructions lead us straight to Venn Farm and the Tizzard family home on the Dorset-Somerset border. Besides running a highly successful racing stable Colin Tizzard is also a working farmer with 250 head of cattle.

"First lot are still on the gallops. "Pauline Tizzard tells me. "They won't be long."

There's a bustle of activity in the yard. Barns and horses and cats are everywhere. Lads, mostly Indians, are mucking out the stables.

"We like it here very much," smiles one.

Terry Hamlin arrives. He's come to watch Mister Quasimodo work. He owns the gelding in partnership with friends Martin Dare and John Snook. A useful animal, it won two decent races last season.

"He'll be out at Exeter for the Haldon Chase. I expect we'll meet one of Paul Nicholls's hotpots there," says Terry with a wry smile.

Avoiding the all-conquering Paul Nicholls team is not easy. First lot is just returning. Cheery

Joe Lively – Joe Tizzard up. (Left to right): Jack Dimond, Colin Tizzard, Richard Dimond. *Picture: Geoff Hill*

greetings from the riders as they bring their charges back into the yard. Washed down and steaming they are led away. Joe Tizzard, stable jockey and son of Colin the trainer, comes back in. Joe's daily counting his blessings after the horrific accident in which he nearly lost his life a few weeks earlier.

"I was helping my brother-in-law, David Gingell, on his farm. The string on the baler went wrong and, stupidly, I crawled under it to fix the problem and got sucked in. I'm so grateful to David, he reacted so quickly. The surgeons at Salisbury did a brilliant job stitching up the gash above my ear. I've spent my whole life on a farm so there's no excuse. All I can say is that I won't ever be doing that again."

One of our very best young National Hunt jockeys Joe risks life and limb in every race so there's acute irony in that he almost lost his life in a farming accident.

Proud owner Richard Dimond has finished saddling up Joe Lively. He leads him out of his box. Richard rides him out every morning. He's not a big horse. Very good-natured, says Joe, as he stands quietly and we all make a fuss of him. Jack arrives looking immaculate in tie and sports jacket. He puts us all to shame. We're all set except for one person. I hurry across to the house to fetch a protesting Colin from the breakfast table.

"My bacon and eggs will go cold! "

But he takes his place. We've got the picture we came for. And surely Pauline will have put Colin's breakfast back in the oven?

(Joe Lively subsequently won two major staying chases at Cheltenham earning Richard a further £50,000 plus in prize money, before unfortunately sustaining a serious cut in a race at Kempton in February, 2009. It was particularly frustrating because plans were afoot for him to run in the Grand National. After a couple of weeks at a veterinary clinic in Salisbury he returned home in good spirits to spend the summer out at grass on the farm. Richard and Colin hope to have Joe back on the racecourse before Christmas 2009. The Grand National 2010 perhaps?)

Bishop's Caundle

In Caundle, vor a day at least,
You woudden vind a scowlen feace
Or dumpy heart in all the pleace.'
  William Barnes

"It's a curious village. You meet scarcely a soul on the street. Perhaps it's all the cars passing through? The pub is really the only attraction, the only reason for people to stop."

Joint managers of the White Hart, Noel Bishop and Sharon Murchie – Clive Dee is the landlord – are attending to their lunchtime customers. Noel looks thoughtful.

"People leave their doorways in the morning, get into their cars and drive off to work, or to the school, or the nearest supermarket, come back and close their doors behind them."

In a sense Bishop's Caundle is a village like so many of its size and composition in the county. Physically it's strung out along the busy A3030 and, like Noel, I've seen not a soul walking. It's certainly not the village William Barnes knew. The church is locked so I walk to the Post Office Stores where I find the key-holder, Elizabeth Porter and husband John, who have run the shop for the past fourteen years. In July, in common with hundreds of others across the county, they will learn their fate and discover if their livelihood is to be removed following the review of our Post Offices. John has long supplemented the family income as a lorry driver but the shop is of vital importance to the villagers. Besides providing a meeting place where locals can socialise, the sheer convenience of the facility is obvious to anyone who cares about relatively isolated communities.

"We have about 330 residents, with nearly a third under the age of 18, another third over 60 and the rest in between. At least we have a lively village school, All Saints Primary, which draws its pupils from a wide area and a pub, a church, a garage and us!" John explains. "At the same time the population is too small to have many clubs or societies."

John suggests I meet Sarah Dean, a former parish councillor and chairman of the Village Hall Committee.

"Sarah knows as much about the village as anyone."

Taking John's advice I call by on Sarah.

"I'm really pleased you have stopped because nobody ever writes anything about us, yet we are typical of so many other villages in the county."

We discuss a document I picked up from John. Sponsored by the Countryside Agency several years earlier it's called the Vital Village Plan.

"Simon Thompson was the driving force behind it, I believe, at County level. It was designed to ensure that villages continue as living entities, not as museum pieces. It did have the effect of getting people together to discuss Bishop Caundle's needs. We consulted as widely as possible and produced a document with a plan of action and dates to implementation. In that sense it was a worthwhile exercise. But, of course, everything depends upon finance. As a village we can only raise so much through jumble sales and the like. I haven't heard anything of it recently. I don't know if the funding still exists. But our village hall is working very well with lots of activities for those who wish to get involved."

Sarah certainly hit the proverbial nail on the head in mentioning the crucial role of finance in so many worthy initiatives. All over the county, at the behest of this or that body, towns and villages are being encouraged to devise plans and strategies to be implemented by specific target dates. No one doubts the sincerity of the individuals engaged in all of these consultations and yet what, I wonder, is the aggregate cost annually to taxpayers and council-tax payers of paying the salaries of all the individuals employed in these deliberations? How many meetings are taking place? What are the transport costs of the various individuals at these meetings – and the rest? I have already handled a number of the documents produced by various public authority bodies? They are invariably glossy, expensively produced, full of coloured charts, couched inevitably in the horrible jargon quite impenetrable to the average reader and full of targets we know are most unlikely to be met. Already, and I am writing still in the first half of the year, it is apparent the economic climate is worsening so the financial support from Government and local authorities is simply not going to be there for a whole host of projects. Meanwhile, we go on paying large salaries to public servants in offices to produce more of the same. I know that often when I go to pay my Council Tax bill, the East Dorset car park at Furzehill is full of vehicles that have brought local government officials to meetings. As a former teacher I doubt one in ten meetings that ever I attended was either of interest or value. A quick phone call or a one-to-one chat was, almost without exception, infinitely more productive. And enormously cheaper! But maybe I'm the odd one out and getting it all wrong. Perhaps that is the future? Ever bigger and more expensive meetings with more and more people on the public payroll enjoying the security of inflation-indexed pensions, financed by a smaller and smaller private sector of producers. I expect some Government statistician somewhere is this very moment working on such a strategy.

(A few weeks after my call John and Elizabeth receive the good news that their Post Office is safe from closure.)

Lydlinch

More than a century ago William Barnes devoted a poem to the five bells of the church at 'Lydlynch', as he then spelt the village.

'Vor Lydlinch bells be good vor sound

'An liked by by all the naighbours round.'

Were he composing now he might dedicate his verse to a lady of the village, Priscilla Vining, for it is to the admirable Priscilla and her fellow conspirator, Michael Davies of neighbouring Bishop's Caundle, that we owe the revival of one of the county's prize assets, Dorset Blue Vinny cheese. At nearby Woodbridge Farm a quarter of a century ago our two valiant alchemists contrived to re-discover the secrets of Blue Vinny cheese-making. It was a long, arduous process but our determined pair pulled it off and so began Michael's Dorset Blue Cheese Co. Alas, Priscilla is now to retire promising never to reveal the secret formula of Blue Vinny's manufacture. Fortunately Michael continues to run the business but these are disturbing days for all Blue Vinny addicts – not forgetting the mice of Bishop's Caundle and Lydlinch.

Caundle Marsh

The Mitford sisters, Hitler and Stalin, Berlin during the Cold War years, our conversation ranges far and wide.If the topics seem unlikely ones, then it's because my companion is an unlikely figure. I've passed by several times on my travels. This afternoon I pull in beside the caravan and introduce myself. Within moments I'm seated by the fire, a mug of tea in my hand and a plate of biscuits before me.

"Any guest must be made welcome. It's a mark of courtesy and custom."

Once a soldier, Moses Willis is today a man of many trades and possessed of an intellectual curiosity that would become a university common-room.

"I was in the REME for 6 years, 130 days and 18 hours and did 3 tours of duty in Belfast at the height of the troubles. Now I'll lay my hand to whatever's needed – sharpening, grinding, tree-felling, plastering, tiling, gardening – you name it! I'll also collect scrap metal free of charge."

And, of course, with consummate skill, he'll fashion a 'vardo', an authentic Romany caravan.

"How many hours do I spend on one? A thousand? I don't count them."

"And I paint them. Like I've painted all these."

Annie's a lady of many talents too. About us sit examples of her handiwork, brightly painted plant containers, watering cans, buckets and lucky horseshoes.

"At Christmas I weave holly wreaths that will last until March. In the autumn I'll pick grapes at John Digby's at Bishop's Caundle – before the first frosts. He's a gentleman."

Moses and Annie have been returning to the same roadside verge at Caundle Marsh for the past 4 years.

"All credit to the Council. The Dorset County Council is the best in England. David Ayres and Mike Evans from the Environment Agency are very fair-minded men too. And the 'gavvers' – the police – they're brilliant. Here it's part common, part highway. I know their job is to get me off as soon as possible, though none of the locals complain. They know I want to stay as long as possible. It's all about a happy medium. They know we play fair by them. We respect this place, leave everything as we find it. No litter. We take a pride. And, contrary to some popular opinion, true Romanies don't steal. Certain 'travellers', well, that's a different story. Another true gent is Terry Pitt-Kirby at Blandford. That's where we pitch before Christmas. I love Blandford. They treat us very well. Sometimes people ask me – what group do you belong to? And I say we don't belong to any group –

Annie and Mary seated, Lisa and Moses standing. *Picture: Geoff Hill*

just to the human race. There are two very good fellows at Kingston Maurward I'm working with on our way of life, Ken Onions and Dave Henty. They understand what we are and what we represent."

Annie is anxious her grand-children will have the education to enable them to have choices in their lives. "Mary, that's our grand-daughter attends the local school. We want to stay here, to give her stability. To make sure she gets a good start. Not to neglect her education. Our daughter Lisa takes her every day in the car. And then there's Judd, her brother."

Moses tells me he only learned to read when he was in the army. Now he reads voraciously, especially history. We're joined at the fire by Mark Smith, a local sawyer. More tea is poured, biscuits passed round. I'd receive no better hospitality in a palace.

"There are some wonderful people about us here. Up at West Hayes Farm, for example, Diane and James Hiscock live there. They foster. They do such a lot of good."

And does the open road still retain its appeal after so many years?

"You know, when I harness up the horse, shake the reins, feel the warmth of the sun on my face, hear the birdsong, smell the plants and trees – it's like nothing else."

But old bones will surely feel the chill of winter more keenly one day?

"I'll put on an extra blanket!"

Stalbridge

'The town, with its radiating streets, sprawls over the hill like a starfish. It possesses a neat row of semi-detached villas worthy of the suburbs of Hull, a place where petrol is sold and shows a general leaning to slate, iron railings, corrugated iron and much bill posting. There are, on the other hand, a few thatched cottages, some fine old roofs of stone outlined by moss, quaint alleys and ancient gardens, and here and there a white bow window filled withy geranium blossoms.'
Sir Frederick Treves, *Highways & Byways in Dorset* 1906.

I cannot claim familiarity with Hull so I am unable to comment on the row of semi-detached villas. As for the corrugated iron and bill-posting I see no contemporary evidence. I suspect our local community police officer would have some apposite words if it appeared today.

Alas, we shall never know what Sir Frederick would have made of my first port of call this morning for it is Dike's supermarket but its dimensions and the contents of its shelves would undoubtedly have astounded him.

"It was my father's dream and five years in the planning. Last summer was awful. The building was going on with water everywhere after all the rain and my father was becoming ever more ill with terminal cancer. Tragically he died in August, just 3 months before our opening on November 5."

It is a story of the triumphant realisation of a dream over-laden with the most desperate and heartbreaking sadness for the entire Dike family which has run a bakery and grocery business since 1851 in Stalbridge. Andrew Dike is the fifth generation of that family and proud of his heritage, not least his father Stephen's role in creating the largest independent supermarket in the county.

"We are a small community and have thought hard about our relationship with other traders in the town. We certainly don't want to hurt or upset anyone."

Such sentiments from the manager of one of the big beasts of the supermarket jungle would be taken with a very large pinch of salt. Coming from the lips of Andrew Dike they are manifestly sincere and heartfelt.

"In order to finance the store we sold 3 acres of land on which nearly 30 houses and flats, including some affordable homes, will be built. That means about 100 extra residents will be spending their money in Stalbridge, in other shops besides our own. We have a free car park with a100 spaces and I will be delighted to see our customers go off after shopping with us to spend money elsewhere in the town. We are ferociously proud of what we have achieved. We're not just another supermarket. We want to be much better than that. We try to source as locally as possible and have over 60 suppliers within a 10 mile radius. We also intend to put back as much as we can into the local community through sponsorship and active support of local charities over the coming years."

It's not for me to advise shoppers or, in general terms, to take sides between rivals but, in this instance, I have no reservations in endorsing Dike's. Besides providing a cheerful and efficient service to the customers over a wide radius, they also provide invaluable local employment opportunities.

"We have a brilliant staff of over 60, full and part-time. Adam Vincent, my manager, is a huge part of the team and, of course, my mother Deirdre is the company secretary. Nor must I forget my debt to my lovely wife Vicky, who comes from just up the road at Bagber and the 'light of my life', my baby daughter Georgina. and her sister Belinda."

I have driven through Stalbridge on my way to Wincanton races but never before, to my shame, have I explored. My first surprise is the extent of Stalbridge's development that is simply not visible from the main road. Already I have discovered a supermarket with a difference, not one more identical link in a nationwide chain but Dike's, authentically local and bedded deep in the community life of the town. Now it is my turn to call in on another local institution- this time one with a national reputation.

Andrew Dike, his wife Vicky, mother Deidre, daughter Georgina, manager Adam Vincent and some of his team.

Fudge's, Station Road

"We simply would not have been able to expand without immigrant labour. Obviously we employ lots of locals but we also have workers from NZ, France, Argentina, Portugal, Slovakia, the Czech Republic and Poland."

Isn't it extraordinary that while few natives of the county will ever have visited Stalbridge, so many young people from distant countries are now living and working in this quiet Dorset outpost? What, I wonder, do they tell their families 'back home' about the town and its inhabitants?

"Tutors from Yeovil College come in to the factory to provide English lessons for two hours a week and we also offer other skills training."

Emma Snead is the assistant general manager together with her colleague Brent Giles and is clearly proud of the success story of the company. Originally a small family bakery at Leigh, founded by Percy Fudge in 1926, the office walls are liberally covered with prize winning certificates and gold awards for products such as cheese wafers, Florentines, Kringle cake and Marmite flatbreads. With 130 staff at the last count Fudges, the Dorset Village Bakery Ltd established 82 years ago, is one of the town's biggest employers.

"And it's still a genuinely family run business. Steven and Graham own and run the company and Graham's wife Sue is a fellow director."

I walk to my car with Pearl White from Milborne Port. She tells me she works in the 'London Room' supplying Fortnum & Mason, Harrods and Harvey Nicholls.

"We even produce a special ribboned Royal collection which goes off to Highgrove."

Wouldn't Percy Fudge have been a proud man?

Coming to Stalbridge also presents me with another opportunity – to renew old acquaintance with Mervyn Frampton and his wife.

Half a century ago we were conspirators plunging our cardboard daggers into Caesar in Albert Maiden's QEGS production of Julius Caesar, I 'the lean and hungry' Cassius and Mervyn as Decius Brutus with Peter Forshaw in the title role. This morning the only plot Mervyn and I are discussing is my chapter on Stalbridge. Mervyn is a well-known face across a wide swathe of the county. For many years he was a PE and Special Needs teacher at Yewstock School in Sturminster Newton.

"Like every teacher I'm forever bumping into my old pupils – and they're always so pleasant."

We decide to call by at the Information Office where we meet Ann Russell and Community Police Officer Kate James. The role of support officers has been the subject of some controversy, both nationally and locally but Kate believes she has a valuable role to play.

"My objective is to establish trust and a working relationship with people so they see me as a first point of contact if they have problems. Likewise they can become my eyes and ears. If they see something they feel needs investigating, they know I am available and in constant contact with Phil Sugrue at Sturminster Newton police station. We can then promptly pick up on their concerns."

As Kate says, policing isn't simply about arresting people and I suspect a really perceptive and efficient community officer can prove a valuable link between members of the public and the police force proper, not least in an era when there are so few 'bobbies on the beat'. As is true in so many areas of life, the critical issue is the quality of the individual engaged. Kate is manifestly a most conscientious officer.

We stroll on past St. Mary's where Mervyn speaks warmly of the local clergyman, William Ridding as 'a very well-respected man', and through the gates of the CE Primary School where his grandchild will shortly be a pupil.

"The school has earned itself all sorts of commendations from the Ofsted inspectors. I understand the headmaster, Michael Allen, is setting high standards which is always good to hear."

We pick up a prospectus which contains information about the school and also the details of the Home School Agreement every parent must sign when their child begins their education. It's the sort of document now obligatory in many of our schools. I must confess it is impossible to resist a smile when I read that parents must ensure their child does not indulge in any 'ageist' remarks. So if a six-year-old shouts out to his teacher that he's a 'boring old blank', not only will he receive a punishment but his parents may be summoned to explain their child's 'deviant behaviour'. I do pose the question – is it actually possible for a six year-old, or any child for that matter, to grasp the abstract concept of 'ageism'? Whoever dreams up these daft ideas?

Mervyn believes one of the strengths of Stalbridge lies in the number of genuine family run businesses that still survive.

"A perfect example would be our excellent butcher Julian Else. His son Martin does a fish round and his other son Nick is set to become the landlord of the Stalbridge Arms. On the other hand, I do feel that Stalbridge may have missed out in that it hasn't seen the number of 'incomers' arriving here that towns nearer the coast have experienced. Their arrival might have given the community an extra boost."

It's an interesting point that Mervyn makes and would apply to a number of localities that have less immediate appeal than Lyme Regis, the Purbeck villages or Sherborne. There is no doubt that an

Now the cows are gone. A familiar story across the county. *Picture: Peter Holmes*

appropriate proportion of 'incomers' moving into a community can act as a beneficial stimulus. We are also very aware of the negative consequences. I am sure that the locals in Worth Matravers, for example, would welcome a campaign by Mervyn to lure some of their recent arrivals to Stalbridge.

At the Crown Hotel I meet Ruth Panton where she and her partner Steve Perry run the pub. We discuss the local employment scene and the presence of immigrant workers.

"There's the William Hughes spring factory, Newton Steel and ASD Saw Mill and various building suppliers. Our trade here is fickle. We cater mainly for the youngsters, lots of builders and scaffolders. They come in wearing their working clothes and they feel comfortable. They're very easy-going and polite. It's so important to know your customers, to build a relationship with them. They expect to see you and appreciate the personal service. As for the Poles and other nationalities living nearby, they tend to keep themselves to themselves."

One legendary figure in the town is Denis Holloway. "Whether or not I'm the oldest DJ in Dorset is uncertain but my first gig was at Hazelbury Bryan in 1946 for the Slate Club."

From such humble beginnings Denis became a full-time entrepreneur supplying DJs and sound equipment across the county. According to local writer John Waltham: 'Denis supplied the equipment for the Yetties' very first concert which took place at Yetminster Women's Institute. Not so long ago, at Sturminster Newton's YFC 70th anniversary dance, the audience was asked how many of the couples had first met at a Denis Holloway event and a forest of hands went up – most of the audience , in fact.'

As for Denis himself, he's still doing the odd gig. "I'm also a regular on a Friday night at the Trooper Inn, Stourton Caundle. I've been going there for 50 years now and I'd like to be a regular for another fifty!"

My last call is upon Brian Spiller, former parish councillor and chairman of the council. Brian remains active in the community through a close association with the gardening and badminton clubs and the Scouts. Brian arrived in Stalbridge for the first time in 1958 and counts himself 'almost a local'. He remembers with nostalgic affection the days when Stalbridge still had a railway station.

"The Pines Express used to travel direct from Bournemouth to Manchester through here. One day we picked up the train, my mother and I, thinking it was stopping at Templecombe but it passed straight through the station. I still recall this old lady saying that if she'd known where it was I wanted to get out she'd have thrown me out of the window. It's funny the things you remember!"

Brian worked both Mr. Dike the farmer and Mr. Dike the baker. "Where the supermarket now stands was originally a piggery before it became a bakery. I believe they're going to call the new development there 'Bakery Field'. I suppose Piggery Field wouldn't have quite the same appeal!"

And Stalbridge today – what does Brian think of the town where he's almost a 'local'?

"Much the same as young Mervyn here, I would judge. It's a good, hard-working, respectable community. Like the rest of the county."

West Dorset 2

Cerne Abbas

I have a choice – to continue eastwards towards Gillingham and Shaftesbury, or to retrace my steps a few miles and then head south towards the coast? For many weeks all my journeying has been inland. I feel a need to see the sea again. I decide to head for Portland taking the A352 towards Dorchester through lovely Minterne Magna, the home of Lord and Lady Digby. No time, alas, to pause here but on instead to Cerne Abbas to renew old acquaintance with one of our county's most celebrated characters? It is intriguing to dip into Sir Frederick Treves again, writing a century earlier, to read of Cerne when he called by here.

'The place is empty and decaying and strangely silent. Grass is growing in the streets; many houses have long been deserted, many have their windows boarded up, or are falling into listless ruin. Here are empty barns, gates falling off their hinges and doorways grown up with weeds. One feels compelled to walk very quietly through the echoing streets, and to talk in whispers, for fear that the sleep of Cerne should be broken.'
  Highways & Byways in Dorset, 1906.

It is a remarkable portrait of dereliction and hopelessness. But what do I find in 2008? Cerne has just been named 'the most desirable village in Britain' by the estate agent Savills! Peter Lane, representing the firm, says: 'We took into account the schools, countryside, quality of housing, historic features, pubs and other facilities. It is a combination of having wonderful historic buildings and modern conveniences like schools and shops. The properties are made from brick, flint and most are listed, so it helps to keep the village looking as it always has done."

His colleague, Antony Lumby, adds: "While much of the county was bombarded with ugly bungalows during the 1970s Cerne Abbas has remained strikingly beautiful. With a waiting list of purchasers for any property that becomes available, the starting price is £500,000."

Officially the village has 732 residents, three pubs, tea-rooms, a new village hall, a school and a post office, reflecting a degree of prosperity Sir Frederick could never have envisaged. At the Village Stores, Andrew Farrow enthuses; "I know there are many wonderful villages but Cerne Abbas is perfect – not just the buildings but the people!"

The local vicar is Karen Curnock and she reinforces Andrew's message: "It's a very compact village and easy for people to come together .There's a great sense of community here."

One of the newest residents is Wendy Charman: "I was in the right place at the right time. People can wait years and still not find anywhere in the village."

One individual, however, is not very happy about one particular aspect of Cerne Abbas – my old friend, the wonderful Rodney Legg, Dorset's most prolific writer – and chairman of the Open Spaces Society. He is not pleased by the state of our Giant.

"Visitors are presently disappointed that they can't really see him. He's gone from being a white icon, through a green man stage, into the invisible man. We need more sheep on the site or it needs the village to trim the grass, weed the trenches and whitewash them."

Rob Rhodes, the National Trust's Head Warden for West Dorset, adds: "It's become increasingly difficult to find the right number of sheep to graze the hills. We can only use sheep because of the steepness of the hill and the fragile nature of this important archaeological site."

It's one of those periodic problems that occur on similar sites, like the figure of George III on the Weymouth hillside. This year, with all the heavy spring rainfall, the grass has grown even lusher and faster.

NT Communications Officer, Maurice Flynn, explains that a 1cm layer of chalk will be removed from the foot-wide outline by hand and then 17 tonnes of fresh chalk crumbled into its place.

"It will then be watered in to form a paste and firmed down to a solid layer."

Helen Mann promises action in the autumn.

"We are expecting to re-chalk him then, which we hope will make him stand out once more."

And put a smile on the face of every visitor.

Abbotsbury

After one Ilchester estate village, so I move on to another. But Abbotsbury, unlike its cousin, has not enjoyed the best of years. In fact it began in a blaze of unwelcome publicity with the news early in January that H5N1 virus, a lethal strain of bird flu, had reached the UK for only the second time, killing 3 mute swans at the Swannery. As a result the Department for Environment, Food and

Left: The Giant, 'One of Dorset's favourite sons?' **Below:** Swans and swanherd, David Wheeler, Abbotsbury.
Pictures: Roger Holman.

Rural Affairs imposed a range of restrictions, including a 20 mile exclusion zone on the area around Abbotsbury, including Chesil Beach and Portland. The scientific conclusion was that the virus had been brought to the locality by migrating birds.

The general manager, John Huston, explained that the 3 dead birds had been found at Chesil and all precautions had subsequently been taken.

"Ministry vets will carry out tests on some of our 800 swans and monitor the situation closely. Our 12 members of staff have been given anti-viral tablets as a precaution."

Unsurprisingly Dorset's farmers were to suffer several anxious weeks as they waited to discover if the virus had spread beyond the Abbotsbury area. A year earlier 160,000 turkeys were culled in Norfolk in a previous outbreak. In recent years the devastating consequences of the Foot and Mouth epidemic, the recent restrictions imposed after the discovery of Blue Tongue in an animal at Lytchett Minster, the impact of bovine TB – each has left farmers asking themselves: 'Just what is it going to be next?'

Fortunately, the restrictions have now been lifted and all seems fine again at the Swannery. It was alarming while it lasted but the breeding season is in full swing and the visitors are back. Everyone breathes a sigh of relief.

South Dorset

Portland

Twinned with Louviers (France)

'From Durdle Pier to Balaclava Bay the shores are rocky and the sea dominated by battleships, submarines and destroyers. The public road keeps away from the east coast and the Navy installations and making for Verne and the Citadel plunges down to Castletown where the Navy have their refuelling station with the gleaming aluminium storage tanks against the waters of Weymouth Bay where once all was coal.'

Monica Hutchings, *Inside Dorset*, 1965.

John Hill, in 1965 a youthful Royal Navy rating, was stationed at the base and remembers it clearly.

"One week the destroyer HMS *Daring* would be in port, another week the landing ship HMS *Fearless*, a month later the frigate HMS *Berwick*. Castletown was full of pubs – The Sailor's Return, The Green Shutters, The Jolly Sailor, The Royal Breakwater and The Portland Roads. At night, the

Looking down from Harbour Heights Hotel on to Chesil, Osprey Quay and Weymouth Bay. *Picture: Geoff Hill*

Master-At-Arms, who was the head of the regulation force, would despatch naval patrolmen or 'crushers', as we knew them, to ensure there was orderly behaviour in the port."

And 40 years on? I am standing on the hill overlooking Verne Common close to Portland's War Memorial. Looking westward towards Chesil and the Fleet or east to Weymouth Bay and there's not a battleship, submarine or destroyer in sight and, no longer, 'any gleaming aluminium storage tanks.'

"It was a political decision. The Government decided it could no longer afford Portsmouth, Plymouth and Portland. In the final reckoning, Portland was the loser."

However, Maurice Stradling, formerly a scientist at the Research Centre at Southwell, recognises the economic logic that lay behind Government thinking.

"There were 3 separate Royal Navy units at Portland, the dockyard which was technically a RN victualling depot though it mostly employed civilians, HMS *Osprey* which was the Navy's helicopter and anti-submarine school and housed naval personnel, and the Flag Officer Sea Training empire which was the NATO – at – sea Training organisation. All three RN bodies left Portland in 1996-7, Flag Officer Sea Training to Plymouth and HMS Osprey's helicopters to Yeovilton. In the same period MOD establishments also relocated from Portland with the loss of many hundreds of jobs. It was a bleak, dispiriting era for the island. I calculated at the time that the loss of salary income to the island was in the order of £20million."

But was Portland, in the longer term, actually a 'loser'? Tim Munro, today the Mayor of Weymouth and Portland and an islander himself, thinks not.

"Was I sorry to see the departure of the Navy? Not really. Portland was, at last, liberated to pursue a different and exciting future. I recall Portland as a boy. In the Fifties and Sixties there might be ships from half a dozen different countries in port. It was a powder-keg of nationalities and these were very young men. There was a lot of heavy drinking, countless fights, prostitution, shore patrols by the naval police and our own constabulary. With the ending of National service, it is true the men were more mature and professional, often with families. But still the presence of the Navy restricted the post-war development of the island."

"I believe Tim Munro is absolutely right when he says the departure of the Royal Navy has liberated Portland. It was a move that made sense for the Navy and it has enabled Portland to look forward to a new and exciting future."

And if there's one man in a position to make such a judgement it is Captain John Harvey, the last Captain of HM *Osprey*, the shore based naval establishment on the island. Yet John's original acquaintance with the island did not augur well for a happy association with Portland.

"The rain was horizontal, our bikes were almost on their sides with a real hooley blowing up from the West. At that moment I caught my first glimpse of Portland. I thought to myself – who on earth would want to live in such a grey, desolate God-forsaken place?"

It was 1964 and the 17 year-old from Thurrock on his Triumph 110 was on a tour of the West Country in the company of a school chum from the local grammar school. Little did young John Harvey guess that 30 odd years later he would return to the island to take up his duties as the last Captain of HMS Osprey. It was a distinguished journey from Thurrock to Dorset – Dartmouth, command of a frigate, the Head of Maritime Intelligence in Virginia and the Commander of the Royal Yacht Britannia. Of his days with the Britannia he speaks with particular respect and affection of HM Queen Elizabeth II. "Her Majesty was an absolute sweetie with a great sense of humour".

And today, what does John make of that 'grey, desolate, God-forsaken island'?

"It has so much going for it – the future looks immensely hopeful."

I've driven down from the grounds of the Heights Hotel and am standing close by where once naval

Ceremony of the Keys, with the Mayor, Sandy West. *Picture: Brian Jung, Dorset Echo*

helicopters flew from hangars and now Poole based boat-builders Sunseeker, the most illustrious name in luxury speedboat and yacht-building in the UK, has expanded its activities to the site. Indeed, Ian Jolliffe, the general manager of the Osprey Quay expansion, predicts an 18 month development costing £8million that will enable the company to expand markedly its range of boats. He anticipates that eventually a further 350 jobs will be created. Jonathan Macklin, Sunseeker's commercial director, hopes many of the positions will be filled by skilled local craftsmen and draws attention to the new training school for apprentices at Osprey Quay. Certainly, all around me is a bustle of activity and preparation. In truth, the moment London was chosen as the venue for the 2012 Olympics and Weymouth and Portland selected for the sailing events the tempo quickened. The second largest man-made harbour in the world, Philip Gollop and his wife originally brought their sailing school across to Portland from Wyke Regis. Today it forms a part of the Weymouth and Portland Sailing Academy. One of the inspirational figures behind the creation and expansion of the Academy was, of course, E.W. 'Bill' Ludlow, whose vision will ensure a magnificent legacy for future generations to enjoy. The great sadness is that 'Bill' will not be here to see it for himself.

(In November, several months after my visit, John Tweed, the Chief Executive, announced that the Weymouth and Portland Sailing Academy had become the first 2012 Olympic venue to be opened. The opening was attended by Weymouth's 2008 Olympics gold medal winner, Paul Goodison, along with Sarah Ayton and Jonathan Edwards. All credit then to developers, Dean and Reddyhoff, and the 100 plus workers engaged on the site for their efficiency and skill in delivering on time and on budget. As Edward Leask, the Sailing Academy chairman, observed: "The enhanced facilities secure the Academy's status as the premier world-class venue for the Olympic and Paralympic Games, as well as providing wonderful facilities for the people of Weymouth and Portland in the longer term." I understand that 5 courses are planned for the Olympics, 4 in Weymouth Bay, and 1 in Portland harbour. The test events will begin in 2010).

If the Navy was one critical part of Portland's heritage, even better known to the wider world was the stone quarried since Roman times and used in many cities in its buildings. Popularised by 2 outstanding architects, Inigo Jones and Christopher Wren, the quarries have always thrived on disaster. The fire that destroyed the Banqueting Hall in Whitehall in 1619 and the most famous fire in our island's history in 1666 which destroyed five sixths of London had not unwelcome consequences for Portland.

In his admirable '*A History of Portland*' (Dovecote Press 1985) Stuart Morris estimated six million tons of Portland stone were supplied to the capital for the rebuilding of the Banqueting Hall, St. Paul's Cathedral and some 50 other London churches and buildings. As for the Great War of 1914-18 Stuart writes '*half a million slabs were shaped, carved with names and badges, and shipped from Portland for planting on the Western Front, together with memorials despatched to every corner of the world. A special quarry was even opened at Wakeham to provide stone for the Whitehall Cenotaph*'. It was the same story after WW2 when Portland stone was not only used for tens of thousands of British and Commonwealth graves, but widely employed to rebuild the blitzed areas of many English cities.

"In the years after WW2 I estimate there were between 700-800 men working in the stone industry," recalls Roly Reynolds, Stuart's brother-in-law. "Portland was then the largest masonry works in Europe. Since that time there has been a rationalisation of the companies involved and much investment in machinery with about 200 still employed in the quarries. Today there is still a steady demand and it's my belief we have enough reserves to satisfy demand well into the future."

Stuart is particularly anxious Portland does not lose any more of its virgin fields to quarrying.

"The old field system is still visible and it is a precious part of the island's heritage. We must save the last of our historic fields."

Portland is, of course, a Royal Manor and Roly has acted as the Court Leet Crown Agent & Bailiff for the past dozen years.

"We are the only court in the UK with such legal powers. Wareham does have an active Court Leet but I believe that's more of an excuse for a good booze-up – but don't quote me!" (Sorry, Roly, I quite forgot your request!)

Once an exclusively male preserve there are now three ladies among its 24 members.

"We are the legal custodians of Crown Common Land. We 'beat the bounds' on the boundary stone along the Chesil Bank when the head boy and the head girl from the Royal Manor Arts Comprehensive participate in the ceremony."

If the Navy and the quarries have played major roles in the economic life of Portland then so too has the fishing industry. And who better to assess its current importance than Ken Lynham who has spent a lifetime in the company of countless Combens, Stones, Whites and Pearces?

Spider crabs – the very name is guaranteed to send a shiver down the spine of the average English female. As for the English diner he or she, it appears, simply doesn't have the patience to eat them. Extracting the flesh from the long, spidery claws can be a time consuming, tedious exercise. But our unlovely friends do have their admirers. The Spanish and Portuguese, in particular, and the Italians too, contrive to turn the eating of the crabs into a highly enjoyable gastronomic and social occasion with the accompaniment of bread, olive oil and, doubtless, a liberal supply of wine. Ken explains the routine.

"The Vivier lorries have large tanks which hold 24 tons of salt water in which 8 tons of crabs and lobsters can be transported live. The lorries travel over on the ferry from Poole to Cherbourg and down to Southern Europe with the drivers dropping off their cargo en route – a two and a half day trip. The trade really began to flourish here in the 1970s and is invaluable to our economy. But it's not only the fishermen who benefit. For every 1 fisherman there are an estimated 5 related jobs on land – in distribution, retail, electricians, engineers, fuel suppliers and the like. I estimate the fishing industry is worth £20 million annually to Weymouth and Portland."

The enduring importance of fishing to the local community is sometimes overlooked, I suspect, because there appear to be far fewer fishing boats along the Dorset coast than in the past.

"You must remember that most boats leave before the rest of the world is up and about and often return in the evening when most people have gone home. Boats today are also very much more efficient than in the past so naturally fewer are needed. But the capital cost of buying and running them is astronomical. As for an indication of how important the industry remains, just draw an imaginary line running 6 miles between St. Aldhelm's Head and Portland Bill and you can reckon there are 26,000 lobster pots alone providing a living for fishermen from Portland, Weymouth, Lulworth, Kimmeridge, Swanage and on to Poole."

Ken Lynham is a true Portlander, liked and respected far afield. Honoured by the City of London Corporation, he's been a part of an industry that has provided him and others like him with a decent livelihood over the years. But being a fisherman can also be a desperately hazardous way of earning a living. Tragedies are all too commonplace and when they occur they can cast long shadows over men's lives and leave a heartache that will know no end this side of the grave.

"It was 2 years ago off the Bill that Peter, my grandson, lost his life overboard. His father and my other son were with him at the time. It hit us all dreadfully hard. Paul was absolutely devastated."

The photograph of Peter, bright-eyed and laughing, full of life and energy, sits on the mantle-piece beside us, a poignant reminder of the daily risks our fishermen face"

"He was just twenty. A wonderful lad. As good as gold. His body was never found. Seven hundred mourners attended the Memorial service and over £7,500 was raised in his honour, which we donated to Portland Coastwatch and the Lifeboat. We were able to provide the funds for another telescope for them."

We all know the splendid work of the lifeboat crews but I'd not previously heard of Coastwatch.

"Geoff Peters is the manager. There's about 60 members of Coastwatch and they provide an invaluable service to all those who are at sea in the locality. I know they've already been responsible for saving lives. They were so good to us at the time we lost Peter – and they're all unpaid volunteers."

Once again, splendid individuals giving freely of their time to the community. What would we do without them?

An office at the Harbour Heights Hotel
There's a hard white hat sitting on her table before me. Perhaps Rachel Barton knows something I don't?

"Don't worry – it's for when I go out on the construction site," she laughs.

At the moment she's enthusing over her role in Portland Gas Storage PLC. The man behind the project is geologist and Chief Executive, Andrew Hindle. When it's fully operational 14 giant caverns a mile and a half under the sea-bed will provide storage for 1,000 million cubic metres of gas which is equivalent to 1% of the UK's total demand, s significant contribution to Britain's energy security. For a scientific ignoramus like myself the concept is mind-boggling. As someone who in his time has failed to construct a rabbit hutch out of an existing wooden box and is baffled by the simplest assembly instructions, I am in awe of men such as Dr. Hindle.

Rachel is also busy campaigning hard to see the Old Engine Shed, a remnant of the Victorian railway and stone quarrying days on the island, reinvented as an 'interpretation centre.' It would reflect Portland's geology and history, provide classroom space and serve as a walker's cafe, all to be financed at a cost of £1.5 million by Portland Gas PLC.

Born in the front bedroom of a house in Queen's Road, Southwell, Rachel Barton, nee Flew, one of the oldest original names on the island, is fiercely proud of her roots, yet she is un-blinkered in her view of Portland. I have suggested to her that the island's rugged bleakness is compounded by the drab, joyless character to the entry to the town.

"I recognise your description. In truth, I think there are several factors at work. Underhill, that is to say Fortuneswell, Castletown and Verne Common do not, in general terms, comprise an affluent area and there are pockets of real deprivation. A number of 'off-island' families have been relocated to Underhill from elsewhere in England, families with problems who sometimes also cause problems. Trouble has been moved from one place to another. I hesitate to put a number on the total but too many certainly for all the respectable, hard-working people in the community. Incidentally, I am also worried about West Cliff, a housing estate to the west of Southwell."

I too have seen the overgrown gardens, the rusting cars, the general air of neglect and dereliction. It must be profoundly depressing, as Rachel says, for all the good people whose lives are being blighted by obnoxious neighbours'. Rachel's previous 'hat', prior to the white one, was as a community officer. She spent a lot of time with the youngsters on the island.

"We do have lots of excellent facilities like the 'drop-in' in the old Methodist Church. However, I am concerned at the number of teenage pregnancies. To my mind the Government of the day seems to aggravate the problem because young girls know they can jump to the front of the housing queue and pick up benefits too easily. If they knew they were going to have to live with their families it might just make them think twice."

But Rachel is excited by many of the changes taking place.

"We must embrace the opportunities the Olympic Games will provide. People like Gary Fooks and his wife Jane are trying to ensure that significant long-term benefits will accrue. Gary is the Olympics legacy officer. We are also looking at the building of new schools and the creation of the Portland Academy which will encourage older people to continue education alongside young people."

(At the year's end it was announced, in the light of the economic recession, the plans of Portland Gas Storage were to be put temporarily on hold.)

On the topic of the Olympic legacy it's interesting to note that local Dorset Echo columnist, Hilda Swinney, would particularly like to see an alternative route from Victoria Square to Tophill constructed, though Hilda recognises Cllr. Les Ames's argument that the likely cost is currently prohibitive. Several local residents such as Southwell businessman, Chris Hornby, and Sheila Bedford of Underhill, would prefer to see the emphasis on the regeneration of areas like Underhill, Castletown and Fortuneswell. Retired RN officer, George Hayhoe of Easton, the Royal Manor Arts College's head boy, Robert Thomas, and deputy head girl, Sorrel McBryde, would prefer that Portland 's sailing and water-sports facilities be expanded for the benefit of local people. Commercial artist, Andrew Joliffe, likes the idea of a dramatic artistic statement to welcome visitors. It will be fascinating to discover what emerges after all the deliberations and quite a challenge for Gary Fooks and his wife Jane to please everyone.

The Southwell Business Park and Portland Spa Hotel

What odds would a bookmaker have offered a few years ago against Portland being the first South Dorset town to boast a 4 star hotel? Yet that is exactly what is happening.

"The Portland Spa will be a venue for conferences, a 'destination' hotel for businessmen and

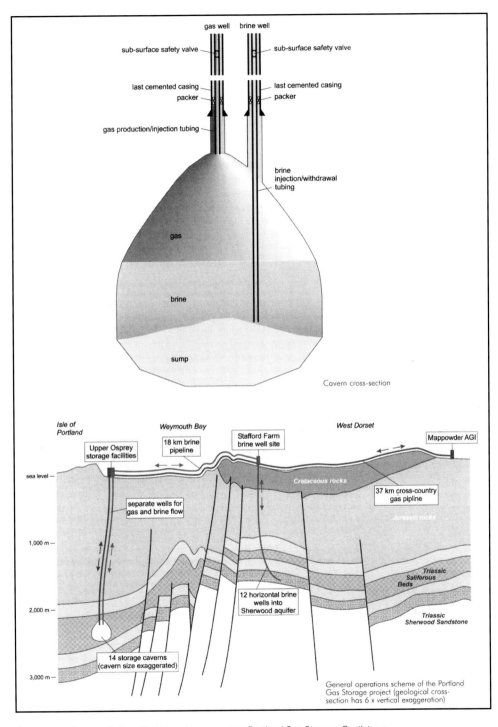

Gas storage diagram. Picture: *David Langham, surveyor, Portland Gas Storage, Castletown.*

those seeking a range of leisure activities in a unique and exciting location- and all under one roof."

Andrew Coupe, a former marketing manager with Devenish and financial consultant, is the Business Director along with four other directors and is clearly passionate about the Portland Spa development.

"The MOD premises were empty for 3 years before the Southwell Business Park was created. We now have 100 businesses employing 500 staff with an annual turnover in the region of £50 million. With space remaining we decided the hotel was the logical next step and we are now in the final stages of slotting in the last pieces of the jigsaw. Unlike practically every similar centre we have car parking spaces for 750 vehicles on tarmac and another 2,000 on grass. The whole area covers 40 acres with 8 acres for outdoor activities. The hotel capacity will ultimately be 200 bedrooms. We have invested £10 million in the Business Park and another £10 million in the whole site. As you can imagine, the input into the local economy will be considerable. We already provide opportunities for skilled local trades-people and the hotel will eventually employ up to 100 with stable all-the-year round employment. Young people will know they don't have to uproot themselves because career opportunities will exist for them here. And just look what Portland can provide within a couple of miles of the hotel – dinghy, yacht and powerboat racing, abseiling, rock climbing, coastal walks, bird-watching. These are just the sort of 'adrenalin team-building' activities many businesses like to foster on such occasions."

It's a brave vision. It is desperately unfortunate for Andrew and his fellow directors that the realisation of their ambitious plans has coincided with the worst economic downturn in many years. I hope they can weather the present crisis without too much difficulty. (Alas, even as we go to print it is announced that the hotel is in the hands of the administrators and its future uncertain. The hotel remains open while a new buyer is sought. The recession is biting deep.)

The Verne Prison

It's Friday lunchtime and work and classes have finished until Monday morning. The rest of the world may continue its labours until late afternoon but the prisoners at The Verne are already spilling out on to the playing field. The sun has, at last, broken through the thick blanket of cloud that has enveloped the island all morning. It's pleasantly warm and several prisoners are already sunbathing, some are kicking a football around and others are strolling around the perimeter of the field chattering in a variety of languages none of which I recognise. A minority of the faces are white.

Back in the admin office a chart records the prison statistics. There are this Friday exactly 587 prisoners representing 72 different nationalities, speaking 50 different languages. Three hundred and fifty are foreign nationals, making 59.7 percent of the total. The largest single national group comprises Nigerians. Five years ago it was Jamaicans who predominated. Many of the whites are East Europeans. Within a few months most will be deported back to their countries of origin.

My guide is Principal Officer, John Masters.

"A large percentage of the prisoners are here for drug-related offences. Organised racketeering, supplying, quite a few are human mules. And if you see a six feet five inches Caucasian, chances are he's a Russian minder."

Most will benefit from hefty remissions in their sentences. Aside from the usual remission awarded for good conduct, a recent memorandum from Jack Straw's Justice Ministry states that foreign prisoners, subject to the original length of their sentences, can get up to 270 extra days removed from their sentences. Those convicted of sex and violent crimes are exempt from this ruling. It's Jack Straw's way of reducing foreign prison numbers and the general overcrowding in Britain's gaols. It has absolutely nothing to do with justice. It's expediency pure and simple.

"We're like postmen," says the young lady in the office with a smile." They'll leave, usually at 8am, though it will depend upon the times of their flights from Gatwick – or wherever. They're taken straight to the airport unless they're appealing, of course, because they want to stay."

There are four categories of prison in our penal system and Portland is Low Risk Category C. D is an open prison like Leyhill for even lower risk offenders. Dartmoor is High Risk Category C. Categories B and A speak for themselves. Any prisoner in a Category C prison is thought highly unlikely to attempt escape. The Verne is also a training prison. John takes me on a tour.

"We have 130 prisoners in the educational block every weekday. Some will be illiterate, others improving their English. Some may be studying for NVQs and the like. Prisoners also have the opportunity to work in the wood-mill learning carpentry skills. They'll make a variety of wooden objects – benches, garden seats, fences, lobster pots even. These are sold commercially. Some of our inmates will learn bricklaying and similar skills. Others will work in the kitchens, as wing cleaners, in the laundry and so on. Working in the kitchens is generally regarded as one of the most desirable and important jobs. Good food plays a vital role in keeping prisoners happy."

John takes me into the canteen where I examine a typical weekly menu. It's cereals for breakfast, together with a pint of milk. A full-English is available on Sundays. Cooked meals are provided both at lunchtime and in the evenings with a wide variety of choice. It's a menu that wouldn't look out of place in a decent hotel. Prisoners fill in sheets at the beginning of each week with their selections. With such a diversity of prisoners, Muslim, Jews, Hindus, Sikhs, and all the other nationalities and religions, all tastes and religious requirements are catered for. I idly wonder if British prisoners eat as well in the gaols of Africa and the Middle East. No bacon on Sundays, that's for sure. I also wonder how the Muslim prisoners would enjoy serving their time in a Saudi Arabian or Iranian gaol?

"The Muslims are eating later this week because it's Ramadan. And, by the way, we did receive a Gold Award a year or two back for the quality of our food."

What is the general regime?

"Prisoners are not locked in their cells. They have their own keys and have free movement about the prison. Their day begins at 8am. On weekdays they will be in classes or in work related activities. In the evenings they can choose what to do with their time – snooker, the gym, TV and so on. A wide range of facilities exist for their recreation. They are expected be back in their own cells by 11pm."

And if they're not, or they're found in another cell in the middle of the night, what are the implications?

"They can be put on a Governor's Report or fined but the range of sanctions is limited. What we rely on in a prison like this is what the authorities call 'dynamic security' which is all about the relationships between the inmates and the staff. We have an excellent, highly professional staff here and I am very proud of them. The truth is prisoners are in your face 24/7 and you've got to build relationships, not only with them, but between prisoner and prisoner. We work very hard to ensure that different nationalities, different cultures, different religions get on together and, generally, we're very successful. Of course, there are problems at times. You're always looking and listening. You might be in your office and you hear a chair go over and you wonder – is it an accident or the beginning of something more serious?"

What do prisoners earn?

"The average would be £8.00 per week but certain jobs like the kitchen would be better rewarded – perhaps up to £12.00."

I am intrigued by the economics of prison life. There are some very wealthy prisoners in The Verne. Even a millionaire or two, I understand. The drugs trade can be a very lucrative profession. Their few pounds of prison earnings are neither here or there. But all inmates do have their own prison bank accounts, ostensibly for their earnings, which can however, be 'topped up' from outside, by family, friends or from their own external bank accounts. The more credit a prisoner has the more freely he can spend on his phone card or on any items he may elect to buy from the 'catalogue' of goods available from the prison 'shop'. Prisoners place their orders which are then delivered on Tuesdays to their cells. Prices are the same as outside and whatever the prisoner spends is duly deducted from his bank account.

I ask John about the use of phones.

"Mobiles are forbidden but a prisoner has access to outside calls up to the limit of his phone card which can, of course, be 'topped up' as long as he can pay."

Are calls monitored?

"Numbers may be recorded. Of course, with so many calls being made by prisoners it would not be possible to monitor more than a small percentage. And then, of course, there would be the difficulty presented by 50 different languages being spoken by the prisoners."

And letters- in and out? Are they censored?

"There is no restriction on the number of letters a prisoner may receive or send. Certain letters might be looked at but the same difficulties exist as with monitoring phone calls."

In the light of the recent changes in the law relating to smoking how are prisons affected?

"Smoking has to be in prisoners' own cells or outside. A shared cell is regarded as a no-smoking area."

I have a look in several cells or 'rooms', as they now often referred to. They resemble a typical student's 'pad'. En-suite, TV, CD player, books, photographs. They bear absolutely no relationship to the era of Porridge. There's no 'lights out.' A prisoner can watch TV or listen to his music into the early hours though he's expected to refrain from disturbing his neighbours.

Back in the office I chat with John and two of his colleagues, Mark Brown and Bob Williams. They're each one of them impressive individuals. Thoughtful, manifestly decent and fair-minded, I'd be delighted to work alongside them any day of the week. I am quite sure the overwhelming majority of prison officers are the same. Are they happy with the present rules and regulations that determine prison policy in general, not specifically those operating in The Verne? I get the feeling they share many of the doubts of society in general about penal policy. John would prefer, I know, rewarding good, positive behaviour by prisoners rather than the granting of 'blanket privileges.' Each of the officers shares the general frustration that they rarely have the time to achieve anything significant with the prisoners. Here today, gone tomorrow. Yes, of course, they must be delighted to see the back of many of their inmates. On the other hand, others have barely settled in to courses preparing them for crime-free lives outside than they are gone. Those with serious drug problems need time and close supervision if they are to be weaned off their addiction.

The image of Portland as a place to serve a sentence has changed. The Verne itself only became a prison in 1949, previously serving as a military citadel. The reputation of the old convict prison of The Grove was not very different from that of Dartmoor. Look at the old photographs and the convicts with their shaven heads labouring in the quarries. It was hard, backbreaking work with few privileges in a grim and forbidding location. Until twenty years ago its population was almost exclusively British. Today it is regarded as one of the more comfortable prisons in which to 'do time' and the presence of so many foreign prisoners and short-sentence inmates obviously markedly affects the nature of the regime.

I bid goodbye to John, Bob and Mark wishing them well in their work. I know they and their colleagues will go on doing their best to rehabilitate whenever and wherever it is possible. Each told me of the letters and Christmas cards they receive from former prisoners who have succeeded in turning their lives around. They can hope for no more.

Portland Bird Observatory

"You won't get it right! You journalists never do get it right!"

Martin Cade, the warden at Portland's renowned Bird Observatory, laughs.

"Alright, I'll amend that. You're an author, not a journalist, but I still doubt you'll get it right!"

After 19 years at Portland Martin has good reason for his general scepticism. When journalists turn up following the appearance of some rare migrant at the old Lower Lighthouse few, in Martin's experience, are able to distinguish between even the most common species. Hence their published reports almost invariably contain glaring and, for Martin, exasperating inaccuracies.

However, I dare to lay down a challenge to our most amiable ornithological expert. Half a dozen bottles of wine for Martin's personal consumption – if I do get it wrong! We shake hands upon the wager. What Martin doesn't know is that I grew up on the edge of the Dorset heath-land and, from the age of 8, was falling asleep either to the churring of a nightjar or the haunting call of a curlew drifting across from the mudflats of Lytchett Bay. Ever since those childhood days I have been a passionate bird-lover myself. Unfortunately Martin doesn't promise me anything whatsoever if I do get it right – not even a cup of tea! Nonetheless, both my pride and professional credibility are at stake. I am, as they say, on a 'hiding to nothing'.

"Our particular interest here lies in the spring and autumn migration. We record movements and numbers and trends in populations. Rarities are, of course, particularly exciting. One of the most fascinating aspects of our work is that you never know what you'll find."

Originally built in 1869 the old Lower Lighthouse was unused and derelict at the end of WW2. It was the kindly father of the remarkable Helen Brotherton who bought the building for his daughter 50 odd years ago. Helen has been a legendary figure in the wildlife and conservation movement for half a century and, thanks to her vision, imagination and generosity, was responsible for the transformation of the lighthouse into an observatory. Sir Peter Scott formally performed the opening ceremony in 1961. Today it provides inexpensive overnight, self-catering accommodation for up to 30 visitors. Aside from ringers the observatory also caters for divers, climbers, artists and a variety of outdoor enthusiasts.

Max Seaford, a regular from Milborne Port, lays down his binoculars this wet, blustery afternoon and whispers.

"Martin is brilliant – one of the finest ornithologists in the country." Raising his voice he adds:" Tell him about the North American Savannah Sparrow, Martin."

Its arrival at Portland back in 1973 was, I learn, the first European record of the bird. This year a thrush nightingale made an appearance which caused no small measure of excitement. There have also been a number of olivaceous warblers, giant white egrets and bee-eaters.

Five years ago Max spotted a red-backed shrike not yards from where we are now sitting. I ask Martin about the dearth of cuckoos.

"Remember they have never been that common but, yes, it's true, numbers were well down but birds like the turtle dove have suffered an even more calamitous drop in the past 30 years or so."

As I prepare to leave I comment upon the splendid views from the top of the observatory, even on a poor day.

"Our views may be fabulous – but our TV reception is absolutely appalling!"

Lyn Cooch, Cotoneaster and 'British Primitives'

Goats and cotoneaster dominate our conversation. They're a distinctly odd pairing but very much in the foreground of Lyn Cooch's thoughts. Yet the young lady beside me looks charmingly normal. Cotoneaster a problem? Rhododendron, yes, and the ubiquitous ragwort. But cotoneaster, surely not. It's decorative, conceals a multitude of sins in most gardens and birds love the berries.

But Lyn, Portland ranger and project officer, is insistent.

"Cotoneaster really is a serious problem in a number of quarries. It shades out other species of plant and it's so difficult to remove or eradicate. Volunteers can spend hours 'cotoneaster bashing' yet make scarcely an impression."

Happily Lyn is more sanguine about the recent arrival of goats on the island.

"We, that is John Stobart of Natural England and our volunteers, introduced 10 'British Primitive' goats, all castrated billies, to the under-cliff on the east side of the island last autumn. Without grazing, areas such as steep, rocky cliffs become overgrown with shrubs which prevent certain plants from growing and that can have an adverse effect on other wildlife, especially insects. We have a team of keepers monitoring their progress."

Years ago I enjoyed a brief, ambivalent relationship with goats, being responsible for 6 months for milking twice daily a small herd of nannies. My employer converted the milk into yoghurt when the product was still unknown to the wider public, save those with allergies. A more contrary beast I have yet to meet. Regularly one or other would contrive to kick over the pan into which I was squeezing the milk from their teats. There was also one particularly obstreperous billy – not that I ever tried to milk him – but, in his case, I think I had the last laugh. Just before my departure he was slaughtered and we ate him. I enjoyed every mouthful! Whether Lyn and her volunteers already have their eyes on any of their introduced 'British primitives' I don't know, but I would recommend roasting slowly in red wine.

Lyn's work is funded by the Portland Coast and Countryside Project among other bodies. She's responsible for 'raising awareness within the community and among visitors of Portland's rich diversity of flora and fauna, preparing leaflets, updating information on boards and similar environmental bodies and liaising with a team of forty volunteers.' She also calls by regularly at the Chesil and Fleet Centre administered by the Warden Don Moxom. It was there earlier in the day that I met volunteer, Derek Fawell, where we watched a party of at least 50 starlings, mostly juveniles, splashing noisily and exuberantly about in a rainwater pool while another 50 or so of their pals looked on enviously. As with the house sparrow, starling numbers have declined in recent years so it's always a pleasure to record healthy broods of young birds.

Lyn is appreciative of the support she receives from many on the island such as Angie at the Heights Hotel, who with binocular specialists Swarovski sponsor their regular news bulletin.

"Bob Ford organises brilliant bird-watching walks from the hotel. And I must mention Nigel Spring, who is responsible for butterfly conservation, and Neal Heanes, another of our volunteers and a mountaineering enthusiast, who has organised buddleia and ivy removing teams."

First of all cotoneaster was a named enemy. Now it's another of my favourites buddleia, the 'butterfly bush', the wonderfully resilient survivor with the 'Never say die' spirit that was so often the first shrub to appear on the old bomb-sites in blitzed cities and cheerfully flourishes in the most improbable locations. Lyn and Neal, how could you?

The Young Offender's Institution

I am with my old friend and Weymouth artist, Duff Pearce, at The Grove outside the wall of the institution. We've been reminiscing about Duff's days as a rugby player.

"We played a few fixtures against the YOI. Usually their numbers would be augmented by several of the warders. They were always 'interesting' games."

Recalling Duff's prowess on the rugby field I suspect 'interesting' is a euphemism for some blood-curdling tackles and fearsome scrums.

Young Offenders Institution. *Picture: Geoff Hill*

"And there, on that wall, that's where I recall some of the local lads would stand and sing 'Born Free'. Or the girls would lift up their tops."

It's not difficult to appreciate that the old Matt Monro hit might enrage the incarcerated youths within, nor that the girls' provocative gestures would stir sexual passions.

"And up there!" Duff points. "That's where the young offenders would hurl insults back – or worse. Sometimes it was packs of excrement. Or they'd spit."

It seems things haven't changed greatly. No one is shouting abuse or throwing missiles this particular afternoon but locals have been complaining they are still occasionally subject to foul language shouted from on high by inmates. Why is it allowed to happen? I will enquire.

The YOI, another day

Waiting in the entrance area for my escort I am the only adult male, other than a couple of burly officers. Half a dozen young women, several with small children or babes in arms, are standing about chatting while their identities are checked. They're all in their early twenties or late teens.

My guide today is the Deputy Governor, David Bourne. David spent a part of his career working with NACRO, the organisation dealing with the Care and Resettlement of Offenders. He is a man committed to the rehabilitation of those who pass through his care though he recognises the re-offending rates do not offer more than limited encouragement.

Some of the statistics are shocking and depressing. Of the 594 prisoners here today – the maximum capacity is 617 – half are black or ethnic. Twenty-nine different languages are spoken. Nearly 60% have been involved in crimes of violence. There are more Muslim prisoners than Church of England and the prison employs a full-time Imam. More than 100 of the young men – and they are between the ages of 18 and 21 years – are already fathers. Their wives, or more likely their 'partners', were the young women I met earlier at the entrance. How many children will they be responsible for by the time they are 30, I ask myself? How many will actually be real fathers to their children? How many of the young women are on benefits? Few of the prisoners are locals. Fifty years ago there might have been the odd Cypriot or Maltese pimp and a few West Indians. Today between 70 and 100 are foreign nationals. Many are from London or other big cities. A substantial number of them are gang members.

"If there's trouble in Brixton, or Lewisham, or Tower Hamlets – a gang killing or knifing – we have to be on our toes for reprisals here. We're watching all the time."

"What are the reoffending rates?"

"Somewhere between two thirds and three quarters. As for the foreign nationals, most will be put on planes at the end of their sentences. Others will appeal to stay. If they have a child it's a bargaining point."

David gives me a guided tour. Physically the place is in good to excellent order.

"Our old gym was inadequate with lots of testosterone filled young men. Today we have a new gymnasium, a new grass and five-a-side all-weather pitch. We do much to encourage sporting activity and we liaise with clubs in the prisoners' home localities so that they can continue their interests when they leave here. Just as developing work-place skills is vital, so participating in sport can turn round lives."

There are 9 accommodation blocks.

"Facilities vary. We have one new unit with 63 mentors who try to play a constructive role in relation to other prisoners. Some of the cells are en suite, others not, but we are constantly working to upgrade our accommodation."

The cells are comfortable enough – TVs, CD players, books, magazines, photographs. The average student bedsit except there is more security.

"We operate on an incentives and privileges basis with TV. We have Enhanced, Standard and Basic. At any one time about 5% will be on Basic – that means they do not have access to TV."

All the officers I see about the compound are in twos or threes. The feeling is very different from The Verne. There's a much greater degree of tension and watchfulness. These are 18-21 year-olds, more volatile and unpredictable than the inmates across the island.

What exactly is the structure of the day?

"8am Wake up call. 8.30 off to work or education. 11.30 Lunch. 12.30 In cells. 1.30 Back to work or education. 4.30 Tea. 5pm In cells. 5.30 In Association. 8pm In cells. Midnight TV and music off. Everyone is either in work or education. We offer a wide range of courses such as Basic Literacy skills, English, Business Studies with examinations in a variety of subjects. We have a 'Writer in Residence', Louisa Adjoa Parker, who encourages literary skills among the inmates. We also offer a range of vocational courses and training – like bricklaying, plumbing, industrial cleaning, decorating, health care, kitchen work and Rail-track. There was a time we used to keep livestock here. There was actually a piggery but that is now commercially run. We have some first-rate instructors and teachers. If someone puts his mind to it while he is here he can certainly benefit considerably. If we can assist them to gain skills and thereby secure decent jobs, they are much less likely to re-offend. But, in the final analysis, however hard we try, it is up to the individual "

I ask David about outside activities. One former officer and old friend, Rodney Hurt, well recalls the days of outside working parties and Sunday morning church visits.

"A few years ago it was a more relaxed regime with fewer difficult offenders. And yes, Rodney is quite right, we would escort prisoners to St. Peter's and take them out on working parties. However, after risk assessment there are so few who are now acceptable for outdoor activities. We cannot afford to take chances. I fear we would not readily be forgiven by the public "

Are there many tensions between the different nationalities?

"It is obviously a very difficult area. We do employ an excellent Imam, Mohammed Saeid, as well a full-time Anglican priest together with other chaplains. We work immensely hard to resolve the issues as they arise. We do take great pride in trying to secure good race relations."

And the inevitable topic of drugs, how are they managing?

"Once again it is something we take very seriously. We are constantly on the look out and I don't believe there is a particular problem here."

What about those good citizens in The Grove who suffer the occasional abuse from the top of the block that overlooks their homes?

"The difficulty arises largely from the location of the building which, as you will appreciate, we cannot do anything about. We have put in windows so offenders cannot readily put their heads out, but there is a problem too with actually identifying those responsible. With the best will in the world officers cannot be everywhere, but the public do need to know we are doing our very best."

Indeed. I am quite sure David and his colleagues will continue to perform their difficult duties to the best of their abilities on our behalf. Society has changed radically in the past half century and, in a number of ways, not for the best. Whilst we all are grateful for the enormous material improvements in our lives, for teachers, the police and prison officers, and for all those dealing with young people, the problems have multiplied. Children and young adults are physically bigger and stronger than at any time in our history. They often tower above those who seek to educate or control them. They are more vocal, self-confident and certain of their rights, if not of their responsibilities, than ever in our history. At the same time many of the social constraints upon their conduct have been eroded or disappeared without trace. Add to the cocktail the consequences of broken homes and families, absentee fathers, few educational qualifications, welfare dependency, drug abuse, cheap alcohol, odious role models, race and religious tensions, to mention but some of the sad realities of contemporary Britain, and it is not a pretty picture. For David Bourne and his officers they are daily in the front line. It is no enviable task.

So I drive down the hill past the Citadel and The Heights Hotel, through Fortuneswell and Castletown and out on to the Causeway, past the Sailing Academy and the Chesil Centre, and on to Weymouth. Has Portland ever known so much change in times of peace as in the past twenty years? How will it look 20 years hence? There is no doubt in my mind that Portland is in a state of dramatic transition and, almost certainly, entering an era of unparalleled prosperity. Perhaps it will not be next year, or the year after that, but I will be very surprised if it is long delayed. The island has so much to offer the 21st century traveller. What will be of critical importance is how the people of Portland respond to the challenges before them.

Weymouth
Twinned with Louviers (France) and Holzwickede (Germany)

I first discovered Weymouth in the Sixties. At that time I could park my little frog-eyed Austin Healey Sprite on the quayside opposite the King's Arms without difficulty. Forte's an institution. Sally Lunn's bakery sold the best bread and cakes for miles around. The aroma of hops still wafted up to Chapelhay from the Devenish Brewery in Hope Square. The Tivoli Gardens pub in Franchise Street was full of beatniks and the best conversation in town, rough scrumpy was just one shilling and eight pence a pint and the music of Bob Dylan, Eric Burdon and the Rolling Stones blasted out of the jukebox. Weymouth FC, one of the most successful non-League clubs in the country, played at the Rec at the bottom of Boot Hill before crowds of three thousand and more. On one occasion, I recall, I walked in the footsteps of Graham Nash, then performing with The Hollies and soon to become a member of the legendary Crosby, Stills and Nash, as he strolled up St. Mary's Street carrying his guitar to the Gaumont, or whatever it was called at the time. I even remember the Brook Brothers, Britain's supposed answer to the Everlys, Phil and Don, as they stood waiting patiently and unrecognised at the bus stop on the Town Bridge, even though they'd just had a couple of major chart hits. How many pop-stars could or would do that today? Was it a golden age? In some ways certainly – has the music ever been even half as good? There was also a degree of innocence that has sadly disappeared. Even my friends among the beach-bum beatniks, who earned their daily crust and drinks money hiring out the deckchairs and floats during the day, were not doing hard drugs. Just the occasional weed, cheap cider and the brilliant music were enough for a good night out. And there was no hint of needless aggression or gratuitous violence.

Today the Devenish Brewery, the Tivoli Gardens and Forte's are but distant memories, parking

'Picture postcard' Weymouth. *Picture: Bill Macey*

in or near the town itself varies between a headache and a nightmare and Weymouth FC, who moved out to the Wessex Stadium at Chickerell to play before crowds a half or even a third of the old gate is, so sadly for all the loyal fans, in the most desperate financial and playing mess in its history. Yet, in many respects, Weymouth remains scarcely altered. The golden sands, the donkey rides and the sand sculptures, the Victorian esplanade, the old harbour, the Town Bridge that lifts on the hour, the bustle of holidaymakers in high season, the Alexandra Gardens, the blended smell of fish and chips and salt air on the quayside, that's still the Weymouth I first encountered 40 odd years ago.

Maureen Attwoll, author of 9 books and one-time manager of Weymouth library, loves the town with all the enthusiasm and passion of a convert to a new cause.

"My niece's children have swum with sharks in the Maldives and explored many other exotic locations. Yet when they came to stay with us I asked them what their best-ever holiday memory was and they said: 'Paddling in the sea at Sandsfoot Castle, finding a dead crab and filling our buckets with little yellow shells.' And that was in mid-winter. Perhaps it's because I arrived here from London when I was a child and saw it first through the eyes of a newcomer for whom the sea was an exciting novelty that I love it so much – unlike my husband David who was born in Weymouth and has lived his whole life here. He just takes it all for granted."

David nods his agreement. "Weymouth's alright, I suppose."

Though Maureen's titles include 'Weymouth, The Golden Years' (Dovecote Press) and 'Weymouth, More Golden Years' (Dovecote Press) she is just a little impatient with locals who resist all change.

"Though much of the town remains unaltered I do welcome those changes that have taken place in recent years. When I worked in the old library, for instance, I would look across at the rear of the Jubilee Hall/Regent/Gaumont in its different guises and what I saw looked like a big, ugly red-brick warehouse. Even though I saw the Rolling Stones and other acts there and had every excuse to be nostalgic, I wasn't sorry to see it demolished. Like many others I was in ignorance of some of its more interesting architectural features when it happened. But I do welcome the shops in New Bond Street. The facilities have improved enormously. It was what the people wanted and Weymouth needed. It's a pleasant square and the Barracuda Bar has been revealed – we couldn't see it properly before. It's been well restored and it's wonderful!"

Maureen is also more sanguine than many about proposed developments.

"At the moment we have 4 large hotels – The Crown, The Royal, The Prince Regent and The Rembrandt. But they are all old buildings that have had to be adapted to meet all sorts of new regulations. That has created difficulties for them. I believe Weymouth needs a modern, purpose-built hotel."

And what about Dorset's libraries since I am with someone who spent much of her working life in them?

"In an earlier age they did grant those in our society unable to afford books, like my own family and many of my friends, access to knowledge and great literature without charge. But it's a different world. With borrowing declining I'm not sure it's viable to keep all our libraries open. Paying staff and maintaining the buildings costs a lot of money. When local authorities are expected to find ever increasing sums for an ageing population, what are its priorities? With access to the Internet more and more people can find all the information they want at their fingertips. And, if you ask people which services they would least like to lose, I doubt libraries would be at the top of many lists, sad though I am to say it."

As I leave Maureen laughs. "I don't suppose Geoffrey Poole, whom I respect greatly, by the way, will be very pleased with me – but there!"

So who exactly is this fearful man Geoffrey Poole who will not be 'very pleased' with the delightful Maureen? He's already been described to me by another friend, Maurice Strabling, as 'At times exasperating, irascible, bloody-minded but, more often than not, absolutely right.'

At this point in the proceedings it is necessary to explain that, at the time of my visit to the town, the single most controversial issue, aside from the building of the new road, relates to the redevelopment of the Pavilion and the surrounding seafront area. To explain it in the most simple and basic terms, the Pavilion Theatre is owned by the Council and needs a large sum of money spent on it if it is to be suitably upgraded. However, the Council does not possess the capital and, to cut a long and complicated story short, engaged a firm called Howard Holdings to present a plan of redevelopment. The company said it would restore the Pavilion to all its former glory and more besides, but this would be on condition that it could build a hotel and apartments adjacent to the site. A new marina would also be constructed. The profits from the sale of the properties would finance the Pavilion redevelopment and mean the Council would have a spanking new theatre free and gratis. I have reduced the matter to its bare bones for fear of boring the reader with the detailed negotiations that inevitably accompanied the whole business. When the plans became public knowledge there was widespread criticism and 7,000 signatures were attached to a petition against the proposal. One of the principal objections was that the building of apartments of several storeys would alter radically the appearance of the whole seafront area to its great detriment. And now it is that I return to the splendid Geoffrey Poole, my companion for the morning.

Sitting in his study with him, surrounded by vast collections of newspaper cuttings, books and files, I soon appreciate this is a man of formidable intellect with a marked distaste for shoddy thinking and incompetence wherever he detects its existence. Geoffrey also writes beautifully and here I will quote in full a piece he sent on the subject to the local press. It is, I believe, a positive gem and worthy of the widest audience – and the judgement of posterity. He begins with a few lines of verse you may recognise.

Goodbye To All That
'*Wiv a ladder and some glasses,*
You could see to 'Ackney Marshes
If it wasn't for the 'ouses in between.'
    Edgar Bateman

'(A Council Official, I will omit the name) suggests comfortingly that while the huge 'Landmark 'block will dominate the Pavilion peninsula and obliterate the Nothe, the other buildings of the scheme have been designed just low enough for us to see the tree tops of the Nothe Walk. We should be grateful! He must know that views are not two dimensional. It is the 'space between' that defines and makes for a view of distinction. Here it is the ever changing activity in the harbour played against the Nothe woods, quays, buildings, out to the stone pier lantern. It is exceptional and iconically Weymouth. To be reassured as we look across the bay...."Is that a tall ship in?" No good telling your visitor what interest lies on the other side of a line of mundane buildings, a carbuncle, and an intrusive folly called a marina. "There's a big fort there, you know, on a headland, built after Napoleon and all that, and guns and searchlights and reviews... No, you can't see it from here or anywhere on the sea front but I'll take you there tomorrow!"

Splendid, Geoffrey!

The Pavilion Theatre

We meet in the foyer. Roger Hogben, a man with 30 years of experience in the private sector, is the recently appointed Business Planning and Performance officer for Weymouth. As we talk so Roger provides me with a guided tour of the whole theatre – backstage, lights and props areas, the bar and restaurant – assessing the life expectancy of certain facilities, anticipating imminent problems, and so on.

"The simple truth is that a lot of money needs to be spent in the next 30 years on the harbour itself and here in the theatre, on the ferry terminal and other projects, and the Council does not and will not possess the means to undertake the work that needs doing. Private capital has to be injected but investors demand, quite understandably, a return on their investment. One of my jobs is to look at everything commercially. The Council doesn't make money on the Pavilion. In fact, it spends money on patching it up. The bar and restaurant has one of the finest views in the town yet we do not provide pre-show food and it's murder trying to get to the bar in intervals. We need to modernise its appearance and, in fact, we have plans for a roof-top restaurant. We should be making money here but, without change, it is impossible. There are many inadequacies in the theatre itself and while we could drift on for a few more years in the same fashion, it is not a rational or economically sensible policy. The complete restoration of the Pavilion will cost £7million."

Roger impresses with the clarity of his thought and his cool analysis of the economic problems that lie ahead for the Council. Even as we discuss the present situation, against the backcloth of a

Weymouth sands, the Pavilion in the distance. *Picture: Bill Macey*

downturn in property prices and sales and their possible implications for the proposed development, he is beginning work on a Plan B. We agree to talk in a few months as events unfold.

(Just a couple of weeks before going to print Roger and I do speak again. Howard Holdings, the intended developers, have recently withdrawn from the proposed development but Europa Capital, a Luxembourg based company with whom the Council negotiated the original deal, has until the summer of 2009 to decide their future plans.) As Cllr. Mike Goodman accurately observes: "This is yet another symptom of the wider economic recession." It seems increasingly likely, therefore, that everything is going to be put on hold for several years with little happening before the Olympic Games of 2012. Roger and his colleagues are reflecting on several possibilities – putting the Pavilion into commercial hands for a limited period while retaining ownership and possibly turning the marina/ferry terminal area into a tented village for the Games. It is indeed ironic that a recession has achieved exactly what those who protested against the Pavilion development scheme wanted so earnestly. What is equally certain is that the whole issue has merely been delayed until another day.

I call by on an old friend Nigel Hodder of Derby Street who, who with his wife Pam, was a signatory to the 7,000 strong petition against the development, and ask him for his feelings on the seeming collapse of the whole enterprise.

"I'm very relieved! And next time, if there's a next time, let them build something everyone in Weymouth can be proud of – just long as they don't expect me to pay for it!"

'There's no business like show business.'

"John lived two doors away. His father, home on leave, sent him down to look at the new baby. He was just six years old – I was the baby! Twenty odd years later he was proposing to me and I became his wife!"

Janet Stockley laughs. It's a good story. But then Janet's life is a remarkable story and a triumph of character and determination over adversity. For some years Westham born Janet was a professional singer, working mostly in the Midlands. 'Songs from the Shows' was her particular forte. Moving back to her home town with John, she applied to join Weymouth Operatic Society and was cast as Nancy in Lionel Bart's magnificent Sixties musical Oliver. From that initial association and, in particular, her relationship with the younger members of the cast, she formed WOW, the Weymouth Operatic Workshop. With musical director Albert Davies and his wife Frances, she began working with 35 youngsters aged 10-18. It was at this time she also began to experience 'a searing pain' and growing discomfort with her movement which the doctors duly diagnosed as osteoarthritis. It was the beginning of years of often acute pain and ever increasing difficulty getting about. But Janet has always been a determined trouper. In 1984 WOW put on a musical compilation followed by Smike.

"My friend Pauline Wootton joined the company at this time in a secretarial capacity and, in the years since, we've staged a host of productions, many of them at the Pavilion Theatre. The shows often attracted as many as 3-4,000 over the 5 performances we usually staged. We engaged a professional director/ choreographer and the only amateurs were the cast themselves!"

Over the years hundreds of local youngsters have passed through the company.

"When we counted recently there were no fewer than 8 former members in West End productions. To name just a few, there's Chris Stanton, Billy Flynn's in Chicago and Kerry Winter is understudying Connie Fisher in The Sound of Music. Obviously we're very proud that we have been able to encourage gifted youngsters from Weymouth and the surrounding locality to develop their talents and go on to careers in the theatre."

It is a wonderful achievement on Janet's part to have accomplished so much, not least when she has often been in great pain and discomfort. Janet pays tribute to all her friends and the supporters

A scene from *Les Miserables* at the Nothe. *Picture: Janet Stockley*

of WOW who have worked in their various capacities to provide entertainment for the Weymouth public for many years.

"My family have been wonderfully supportive and patient. John, my husband, has acted as Treasurer and Stage Manager and my daughter Zoe has assisted so much with the props for our productions."

For every one of the young performers who have graduated to the professional stage, there are scores of individuals in Weymouth and around the locality whose talents as singers, dancers and actors have blossomed thanks to Janet's encouragement. That has been a very special achievement by a very special lady.

Another Weymouth resident for whom the Pavilion Theatre has played a central role in her life is another remarkable lady, not that she would ever see herself in that light. Alas, the Pavilion was not merely the backdrop to some of the happiest moments of her life, it also provided the setting for one of the saddest.

Peter Cotton was one of the best-loved figures in Weymouth and, when he passed away in 2004 at the all too early age of 58, hundreds of his friends, including this writer, packed the Pavilion for his Memorial service when they heard Bill Macey's moving tribute to a truly good and most unassuming gentleman.

It was Peter's grandfather, Edward Ainsworth-Cotton, who founded the family business of funeral directors in 1912, later managed by Peter's father John, or Jack, as everyone knew him. Peter himself took over the business in 1990 following his father's retirement. To most of us, being an undertaker and dealing on a daily basis with the dead and the grieving remains an unappealing, even grim profession. But, if inheriting the family business and its traditions ever depressed Peter, he never let it show. Besides, there was a very different side to his life. Peter was bitten by the 'theatre bug' at an early age and thus began a life-long love affair with the Pavilion, graduating from 'sweeper-up' to electrician, designer, lighting director and, finally, to his great delight, to Stage Manager. Standing in the wings or at the back of the hall, listening to the laughter or the hushed silence of an audience, must have provided the perfect antidote to more stressful events in his day-to-day profession.

There was another love in Peter's life, the young teacher who regularly brought her pupils from the Covent of the Sacred Heart to the theatre for the annual Christmas production. Jane and Peter married in 1993 but their happiness ended when cancer cruelly cut short Peter's life. So it was that Jane was faced with a difficult decision. Though she had been helping Peter in the family business, mostly in the office, she had never visualised making it a career and involving herself with funerals and burials.

"I'll give it a year, I said to myself. I suppose I felt I owed it to his memory and it was what he would have wanted me to do."

However, she did fear that clients might be put off by a woman running the business. She need not have feared. Appointing Margaret Sharratt as her fellow director proved an inspired choice.

"Fifty years ago I doubt it would have been possible. Even a few years ago there were not many women in the profession but today it has become acceptable and for that we are both grateful."

On broader issues relating to death in our society, to what extent does it remain a taboo subject for most people?

"There is no doubt that as a society we have become much more clinical in our treatment of death. Far more people die in hospital than at home. A few generations ago it was the reverse and death was more matter-of-fact. Life was shorter and cheaper and contagious diseases were commonplace. Now life expectancy for both men and women extends well into the seventies and, of course, many are living way beyond that."

What about the ratio of burials to cremations?

"About 80% are cremated. Burials in town churchyards are almost impossible due to lack of space. One or two churches in Weymouth will accommodate the partner if a double plot has already been acquired but, at St. Andrew's at Preston, St. Ann's at Radipole and St. Mary's at Chickerell, space is severely limited or non-existent. It's a similar pattern in many areas of the county, especially the bigger towns."

How does Jane feel at the end of a typical working day?

"Do I enjoy my work? Enjoy would be the wrong word. Do I derive satisfaction from assisting people through a very difficult period in their lives? Yes, that does bring its own rewards."

In their very different ways Janet Stockley and Jane Cotton continue to play significant and invaluable roles in the community life of Weymouth. A common thread to both their personal lives has been the Pavilion Theatre during a year in which the building's redevelopment has been at the very centre of so much debate and division.

One other lady in Weymouth very aware of the significance of the Pavilion in the community life of the town is the former Mayoress, Jenny Harris, who during her recent term of office, was very surprised to discover just how many events are staged in the whole Pavilion complex, not least in the Ocean Room. She mentions various presentations, educational activities and sporting gatherings among others. Jenny's conclusion is an interesting one.

"While a number of the activities may show up as losses on the balance sheet, they play an important part in the life of our town and entirely justify the subsidies which we provide towards the running and upkeep of the Pavilion."

By the year's end we should have a clearer picture of its future.

This morning it's across town to see a man who has been at the heart of Weymouth's public life for many years. Doug Hollins is a man of many parts, ex-Mayor, councillor and author. He's currently the environmental brief officer.

"The simple truth is that parts of the town are looking tired and shabby. We urgently need to refurbish and regenerate without destroying our inherent character and appeal. We have wonderful sands, a fine Georgian seafront and Victorian esplanade. But nothing lasts forever. Remember one third of our economy depends upon tourism and we are in competition with other resorts. I appreciate there is a serious divide within the town. One half, mainly the older generation, intelligent and articulate, is comfortable with what we've got. The other half, mainly the younger element, welcomes change. It's a balancing act but, at the same time, as a councillor you have always to be looking forward, thinking ahead. Because we are so dependent upon tourism which is a low wage industry, we must attract other forms of high-tech enterprise, especially marine-based, that will provide jobs and raise incomes. English Heritage gave us half a million pounds to restore the three statues, George the Third, Queen Victoria and Sir Henry Edwards – he's in the Alexandra Gardens – and the sea-front shelters. We also need to improve the 'gateways into the town', to use the modern jargon, the pier bandstand and the area between the railway station and the town which looks dingy. We want to develop a cafe culture with more pedestrian friendly areas. As for the proposed Pavilion development, critics must appreciate the Council has no money to do anything itself. Were it all to go ahead the scheme will cost in the region of £150million to the developers. As a Town Council we would have £20 million handed back at the end in the form of a rebuilt Pavilion Theatre and a new marina. I do agree with the critics that we must be careful with the architecture. It must be something that truly blends with our historic traditions. Modern architects, of course, do want to build something which 'makes a statement about modern Weymouth' It's a great challenge to get it right. I would like to think that in 10 years time we will have a Weymouth of which the townsfolk will be proud, the best of the past restored and enhanced and the facilities to appeal that will take the town forward."

Doug Hollins is well regarded in the town. He's a transparently honest, intelligent figure who sees very clearly the whole picture. The problem for Doug and other councillors is that architectural plans on the drawing-board are one thing, their realisation in bricks and concrete and glass are often something else. It's an unenviable responsibility.

Next I'm off to Westham to see another gentleman who's been at the centre of Weymouth civic life for as long as most people can remember. Alderman Andy Hutchings is a big man with a big heart and has been a councillor for his beloved Westham for a quarter of a century.

"I wouldn't want to live anywhere else. My holiday is my beach chalet up at Greenhill. I did go up to Blackpool but, you know, the place isn't a patch on Weymouth. It's full of tatty rock-shops, though I did like the tramways."

Recently Andy published a collection of Weymouth postcards in the Images of Britain series in collaboration with his friend Geoff Pritchard. All the scenes were captured by the brilliant local photographer, Edwin Seaward, who died in 1955. Such collections of old postcards are so evocative of a bygone age and I appreciate Andy's enthusiasm. Surrounded by railway ephemera, he's also one of the Friends of Upwey Station together withTerry Putnam, Peter Meech and John Trevett.

"It's both a Great Western and South West Trains station but, of course, it's unmanned. We like to maintain it in good order – litter picking, general tidying up, that sort of thing. We like to feel we are the 'eyes of the local residents.'"

Like Doug Hollins, Andy would dearly like to see the development of a first-rate transport interchange at Weymouth station.

"You know when people first arrive in the town at the station, they walk up the road to the sea-front, see the Clock, shake their heads and disappear down the subway thinking they'll finish up near the sands, only to emerge on the same side of the road. It's quite comical to watch though I' m not sure they all see the joke!"

Next it's off across the town, past Lodmoor, to Preston to meet another of the old guard of Weymouth's community though he's not a councillor this time.

"The older generation will remember when Jersey potatoes and Guernsey tomatoes came in through the port in vast quantities – now they're flown in. The cargo boats have all but gone too. Then there were the ferries like the SS Caesarea (Jersey) and the SS Sarnia (Guernsey) plying their services down to the Channel Islands. Now it's the Condor ferries."

Brian Searle's reflections of Weymouth will stir many memories. Brian is a retired 'preventive officer', more commonly known to us as a custom's officer. For the better part of 20 years Brian trained a beady pair of eyes on the long queues of passengers passing through the barriers, the guilty and the innocent.

"Those were the days of purchase tax and excise duties before Britain joined the Common Market. I know most people would see it as progress that there's now free movement between European states, but I feel it's another element of social control that's gone and people do still take advantage, of course."

But it wasn't always a matter of Brian scrutinising the passengers. There was one particular instance he recalls as if it were yesterday.

"When a thousand pairs of eyes were suddenly trained on me. My old pal Bill Macey spotted me on duty one day and shouted out at the top of his voice, 'Are you still sleeping with the same woman, Brian?' How embarrassing was that – and me a respectably married man? But they didn't know that, did they? But that was also the old Weymouth – families who knew one another and laughed together."

Chickerell

I'm really not sure I'm doing the right thing by including my section on Chickerell in my chapter on Weymouth. It could mean big trouble for me. But I like living dangerously!

"What exactly constitutes a town? There's an interesting subject for debate."

Norman Carter, most amiable Mayor of Chickerell, laughs. It's certainly a subject to which I will return another day.

"Whatever does, the reality is that Chickerell is now officially a town in its own right. Remember we never were a part of Weymouth. The old parish boundary lies down the road and we come under the umbrella of West Dorset District Council. Curiously enough, most of Weymouth's industry today lies within OUR boundaries on the Granby Estate, together with the schools, the army camp, the football ground and even the Dorset Echo Office. And we have our road signs proudly proclaiming

'Welcome to Chickerell. Please drive slowly.' "

In such circumstances perhaps Weymouth should be absorbed into Chickerell! ? It's certainly an oddity that Chickerell's revenues pass to an authority extending to the far west of the county, as far north as Sherborne and Crossways to the east.

"In the next 10-15 years another 250 houses will be built between us and Weymouth so we do need an improved infra-structure to satisfy our growing population. My goal as Mayor must be to continue to press for just that."

Norman certainly presents a persuasive case for the 'town' in which he has lived for the past 40 years and whose population he has seen grow to its present 6,500. Though I don't mention it out of sensitivity to his feelings, I suspect that if Norman's beloved Chickerell were, by some freakish historical accident, to be dropped into the 19th century Balkans, its larger neighbour would simply annex the impudent adjacent territory without a second thought and Norman's head, minus his body, would be displayed on the town's gate. Neither would I give much of a chance for the survival of John Dean and his fellow councillors, unless they chose the path of collaboration with the ancient enemy. As for the town of Chickerell's historian and local patriot, Charles Aldridge, notwithstanding his advanced years, I fear he would finish his days in the equivalent of the Nothe Fort, like an ancient Monsieur Manette awaiting his Sydney Carton.

In the Dorset Echo offices

With trilby hat, bitten down nails and a half-smoked cigarette dangling from his lips, Harry Walton's world-weary cynicism would fit Humphrey Bogart in a b/w Fifties movie to a tee. But our man is tall, strides purposefully down corridors, doesn't smoke and looks 15 years younger than his age. Harry Walton, chief reporter with the *Dorset Echo*, has been with the paper nearly 30 years. Besides, Bogart wouldn't have been married and Harry's married to a Weymouth girl and a devoted family man.

"But show me the reporter who's not at least mildly cynical."

We've been discussing Weymouth's relief road which has just been given the go-ahead.

"Do you know when the topic of the relief road was first voiced? 1923 !Of course, it wasn't the same road and conditions were very different. But 80 years have gone by since that moment. Let's see it built first. Then we'll judge it – at the end of the summer season of 2011. If it's deemed a success, I'll be the first to cheer. In the meanwhile, I'll watch and wait. And the same goes for the Pavilion development. What does concern me and it seldom seems to get a mention is the demolition of so many large houses set in big gardens, as along the Preston Road, and their replacement by blocks of flats. I'm also worried by the loss of 'character' shops in the town itself. In troubled times like these, the multiples can withstand a lot of grief. For the small independents it can be the end."

So Harry is like Bogart after all – his first concern is for the small man.

"And if, by way of contrast, you'd like me to throw in a real success story, let me suggest the Nothe Fort. It's brilliant and great value for money. And Weymouth in general? It's a great place, especially to bring up a family."

Of course , the Nothe Fort, it's where many of my old beach-bum, beatnik friends used to sleep back in the Sixties before it was restored after they'd staggered out of the Tivoli Gardens in Franchise Street. Then there are the Nothe Gardens, Harry, of course. Though they had a wild charm years ago, along with plenty of brambles, I suspect most locals welcome the 'improvements' of recent times. The fact that few visitors ever venture far enough to discover them is an added attraction.

The news that Weymouth's Relief Road, from the Manor roundabout to Ridgeway, has been given the Green Light by the Department for Transport is greeted enthusiastically by practically everyone who has had to endure the misery of queues and tail-backs on the A354 Dorchester-Weymouth road in recent years. Angus Campbell, the leader of the Dorset County Council, welcomes the confirmation that the £80 million road is, at last, to be built.

"It's great news for the area and will help to support the economic and employment needs of Weymouth and Portland."

The Broadwey ward County Councillor, Harry Burden, enthuses.

"The road has overwhelming local support. It really is an occasion to celebrate."

So, let's hope Harry Walton is cheering, along with the rest, and the road is a success. One word of caution, however. Isn't it amazing that for every road that's built, there always seem to be more than enough cars to fill it?

If AFC Bournemouth's result is the first one I look for, Weymouth FC's is one of the next. There was a time in my life I often stood on the terraces at the old Rec and cheered on the Terras. Tony Hobson, whose parents ran the Tivoli Gardens, was one of the finest centre halves outside the Football League. Micky Cave, later to become a legendary figure at Bournemouth, was in the side, along with Terry Gulliver who also journeyed forty miles eastwards to Dean Court. Richard Hall was a popular local lad who always played his heart out. The forward line which included Hannigan, Spratt and Hutchinson was one of the most lethal in the league and in the club's history. At that time a large number of the supporters walked to the ground because it was situated in the heart of the town and the gates, especially for the big games against local rivals like Yeovil and Bath, often exceeded the 3,000 mark. The players were semi-pro which meant they all had ordinary jobs and what they received as footballers was a welcome addition to their income. The club was solvent as were other similar clubs. They operated within their means. It was a period of financial sanity and limited ambitions. A good FA Cup run was the icing on the cake and Weymouth enjoyed several of those. When the ground was sold for redevelopment and a supermarket moved in, hopes were high that the Wessex Stadium would provide improved facilities for the spectators, ample parking and, possibly in the longer term, even the chance of League football in the town. But, there's an old saying, 'Many a slip twixt cup and lip' and another 'Cut your cloth according to your coat'. There is one more which seems particularly apposite. 'Those whom the gods would destroy, they first make mad.' Right across the football world we are now seeing the consequences of grandiose ambition unaccompanied by common sense and financial probity. Even the most successful clubs in the kingdom carry enormous burdens of debt which, sooner or later, will bring ruin to many of them. We have seen it all too clearly in the world of banking in the past year. Sadly, all the clubs along the South Coast are now mired in the horrendous consequences of inflated ambition, greed and financial incompetence. Only when a wealthy backer comes along with unlimited resources is there temporary relief. When no 'shining knight' appears, the result is disaster. But I am pre-empting the story of the season of 2008-9 for Weymouth FC. And it all began cheerfully enough.

The Wessex Stadium, Weymouth FC

"When I was a lad – I came from Bethnal Green – I'd go to Hackney Marshes and it was a sea of colour, hundreds of players, matches going on all over the place. Of course, there'd be the odd scuffle but I remember no really bad behaviour. The referee's word was law. And in March, 1938, when I went to see Spurs playing Sunderland in the FA Cup at White Hart Lane, there were 70,000 spectators and, though I was just a nipper, I went un-chaperoned and I felt safe. That's how things were then. They were ordinary working people but they behaved themselves and took care of me."

Bob Lucas pauses. It was a long time ago. It was a different age with different values. There was a working-class poor materially but proud, dignified and self-disciplined. My own father was a part of that class and that era. He stood in similar crowds at The Valley because he was a Charlton Athletic supporter. He may even have stood alongside Bob Lucas at one of London's grounds. When one reflects on some aspects of the contemporary world, though we are so much materially better off, there is no shadow of doubt we have also lost much that is precious that our fathers and their fathers knew and took for granted. Bob's 83 now, yet still remarkably agile and spry.

"I started my career with Crystal Palace, then came down to join Weymouth in 1949 when the club was playing in the old Southern League. In my first game at the old Rec, watched if you can believe it by 11,000 spectators, I conceded four goals. That followed a 3-0 defeat in my first appearance. Seven times I picked the ball out of the net in my first two games. Not a good start!"

Bob chuckles at the recollection.

"But we then went 22 games without defeat, a club record that still stands today. The highlight of my career came at Old Trafford in January, 1950, in the FA Cup. We lost 4-0 but it was no disgrace. United were a great side."

Bob played 79 games for the club in two seasons before injury sadly forced an early retirement.

"There was no protection in those days for goalkeepers and we all suffered some terrible knocks. And, of course, there was a lack of medical understanding and care. That was when I decided to become a physio because I wanted to help players who were injured. I attended a course at Lilleshall and became the club physio for the next 30 years."

For the last six years Bob has been president of Weymouth FC.

"Why do I love Weymouth so much? It's not just been the football. I'll tell you – because if I hadn't come down I'd never have met my wife Jean – and she's been the most wonderful wife and the mother of our children."

And the feeling at the club this morning is one of quiet optimism. There's a new owner with Malcolm Curtis having replaced Mel Bush. Jason Tindall has departed to Bournemouth and a new manager has been appointed in the solid form of John Hollins, once of Chelsea and England and a man with a distinguished career on and off the field. Even the girls in the office, Jaz Curtis, Sarah Eastby and Carol Biggs, are full of good cheer. The first few results have been satisfactory. I drive away from the Wessex Stadium little guessing what is to follow a few months later. (Continued at the end of the chapter.)

It's back across the border, fortunately spotting no sentries, dogs or look-out towers and I arrive unscathed at Weymouth's glorious old harbour.

The Nothe Parade

We met and talked earlier of his days on Portland at HMS Osprey and the transformation of the old naval base. This morning Captain John Harvey and I are sitting in his superbly located house next to the Lifeboat Station overlooking the old harbour.

"When I retired from the RN Bill Ludlow asked me if I'd care to be involved with the lifeboat. I felt privileged to be asked and I was delighted to accept. These days I am the Lifeboat Operations Manager and one of the six launching officers. We're all unpaid, I hasten to add. If we get a call, I ring the coxswain, Andrew Sargent, and we discuss the situation and what action to take. To summon a crew, if we need to put to sea, we launch two maroons and then all hell breaks loose with the cars hurtling down to the quay. The authorities are not keen on the firing of maroons these days after an unfortunate accident, not here, I hasten to add, but it is essential in the holiday season with all the holidaymakers' cars around on the quay. We have a pool of 30 volunteers and there will seldom be fewer than 15 here within 5 minutes. They're a brilliant team and society in general owes so much

Weymouth old harbour with Georgian front. *Picture: Bill Macey*

to our life-boatmen who risk their lives on our behalf. Usually it's 6 or 7 who actually put to sea in either 1 of our 2 boats which will, of course, be determined by the nature of the mission. We have the all-weather Ernest & Mable that cost £1.8 million, or the Atlantic rib inflatable, the Phyl Clare that cost £100,000, both named after their generous benefactors. And I must not forget to mention the part played by our invaluable mechanic, Hefin Roberts."

I've several times heard the name Bill Ludlow mentioned – who was Bill?

"E.W. 'Bill' Ludlow was often referred to as 'Mr.Devenish'. He was a splendid and much-loved figure in the town and chairman of the Lifeboats for 30 years. He was a JP, the chairman of the Bench and he set up the Sailing Academy. When he died a few months ago his ashes were scattered in the harbour from the lifeboat. His wife Di, by the way, has been closely associated with Riding for the Disabled."

John is also the president of the Sea Cadets in Portland based at West Cliff and a trustee of the Chesil Trust that promotes a scheme to encourage young sailors called 'Sail for a Fiver'.

"Some of the kids are on a hiding to nothing with their backgrounds. To give them an interest and a skill can transform their lives. There are some brilliant individuals supporting the Chesil Trust and it's a great idea."

John has also recently been invited to work alongside the new harbour-master Peter Mole.

"Peter's an ex Merchant Navy man who's recently succeeded Bill Chambers and an excellent appointment."

John is much concerned at the deteriorating condition of the harbour walls.

"The metal pilings are suffering from low water corrosion. The longer restoration work is

Weymouth lifeboat. *Picture: Allan Birch*

delayed, the more expensive it will ultimately be. I believe the £500,000 income from harbour fees needs to be ring-fenced. At the moment the money simply goes to the Council. The ferry terminal is very much in need of upgrading too. It's old and scruffy but, of course, we're in a period of economic stringency."

As I leave I remark again on the wonderful, ever-changing prospect from John's window of the passing craft, the life-boat moored just yards from his front-door and the general bustle of harbour-side activity. It could hardly be more fitting for a man who has spent so much of his life at sea in the Royal Navy and, even today, loves nothing more than 'messing' about in his boat in Weymouth Bay unless, of course, it's roaring around on his motor-cycle with his very brave wife Lesley on the pillion!

"I do realise how fortunate I am. When my elderly mother comes to stay, she loves just to sit at the window and watch the world. It is the most perfect place."

John has achieved much in his life and continues to employ his energy, enthusiasm and knowledge on behalf of the community. He hasn't done too badly for a grammar-school lad from Thurrock.

Chapelhay

A few months ago and he would have been putting the finishing touches to his column in *The Mail on Sunday*.

"To tell you the truth, I'd grown weary of my weekly rant. After 11 years I did feel I'd just about exhausted the topics for the column. Thursdays, when I usually prepared my pieces, had become something of a strain."

We're sitting, this uncharacteristically sunny day in this sunless summer, in the lounge of Peter and Geraldine Dobie's house in Trinity Terrace gazing out across the old harbour. It's a tranquil scene. Not really a place for ranting, though Geraldine is not at all happy about the proposed Pavilion development – like the 7,000 other signatories to the petition against it. Peter, a former *Telegraph* man and broadsheet Political Editor, found the property in 2001. He lives in London but he and Geraldine return regularly. Miraculously he's a racing man. I come upon so few that it's a joy to find a kindred spirit. We agree to go to Wincanton or Salisbury when the book is done, if ever it is done. Peter loves Weymouth.

"It's much more than a second home. We feel we've been enveloped within a warm community of friends and neighbours. People here do look out for one another."

Chapelhay – Another day

From the window in Trinity Terrace it's a similar view across the old harbour to that from Peter and Geraldine's window. Today the weather, however, has reverted to the sullen, drizzly murk so characteristic of this dreadful summer.

"Our veneer of civilisation has made us ever more sceptical."

The lady beside me is seventyish, lean with alert eyes and clearly undiminished vigour. Many of those three score years and ten were spent in the company of children with 'learning difficulties.'

"My greatest joy was teaching a child how to read and to write."

She opens a pack of cards and places them on the small table between us.

"The cards talk to me. Even as a child I realised I possessed a gift."

Neighbours Duff Pearce and Peter Dobie tell me Mary Miller's clients sometimes travel from far afield, even abroad, for a consultation.

"I lived in Sherborne for 60 years. Once I was invited to the church fete to do some psychic readings. I read palms as well as the cards. Then a friend told me they'd planned a grand finale to the day's entertainments – they were going to burn me at the stake as a witch!"

The lady chuckles at the memory. She's only half jesting, you think. Innumerable cats sit about us. They're on every chair and cushion in sight, as enigmatic andscornful, as only cats can be.

"Would you like a kitten?"

I politely decline. Much as I love cats they are scarcely compatible with the colony of 40 cheerful house sparrows I've built up in my garden since the sad demise of our last two family cats, William and Harry. Though the cats remain resolutely indifferent to my presence I am more concerned about the lady's dog. The animal is decidedly boisterous. It's also sniffing ever more curiously at my bag. I begin to fear for the survival of the Belgian bun I bought at Sally Lunn's on my way through the town. Mary suggests I place the bag beyond the dog's reach. It's a wise precaution.

"Now, if you'd care to cut the cards. That's it – and then once more."

I cut the cards several times as Mary arranges them about the table

"You know what they plan to do with the Pavilion? It's appalling. And all those dreadful flats they propose."

Mary tells me she still loves to dance at the Pavilion. Wherever I go the topic is raised. For so many the Pavilion has been, or remains, an integral part of their every-day lives. I tell Mary, Yes, I am aware of the concerns. It seems she's also fallen out seriously with the Council over local parking issues. She shows me the letters and press cuttings and emails. She's on another collision course with authority, I think. The cards are now laid out around the table. Mary offers a character analysis and makes a prediction or two. Am I really that bad? Beyond all reasonable hope. Ah, well.

"The Pavilion development? I see serious financial problems ahead and likely failure. Your book? That will be a success."

But are you quite certain, Mary, you haven't got the two predictions the wrong way round? It is very important to me. I depart, not forgetting Mary's stern injunction to shut the gate behind me. The dog has escaped before and led her a merry dance down the Chapelhay steps I check my bag. My Belgian bun is safe. It's still drizzling. Will it ever stop?

Shall I tell my publisher about the prediction?

Radipole and Lodmoor, Late autumn

It must have been in the Sixties that I first walked around Radipole Lake and Lodmoor. At the time Lodmoor was being seriously discussed as a possible site for one of Sir Billy Butlin's Holiday Camps. I couldn't believe that so many locals were even prepared to consider the possibility but it was true. It was regarded by many as a drab, unappealing, worthless wilderness. Dumping of refuse was already seriously eroding the western edge. I can only suppose that the locals sympathetic to Sir Billy imagined it would bring more people and money into the town. As for Radipole, though it was used by residents living nearby for walking their dogs, far fewer bird-watchers used it compared with the present. Bird-watching was then far less popular as an activity. I was one of the few people in my circle of friends who owned a pair of binoculars. One or two were more inclined to shoot a bird of prey than watch it through a pair of glasses. We've come a long way since that time and obviously I'm pleased that there's a far greater awareness of how precious our wildlife is and how we must protect it carefully. Even so, there are moments when I am ever so slightly irritated by a misplaced sentimentality, or a stridency amongst conservationists that does not help anyone.

Quite my most memorable visit to Radipole must have been 30 years ago and it happened in the car-park not far from where the RSPB building stands. It was one of those freakish, chance events that every bird-watcher has experienced when you happen to be in the right place at the right time. There was no possible way I could have anticipated or planned it. Having parked the car I realised I was entirely surrounded by wagtails, not the familiar pieds, but rather a mixed party of yellow, blue-headed and grey-headed wagtails. There were probably 100 or so birds just beginning their autumn migration. I've seen only a handful of yellow wagtails since that day – and none for at least ten years – and certainly not another blue-headed or grey-headed. And extraordinarily, on that afternoon, absolutely no one else was paying the birds the slightest attention, not at least whilst I was there.

This morning my companion at Radipole is Nick Quintrell, the full-time RSPB warden. Nick works in close co-operation with site manager, Nick Tomlinson , in defining work programmes, refining general ideas and finding the most economical and practical ways of implementing day-to-day operations. It's a job that varies enormously from organising volunteers and estate workers, being engaged in hard physical graft like scrub clearing and reed cutting, to writing reports and producing ecological surveys.

In truth, I'd thought to visit the reserves earlier in the year to coincide with my general visit to Weymouth, but it proved impossible to arrange a suitable date, such was Nick's workload. As it happens, I am now rather pleased about the delay because there are far fewer people about and there's also an austere grandeur about mudflats and reed-beds on a grey autumn morning. Rain before noon is the forecast. Nick and I set off along the path skirting the lake on its western side. We've barely started before we meet estate worker, Anne Simpson, who's cutting the path-side vegetation using a brush-cutter. Nick explains the general strategy.

"In October and November we cut the paths back severely so that they remain clear throughout the winter. This enables us to get on with the habitat management of the sites. From spring through to late summer, however, we cut the verges very selectively to maintain and enhance the botanical diversity allowing, as far as possible, the native plants to flower and seed before cutting and removing the arisings."

I ask Nick about the other principal autumn tasks.

"At this time of the year the priority is habitat management which really means working to maintain reed-bed and wet grassland as the dominant types here at Radipole. Reed-beds are essentially an ephemeral habitat. Left un-managed they tend to dry out allowing other species to establish themselves. This will eventually lead to willow dominated woodland. We cut reed on Radipole on a 5 year rotation so that a mosaic of differing age structures is established within the reed-bed to satisfy the specific niche habitat requirements of key species such as the bearded tit. We then rake up the reed and leaf litter together with the willow and the sallow to prevent the drying up process that would otherwise occur. To allow us to get into the reed-beds to carry out this essential work, water levels are gradually 'drawn down' in late summer, after the reed-bed birds have fledged, and raised once again in February to discourage more vigorous competitors from getting a foothold to the detriment of the reed-bed."

The weather-men were right. It's already started to rain and it's barely ten.

"By the way, I'm hoping we may glimpse a bittern."

Since I've never seen one of these rare and elusive birds, nor heard its famous 'boom', that would be something special. We spot some goldfinches and chaffinches and a solitary bullfinch.

"My favourite bird," says Nick.

They're certainly handsome creatures though I must confess I'm never too keen on seeing them in my garden in late spring tearing at my blackcurrant buds, but they're far less common than a few years ago and I've not seen one in the garden for years.

"Look! Up there!"

It's November 13, it's raining and not especially warm and two swallows are still with us looking for a meal among the raindrops. This time it's my favourite birds, along with house-martins and grey wagtails. We discuss the options. Where would we rather be this November morning – here at Radipole or in the sunshine over Capetown? It's not a question that requires an answer, we agree.

We hear the 'pinging 'of the bearded tits but there's no sighting, not even a fleeting glimpse of Nick's friend, the reclusive bittern. It's fast becoming the sort of day when any self-respecting bird will keep well down out of the wind and rain. We press on to the relative comfort of the Visitor Centre.

Clive Dudderidge, a veteran of many ornithological campaigns, recalls one particularly memorable day.

"Snow had stopped play in a Test Match at Trent Bridge and I saw a flamingo here at Radipole standing among the falling snowflakes. I also saw a pelican at Lodmoor. Both escapees, I dare say, but interesting."

Dan Bartlett muses over the comment he once heard by a lady about Lodmoor.

"'A mosquito infected swamp', she said. She was, no doubt, one of those who wanted Sir Billy here. When they turned him down he went to Paignton instead. What a shame!"

Allan Neilson and Andy Taylor are discussing Allan's latest project, a fresh edition of *The Birds of Radipole & Lodmoor – Birds of the Weymouth Reserves,* building on an earlier work by Doug Ireland. I look forward to its publication.

Lodmoor in autumn. *Picture: Geoff Hill*

'Everyone with a gun and a taste for letting it off knew Lodmoor'

John Meade Falkner(1858-1932), The author of *Moonfleet*

It's time to cross town to Lodmoor. Melancholy shades of grey, brown and black predominate. The rain is steady now and the wind is freshening – teal, wigeon and mallard by the score, various waders probing for a tasty morsel. A solitary snipe flies up and darts away with its familiar zigzagging flight. There's no sign of anyone with a gun. They would get very wet this afternoon – and short shrift from Nick.

"Here and at Radipole we carry out cyclical scrub removal, coppicing, pollarding and clear felling with chainsaws. The wood is then hauled out of the meadows and either burned or stacked to form habitat piles to benefit invertebrates. It is particularly gruelling work given the underfoot conditions and so, to lighten the burden we rely heavily on volunteers, in particular our regular Rethink (a mental health charity) work parties to whom we are enormously indebted. The rest of the year is full of variety – cattle fencing, gates and cattle bridges to replace or maintain, 70 head of cattle to look after, signs to renovate, excavating scrapes and pools, hand-pulling ragwort, planning and carrying out wildlife surveys. We're never idle!"

Nick counts himself a fortunate man.

"Almost all that I love in life involves being outside. The nature of my job brings a reward and satisfaction beyond money and material acquisitions. To get up on a Monday morning and go to a place I would choose to go to, even if I were not being paid to do so, is a richness that most people do not enjoy. I am a very lucky man."

(Just a few days before going to print, Nick telephones to say that a pair of Marsh Harriers appear to be preparing to nest at Radipole. If it happens it will be the first time in half a century or more.)

One famous resident in the town has an unsurprising bee in his bonnet. He is Mervyn Sharp, the first person to be crowned King of the Channel after completing the Channel swim for what was the world record 7th time. Mervyn worked for 25 years at Weymouth swimming pool and is eager to see every child leave school able to swim. At the moment he is not at all happy about the Town Council's decision not to support a Government project to get more under 16s and over 60s into the water. If any man can change minds, it's surely Mervyn.

One of the more heart-warming stories of the year relates to a young man named Seb Green. It was in 2004 that Seb and a friend 'borrowed' a dinghy from Weymouth harbour late one night, became stranded in mud on the Fleet lagoon , necessitating a major rescue effort involving police and naval helicopters, 2 coastguard teams and 2 RNLI lifeboats – the whole exercise costing £20,000. Seb's conscience was sufficiently troubled by the incident that earlier this year he set off on a round Britain sponsored walk to make recompense. Now a member of the Territorial Army with a military career ahead of him Seb is hoping to raise a handsome sum for his chosen charities.

Weymouth FC, Everything that can go wrong – does. (Written at the season's end)
To the outsider – and that means me – the first few months of Weymouth FC's 2008-2009 campaign seemed to be going along normally enough. I checked the scores each Saturday and though the team was not among the top six in the League, neither was it doing too badly. What I, and the supporters who trek out to the Wessex Stadium on a regular basis, didn't know was that the club was losing £9,000 a week with total debts amounting to £500,000. Then I learned that the manager, Dave Hollins, was going 'on indefinite gardening leave'. In other words, there'd been some major fall-out backstage and the romance was over. Now I don't live in Weymouth and I do not pretend to know exactly what was going on. I suspect that even if I knew some of the details, I would not be in a position to print them.

What has happened since is so extraordinary that any novelist who submitted such a story outline to a publisher would probably have it rejected for being too fanciful. I must, of necessity, keep it brief but the resignation of the club's chairman, Malcolm Curtis, allied to the departure of John Hollins and the revelation of the mountain of debt, growing weekly by an eye-watering sum, leads inexorably to talk of take-overs and, even more seriously, of a player walk-out because they are not being paid their wages. Meanwhile Malcolm Curtis, revealing that the club owes him £250,000, insists he won't be 'banging the door down' to recover his debts if a buyer can be found. Having bought and then sold the land surrounding the stadium at Chickerell during his term as chairman, Mr. Curtis says he just wants a satisfactory outcome to all the wrangling and negotiations.

As for the loyal supporters of the Terras they are as bemused as the rest of us. Gerald Mabb writes an eminently sensible letter to the *Dorset Echo*. *'To attract investors a properly costed business plan with realistic projections of income needs to be drawn up. Costs have to be critically appraised and, if they exceed income, a further examination needs to be carried out.'*

The Chief Executive, Gary Calder, has meanwhile issued an appeal to supporters to buy 50p shares in the club to raise funds to pay wages and meet the day-to-day running costs. Heroically the fans rally round with £30,000 pledged in just one day, with even hard-up pensioners and school-children raiding their bank accounts and piggy banks to help the club they love. Ian White, the Supporter's Club chairman describes the response as 'absolutely unbelievable.' An 11 year-old school-boy, Jordan Luxton, sums up the mood of many supporters: 'I've bought £10 worth of shares.

'Men against boys'. A brave but vain
performance. *Picture: Dorset Echo*

					LAST SEASON'S STANDINGS						
	HOME				**BLUE SQUARE PREM**	**AWAY**					
Pl	W	D	L	F	A		W	D	L	F	A	Pts
46	15	5	3	48	23	Burton (C) 12	2	9	33	29	88
46	14	6	3	34	15	Cambridge U..10	8	5	31	24	86
46	14	8	1	41	18	Histon 9	6	8	37	30	83
46	11	7	5	38	23	Torquay (P) 12	7	4	34	24	83
46	12	8	3	41	23	Stevenage......11	4	8	32	31	81
46	16	2	5	40	18	Kidderminster 7	8	8	29	30	79
46	16	3	4	42	20	Oxford 8	7	8	30	31	77
46	12	5	6	26	19	Kettering 9	8	6	24	18	76
46	13	5	5	48	26	Crawley 6	9	8	29	29	70
46	11	7	5	39	22	Wrexham 7	5	11	25	26	66
46	11	5	7	30	24	Rushden..........5	10	8	31	26	63
46	14	5	4	35	19	Mansfield........5	4	14	22	36	62
46	11	3	9	29	27	Eastbourne......7	3	13	29	43	60
46	10	9	4	28	19	Ebbsfleet 6	1	16	24	41	58
46	9	7	7	30	29	Altrincham 6	4	13	19	37	56
46	8	6	9	29	33	Salisbury 6	7	10	25	31	55
46	8	9	6	26	20	York 3	10	10	21	31	52
46	7	6	10	39	40	Forest Green ..5	10	8	31	36	52
46	12	5	6	31	24	Grays 2	5	16	13	40	52
46	7	10	6	27	26	Barrow............5	5	13	24	39	51
46	6	8	9	21	29	Woking (R) 4	6	13	16	31	44
46	7	5	11	29	26	Northwich (R)..4	5	14	27	49	43
46	5	6	12	27	53	Weymouth (R) 6	4	13	18	33	43
46	5	2	16	15	41	Lewes (R) 1	4	18	13	48	24

Deductions – Oxford 5pts, Mansfield 4pts, Crawley 1pt

I really want to try and help the club. I watch them at every home game and near enough every away match. I'm Terras through and through.' Terras Trust press officer Connor Kinsella announces the Trust has pledged £5,000 towards the purchase of shares. Speaking on behalf of Trust board members, Matt Barton, Mark Golsby, Tony Baylis and Steve Walkinshaw, Connor explains: 'Considering we have just £7,000 funds, it's an awful lot of money but we must do our best for the club we all love.' At the same time the manager, Alan Lewer, says he is thinking of stepping down. Can things get any worse?

Yes, they can and do. The players, unpaid and no longer protected by club insurance, decide they have had enough. They walk out. The rumour is soon circulating that the club will be fielding its youth team for the fixture just 24 hours later. Getting wind of what is happening at the Wessex Stadium and, for probably the only time in their lives that their 'intelligence' is one step ahead of the bookmakers, those 'in the know' hurry to back the opposition, Rushden and Diamonds, in the Blue Square Premier match against Weymouth FC. Opening at odds of 15-8 on the Friday evening, Rushden are backed down to odds of 4-6 before the bookies, their suspicions now thoroughly aroused, decline to accept any more bets. On the major betting exchange Betfair, an estimated £680,000 is wagered on the result and bookmaker's liabilities run into hundreds of thousands of pounds. Terras fan, Keith Avant, is typical of those who take advantage of the 'inside' information. "I wagered £100 though it was hard to back against the team I support and I got £237 back. I was a bit emotional about it but it was a good investment!"

Indeed, it proves an excellent investment for our 'shrewdies' and an expensive afternoon for 'the old enemy'.

Weymouth 0 Rushden & Diamonds 9

Adam Summers, writing in the *Dorset Echo*, describes events at the Wessex Stadium. *'It was a case of men against boys as Rushden & Diamonds put a brave Weymouth youth side to the sword as the Terras' deepening crisis sank to an all-time low......... At the final whistle the home fans once again showed their respect for their young team by putting their hands together and clapping them off the field but how long such a situation is allowed to go on remains to be seen.'*

Surely things cannot get worse still? Indeed, they can. Enter one West Country businessman, Stephen Beer, who appears as the shining knight on the white charger' riding to the club's rescue with the promise of £300,000 to put into club funds. Hopes are raised sky-high. Alas, only after a misspelt cheque splattered with correcting fluid is rejected by the club's bank, do doubts begin to surface about Mr. Beer's credibility. The truth is soon revealed. Our Torquay businessman is himself in serious financial difficulties with debts exceeding £20,000.The fans who have been hailing Mr. Beer as their saviour would now cheerfully heave him over the sea-wall into the harbour. What has been high drama has degenerated into farce.

Former players and officials express their dismay at what has happened to the club. Stuart Morgan, a former manager, and Chris Steadman, once the company secretary, who were associated with the club in happier days, are angry at what has happened to the administration of club affairs in the past 10 years or so. At the same time, both wish to be constructive and look to the future.

"Whatever has happened there are a loyal bunch of supporters who have stuck with the club. We must take a positive attitude in its bid to retain its very existence. Let's get football people back involved with the club and we would be very happy, like many others, to offer ways to move forward. Living within your means is achievable but the dreams will have to be kept on hold – survival is paramount."

Wise words but, sadly, the remainder of the season is best forgotten. In spite of valiant efforts by all those associated with Weymouth FC, players, supporters, staff and officials, no further victories are achieved and the club is relegated to the Blue Square South.

Maggie Aldridge's donkeys still delighting the children, Maggie with Jessica Grice. *Picture: Bill Macey*

As someone who loves the game and retains a particular affection for Weymouth FC, I hope the club will emerge from this nightmare and regain its status as one of the best non-League clubs in the country. As a supporter of AFC Bournemouth, I understand all too well the difficulties facing the smaller clubs across the UK. A small part of the wealth swilling around in the Premiership directed towards the lower divisions would help greatly – but one lesson must be learned.

'Annual income twenty pounds, annual expenditure nineteen nineteen six, result happiness. Annual income, twenty pounds, annual expenditure twenty pounds ought and six, result misery.' (Mr. Wilkins Micawber. *'David Copperfield'* Charles Dickens)

Quite what the season 2009-2010 will hold for the Terras is unclear. For the sake of all those good people associated with the club, it is to be hoped that a period of retrenchment will be followed by renewed success. After I have checked the AFC score for the day, Weymouth FC will be my next. (Just days before going to print I speak to Terra's supporter Paul Roper at the Dorset Echo. Paul tells me that Matty Hale is the new manager and the splendid Ian Ridley, the sports journalist with *The Mail on Sunday*, is trying to raise funds for the club through a rights issue. Good luck to everyone concerned! They will need it as the club begins a new season in the Blue Square South, the same league as neighbours Dorchester FC.)

It's almost the moment for departure. A few reflections before I leave from my old friend, Maurice Strabling, which crystallise many of the major changes of recent times.

"When I was a boy hundreds of factory workers would arrive from places like Cardiff, Bristol and Swindon on weekend 'Seaside Specials', stay for a week and then return home. People with cars stayed in houses along the Dorchester Road that advertised bed and breakfast accommodation, some with 'hot and cold' water in the bedroom, the house owners often sleeping in garages or garden sheds to maximise their income. Nowadays, most visitors to Weymouth arrive by car returning home the same day. The seafront hotels now group together to provide accommodation for coach parties – mostly elderly people – for whom the season is not restricted to school holidays. The town's main trade – tourism – has adapted to changed social patterns.

Weymouth's harbour, now largely retired from its previous commercial freight activities, is still the base for the Channel Islands ferry service, now using a fast roll-on-roll-off Wave-Piercer, which provides a daily service during the summer season. There is still some commercial fishing but now angling parties and wreck diving groups are more commonly seen and large yachts and motor cruisers occupy serviced pontoons where once open fishing boats swung on buoys. Weymouth's harbour has likewise adapted to changes within the leisure industry.

Paddle steamers used to operate out of the harbour, providing trips along the coast to Lulworth and Swanage, operated by Cousins a marine and engineering firm with huge workshops on the upper harbour quayside. Its former site is now a block of expensive apartments. Whiteheads at Wyke was another engineering firm employing many hundreds of men. The site is now a housing estate. Again Weymouth has been obliged to adapt.

Once town centre shops provided everything required to run and set up a home, providing carpets, furniture, curtains, kitchen appliances, cutlery, crockery and, of course, fresh food. Weymouth had a choice of grocers, butchers including a specialist pork butcher, fishmongers, greengrocers, dairies and bakers. Competition with out of centre supermarkets, trading estates and the growth of internet shopping have all had their effect. So have pedestrianisation, expensive car parking and vigorous car parking enforcement. The more difficult it is to shop in a town, the fewer the people who shop there, so Weymouth's shops no longer provide a full range of goods. On the other hand, it now has many providers of coffee and fast food and wine bars and clubs aplenty. For good or ill, the retail world has altered markedly and Weymouth has adapted to those changed circumstances."

There is an air of wistfulness in Maurice's reflections which I understand perfectly. There were a number of features of the old Weymouth that I preferred – Weymouth FC at the old Rec was just one – but the world moves on and, as Maureen Attwoll persuasively argues, certain changes have been for the best. Besides, there's nothing we can do to resurrect the 'golden age' of our youth. It will be for the next generation to decide the future of the town.

So the time has come for me to leave Weymouth, to cross the Town Bridge and cast a final look at the old harbour and make my way up St. Mary's Street towards the esplanade. But there's one last call to make. It's a call we've often made before and it's always a pleasurable one – fish and chips on the quay from Bennett's. No, I don't have a financial stake in the business and, No, we're not related, but how could I leave without putting my head round the door, as thousands of others do every year? It is a family-run business and they've been there for 20 years which is a good enough recommendation in itself. Terry and Jan Bennett and their son Mark are a good team. Jan's always so polite and helpful and cheerful.

"We buy good quality fish, always Icelandic because it's the best, and we make our own batter. The secret is not to have the batter too thick – just as thin as you can make it because then the fish doesn't shrink."

"Cod and chips twice, please, Jan."

Dorchester
Twinned with Bayeux (France), Lubbecke (Germany) and Holbaek (Denmark)

The King's Arms

"You see the old fellow with the stick just across the road. That's Henry Locke, his father Arthur was Hardy's solicitor – it's now Porter & Dobson's – he would have handled all his legal affairs. Henry's 85 now and a splendid chap."

I'm sitting in the lounge of The King's Arms with Mike Nixon, secretary of the Hardy Society, awaiting the arrival of Alistair Chisholm whose evening ghost tour of the town is advertised on a board outside. We follow the progress of the grey-haired figure up Higher East Street and I wonder if Henry, who would have been 5 when Hardy died in 1928, has any recollections of the great man. But I can hardly chase up the street after the dear fellow so I doubt I'll ever discover.

It's always intriguing to learn how, why and when readers fall in love with a particular author's work.

"My first association with the county was in 1957 when a favourite uncle, who was evacuated to Bowleaze near Weymouth during the war, invited me down for a holiday. I heard all about Hardy, read *The Well-Beloved* and was hooked from that moment on."

"Which only happens to be one of the most obscure of Hardy's novels and certainly not the easiest read!"

Alistair Chisholm, Town Crier, Chairman of the Chamber of Trade, Mayor's Escort, Ghost Tour

Thomas Hardy. (1840-1928)

The Hardy Players – 'The Mayor of Casterbridge' (adapted by Devina Symes) with Carole Redhouse, Gary Chilvers, Chris Pullen, Hilary Charlesworth, Keith Graham and Mark Kelly. *Picture: Alan Hodge*

Guide and a man of a dozen other parts, arrives with his customary flourish and quip. In his footsteps follows another of Dorchester's familiar faces, Roger Parkes, a gentleman of ruddy complexion and twinkling eyes, who has for as long as most can recall, delivered the *Dorset Echo* about the town.

"Fifty-two weeks of the year, every day bar Sundays and Christmas Day. I've worn out two trolleys and eleven pairs of shoes. When I heard the Olympics were in England in 2012 I thought to myself they've chosen well because I'll be 65 and that'll my retirement year."

No sooner have I shaken Roger's hand than I am on my feet again being introduced to two ladies. It is a pattern of events with which I will soon become familiar in Alistair's company. Alistair knows everyone and everyone knows Alistair.

"Allow me to introduce you to Helen Gibson and Lilian Swindle, past and present Hardy archivists at the Town Museum. Helen's late husband Jim was responsible for assembling all of Hardy's poems for Macmillan's. And they are the most splendid of ladies, I assure you."

So, within five minutes I have seen the son of Hardy's solicitor, met the secretary of the Hardy Society, two charming Hardy archivists and Alistair, a man dedicated to the cause of promoting Hardy's cause within the town and to the wider world. I can only be in Dorchester! So are the county of Dorset and the town where the great man spent most of his life making the most of their associations with one of the nation's greatest writers? Alistair responds first.

"Unfortunately they're not. For visitors arriving at either of our railway stations, or by car in the town itself, there is almost nothing to inform them of Hardy. Most fortunately we do possess an excellent Town Clerk, Dennis Holmes, and Cllr. Peter Mann who are doing their very best to keep the Council informed and actively involved in Hardy events about the town. There's also Andrew

Wadsworth, the developer of the brewery site, who has asked us to select some lines from Hardy that can be engraved on the pavement slabs near the site – preferably on the theme of the virtues of good ale!"

Mike Nixon highlights the absence of even basic amenities for visitors to those locations associated with the great man.

"We urgently need a public toilet at Bockhampton. It's way out in the wilds and, for many of our visitors, that is no laughing matter. I'd also like to see a dedicated transport service operating between Bockhampton, Max Gate, Stinsford and the Town Museum. If someone doesn't have a car such visits are impossible. And, if someone does have a car, there's the problem of parking. How much easier it would be for everyone to have a transport link between his birthplace, his home, his final resting-place and the Town Museum where so much Hardy memorabilia exists."

"What is absolutely vital is that the town of Dorchester itself remains the focal point," stresses Alistair. "With all due respect to Poundbury, we don't want a visitor centre out there. Hardy, I am quite sure, would have wished it because the town meant so much to him."

And what of the Hardy Society, I enquire of Mike? Is it flourishing?

"We have more than 1,200 members worldwide in 31 countries with about a third of our membership in this country. There has been a certain division in the past between the academics, who love to argue about the significance of a particular comma in Hardy, and the ordinary enthusiasts. Much to my delight we've recently forged close ties with the New Hardy Players and the Barnes Society. Devina Symes is busy writing a script for the next production *The Mayor of Casterbridge* which will be staged next summer. We also have an enthusiastic new chairman in Dr. Anthony Fincham who recently published a fascinating new book on Hardy – *Hardy the Physician, Medical Aspects of the Wessex Tradition*. I am also delighted that the writer and film director Julian Fellowes is now our president. One of our recent achievements of which I am particularly proud was to secure a painting, sold in 1937 by Florence Hardy, which originally hung in Max Gate. Thanks in no small measure to the fund-raising activities of Julian Fellowes and a number of other dedicated supporters, we were able to raise the necessary £5,000 to purchase it and it will be returned later in the year to its precise place in Max Gate."

Out and about in the town – Another day

Alistair, Dorchester's charming new Mayor Kate Hebditch and I, begin our morning with coffee at Napper's Mite where he relates to me the history of 'The Bid'. As the President of the Chamber of Commerce, Alistair is anxious that Dorchester should properly punch its weight in the very competitive market place of modern-day tourism and business.

"As a town we need to promote ourselves, to draw people here. Everyone benefits from an improved 'foot-fall'. It's about shopkeepers, the restaurants and pubs, the Town Museum, businesses of every kind. To market ourselves, to promote attractive events, to persuade people to come here – it all costs money. From a variety of sources, the Town, District and County Councils, the Duchy, voluntary contributions and Rural Renaissance, we raised the sum of £50,000. Phil Gordon was the Bid Project Manager. Then we had to go out and persuade local businesses to agree to contribute in total £100,000 a year for the next 5 years. There was an overwhelming vote in favour and they have agreed to contribute 1% of rateable value. The intention is to smarten up different areas of the town, to advertise the town to the wider world and to promote a variety of events. I believe it will pay for itself many times over and everyone will benefit. It is really a vote of confidence in the town and an investment in its future."

We discuss the various developments presently underway in the town – like The Maltings. One

HRH Prince of Wales and the mayor, Kate Hebditch. *Picture: Peter Holmes*

of them is the projected theatre.

"When it's completed – and it absolutely must be called the Hardy Theatre – there is no doubt it will attract an audience from far and wide for top-class productions. There could be a gallery and rehearsal facilities to draw the finest talent. And everything must blend harmoniously into the landscape. Further, as a necessary part or revitalising the town we must tackle the problem of the traffic. We need, I believe, to pedestrianise High East Street so that the town is not cut in two by traffic. We have a brilliant museum that doesn't get half the visitors it deserves because people have to run the gauntlet of non-stop traffic to get there. The street could be closed between 8am and 5pm. People would immediately feel more comfortable."

Alistair Chisholm's enthusiasm is un-bounding. He has views on everything relating to the town he loves. Although I know the town modestly well myself, it's fascinating to see it through the eyes of someone who walks its streets every day of the week. And that is what we now do – walk its streets.

"I believe my 18th century forebears drank and gambled away the family fortunes in Lincolnshire. Does that explain away my presence in Dorchester? Not really."

Alistair introduces me to the speaker. "Nick Wimberley. Nick arranges the Summer Saturday Live Music in South Street throughout the summer."

"This week is the Veterans' Festival. Ray Piper will be playing songs from the Forties."

It's an innovation that enlivens the town, putting a smile on the faces of the shoppers. As Nick leaves us, so Robin Potter arrives wearing a broad grin, a Sunderland FC tie and a crash helmet. A former Mayor and a maths teacher at Hardye's, Robin is on his way to the Carer's Group. There's the usual banter and verbal sparring, mostly relating to Roy Keane and Sunderland FC. How does the good fellow square supporting both the Carer's Group and Roy Keane?

Outside the Corn Exchange we meet Pete Hopkins. As always Alistair provides the introduction.

"Pete's one of those brilliant guys, like several other council employees, who does so much over and beyond the call of duty. If the Exchange isn't booked, Pete will take it upon himself to organise an event and raise money for charity. We've had Chris Jagger, brother of Mick, among others. Perhaps the most unusual was the Leider School of Music, a full Dutch symphony orchestra, who were on their way to Ireland. It took a week to organise but we raised £3,500 for the Tsunami victims. We've also raised funds for the Dorset Air Ambulance and other local charities. And I must mention Julie Holling and Steve Charles who give so much of their free time on behalf of good causes."

Anthony Moger is wearing another tie I do not recognise. It bears the image of an English partridge.

"It's the tie of the Game and Conservancy Trust based in Fordingbridge. We're engaged in a project to encourage the return of the English partridge to our countryside."

We're looking at the Charles Street project and discussing its long-term future? Alistair has his say first.

"An underground car-park, the District Offices above ground and a mix of commercial and housing – if the Council rationalises its offices it would bring greater efficiency and savings."

Anthony doesn't entirely agree. "Personally, I think the offices should be at Poundbury. But what did a girl who works for the council say to me? 'There'd be nowhere for me to get a sandwich, whereas in town I can do my shopping in my lunch-hour or after work.' Those arguments carry a lot of weight with councillors. And, by the way, I disagree with Alistair about the pedestrianisation of High East Street. I remain in favour of cars having access to the main streets."

The Hub and matters arising

Dorchester is the county town of Dorset. It is, by common consent, architecturally handsome, abundantly rich in its historical and literary past, and possessed of a civilised, gifted and industrious populace. However, beneath its surface prosperity and apparent social unity, there exists another world. It is true of every town and city in the land. Its presence may be small, unseen and unheard most of the time by the average citizen, but it is there and how the county town responds to the challenge of that world is of importance.

"The Government says there are just 459 across the country. We know that's nonsense."

When a Government which has long since lost count of the number of immigrants, legal and illegal, who have arrived in the UK in recent years, claims to know the exact number of rough sleepers nationwide it's impossible to suppress a laugh. Just who's kidding who? How can anyone be sure they haven't missed someone beneath a railway viaduct or in a promenade shelter?

In my far-off days of childhood in the very Sandy Lane that joined the parishes of Lytchett Minster and Upton, I do clearly recall the occasional knock on the door when a passing tramp would very politely request a glass of water which my good-hearted mother would, with equal politeness, cheerfully provide. Even then these ragged, be-whiskered, enigmatic figures were a diminishing band, much reduced in number from the days so vividly described by George Orwell in *Down and Out in Paris and London*. But if the 'traditional' tramp has largely disappeared from the highways and byways, we see instead in most towns those now categorised as 'rough sleepers' or even, a phenomenon I never witnessed as a child, the beggar. What should be the appropriate response of our humane, liberal society to these wretched individuals? Of course the police can and often do merely 'move the problem on' from one town to another, just as The National Trust and landowners still 'encourage' travellers to 'move on' from one site to another in a neighbouring county. While it is entirely understandable the policy, for some in our midst, is both un-Christian and, in the final analysis, ineffective.

Margaret Barker, a Quaker since the early 1980s though she still likes to play the organ for congregations at Broadmayne C of E, is the chairman of the Dorchester Poverty Action Group, a body set up by Churches Together, to tackle the 'pockets of deprivation' in the local community in the postal districts of DT1 and DT2. She and her friends have also been much exercised by the matter of those individuals who, for whatever reason, have become the homeless wanderers of the modern world. Dorchester is on the main road and it attracts its share of these drifters.

"There have always been wayfarers, tramps most people would call them, but that older generation are now most of them dead. Today drug addiction has compounded the problem of the rough sleeper. With drunkenness there was a public nuisance but, when drugs are a part of the equation, there's the added danger of violence and public revulsion and fear. Theft to feed the addiction becomes a routine part of existence."

In 2000 the Government launched its 'Rough Sleepers Strategy'. Volunteer groups were drawn together to discuss the issue and, as a result, The Hub was opened by Margaret and like-minded friends in the Salvation Army Hall in 2002, subsequently moving into new premises near Dorchester West railway station in property leased from businessman, Peter Bolton.

"One of the problems for such individuals has always been that they have no fixed abode which creates problems when they wish to claim benefits. The Hub provides a correspondence address from which they are able to telephone the Benefits Office in Weymouth. Currently they are able to claim £52 a week in benefits. You must remember that some individuals are so alienated from society that any kind of contact with officialdom is difficult. We began providing laundry facilities and showers and a hot meal at lunchtimes. Representatives from Shelter, Health Care and the Job Centre also regularly put in an appearance. By the spring of 2007, however, serious problems were surfacing. Local residents were becoming ever more disturbed when it became apparent The Hub was becoming a beacon for 'rough sleepers' from far afield. When we closed our doors at 2pm each day some individuals became a real nuisance about the town. Their behaviour was upsetting even people sympathetic to what we were trying to do. Local criticism was entirely justified. So we had to rethink our strategy. We didn't want The Hub to be used by travellers who were living in a van nearby, nor did we wish to be seen as some sort of club. We began by charging for food. Only a modest 50 pence for a meal but it does mean that everyone has to accept some responsibility for their own welfare. At weekends we provide a meal ticket which they can exchange at the Top of The Town Cafe. Dennis Perrott, the owner of the cafe and his son have been splendid in the help they have given. We have also now restricted numbers here with an absolute limit of twelve. Of course, it is very difficult to strike a balance between helping people with no roof over their heads and all sorts of personal problems in their lives, and being used by manipulative and often very difficult individuals."

At The Hub, Later in the day

"One day at a time. I think I'll have it engraved on my tombstone."

Chris laughs though you know there's almost certainly some complicated, unfunny story behind the careless laughter. Chris is clear-eyed with a good complexion, unlike most of those about him. He's also smartly dressed in a clean shirt and jeans, his hair tied in a neat ponytail, late twenties, well-spoken, manifestly bright. He's already eaten and leans back in his chair. Lunch-time is almost over. Just half a dozen are still sitting at the tables.

A voice from the back. Bob Matthews, who with another part-time worker Ann McDonald runs The Hub on a daily basis, calls out to Chris.

"I've found somewhere for you. Are you interested?" It seems Bob has found a bed-sit in

Weymouth. Chris nods although he's not sure he really wants to go to Weymouth.

Stuart is setting out for Pilsdon. Stuart's from Greenock, 12 years in the army, he tells me, the last 17 on the road.

"I used to be able to walk from the station at Bridport to Pilsdon in 2 hours. I had an accident a few months ago. Now it takes me four."

Stuart's got an unpleasant cough. I've heard the same sort of cough before. It's a common condition among those sleeping rough for months on end. He also smokes, painstakingly folding a wafer-thin roll-up.

"I was a resident at Pilsdon for 2 months. I got itchy feet and left. Jonathan (Herbert) said I would always be welcome to return. Maybe I've had enough of the travelling?"

Deliberate of speech with an almost impenetrable Scottish accent, patently sincere, Stuart is also instantly likeable. As he exits, his weighty pack strapped to his back, I ask him to remember me to Jonathan.

Chris has emerged from his conference with Bob. He's still not keen on re-locating to Weymouth but he's ready to consider it. He returns to his seat.

"The people you meet here are no better and no worse than in any boardroom. Probably better. Less ego."

Hazel and Graham Melling are just leaving after their morning's voluntary stint. They were introduced to The Hub by their vicar, Graham Perryman, a member of the Melbury team.

"We both lost our partners a few years ago. Then we found one another. We've been so lucky in our personal lives. Helping here is a way of saying thanks for our own good fortune. There but for the grace of God, we say."

I walk back into the town with Bob.

"When we were providing free sleeping bags and free food, the police and the Council said it meant our clients had more money to spend on alcohol and drugs. Now I say to my volunteers 'Don't give money.' If they run low on funds they are allowed up to £5 'on the slate' but no one has ever exceeded that figure. We need £200 a day to cover our running costs. The money comes from various charitable trusts. And, of course, without our volunteers, it would all be impossible."

Chris has followed us down the road. "I'm off to the library to read the papers."

Chris doesn't fit the image of the 'rough sleeper'. He's still got a pride in his appearance. But appearances can be deceptive. Something is not right in his life. I heard the other day that one quarter of the population will suffer with mental health problems of some kind in their lifetime. Most of the individuals who use The Hub have some such difficulty, be it caused by or compounded by alcohol or drug abuse. As Hazel and Graham Melling said, 'There but for the grace.....'

At least some fine people of Dorchester and district are doing their valiant best to prove we really are a caring society. I cannot help but think it is entirely fitting that the county town of Dorset cares as much as for the unfortunates of our society as the privileged.

(Stuart referred to an accident which had affected his ability to walk. Not long after our conversation I understand he was involved in another incident with a car which necessitated a further spell in hospital.)

Poundbury

I always try to talk to the local journalists. They know their communities far better than a passing stranger. It would be insulting not to draw upon their knowledge of the locality they write about on a daily basis. I find they are also extraordinarily generous in their willingness to help for which

Holmead Walk, Poundbury. *Picture: Tom Lane*

I am very grateful. Dee Adcock of the *Dorset Echo* is no exception. She's a lovely lady, bubbly and sympathetic. We've been discussing the area in general terms.

"The relationship between Dorchester and Poundbury is probably the single most controversial issue locally. It's certainly been a difficult relationship at times. There is little doubt that Prince Charles's involvement complicates peoples' feelings. On the one hand Poundbury is his vision. It's being built on Duchy land. He cares passionately about the project and desperately wants to get it right. Much of it is right though people have their reservations. On the other hand, the Prince does have his critics and detractors. Some of the comments on Poundbury stories on the newspaper's website are very personal and offensive. I believe we need to reserve judgement until the site is completed and that will be many years into the future. It was described in the early days by some as Poundbury model village though the word 'village' has been dropped as it has grown and it is now usually described as an urban development. It is seen as an 'extension' of Dorchester, a big extension. There does remain among some members of the public a feeling of 'Them and Us' but it's impossible to say whether that's a majority view. Sometimes you hear the word Poundbury pronounced in a deliberately snooty and rather mocking way as 'Pownd'bry.'"

Alas, I am unable, phonetically or in any other way, exactly to capture Dee's pronunciation. It is the best I can do but readers will get the general gist. Following my conversation with Dee there is but one path I must tread.

Everyone in the county was intrigued when we first got wind of Poundbury in the late 1980s. For years HRH, Charles, Prince of Wales, had been railing against the monstrosities of modern architecture. Now he was going to build his own village, or whatever we should call it, on 400 acres of Duchy land just outside Dorchester. There were to be 250 acres of mixed-use building and 150 acres of landscaping. Leon Krier, the renowned architect and urban planner was appointed to create an autonomous new extension to Dorchester. The Masterplan divided Poundbury into 4 distinctive quarters with each quarter corresponding to a Phase. At the end of Phase 4 an extra 5,000 people would be added to the population of the town with a total of 2,300 extra homes. Ever since the original plan was announced the interest has never faltered. We've all been there to have a look. It's fair to say that opinions have been divided. I have no idea of the percentages for or against. Besides, it's unfair to prejudge. If Rome wasn't built in a day, then Poundbury wasn't going to be built in a day. Construction actually began in the autumn of 1993 and the aim is that the final phase will be completed by 2020.

Simon Conibear, the development manager of the site, explains: "While many people imagine Poundbury is mainly about architecture, it's true to say that it's as much about creating an area in which the residents can not only live, as on most modern estates, but also shop, play and work. The architecture is traditional which clearly will not come as a surprise, and our builders use local Dorset materials whenever and wherever possible, such as stone, slate and render. Many of the architects themselves are based here in the county in Dorset. In Phase 1 C.G.Fry & Son Ltd from Litton Cheney and Morrish Builders of Poole undertook our building work. In Phase 2 the same companies together with Westbury Homes have been completing various projects, both residential and commercial. What I do know comes as a shock to many people is that a fifth of the housing is being built by housing associations for rental by people on the local housing list. Integrating social housing is a challenge but we did not wish to perpetuate segregated housing development. Yes, there may be problems but our intention is to create a generally benign environment in which people can live comfortably together."

It's a commendable vision. Walking around Poundbury I wouldn't know where the social housing is or isn't, though I have no doubt that the residents are aware. Will those on the waiting list be carefully monitored before they move in and, should the odd family become a nuisance to their neighbours, will they be moved out again? After all, if you have spent the better part of half a million pounds on a property, how would you respond to having 'a neighbour from hell'?

'A Vision of Britain', written by HRH Prince Charles, sits on the coffee table in the lounge of Mike and Jen West's apartment.

"For both of us Poundbury is the expression of fundamental ideological beliefs."

Mike was the previous Chairman of the Poundbury Residents Association.

"Remember the horrible old ribbon development along the main roads that characterised so much pre- and post-war building with absolutely no sense of community? Remember too the zoning of industrial areas well outside or on the fringe of residential areas. Yet if you look at the growth of London in the eighteenth and nineteenth centuries, for example, when innumerable villages were gradually joined up, there was a real mix of housing for all classes alongside industrial enterprise – and it worked."

I pass across a newspaper cutting headed 'Vanity Village.....Minister attacks Charles's model community.' In an address to the Fabian Society in April the Communities Secretary, Hazel Blears, refers disparagingly to the various 19th century industrialists' housing schemes such as those at Saltaire and Bournville. Ms. Blears adds: 'They owed more to paternalism and the aggrandisement of the benefactor than real concern for the residents. If I were feeling cheeky, I might add Poundbury to the list.'

Citing Aneurin Bevan's vision of 'Towns where the doctor, the grocer and the labourer all lived in the same street', Ms. Blears continues her diatribe with the following words: 'As a Government we want to see different types and sizes of property mixed together, rather than the wealthy in gated communities and the poor in sink estates.'

"Doesn't the silly woman appreciate that's exactly what we have already got here in Poundbury?" Jen West is clearly both incensed and exasperated by the Minister's remarks.

"Besides her lamentable ignorance of history – actually Saltaire and Bournville hugely improved the lives of the workers who lived there – if she looked at Poundbury today and Phases Three and Four of the Development Plan, she would realise that is precisely what the Prince and his team have in view."

Jen is absolutely right. The appalling historical ignorance of most of those in Government and, quite possibly among Opposition spokesmen as well, never ceases to infuriate. The words 'half-educated' spring to mind. But one only has to listen to the level of parliamentary debate on Yesterday in Parliament on Radio Four and it is impossible to escape the conclusion that the Commons is stuffed with third-rate minds, party hacks and self-servers. How many have ever had real jobs? There are splendid exceptions in every party, of course, but Ms. Blears is certainly not one of them.

Mike and Jen's vision of the 'New Urbanism' and 'Sustainable Development' is an integral part of Poundbury's future.

"Poundbury is being built in overlapping circles of 200-500 dwellings. The idea is that when it is completed it will be possible to walk from one side to the other in 10 minutes. It's also hoped many people will dispense with their cars and walk to their places of work within Poundbury and to the shops. Or even into Dorchester itself. In an age of escalating fuel prices this seems very sensible."

Toad Hall, Peverall Road East

If I attributed the above words and views of the Wests to my present companion, Fran Leaper, I suspect she would scarcely disagree with a syllable.

"As members of the Residents Association we have always tried to welcome incomers to the Poundbury community, to acquaint them with the activities they may care to join in with, to introduce them to neighbours and a wider circle of residents. One of the ideas behind the actual design and lay-out of the houses and streets is to put people in touch with a social circle of 50 or so others nearby. After all, it can make so much difference to peoples' lives, especially when they first arrive, to be greeted in the street with a cheerful smile and a Hello. "

What about future developments?

"We already have a splendid doctor's surgery. Will we eventually have a primary school? That will obviously depend on demographics but it is a possibility."

So what tentative conclusions may we draw? My visit to Poundbury has, of necessity, been brief. It is evident that those who live here, certainly all the individuals to whom I have spoken, remain very enthusiastic and there is clearly much to admire. Since I do not live here I cannot write of how it feels to wake in the morning, draw the curtains and look about, to walk to the shops or visit the pub in the evening and stroll back home. When I contrast Poundbury with many of the housing developments I have seen on my travels, it is so different that it is difficult to draw comparisons. But, as I wrote earlier, let us return 10 or 20 years hence. Only then will we be able properly to judge. In the meanwhile, let us commend HRH, Prince Charles, for the courage and imagination of his vision. Here is a man who cares passionately about his country, who manifestly wishes to do good and bequeath to future generations a legacy they will value and respect. I am certain history will be kind to the Prince and, I have little doubt, to Poundbury.

Still in Poundbury, but the subject is local government, not housing

"There are altogether too many political shenanigans in local government. Policies are too often judged not on their merits but the politics of the group advocating them. And it's getting worse. There's ever increasing politicisation of local politics and it's a trend I deplore."

So speaks David Barrett, a former Dorchester Mayor and the leader of the Independent group on West Dorset District Council.

"We need to simplify the tiers of government. We also waste too much time and energy producing report after report, sometimes on the same subject, when so often nothing is done. How many peoples' salaries are being paid churning out these reports? And who foots the bill? It's the Council Tax payer, of course. Dorset needs some joined up thinking. It suffers from being a fragmented county. There's absolutely no point being a councillor unless you can do something."

But there's one group of local activists David does passionately support and they are all the voluntary workers in the community.

"Like my wife Lynda and so many of her friends. They are worth their weight in gold. No local authority could do without them."

You are so right, David. Everywhere I journey it's the same heart-warming story.

The Weldmar Hospice Care Trust, Herringston Road

We meet on the stairs, a black and white collie called Trixie and her owner Pam Elliott. Trixie's an exuberant bundle of life enhancing warmth and fun. Pam is wearing a badge bearing the words Pets for Therapy.

"Trixie comes along to cheer the patients."

The Weymouth midnight walk on behalf of the Weldmar Trust. *Picture: The Weldmar team*

I am sure she does it brilliantly. She's put a smile on my face, that's for sure, without even trying.

"Actually we can and do arrange for patients to have their own pets brought in to see them."

That is imaginative compassion in practice. I bid Trixie and Pam a reluctant goodbye and follow Caroline Nickinson up to her office. Caroline is the Director of fundraising for the Trust. With annual running costs alone of £5 million, it's a formidable challenge.

"We receive a NHS grant of about one third of our expenditure, 20% plus from our shops and about 10% from our investments. My personal fundraising target for this year is £2.7 million. Fortunately there are so many wonderful people who help me. I know for some of my volunteers that this is their life. There's a lady who soaks stamps off envelopes, another spends hours doing jigsaws to make sure that those we sell are correctly labelled. 'No pieces' missing is her favourite description! Often I don't know their names, many I've never met. But their efforts transform so many lives."

There have already been moments on my journey when I have felt especially humble and of little consequence and this is another. A succession of nurses come and go in the office, pausing briefly to make a quick cup of tea or coffee and momentarily relax from the busy routine of their lives.

"The Weldmar Hospice care Trust evolved over a period of 20 or so years from a group of similar, overlapping bodies – the Dorset Health Trust, MacMillan, the Trimar Hospice, Cancercare Dorset and the Joseph Weld Hospice. Half of our patients go home again from the hospice. Our nurses and doctors provide respite care, pain relief and symptom control. And for those who do end their days here, everything is done to ease their passing and to assist their bereaved relatives."

Caroline was actually one of the founder members along with the late Major John Greener and the late David Revill.

"The land here was bought from the Duchy and Prince Charles is our patron. He calls by informally from time to time and just sits and chats with the patients. He has a lovely way with them. But there are just so many splendid people working in so many different areas for us."

Caroline must have some very special memories of her own.

"Sir Joseph Weld was very closely associated with our work throughout. He cut the first sod of turf here before the building work began. I remember seeing tears in his eyes as he did so. My young son, Andrew, remarked to me when he met him that he was like a big 'Grandpa figure' and it was true. He was such a lovely man. Sadly he died a few months later. Then there's our old friend, Roger Holman, who comes over every year with a selection of his photographs for our calendar which he generously provides for us. Two of the biggest fundraising events are the carol service at Brewer's Quay in Weymouth when we have a large Christmas tree decorated by lights and, of course, our sponsored midnight – walk across the town. Over 1,000 ladies set out at midnight on August 30 from the Pavilion Theatre to Overcombe and back, a distance of 4 miles. That's a very special occasion."

Does Caroline ever get weary or depressed after a particularly difficult or frustrating day?

"You know, if ever I have a bad day, I just walk through the ward and it really touches my heart and gives me fresh strength. I feel I am privileged to be working with wonderful people and for such a good cause."

I will leave Weldmar with the words of Dr. Geoffrey Guy, the chairman of the Trust and Alison Ryan, the chief executive, as they are expressed in their Newsletter.

'All we have done this year is thanks to you and our plans for the future are ambitious. With your continuing help and loyalty we will do even more in the future.'

County Hall
He farms 90 acres at Iwerne Minster, mostly cereals. He's a former soldier representing Hambledon as a Conservative. He's also the chairman of Dorset County Council and a most affable individual –

his name is Angus Campbell.

"I was elected the leader of the Conservative group 3 years ago. We are the largest party on the Council but, to be honest, party politics are fairly muted at this level. There's a Cabinet of 7 members with particular responsibilities for areas like Environment, Children's services, Community Safety, Adult Social Care, Highways, Resources & Efficiency and so on. As others will have told you, we are a relatively low funded county so we are obliged to make more direct financial demands on the people of the county. We have an annual budget of about £600 million and we have to spend that money cautiously."

For most of us, the image of Dorset County Council is of a remote body operating at County Hall which employs a large and expensive staff. There's also a widespread feeling that bureaucracies tend to be self-perpetuating, self-satisfied and immune to the general economic difficulties of the average citizen. It may be an unfair perception but it is one that undoubtedly exists. Taking the issue of large salaries paid to officials in various departments, I ask Angus for his response.

"We have to pay the going rate for the right calibre of staff. We are competing in the market place with the private sector for the best talent in the land. "

It's a thorny issue, I know, especially with so many people employed in the public sector today. I do recall as an economics student at the LSE learning from Robert Peston's father, Lord Maurice Peston, about 'imperfect competition' in the market place and its effect upon distorting price, whether it be that of labour or commodities. I suspect that's exactly what we have in modern Britain. The 'fat cats' in parliament, public service bureaucracies and the BBC, to name but three areas, are able to vote themselves huge salaries and bonuses secure in the knowledge that the burden will be born by the public purse or the licence payer. Likewise in the private sector, as exemplified by the bankers, directors determine pay structures and pass the cost on to consumers. There is, very simply, no proper competition, which would have the effect of bringing down salaries to more realistic levels. Meanwhile, ordinary mortals scratch about as best they can, unsubsidised by anyone. But Angus Campbell is such a pleasant fellow I do not have the heart to argue with him today.

"I promise you we are very concerned about value for money in providing services. In Fit for the Futurewe are employing all the modern technology, getting departments talking to one another – there is a real emphasis on efficiency."

And what is the County's relationship with Central Government?

"We are under constant pressures of all kinds. We cannot be detached. We can fight our corner but Central Government will have the final say. We do, of course, have particular difficulties in Dorset. Though in many ways the county appears affluent, actual salaries /wages are 11% below the national average, employment opportunities are limited, housing costs are high and the number of people retiring to the county does 'skew' the general economic picture. A larger than average population of retired people does raise the cost profile with our limited resources."

Angus is a farmer, a political representative of his constituents and he plays an important role, along with his Cabinet colleagues, in determining policies within the county – what are his guiding principles?

"Dorset is a beautiful county. I believe 50% is designated as being of Outstanding Natural Beauty. We must preserve that landscape for future generations. At the same time we must support and encourage business enterprise because it's the powerhouse of our economy. Dorset is also a county with a rich history. There are sometimes tensions between each which we must seek to resolve as satisfactorily as possible. If I can play a small part then I will be content."

I am sure Angus will work hard on our behalf, though I am still not happy about those big salaries.

Dorchester Police Station

I decide to call by on a man who, by common consent, succeeds daily in giving the Dorset Police a good name. He's not just popular with his fellow officers; he's respected and well-liked across the local community. His name is Inspector Les Fry.

"Dorset is where I was born and brought up. To be where I am in the county town doing what I do makes me very proud. I wouldn't want to be anywhere else."

We talk about the 'image' of the police in general terms and a number of the reservations expressed by the public.

"I recognise everything you say. I do cringe sometimes when I read about certain incidents but you must realise that policing has changed dramatically since the days of Dixon of Dock Green. It has changed because crime has changed in character in many ways. There's computer fraud, paedophilia on the Internet, terrorism, criminals travelling further and faster than ever in the past to commit their crimes and make good their escape, the complexities of the drugs world. The village bobby of the past would not recognise today's world. The police have had to respond to meet society's different needs. But I agree with you 100 percent that officers must treat members of the public as they would wish to be treated themselves. It is something I constantly remind my officers to practise – civility and good manners at all times. I would add that I am immensely proud of my colleagues. They are very professional and committed and capable. I have never felt obliged to reprimand any one of them for unsatisfactory conduct."

And all that paperwork we hear so much about? Les grimaces.

"Even if you take the most minor of offences, that of being drunk and disorderly, it represents an hour of form-filling. I feel we could and should reduce our time in the office by 50%, if only the politicians would let us! That would free a lot more policemen for everyday duties."

What about the impact of the European Court of Human Rights and its impact upon policing?

"Broadly I approve of many aspects of the Human Rights Act but it is being exploited by criminals and their lawyers. We have to be whiter than white and they will exploit every loophole to escape justice?"

Does Les feel frustrated when the forces under his command have caught criminals only to see them being treated leniently by the courts?

"To tell you the truth, we do our job as professionally as possible. If we obtain a guilty verdict that is our job done. It's out of our hands then."

That's a suitably diplomatic answer, Inspector Fry.

One of Dorchester's legendary characters is Les Phillips MBE, thrice Mayor, chairman of Dorset Association for the Disabled, chairman of Care Line, an emergency monitoring and alarm system for the elderly serving over 6,000 people, for many years one of the leading farriers in the district and so many other things besides, that it's impossible to include more than a handful of his remarkable achievements. Besides which, he's a much loved, highly respected figure in the community. Married to talented artist Yvonne, or 'Vonty' as she is widely known, with 2 children, Jane and Richard, Les was awarded the MBE in 2000 for his services to the town and its people. It's an honour richly deserved for one of the most public-spirited, big-hearted men not only in Dorchester but in the county itself.

A Magistrate's lot

"It was Sir David Ramsbotham, a former Chief Inspector of Prisons, who addressing a meeting of the local Magistrates Association, observed that one third of those imprisoned are 'sad' with difficult and desperate backgrounds, one third are 'mad' and suffering from a variety of mental illnesses, and one third are plain 'bad'. Of course, it's a crude simplification but, as a judge or magistrate, when a verdict is passed, you have to decide the most fitting sentence for that particular individual. Every case is subtly different. The sentence must reflect the nature of the crime and the personality of the offender, whilst satisfying society in general and the victim in particular that justice has been seen to be done."

Educated at Hardye's and St. Luke's, Exeter, Adrian Downton spent 4 years in the film industry before entering teaching, eventually becoming a headmaster, first at Wareham Middle and then at Dorchester Girl's Grammar which duly metamorphosed into the local Middle school.

"It was Lady Williams, the chairman of the Bench, who suggested I might consider becoming a magistrate and, after some intensive training, I became a JP in 1987."

Recently retired a number of changes have saddened him.

"In the last few years we have lost our Magistrates' Courts at Dorchester, Gillingham and Sherborne. Magistrates' Courts deal, of course, with the lesser offences, the more serious go on to the Crown Court either in Bournemouth or here in Dorchester. The most serious will be heard in Winchester. The whole process was called rationalisation, but was actually a cost-cutting measure and a regrettable one, I believe. It helps enormously when a magistrate is familiar with the community where he is sitting. It's no different from an experienced teacher or policeman who is all the better equipped for his job when he knows the locality. You get to know families and the backgrounds of individuals which can help enormously in making correct judgements and deciding the most appropriate way in which to deal with certain offenders. The further you remove a judge or magistrate from his community the more difficult it becomes."

Inevitably the subject of drugs is at the forefront of much discussion between police, magistrates, prison authorities and the probation service.

"I agree with those who say that short-term sentences for drug offences are almost valueless. It is impossible in a short period to achieve anything useful. What is needed is longer-term attendance at treatment centres. It's a depressing fact that methadone which is often prescribed for addicts has just a 7% success rate. Ninety-three percent return to their habits. What they really need is a period of 'cold turkey'. There has been some success in different parts of the country, originally piloted in the USA, with 'dedicated drug courts' and this may be the way forward. Offenders are obliged to attend regularly and they are very closely supervised and in regular contact with the same magistrates and social workers. Drug rehabilitation sentences are effective if the addict is supported by friends and family and employment. During this last year, here in Dorchester, I know of at least 6 deaths as a result of acute addiction. A deeply addicted heroin or cocaine user is most likely to end up dead!"

Finally, the Human Rights Laws, what should we do?

"I don't think it is so much a matter of European judges interfering with our judicial affairs but, once signed up to a set of 'rules' or 'articles', we have to abide by their interpretation. I believe a thorough re-examination and possible revision of several 'articles' could be beneficial."

Knowing Adrian of old and the familiar twinkle in his eye, I ask him what incidents have particularly amused him on the Bench over the years?

"Anecdote number 1 – a defendant on a theft charge was asked to 'take the oath' in one of our local courts which he duly did. When he was eventually taken back to the cells, it was found that he had taken the bible with him! He'd nicked it! Anecdote number 2 – A homeless young lad living in the Bridport area a few years ago was prosecuted for stealing food from a supermarket. The chairman asked him whether he had any dependants or family, whereupon our young lad produced from his baggy trousers with large patch pockets a couple of ferrets and stated he was their carer!"

Hangman's Cottage

Hangman's Cottage. There's a name for the family home. Not a Rose, Honeysuckle or Wisteria Cottage, The Old Rectory or even a modest River View, rather it's a name to pluck from the pages of a novel by Dickens, Doyle or Edgar Allan Poe. How can I resist discovering who dwells in such a place?

I ring the bell with an eager curiosity. A dog bays loudly within. It sounds distinctly promising. I wait for the creaking door and a bent old man garbed from head to toe in black with broken teeth and bloodshot eyes, or a hideous, cackling old hag with matted hair and broomstick. Instead, I see before me a most attractive young woman – and a basset hound. With a charming smile I am ushered into the lounge where a plump black rabbit that looks, to my eyes, as if it should be in a gently simmering stew-pot with carrots and bay leaves, squats unconcernedly in a basket. The basset hound continues to bay loudly. The creature clearly possesses the lungs of a Pavarotti or Caruso.

"I'm afraid the dog is absolutely terrified of the rabbit."

My illusions are being shattered by the second. Ghosts then surely and things that go bump in the night, unexplained screams and sobbing? Alas, none, the lady regrets.

There were originally three cottages, she explains. Two were agricultural dwellings, presumably where the 'drowners', who once so skilfully managed the water meadows for Coker's farm, must have lived. The hangman lived at the far end on the right as you face the building, she adds. I sit in quiet reflection and stroke the rabbit. There's certainly plenty of meat on the creature, enough for two nights and some left over for supper, I would judge.

Hangman's cottage.

The lady returns with a tray of coffee and biscuits as her husband returns from their tobacconist/sweetshop in the Arcade. The ratio is two thirds tobacco sales to one third confectionery, I am mildly surprised to learn in an age when smoking is regarded by the health fascists as morally on a par with grievous bodily harm or kidnap.

"When the cottages were modernised they found the hangman's ropes in the roof-space. They are now in the County Museum, I believe."

The garden is glorious, full of flowering shrubs and trees, doves and exotically coloured bantams. Should I perhaps return one winter's midnight when the wind is howling through the trees and a full moon casts sinister shadows about the cottage? As I take my leave of Hangman's Cottage and thank Lesley Martin and her husband John for their hospitality, two other questions occupy my mind. How can it be that a basset hound is so fearful of a rabbit? And would the rabbit possibly be better beneath a pastry crust rather than casseroled?

Cokers Frome Farm

"I farm sheep and I farm people," laughs John Mayo.

It's a far cry from 1848 when John's great grand-father, George Mayo, acquired Cokers Frome Farm, including the 50 acres of water meadows bordering the Frome, a stone's throw from North Square and the prison. A full history of England's water meadows, their significance and decline, must lie elsewhere than in this volume though for John it is a sad story.

"The farm employed 2 highly skilled 'drowners' whose job it was between mid-October and mid-April to 'manage' the river, ensuring a water temperature that maintained the permanent growth of the grass through the winter, without the use of fertilisers, of course, and allowed the meadows to act as a sponge. The Environment Agency which took over the responsibilities of the riparian owners simply doesn't know as much about river and meadow management as the old 'drowners', I'm afraid."

As for 'farming people', I understand John's comments when I look across the fields from the farmhouse towards the town. In all my life I have never seen, nor would expect to see again, so many girl guides. Their tents are everywhere and small, bustling figures appear to fill every square yard of grass.

"The security there is so strict that our son Richard who works the farm with John had difficulty getting back to his home last night, "says Irene Mayo. "There are actually over 1,000 guides, I believe, and our grand-daughter is among them. Yesterday she poked her head through the hedge to greet us! They come every 5 years for a week's camping. How they manage without all their modern trappings of mobile phones, i-Pods and computers, I wouldn't know!But they're off on visits all over the county every day and I'm sure it's a wonderful experience for them."

"And after they've gone the Dorchester Show will be taking place here in September. The Dorchester Agricultural Society has a 21 year lease and occupies the field for a month. Last year the show which features livestock, trade stands and a host of activities for the whole family attracted 58,000 visitors. So you see what I mean about 'farming people'," adds John with a laugh.

And what about the sheep – are returns improving as with beef and dairy?

"Prices have picked up. We've got 800 sheep, 500 ewes and 300 lambs. Obviously lambs are the most lucrative. Unfortunately there's absolutely no money in wool. It actually costs money to have them shorn!Mutton has become a little more fashionable of late, thanks to the celebrity chefs and Prince Charles who often give it a mention. But mutton does need to be cooked very slowly to get the flavour and the modern housewife, I'm afraid, won't touch it!"

Walking across the fields to the river joining John Mayo's farm I pass the Bemlett family's Frome Whitfield Farm and find myself wondering if 50 years hence this lovely patch of old England will still be green, or built upon ? It will be a sad day for Dorchester if ever it should come to pass. Planners would have to face the wrath of the allotment holders certainly, for here are the most immaculate allotments I have seen anywhere on my travels. John Mayo tells me the Council acquired the land from Cokers farm in 1962. It was in these same meadows, not so far along the banks of the Frome, that spectators once gathered to watch the hangings outside the prison as described by Hardy in The Withered Arm. Today it is a tranquil, untroubled spot and thoughts of hangings are far removed. But I am still reflecting upon that rabbit – should the pastry crust be puff or short?

Dorchester FC

From Weymouth to Dorchester, from Bournemouth to Southampton, from Portsmouth to Brighton, every football club along the South coast is suffering from an identical malaise – financial problems of an acute nature with no obvious cure.

I call by at Dorchester FC's Jewson Stadium in the first weeks of the season. There's quiet optimism as there always is at these times. Eddie Mitchell, Sandbanks resident and self-made building millionaire, is the chairman and chief share-holder and Shaun Brooks is the manager. Shaun, of course, is the son of that most gifted ball-playing Spurs star, the late Johnny Brooks, and no mean creative player in his own right. I saw Shaun many times at Bournemouth and it was always a pleasure to watch an intelligent player of his calibre handle the challenge of more physical opponents. Eddie Mitchell has already spent a lot of his own hard-earned cash supporting the Magpies but he is anxious that more supporters turn up at the stadium to improve the club's finances. I understand Eddie has recently undergone a serious operation. Everyone at the club wishes him well in the coming months.

(In the event Dorchester struggle but escape relegation by a hairsbreadth, Shaun Brooks parts company with the Magpies and everyone hopes for better fortune next time around. Eddie Mitchell steps down from his position as chairman as he moves to AFC Bournemouth in early summer to assume a similar role there.)

Dorchester Prison

'You're going to prison to be punished'. Prison Officer Mackay (Fulton Mackay) to Ronald Stanley 'Fletch' Fletcher (Ronnie Barker) .The pilot episode of 'Porridge' BBC TV made in 1975.

'Deprivation of liberty is the punishment – being separated from family, friends and society. It is not our job to punish prisoners when they are in prison'. Tony Corcoran, Governor, HM Prison, Dorchester, words spoken to the author in 2008.

There are, on the day of our meeting, 218 prisoners of whom one half are on remand awaiting trial and sentence. With the majority of prisoners sharing a cell, Dorchester is one of the most overcrowded gaols in the country. Like many Victorian buildings the roof has been causing problems for some years and a new one is under construction so there's scaffolding everywhere, inside and out.

Tony Corcoran, Governor of HM Prison, Dorchester, for the past 18 months, is an amiable, manifestly dedicated man with a Master's degree in Management Criminology from Cambridge.

"I am proud this prison has been given Level 4 status for reaching Key Performance targets. It reflects much credit upon the staff."

I'm quite sure it does. The members of staff I meet appear highly professional, briskly efficient and pleasant.

"When a prisoner arrives after sentence he is assessed. As a matter of principle we try to place him in the institution most appropriate to his needs. The low-risk Category D are transferred to an open prison like Leyhill, young offenders to Guys Marsh, the more serious offenders to Long Lartin."

There is a scarcity of meaningful jobs in Dorchester. The kitchens, laundry, reception and orderly duties occupy most inmates. Attending educational classes counts as work.

"An employed prisoner receives £6.00 weekly, a prisoner who chooses not to work receives £2.50. There is, therefore, a clear incentive for a prisoner to work."

Prisoners may choose to work, or not to work?

In the company of PO 'Steve ', I get to look at a cell. It's a typical Dorchester cell, Steve tells me, with a barred window, bunk beds, a WC with a screen for privacy together with a wash-basin, TV, CD player, toiletries, books, and family photographs. A Father's Day card is propped up on a table, a poignant reminder of the world outside and the family this particular prisoner chose not to consider when committing the crime(s) he committed. It's not a spacious cell for two occupants, but the height of luxury compared with the cells I saw years ago in Winchester, Wormwood Scrubs and Lewes. 'Fletch' and 'Lennie ' would definitely have likened it to *The Ritz*. No chamber pots, no 'slopping out', no bare floors to be scrubbed daily, no bed-rolls to be inspected each morning, no 'Lights out' policy at 9pm. Nor do TVs have to be switched off, so a prisoner can watch into the early hours. In human relationships there's usually a dominant figure. In a prison cell presumably that figure will determine TV viewing. Pity the poor prisoner who wants to sleep.

"There's no shouting at prisoners. We treat our inmates with respect."

Generally, it's a commendable principle. However, I taught for a number of years and, sometimes, like every other teacher I knew, I shouted. When I did the pupils knew I was angry and they had overstepped the mark. Was I wrong to do so? Were all my colleagues wrong? Were we infringing their human rights and dignity?

"Re-offending rates are 50% for adult offenders, about 75% for young offenders. However, it's impossible to judge the success rate of any individual prison because prisoners do get moved about so much."

And the inevitable subject of drugs inside and out?

"Many offenders commit offences to fund their drug habits. Probably 70% or more of our prisoners have drug related problems and we do have to keep a watchful eye on visitors trying to bring drugs in. In addition, many of our inmates are illiterate or barely literate and lacking workplace skills. Many have damaged personalities. Society has to accept its share of responsibility."

Unfortunately my conversation with Tony Corcoran was restricted by several calls upon him during my visit and I was unable to ask many questions I intended. The Governor was unable to offer me the opportunity of another visit.

Reflections on my visits to Dorset's prisons.

I have now visited 3 Dorset prisons and so far I have refrained from making judgements, aside from the occasional literary equivalent of 'raised eyebrows'. But the time has arrived when I feel it is not unreasonable to express a few considered thoughts. First of all, I would like to thank Tony Corcoran, the Governor of HMP Dorchester, David Bourne, Deputy Governor of YOI, Portland, and John Masters, Chief Prison Officer, HMP, The Verne, Portland, for their time and courtesy. I would also like to praise unreservedly all those officers I met during the course of my visits together with their colleagues. I know they are good people performing their onerous duties conscientiously. I would go further and add that it is clear many officers are investing an enormous amount of their time and emotional energy into helping prisoners to return to the community better people with improved prospects of turning their lives around. Together with their instructors, chaplains and other religious advisers, prison visitors and support staff, much excellent work is being done.

However, I do have a number of serious reservations relating to what I have seen and heard. Of course, neither Governors nor officers have any control over most of these matters. I suspect, like many readers, they inwardly rage at the failure of Governments to build enough prisons to house those individuals the courts find guilty of committing crimes that merit a custodial sentence. (See page 224 – Lord Phillips of Worth Matravers) The ensuing over-crowding produces lamentable consequences in so many areas. Early release should be an earned privilege for the most deserving of prisoners, not a cost-cutting expedient that makes a mockery of the law. As others observe elsewhere, it's difficult enough to get into prison these days without compounding the farce by early release. While it may be tempting to rid the country of foreign nationals in our prisons by this method, what message does it send out to their brothers-in-crime outside? One is that if they are thinking of committing crimes, the British system of justice will ensure they serve very much reduced sentences in the most of congenial circumstances. I wonder too how many of those sent back to their country of origin will be returning to the UK by the backdoor within a short space of time?

I am not alone in my opinion. I will quote directly the words of Clive Chamberlain, Chairman of the Dorset Police Federation.

"The Police Federation has long warned that more prisons are needed. If prison overcrowding is resulting in sentences being cut even further then the criminal justice system is failing victims of crime and further demoralising front-line officers who see those they have arrested flying out through the revolving door of justice. The public need to be safe and criminals should serve their full sentences."

In the light of the fact that so many prisoners are drug-users and their crimes are drug-related, it is self-evident there is no point in sending offenders to prison for such short sentences when there is insufficient time for their drug recovery programmes to be completed. It is a waste of money and scarce resources. The answer would appear to be many more effectively monitored drug-treatment centres outside prison, or sentences of such length that a recovery programme may be completed before release. There are no guarantees in any policy but it is clear that, at the moment, we are not tackling the problem with any degree of success.

But let us look at certain aspects of prison life that leave me feeling very uneasy. I realise our prison officers have a difficult job and that having a largely acquiescent prison population makes their lives easier. Were I in their shoes I would want to avoid confrontation with angry, bored and, in a number of cases, dangerous and violent prisoners. Filling their bellies with good food, letting them watch TV as a right, all through the night if they so wish, having their own keys (as at The Verne) with the consequent freedom to roam the prison at will – such privileges do make for a more or less contented prison population with the minimum of aggravation. But do they have the effect of making prisoners fear another prison sentence? Where is the deterrent element that should be a part of the equation? If 'doing bird' is that comfortable it simply becomes a routine part of the professional criminal's way of life. And the knowledge of 'soft' gaols permeates the consciousness of the whole of society so that committing crime, even if it means getting caught sometimes, is seen by many as 'no big deal'.

There was one aspect of modern prison life that did shock and disturb me on several counts. Though mobile phones are not permitted, prisoners are effectively allowed unlimited access to the outside world by the use of land-line phones – up to the limit of their card credit. For most of them, of course, this detail presents absolutely no impediment because they can have their prison bank accounts topped up from outside. As a consequence, it means they can speak to whoever they please for as long as they please. With the enormous number of languages now being spoken by prisoners, the ability of the prison authorities to monitor calls or maintain any sort of control has effectively gone. I witnessed one individual prisoner, nationality unknown, speaking for at least 15 minutes and he was still talking when I left the area. For all anyone knew he could have been running his outside criminal racket right under the noses of prison officers and they would have been powerless to do anything about it. Does anyone doubt that many do precisely this? Presumably it would have been in breach of his 'human rights' if he was denied access to the phone. But what about the rights of society to ensure no such abuse occurs, I would ask? Maintaining family contacts through controlled visits, or granting a strictly limited number of phone calls, the right to which would be earned by exemplary behaviour, is one thing. What now exists is anarchy. I know there will be those who argue that speaking on the phone to a loved one may sustain a relationship. I would suggest that as many misunderstandings and suspicions can arise through phone calls, or an inability to make contact with a loved one, that such an assertion is highly questionable. Anyway, in a less indulgent age, prison authorities strictly controlled visits, letters and phone calls which were permitted only on compassionate grounds in rare circumstances. Were they wrong?

Finally, we come to the reoffending rates which are disturbingly high. I count myself a liberal with a small 'l' but I am not in favour of licence. As I have travelled across the county very often the conversation has strayed on to subjects other than those I have recorded in these pages. There is no doubt that there is a widespread feeling that those in high places in our society too often forget the victims of crime and make excuses for the criminals. It is quite true, as Adrian Downton remarks, that prisons contain a mix of 'The sad, mad and bad'. It is important that we distinguish, where we can, between the categories. Each needs a different approach. I fear, at the moment, we are often confusing them and, in the process, confusing ourselves.

Is Tony Corcoran correct when he says that 'deprivation of liberty is THE punishment'? It is undoubtedly true, as David Bourne remarked to me, that being in the company of some very unpleasant individuals may in itself be a form of punishment but that is an incidental factor. It was not the view of PO Mackay in Porridge that 'deprivation of liberty was THE punishment', nor the view of the majority of previous generations of prison officers and Governors, nor most Home Secretaries. Nor was it the judgement of society in general. Of course, humane treatment must be accorded prisoners but most people believed prisons should also be sufficiently disagreeable to act as a serious deterrent to further wrong-doing. When life is very comfortable 'inside', when sentences are seldom completed, when a range of 'blanket' privileges exist, when sanctions for misdemeanours are trifling, when Fixed Penalties and Cautions are used for a variety of serious crimes, including acts of violence, and the fines ignored and unpaid without consequences to the offenders, are we not undermining the public's confidence, quite understandably, in our whole judicial system? For the past 25 years or so penal policy and the Criminal Justice system has been largely shaped by the 'liberal intelligentsia', exploited by lawyers and the criminals they represent and, in the past decade, further influenced by the dictates of European law-makers and the Human Rights 'industry'. I will repeat a statement I made earlier. I count myself, in most senses a liberal with a small 'l' but I also care passionately about justice for the victims of crime and the general health and safety of our society. Just days ago the trial ended of one of the most horrific murder cases in the annals of British criminal history. Two brilliant young French students were murdered by Dano Sonnex and an accomplice in the most horrible circumstances, being stabbed more than 200 times in a frenzied assault. At every stage it appears that our judicial system failed those young men and their heartbroken parents. It was a crime that brought shame on our country. Sonnex had a record of brutality and violence that should have seen him already behind bars for many years. Yet he had not long been released after serving just 4 years of an 8 year sentence. Sonnex served a part of that sentence in the YOI at Portland. If Sonnex had still been in prison two brilliant young Frenchmen would still be alive and their parents would not be facing lifetimes of permanent grief. Incidentally, nearly 60% of those now held in the YOI were convicted of crimes of violence. The case further

Rebecca Lardner and two of her pictures 'Fish Supper **(left)** and 'Checking the Catch' **(right)**. *Pictures: courtesy of DeMontfort Fine Art*

demonstrates the demands upon our prison staff that they have to deal daily with such young men. The failures that led to Sonnex's crimes highlight many appalling deficiencies in our wider criminal justice system.

Dorset is fortunate in that it is relatively free of serious and violent crime but even here there are not dissimilar examples to the one I have highlighted. I will not name 'names' but every reader will know instances in their own communities of thugs escaping with pathetically light sentences after committing acts of extreme violence, or even walking free after serious crimes. Is this the society we wish to bequeath to our children?

If I have used my chapter on Dorchester to raise some controversial issues, I must leave this splendid town on some lighter, happier notes, or its citizens may accuse me of depressing them and that would not be fair.

There is a young lady who now lives in Fordington I knew first 20 years ago as a student in my classroom. Today she is a most accomplished and successful artist. Her father was the gamekeeper on the Encombe estate in the Purbecks and she was brought up as a good country girl with impeccably good manners and possessed of a work ethic which made her determined to make the use of her talents. When I call by on her she welcomes me with the smile I remember and shows me some of her drawings, prints and canvasses. The range of her work is extensive – from jazz musicians to birds, from conventional land and seascapes to her quirky, highly successful scenes of animals and other creatures in amusing situations. Already she has sold a painting to Sir Paul McCartney and she has a waiting list for her original work. I have great pleasure in including, with Rebecca's kind permission, two of my personal favourites. Artistic success could not come to a more charming and

Claire Robertson, and staff of Wellworth's. *Picture: Geoff Moore, Deep South Media Co*

unassuming young lady.

One of the most heart-warming stories of these troubled economic times to capture the imagination not only of local people but the national press, is the re-opening of the former Woolworth's Store in the town. After the financial collapse of the Woolworth chain with debts of £385 million and the closing of 815 stores across the UK, the former manager of the Dorchester store, Claire Roberston, responds to the challenge by persuading an Ireland based consortium to give her the financial backing to re-open. Explaining that the Woolworth's store had always been profitable – and with the enthusiastic support of her staff – Claire has contrived to pull off what many would have thought impossible. The DJ Chris Evans, who'd read about the story in the newspapers, gallantly volunteers to 'open' the store for Claire and, with my good chum Dorchester's Town Crier, Alistair Chisholm, providing lusty vocal support, Wellworth's is opened less than 3 months after Woolworth's closed amidst scenes of great enthusiasm. Claire, the mother of Daniel and Alice, is delighted with the store's early weeks of trading. Absolutely brilliant, Claire, and congratulations all round to everyone involved!

Max Gate with the wonderful Norrie Woodhall, In the spring of 2009

We've not met before this very special afternoon in Max Gate. Devina has helped enormously in setting it up, arranging with Norrie and the various members of the cast I said I'd love to have in our photograph. For several months we feared it might never happen because Norrie was ill and in hospital for quite a few weeks during the winter and, when you're 103 years-old, you need to be mentally and physically tough to battle on. But now the cast is assembling, Brian Caddy from the Barnes Society, Mike Nixon from the Hardy Society and Alistair Chisholm, of course, fresh from his TV appearance at Wellworth's and his triumphant cameo role as an expert on lavatory

At Max Gate with the wonderful 'Norrie'. (Left to right) Alistair Chisholm, Mike Nixon (Hardy Society), Devina Symes, Brian Caddy (Barnes Society), Andrew and Marilyn Leah (tenants of Max Gate). *Picture: Geoff Hill*

fittings. The NT tenants of Max Gate, Andrew Leah and his wife Marilyn, have been very kind too in accommodating us. Andrew and Marilyn have lived at the house since 1994 when they were chosen from a list of 160 applicants to administer the day-to-day running of the house and deal with the press. In recent years they have welcomed 4,000 visitors annually, besides organising educational courses and seminars throughout the year. Andrew shows me the painting the Hardy Society recently purchased and re-hung in the original position it occupied when the great man lived here.

And now here's the lady herself, our celebrity guest, on Devina's arm, looking cool and composed and so very prettily dressed. I've seen the photos of her when she was young. She was a beautiful girl. She still looks radiant and alert. We speak of Hardy and her memories. She's answered the same questions a thousand times but you'd never guess. It was in 1924 that Hardy presented the Hardy Players with his own dramatisation of *Tess of the D'Urbervilles*. Norrie's sister, Gertrude, 10 years her senior, was cast as Tess and Norrie as Liza-Lu. At rehearsal, Hardy sympathetically added an extra line for her. Instead of the two words, 'Tess, Tess', it became 'Tess, Tess, I'm so glad you have come home.' Norrie recalls it as if it was yesterday, her memory unimpaired more than 80 years later. And it's all there, her memories of Hardy and his wife Florence, her country childhood, her relationships with her sisters, her very happy marriage to her beloved Frank Woodhall, her battles with serious illness, her 100th birthday – in her book *'Norrie's Tale'* (Published by Lullworde Publications, 2006). Norrie's also an accomplished painter and no mean poet as the book confirms.

It's photo time. Geoff even persuades the badly behaved Alistair to behave. It's a unique gathering here in Max Gate. I'm so grateful to Norrie and Devina and everyone else for coming along. Andrew and Marilyn have been superb too in accommodating us. None of us will ever forget the moment. Norrie permits me a decorous kiss on the cheek. Thank you, young lady.

I remember many years ago the wonderful John Arlott observed that even if one didn't know it as a fact, Dorchester feels like a county town. Of course, when he was alive Dorchester still retained the long avenues of sycamores, limes and beeches lining the roads leading into the town. Many of those trees have since been felled but, in spite of the changes, he was absolutely right. It is unlike anywhere else in the county. It has known civilisation for more than 2,000 years. It has an air of assurance and dignity befitting the capital of our county. Whatever changes are now taking place Dorchester will quietly absorb them and make them its own. Have I done the town justice? After all, I've written nothing of Maiden Castle, Maumbury Rings or the town's rich historical and archaeological past, but that has all been admirably documented by others better equipped then myself. When I arrived I knew scarcely a soul but I feel I am leaving behind a group of friends. They will be my judges – with kinder hearts, I trust, than another who visited the town more than 300 years ago.

Winfrith

Dorset Police HQ
These are not easy times for the police. The public, in general, doesn't quite know what to think. All men and women of goodwill want to respect and admire our police service. The good old English copper, after all, armed with just his truncheon and whistle, was for generations a model envied across the world. We know there are thousands of brave, principled, conscientious officers carrying out their duties today, often in very difficult circumstances, in the finest traditions of the British police force. Yet there remain serious misgivings too. Some senior figures have not distinguished themselves. Grave difficulties clearly exist within the Met, both at a personal as well as operational level. More general criticisms include a lack of visibility on the streets, a failure to respond to calls and incidents or turning up too late for effective action to be taken, an obsession with political correctness, form-filling, ticking boxes and meeting Government imposed targets, failing on occasion to distinguish between the criminal and the victim and, all too frequently, forgetting to use old-fashioned common sense. The unfortunate consequence is that every police officer in the land carries the burden of public perception, even if it is mistaken or muddled. And that is grossly unfair to many splendid men and women in the force.

It is against this background that I am sitting with Martin Baker, the Chief Constable of Dorset, in an office at Winfrith Police HQ to discuss such matters and, in particular, policing within the county.

Reassuring is the first adjective that springs to mind as I survey my companion across the table. Genial, physically imposing, articulate and clearly highly intelligent, Martin joined the service as an eager young cadet in 1974 and spent 13 years with the Met, much of it with the CID and the anti-terrorist branch then engaged in the struggle against the IRA. Married to Trudi and the father of three daughters, Martin is a well-liked figure within the force and the wider public. Years ago he'd have made an excellent village bobby for he's someone the local community would have instinctively warmed to and trusted. As it is, in a much changed world, he's risen to the lofty heights of Chief Constable and is regarded, to use a modern colloquialism, as 'a safe pair of hands'. On the topic of Chief Constables in general, he has definite opinions.

"I abhor the 'celebrity' Chief Constable. It's not our place to be flamboyant, nor to be involved

The Chief Constable, Martin Baker'.
Picture: Dorset Police

in public or political debate. Least of all, when political begins with a capital P. We should not step outside our fields of expertise. No Chief Constable will ever win a battle with the media. My job is to create an ethos within the force that will bring out the best in everyone."

He's not happy with Dorset's finances and feels the county is short-changed.

"We are not financially well-treated by Government. Dorset is the second worst funded county in the country. The National Funding Formula fails to recognise two facts. It doesn't allow for visitors coming into the county. While the ratio of police to residents is slightly higher than average, our 19 million visitors count for nothing. Last year, for example, 20% of the offences committed in Bournemouth were by outsiders to the town. We have the major problem too of 30,000 stand-up drinking places in Bournemouth alone every week-end. The number of pubs and clubs are averaged out over the whole county but in Bournemouth we have one of the biggest night-time economies in the UK. The net result is that if Dorset had the average funding of a non-metropolitan police force we would receive from Central Government an extra £15 million a year – and that would buy a lot more cops!"

One of the greatest anxieties of our age is the drugs issue. When I was a boy the only individuals who thought drugs 'cool' were American jazz musicians like Chet Baker, Stan Getz and Miles Davis. As a young man in London in the Sixties when drugs began to surface as a problem I and my student friends uniformly regarded the habit as moronic, unhealthy and a waste of money. It might be a habit prevalent among rock musicians but, for the student population subsisting on modest grants – and our numbers in those days were relatively small compared to today – beer, cider and a few cigarettes were our greatest extravagance. Of course, we knew where the trafficking took place. Seedy clubs in Soho always contained a pusher or two though they mostly dabbled in pills that enabled the user to remain awake all night and party into the dawn. I even had a pill-popping, drug-pushing girl-friend briefly whom I met in a club in St. Anne's Court. My efforts to change her ways proved completely futile and our relationship came to an abrupt end when she was arrested and finished up in Holloway prison. The truth is that drugs were not a serious problem outside London and the big cities. Today, it's fair to say drugs are everywhere and a major social evil. And I use the word 'evil' deliberately because I cannot condone their use when I see their effects on so many tragically blighted lives. I feel particularly angry that certain pop-stars and so-called 'celebrities' not only indulge – that is their misguided prerogative – but, by glorifying the habit, encourage others to do so. Their crass stupidity and self-indulgence is compounded when certain companies choose to employ such individuals to advertise and promote their products. Their cynicism and social irresponsibility is beyond belief. Martin Baker does not disagree with my feelings.

"There is no doubt drugs are a major cause of illness and crime and they drive a huge criminal economy as well as running people's lives. Unlike alcohol about which we know a great deal there are such divergent views on individual drugs and their effects. If history tells us anything it is that the product constantly mutates. I do not believe we understand enough to legalise or decriminalise. Meanwhile, there has to be a subtle balance between enforcement, treatment and education. I believe the key question is this. What would you say to your child – and I have three young daughters – if drugs were decriminalised? Would you say that it's OK to take them? I wouldn't want to say that and I doubt many parents would. And, once the genie is out of the bottle, how do you put it back?"

I ask Martin what he thinks of the extended opening hours legislation which was supposed to ease the problem of binge-drinking?

"Last year 38% of the people arrested for being drunk and disorderly were picked up between 1-2am. Now people are being brought in as late as 5am. We have been obliged to alter shift patterns as a consequence – with some real staffing gymnastics. Our forces are stretched and obviously it does take us away from other activities. As for the local authorities, how can they be expected to cope with cleaning up the mess before ordinary citizens come out on the streets in the morning? Unfortunately we have a long way to go before we achieve the continental cafe style culture combined with responsible drinking. I deplore the cheap drinks promotions of the supermarkets and the fact that an awful lot of parents are giving their children money to buy alcohol. Such activities just aggravate the problem."

And what of the endless form-filling we hear so much about?

"We do have to be accountable and we must keep proper records to protect the ordinary citizen but everything we do must be looked at carefully. I do encourage the force to make suggestions for improvement in our practices and we consider thoughtfully the ideas that come forward. At the same time we in Dorset police believe we are as efficient as any force nationwide. We have a computer system linked to one data base and we will shortly have the facility that will enable officers to write up their reports on their computers when they are in their cars, thus obviating the need to return constantly to their offices."

What of some of the broader criticisms about not appearing to care about a range of 'lesser' crimes?

"The public do clearly lose confidence if we do nothing – or appear to do nothing. We must try hard to explain exactly what we are doing. We employ a team of trained professional analysts who are looking constantly at reported crimes. Can we establish a pattern of some sort? Has there been a spate of such crimes? Are we likely to know the probable offender from the methodology employed? With the aid of modern technology we are trying to discover links. In short, we are using a number of such procedures that are unseen by the public in order to detect the criminals."

And crime statistics? This is an area riddled by manipulation and spin of the most deplorable kind. The public is legitimately incensed if it feels it is being hoodwinked by Government or the police.

"Statistics are often confusing. Take assaults – most are between people who know one another. They are in some sort of relationship. If one of the parties doesn't wish a prosecution we cannot claim it as a detected crime even though we have effectively sorted it out. There are many other areas where statistics simply don't tell the whole story."

I invite Martin to sum up the Dorset Police Force, as he sees it.

"I've worked in five different forces and Dorset is by far the best. On various counts I believe we are performing outstandingly. Overall crime is at an all-time five year low, the calibre of my colleagues is exceptional, public confidence has grown and we are now achieving the highest level of confidence of any force in the country."

Martin was recently in China on a fact-finding mission examining security arrangements at the Beijing Olympic Games.

"The sailing events were staged 500 miles from the capital and the Chinese erected a 35 square mile exclusion zone round the venue at Qingdao. They were taking no chances!"

China, of course, remains a dictatorship, albeit a more benevolent one than in the days of Chairman Mao, and can more readily impose draconian restrictions. The same measures are hardly open to Martin and the Dorset police when they are arranging security for the 2012 Sailing events at Weymouth and Portland. Whilst the competitors are, I understand, staying on board cruise liners anchored in the harbour, large numbers of spectators will be converging on the Dorset coast to watch on the giant screens erected on the sands. If not presenting quite the logistical difficulties the Met face in London, Martin and his colleagues will certainly face some major challenges.

"Success will be some gold, silver and bronze for the competitors and a peaceful and enjoyable time for the spectators and, hopefully, some warm sunshine!"

And we can all say Amen to that, Martin.

(A Post Script to my conversation with Martin. I am disturbed to read in the Echo, not long after our meeting, two separate pieces by reporters Darren Slade and Paula Roberts in which they reveal that, under the Freedom of Information Act, the paper has discovered a number of curious anomalies in the published statistics of Dorset Police. Taking the month of October as an example, Darren says that Dorset Police gave details of fewer than 35 crimes when there were 3,573 crimes committed; just 12 cases of violence against the person were revealed compared with 800 recorded; no sexual offences were revealed when 70 were recorded; 5 robberies revealed against 26 recorded. Bob Satchwell, the director of the Society of Editors, comments: "It just beggars belief that the police are withholding information on this scale. The public have a right to know what's going on in their midst and in their communities." The Bournemouth councillor, Nick King, a member of the police authority, suggests a part of the problem might be 'the target based culture imposed by the Government.' He adds: "There's something built into the system that discourages people from being up front about what's happening. But the fact is that withholding information is unwise because it only makes people suspicious."

Disappointingly, although Dorset Police employs a dozen full-time PR staff, when I speak to Darren he says no one from the authority is prepared to comment on his findings.

I would make an appeal to our Chief Constable. I have no doubt there are explanations for the discrepancies in the figures provided. I also know that 'crime statistics' can be misinterpreted and misleading. But, insofar as it is possible, please let us have transparency. Let not niggling doubts remain in the public's mind. We prefer the truth. We know you are working hard on our behalf and doing an excellent job. Have enough confidence in the common sense of the Dorset public to let them make reasoned judgements on the actual figures. In the past year we have discovered many ugly truths in our public and business life. Honesty is the only way forward.)

Winfrith UKAEA

I must confess I have no understanding of the science but the current plan is that the old nuclear site will be 'fully decommissioned' by the year 2018 and returned to non-nuclear use by 2020. A substantial funding cut affecting both Winfrith and its sister site, Harwell in Oxfordshire, has apparently slowed down the whole process of 'decommissioning' and its return to its original heath-land status. Notwithstanding the delays, the head of the site, Andy Staples, reports continued progress.

I understand all the above ground structures of the A59 building have now been demolished and work continues on the removal of below ground structures When it is completed a remarkable era in the history of Winfrith will have ended.

Whitcombe

Whitcombe Manor

"How do I see Dorset? The Ridgeway, the valleys, the big houses, the small communities – the same ones Hardy and Barnes saw and wrote about. As a writer I find it easier to write about the small community with its claustrophobic element, the dysfunctional families, the clashes of personality, the wife with nothing better to do than criticise her husband or children, a psychopathic figure in their midst. I love to plant red herrings, persuade the reader to like the bad character. Since I was a child I have immersed myself in crime fiction – writers such as Patricia Highsmith, Agatha Christie, Conan Doyle, Georges Simenon."

With 25 million books sold and translated into as many languages, Minette Walters today enjoys

Minette Walters 'I love to plant red herrings, persuade the reader to like the bad character'. *Picture: Geoff Hill*

a reputation as one of the most popular 'psychological thriller' writers. Yet it was not a success easily gained. The daughter of an army officer she graduated in French at Durham before embarking upon a career as a journalist writing romantic and serialised fiction, all the while honing her literary skills.

"My first novel *The Ice Age* was with an agent for two years before Heinemann bought it. I was advised to reduce my original 105,000 words to 80,000 so I removed a peripheral character and, to my delight and astonishment, I won the John Creasey Prize for Best First Novel."

The material rewards of Minette's worldwide success are all around her. She shares Whitcombe Manor and its 100 acres with her husband, Alec, a former finance director, internet businessman and part-time farmer. It is a superb property, tastefully extended to accommodate its latest addition – an orangery.

"Each book pays for something else in the house," she laughs. "Actually Whitcombe was in the Domesday Book. There were just 7 villagers, 2 slaves and 5 smallholders."

Alec is the historian and locates the entry in his modern copy of the great Norman volume.

"It hasn't changed that much. About the same number of people and Alec and I are the 2 slaves!"

Minette laughs frequently, often most engagingly at herself. We discover we even share the same academic qualifications – 2.2s from our respective universities.

"Mind, those were the days when not many got 2.1s and scarcely anyone, except the geniuses got a First!"

Monica Hutchings described Whitcombe *'as being almost too good to be true, especially when it is located right beside an A road.'*

"Actually Whitcombe's a remarkable little community. At our Christmas festival we have over 100 in the church and there's a wonderful feeling. William Barnes was, of course, the curate here for 4 years. And in the locality we have some great characters – like Paul Moxon, for instance, who recently celebrated his sixtieth birthday. He lives at Number 1, Whitcombe. He was the poultry-man here. He introduced me to so many people. Alec couldn't have succeeded with the farm if it wasn't for Paul. He hasn't got a passport and he's only been to London once. But what a marvellous man! And not far away there's John Randall and his wife Dorothy- he's 92 and the Dorset downs guru. There's nothing he doesn't know about the Dorset countryside. And his wife cooks the finest beef I've ever tasted. Then there's Tony Swain, an amazing shepherd, and Fred Mabey who held the poacher's franchise!'London's up north', he would say. A typical old-fashioned truly Dorset person."

Back to literary matters. Does Minette entertain hopes of winning one of the more 'serious' highbrow awards?

"The Booker Prize? Too often intellectual snobbery invades. Besides, how many people actually read some of those books?"

Minette admires enormously a number of her contemporaries – Ian Rankin, Colin Dexter and Ruth Rendell.

"I believe Ruth is quite capable of writing 'a great novel.' But Ruth prefers to pursue her own particular genre. The best books anyway transcend the category the publishers choose to put them in. Writers like Harper Lee and Daphne du Maurier's work will stand the test of time because it is, by any standards, very good work. As for myself, I will continue to do what I do best and try to produce a book every year. We'll have to see what happens."

The little girl who first saw Dorset from her father's boat – Chapman's Pool and Weymouth were particular holiday favourites – has journeyed a long way in the past twenty years and entertained a great many readers. Long may she continue to do so.

Whitcombe Racing Stables

Jo Crowley meets me at the door. Jo is Liz Nelson's trainer at Whitcombe. She ushers me into the office where Liz is on the phone. Seated in her wheelchair beside the window the lady is laughing loudly. Photographs of racehorses hang from every wall, form and breeding books line the shelves, back copies of the Racing Post sit in a pile on the table. Liz finishes her conversation.

"I'm off to Doncaster Sales next week. With the economic recession I'm hoping it'll be a buyer's market."

Liz has spent a lifetime with horses – hunting, breeding, owning and training. Two years ago she realised her dream by buying Whitcombe outright. Originally developed by Peter Bolton 20 years ago, it had fallen into a state of disrepair. Its new owner was under no illusions that a large investment of time and capital were essential if former glories were to be restored. Big names have trained here like Toby Balding, David Elsworth, Reg Akehurst and Gaye Kelleway. Equine legends like Morley Street and Cool Ground have paraded their talents here.

"We've got 14 in at the moment. Jo's brilliant and we've already enjoyed success. When everything is finished there'll be 5 yards. Three of them I'll let to other trainers. Failing that I'll use them for retired racehorses, or as rehabilitation or equestrian centres. Besides the grass and all-weather gallops, we also have 86 acres of corn, 14 acres of woodland and 107 acres of paddock."

The phone rings again and there's more exuberant laughter. The lady clearly possesses a great zest for life despite breaking her neck in a car accident in 1974 and spending much of her life since confined to a wheelchair. Residents of Higher Eype, where she still lives, will remember her days at the Eype Mouth Hotel. In Bridport she ran The Bull Hotel. She's also a gifted musician, having trained as a harpist at the Royal Academy of Music. She reminds me a little of my old friend Louie Dingwall, the Sandbanks racehorse trainer, one of the first three ladies to hold a licence to train in her own right. Liz is possessed of the same dogged determination to ignore physical disabilities and make the most of every waking moment.

"We're launching a bid with Kingston Maurward to provide an equestrian centre for competitors for the 2012 Olympics. It has to be situated within a four hours drive of London. Many will be bringing their animals over a couple of years before the event. Last year I bought a lovely eventer in Ireland called Oslo that I've sent to our Olympic bronze medallist, William Fox-Pitt. We've high hopes of him for 2012."

The phone rings again. The lady is a human dynamo. Notwithstanding her innumerable interests what impresses me most is her commitment to help others less fortunate than herself. She's on a 24 hour call for Motor Neurone disease patients – at any time of the day or night she might get a call.

"It helps that they can talk to someone when they feel lonely or depressed. As often as I can I go to visit them."

She's also an active member of the Weldmar Trust hospice where I know she's warmly regarded. She's also a Friend of the Mountjoy Special School for severely handicapped children at Bridport.

Liz Nelson is a special lady and I feel privileged to have made her acquaintance. I hope she finds a bargain basement equine star at Doncaster and a horse to put Whitcombe back on the map.

Tolpuddle

Just days before the July rally

"I can remember when we'd have 4,000 farm-workers here for the July march. This year I doubt there'll be fifty."

We're in Oliver Trevett's vegetable garden at Number 6, Memorial Cottages, erected in 1934 to commemorate the centenary of the Martyrs' transportation to Australia, admiring Oliver's tomatoes

Tony Gould and friends, Tolpuddle, 2008.

and onions. With me is my old friend of QEGS days and retired trade union organiser, Tony Gould, and 84 year-old Ron Dyer who lives at number 5. It was way back in 1962 that Oliver was elected branch secretary of the National Union of Agricultural Workers at Winterbourne Stickland. At 81 he's still the branch secretary of what is now the Agricultural section of the Unite Union, even though the number of farm workers and union members has shrunk to a tiny proportion of their former totals. In my youth I made the acquaintance of Arthur Jordan, then the secretary of the Dorset branch of the union and an active Communist in the days when the British Communist Party could still boast 40,000 members. At the time Jordan represented several thousand farm workers in the county. Half a century on with farming changed beyond all recognition, one man and a single employee and a team of seasonal contractors can harvest hundreds of acres in a matter of days. The size and nature of the labour force has changed too and, though the union can still play a valuable role is assisting its members, its broader influence is much reduced.

Just 4 days remain before the annual rally and Tony and I tramp across the adjacent field to exchange pleasantries with Dick Muskett, a Tolpuddle rally veteran, busily preparing the area for the imminent arrival of several hundred campers. For once this miserable summer a fine week-end is promised and, as one of the founders of the Worker's Beer Company, Dick anticipates a hectic weekend. Tony's wife Liz, the secretary of the Village Hall committee, is no less occupied with a band of helpers preparing for the many hungry mouths that will be in search of sustenance – all profits, quite appropriately, to the Village Hall fund.

How did my old chum Tony arrive back in the county after so many years in exile?

"There was an element of chance about it really. Had another property in a different village caught our imagination we might well have settled elsewhere."

But when Number 1, Manor Farm Cottages, Tolpuddle, appeared on the market it proved, unsurprisingly irresistible. I suggest Tolpuddle must feel like his spiritual home and he doesn't disagree.

But what, I wonder, would George and James Loveless, John and Thomas Standfield, James Brine and James Hammett make of the village today? Certain physical features they'd recognise without difficulty – the main street winding through the village past the sycamore (a younger specimen) and the church of St. John's on its way to Dorchester. What would astonish them, however, are the properties lining the main road and a number of the new developments lying to their rear. Three hundred thousand pounds would buy very few. Half a million would be nearer the mark in many instances. Although inflation has made a nonsense of comparative prices, the reality is that Tolpuddle is manifestly no longer a poor village. It is, in fact, a gentrified village, highly desirable, with properties much sought after. Since the by-pass was opened through traffic is negligible, yet access to neighbouring Dorchester, Poole, Bournemouth and the coast is easy and quick. The transformation is almost complete. Hammett's grave in the churchyard – he was the only one to return to the village- and the tablet on the side of the Methodist chapel honouring the 6 men, the Memorial Cottages and the Martyr's Inn (once the Horse and Groom) are all reminders of Tolpuddle's historic significance in the Labour and trade union movement. There are few today who would not acknowledge the courage of George Loveless and his friends, nor the justice of their cause. They were good men cruelly treated by representatives of a landowning class who heartlessly abused their power and privilege. Though we live today in a society in which most of the remnants of that old power have thankfully disappeared I, and no doubt most of the readers of these pages, will from time suffer the misfortune of meeting an individual who clearly shares the mentality of that bygone age when the whim of a rich man, or woman, could lead to dismissal, eviction, or worse. On such occasions I find myself thanking my lucky stars that I live in a democratic age when my vote is as good as that of anyone else and I can speak my mind freely. But, back to the Tolpuddle of today, for in some ways it is curiously at odds with its heritage.

"Tolpuddle does reflect," says my friend Tony, "the wider changes of contemporary society."

The annual rally presents a different face too. There was a period in post-war Britain when it was all but obligatory for the leaders of Old Labour to establish their Socialist credentials by joining the march and speaking on the platform. Messrs. Healey, Kinnock, Foot and Benn all attended. Many Labour MPs were sponsored by the unions and owed their seats to their paymasters. But New Labour is a different kettle of fish. It is impossible to imagine a day when David Miliband, Ed Balls and Lord Mandelson would ever link hands and march in solidarity through the village.

"What sort of reception would they receive?" asks Tony with a wry smile. "And, as importantly, what would Middle England think?"

One figure alone reappears with absolute regularity. Tony Benn may be widely regarded as a misguided, political 'daydreamer' but, at least, he has not betrayed his principles and he is equally known to be a thoroughly pleasant and kindly man. Each July his speech is the best received and he is warmly welcomed by the representatives of left-wing Labour Party branches, trade unionists, eco-warriors, CND, Friends of the Earth, Amnesty International and similar focus groups who make up the bulk of those who attend the rallies.

Tolpuddle retains a romantic resonance for many who come down every July, often to renew old acquaintance. Not that there was anything remotely romantic about the events of 1834. It is entirely appropriate that the Six Men of Dorset should continue to be remembered for the sacrifices they made on behalf of working people everywhere. But I find creeping insidiously into the contemporary equation certain inconvenient questions such as – what on earth do some of the 'fat-cat' union bosses like Derek Simpson, Dave Prentis and Brian Caton, with their six-figure salary and pension packages have in common with George Loveless and his impoverished companions? Precious little, I fear. And what does the man who will carry the Tolpuddle banner at the march this year, my old friend, Tony Gould, think of the future of Tolpuddle and the rallies?

"I believe Tolpuddle will remain, certainly for the foreseeable future, as a festival for Socialists and radicals of all descriptions."

And the good citizens of the village – what is their attitude?

"One of benign tolerance," smiles Tony. "And, of course, the pub will do good business."

(In the event this year's rally attracted thousands to the village which was staged in near perfect weather conditions. It was described by one of the organisers, Nigel Costley, the TUC South West Regional Secretary,as 'brilliant, by far the best yet, a triumph.' And Liz Gould and her valiant team of helpers raised nearly £1,700 for the Village Hall Fund!)

Wool

Monkey World

How to begin, for I want to get this right, both for Jim Cronin and Alison? One was a very remarkable man, the other is a no less remarkable woman.

I suppose I first learned of the madcap venture when I picked up a copy of the *Echo* 20 years ago and read about an American who planned a monkey sanctuary near Wool. I knew the general location well enough – though not the detail that it was actually on the site of a derelict pig-farm. That won't last long, I recall, was my initial response. I knew nothing of the economics of the situation, of course. Did the fellow have any capital behind him? Probably not, I suspected. But it was a story for the *Echo* journalists to cover so the reports continued to appear. It was probably quite a pleasant escape from the offices on Richmond Hill to get out into the Dorset countryside. I don't remember the exact date we first went over as a family to have a look at Monkey World but it was probably about 18 months after Jim Cronin openedup. The weather was, as it so often is in the UK, nothing very special. The site looked particularly drab that day, the enterprise seemed barely up and running and we saw disappointingly little of the monkeys. Unlike some more fortunate souls, I didn't meet Jim. I understand he actually escorted some sceptical, disappointed visitors around the site himself, explained his vision, filled them with his own enthusiasm and they left converted. My first impressions were not so much unfavourable, rather I left waiting to be convinced. Besides, my daughter liked the monkeys she did actually get to see.

So the years passed and, like millions of others, I was entranced by the TV series Monkey Business. We got to see and know the characters who lived in the sanctuary, both primates and staff – like Charlie the chimpanzee and the 'Bachelor boys' and, of course, Jim's right-hand man, the ever dependable Jeremy Keeling. Naturally, the Echo continued to cover the events in Wool. We learned of the journeys Jim was making across the world to rescue primates from a variety of unhappy situations. Another name began to appear too alongside Jim's, that of his new wife Alison.

"I grew up in Southern California. I always loved the outdoors, the wildness, the overgrown scrubland, riding horses, swimming – there were no Barbie dolls in my childhood. That just wasn't me. My parents were always very supportive. I was passionate too about archaeology and I also found myself becoming ever more interested in anthropology. After graduating from High School and university I applied to come to Selwyn College, Cambridge for a year as a foreign student. I guess I impressed them enough to let me stay for another 3 years to read biological anthropology."

We're sitting in Alison's log cabin office this morning in Monkey World – Alison, Sarah Lambert, her personal assistant, and me. Alison is tanned, dressed in a tee shirt and shorts, slim, pretty, feminine. She's also courteous and charming.

Johni, Jeremy Keeling, Jim Cronin and Alison. *Picture: Monkey World*

"I emerged from Cambridge with a BA and MA. I finished at Selwyn in 1989. I met Jim in 1991."

In a sense we know much of the rest of the story because the lives of Jim and Alison and Monkey World became public property through scores of newspaper and magazine articles and, above all, through the wonders of television. Their record is there for us all to see, rescuing capuchins from solitary laboratory cages in Santiago where they were confined for up to 20 years, only being removed for medical experiments, saving chimpanzees from photographers in Spain where they were used as tourist props, liberating a chimp being cruelly exploited in a Bangkok zoo – the stories are legion and unfailingly heart-warming. Monkey World is home also to 2 thriving groups of Woolly Monkeys which originate in the area of the Northern Amazon but are declining fast because of habitat loss. In fact, Monkey World is also playing an important role in world-wide breeding programmes, not just of Woolly Monkeys but other primates such as orang-utans and golden-cheeked gibbons. It is a record of enormous achievement that justly earned Jim an MBE from Her Majesty 'for services to animal welfare.'

So much then for all our initial scepticism about the staying power of this American and his eccentric but brilliant vision – he confounded every one of the doubting Thomases, including this writer. So just where did the man originate and what was his background? Born in New York in 1952 Jim was the son of Irish-Italian parents and first became involved with primates while working at the Bronx Zoo, before moving to Britain in 1980 to take up a position at John Aspinall's wildlife park Howletts. There he set up a primate breeding programme before deciding to develop a monkey conservation park along with business partner Steve Matthews. It all sounds so straight-forward now, doesn't it? Except that no one had ever undertaken such an ambitious programme before with primates, least of all in such an unlikely location as Wool in the heart of the Dorset countryside.

And Jim's timing was crucial coming at a moment when the very survival of many species across the world was threatened as never before.

So, at Christmas, 2006, everything seemed set fair. Jim and Alison were working on an exciting new project in Vietnam at the Dao Tien Rescue Centre besides a host of other imaginative ideas for the future at Monkey World, when suddenly their world was turned upside down. They had just completed a mission in Mexico to rescue a young chimpanzee being used as a photographic prop and were unwinding in Australia when Jim began to feel ill. He was experiencing increasing pain in his side. Within days tests confirmed advanced liver cancer. Intending to return to England in stages, they reached Los Angeles before travelling on to New York. By now Jim was desperately ill and, on March 17, aged just 55, St. Patrick's Day, Jim died in the Cabrini Medical Centre at Mount Sinai hospital in the city in which he was born. Everything had happened so quickly.

The word 'tragedy' is used so carelessly in the modern world that I will return once more to my *Shorter Oxford Dictionary*. 'Tragedy' – 'An unhappy, terrible or fatal event in life. A calamity, a disaster.' By any standards, Jim's death was truly a tragedy. At a personal level, for his wife Alison, it was the most dreadful, agonising loss. After all, Jim died long before even the proverbial three-score years and ten he might reasonably have expected. When so many in today's world live way beyond that age, Jim's life was cut cruelly and abruptly short. And here was a man, not on the verge of retirement, but one who still had so much to do with his life, so much to give, so many projects buzzing around in his head, so much energy and passion.

The shock of Jim's death was reflected in the national and local papers. Neil Butterworth, the Echo's Editor and a personal friend of Jim and Alison, ran the following headlines on successive days 'Monkey World's Jim dies. Liver cancer claims the life of the man who saved the apes.' And 'Jim Cronin, Monkey World founder 1952-2007. Your work will live on. Wife Alison's pledge to continue 20 year legacy.'

At Monkey World the letters of condolence poured in from across the nation and beyond. The tributes flowed in too from many of Jim's distinguished friends and supporters in the world of conservation – individuals like Ian Redmond, Will Travers, Robbie Marsland and Cyril Rosen. Jez Hermer, the spokesman for Monkey World commented:"Jim was larger than life. If he hadn't been so full of energy, he couldn't have achieved the things he did."

And now here I am 18 months on sitting with his widow wondering how on earth I can possibly do justice to a man who really did stamp his mark on the world and leave it a better place? I am sad that I never met Jim for then I would have my own particular image and would better be able to conjure up the right formula of words. And then, of course, there is Alison herself. Even as we chat the telephone is constantly interrupting us. She's just making plans to fly to Spain on another mission. When she returns it will be with another very fortunate primate who will live out his life with his own kind and receive the very best of everything Alison and her staff can provide. Next month it might be another batch of primates from animal labs or a call from another pet-owner unable to cope. Who knows what's round the corner? The only certainty is that Alison and her team will respond.

I decide to ask her the question though we both recognise the difficulty of the answer. In fact, Alison reads my thoughts, not for the first time this morning, with uncanny accuracy even as I begin my circuitous approach.

"Animal experiments to benefit mankind?"

I don't say the words but she knows exactly what I'm driving at – I'm asking her for her views on the ethical justification of experiments to discover cures for terrible illnesses like cancer. The cancer that killed Jim, for example.

Alison pauses. I know she's thought through these matters in her own mind a thousand times before. Is my question even fair in the circumstances?

"We don't take a moral stand. Rather we start with the premise that medical research is happening all around us. We offer our services to re-home those primates which are no longer required. Labs do contact us directly. I also believe passionately that Government bears a great responsibility to ensure that all animals are kept in the most humane conditions. There should always, for example, be companion animals. Loneliness can be as distressing for any animal as a human. No animal should be kept in solitary confinement."

The future of Monkey World – where does it go from here?

"What are our priorities? Welfare clearly is number one – that and education. And by education, I mean, reminding the public about the cruelties of the pet trade, about habitat destruction, about preserving species. We want to continue to develop that area of our work here – to educate young people, above all, for they are the next generation. We must inform them so they will, in turn, continue the work we are doing now."

How many primates are in the sanctuary at the moment? And staff?

Alison rustles through the papers on her desk. "As of this moment the figure is 235 and 80 staff – approximately."

Aside from bearing the ultimate responsibility for 235 primates and 80 staff, what about the mundane but not inconsequential issue of the financial ledgers, balancing income and expenditure, keeping the very expensive ship that is Monkey World afloat?

Alison laughs. "That's down to me too. That's my responsibility. But we do try to be efficient. We recycle a lot."

And 'leisure time' – whatever 'leisure time' she permits herself which is, I suspect, very little?

"I do love my garden. And I read – detective fiction like Patricia Highsmith. I listen to music. Mostly rock n' roll – the Rolling Stones. They were my era. Sport? I am quite interested in soccer. I was actually the captain of Cambridge ladies soccer XI. In the States soccer is actually more of a girl's game. And I love travelling which is fortunate because I do a lot of it. Naturally too I love seeing my family. My parents come over once a year. My sister Eleanor is presently in Papua, New Guinea. And you've met Bella my Great Dane."

I'm not going to ask the obvious fatuous questions for Alison and I both know the answers. But she does volunteer a thought or two.

"It does make it easier working here every day – being constantly occupied. Jim's presence is everywhere. And I love seeing him on film, seeing his smile. I embrace all that. We were so perfect for one another."

As I walk back to my car, the day's visitors are filing in. They're all ages, all colours and creeds and nationalities. Lots of eager-eyed children inevitably, lots of smiles generally. Even the bold visionary Jim Cronin would never have dared to dream 20 years ago his idea would come this far. Monkey World, nationally and internationally known and respected – and loved. It is desperately sad that Jim has gone. He deserved better. His memory will live on though that is but small consolation to his friends and, above all, to Alison. But his legacy is tremendous and I do not exaggerate. Monkey World is not a zoo. That's something that Jim taught us. It provides a happy home for primates living as close to a natural life as possible. It's also a place of serious scientific study and learning and a location where a number of breeding species may be saved from extinction in the wild. It is also fun and education for the tens of thousands of visitors each year and provides entertainment and enlightenment in equal measure on our screens. It is an extraordinary creation.

I leave with another thought. Jim made lots of decisions in his lifetime. Like all of us, some were right and others were wrong. Just occasionally we make a decision in our lives that is touched with inspiration and even genius. In 1991 Jim Cronin met Alison, and later asked her to become his wife. At that moment Jim could have no idea how his life would evolve or how many years he had remaining to him to continue his great work. But, what is beyond all dispute and self-evidently true, is that in choosing Alison he found someone both intellectually capable and possessed of the necessary courage and determination to continue his life's work after he was taken from us so suddenly and so prematurely. I will repeat the words I wrote at the beginning.

One was a very remarkable man, the other is a no less remarkable woman.

Bovington

The Army camp

"The Roman centurion used his shield and helmet, the knight of old employed his body armour and vizard, but there always existed a critical balance between protection and mobility."

We have been discussing the role and effectiveness of armoured vehicles in Iraq and Afghanistan and the criticism levelled at the MOD that it has been too slow in providing adequate protection for our servicemen in conflict areas. My companions are experts in their fields, Colonel David Swann MBE, Commander of the Bovington Garrison and the Armour Centre, Lt. Col. Richard 'Sid' James, Chief of Staff of the Armour Centre and David's right-hand man and Lt. Col Chris Donoghy, formerly of the Royal Signals, now the civilian Commander of the Training Areas of Bovington and Lulworth. Richard continues his analysis of the dilemma.

"It is possible to manufacture an almost impregnable tank but it wouldn't be sufficiently mobile for a variety of situations – for use in narrow streets, for example, or where speed is of the essence."

David highlights the difficulties that confront the MOD.

"They have to commission, manufacture, and get into service the appropriate vehicles for a variety of very different situations. The theatres of war vary so greatly. Such a procedure takes time whereas insurgents and terrorists can and do speedily exchange information on the Internet, swopping tips and giving advice on how to exploit any vulnerability in our (the Allies) equipment."

"The Armed Services need a 'golfbag' of vehicles to respond to these challenges -anything from lightly armoured vehicles to heavily armoured tanks," adds Richard. "It is easy to criticise but criticism is not always fair, though if you are the parent of a young man killed or injured in combat, anger and frustration are easily understood. Public money has to be spent wisely and a tank can easily cost £5 million and upwards."

There is no doubt that of our contemporary institutions the Armed forces are the most widely admired and respected, so it is with particular pleasure that I am today sitting in the office of Col. David Swann at the home of the Royal Armoured Corps at Bovington.

"Not only our physical but our spiritual home," David adds with a smile.

Bovington, of course, is where it all began in the early months of WW1 before the first of the great lumbering giants, initially labelled 'mobile forts', made their presence felt in the closing stages of the Battle of the Somme in 1916.

"There are 11 regiments, each one recruiting in different areas of the country," explains Chris Donoghy. "Here young soldiers arrive to undergo preliminary training in tanks and reconnaissance vehicles, and more experienced soldiers learn to use new equipment and gain additional skills – all a part of their career progression."

Today the MOD training grounds cover 2,661 acres of Bovington and a further 7,338 acres of Lulworth which is used for gunnery training, a combined acreage almost equivalent to any of the four largest landed estates in the county.

I ask Chris about the general arrangements relating to recruits in the modern army.

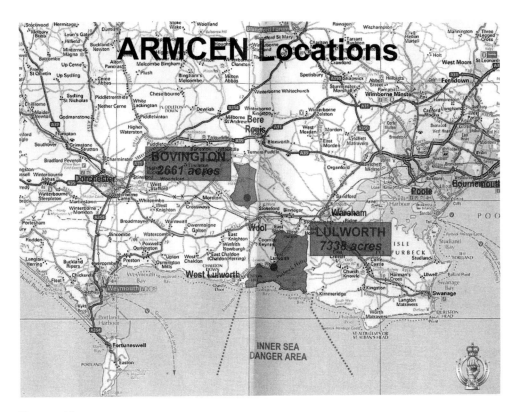

The map of the army ranges

"In Phase 1 after a soldier joins the Army he or she has 14 weeks initial training elsewhere. Within that period they are free to leave if they feel the service life is not for them. Phase 2 is the point at which soldiers begin their training here, learning to operate armoured vehicles, on average spending 3-4 months in training. About 600 pass through that procedure each year. In addition, we have another 5,500 arriving for advanced training. At any one time we'd have 450 soldiers here. Everyone initially learns on our all-weather circuit before progressing to public roads. I think most members of the public prefer it that way! We also practise low-level war games. Lulworth, of course, is for gunnery training when the ranges are closed to the public and an offshore exclusion zone comes into force."

David, Chris and Richard, affectionately known as 'Sid', have all enjoyed their military service enormously. Sandhurst educated David, who married a Winfrith girl, extols the virtues of the variety provided by service life.

"I've travelled widely and it's tremendously stimulating to meet fresh challenges every 2 or 3 years. We are all constantly learning new skills."

For Richard and Chris, being a soldier means being a part of 'a highly respected profession' in which they have shared the company of splendid colleagues and found a great sense of fulfilment.

And what of the camp itself and its relationship with the local community – is it an integral part? Chris picks up the threads.

"There's a smaller number of soldiers here than in the past, of course. Many people remember the Junior Leaders and their association with Bovington but they departed 15 years ago. Many of the former army houses have been sold off. Those here with their families today are generally training other soldiers. We do try to foster a good relationship with our local community and I believe we succeed. An example would be the OAP lunches at the Memorial Hall and there's a youth club where the facilities are shared between the Army and local young people. Colonel Swann is a governor of a couple of local schools and also the Vice-President of the Dorset Youth association. There's also the Saddle Club with about one third Army members and two thirds civilians enjoying the riding. That represents a very important link between the Army and the community."

How does see Chris relations between Army personnel and the wider public? We've all heard appalling stories in recent times like the one in which a young soldier was denied a hotel room precisely because he was a soldier, and other examples of servicemen being abused by extremist sections of the Moslem community – though not in Dorset.

"Reinforcing links with the public at large is, I believe, of great importance. We actively encourage our men to wear their uniforms on their way to and from work, or when going to a shop or filling station, or to the station. We also expect them to wear their uniforms at public functions."

At a time when a large swathe of the British public are heartily sick of over-paid, foul-mouthed 'entertainers' and too many ill-disciplined, uncouth and obscenely rewarded footballers, I sense a widespread feeling that we should swop our role models, abandon the obsession with 'celebrity', and recognise those in many walks of life who are the true, often unseen heroes of our country. The British Armed Services have consistently earned our gratitude and respect by the manner in which they have, almost without exception, conducted themselves in modern times. It has been a pleasure and a privilege to be with David, Richard and Chris this autumn afternoon.

The Tank Museum

Work continues apace at the Museum for the grand opening next year of the £16.5million redevelopment project, aimed to coincide with the 70th anniversary of the Bovington based Royal Armoured Corps. Of course, the man who deserves so much of the credit for the original Museum is still with us, Lt. Col George Forty who, after a very distinguished military career, became the director and curator in 1981.Having visited the Museum many times over the years, often with school parties, I know just what a brilliant job Lt. Col Forty performed in expanding the collection of tanks and armoured vehicles and he deservedly was awarded an OBE for his services. As if doing this wasn't enough, the gentleman from Briantspuddle has also contrived to write 50 books and he edits the magazine *Tank* with his son Jonathan. I suspect he's still running 10 miles a day, milking a couple of cows and looking after a very large garden with his wife Anne. Meanwhile, Nik Wyness, the spokesman for the Museum, is looking forward eagerly to the opening in 2009.

"The new exhibition looks absolutely amazing. I know visitors will be delighted."

We all look forward to seeing it next year.

East Stoke

My first acquaintance with East Stoke was many years ago when I used to deliver one of the finest students it has been my privilege to teach, Alistair Matcham, back to the small cottage that stood by the level crossing. Alistair's father manned the local box as the trains passed to and from Dorchester and Weymouth, and we were rehearsing extracts from a school production of Goldsmith's *She Stoops To Conquer*. With buses few and far between it wasn't easy for many of our pupils to get home if they stayed after school. In those days the village still had a primary school, a functioning church and a post office – and prior to that a village shop – all are now memories. But, even with those facilities, it was still a quiet backwater. It's even quieter today, so imagine my surprise when I saw the headline just a few months earlier in a major daily 'The Mouse that Roared'. It was an account of a referendum conducted by the Parish Council on the question 'Do you want a referendum on the EU Constitutional Treaty?' Discovering a little-known clause in the Local Government Act of 1972 the Parish Council had succeeded in doing what no other similar body in the whole of the UK had achieved. Of its 369 residents 80 voted with a resounding 90% casting their votes in favour of the proposal.

As Darren Patterson observed: "This is a massive turnout for the parish. Hopefully it will be the start of bigger things to come. Surely the Prime Minister Gordon Brown will listen."

Villagers Jim and Iris Boll, Gemma Malbon and Imre Niedermayer, landlord of the Stokeford Inn, all enthused that the democratic process was being used by local people in an issue of importance to them. Alas, Darren Patterson's optimistic reflection has produced no discernible result as yet.

Now, as I drive through the parish, the village is debating the possibility of a wind farm at Master's Pit, off the Puddletown Road. Will 6 x 125 metre turbines capable of generating 18 megawatts of electricity, sufficient power to serve 10,000 households, be permitted to be built? The landowner, Will Bond, believes the site is entirely suitable. Barry Quinn, East Stoke Parish and Purbeck District Councillor, who lives in adjacent Binnegar, wants to know more about the implications. Unsurprisingly, in the light of East Stoke's recent democratic foray, no fewer than 150 residents and others possibly affected by the development have just packed the D'Urberville Hall in Wool to listen to the arguments for and against the proposal. Peter Barker, a founder member of the group called Say Yes to Wind Power, recently launched in Wareham, believes the public response is overwhelmingly in favour. However, Terry Stewart, chairman of the Dorset Campaign to Protect Rural England, is sceptical. An ally of DART, Dorset against Wind Turbines, he believes it is imperative that everyone is fully aware of the implications of any such development in the vicinity.

Forty years ago, when first I came to East Stoke, coal-fired stations were still producing much of the UK's energy with coal mined in British mines. Atomic energy was in its infancy. We'd never heard of global warming or solar power, renewable and sustainable were adjectives as uncommon as obese and to be 'gay' meant to be light-hearted, and the idea of wind turbines at East Stoke would have been regarded as unlikely as a black President of the USA.

Piddletrenthide

The Manor House

"Dear Kenneth Grahame could never have realised some of the consequences when he wrote *Wind in the Willows*. It was a wonderful book and generations have enjoyed it but, ever since, everyone has been influenced by the character of Mr. Badger. Gruff but good-hearted and kind, every reader loves him. And, indeed, the badger is a very handsome animal and none of us wish him harm. But there is a real problem in the countryside. It's beyond dispute, I think, that he carries bovine TB and there is cross-infection with cattle, deer too in all probability. 'Closed herds', that is those with no contact with affected cattle, are picking up the infection. And while we are dealing with affected cattle through skin testing, isolation and slaughter, we are not dealing with the problems of the badger population. The disease is now endemic. And they must be suffering too. Are we really helping them by refusing to cull?"

I'm at the Manor House at Piddletrenthide with James Boughey who has farmed the 2,200 acres estate since 1978.

"We did have 400 head of cattle here but my farming policy has been determined in part by the problem of bovine TB. Frankly, for any farmer who is predominantly cattle, it's a very serious problem. Unfortunately Government compensation doesn't solve the fundamental issue."

I've come to talk farming in general with James and we have found ourselves dwelling on the particular. It's been a feature of all my discussions with farmers on my travels that each has his own particular concerns whether they are milk returns, lamb prices, organic or non-organic, GM, small-scale sustainability or, in James's case and that of a number of other farmers in the county, the impact of bovine TB. I also have my own particular reason for calling upon this most affable of farmers – to find the answers to several questions that have long intrigued me. But first, we leave the Manor House and set off in James's Land Rover, bumping and squelching our way up the slope to the highest point of the farm. I am amazed at the ease with which the vehicle negotiates the thick mud and pools of standing water though I suspect having a highly proficient driver at the wheel does help.

"My father bought the estate in 1956 when the land was largely farmed by tenants. Now just a couple remain with 25 acres apiece and we farm the rest 'in hand'. We farm the west side of the valley. It's mostly arable with a beef suckler herd of 75."

Besides providing me with an opportunity to see the farm for myself, I am on my way to pick the brains of one of James's employees.

"Chris Cuff is not only a brilliant worker; he's also very knowledgeable and should be able to answer your questions."

Ever since I discovered that the legendary figure Ralph Wightman grew up in Piddletrenthide, I have been determined to discover the great man's precise association with farming and the locality. Ralph Wightman was one of the radio voices of my generation. In his gentle Dorset burr he articulated the concerns and thoughts of farmers everywhere, during a period when the nation was still very conscious of the profound debt they owed the farming community for their efforts in feeding the British public during the long, dark years of the war.

James switches off the engine. "There's your man."

Chris Cuff is hedge-trimming. Seeing our approach he opens the window of the cab and leans out. It must be a lonely job but Chris has the compensation of glorious views across the open country and the satisfaction of seeing his handiwork all about him.

"So, Chris, what do you remember of Ralph? Was David his nephew? Did he ever actually farm himself?"

Chris rubs his chin thoughtfully.

"My guess is that, yes, he was David's uncle and, no, he never actually farmed himself. I do remember him well though driving off in his car back in the Fifties. To Bristol sometimes, as I recall, for the broadcasts."

James remembers David well. "David Wightman was one of our last tenant farmers on the estate. He farmed the 500 acres of Bellamy's Farm with half a dozen employees. Sadly he died while out working on the farm."

The pieces of the jigsaw are fitting together. Chris offers a parting thought.

"But give his sister Marian a ring or David Abbott. They'll put you right."

James explains the rotation on the neighbouring fields.

"It's a 6 year rotation. Two years of grass, then spring wheat, 2 years of winter wheat, followed by spring barley under-sown with grass. The latter is the most economical way of re-introducing grass and grazing."

James is a countryman as well as a farmer.

"The Piddle rises at Alton Pancras and runs through the estate. We've planted small copses to encourage bird life and we are conscious of our responsibilities, not only to feed the nation but to maintain the landscape and the habitat. The South Dorset hunts over the estate in the winter months."

Besides Chris Cuff, James employs Jake Barnett and Andy Curtis. It's certainly a reflection of the changes that with such a vast acreage, James can efficiently manage the farm with such a small workforce. There's also a racing stables on the estate.

"Nick Mitchell trains out of East Hill Stables. Nick's the son of Richard, of course."

For years Richard was no mean force in NH and point to point racing. And Nick has recently taken charge of The Listener, one of the major players in 3 mile chases in recent years when with Robert and Sally Alner, where Nick himself worked until setting up on his own. James has a horse of his own with Nick, a 5 year-old gelding named Grand Sefton.

So I take my leave of James, husband of Katy and father of 4. It's been both informative and enjoyable. Now I have just a phone call or two to make and my quest will be over.

Marian Wightman, niece of the splendid Ralph, confirms Chris Cuff's opinions.

"Although it was a long time ago, I remember my uncle Ralph very fondly. He was a thoroughly nice man, very kind and pleasant. I do remember going for drives with him in his car. He was born here in Piddletrenthide and grew up in a farming family but he never actually farmed himself. He was educated at Beaminster Grammar School and went off to Durham University. Later on, as you will know, he became famous for his broadcasts on Any Questions."

I am so pleased to have traced one of my boyhood hero's roots and to have made contact with a surviving member of the family. I am also delighted to learn that he was 'such a nice man', as I always believed him to be. Ralph Wightman, 1901-71, writer and broadcaster, the voice of farming and the countryside in my youth, one of Dorset's great 20th century figures and a gentleman in the true sense of the word, you are remembered with great respect and affection.

Bere Regis

One of the locality's major attractions these days is the farm of Kevin and Amanda Crocker and their farm-shop, recently voted in the Taste of Dorset Awards the 'best food producer 'in the county. As I can cheerfully confirm, Pampered Pigs is an outstanding shop and Kevin and Amanda deserve great praise for all their hard work in recent years.

As Amanda says: "Winning this award means a lot to us. We try very hard to produce very high quality products that really taste excellent. We employ local staff and we only use local produce. We are an authentically Dorset supplier for Dorset people."

Pampered Pigs have just acquired two more major attractions in the form of 2 magnificent shire horses named Sherman and Speculator. Next summer they'll be pulling a hay-cart for children and families to ride on. I'm sure they're going to give a lot of happiness to people. Am I a bit old for such novelties? Surely not.

West Stafford

West Stafford Manor

"The play was *A Touch of Spring* by Sam Taylor. It was my first venture into the West End. I had to fall down a flight of stairs every evening – twice daily on matinees, of course. I was in the play for a year and I had a few bruises and strains when I finished but, at least, I'd made it to the West End!"

Julian Fellowes laughs at the memory of it. Educated at the Catholic school Ampleforth, he read English at Magdalene, Cambridge, from which he emerged with both a BA and MA, before studying drama at the Webber Douglas Academy.

"My father said he'd see me through my training and I was always welcome to live at home but,

Julian Fellowes and Hardy Society friends at Max Gate. The return of the painting Emma Hardy sold to its rightful home. *Picture: courtesy of Dorset Echo*

from the moment I'd finished at drama school, I had to stand on my own feet financially."

As with so many young actors it was off to rep at far-flung Northampton and Harrogate before the big break in London. It has proved a fascinating career ever since with theatrical roles alongside Hayley Mills, Leslie Phillips and Donald Sinden, to mention but 3 household names and a spell at the National Theatre. On film he's appeared with Anthony Hopkins in *Shadowlands*, Jeremy Irons in *Damage* and Pierce Brosnan in *Tomorrow Never Dies*. On TV he has been a familiar face with one his best-known roles being that of Lord Killwillie in Monarch of the Glen.

"In some ways I became a writer by default. I was writing scripts for TV – children's stories like *Little Lord Fauntleroy* and the *Prince and the Pauper* – that were kindly received by the critics. I'd also spent a couple of years in Hollywood where I found myself becoming ever more fascinated by film-making."

The rest is history, as they say, for this most unassuming and amiable of English gentlemen. His film screenplay debut was the Robert Altman directed *Gosford Park* which, besides gaining a number of awards in various categories, won for Julian an Oscar for the Best Original Screenplay.

I mention a film directed by Julian that I saw at the Tivoli 3-4 years ago which kept me on the edge of my seat throughout, a film reminiscent of my early days of cinema watching. Superbly acted with an intelligent script and a clever twist at the end, it belonged to a genre now largely neglected.

"Yes, that would be *Separate Lies* and I'm pleased you enjoyed it. It was a very satisfying film to make."

Juggling all the demands on his time cannot be easy. With two recent novels to his credit, *Snobs* and *Past Imperfect*, *The Young Victoria* his most recently released film playing to enthusiastic audiences, another film *From Time To Time* recently completed awaiting a release date – much of it shot at Athelhampton House – and other projects in the pipe-line, it's a hectic schedule. And I haven't mentioned the single most important part of Julian's life.

"I married late – I was actually forty."

To spend a few minutes in the company of Julian and Emma it's clear to see the pair think the world of one another. It's also an intriguing union. As I discover when examining the paintings hanging on the walls about me, Julian is descended from a long line of distinguished naval officers, including more than one Rear-Admiral, quite possibly an Admiral or two, while Emma is related to the gentleman whose face and pointing finger featured on thousands of posters nearly a century ago, Lord Kitchener of Khartoum and of Broome.

"We have a son, Peregrine, who's absolutely lovely," says Emma. "He's just finished Winchester and he's having a gap year before going off to university."

While Julian is at work on his varied projects Emma is a lady-in-waiting to Prince Michael of Kent. But it's not just Julian's artistic career and his family I've come to discuss, it's his relationship with Dorset.

"We actually moved here in 2002. We both felt it would be good for Peregrine to know something of country life and so we started looking. Emma actually visited a number or properties but this house was just the second I saw. I fell in love with it immediately."

It's not difficult to understand why. Described by Monica Hutchings as *'Georgian and of quite arresting appearance, set well back from the by-road, steep-roofed and with a double-storeyed porch'*, it stands in extensive grounds and must be an oasis of tranquillity for a couple with so many commitments amidst the bustle of city life during the week.

"It was a most curious thing. As you will have noted, I have long collected the paintings of Arthur Shirley. In the church at West Stafford I discovered that he was actually my great, great, great uncle. So I am, in truth, much more connected to Dorset than ever I had imagined. Interestingly, the vicar here was engaged in a long-standing feud with Hardy. Hardy also apparently used to borrow the butler from West Stafford Manor for certain functions at Max Gate."

Since Julian and Emma arrived at West Stafford there have been many invitations to become involved with local charities.

"It's always flattering to be asked but we do have to restrict ourselves. There are only so many hours in any day. I was very pleased to become involved with the admirable Weldmar Hospice which, as you know, does the most wonderful work. I was particularly thrilled to be able to offer them the opportunity to benefit from the world premiere at Bridport's Electric Palace of *Young Victoria*. I believe we raised the grand sum of £9,500. I am also associated with Age Concern. On the social side I was invited to become the president of the Hardy Society which I regard as a great honour."

What next, I wonder, for this versatile and energetic English gentleman? More films, more books?

"To tell you the truth, I find writing novels very relaxing. I unwind as I write. The world of film-making is obviously more stressful and I never can tell where I will be from week to week, but there are always projects in the air. Who can tell?"

I know Julian and Emma are regarded with great affection in the county. Wherever I have journeyed I hear the same sentiments. Kind, considerate, generous and constantly willing to give whatever time they have left over at the end of their busy days to the community about them. I have admired Julian's work from afar for a number of years. It has been a great pleasure to meet Julian and Emma this morning. It is typical of their warmth and old world courtesy that they stand in the doorway of their splendid house and wave until I am out of sight.

Swanage
Twinned with Cerisy-La-Salle (France) and Rudesheim (Germany)

"When you get a bit older, it's good to find a place that's 'a little bit in the past', if you know what I mean. Swanage doesn't change, does it? You feel comfortable here."

We're standing outside the Mowlem Theatre. Now the schools have gone back the sun has, inevitably, emerged from behind the sullen cloud cover of recent weeks and there's a bustle of late summer activity. Local mums with under-fives, carrying buckets and spades and rubber rings, mingle with senior citizens walking ancient dogs and office workers munching their sandwiches. Paul Goodger and his wife Diane are down from Buckinghamshire with Diane's elderly parents, George and May.

"We've been coming for years and we absolutely love it. The people are friendly and you can trust them. We dozed off in one of the sea-front shelters and anyone could have walked off with our bags – but they didn't."

'A little bit in the past'. It's true, of course. The town has scarcely changed since I was a boy. The names above some of the shop windows may have altered and there are far more cars. But Swanage is reassuringly familiar. As Paul Goodger said, as you get older you do welcome the comfort of the familiar.

When did I first see Swanage? Curiously I remember with clarity. Not the exact date of course, but the occasion. A Mr.Pople ran evening coach trips from Upton. Scarcely a family I knew owned a car and my father was no exception. It was almost certainly a Saturday with departure at about 6pm and the coach was usually packed. Mr.Pople's trips were to local beauty spots like Lulworth Cove, the Blue Pool or Swanage. I don't ever remember going as far afield as Weymouth. The travelling would have taken up too much time. So what was the memory that still lingers after so many years? It was of the amusement arcade on the sea-front where you slid your pennies into a machine and prayed the long arm would scoop up one of the piles of coins and send it tumbling down into the brass cup at the bottom and you would be rich beyond avarice. At least, that's how it seemed to a boy of eight. Sometimes you did succeed in getting a few pennies back but that was the best that I recall ever happening to me. But those coins were, of course, all the encouragement you needed to persevere until you'd exhausted the coppers your mother had given you. It was so exciting and quite unlike any comparable experience I had known, and that is why I remember that Saturday evening when I first saw Swanage.

There is only one possible person with whom I can begin my days in the town – with the great man himself, 'Mr.Swanage', my old friend, George Willey.

"I've often said I count myself blessed having been born weak-willed and of an indolent nature. It's meant I've never felt guilty about not writing a book when so many people have urged me to do so."

George Willey chuckles mischievously. Yet this man who self-deprecatingly describes himself as a born sloth has yet contrived to write his own weekly column in the local press for the past 54 years – and he hasn't missed one single week in all those years. It is, by any standards, an astonishing achievement.

"Actually I do rather suspect my Tilly Whim column which began in the now defunct *Swanage Times* and now appears in the *Swanage & Purbeck Advertiser* could well be the longest running weekly column written by one individual anywhere in the UK. It is, in truth, an affectionate, cosy piece appealing to an older readership. I've never sought to raise blood."

George Willey, Mr Swanage. *Picture: Pat Timmons, Bournemouth Echo*

The youthful George began his life in Newport, South Wales, where his first job in journalism was with the *South Wales Argus* before he journeyed south to join the *Western Gazette*. For half a century he has earned a crust writing for the local press and, when the opportunities arose, selling stories to the nationals. His wife Bea for some years ran a successful guest-house.

"Bea's contribution was immensely important to us when our children, Wolf-Christian and Katina were growing up."

And the Swanage he loves so dearly. Would he change it?

"Certainly not. In fact, I am very pleased there have been such rigid planning controls. We owe a great debt to the planning authorities. Their constraints are our best safeguard. Very unusually, because of the sweep of the bay, Swanage actually faces east. Any further development must, therefore, be on the western edge of the town. The one tragedy of Swanage – and it is a situation common to a number of similar towns and villages in the county – is that our children grow up in a wonderful environment and then find it all but impossible to buy property in the locality and are compelled to move away."

We discuss many of the advantages of the locality – and one in particular.

"Crime is minimal here. The inaccessibility of Swanage is very useful. Only the most stupid of criminals would commit a major crime here – such as a bank robbery. We are 12 miles from anywhere and the roads are not suitable for a quick get-away!"

As a journalist George has met practically every famous name who's come to visit or live in the area.

"I have always been most cautious in approaching 'celebrities'. Many come here to escape from the press and value their privacy, so I have always sought to respect theirs. I do remember Enid

Blyton very clearly. Actually the Enid Blyton effect is still quite potent in Swanage. Middle-aged ladies, though they might not admit to it, love to come down and visit for themselves locations where she set many of her stories. I recall when she would accompany her husband, a Harley Street surgeon, to the Swanage and Studland golf course and set up her typewriter and write her *Noddy* or *Secret Seven* or *Famous Five* stories while he was playing a round of golf. She was possessed of a very astute business brain. She used to scribble me little cards inviting me along when she did her book signings knowing I would give her publicity. Quite one of the most delightful men to live down here was Brian Johnston, the cricket commentator. He really was the most charming and kindly of men."

Just a few months ago George's likeness was captured in a bronze bust by local artist, Freya Boyesen. It was the idea of Keith Roker, the director of the Quarr Gallery in the High Street.

"George is a local treasure," Keith said. "He has an unrivalled reputation that we think requires both recognition and memorialisation."

('A local treasure' is a description everyone would attach to George 'Mr.Swanage' Willey. I first became acquainted with George and Bea at parent/teacher meetings many years ago at Purbeck School. I knew their son Wolf-Christian who went off to pursue an acting career at the Central School of Speech and Drama. I last saw Wolf at the Lighthouse in Poole after a performance of *Jamaica Inn* in which he appeared with William Gaunt when we enjoyed a drink together. Wolf now teaches at a special school in Swanage. I also knew George and Bea's daughter Katina who was a delightful student in my classroom for several years and of whom I was very fond. When I conducted my interview with George in late summer, Katina was already desperately ill with cancer. George and Bea were visiting her daily and praying that there would be a miracle. Sadly, shortly afterwards, Katina passed away, still a young woman with 4 children of her own which included triplets. The whole of Swanage was deeply saddened by the news for Katina was a very popular young lady and George and Bea are both much loved and respected within the community. At school Katina invariably brightened up my classroom with her presence just as she lit up the lives of those around her in Swanage. She will long be remembered in all our hearts.)

Michael Pratt, most honourable Mayor of Swanage, may no longer possess a blinding turn of foot, nor the elasticity of movement to compete with the likes of Theo Walcott or Ronaldo, but there was a time he was regarded as one of the most promising 25 young footballers in the land. The year was 1959 and among the remaining 24 are 2 names everyone will recognise, Sir Geoff Hurst and Nobby Stiles, members of the World Cup winning squad of 1966. Today the former Swanage Grammar cricket and soccer captain is a member of a different august group, the 'Mayoral Chain Gang'. A former accountant and hotelier Michael retired in 2000 and, despite some major health problems, is doing his best 'to put something back into the community I love.'

"Being Mayor is a great honour but it is, of course, essentially a ceremonial role. As a councillor, I have been concerned that planning for the town is determined in Wareham by the Purbeck District Council. We can express opinions but whether we are listened to is something else."

Michael has been most troubled by the loss of many small hotels and their replacement by flats.

"What we don't want is to become an overspill from Canford Cliffs where they've all but run out of space. Now developers are coming along to tempt householders into selling their properties here so they can be demolished and replaced by flats."

But Michael remains optimistic about the future of the town. "There's so much natural beauty around us and it benefits from the 'blue flag' for safe bathing designation. In fact, just a couple of days ago Alison Holmes, our Tourist Information Centre Manager, announced that we'd received another major award for our central beach – the 'Quality Coast award.' We've got good facilities for youngsters like the skateboarding park, thanks in no small part to Lorna Haynes who ran the

London Marathon to raise funds for it. And it's a very warm and friendly place."

Something Michael does miss from his days as an hotelier at the Corrie Hotel is the relationship he built with the visitors.

"I remember one particular group of 6 families who struck up a friendship and came back year after year to renew old acquaintance. They still meet up, I believe, for an annual reunion even though the children are long since grown up. One lesson I learned as an hotelier was always to get the children on your side, to make sure they had a wonderful time, because then they would insist upon coming back time after time. It was a good formula"

And a valuable piece of advice for every hotelier who may read Michael's words.

Michael does find some of his mayoral duties tiring and is grateful for the support of Constance Gainsborough and, of course, his wife Margaret and daughters Deborah and Julia. As so often on my travels I have found another good man 'doing his bit' for the community he loves. It's just a pity he's no longer one of the most promising young footballers in the kingdom. One or two of our local sides could do with his talents.

Gloria Marsh has twice been Mayor as well as a councillor for twenty years. Her late husband Vic was once the full-time coxswain mechanic of Swanage lifeboat and one of the legendary figures of the local community. Gloria is proud of the traditions of Swanage, not least its support for charitable causes and its current status as a Fairtrade town. We've also been discussing the young people of the area.

"There's a small nucleus of troublemakers who rebel against authority but I believe there's no excuse for bad behaviour in the town. We have excellent sporting facilities – football, cricket, rugby, rowing, skateboarding – and there's the beach. What more do young people want? Earlier generations had far less. It's very disappointing when young people let themselves and their parents down."

Gloria reminds me of a recent incident involving vandalism in the town and the introduction of a new police and community strategy to bring offenders face to face with the consequences of their actions. It seems an appropriate moment to bring in another well-known face, that of Cllr. Mike Whitwam, a former customs officer and presently the chairman of both the Swanage Railway Trust and the Swanage Railway Co. Mike was closely associated with the vandalism case and was interviewed on TV afterwards.

"A railway carriage window was smashed and the youth concerned was identified and interviewed. The idea of 'Restorative Justice' is to get the offender or offenders to acknowledge what they have done and, so far as it is possible, to do something to make amends for the crime they have committed. They also have to apologise and sign an agreement not to repeat such acts. Of course, its success will depend very much upon the individual's response. But it is a step in the right direction, I believe."

Mike and I talk too of his great passion for the Swanage Railway.

"It's all about reliving one's childhood, I suppose, a feeling of nostalgia for a lost age. There is something very special about the age of steam railway."

I ask Mike to tell me something of the various bodies.

"The Railway Trust is a charitable body with 4,000 members and a Management Council of sixteen. The Railway Co is not a charity and is charged with the duty of making the day-to-day arrangements, while the Trust makes the long-term strategic decisions. All our engine drivers are volunteers but we do have about 30 paid staff, mostly part-time, many of them working seasonally in the catering areas. The Railway Co is supposed to make a profit – in fact, it just keeps its head above water."

What about the longer term? What ambitions do you entertain?

"We have been in long-term negotiations with Rail-trackObviously there are complex details relating to the 3 miles of track which belongs to them that we might lease or purchase. There's also the small matter of the re-signalling of the line to Wareham. In the fullness of time we would love to see the passenger service fully restored. It would be brilliant for the town."

The Swanage Railway, Corfe Castle Station – A Sunday morning

The bells of St. Edward the Martyr are summoning the faithful. A dank mist hangs over the Purbecks on this most dismal of summer Sundays. On the platform of Corfe Station a score of travellers are patiently awaiting the arrival of the next train to Swanage under the watchful gaze of acting station master, Peter Foster.

"My grandparents' garden in Beaucroft Lane, Colehill, bordered the old Wimborne – West Moors line, the 'Castleman Corkscrew' as it was affectionately known, and I would stand by the fence watching the trains pass by. That was when I became fascinated by railways. They've been my passion ever since."

The train from Swanage arrives and Peter, together with his wife Heather, attend to enquiries from passengers. A middle-aged couple are eager to inspect the former station master's living-room which is furnished much as it was when the last occupant lived at the station with his family. Cups and plates sit on the table, only a match is required to light the fire laid in the grate.

The line linking Wareham to Swanage was opened in 1885 and closed in the economy cuts of 1972, before being resurrected thanks to the heroic efforts of the volunteer members of the Swanage Railway Society. The completion of the link to Norden in 2002 enabled trains once again to pass directly from Wareham to Swanage, albeit on a strictly limited basis.

"The Swanage-Corfe line is described as a 'heritage' railway which means that it's a 'preserved, once functional' system. It is dependent, of course, upon our splendid band of volunteers with the minimum of paid staff – and we are like one big happy family with a wonderful team spirit. The nearest comparable line is between Alton and Alresford in Hampshire which is popularly known as the 'Watercress Line'. It is improbable, to say the least, that any other line in Dorset could be restored. Nothing is left of most of the old lines."

Though Peter admires a number of the features of the modern railway system he does regret the impersonal nature of the unmanned stations, though recognising the economic pressures.

"Many people, especially women and the elderly, do feel vulnerable, not least at night. And then there are all the notices – 'Don't do this' and 'Don't do that' and 'You will be fined unless...'. It can all feel very intimidatory. There is the loss of the personal touch which may be inevitable but it is a shame. Perhaps I should have been born in an earlier era. I do feel a sense of affinity with the stationmasters of old with their brightly painted stations, the hanging baskets and the snug waiting-rooms – like Perks in *The Railway Children*. It brings back a warm glow of nostalgia. What we have today, if you think of most stations, doesn't exactly feel like progress."

Peter and Heather also retain close links with Dorchester Hospital Radio though he's recently handed over the role of programme organiser to his friend John Coleman.

"We have a brilliant team including Dorset's most decorated scout, Jim Davis, and we've received wonderful support from people like Alistair Chisholm and Paul Atterbury. Heather and I are also involved with *West Dorset Talking Newspapers* which provides a service to the registered blind in the area. Audrey Stubbs does a fine job as our secretary."

I came to talk railways with Peter and Heather and we've done just that but, as so often on my journey, I discover the details of other selfless, big-hearted individuals performing great acts of kindness for others less fortunate. What some exceptionally good people we have here in the county.

The first train since 1972 from London Victoria to Swanage. *Picture: Richard Crease, Bournemouth Echo*

(The dreams of Mike Whitwam, Peter and Heather Foster, and all the other valiant members of Swanage Railway Trust, are realised even as we go to print. On April 1, 2009, the diesel hauled 12 carriage Purbeck Pioneer left Victoria Station at 8.45am bound for Corfe Castle and Swanage. Driven by Dave Gravell from Poole, it arrived at 2pm to an applauding crowd of 1,000 spectators. One of those on the platform was 87 year-old Moyra Cross, a veteran campaigner, who had never lost hope that one day all the hard work of the volunteers would be repaid by success. Among the 400 passengers were father and son, Frederick and Peter Sills from Wareham, who rode on the last BR train to run on the line on January 1, 1972. Frederick, now 86 years old, summed up everyone's feelings.

"All credit to the Swanage volunteers, they have performed miracles!"

If what happened on April 1 was not enough, on May 2 the first steam train for 42 years made an identical journey to Swanage from Victoria. This time the 11coach Dorset Coast Express, hauled by the 1940s built engine Tangmere, arrived just 2 minutes late at 1.17pm to rapturous applause. Among those on the platform was the railway enthusiast and 'pop supremo', Pete Waterman. I seem to recall one of his hit compositions for Rick Astley was 'Never gonna give you up', which seems an eminently appropriate anthem to be adopted by the Swanage Railway Trust.)

One Swanage resident, Chris Phillips, who retires shortly has been a town council groundsman for the past 33 years and primarily responsible for the superb quality of the bowling green at Beach Gardens which has provided so much pleasure for visitors and locals alike. Chris now intends to spend more time on his duties as the verger at St .Mary's. It is so easy to overlook, or take for granted, the splendid work of many public and local government employees. Swanage is grateful for all of Chris's efforts over the years.

There has been a long-established association between Swanage and the 11th Signals Regiment, based at Blandford Camp, and the man responsible for co-ordinating the link for the past decade is Frank Roberts. It was in 2005 that the Mayor of Swanage granted the liberty of the town to the soldiers of the 11th Signals in recognition of their much valued contribution to the life of the town, particularly for their work on the railway restoration project. Most recently the soldiers have been responsible, along with Swanage electrician Dave Barrow, for repairing the floodlights on the War Memorial and undertaking landscaping and roof repair work at Herston Halt railway station. The name of Frank Roberts is, not surprisingly, a very popular one in Swanage. The year 2009 marks the 25th anniversary of the association between the 11th Signals and the town and will be marked at the end of May by a series of events. The organiser of the Armed Forces Weekend, Steve Churchill, comments:" I feel it's a way of showing our appreciation of all they have done for us and I think most people feel the 11th Signals is the town's regiment."

Two widely contrasting figures from the world of entertainment currently have homes in the town. One is the former Coronation Street star, Thelma Barlow, who played the role of Mavis Riley for an extraordinary 26 years and a certain Jonathan Ross. Thelma is a popular, affectionately regarded and dignified figure in the town who recently opened the Swanage Area Senior Forum aimed at giving a voice to the over 50s in the community. Of the painfully unfunny, tasteless, grossly overpaid Jonathan Ross, it is impossible to excuse his vile behaviour towards the respected and much-loved actor Andrew Sachs. The spineless moral cowardice of the BBC in failing to dismiss Ross following the incident is scarcely less reprehensible. It is just as well that I have not spotted Ross during my travels in Swanage for I know I would have given him a piece of my mind.

The Mowlem Theatre

"The old dear was very irate. She thought the language appalling and the nudity quite disgusting. I tried to placate her but she simply stormed out of the building."

The occasion was a showing of *The Full Monty* at The Mowlem and Brian Travers still chuckles at the recollection.

"She'd convinced herself the film was the life story of Viscount Bernard Montgomery of Alamein. How she'd missed the reviews I'll never know but there you are!"

The administrator of The Mowlem, Brian Travers Is one of those transparently decent, kindly, infinitely good-natured individuals everyone warms to within moments of first meeting. We first made acquaintance 20 summers ago when he was a pupil in one of my history classes at Purbeck School. For some reason neither of us can recall I gave him the nickname of Tommy Traddles after the young lawyer in *David Copperfield* who assisted Mr.Micawber in exposing the loathsome Uriah Heep. Brian even took to writing the name of T.Traddles Esq on the front cover of his exercise books and test papers which probably goes to prove we are equally mad. I also witnessed his first stage appearance as a character in Alan Ayckbourn's comedy *Confusions*.

"I blame Barbara Acres for everything's that's followed!"

Barbara was Brian's popular drama teacher but, as he readily acknowledges, it is very much to Barbara's credit that she both spotted and nurtured Brian's love of the theatre. Over the years Brian has played many roles both on the stage of The Mowlem and in furthering its development as a much valued and integral part of Swanage's cultural life. He's been a barman, front of house, assistant and now full-time administrator.

"Many people assume The Mowlem is run by the Council but, in fact, we are entirely independent and governed by a nine member Charitable Trust. There are 3 full-time professionals here, myself, Ian Cheeseborough, the chief technician, and his assistant Tom Curtis."

Though superbly situated by the water's edge with spectacular views from the upstairs bar and

Brian Travers. An old-fashioned actor manager!

restaurant across Swanage Bay, the 378 capacity theatre's greatest admirer would not describe the building as anything other than functional. Built in 1966 the popular judgement is more likely to be 'downright ugly' but, whatever its lack of aesthetic appeal, Brian and his team work very hard to provide uplifting entertainment within its four drab walls. The old saying, often used in the world of horse-racing, 'Handsome is, as handsome does' seems entirely applicable to The Mowlem. Not every Epsom Derby winner would win a prize for looks, and likewise the depressing appearance of the building cannot negate the magic and charm of live theatre or film.

The Mowlem is also home to a yearly panto in which Brian alternates as the panto dame or 'baddie.' His own company Knollsea Productions stage two plays every year and June Ranger's exuberant dancers take over the stage every other year for several performances. Various other community groups use the room above the theatre as a meeting -place. Brian does entertain one cherished hope though he fears time may be running out for its realisation.

"I'd love to get Ken Dodd here. He's often said he'd like to appear in every British theatre but he's 80 now and in constant demand all over the country. I'm quite certain that if ever he did come it would be the longest stage performance Swanage had ever seen!"

For Brian and his sisters, Becky and Claire, the last few months have been full of sadness, losing both their mother and father, Rachel and Les, within weeks of one another to cancer. The whole Travers family, uncles, aunts, cousins and friends are taking part in the London Moonwalk charity event in their memory. We wish them well.

One of the town's strengths is undoubtedly the variety and number of its independent shopkeepers and small business people. One such is Peter Hayman whose splendid bakery and coffee shop attracts locals and visitors alike in large numbers through its doors.

"The date was May 14, 1941. Whether the German bomb aimer was simply anxious to dispose of his cargo which was most likely intended for the radar installations at Lulworth, or his target was more specific, the effect was the same. The bank in Institute Street was on the receiving end and my grandfather, Edward Hayman, who was standing in the front of the shop opposite the bank quietly minding his business, was blown by the force of the explosion right across the building to its rear."

It is, at such moments, that family histories, besides those of nations, can be dramatically altered for good or ill. In this instance, Edward Hayman thankfully lived to bake another day and duly, with his son, rebuilt the business that had been founded in 1920. Today the third generation of the family Peter, assisted by his wife Janice and son Jonathan and when they are at home, by daughters, Anne, Lucy and Sarah, run a thriving bakery and coffee shop business.

"We have an excellent team. Eddie Stockley looks after the bakery which we moved out on to the industrial estate at Victoria Avenue with a young lad, Andy Strong, he is bringing along. Eddie is what I would describe as an old-fashioned baker and confectioner in the best sense of the word."

Having grown up in the bakery business myself I am always curious to learn any trade secrets.

"It's long established good practice. We make up the dough, scale it into 1 lb or 2 lbs loaves, allow it to prove up, then remove from the tray and mould into whatever shape is required. Then some loaves will go into tins or on to a tray before being proved up for a second time. Then they're ready for the ovens. Of course, it's much more time-consuming than factory practice but the bread has a proper crust, a better texture and it lasts longer. Fortunately we have, like a number of other small independents, built up a loyal clientele who are prepared to pay extra for a better product."

Peter is representative of many small traders in Swanage who rely heavily upon the summer trade to cushion them against the leaner winter months.

"I do love the town and wouldn't want to live anywhere else but I do feel there exists, at times, a certain tension between the traders and the Council. One particular bone of contention would be the obstacles placed in the way of the coach trade. Parties who come to the town are mostly older people who want to see the sea, have a cup of tea and a potter around the shops. They don't want to walk a long way into the town. In my opinion and that of other small traders, the Council could alter the dropping-off and pick-up points without any major problems. It would benefit the town and help to keep the shops busier during the winter months. We are in competition with other seaside towns and the coaches will go elsewhere if it is easier for the drivers and passengers. I have a staff of 22 and I like to keep them all on during the winter though their hours will, of course, be shorter. After all, all these people do need the money and they do spend it in the town."

Incidentally, I do warmly recommend the bread and cakes at Hayman's. Both are quite excellent.

Durlston Country Park

One of the great pleasures of visiting Swanage is to spend a few hours in the 300 acres of the Durlston Country Park. I first discovered it 20 or so years ago and I love the variety of natural history experiences the different seasons offer. The most memorable for me was 3 or 4 years ago in late September when, for hour after hour, thousands of swallows passed ceaselessly overhead flying eastward before Channel-hopping over to France on their annual migration to the African continent. Created in the 1890s by George Burt, with its Castle and celebrated Globe, the park became a Mecca for Victorian artists and tourists with its wealth of imported plants and spectacular views. The RAF occupied the site during WW2 and the last huts weren't demolished until the early 1970s. Today the reserve is managed by the Dorset County Council.

Like an autumn migrant himself, our central character, Hamish Murray, Dorset Countryside head ranger and Durlston project leader, moved south from his native Inverness, pausing only for a fuel stop in Rochdale where the notable song-bird, Gracie Fields, was fledged many summers ago, before the final leg of his journey to Dorset. Just days before our meeting, Hamish received

Durlston Country Park. *Picture: Roger Holman*

confirmation that the Heritage Lottery Fund had agreed a £3 million grant towards the restoration of the Castle and Park, bringing the total cash injection into the project to over £5million.

"It's our newest, shiniest national nature park," enthuses Hamish.

In official language, it was declared by Natural England a National Nature Reserve, the first such designation since the conservation body was set up in 2006.

Where did a passion for wildlife and the great outdoors begin for Hamish Murray?

"I was just 8 years-old and out walking when I heard this bird singing. I was intrigued to discover what bird it was that was making this noise so I tracked it, looked it up, and that was that. In fact, it was a dunnock."

There are a number of words which have crept into recent everyday usage that I freely admit to loathing and one of them is 'birder'. It is crude, ugly and insultingly narrow in its implications. Would we refer to a dermatologist as a 'skinner' or an orthopaedic surgeon as a 'boner'? Of course not, and I refuse to use the word 'birder', even as a shorthand term. I know ornithologist is longer but, as the Shorter Oxford defines it, one who studies 'the branch of zoology that deals with birds', it has a dignity and precision sorely lacking in the term 'birder'. All of which brings me to the point which is that, by common consent, Hamish Murray is a quite outstanding ornithologist with an astonishing ability to identify even the rarest of birds not only by appearance but by song and call. This particular talent is of huge value at Durlston for, like Portland, the locality is a migration station for millions of birds every year. For most amateur bird-watchers it is one thing to identify a stationary bird in reasonable light, quite something else to recognise a species flying overhead at several hundred feet in the gloom of dawn or dusk. Hamish dismisses the notion that he possesses a rare gift.

"It's much more a matter of hard work and practice," he insists.

Besides which, he says, there are species which cause even an experienced individual like himself considerable difficulties.

"Tits are a particular nightmare," he confesses with the barest flicker of a smile. "The great tit alone has seventy-odd different calls."

I discover that Hamish is also a talented musician and sound has always fascinated him. I suspect, whatever his modest protestations to the contrary, that he does indeed possess a rare gift which enables him to distinguish between such a wide variety of species.

What has been the most exciting moment for Hamish at Durlston?

"A very difficult question but, if I had to choose just one, it would be Dorset's first recorded 'common rose finch' singing in the gully – a bird most usually found in Eastern Europe."

Ben Wallbridge is his name. It's a name that triggers associations. Is the young fellow sitting beside me at a table outside the Visitor Centre a member of that remarkable family whose history has been inextricably bound up with the life of the Toller Valley for the past 300 years – Toller Porcorum, Kingcombe and Powerstock?

"Yes, it's true. My great grand-father farmed at Kingcombe until his nineties."

And, of course, because John Wallbridge didn't use chemicals but farmed using traditional methods, it made Kingcombe a uniquely valuable acquisition for the Dorset Wildlife Trust. It seems, therefore, entirely fitting that 4 generations later another member of that distinguished family should be involved in countryside conservation. Ben's role is that of coast and marine ranger for the locality.

"My particular brief is to encourage a greater degree of public understanding of the marine environment. With a new Marine Bill coming out next year I hope for a co-ordinated approach drawing together all interested parties. Peter Tinsley has been responsible for a sea-floor survey on behalf of the DWT. With the depth of information now available we will be able to have public discussion based on solid scientific evidence. But there must be compromise between wildlife groups and those whose livelihoods are affected. To give a couple of examples, we need to protect breeding and nursery areas. With a thorough appreciation of cause and effect, everyone stands to benefit from a co-ordinated strategy – fishermen and the marine life. Along the coast we have an important colony of kittiwakes whose numbers are declining. Is it because their food stocks are being reduced? We know that 80% of catches is often thrown away. What can we do to remedy the situation? I believe passionately in compromise between all affected interests. It's absolutely no good people on one side or the other side being dogmatic in their approach. All that happens is that people are needlessly alienated."

It is apparent to me that Ben has exactly the right credentials to make a success of a very complex issue. A readiness to find the middle ground and draw different factions together is of critical importance.

Katie Black arrived at the Centre fifteen years ago.

"Not intending to stay. But Durlston is such a wonderful place and we have a brilliant team here."

Katie's a ranger with particular responsibilities for land management.

"I carry out counts of our species. Despite anxieties elsewhere moth species and numbers appear healthy. We have lost some but other species have arrived. We also have a good colony of bats, mostly pipistrelles. I recently conducted a midnight survey of glow-worms and we found over a hundred."

Of Katie's most exciting moments at Durlston the most extraordinary was the count of 70,000 plus wood pigeons making a mass exodus from the mainland one day.

"It was absolutely astonishing. The sky was absolutely full of them."

A few pigeon pies for our continental sharp-shooters, I would guess.

Katie's looking forward to next February to see if her favourite guillemot returns for its 15th summer.

"I call it Tufty. It must have had an accident when it was young because its head feathers stick up very conspicuously. I believe the oldest recorded guillemot was 32 so it's got a long way to go yet."

Ally Tuckey concentrates hard. I've just asked him what led him to a passion for natural history?

"I was just 5 and walking with my dad in Epping Forest. There was this wonderful grove of hornbeams and I vividly recall seeing hundreds of caterpillars on the trees. I just wanted to know all about them."

From estate worker to country ranger, Ally loves his present role at Durlston in education and interpretation.

"Adults, school-children in group parties.- the questions often come thick and fast, but it's constantly interesting with new challenges."

And his most memorable experience at Durlston?

"It was mid-October and there'd been a terrible night of storms. Suddenly the sky was full of thousands and thousands of redwings. It was an amazing spectacle."

I cannot leave Durlston Visitor centre without a reference to the wonderful diary our wardens maintain throughout the year. It's a topic I raise with each one in turn amidst much good-natured jesting. In fact, the diary hangs in the Visitor Centre and is always my first point of call, as I suspect it is for many other visitors. The wardens have a rota for writing it up every morning between 8 and 9 am. I never cease to be entertained by the entries. Do I detect a degree of amicable rivalry between our diarists to achieve the most poetic, descriptive entries? At moments too I am astonished by the remarkable precision of their counting of the species recorded on their morning walks. There cannot be much wrong with the maths teaching in our schools when one entry reads, 'Over 1,000 linnets this morning, 11 bramblings, 135 meadow-pipits, and 1Lapland bunting ' Or, on another day, '10 crossbills. 3 tree sparrows, 400 linnets and 340 goldfinches'. Or on a third day, '81 redpoll, 92 siskins.'

Are they never tempted, especially on particularly vile mornings, to invent a few figures? After all, who would know whether it was 298 or 299 willow warblers that made landfall one late March morning in the gully? Am I thereby most unfairly imputing they play the sort of mischievous game I would be sorely tempted to play in their position? But let me give an example or two of the splendid literary flourishes of our diarists.

'Very atmospheric, a swirling mist, the top of the lighthouse making brief appearances as zephyrs of breeze cleared the view.' Robin Plowman (Robin is Number 2 to Hamish, I believe.).

'A still, grey morning, with a dramatic grey-blue landscape looming ominously overhead.' Ally Tucker.

'The loud, pathetic cry of a peregrine falcon, the noise traced to a bird perched forlornly in the rain on a cliff edge'. Katie Black.

'The deep red berries on the hawthorn being eaten by a flock of greenfinches. A tinkling sound as a

charm of 25 goldfinches landed in the wispy white flower heads of the Old Man's Beard, the sun's rays highlighting their wonderful gold feathers and red smudges on the forehead.' Katie Black.

Not only do we have wildlife experts but a burgeoning literary talent at Durlston.

I ask Hamish if his diarists ever indulge in a little poetic licence with their numbers and sightings? He smiles amiably.

"I do recall an entry we included one April 1 which referred to a *'dangerous, dog-eating rabbit which it would be advisable for dog-owners to be on the look-out for.'* We actually had several anxious ladies making enquiries about the rabbit and asking if it was safe for them to walk their dogs."

You have been warned.

The Yacht Club– A Saturday evening

The lights of the town flicker brightly across the calm grey waters of the bay this late summer evening. Within the Clubhouse there's a sense of expectancy. A good crowd has assembled for the entertainment, including old friends Barry and Phyl England whom I've not seen in years. Barry was a member of a bat society but he became disillusioned by all the rules and restrictions. Phyl 's specialist interest is moths. She tells me she has a foolproof technique for ridding herself of bores at parties.

"I just begin to relate the details of what I found in my moth trap the previous evening. You can see their eyes begin to glaze over."

It was another old friend who invited me over, Mike Etherington, former maths teacher at Purbeck, musician and brother of Jim. Mike's here with Jean and Jean's sister Frances who's down from Aldeburgh.

"Actually I don't care for Britten's music. Do you?" she whispers in my ear.

Mike introduces me to Chris Haw, former lifeboat coxswain, raconteur and wit. The stories Chris relates are, I understand, the stuff of local legends but there's not time enough tonight because we have assembled to listen to another. Besides, are they 'before the watershed' reading?

The handsome young man with the curly hair across the table pushes aside his plate. He's barely touched the generously sliced wedges of ham and Stilton and salad.

"I never have an appetite on such occasions."

A notice sits beside his plate 'Reserved for the poet.' At least the poet is not reserved. In fact, he's quite chatty. Why the name Elvis McGonagall?

"I needed a stage name. I noticed someone had called himself Bing Hitler. Elvis McGonagall is quite modest by comparison."

Our hero goes off to change.

"I've heard him on Radio Four on Saturday mornings. He's very good," I hear someone say at the bar.

Now he's back complete with a tartan waistcoat and a book which he flicks through. Does he actually need to refer to it? Or is it just a reassurance, should he dry? Or a mere prop? The lights dim. Conversation ceases. Our poet begins. Slowly and softly at first, quickening the tempo and volume as he progresses. Political and social satire, it's refreshingly even-handed and genuinely funny. No one is spared – George Bush, Gordon Brown, Tony Blair, David Cameron. Why should they be spared? They profess to know what is best for us after all, but seldom do. The arrows are fired straight and accurate, the intonations and nuances of speech are precisely captured. Laughter erupts all about us. Warm applause each time he ends. He has us in the palm of his hand.

All too soon he's done. He's back in the seat marked 'Reserved for the poet' alongside Helen 'his muse', who works at the Margaret Green Animal sanctuary at Church Knowle. He's off to the

Soho Theatre shortly for 2 live performances. More radio work later in the year, he tells me. Elvis McGonagall is a considerable talent. He needs only a little good fortune to become a star and a household name.

It's almost time to move on. I wonder, setting aside the young people who quit the town in pursuit of fame and fortune or because they cannot afford the property prices, how many older people leave Swanage? Let me give you a case study. He arrived as a young teacher in 1970, a Hull boy, with old-fashioned romantic Socialist leanings. He told the headmaster at the Modern School, Eddy Corben, he intended to stay for no more than a year.

"I arrived in January and, at first, I hated it. I knew no one. I couldn't get a flat, the beer was ghastly and the fish and chips were worse. I found the locals very unfriendly and suspicious, and I was amazed to find the 'squirearchy' alive and well in the Dorset countryside. A Yorkshireman tugs his forelock to no one!"

Nearly 40 years later Mike Etherington is still in Swanage and a part of the furniture. His daughter Hannah is a teacher here too. After being educated at the Purbeck she returned to the town. He's even become a grand-father. So what has Mike found in the town that's delayed his departure a mere 38 years?

"A variety of reasons, I suppose. Teaching in the north-east was tough. Even then a lot of the kids were a handful. It would be tougher still today. Down in Dorset if they get bored, they mostly want to sleep. It's also a great place to bring up your kids. It's pretty safe, everyone knows one another and, in common with all small communities and small schools, they look out for each other. Also I don't know many places in the world where you get such a variety of scenery in one small area. Hills, woods, sea cliffs, chalk down-land, heather down-land, it's all right on your doorstep. The Dorset coast east and west of Swanage is magnificent. I've spent years messing about in canoes and small sailing boats and never tire of the views of the shore. I think one of the best things I've ever done was to help set up Swanage Sea Rowing Club. Soon after we started I took half a dozen ladies who had never been out to sea before and we rowed to the end of Ballard Down. There's a cave at the end of the cliff big enough to take a 32 foot pilot gig, and I shall never forget the look of wonder and delight on these girls' faces as they sat in the cool dark of the cave looking out at the bright sunlight on the sea."

Mike's got his reservations, of course. The architecture of the past 50 years hasn't enhanced the town and there are several really ugly buildings the planners should never have allowed. He suggests some 'Spanish Costa-style houses next to the fishermen's huts at Peveril Point' as an opportunity to build something that would enhance rather than detract from the aesthetic quality of the town. But, whatever its shortcomings, Mike regards Swanage as 'a great place to live'. And with another grandchild on the way he has no plans to leave. It's a story that could be repeated with innumerable variations, I suspect, hundreds of times across the town.

There's a final point, I guess. As Paul Goodger observed right at the start, as we get older, most of us appreciate things that are 'a little bit in the past'. And, undeniably, Swanage is 'a little bit in the past'. But, in many ways, that is a real strength in a world that often seems to be changing too quickly and not always for the better.

Lulworth

*Lulworth Castle Estate With Wilfred Weld,
where the priorities of conversation are swiftly established*

"I remember being at Dean Park – it would have been 1948 or 1949, a game between Hampshire and Somerset. And this announcement came over the loudspeaker, 'Please would Harold Stephenson come out of which ever beer tent he is in as he is wanted on the field to carry out his duties as Twelfth Man.' A different world!"

Though I've come to talk estate politics and economics with Wilfred Weld, with our shared love of Hampshire cricket, it's scarcely surprising our conversation strays. Wilfred, of course, has been president of Hampshire CCC since the coronation of Edward VII – or something like that anyway.

"As a small boy I used to cycle down to Wool station, get the train to Bournemouth, then walk up to the cricket ground in Cavendish Road."

It's an engaging image, the small boy with his packed sandwiches – lettuce and caviar? – tramping up Richmond Hill to watch a day of old-fashioned three day county cricket in those immediate post-war years, when thousands flocked to the county grounds to renew their relationship with the game they loved. There must have been many occasions when Wilfred and I sat in the same crowd watching our heroes in those halcyon days before 'central contracts' and all the stars of the cricketing world, Len Hutton and Denis Compton, Peter May and Tom Graveney, Freddie Trueman and Jim Laker played regularly for their counties. Wilfred and I saw them all in those far-off childhood days. Certainly we established we were both present at Dean Park when Hampshire won their first County Championship in 1961. The names of Colin Ingleby-Mackenzie, Derek Shackleton (who went on to coach at Canford and sadly died earlier this year), David 'Butch' White (who was doing his National Service at Blandford when spotted by Hampshire), Roy Marshall and Peter Sainsbury are indelibly etched in our consciousness. Extraordinarily, many of Wilfred's heroes did in fact play in later years on the cricket square that Wilfred created in the grounds of Lulworth Castle, when he built the house in which he has lived for the past 30 years, soon to be vacated for his son James. Wilfred and Sally's other children are William, Thomas, Rose Mary, Lucy, Henrietta and Sophie.

"Generally we'd play on Sundays against a variety of club sides. We'd begin with coffee at 10.30 and often play on into the evening. Then it was back to the house for eggs and bacon at 10pm. They were wonderful days but very demanding upon my poor wife Sally!"

Wilf did actually play a game or two for Hampshire's Second XI so he must have been useful though he modestly dismisses the notion. Who was captain in the epic games at the Castle ground?

"Who do you think? It was my bat, my ball, my ground – it would be a poor show if I wasn't captain!"

We could talk cricket indefinitely but it's back to the serious matters – owning and managing one of the last surviving great estates in the county. A mere 12,000 acres or so. What do I own – one eighth of an acre, if that? But how could I be envious of such an affable man? Besides, what a responsibility, I say to myself, though Wilfred seems to wear his cares lightly enough.

"The estate then? We farm about 4,000 acres in all – that's about 50% 'in hand'. The MOD has about 1,000 acres, then there's 100 acres of traditional heath-land, 1,200 acres of woodland, tenant farmers occupy about 4,000 acres. Finally, we set aside about 500 hundred acres plus of down-land for events and parking."

Times have changed since Wilf assumed responsibility.

"When my father was here 50 years ago, there were 34 tenant farmers and Father farmed about 200 acres. Over the years as various individuals have given up their tenancies we have amalgamated farms and brought them 'in hand'. We're mainly dairy with about 1,000 cows. We have a contract to supply Marks & Spencer. We farm about 2,000 acres of arable, mostly wheat and we are engaged in various conservation projects, re-establishing the English partridge, for example, and other schemes to encourage breeding sites for lapwing, stone curlews, dormice, butterflies and so on. We're also committed to opening up footpaths. In all, we employ 3 rangers to deal with these responsibilities. Land management has changed dramatically over the years."

In fact, it was only a few months earlier that an ancient path from East Lulworth to Arish Mell was reopened almost 70 years after its enforced closure when the Army decided to expand its firing ranges. It was a fine team effort by the Lulworth Estate and the Army, as represented by Lt. Col. Charlie Lambert. James Weld observed at the reopening: "The last time this route was used by the Estate was in 1929 when the fire service attempted to draw water from the Arish Mell Gap to extinguish the devastating fire at Lulworth Castle"

And the splendid Lulworth Castle?

"The Castle attracts 75,000 visitors a year and is also available for events such as weddings and musical concerts. This year we hosted the Bestival which proved a great success. Financially, it also helps considerably that we have an income from the car-parks at Durdle Door and Lulworth Cove. To sum up, as a family, as an estate, we've simply had to become ever more commercial to survive, just like every other big estate in the country."

The formal discussion ended, it's back to the cricket and the Winner Takes All big match in the Caribbean which Wilfred will be watching with keen interest that very evening. (The Stanford fiasco). And, of course, his beloved Hampshire CCC.

"It's a great shame that Shane Warne didn't return to the club this summer, you know. I found him such a pleasant fellow – and what a cricketer!"

(Of course, Wilfred's son, James Weld, is today more often the 'public face' of the estate with Wilfred increasingly taking a 'back seat', but the temptation to talk Hampshire cricket with the great man himself was irresistible. I trust James will excuse my self-indulgence!)

Worth Matravers

It's a major problem across the county but nowhere as serious as here in Worth for this is the land of second homes. Estimates vary wildly between 20% and 50%. Local resident Colette Drayson suggests the figure may be even higher. Whatever the exact total, inevitably the principal anxiety of the local community is to find houses for the young who want to live in the area where they work and belong at prices they can afford. Here the difference between annual salaries and property prices is in a ratio of 20-30 times. One response has been the creation of the Worth Community Property Trust, run by volunteers, which aims to build low-cost homes for villagers on a shared ownership or rental basis. The chairman Bob Kenyon is hopeful the houses will be built on the northern side of the village with a binding legal agreement in place to ensure the properties remain 'affordable' in perpetuity. It is a bold and commendable initiative.

The Square and Compass

At least the good folk of Worth have a pub of their own, unlike so many villages. It is also a most remarkable pub. Few pubs have books written about them but this one has – *The Square and Compass: A Newman Century*. Its author is Ilay Cooper with illustrations by Jack Daniels. It's a pub that has been visited by more than its fair share of famous names from Augustus John to Amy Johnson, Sir Bernard Lovell and Alvar Lidell. The Square and Compass is owned by one of the great

Purbeck characters of modern times in Charlie Newman and has been in the family for nearly a hundred years. These days Charlie lives nearby with his partner Cath Bradshaw. One of the quirky features of the pub is that it boasts its own museum. It has just been crowned national cider pub of the year by CAMRA, the Campaign for Real Ale. The pub has been brewing its own ciders for a couple of years and stocks a range of others. As the manager Kevin Hunt observes:"We're very happy about the award. It's a pleasing recognition of what we are doing here."

Incidentally, this writer enjoyed the finest hot Cornish pasty of his travels at the Square and Compass.

The village even has its own Lord and a most distinguished gentleman he is for Lord Phillips of Worth Matravers is the Lord Chief Justice, the most senior judge in England and Wales. Lord Phillips has recently been expressing grave anxieties about the dangers of the early release of prisoners, the increasing reliance of the courts on fixed penalties even for what of us would regard as serious offences and the general problem of prison overcrowding. As Lord Phillips correctly observes there must be further investment in prisons if longer sentences are generally to be imposed for the more serious offences. Three hundred years ago another Lord Chief Justice bluntly spoke his mind in Dorset. I suspect his answer to prison overcrowding would have been a simple one for Judge George Jeffreys (1648-89), of course, presided over the 'Bloody Assizes', which included a visit to Dorchester, when 300 were hanged after the Monmouth Rebellion and several hundred more transported to the West Indies. For Lord Phillips of Worth Matravers the remedies of hanging and transportation no longer exist.

Tyneham

Not far away at Tyneham, Swanage-based artist Lynda Price and her husband John, are engaged in a fascinating and imaginative project to restore the Great Barn of the farm in the village as The History Barn, to be used when it is ready by school and community groups. Linda would like to be able to show how the farm worked and, for that reason, she is busy collecting old farm machinery. I look forward to seeing the result of Lynda and John's efforts on my next visit. Time and again across the county we see what passionate enthusiasts can achieve – from restoring old railway lines, creating 'living churchyard' projects, building up museum collections, conducting invaluable scientific research into butterflies and bats, and so on. It's brilliant and it's impossible to praise the individuals too much.

Church Knowle

The Margaret Green Animal Rescue

"For an old person obliged to enter a nursing home or hospital, the welfare of a much loved pet is of paramount importance in their lives. Or it might be a case of a family break-up, or a bereavement? Anyone who has ever had a pet and loved it very much will understand the dilemma facing individuals in such situations. What do you do for the best? Sometimes they know it will either be a matter of having their pet put to sleep or finding a new home. In such circumstances we are often able to help."

Donna White, the Trust's Marketing Manager, not only loves the animals who find their way to Church Knowle, she cares profoundly about the service the Trust can offer to those in need.

It was in 1965 that a wealthy Bournemouth businessman, Jerry Green, acquired the 35 acres in the quiet village of Church Knowle, set amongst the rolling hills and fields of the countryside just a mile or so east of Corfe Castle, and founded the sanctuary. In the years that followed his daughter Margaret developed and expanded its activities whose name it bears today. I've arrived on a Thursday lunchtime just in time to see a group of youthful, smiling teenagers departing.

"We have groups come out every Tuesday and Thursday. They relate to the animals and it's a very valuable and rewarding experience for them. "

Donna and I walk around the barns and enclosures and she introduces me to a number of the characters who occupy them, horses, dogs, rabbits, pigs, donkeys, not quite Noah's Ark but a good cross-section of the animal kingdom.

"We've also got a feral cat colony which lives nearby. We put food out for them. They sleep in the barns and stables."

Before I came I hadn't given thought to the range of services the sanctuary provides. Caring for abandoned animals and the victims of cruelty, finding homes for strays, I understood that, of course. But granting peace of mind to the aged or the sick, unable any longer to care for their pets, by taking them in temporarily or for longer periods, even sometimes for the rest of their lives, that was an invaluable role I hadn't considered. In the general scheme of things, the Rescue Centre is but a small oasis of kindness and compassion and love, but what a brilliant service it provides to the wider community. Rescuing and re-homing more than a thousand animals of all kinds every year, providing a permanent refuge where it is necessary, the Margaret Green Foundation Trust, like so many small charities, finds it a permanent struggle to balance its books and meet its costs. In the current economic climate it is going to be even tougher for so many similar worthy bodies. We must not forget them.

(Since the number is small I shall make space for the names of the five patrons of the Trust – Edward Fox, the actor, Lady Saunders (formerly TV's Katie Boyle), Claire King of Emmerdale Farm fame, Anthony Head and Sarah Fisher. Aside from all the splendid volunteers, the other employees include Ellie Makin, Alister Beardmore, Julie Ford, Vicki Frampton and Alex Evans.)

The Purbecks

Other matters

Many farmers on the Isle of Purbeck are very concerned about the huge increase in deer numbers, especially the herds of Sika that are now causing serious crop damage across the locality. Though they can be shot legally by landowners who find them eating their crops, a number of local landowners have sold the shooting rights to deer stalking companies so the tenant farmers are unable to take action. Malcolm Elford, of Kingswood Farm, is one such individual affected. He says the deer are putting his livelihood at risk eating up to a tonne of his crops each night. Another tenant farmer, Julian Cranton, says the existence of the MOD ranges and the absence of humans from large tracts of the land, makes It easier for the deer to flourish undisturbed. He adds that the MOD is doing all it can to help but the sheer numbers of deer are continuing to present a serious problem. He reports herds up to 200 in size with an estimated 3,000-4,000 in the Poole basin today.

As a part of the £2million Keystone Project a set of 19th century sheds and quarry buildings are to be renovated in Langton where it is hoped the traditional stone-carving skills can be kept alive. As the project manager, Jo Bowry, observes:"It's intended that the centre will ultimately teach the skills of the past and promote traditional stone sculpture. There are still a number of quarries here in Purbeck and we don't want to lose that invaluable link with the past. The Centre will be open to students and visitors alike and we will provide apprenticeships as well as recreational stone-working."

As another aspect of the Keystone Project, Richard Caldow, the bio-diversity officer, is overseeing an important conservation scheme in the area of the Frome Valley intended to improve wet grassland

Clive Hannay's 'The Heart of Dorset'. Clive's work is available through Peter Hayton at Towngate Gallery, Poole

habitats and so encourage the return of birds like the lapwing, redshank and snipe. Sluices have been built at Priory Farm, East Holme and Manor and Bindon Farm, Wool. With so many bird species under threat because of the loss of habitat, it will be fascinating to see the outcome of Richard's work in the coming years.

In another splendid project the 16.272 stones of the Clavell Tower, built in 1830 by the Revd. John Clavell, have been moved brick by brick from its perch on a cliff at Kimmeridge Bay 25 yards further inland, by means of a grant from the Heritage Lottery Fund and additional support from the celebrated crime writer, P.D.James, who featured the tower in her novel *The Black Tower*. The Landmark Trust, which has been involved directly in the painstaking and highly skilled work deserves much praise – from Adrian Tinniswood and Peter Pearce, who have overseen the project, to each one of the fine craftsmen who have helped to save this celebrated Purbeck landmark.

Corfe Castle
Twinned with Pont Hebert (France)

It's one of the ruins that 'Cromwell knocked about a bit'. On any day of the year it looks magnificent, as does the village itself. Every year tens of thousands visit. If the roads in summer now are often congested, how many would be visiting if the Roundheads had simply decided to garrison it with their own men and leave it alone? It was vandalism on a scale scarcely paralleled anywhere in the kingdom. I've visited scores of times, walked up and down and all around it. It never fails to excite the imagination. So much history, so much drama, and so many characters, good and bad, have dwelt within its walls. Almost invariably, before I leave, I pop into Dragon's the bakers. Years ago I taught Clive and Hilary Dragon. Each week, usually on a Wednesday, one or the other would bring into my classroom in Wareham a 'Dragon' loaf, freshly baked, crusty and often still warm from the bakery. It was a standing order, as good as any bread in the county. I knew Mum and Dad Dragon and very nice people they were – good-hearted Salvationists. Clive blew his trumpet in the band every Sunday. Now Nigel, the eldest son upholds the family tradition, and a fine baker he is. One of my favourite characters in the village was Tim Stockley whose house overlooked the churchyard. The first sight every morning when he drew the curtains was that of the headstones in the churchyard. 'TCP', as I knew him, was as solid and dependable as the stone in the castle itself, kind-hearted, reliable, unfailingly cheerful, like his sister Mary – but neither are about this morning as I explore again. Besides, would I still recognise them? Tim must be in long trousers by now, after all.

Across the road at The Castle Inn is hotelier Andy Hageman, better known as the Basil Fawlty of Corfe, though there's a kind heart beating somewhere within, I'm assured. They hold a family fun day there and landlady, Laurice Turner, explains that all the moneys raised go to the local primary and the football club. Up the road is the Ginger Pop shop which is devoted to the works of Enid Blyton. Though some may affect to look snootily down upon the lady's work, she remains enduringly popular. At different times I have run school libraries and I know how many children enjoyed her stories. And if they fell in love with reading as a result, they could progress to other more demanding literature as they got older. Why despise what is innocent, free of bad language and gives pleasure? Of course, the shop is here in Corfe for this is Blyton country. Miss Blyton wrote many of her stories just a few miles down the road at the Isle of Purbeck Golf Club. The settings of a number of her stories are all around us. Viv Endecott, the shop's owner, is planning to celebrate the 40th anniversary of the author's death in November at Earth House in Cranborne with readings of some of Miss Blyton's stories. Viv has also recently commissioned a new portrait of Miss Blyton by her friend Hannah Avery wearing one of her Famous Five badges with Corfe Castle in the background. Good luck to Viv, say I.

Castle Inn, Fun Day. *Picture: Pat Timmons,*
Bournemouth Echo

Back in the tiny square, in the shadow of the castle, sits the Greyhound Inn, said to be the most photographed pub in the kingdom. Elen Lesourd, who works in The Greyhound, says visitors particularly love to sit in the garden which backs on to the castle itself. And Corfe itself ranks among the top ten of the nation's favourite views, which comes as no surprise to Steve Hitchens, chairman of the Corfe Castle Town Trust. As he says: "There are so many different positions from which to view the castle. It's all good publicity which helps all our traders."

Now the scaffolding is gone and the restoration work of the past 2 years is done. It was a protracted and demanding job for the National Trust and public safety is always a major concern. Pam White, Corfe's community and learning officer, explains some of the techniques used. "We've used turf to cap many of the walls. The turf is made of lime-tolerant grasses and native wildflowers. This will stop much of the rain from getting into the stonework. Combined with breathable joints, this in turn will allow the water that does get in to evaporate through the lime mortar rather than the stonework."

Doug Whyte, property manager for the NT in Purbeck sums up:"It's no exaggeration to say the work has saved the castle from closure."

Edward Fox OBE lives not far away with his wife Joanna David, both most distinguished members of the acting profession. Their daughter Emilia has followed in their footsteps. They also have a son Freddie. I have admired all three actors enormously in their various roles over the years. Edward has often involved himself in local community affairs, his association with both the Rex Cinema and the Margaret Green sanctuary being just two examples and he and his family are regarded with much affection and respect in the district.

It's time to move on but not, of course, before a visit to Dragon's Village bakery!

Studland

'Naturists may be seen beyond this point'

It's a rum old world, as they say. When a group of naturists insisted upon walking along the Jurassic Coast coastal path between Swanage and Lulworth Cove wearing only walking boots, aside from the rucksacks strapped to their backs, they were indignant that the police insisted upon accompanying them in order to allay any objections from fully clothed members of the public they might happen to meet. Personally, I would have found it interesting to have watched them clambering over stiles and negotiating any thistles en route, but I suspect humour is not a commodity in great abundance on such occasions.

Studland, as we have all known for many years, is one of the favourite places in the UK 'to let it all hang out'. In fact, the National Trust has recognised a half-mile stretch of Knoll beach as an official naturist area, indicated by marker posts, formally recognising a practice that has gone on in the locality for almost a hundred years.

As Emma Wright, the NT's visitor services and enterprise manager for Studland beach, remarks: "The road came in 1923 and then the ferry which opened up the area to people not only from the UK but all over the world. Studland was full of arty people who were exploring alternative life styles and different sexual relationships."

While 'exposure' was once a criminal offence, now only 'aggressive exposure' is illegal but not nude sun-bathing. Interpreting the law cannot, at times, be easy for those seeking to enforce it. Inspector Ashley Adams, the Purbeck section Commander, and his team have had to cope with a variety of questionable activities both embarrassing and offensive to most visitors, especially family groups with children. The Studland Beach Users Action group was formed to protect the image

The bottom line!

of the area from 'the inappropriate behaviour of a minority.' Another body, SUN or the Studland United Nudists comprising 100 members or so, are anxious to co-operate with the police, the NT and SBUAG, fearful that offensive conduct by that minority might lead the NT to reconsider its position.

Considering the appalling weather this summer, the absence of sun and the deluge of rain, there must be some very bedraggled, sodden naturists crouched between the dunes.

WAREHAM
Twinned with Hemsbach (Germany)

He was my favourite author. I preferred him even to Captain W.E.Johns. I have a list still of exactly how many and which of his books I read, copied into an ancient, red exercise book in my childhood hand. The aggregate was 15 with a further 3 written by his brother J.F.C.Westerman. Many were venerable, battered, pre-war editions for there were few newly published books on school or public library shelves in the 'Austerity' years after the war. I have no idea how much the librarian at Wimborne Grammar had to spend on books but it could not have been much, a pitiful sum compared to what school librarians are allocated today, no doubt. But how we valued those books and how keenly I enjoyed those dark winter nights reading in bed the stories of Percy F.Westerman. And, all the while, unbeknown to me, my literary hero was living on board his boat 'Dot' on the Frome not a dozen miles away at Wareham.

So, this morning, sitting in the club house of the Redclyffe Yacht Club beside the river and

Wareham Quay. *Picture: Pamela Bowyer-Davis*

beneath a photograph of the great man, brings the memories of my boyhood flooding back. Percy F. Westerman, (1876-1959), the founder of Redclyffe Yacht Club in 1933, is largely forgotten today. I fear his adventure stories, many of them set in the years of the Great War, with titles such as *With Beatty off Jutland* and *A Lively Bit of the Front* do not read too well today. Incidentally, when the damp of the river Frome became disagreeable to ageing bones Percy F took refuge at Eastcote, Bestwall in the town itself. Today I am in the company of Ruth Solomon, the Hon Sec, and Colin Page, father of Tim and Vicky, a marine engineer and former freelance Fleet Street illustrator. Colin joined the Yacht Club back in 1965 and this summer joined in the 75th anniversary celebrations along with its other 125 full members and friends.

"We are a 'dry' club, of necessity really. We're well off the beaten track here at Redclyffe, as you can see. We couldn't possibly safely store alcohol. As it is, there's nothing here that thieves would be interested in."

It is a splendid location. Monica Hutchings wrote of the club house as situated *'where a bluff of hard red hillside juts above the river'* and I cannot improve upon her description. Indeed the stroll from the town along the river bank is one of the most agreeable of so many fine walks in Wareham. With views across the river to the church of Lady St. Mary's, the Granary restaurant and The Priory on one side, and the flat expanse of water meadows extending towards Stoborough on the other, with the ruins of Corfe Castle in the distance, it is a unchanging scene of great beauty and tranquillity.

"We're 11 miles to the harbour entrance, an hour and a half to The Haven, "says Colin.

It would be tempting to join a leisurely cruise on such a morning but there is, alas, no time for 'messing about on the river' with so much to be done. It's back into town and another call.

"More than 1,000 years ago Wareham was said to be one of the 3 most important towns in Wessex – along with Winchester and Southwark. And we're 400 years senior to Poole and Wimborne, as I constantly remind the Mayors of those towns."

Malcolm Russell, Wareham's Mayor, laughs. "Nothing like a little local pride to stir the blood!"

Former REME officer Malcolm was first motivated to become actively involved in local affairs when he joined those arguing their case for the Sandford by-pass – 'the A351 campaign.'

"The simple truth is that Sandford needs a by-pass. As anyone who uses the road will know, there are acute traffic problems which are getting worse year after year. Unfortunately we were constantly obstructed by two individuals in particular representing English Nature, or Natural England, as it is today. We all love the countryside – not least myself – but they displayed what I would describe as the 'lance-corporal attitude '. By that I mean they were like the L.Cpl. who's in charge of the stores and just slams down the flap when a soldier asks for a piece of kit. He's showing his authority just for the sake of it – in short, being thoroughly bloody-minded. The two individuals constantly put obstacles in our way. We'd no sooner found one solution than they discovered another reason to be awkward. At one point a snail measuring just one millimetre, which is invisible to the naked eye, was under threat, so they claimed. I pointed out that every time I put my foot down in the area of heathland where they live I must be murdering hundreds! But that's how they were – unreasonable, uncompromising. When the welfare of a minute snail takes precedence over the needs of tens of thousands of humans I believe we have taken leave of our senses. Besides which, nature is very resilient and the creature was certainly in no danger of extinction. How on earth would Stephenson and Brunel and Brindley ever have built the railways and canals in modern England?"

Is the issue therefore dead and buried?

"How can it be when the need remains? Unfortunately the cost has escalated to at least £250million today. No Government is going to provide the funds in the current economic climate, but the matter will return. That is absolutely inevitable."

Malcolm is enjoying his year in the civic 'hot seat' but he is, he confesses, constantly looking over his shoulder.

"Every year there's some horror at some stage. I'm just keeping my fingers crossed."

Though Malcolm is a Conservative by persuasion he has reservations about politics in local government.

"Do we really need a political animal as a councillor or Mayor? It's about serving the community as best one can, isn't it? Judging issues on their merits?"

We also establish that I met Malcolm and his wife Dawn more than 20 years ago when I taught their daughters, Sheena and Bernice. It's a small world.

The Centenary Year of Wareham golf club

"The day before the judging of the Small Town In Bloom finals I noticed that one of the hanging baskets was looking rather sorry for itself. It hadn't been watered properly, I suspect, so I switched it with one from around the corner."

Was that the critical moment, I ask myself? Was my home town of Wimborne outflanked by the Machiavellian cunning of this otherwise charming lady sitting beside me in the clubhouse of Wareham Golf Club this autumn morning? Audrey Tighe, Deputy Mayor, is friendly enough in all conscience, but there are limits to friendship. Besides, I ask myself, how can Wimborne compete on level terms with a rival that invites judges to view hanging baskets from the ninth hole of such a magnificent location? And what were they fed on, I wonder, these judges – cream cakes and doughnuts from Dragon's of Corfe Castle, lardy cakes and Belgian buns from the award-winning Clive Williams of Wool? Or did this lady beside me turn her fair hand to cake making besides her other skulduggery?

Wareham golf club is Audrey's second home these days. Her name is even inscribed in gold lettering on the board above my head – a ladies' champion in her pomp, no less. For years Audrey lived at Sandford, moving into Wareham in 2000 after the death of her husband Jack. She's the only Labour councillor which speaks volumes for her personal popularity. Audrey would like to see young people in the town have premises of their own. Many of them are reluctant to go up to the Purbeck Sports Centre, she says, associating it too closely with school. It's always a delicate issue, of course, young people having a place of their own when there are pubs near at hand. Most may be sensible enough, but there's often an awkward minority. I would guess those are the reservations of those uneasy about the proposal.

Audrey attends the local Catholic Church which attracts a regular congregation of a hundred or so, she says. Always ready to embrace change, she would welcome one reform in particular.

"I do believe in this day and age the clergy should be free to marry."

Audrey picks out two names for me particularly worthy of praise for their selfless efforts on behalf of others.

"Mary Wainwright has worked very hard for the community. Mary sits on innumerable committees. And Ann Selby, she's a wonderful lady in all sorts of ways. She saved up and collected enormous quantities of papers, raising money for the Carey Hall. She's the mother of Paul."

Of course, Paul Selby, I remember him very well – a splendid young man, always courteous with a quiet dignity that impressed everyone. And Audrey's has children of her own too – Michelle, a policewoman, who won an award for bravery, Martine, Patrick or 'Paddy' who teaches sport, and John, a member of my old Wareham School Cricket XI. I taught them all at one time. My former pupils are everywhere.

"My father, the Revd. Peter Matthews, was at one time the curate at Lady St. Mary's."

If only the Revd. Matthews had lived to see the event, he would have been very proud of his daughter Susan (Elmes) last year when she was chosen to be the Mayor of the town. I ask the former Parkstone GS student Susan what projects she would highlight among the local community's principal achievements of the last year or two.

"A mobility shop was opened in the town and the Hauses Field project on Northmoor – both have proved to be successes. Les Burns and Kevin Randall were the driving forces behind the clearance of Hauses Field. It's a 5 acre site and lots of volunteers, like tree surgeons and plant hire people gave freely of their time and skills to create an attractive open space for children to play. We also raised a grand total of £5,640 last year for charity which reflects so well upon the many kind, big-hearted individuals who worked to raise it."

Susan supports Audrey Tighe in campaigning for a 'youth cafe' in the town which, she believes, would be much appreciated by Wareham youngsters.

"We could let them decorate the premises so they would feel a sense of ownership and responsibility for it. There could be a pool table, computers, a large TV screen, coffee and soft-drink facilities. The police would know where they were and it could be properly monitored. Many young people simply don't want to go back to school which is what they feel they are doing if they go up to the Sports Centre."

Sue is, of course, married to one of the town's great, born and bred Wareham 'characters' Hughie Elmes. To describe him as 'larger than life' would be no more than the truth. The bailiff to the Court Leet, Hughie is also no mean author and his latest literary masterpiece is *Ye Olde Wareham Pub Crawl* in which he describes no fewer than 27 local taverns that once existed about the town. He's also arranging 'pub tours' about the town but not, I hasten to add, to all 27 since most of them have long since closed their doors. Quite what condition even dear Hughie would be in after visiting that little collection, one shudders to think. Susan would be attending to the man with the biggest hangover in Dorset's inebriated history!

Wareham in Bloom

"To tell you the truth, I rather suspect Anthony (Oliver) is just a little envious that Wareham is physically so compact whereas Wimborne is rather more spread out. It does make it a more difficult for them."

As the mastermind behind Wareham's recent successes in the Britain in Bloom competition, Eric Osmond, has a clear strategy when it comes to spiking the guns of his competitors.

"It is vital that as people enter the town a good impression is immediately created. Maintaining the verges, planting bulbs and flowers persuades visitors that here is a town that cares about itself. Seeing St. Martin's Church well decorated reinforces the general impression. Keeping as many of the displays as possible at eye level is also important. They shouldn't be placed too high or they lose much of their impact. We also have to remember these days 'Health & Safety' regulations, so watering must be possible when standing on the ground and not perched up ladders. Altogether we have a team of 40 volunteers and 80 units – stands, troughs, baskets and so on. The pubs look after their own displays and they make an excellent fist of it, especially Julia Ballard at the King's Arms and Kevin Mitchell at the Duke of Wellington. Of course, it's all excellent advertising for the town. When a town looks attractive and inviting, visitors are much more inclined to stop and wander about, look in the shops, call in at the pubs and cafes and generally spend their money here. And, on a daily basis, it's so much more pleasant for all the local people when the town looks really pleasing to the eye. It all started in a very small way back in 1991 when we planted bulbs in the verges and we've gone on from there. I must give credit too to individuals like Simon Goldsack at Holme Nurseries who initially supplied the bulbs and Jorg Annaheim , a Swiss nurseryman at Sandford, who today supplies the flowers for Wareham in Bloom. 'Wareham flowers are my reputation', Jorg said. And he's proved just how good his flowers are. Our Town Clerk, Rod Curtis, is also very supportive. It is very much a team effort."

Winfrith born Eric, married to Renate, joined the Council in 1991 and served two terms as Mayor in 1995-6. He is also keen to compliment the work of several other individuals who have helped to make Wareham a better, brighter place in recent years.

"John Scott, the Project Manager behind Wareham & District Development Trust, has been responsible for improving footpaths, work on the Priory meadows, putting in stone benches and seats and information boards and the 'Lifewheels , Hire and Buy' at St. John's Hill. Steve Brett has also been brilliant in his capacity as Senior Supervisor at Community Payback which has its County HQ at Sandford Lane. Steve organises offenders who wear yellow tabards, so that people can see them, and they've done not just litter-picking but cutting back hedges, painting gates and railings at the Cenotaph and St. Martin's .An administration fee is paid by way of recompense. When I see Steve he'll call out: "Can we help? Any jobs need doing?" And, of course, Les Burns and Kevin Randall who are always so involved – the community cannot thank such people enough for all they do."

A centuries old tradition kept alive in Wareham every year is the inspection carried out of the local pubs by the members of the Court Leet. The inspectors regularly include bread weighers, ale tasters, leather sealers, carniters who check meat, and scavengers who have the dubious distinction of making sure the toilets are all in good working order. Any landlords in the town failing to comply with the requisite standards are obliged to provide a drink for the 'common pot'. As the respective 'officers' gather at the Town Hall to produce their reports, the chimes of noon are followed by the traditional 13th stroke of the newly restored bell in the building opposite. Earlier in my travels a certain Roly Reynolds in Portland passed a somewhat disparaging judgement on the 'goings on' of Wareham's Court Leet. However, as my old friend, the bailiff Hughie Elmes, observes: "I think it's very important to maintain the tradition. I'm the third generation of my family to take part."What is certainly true is that Hughie is not going to be corrupted by the scale of his salary or any expenses he might receive, unlike a number of our not so honourable Members of Parliament. He receives the princely sum of £1 per annum.

A passing thought, Hughie. Why not invite the good Roly over for the occasion next year?

My own earliest acquaintance with Wareham and district came as a member of a party of ten year-olds from Lytchett Minster School on a week-long stay at Carey Camp. My most vivid memory is of being rudely awoken just after dawn, along with my friend John Selby, now a conservation worker, on a bitterly cold morning and instructed with a dozen others to pick up stones. It was a collective punishmentmeted out for the misdemeanours of certain precocious individuals who were rumoured to have visited a neighbouring girls' tent in the early hours. We innocent ones who had slept through the entire episode weren't sure whether to feel angry or envious. Mentioning John's role in conservation reminds me of a comment made to him recently by his daughter.

"Dad, you say you are a conservationist, but you always seem to be destroying something, burning it, cutting it down or digging it up! "

Of course the old Number 89 rumbled along the Dorchester Road bearing left at the Baker's Arms and on through Holton Heath and Sandford to Wareham. But the general opinion in those far-off days was that there was absolutely no reason for anyone to journey to Wareham because there was nothing there unless, of course, it was to visit an ancient grand-parent or elderly aunt. Even

The centuries old tradition of the Court Leet is celebrated. *Picture: Pat Timmons Bournemouth Echo*

then, we felt sorry that they had to visit such a dismal place. Such an opinion remained unchanged even when I bought a car and journeyed there with a group of friends for a night-out. Invariably we left feeling depressed with a feeling we had wasted our time. 'Wareham was a bit of a dump' was the general view but, of course, we were teenagers at the time and no doubt the good citizens of the town felt rather differently. There was a certain irony then in my acceptance ten years later of the offer of a teaching post at Wareham Modern School in Worgret Road by the headmaster, Don West.

What was true, however, was that by the late Sixties the town was undergoing change. New housing developments at Northmoor and elsewhere in the area were bringing more professional people and more money into the local economy. New restaurants were opened, the pubs were serving food and more imaginative shop displays were brightening up the general appearance of the town .The former drabness was beginning to fade into memory.

At Wareham Modern legendary figures were still teaching, masters who had been a part of the fabric of the town for generations. Jack 'Shady' Armstrong, Geography Master and lifelong Socialist, had arrived at the school in September, 1939, to find his first task was to welcome a train bearing 'evacuees' from London who were initially accommodated at the school before being farmed out to local families. One of the most popular teachers was 'Bill' Price, the Head of English and quite one of the most civilised and courteous of men I have been privileged to know. His school assemblies were the best I ever heard and full of gentle wisdom and common sense. 'Bill' sought valiantly to cultivate an appreciation of literature and poetry in youthful rustic minds. 'Doug' Mellor, Mathematics teacher and the father of David, the Conservative politician and football pundit, was another. The young Mellor, of course, was a pupil of Swanage Grammar before entering politics where he was described by an old colleague, David Saville, as 'probably the sharpest mind I ever encountered in any classroom.'

In the town itself one of the fixtures was Oliver 'Rusty' Irons who ran the Rex Cinema from 1963 to1986 when he decided unsurprisingly, at the age of 78, to retire and sell it to a small local consortium 'The Friends of the Rex'. The history of the cinema, which began life in 1922 and still has its original gas lights, is related by the redoubtable Hughie Elmes in his admirable '1980 to the Millennium with the Local Yokel'. In recent months the future of the Rex has been in question owing to the departure and retirement of a number of the members of the consortium. Of the original 9 just 2 remain active, one of whom, Dougal Dixon, observed that 'it had become too hot to handle.' Sadly, at the same time, one of the best loved figures associated with the Rex and the annual Film Festival, Sir Bill Cotton, the former Head of BBC Light Entertainment, passed away. Happily, recent months brings the infinitely more cheering news that the Purbeck Film Charitable Trust which runs the annual Purbeck Film Festival, backed by Viridor Credits, the Town and District Councils, has completed the purchase of the cinema. The jubilant chairman of the Trust, Tony Viney, Neil Child, Hilary and David Evans, the director of the Festival, Town Mayor Malcolm Russell, Gary Suttle, leader of the Purbeck Council and Patrick Capper, Viridor's chief executive, have expressed their collective delight at the successful outcome of campaigning and fund-raising. I am sure the good burgers of Wareham will share their pleasure. The Rex is an irreplaceable asset to the town.

Another of the town's familiar faces in years past was that of Arthur Grant, father of Geoffrey and Annette, who photographed just about everyone and everything that moved with unfailing patience and good-nature. Arthur was a schoolboy at Tyneham when it was taken over by the military in the war and he often spoke of his days in the village. His school-desk can still be seen in the village school-room.

Christmas in Wareham

"It all began with a successful bet at Wincanton races in December, 1958, exactly 50 years ago. Four local businessmen, Jack Spiller, George Burt, Cecil Mears and Tony Gurner-Jones, then the Licensee of the Red Lion Hotel, were celebrating a £300 win on a bet they'd placed. They resolved to use the money to erect a Christmas tree outside the hotel and to arrange for Father Christmas to give a present to local children. From this beginning has grown an annual parade watched by 4,000 plus every Christmas. It's now a tradition for Father Christmas to arrive in his golden boots on a different form of transport each year. In previous years he has used the James Bond boat, a dog sledge and camels – real live camels x 3 – we try to keep them guessing! He then climbs on to the roof of the Red Lion. Of course, he is properly harnessed – we don't want any accidents. Nigel Spiller now plays Father Christmas, for years it was his father John. We like to be able to give all the children special gifts each year. It really is something brilliant and very special. The whole event is now organised by a Father Christmas Committee."

I knew Les Burns long before he became a councillor and later the Mayor of the town. In those days he was Inspector Les Burns, finishing his days as a Chief Superintendent. Les was hugely respected by his colleagues and the public who knew him as eminently approachable and fair-minded.

"I don't envy the modern bobby's lot. Not one bit. It's so much more difficult than in my days with the drugs, violence, verbal abuse and, of course, political terrorism. Then there's that gigantic burden

Christmas, traditional style at the Red Lion, Wareham. *Picture: Pamela Bowyer-Davis*

of paperwork that militates against fighting crime and efficiency. Like magistrates the modern policeman is far less likely to know his community. I began by living in a police house in the locality I served. Magistrates were likewise likely to be appointed locally, so there was much closer liaison between the bobby and the courts. Now I might live in Ringwood and motor to Wareham every day for my 8 hour shift. And many of the courts have moved away from the small towns. Years ago we weren't community policemen – we were policemen living in the community. The whole process has been centralised. Local police stations have been closed or their opening hours severely reduced. As for criminals, it really is very difficult to get into prison these days. Some crimes are more acceptable – like theft. Providing you don't steal more than £200 as a shoplifter you'll be punished by a fine. Criminal damage below £500 is also punishable a by a fine of just £80! Even many offenders guilty of threats or conspiracy to murder and arsonists often receive only a caution. Juveniles have to commit many more crimes before they appear in court – and the average age for youth crime is steadily dropping. Instead of being dealt with severely from the start they are encouraged by the system to expand their criminal activities. By the time they actually appear in court they are often hardened criminals. Even when they are convicted the Home Office wants to keep them out of prison because of overcrowding. As for the crime figures they have to be taken with a pinch of salt. Much crime is not recorded because it is too much trouble and too time consuming for the overworked policeman. We've watered everything down – the courts cannot cope with the numbers of offenders. People just don't realise what it feels like to be at the sharp end. There have to be proper sanctions in place. People need to know where they are."

I know Les speaks for a huge number of police officers, past and present, in articulating his concerns. We would do well to pay heed for it is the voice of long experience and mature judgement. It has been a great pleasure to meet Les Burns again, his wife and their daughter Michelle, another of my former students, who now paints for a living including the signage for country paths and local nature reserves. How fortunate I have been to know so many fine young people – and their parents.

One much deserved award made at the year's end is to Roy Anderson and his wife Nancy as' Volunteers of the Year' for all their many services to the community over a long period. Roy is a former long-serving councillor and Mayor of the town and a Justice of the Peace. Sadly, not long after the award, Roy passed away. I will simply quote the tribute paid to him by a former colleague on the District Council, Bill Trite. 'Purbeck has lost one of its finest and most dedicated public servants – always fair, even-handed, with an unruffled calmness and a desire for inclusivity towards all members.'

Art in Wareham

It's always a pleasure to call by at Peter Hedley's Gallery in South Street. Peter invariably stocks an attractive collection of original paintings and prints. Often I call by at some small gallery and emerge reflecting that, even with unlimited cash in my pocket, there's absolutely nothing that I would buy. That doesn't apply at Peter's for there are always many paintings that reflect genuine artistic ability, rather than mere daubs of paint splashed over a canvas accompanied by some pretentious wordy rubbish telling us what the artist is supposedly communicating. Everyone has seen the canvas that, for all the world, could have been painted by a small child or a cat with a brush tied to its tail, with a text explaining that the painting reflects 'The nature of rural life in post-Stalinist Bulgaria', or 'Here the artist is expressing her sub-conscious desire for motherhood frustrated only by the wicked economic policies of Mrs. Thatcher.'

But there are talented artists in Wareham and district. Alas, I have only time to mention two. One is a young man called Mark Farmer I knew some years ago whose canvasses decorate the walls of the Duke of Wellington. The other is known to a much wider public and lives at Sandford with his wife Terri and daughters, Ashleigh and Rowan. By profession he is actually a painter and decorator- and I have no doubt a most splendid one. But what I would do first is to step back 25 years to a history classroom and an earnest young fellow sitting at his desk drawing the most meticulous pictures of historical scenes and locations in his exercise book. They were the accompaniment to his written work which was completed with an equal degree of conscientious application. The boy's name was Clive Hannay and his privileged history teacher was this author. Today Clive's drawings and paintings appear regularly in *Dorset Life* and his canvasses hang in many living-rooms around the county. As all those familiar with Clive's work will know, his attention to detail in his scenes from the Dorset countryside or of churches and houses is nothing short of astonishing.

"To tell you the truth I was doing my head in. I needed to step back, to relax, to paint with more freedom."

Clive laughs but I know exactly what he means. When you are his kind of artist, where do you stop in your search for perfection – another brushstroke here or there, a few more tiny dots of paint somewhere else? Gaze at his work and you wonder how on earth he manages the subtlety and the detail. But it was all there in that small boy I knew many years ago – so diligent, intellectually curious and unfailingly courteous in the class-room. With typical kindness Clive tells me I may use any of his work in my book and I am delighted to feature one of his finest paintings *Heart of Dorset*.

One lovely young lady from Northmoor Park whose face appeared in all the newspapers and on TV 20 or so years ago, who still regularly returns to the locality is Shelley Preston. When the chart-topping group and Eurovision Song Competition winners, Bucks Fizz, were looking for a replacement singer they ran a national competition of their own. Shelley, a former Sixth Form Purbeck pupil, successfully auditioned and so began a musical career that saw her touring with the band and stars like Jason Donovan and Michael Bolton. Unspoilt and unaffected by success, Shelley remains the delightful girl her teachers and friends knew 20 odd years ago. Without fail, each Christmas the first card to arrive through my letter-box is from Shelley and her son Ben.

Alas, for I am fond of Wareham, it is already time to continue my journey and leave behind this town where I have so many friends and acquaintances. More than most, I believe, Wareham has changed for the better in the past half century. It is brighter, more welcoming and certainly more prosperous, yet it has contrived to lose nothing of its inherent aesthetic appeal. It remains a small market town surrounded by water meadows and fields and trees with, of course, the splendid Frome flowing gently and quietly through its very heart. I know I shall return many times in the years ahead which eases the pain and regret of departure today.

Education in Dorset

With particular reference to south-east Dorset and the grammar/comprehensive debate

It's a topic as complex as any in the book – the story of education in Dorset these past 50 years (and elsewhere in the UK for that matter). It is a theme we should surely put under the microscope because it is of such monumental importance to our children, our grandchildren and all their futures. I have only ever read in Dorset publications the facts of the changes as they took place. I have seen no serious evaluation of those changes. It is almost as if they were an Act of God and the absence of subsequent discussion definitive proof that the architects of change in the 1960s and 1970s were correct. I am neither saying they were right or wrong, but let us try seriously to examine certain aspects of what happened and any lessons we may usefully learn. I appreciate fully that what follows is barely scratching at the surface of the subject. In truth, a whole book could usefully be devoted to a most thorough examination of education in Dorset. Perhaps one day someone with the time and energy may have the ambition and patience to take up the challenge. In the meanwhile, let us talk to a number of those who witnessed and participated in the changes at first hand. I have no doubt but that the shades of opinions expressed in this study would be replicated, with only modest alteration, in other locations about the county.

Fifty years ago every Dorset town still retained its own grammar school which, by means of the 11 plus, selected approximately 20% of the children of that age group to follow what was regarded as an 'academic' education. The remaining 80% attended secondary modern schools with a small number at technical schools such as the one at Weymouth. By the 1980s, following reorganisation, all the grammar schools outside Poole and Bournemouth had disappeared to be replaced by comprehensives. In some areas of the county 'middle schools' were created educating children between the ages of 9-13. Elsewhere the age of transfer from junior to secondary varied from place to place and is still the subject of review and change. Some of the new comprehensives evolved on the old grammar school sites as at Lyme Regis; some on the old secondary modern sites as at Wimborne; in other places brand new, purpose built schools were built as with The Purbeck at Wareham and Corfe Hills at Broadstone/Corfe Mullen. Only in Poole and Bournemouth did the grammar schools survive in the form of Poole Grammar for Boys, Parkstone Grammar for Girls, and the two single sex Bournemouth schools. Public schools, meanwhile, such as those at Sherborne, Canford, Bryanston and Milton Abbey continued to go their independent ways.

One of the most significant figures in the changes in East Dorset was Don West, now 86, who arrived in Dorset in 1967 with his wife Delia and their young family to become the headmaster of Wareham Modern, fully aware that an educational revolution in the Purbeck area was imminent and eager to play a leading role in the reorganisation. With a wealth of experience in education both in this country and post-war Nigeria, as well as service in the RAF, Don had no doubts that comprehensive schools were the way forward.

"At the heart of the matter were the inadequacies of the Butler Act of 1944, the existence of the tripartite system and the failure of the eleven plus to differentiate accurately between pupils of different abilities. Many able pupils failed and still fail the test, wherever it exists. That is the simple, incontrovertible truth and there is no escaping it."

The Purbeck School began life in 1974 combining four schools, Swanage Grammar and Swanage Secondary Modern, and the Wareham and Bovington Secondary Moderns. Don West was the headmaster of the new school and responsible for overseeing the momentous change.

"However good the smaller schools were, The Purbeck School offered opportunities never previously available in the locality to ALL of our students. The facilities we were able to provide in Science, Music, Sport, Technical subjects and Careers were infinitely superior. New job prospects were opening up and we had to prepare our students for this new world."

David Parry-Jones who, as the deputy head worked alongside Don both at Wareham and The Purbeck, felt no less passionately at the time about the injustice of the old system.

"Not only was it an inaccurate guide in many instances, it was often particularly socially divisive. The stigma of failure really rankled with those who did not pass the exam. I believe it was most acutely felt in the small village communities which existed across Purbeck."

Carol Turner, an East Stoke girl and today a councillor (soon to be Mayor), recalls that though she passed the eleven plus her father did not want her to go to the grammar school. Many parents remained confused by the system and its possible implications.

Maurice Turner, the head of careers both at Wareham Modern and The Purbeck, agrees with his former colleagues.

"I believe the remarkable success stories of so many Purbeck students in their subsequent careers vindicate the change to a comprehensive system. Many of the students would simply not have enjoyed the breadth of educational opportunity in their former schools."

Maurice was also an accomplished pianist and participated in a number of musical productions.

"With the numbers of children in Purbeck we were able to stage artistically highly successful productions that would have been impossible in the smaller schools."

However, Maurice recognises flaws that existed in the new structure – and quite possibly remain today.

"It is so important to motivate students – for them to see a purpose in what they are doing at school. Are we trying hard enough to differentiate between the needs of students? I believe we must provide more technical and vocational courses."

The Square and Compass, Worth Matravers – Another day
Today I have invited a number of other teachers present in 1974 when The Purbeck School was established. Nearly all taught previously at either Swanage Grammar or the local secondary moderns. All taught at The Purbeck for the remainder of their teaching careers alongside their colleagues in

the previous section. While acknowledging many of the positive achievements of the new school and the professionalism and dedication of the staff, not least its leadership under Don West, there exists an almost unanimous feeling that as teachers they actually enjoyed their teaching much more before the advent of the 1,400 comprehensive at Wareham.

Ken Saunders, a year head, expresses the general sentiment: "I didn't really enjoy the later years of my teaching career. In the smaller schools you knew everyone and everyone knew you. Nor was there the parental involvement in the big school. Often parents lived many miles away and felt detached from the school. If you compared the attendance on Sport's Day, for example, lots would turn up at the small local school, whereas scarcely a person attended those at Purbeck. It was also impossible to have the whole school together for an assembly which was very unfortunate. How could you build a feeling of one community? Like other Year Heads I also knew really well only the very best pupils and the very worst – especially the latter which, in itself, was rather depressing. Was I able to devote as much time as I would have wished to those in the middle – the majority, in fact? No, I wasn't."

Mike Etherington, who taught maths, saw disadvantages in the inevitable inequalities in the status of staff. "In the small school virtually everyone, save the headmaster and perhaps his deputy, enjoyed more or less equal status. Staff were paid according to age and experience. In consequence, everyone mucked in. No one did things merely to enhance their career prospects. There was a sense of a school community. However, when some people are earning significantly more than their colleagues, there's more of a feeling of 'Well, let them do it.'"

Noel Donnelly, who taught geography and was much involved in a variety of extra-curricular activities, looks back at the original creation of The Purbeck with his customary blunt Yorkshire realism. "Purbeck was seen by the county authorities as being cost effective. A large number of pupils, 1,400 or so, were to be bussed in from all over the area and taught in the most economical way – by specialist teachers all on one site. It wasn't really anything to do with what was best, but what was cheapest!"

Barry England, a technology and outdoor pursuits teacher, reflects on the cost of the buses over the 25 years since the school began life – fuel and staff wages.

"Two hundred days a year for 25 years – what does it add up to? Of course lots of children were bussed before and Purbeck is a rural area but, if there had been two smaller schools, one in Swanage and one in Wareham, what resources could have been devoted to them?"

Dave Sagar, a science teacher, was particularly upset by a change in the curriculum, lamenting the day that individual sciences were replaced by a general science course. "I realise this is a broader criticism of educational trends but It should never have happened. It's not the way to educate young people in science. And having children spend just one year and a bit in a school before they have to choose their examination option subjects is unsatisfactory."

The children moved (and still move) to The Purbeck at the beginning of Year 9 when they are aged 13.

Mike Etherington develops the theme. "At times it felt It more like an educational factory than a school. It lost the personal feeling that I valued so much in the smaller school. And how could children stay behind for extra-curricular activities when it was so difficult to get home afterwards, if not downright impossible. I could no longer say: 'Hey, kids, it's a nice evening. See you on the beach at five and we'll paddle into Poole harbour.' The kids had to catch their buses straight after school. I had to borrow a minibus and a trailer. After a while these things ceased to happen. I am absolutely convinced that schools should be local and a part of the community."

Barry England, with similar experience of after-school activities, concurs with Mike on this serious weakness of the non-neighbourhood school.

John Howitt, who taught maths, sums up his own sentiments very succinctly. "I really wouldn't want to begin a teaching career in the present set-up. I am also far from convinced that we were able to stretch the most able sufficiently as in the grammar school system."

It was certainly true, in my own experience, that having children of such diverse abilities in the same classroom made it extremely difficult, if not impossible, to adapt one's teaching accordingly. I recall one classic case where I was teaching one of the most brilliant academic boys in the school – a young man who later achieved distinction at Oxford – in the same history examination group as pupils who were barely literate and quite unable to grasp any difficult concepts.

Another regrettable consequence of merging four schools into one was the loss of opportunity for many pupils to represent their schools at sport. Where once there had been four school teams representing four different schools in sports like football, cricket and rugby – the same applied, of course, to the girls – with the creation of The Purbeck there was only one representative team. Where once 44 boys, plus all the fringe players, played for their school XI soccer teams, now there were only eleven. It is true the selected XI was a stronger unit in the bigger school, but what of the unfortunate effect on the boys who could no longer proudly claim they represented their school with the status and confidence such achievement gave them as individuals? I know that only 2 or 3 of the school cricket XI who represented Wareham Modern when I ran the school team would have played in the Purbeck XI but what fun our team enjoyed and how good the experience was for the boys. While acknowledging the range of sporting facilities in the bigger school was expanded, such a change could only be seen as retrograde. As a general principle how much more significant is it in the inner cities today in the giant comprehensives, where achieving status through sport may redeem the lives of alienated youngsters? In small schools they would be stars with status and self-belief, in the big schools they are often anonymous, alienated and indifferent or actively hostile to schooling. Incidentally, I must here pay a particular tribute to my old friend, Bob Croom, the games master at Purbeck, who for the past 30 years has, despite all the obstacles, fostered a love of sport in the locality and set standards of excellence that are recognised by all his fellow teachers in the county. Like Tim Hall, the former games master at Poole GS, teachers such as Bob Croom deserve so much credit for all their unstinting service to their students, the time they have so freely given out of school and the sporting values they have inculcated.

Have I fairly reflected the views of my former colleagues? Do we sound excessively jaundiced? Although we all continued to do our very best for our pupils and, of course, there were many enjoyable moments at Purbeck, what most of us as classroom teachers missed most in the big new school was the family feeling that we once experienced in our smaller schools – building the close relationships on a daily basis with our colleagues and our pupils and their parents that can make so much difference on all sides. So are we lamenting the arrival of the comprehensive system or merely the size of the school, or is it something of both?

Let's move a few miles to the east to another school with which I am very familiar having spent the last 10 years of my teaching career there.

Poole Grammar School, Gravel Hill
'I really couldn't guarantee how long your position in this school will last, nor how long the school will survive as a grammar school. If I had to predict, it could be a comprehensive within the next 10 years.' Words spoken by a former headmaster, Nigel Gilpin, to the present head of Art, Rob Mouzer, when he was appointed in 1984.

Twenty-five years later and not only is Poole Grammar School still with us, its numbers are at a record high when a number of local comprehensives are suffering falling rolls, and its academic success makes it one of the finest schools in the south of England.

Ian Carter is the present headmaster. He begins with a statement that is fascinating and profoundly important in its implications.

"There are certain objective criteria employed when analysing a school's social and ethnic composition and yes, I understand that Poole Grammar in 2008 does indeed have the greatest social and ethnic mix of any local secondary school."

Yet one of the arguments often advanced by the supporters of the 'comprehensive ideal' is that the grammar schools are just middle-class institutions perpetuating privilege.

"The truth is, of course, that traditionally grammar schools have been the most important vehicle of social mobility in the post-war years. A whole generation of talent from working-class backgrounds emerged through the grammar schools and the latest research shows it is still true today. Naturally I recognise the fallibility of testing at 11 or 12 but, as long as there exists every opportunity for children to transfer between schools at a later date I do not feel defensive about the grammar school system. At 16 there will be students who come here, or they may choose to remain in the excellent Sixth Forms of their own secondary schools. There are, of course, a number of fine comprehensive schools in the locality that also do a splendid job for their pupils. I believe that East Dorset is very well served by its schools. Incidentally, I would also fly the flag for single sex schools. I believe that up to 16 both boys and girls do benefit from this form of education. In the Sixth Form, we do enjoy a close collaboration with Parkstone GS in a number of areas."

Does Ian have any particularly strong feelings about the size of schools in the light of the steady increase in numbers at Poole GS in recent years?

"I do believe strongly in cohesiveness. There is a point at which a school can become too big. However, I would hesitate to put a precise figure on it. I suspect there is a far greater need for smaller schools in areas of economic and social deprivation where a school can provide a measure of support and stability for those students from broken homes and poor backgrounds."

One interesting aspect of Ian's work is the 2 afternoons he spends with the pupil referral unit in Poole.

"There is an excellent head and I am one of the associate heads. It's terribly important to do something worthwhile with these children, some of whom have been excluded from their own schools, perhaps for violent or disruptive behaviour. We all work together and support each other as best we can."

John Cutler is the head of English and I ask him first about selection in education.

"I am happy with selection as long as it is viewed like a set of traffic lights indicating the most appropriate route for a child to follow. At the same time, it should be divorced from the idea of succeeding or failing. Every child is different and deserves the very best education, so each school should be equally funded and recognised as having equal status. There must also exist, to use again my earlier analogy, the opportunity for a change of direction at a later date."

With much anxiety being expressed about education in general and, more specifically, standards in written and spoken English, what does John feel on that score?

"First of all, I believe passionately in the liberating value of education. Education is freedom. It means the freedom to choose. The more educated you are, the more choices you have in your life. As far as English is concerned, whilst I am totally opposed to the misuse of words, I do believe we should be more tolerant of change in our language. I belong to the Stephen Fry rather than the John Humphry's school of thought. I don't object, for instance, to the verbalising of nouns. Language is constantly evolving. It should be lively and innovative. Shakespeare – and there was no greater master of the English language – used it boldly and imaginatively. It's like etiquette. Is there really a proper way to eat a pear? Why does it matter if it's called a toilet or a lavatory? I'm afraid the class

Students from Poole Grammar School on a paintballing expediton in the New Forest. *Picture: Poole Grammar School*

thing does intrude here. In the big, wide world, do some of our grammatical 'rules' really matter terribly?"

And John's final observation?

"Whatever educational system we follow there is one simple truth. The single most important part of the equation is the support, or the lack of it, that a child receives at home. The role of parents is absolutely crucial. Mum and Dad may have received little education themselves but, if they support their children and respect the value of education, then anything is possible for that child!"

Of course, this has been but a cursory look at the subject of selection and the growth of the 'big' school. What is a reasonable observation to make, I believe, is that a very large number of teachers who have experienced both smaller and larger schools have considerable reservations, for various reasons, about the changes of the past 40 years. Personally, I disliked intensely the impersonality and anonymity of the large school. To walk down the corridor of a small school and recognise every face, to share in good-natured banter with pupils and exchange often valuable information, is a joy and advantage unknown in the big school. I believe it is the view of almost every colleague I have worked with in my career that it is what they as teachers greatly prefer. Of course, what is increasingly true is that few teachers under the age of 40 have any experience of smaller schools, either as students or teachers.

On selection, clearly opinions are divided but, if academic excellence, social and ethnic mobility are seen as highly desirable goals, the destruction of the grammar schools can be seen as a grave mistake. As long as the opportunity exists for transfer, as long as investment in every kind of school is comparable, then the argument for the retention of the 164 existing grammar schools in the UK – even their expansion- is compelling though I know some of my former colleagues at Purbeck would not go that far. I spent my first ten years in education teaching in secondary moderns, as did a number of my colleagues present at our discussion in the Square and Compass, and they were good schools. Who is to say that they would not have been outstanding schools with the same level of investment that was devoted to the introduction of the comprehensive schools? Vast sums of money would have been saved in transport costs. There is absolutely no reason why any school needs to be regarded as inferior. One school may be brilliant in encouraging academic excellence, another similarly regarded for the outstanding quality of its vocational training. One area where there is almost unanimous agreement is that, beyond a certain point, schools can become – and have become – too large. The argument that large schools provide economies of scale and are able to offer a wider curriculum is questionable. There is no reason why as many subjects should not be available in smaller institutions since specialist teachers could well divide their time between schools, just as peripatetic music teachers already do. It is far cheaper for teachers to be mobile than many hundreds of students. It is just possible to 'get away' with a larger school – up to a certain point – when the pupils are uniformly well-behaved and motivated. That is certainly not true where there is little parental support and many pupils are disruptive. In such circumstances I believe the large school simply compounds the problems, despite the best efforts of the most dedicated staff. Unfortunately, in this writer's opinion, it is impossible to be optimistic about the future. We have travelled too far in the wrong direction for too many years. Ask any teacher in the land and they will agree – children are becoming a percentage point or two noisier and more difficult as year succeeds year. Fortunately in Dorset we still have many excellent schools, pupils who are mostly keen to learn and broadly supportive parents. But are our schools as good as they could be? Regrettably, I fear there is only one conclusion.

I did ask my colleagues, Mark Partridge, Peter Coles and Steve Smith – each one a language teacher – for their knowledge and experience of academic standards and selection in our neighbours France and Germany. In France, of course, which is a secular state without faith-based and independent schools, there exists effectively a comprehensive model. Clearly there will be marked differences in both the quality of education and discipline depending upon the locality of the school. However, Mark felt unable to offer any definitive opinion on standards. Steve explained that in Germany, which is often held up as a model of excellence, there are 3 types of secondary schools – the Gymnasium (the equivalent of our grammar schools) which selects 40% of the school population, the Realschule which takes 20% in the middle range and is part vocational and part academic, and the Hauptschule which caters for the remaining 40%. While the typical Gymnasium is a source of excellence, the same cannot be said of the Hauptschule where both the education and discipline leaves more than a little to be desired. The latter type of school tends to contain a higher proportion of Germany's immigrant population, often those with language difficulties besides low academic achievers. One headmaster of a Hauptschule in Berlin in 2006 wrote an 'open letter' to the press complaining bitterly that discipline had broken down in his school and it had become impossible to function normally. Steve added that within Germany many observers were critical of the educational system which was said to restrict social mobility and reinforce the existing class structure. What is clear in general terms is that nowhere is there a perfect system or one particular model to be followed.

Leaving aside for a moment the question of 'To select, or not to select', one hugely important topic for every young person and parent today is that of university education. With the Labour Government setting a target of 50% of young people attending university, there is increasing anxiety about the cost and value of such education, both to society and to the student. Anyone over almost any age, certainly for those over 40, knows how examination standards have changed in recent times at every level, GCSE, A Level and Degree level. Where once if a student secured even half a dozen passes at GCE O Level they had excelled, now even the most modest students will often 'pass' ten subjects, not infrequently with high grades. Grade inflation has devalued our examination system. Very good students actually used to fail examinations. In my own GCE and Sixth Form days failure was commonplace, even for the most able of students. Only blinkered politicians and the most naive would deny the harsh truth. If our driving examiners applied identical criteria to those marking school and university examinations and passed almost everyone, our roads would be full of drivers without motoring skills. Would we as a society for one moment tolerate such dangerous absurdity? It is not the fault of the students that standards have changed. I know it hurts them to hear the older generation speak in such terms. It seems as if we are decrying their hard work and achievements when no such slight is intention. Often the most academically gifted and the average are scarcely differentiated. Only at some later stage will it become apparent, often when it is too late. Employers know the truth about our examination system and that is why increasingly they are setting their own tests for applicants for posts. Sadly, tens of thousands of students possess almost meaningless qualifications .What they do very definitely possess, however, are debts of such colossal proportions that they will be crippled financially for years to come. Many will never be able to repay more than a tiny proportion of such debt. It is lunacy. As a society we are duping every year vast numbers of young people by persuading them to follow courses for which they are ill-equipped in order to obtain qualifications that possess precious little value in the market place. For a large number of young people 'Going to uni' has become 'a rite of passage' rather than a demanding intellectual challenge. It would be brilliant if our society could afford it and it cost the students nothing, or next to nothing. But that is not the reality – far from it. Lots of young people would be better off finding a job and attending courses on day release or securing proper vocational training. Of course, there are particular problems finding employment at the present time because of the economic recession, but 'going to uni' for the wrong reasons could prove a disastrously expensive choice for the unwitting. There is nothing to stop someone returning to education at a later date when he or she is more mature and financially able to do so. As someone who has spent a lifetime in education, I am all in favour of it but the present situation is absurd and dishonest. We now have many second and third-rate universities (often the old polytechnics) offering meaningless courses with high drop-out figures, precious little tutor/student contact time, and all the while horrendous debts are accruing in the student's bank and credit card accounts Ultimately such financial burdens will demoralise and occasion great distress to the victims of our collective irresponsibility. At the same time, not least in a period of acute economic difficulties, we are starving other vital services in our society of badly needed resources. It is against this background that I pose some questions to another former colleague.

In the Career's Office
"Be informed. When a Sixth form student sits before me to discuss his future that would be my first piece of advice. There's an absolute treasure trove of information in every Career's room in every school in the county."

David Darch, Careers Master at Poole GS, knows his responsibility to the modern student is probably greater than in any past period of our history. Like most of those who are over the age of 40 David's own university days were financed by a grant sufficient to meet his living expenses with no tuition fees to be paid.

"These days we're looking at a likely student debt of £25,000. In consequence, the student needs to make a thoroughly informed choice of course. If he, or she, is seeking entry to one of the traditional professions like medicine, law, accountancy or teaching, then university is the necessary and inevitable route. However, no one should go to university just for the sake of it – not because of pressure from any quarter, parental, peer or simply because he or she just doesn't know what else to do. It should be a calculated assessment of what that person really wants to do as a career and how to secure those necessary qualifications or skills. There is another cost too. The student will have foregone earnings during those 3 or 4 years of study. My role must be that of the dispassionate adviser, to take an objective and constructive position."

I know that David regards my views as excessively critical of present trends, but how can one be complacent when it is so evident that we are drifting, just as we have drifted as a society towards other treacherous rocks in recent years, towards a situation where we have a population of young people hopelessly enmeshed in a world of debt with no possibility of escape? And that is before they want to secure mortgages and families. It is not the road to peace of mind and human happiness.

Lytchett Minster

Little Chimneys

Fifty years ago we would have met at the Manor House. Today the old Manor is the local comprehensive school. Post Green where we might alternatively have met is let to a tenant. So it is that I am sitting with Sir Thomas Lees at his pleasant but unpretentious farmhouse Little Chimneys that he shares with his wife Jefsimam.

Sir Tom, as he is affectionately known, has just told me a most remarkable story. But, before I relate the detail of it, I will travel back in time more than half a century to the days when a small boy lived with his parents in a small bungalow in a pot-holed, very sandy lane at the Lytchett end of Upton. After a serious illness the boy's father, a baker by trade and unable to walk the mile to the bus-stop and still convalescing, decided to bake a tray of lardy cakes in the kitchen oven. The boy's mother placed the lardy cakes in a basket, covered them with a cloth, and tramped the lanes and roads nearby selling her wares at the door. As the weeks passed so the boy's father began to add to the range of cakes and pastries and buns. A local craftsman, Mr.Hockey, built a small handcart which he fixed to the chassis of an old pram, painted it green and Upton Bakery was born. In due course, the boy, by now 12, took over the round from his mother and for the next 6 years and for the next 300 or so Saturdays – missing just one in all that time – walked around the village pushing the handcart from door to door selling his father's cakes. During those early years one invaluable source of income for the bakery derived from the sale of cakes to a certain Lady Lees of Lytchett Manor who had opened a roadside cafe for coach parties and motorists on the Dorchester Road, about half a mile from the village school where today there is a caravan park. Usually Lady Lees would collect direct from the bakery. She'd arrive in her old black saloon, followed by half a dozen of her dogs barking loudly which followed behind her through the lanes.

This morning the small boy whose father baked the cakes is sitting with the son of the redoubtable Lady Lees and listening to a tale which, even at this distance of time, moves both the teller and the listener in equal measure.

"I had an elder brother, James, who served with the SBS and was killed in action off Dalmatia. Actually he was seriously wounded by a grenade thrown by an Italian soldier who was also gravely injured in the explosion. The two men were both cared for by local nuns. Curiously, it was my brother who was thought the most likely to survive. In the event it was he who died and the Italian who lived. James was buried on an island off Dalmatia. After the war my mother travelled to the island and found the nuns who had nursed my brother and thanked them most warmly for their kindness. She also elicited the name of the Italian and his family in Salo where she discovered the soldier's mother was almost exactly the same age as herself. My mother also met the young soldier, Roberto Comotti, and in an act of reconciliation, she forgave him for what had happened to her own much loved son. She understood very clearly that in war soldiers are fighting for their country. The town of Salo awarded her a gold medal for forgiveness. My brother's body was later moved to Belgrade by the British War Graves Commission. A little later, when a memorial to my brother James was unveiled at Lytchett Minster church, Roberto Comotti came over to England to attend the service. As you can imagine, it was a deeply moving experience for everyone involved."

I had no idea all those years ago that the lady from the local manor house who came to collect cakes at my father's bakery had endured so much grievous pain and shown such compassion. After I left the village and went to London, she switched her boundless energies into Christian film-making projects.

"Originally our family owned cotton-mills in Oldham. They had deep evangelical roots with a strong social conscience. I understand that even in depressed times they kept the factories working for the sake of their employees. The family acquired the Lytchett estate and manor house in 1885. My grandfather was the Conservative MP for Oldham and later for Birkenhead. During the Boer War he served in the Dorset Yeomanry where he gained the DSO. When he returned to England he received a baronetcy for political and public service and proceeded to rebuild the estate here which my father Sir John inherited in 1915 after my grandfather's death. As for my mother's film-making ventures, for which incidentally I was roped in as the camera-man, she actually made two films in which our local GP, Dr.Chown, played Christ on both occasions. As for the manor, it was sold to the County Council in 1953 for just £10,000 to become a school. But if I tell you it had 39 bedrooms and 13 bathrooms, you'll understand why we decided to sell it. I didn't want to see it become a country house or club. I preferred the idea that it was put to be put to some good use. Since that time I imagine the figure spent on it is in the region of £10 million – and it has become a fine school. As for my mother, she died in 1967."

Sir Tom, who joined the RAF in 1943 and later attended Cambridge, ran the estate for many years before passing over the day to day responsibilities to his son Christopher. But, like his forebears, Sir Tom did not merely inherit land and the attendant responsibilities. He also absorbed the Christian values that have clearly permeated the Lees family life for generations.

"We began running Christian camps initially at Post Green in the late 1960s. Then we found we'd outgrown Post Green and so we took over a field at East Holton Farm organising camps at the Bank Holidays. We'd organise discussion groups in a big marquee. Then one day the head-teacher at a school in Parkstone, Mrs.Van der Veere, which catered for children with a range of physical disabilities brought the whole school , staff and children, over for a break in our country setting. It was a chance for the children to experience new horizons, see animals like deer and rabbits and birds. Many were in wheelchairs. It all went very well but the head said to me afterwards, 'We (the staff) are absolutely shattered. Have you anywhere inside, specially equipped for residential accommodation, where the children can experience all that you have to offer here?' There was, in fact, just one place, Churchtown Farm in St. Austell in Cornwall, which provides this sort of facility for which there was a 3 year waiting-list. It was what I would describe as a 'Damascus moment'. I realised there was an enormous need for accommodation for disabled people providing this sort of experience. It would provide a respite for them and their carers, a place where they wouldn't be patronised and put down. There was a girl Jenna Edwards who wanted a place to practise, teach and display ceramics. In recent years Holton Lee has evolved as a day care and residential centre for those

The East Holton Driving Centre at Holton Lee.

with Downs Syndrome, the physically disabled and so on. We have a barn that can accommodate between 10 and 20, depending upon circumstances, and 2 cottages with room for 2 families. There is a strong emphasis on making full use of our countryside environment. For example, we have a very popular and successful pony and trap driving facility for the disabled under the aegis of the East Holton Driving Centre. It is a team effort involving 2 excellent gentlemen in particular, Wally Pitt from Wareham, late of the Household Cavalry, and Johnny Colville, the chairman of the committee, from Swanage in conjunction with Riding for the Disabled. We are able to provide stabling facilities and access to the paths through the countryside. It's absolutely wonderful to see the faces of those participating. For a number it will be the first time they have been in control in such an activity."

It's unreservedly brilliant, Sir Tom. Your dear mother would have been very proud.

Lytchett Matravers

Race Farm
"For 43 years I've worked on the estate. I did the ploughing and combining and dairying. I live down the road at Newton Farm."

Gordon Cleall is brushing up the driveway.

"No, you don't see many of those about today."

I've knocked the door and I'm inside the house now peering out of the window. They're certainly an unfamiliar sight in an age of almost universal uniformity. Twenty or so longhorns are cheerfully squelching around in the mud and their feeding troughs.

"Originally my wife bought me the one animal. I had to buy a few companions. The story's gone on from there. As you can see, they do need special troughs. They tend to get their horns locked in the conventional ones."

Christopher Lees, the son of Sir Tom, administers the 2,500 acres estate his family has owned for the past 150 years. These days Christopher farms two thirds of the acreage 'in hand' – six farms in all.

"There are two remaining tenanted farms – French's and Hill Farm."

It's not been the easiest of years in more ways than one. French's Farm, past which I walked every morning and afternoon for three years of my life as a pupil at Lytchett Minster village school and is

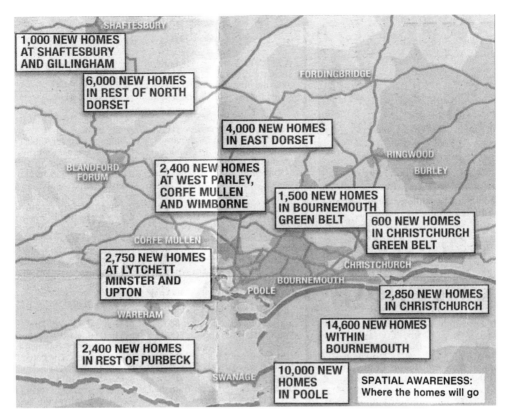

Western extension map, will it become a reality?

now farmed by tenant David House, was where Blue Tongue was discovered in a single animal at the end of last winter.

"Now we're jabbing away like mad. It's worrying when it happens but hopefully there'll be no recurrence with the vaccination programme established."

If Blue Tongue was yet another unpleasant scare for every local farmer with all the attendant restrictions on movement of livestock, another matter altogether has been exercising Christopher this past year or two. The proposed Western Extension to the draft Regional Spatial Strategy identified the Lees estate as the possible location for 2,750 new homesChristopher's studied response has not endeared him to various groups vehemently opposed to development but he is unrepentant.

"We are confronted by the reality of population growth. Where are the young people of Poole and Bournemouth going to find homes? We must retain these people – their presence is vital for the economic and social well-being of the locality. By a greater density of development? Yet more high-rise blocks of flats? Do we simply sanction piecemeal sprawl, which is a real danger, without proper planning and infra-structure? Or do we try to provide the best housing possible, embracing modern technologies, in an imaginatively designed environment?"

Christopher passes me an article reproduced from the Health and Science page of The Week which closely reflects his own thinking. The study undertaken provides convincing evidence of the general health benefits, both physical and mental, of living in a location with greenery and space.

A demonstration against further housing development. *Picture: Sally Adams, Bournemouth Echo*

"The argument to my mind is irrefutable. We need housing that is mixed with parkland, even farmland, incorporating recreational facilities, a lake or ponds, cycle-ways for children and adults so they cam move around safely. How much of our post-war development even comes close to realising this vision?"

I reflect upon the locality I knew as a child 50 or so years ago. Aside from all the 'in-filling' of new housing in its different forms within the boroughs of Poole and Bournemouth, the areas of Canford Heath, Upton Heath, Turlin Moor, Northmoor and Corfe Mullen were then heathland, reclaimed marshland or poor quality farmland. Only the familiar ribbon development of the Thirties lined the roads through Upton, Lytchett Minster and Lytchett Matravers, Hamworthy, Wimborne, Wareham, Corfe Mullen and Ferndown. Many thousands of homes have been built on land where, as a boy, I knew only trees, heather, grass, pasture or arable crops. As Christopher Lees argues, we are now faced with an explosion of population. It is no use lamenting it. We are where we are. Bill Bryson might argue that we should build on 'brown field' sites in the North of England. In a Stalinist dictatorship the compulsory movement of population might be possible but Britain is a democracy. Even with the most imaginative financial inducements, it's difficult to conceive that many young people from Poole and Bournemouth will be persuaded to uproot hundreds of miles northwards. It is axiomatic that we must encroach no further on heathland or floodplains. Few 'brown-field.' sites remain in this locality. We all pay lip-service to providing 'affordable housing'. Most of my generation clambered uneasily on to the property ladder borrowing three, certainly no more than four times, our annual salaries and we were not burdened by massive student debts. Today the gulf between local property prices and salaries , even combined ones, is often six, eight or even ten times annual salaries. And what happens when a couple decide to start a family? And we are talking of the responsible couples who have postponed starting families until their thirties, not the feckless young women impregnated by equally feckless young men who know a child or two will gain them a council flat. What would I prefer of my childhood locality? No discernible change? Of course I would. We all love the signposts of our early years, the recognisable landmarks. But what is the likeliest scenario fifty years hence? That there will have been change as great as that which I have witnessed in my lifetime is a certainty. Our population is growing and people have to live somewhere. Twenty miles westward Prince Charles and his advisers have embarked on a bold, imaginative project at Poundbury. Whatever the reservations it is an honourable vision, and not even the sternest of its critics would deny that on every count it is a huge improvement on every other large-scale development Dorset has ever seen. So, what conclusions can we draw? I know Dave Wells believes that at least a part of the solution must be to build up and Poole and Bournemouth 50 years hence will, of necessity, contain many towering blocks of flats. But how suitable is high-rise development for families and children? I knew Lady Lees, Christopher's grandmother, as a lady of high principle and moral courage. Sir Tom Lees, Christopher's father, has established a no less honourable reputation in the locality. He has created Holton Lee which will be a lasting memorial to him. I also believe Christopher to be a man of decency and principle. He has spent the past 35 years farming the land around Lytchett Minster and Lytchett Matravers. It is not good farming land and its comparative yields are less or no better than average. He has worked long hours and raised a family by his labours.

As his land agent, Oliver Chamberlain of Chichester's, recently explained: "The Lees estate will only agree to the development on its terms – if it retains as much control over the plans and design as possible."

So I am not going to castigate Christopher for believing that a properly planned development on this Western Extension would be an improvement to the likely alternative – that is, if in spite of local opposition, building is indeed sanctioned by Westminster. Whatever the Conservatives may promise from the Opposition benches now, the fundamental problem will remain. Where is the overspill from Poole and Bournemouth going to live in the longer term? Christopher is in an invidious position. Damned if he supports planned development by the present generation and probably damned by later generations if he doesn't. It is a genuine dilemma. At a personal level, I hope the locality will be preserved in its present form. I have great sympathy with those campaigning against this Western Extension, but I fear the probable outcome will be exactly what we – and by 'we,' I mean Christopher and I and the campaigners – most dread. The land will simply be built upon over the years in a piecemeal sprawl, north and west, with none of the features Christopher recommends. In the past half century Christchurch, Bournemouth, Parkstone, Poole, Hamworthy and Upton have, in all essentials been joined up. Why should we suppose with an expanding population and growing housing needs the next 50 years are going to be any different?

Elsewhere in the village one particular award winning establishment is honoured by a visit from Her Majesty, Queen Elizabeth II. Only days after being severely affected by a blaze on the premises, Jenny Goldsack at Goldy's Farm Shop receives the ultimate accolade of a royal visit. A host of local and national awards have come Goldy's Farm way in recent months which reflects the imagination and energy of Jenny and her team. What is particularly interesting in the award from Own and Local is that half of the foods for sale in the farm shop must be produced by the retailer, with the other half emanating from a local supply chain. With the variety of restaurants and the many excellent pubs offering food in the UK today, the quality products of our farm shops and small independent retailers, the days when other nationalities could laugh at British culinary ignorance are certainly a thing of the past.

The clock tower, Upton. A fine example of Brian Cooper's talents.

Upton

"When an old lady comes along and admires one of my floral displays and says, 'Brian, that looks really lovely', that's my greatest reward. A kind, complimentary word or two means much more than certificates or presentations."

Brian Cooper is, in his own quiet, unassuming way, an extraordinary man. At 75 he's not only working two and a half days a week as the contract grounds-man for Lytchett Minster and Upton Council, he also finds time for other gardening jobs around the locality. Most remarkably, however, he continues to indulge his passion for competitive grass-track racing – no brakes, remember – at speeds of up to 70mph! His house is overflowing with mementoes, cups and photographs, reflecting his successes in his beloved sport and as a gardener par excellence. A self-confessed dunce at the village school in the days of the formidable Chas Burton, Brian was an apprentice gardener at Upton House in the day of the Llewellin family, and an award-winning head grounds-man at Poole Park. Curiously he and his wife were actually the last residents of the lodge in the park. He also owned Upton Nurseries, keeps bees, and is as knowledgeable about flowers and shrubs as any man I've met. Not bad for a self-confessed dunce!

I call by at the council offices in Moorland Way to make acquaintance with the chairman, Cllr. John Small. John has several matters on his mind, one of them being The Greenridge Hotel, formerly the Upton Hotel, at the cross-roads.

"It looks dreadful, of course, and it's a real problem. Hall& Woodhouse are talking of having it converted into a care home. Is it the right place for a care home? Besides which, many people still want it to remain a public house."

I know Simon Thomson, the chairman of LM & Upton Community Association, Simon Williams, chairman of the Upton residents association, and individuals like Shirley Benjafield are campaigning for its retention as a family orientated pub, or at the least, for its continued use as some kind of community building. I also know there have been serious problems at The Greenridge. With changing social habits, a very competitive market-place, certain elements among its clientele causing difficulties and the highly successful Hall& Woodhouse owned St. Peter's Finger just a mile and a half down the road at Lytchett Minster, it's not entirely a surprise that 'time has been finally called' on what was, in my youth, a thriving and popular pub. A very large investment would be required by the brewery company to rejuvenate the 1935 building with no guarantee of success. It's very unfortunate, especially for everyone in Upton who used to walk to The Greenridge for a drink and walk home again afterwards. Unless you live at the Seaview Road end of Upton it's highly improbable you're going to walk to the St. Peter's Finger, certainly not in bad weather. And Upton is now officially a town with a population of 8,000, yet how can you possibly have a town without a pub at its heart? There is no immediate resolution of the problem in sight. (Even as we go to print, it's announced the District Council has thrown out plans for the rest home. The problem remains. My sympathies are with the people of Upton but I do also understand Hall & Woodhouse's situation.)

Charles Small is pleased with one imminent innovation – the creation of a one-stop shop at the building where we are now seated.

"It will be the first of its kind in the county. The police, planning, the council, CAB, youth advice, council tax payment facilities – everything will be here. It will be convenient for everyone and we

The Green Flag Award, Upton House. *Picture: Penrose Photography*

Prince Carol
and Princess
Jeane. *Picture:*
Bournemouth Echo

are rather proud of that."

Certainly the Upton Police team of Supt. Gary Smith, Sgt Jon Wasey, Insp Chris Weeks, PC Craig Tatton and PCSO Robin Morgan look cheerful enough at the prospect of having a local base, rather than travelling to and from Wareham when on duty. It will be so much easier for the locals to pop in and discuss any problems that arise. The Council deserves praise for such a sensible initiative – what is fashionably labelled, I believe, 'joined up thinking.'

Upton House

It was a late summer's day in the Sixties that, responding to an advertisement in the Echo for a private tutor, I found myself walking up the drive to Upton House. I was greeted at the door by Princess Jeanne, the second wife of Prince Carol of Rumania, who with her husband had 2 years earlier become the tenants of the property after it was given to Poole Council by the departing Llewellin family. Having just graduated from the London School of Economics I was young and tolerably confident in my abilities, but this was my first brush with 'royalty', albeit of questionable East European stock, and I was uncertain quite what to expect. I was ushered into a large room to be courteously received by Prince Carol. I was then both surprised and entertained by the sight of Princess Jeanne walking uneasily backwards all the way to the door. Prince Carol explained that his son was to be prepared for the Common Entrance examination to Public School. The young man, a pale, shy, inoffensive, little fellow mumbled a few words before the Prince accompanied us both on a tour of the grounds; including the greenhouses, where we paused and discussed further the nature of my possible responsibilities. We parted on undefined terms. I was far from sure I wanted the post.

Peacock tea-rooms, Lucy Townsend, Carol Hill and the team. *Picture: Geoff Hill*

I still entertained ambitions to return to London and become an actor, but I was broke. Equally, I suspect the Prince was looking for someone more mature and experienced. In the event the matter was soon resolved.

Just 48 hours later my friends, Jill and Keith Harvey, showed me a cutting from a national daily. It read something like this, 'The former Oxford tutor to the son of Prince Carol of Rumania is suing the Prince for non-payment of tuition fees.' I escaped unscathed, but during the next few years the Prince contrived to run up substantial unpaid accounts with a number of unfortunate local trades-people. When he and Princess Jeanne departed Upton House, they left unlamented. I heard no more of the pair until I chanced upon a piece by Brian J.Galpin, writing in this year's Dorset Yearbook. It seems Prince Carol died in 2006 at the age of 86. Of his son and heir, however, I have no knowledge.

Upton House, One day in late summer
"Roger Brewer is actually the manager of the House and Country Park. I'm employed by Poole Council to oversee the leisure, business and events side."

The view alone across the parkland to Poole harbour from the office window is worth a few thousand pounds a year but I doubt Colin Gundry would agree to a salary reduction on those grounds though he doesn't dispute my general assertion. It's no sinecure, however, and Colin's responsibilities are extensive. Besides maximising the usage and income of the House through meetings, seminars, weddings, concerts by the BSO, country fairs and countless other events, he's also responsible for managing 24 events sites in the borough, such as Baiter and Poole Park, 23 roundabouts and over 700 public seats! I am surprised he's not worn out though he does appear amazingly upbeat and spry.

"We're all working hard on our refurbishment programme here. The second floor of the house and the basement remain as yet out of bounds. We also have ambitious plans for the walled garden but everything takes time and money."

But possibly Colin's most conspicuous and highly praised handiwork is to be seen every day by thousands of motorists – on the various roundabouts which are his responsibility, such as those at Holes Bay, one with fishing boats and another with buoys and anchors, and at Hunger Hill with the Poole canoe, a craft specially built for work in the shallows of the harbour. As Colin explains:"Each reflects Poole's nautical heritage."

The Peacock Tea-rooms

It's patently obvious the members of the team on duty this morning think very highly of the lady who organises their world here. Cheerful greetings and warm smiles abound together with politely worded enquiries if there's a problem. Maria Cobb, whose great uncle owned Cobb's Quay at Hamworthy, hands me a copy of the Poole Council Mission Statement. Normally I'd run a mile to avoid one of these statements full of trite declarations of worthy intent couched in the language of the bureaucratic ideologue, but not on this occasion

'The Peacock Tea-rooms are a Borough of Poole Enterprise, set up to assist in the vocational training of people with learning disabilities.'

"Most of our team of 15 are in residential homes but some do live at home with their families. Several even travel here independently. It is so good for their morale. They feel wanted and valued. They have become real members of the community."

It's all too easy to be patronising in such circumstances but such sentiments are entirely out of place here. The team are all trained in basic food and hygiene skills and customer relations. Their friendliness and warmth put to shame those uncouth, indifferent individuals we all too often meet in the service industry.

"Our customers are wonderfully supportive. They become their friends. The team especially value complimentary remarks in the visitor's book."

Upton House and Country Park and the Peacock Tea-rooms are a splendid asset to Poole Council. Like so many others I always enjoy my visits here. Remembering those far-off days of my childhood when the Llewellins lived here and later, the chequered tenancy of Prince Carol, I think it fair to observe, without fear of contradiction, that never in its history have Upton House and its splendid grounds given so much pleasure to so many people. I congratulate everyone involved.

North Dorset (2)

Shillingstone

There are many worrying trends in the countryside. A dearth of cuckoos, declining numbers of previously common species of birds, a sharp reduction in the number of many moths, butterflies and insects, fewer hedgehogs – the list is long and deeply disturbing. To add to the picture, serious worries about our bee population have not only caused much anxiety among bee-keepers everywhere, but among all those who rely on bees to pollinate their crops.

Lesley Gasson is not only a local politician and Shillingstone reisident, she is also an apiarist who has trained many aspiring bee-keepers.

"Numbers of bees have dropped nationally between 10-20% in the past couple of years. Much of the blame can be attributed to the mite verroa destructor. It can absolutely decimate hives. We have also endured two poor, wet and cold summers. I have 8 hives and would normally expect to harvest around 60lbs from each hive and nearly 500lbs in total. This year I have harvested just 200lbs. But we also must ensure that bee-keepers are trained properly so they can handle their hives and colonies effectively."

Stephen Cheleda, secretary of the Sherborne Division of Dorset bee-keeping, is frustrated at the Government's attitude.

"The economic value of honeybees and bumblebees as pollinators in the UK has been estimated at over £200 million a year. We are asking for £8 million to be invested in research. The Government spends just £200,000!"

Terry Payne, who is a bee-keeper in Iwerne Minster and the secretary of the Blandford and Sturminster Beekeeper's Association, is no less apprehensive.

"I have had no honey for harvesting for the past 2 years. The dreadful weather has been largely responsible and obviously we can do nothing about that, except hope that next year it's better. At the same time, the Government simply must put more resources into funding research into bee health. It is not something we can be complacent about. Bees pollinate a third of all that we eat and they are responsible for 50% of the pollination of wild plants and flowers on which the animal world relies for its survival. We need to investigate thoroughly what is killing bees and the best way forward."

We all know that in times of financial stringency many research projects can be cut. This particular one must be funded adequately. It is of huge importance to us all. Lesley Gasson, Stephen Cheleda and Terry Payne are absolutely right to draw our attention to this worrying situation.

The Shillingstone Station Project, Supported by the North Dorset Railway Trust
"Jeff Waring's i/c the kettle this afternoon."

It's a fine winter's day and there's a steady trickle of visitors coming in both directions along the track to the station. Jeff, a Belfast man with a broad Northern Irish accent, is brewing tea for some of the inquisitive visitors. Bill Munden's the cheerful 'stationmaster' on duty this afternoon answering enquiries and selling the odd memento.

Shillingstone is a station with a history. Here it was nearly 100 years ago, February 27, 1915, to be exact, that Rupert Brooke and his battalion joined a train to Avonmouth before boarding a troopship bound for Gallipoli, never to return. Even standing on the platform, surveying the countryside which will scarcely have changed in a century, is to experience something of that fateful moment. How many of his battalion returned to Dorset, I wonder? Here too King Edward VII would alight on his way to Iwerne Minster House, the royal visits being responsible for the ornate canopy. The only surviving member of the former staff, Bob Downes, describes how they used once to handle all the suitcases and trunks for the various private schools in the area at the beginning and end of each term.

I've often driven through Shillingstone but, like most travellers, I have never previously paused here. It is a remarkably long village, extending a mile in length. I'd heard about the station restoration project, of course, but this is my first visit. Bill Munden is passionate about recreating something of the station's old glory.

"It was Mike Pauley's brainchild in the first place and he's our chairman. Our general secretary is David Mouser and Dereck Boyte and I make up the committee."

These are early days but already the team have made some excellent progress. Tony Ward, another member of the restoration team, says the longer-term plan is to extend the track north and south, rebuild the signal box, the down platform and engine room to create a working museum.

Bob Munden has a particular wish. "I'd love to recreate a really attractive garden here. The old stationmasters had so much pride in their stations."

It's splendid that once again a small band of volunteers is preserving something of historic value and genuine interest from the past. In years to come I have no doubt the names of our good friends here will be spoken of with gratitude and respect. Call by and see them. You're sure of a welcome. With a bit of luck you may even get a cup of tea!

Childe Okeford

As in many similar villages, the parishioners of Childe Okeford have in recent years been particularly anxious that the essential character of their village should be preserved in the face of insidious, unwanted 'creeping development.' Lying as it does under the prow of the earthworks at Hambledon and containing a great many attractive properties, it is absolutely essential that any additional housing should be subject to the closest scrutiny. It's the same old story of developers preferring to build large, expensive, four-bedroom properties, on which they can make more profit, rather than the smaller, well-designed 'affordable' dwellings that any thriving village community desperately needs if it is to retain a nucleus of young couples. A key figure in the effort to safeguard the village's character has been parish councillor, Derek Duke. The Child Okeford Village Design Statement has now been approved by North Dorset District Council and will, as long as it is adhered to, ensure that all future building within the village meets the wishes of the whole community. As Derek confirms:" This result is down to the dedicated efforts of a whole team of villagers and planners."

Once again, it shows what can be achieved by determination and hard work. Well done, Derek, and all your supporters.

Droop

Near Hazelbury Bryan, Sturminster Newton, Lockett's Farm

At 5am on a dark winter's morning in November, 2007, Robert Alner, the distinguished racehorse trainer and much loved family man, suffered grievous injuries when the Peugeot 406 he was driving collided with a telegraph pole not far from his home. It was an accident that devastated not only his family and friends but the whole racing community. Very simply, Robert Alner had long enjoyed a reputation as one of those people absolutely everyone liked and respected. To learn as the days passed of the full extent of his injuries was to compound the distress occasioned by the news of the original accident. Though thankfully mentally as sharp as ever, it soon became apparent that Robert, barely able to move or speak or even to eat, was destined at best to a life confined to a wheel-chair. Thanks to the remarkable skills and dedicated care of surgeons and nurses at Bristol's Frenchay hospital and Odstock near Salisbury, the quality of Robert's life has very slowly improved over the months. Meanwhile, with great courage and determination his wife Sally, supported by her family, jockeys, stable staff and the wider racing community, has contrived to keep 'the ship afloat'. In December, 2007, just weeks after the accident, one of the horses from the Alner stable, Miko De Beauchene, ridden by Andrew Thornton and owned by Andrew Wiles, won the Welsh Grand National at Chepstow. It was one of the most emotional occasions I, as a racing enthusiast for half a century, have ever witnessed. A gala ball staged at Wincanton racecourse, attended by 550 guests including a host of racing celebrities, subsequently raised over £200,000 on behalf of Robert, proof enough of the great esteem in which he and Sally are held. This morning I have arranged with Sally to call by at the stables in order to take a photograph of the stable star Miko de Beauchene and meet the stable team.

Robert Atner has long enjoyed a reputation as one of those people absolutely everyone likes and respects.

Sam Johnson, Miko de Beauchene, Robert Walford and Sally Alner. *Picture: Roger Holman*

It's a dank, dismal, misty morning. The narrow, twisting lanes out of Blandford are liberally strewn with the last leaves of autumn and a coating of slimy mud. It's not a locality I know and I'm relieved my friend Betty Read is navigating. Around a corner and I narrowly avoid the figure of a middle-aged, over-coated man stoically pushing a pram stacked with his worldly possessions. It's a long way from anywhere. I wonder where he's bound? I hope he knows and that it's not too far. It's not really a day for wayfaring.

Though I have not travelled this road before my friend and master photographer, Roger Holman, seems familiar at least with parts of the route. Is there anywhere in the county the man hasn't photographed – or considered photographing? We arrive and park outside the entrance to the farm and tramp up the drive to the house and stables. First lot is just returning. Sally Alner greets us warmly as we approach. Sally's a jolly, matriarchal figure though I have no doubt she'd give me a good dressing-down if I deserved it. She and Betty Read are old pals. A box nearby is disgorging its equine cargo, back from the gallops. The season's now in full swing, the tempo quickening all the while. It was the Paddy Power at Cheltenham last Saturday, the Hennessy at Newbury on Saturday week.

We've arrived on a hectic morning though no morning's less than busy at this time of the year. Declarations to be confirmed for forthcoming meetings, horses to be organised, second lot out in half an hour. Sally beckons our quartet through into the warm kitchen and puts the kettle on. I introduce Roger and my old school-friend, John Hill, who's never seen a racing stable before. Sally looks cheerful enough though the events of the past year would have broken lesser spirits.

Avril Griffin, Sally's secretary, is at the computer, her grandson Kyle beside her. He's dying to help but he's only three – it's probably best if he just watches this morning. Sally hands round steaming mugs and we admire the photographs occupying every vacant space on the walls. Flyer's Nap, Cool Dawn, Kingscliff, The Listener – it's a distinguished roll-call of equine heroes, past and present. Robert and Sally have tasted success at the top table of National Hunt racing.

"Where did we meet? It would be pointing. It just went on from there."

There's a wall-clock decorated with the Cerne Abbas Giant. A wedding present, I idly wonder?

"Robert's coming home at the weekend – just for the day. And, yes, he'll be home for Christmas."

Robert's the unseen presence but he's everywhere – in every room of the house, in every part of the yard, in the tack room, in the boxes, out on the gallops. He was born here. It's where he belongs.

Robert Walford, courteous and softly spoken, a very promising rider of the new generation of that mad breed of jump jockeys who daily tempt the gods for precious little reward of a material kind, newly engaged to Louise Alner, is on the phone discussing stable plans, confirming entries, cancelling others. Robert's father Tim trains at Sheriff Hutton in Yorkshire. Robert divides his riding between his father's horses and the Alner's.

Outside in the yard Miko de Beauchene, the hero of last year's Welsh Grand National, stands patiently with his lass, Sam Johnson. We all cheered like mad and shed a tear or two when Bob Champion won the Grand National on Aldaniti after conquering cancer. Last year at Chepstow the same raw emotion engulfed every watcher when Andrew Thornton returned triumphant on Miko. No one who saw it will ever forget Andrew's tears.

"Must I be in the photo?"

Please, Sally, If you would be so kind. Besides, you know Robert would want you there.

We tramp outside and Roger points his camera. Sally smiles, barely able to disguise her reluctance, though I did notice she was brushing her hair in front of the mirror before we came out. Sally hates fuss and this is fuss, but she's an angel this morning. Rob joins the photo grouping. Roger's satisfied, insofar as any perfectionist is ever satisfied. Sally and Rob hurry off and we explore the yard and the boxes. Miko's full brother, Nicto de Beauchene, hangs his head out of his box as we pass.

As we leave we see Sally pulling out on Miko. We wave our goodbyes. It's been a morning we'll not soon forget. Thanks, Sally, for your patience and kindness. Give our love to Robert.

(It proves an exasperating season for Miko de Beauchene.- a fine third under a big weight at Haydock and three uncharacteristic tumbles. But Nicto won twice. That's the glorious uncertainty of racing. Meanwhile, thankfully, Robert's back home though he does need round-the-clock care.)

Sturminster Newton
(Twinned with Montebourg in France)

It was always my intention that my visit to the town should coincide with its tenth annual Cheese Fair in September but, following torrential rains in the preceding week and with the recreational field waterlogged, to the great disappointment of countless producers and visitors alike, the fair was unavoidably cancelled. Having visited the event the summer before I know what a bitter blow it must have been to the hard-working organisers and all the small producers for miles around. So it is that I have arrived later in the year than intended but, fortunately, on a fine day and I am taking the opportunity to wander idly about the locality and savour what the town has to offer. My first stop is at the Bull Tavern where I make the acquaintance of former councillor Denise Roome who runs the inn with Neil. It proves to be an eminently civilised place to begin my tour.

I set off from The Bull across the handsome fifteenth century bridge over the Stour towards the town, with a view in one direction over the water meadows to the Old Mill and the other to Riverside House. Sturminster Newton is, of course, a town replete with literary associations. It was

Cllr. Charles Fraser, chairman of Sturminster Newton Town Council, lays a wreath on the grave of Dorset poet, Robert Young. *Picture: Pat Timmons, Bournemouth Echo*

at Riverside House that Thomas Hardy wrote what many consider his finest novel '*The Return of the Native*'. It was also Hardy who aptly described the Blackmore Vale as 'The Vale of Little Dairies' and certainly Sturminster's own history was long associated with dairy farming and its products. William Barnes was once employed by a local solicitor and wrote the poem '*The Maid of Newton*' in honour of the '*fairest girl in the town*'. The dialect poet, Robert Young, writing under the name of Rabin Hill, passed most of his 97 years in the town. The centenary of Young's death on 7 April, 2008, was commemorated at the cemetery just a few months ago. Most sadly a man I'd hoped to meet, the teacher, guitarist and graphic artist Paul Hart, who was closely involved in the anniversary celebrations and responsible for the repainting of Young's metal grave marker, passed away not long afterwards. In more recent times my good friend, Roger Guttridge, himself a native of the town, has upheld its literary traditions with a succession of fine books on the county.

"When I was a lad in the 1960s you could lie down in the middle of the street on a Wednesday which was then early closing. You'd be ill advised to try it today."

The first baby to be born in Mappowder at the end of WW2, Victor Fox is this year's Town Chairman. A gentle, kindly man possessed of a lilting Dorset accent and a charming wife named Elizabeth, Victor daily counts his blessings.

"It's such a wonderful honour to represent this town. I love meeting people and trying to be of service to them. Of course, in the past year or two we've seen some remarkable changes here. When the old cattle market closed down in 1996 it left a big development site in the middle of the town. We also lost a major employer when we lost the Sturminster Creamery in 2000. These were body blows to the town but we had to pick ourselves up by our bootstraps. There's nothing to be gained by sitting around moaning. We decided we needed new community and medical centres and a supermarket. It became a real team effort. Three years ago we had a day-long marathon signing session of legal documents involving the town council, Taylor Wimpey and the Charles Higgins Trust, the district council and SW England RDA. We employed Philip Proctor, a most helpful architect from Shaftesbury and a local builder named Philip Hammond. All the ducks had to line up together. The net result is what you see before you today. Philip Hammond, to his credit, completed the job 'within budget and within time'."

We've left Victor's cottage in Church Street and I'm now on a conducted tour of The Exchange where he introduces me to Pam Naylor, the most helpful admin assistant to the council. I understand the pride in the Chairman's voice. It's an impressive building that now stands on the former site of the old cattle market.

"It was opened by the actor and film director Julian Fellowes at the end of last year. He especially liked the balustrade design of the staircase which was created by our local blacksmith Ian Ring. The stone carvings over the entrance are by Pippa Unwin and up there is the old market bell which had been looked after by a local farmer since its removal from the market. A young lad by the name of Joshua Twigden was given the honour of ringing the bell, exactly ten years to the day after it was last sounded to mark the closing of the cattle market after 700 years of trading in the town. It's been a fantastic achievement by so many people in the town."

Victor takes me inside and up the stairs to the 300 seater auditorium which can be used for shows and a variety of cultural events.

"The seats can be easily moved so that it can become a ballroom or whatever is required. Outside you can see the Elizabeth Frink sculpture that we have on permanent loan. The whole project has cost £2.6 million which is a lot of money but we believe it's a huge asset for the town."

What's the population of the town these days and its employment opportunities?

Joshua Twigden pulling the rope to ring the old market bell, marking a new era in the town's history: *Picture: Corin Messer*

SNADS production of Lady Windermere's Fan. *Picture: Graham Baseden*

"We're about 3,900. I'd describe Sturminster as big enough to get nearly all you want on a daily basis but small enough that most people know who you are. As for employment, we do have the North Dorset Business Park and Butts Pond, both of which are home to a variety of businesses. Obviously we've got the shops and Health Centre, Sturminster High School, the William Barnes Primary and Yewstock which caters for children with learning difficulties. Clearly there are a fair number of self-employed craftsmen, but a great many folk do go off to work elsewhere each day. Of course, one of the problems, as with so many places, is property prices. The difference between average salaries and house prices is in a ratio of ten times which does make it so very difficult for our young people."

My next call is upon Robert Cowley at Rixson's Cottages. As a boy Robert attended the local primary with Roger Guttridge before going on to Hardye's and Magdalen College, Cambridge, where he read English. At this point our tale takes a curious and unexpected twist that saw Robert returning to Sturminster, instead of following the academic career he might initially have anticipated. Robert's grandfather had established a plumbing business way back in 1898 which his father subsequently inherited and developed. When Robert's father became ill and unable to run the business, Robert returned to assume responsibility. He soon found himself enjoying the challenge. Besides which, he was able to pursue his academic career by lecturing. His brother Peter, likewise a graduate, later joined forces with him to form probably the most academically qualified team of plumbers in the county, if not the kingdom. Robert's return to his roots was not only a blessing for all those householders in the locality in need of a skilled plumber but for the community at large, for he duly found himself the youngest member of a planning committee involved in the building of a new hall in the town. But it was the dramatic change in the town's fortunes with the closure of the cattle market that saw Robert and his wife Linda become involved in a major project to revitalise the town. Though a part of the process was described earlier by Victor Fox, it is interesting to view the action through another pair of eyes.

"We had this 7 acre site in the middle of the town left empty – a couple of auction rooms and cattle pens, practical in their time but not very beautiful. The site was owned overseas in the Cayman Islands by a South African, I believe. There were various initiatives. At this point we had a very good community worker named Lynn Saunders who played a very useful role in getting everyone talking. Harry Dawes, the former headmaster at the secondary school, sadly now deceased, played his part too along with Alan Bruce, also deceased, who was especially interested in the ecological aspect of any future development. Individuals like Pat Johnson and Jackie Upton played crucial roles. If we were to achieve anything we had to pull together as a community. Sturquest was created which was an amalgam of community groups, the town council, district and county councillors. We met once a month, everyone participated with no one pulling rank. It was a remarkable set-up. We drew up plans and put them before the town together with a planning application. Between 350-400 people turned up. John Dunne, our enabler, came up with the money from a variety of sources. The brilliant reality is that The Exchange belongs to the community and it's the home to all the clubs and societies in the town – and it starts with a clean sheet. We have a wholly volunteer staff supporting a full-time general manager, Robin Savill. We also have the superb new Charles Higgins Medical Centre. I believe what we achieved is an example of what can be done collectively. It's a model for others to follow."

It clearly is just that. Barely a decade ago Sturminster was still reeling from the shock of the closure of the cattle market. It is a tribute to the resilience of the local people that they have created in its place something as splendid.

Another recent addition to the town's attractions is the newly opened museum in the Old Market Cross House. With a grant of £50,000 from the Heritage Lottery fund it has been possible to relocate the contents to the thatched 16th century building from a location on the fringe of the town. At the opening ceremony just a few days ago three ladies, Margaret Score, Audrey Fox and Gwyn Rogers 'cut the ribbons' so marking the roles their late husbands, Stan Score, Tom Fox and Ray Rogers, had played in establishing the original museum. As David Fox, the local councillor and president of the Museum and Mill Society remarked; "This grant gives us a wonderful opportunity to create a superb new heritage centre here which will be able to reflect not only our town, but the villages around, and the great changes that have occurred over the years."

With the successful completion of The Exchange project the thoughts of Sturminster's citizens are turning increasingly towards the most appropriate use of the old Unigate Creamery factory site off Station Road, closed in 2000 when the company was integrated with Dairy Crest. It was in 1913 that a co-operative of local farmers created the creamery with the aim of supplying cheese and milk locally. Speaking on behalf of Sturquest, Hugh de Longh confirms that lots of general ideas are being circulated but no decisions have yet been taken. The most popular seems to be a mix of affordable housing, car-parking provision and facilities for young people in the town. After the success of their previous deliberations I have little doubt but that the quiet, reflective wisdom of the locals will again produce a wise outcome.

The Vicarage, St. Mary's Church

"I didn't see Jesus making judgements before meeting people. I must meet people where they are, accept people where they are. I will baptise the child if the parents are not married. It would be very unfair on the child not to do so. If I know they are not married I may ask them: 'Would you like to get married here at St. Mary's?' I believe the Church has to go along with the changes in society. At the same time it must not lose its moorings. It must retain its fundamental teachings."

The Palm Sunday procession in Sturminster Newton. *Picture: Winston Fane-Bailey*

The Revd. David Seymour arrived at St. Mary's 7 years ago from Bradford-on-Avon. Born near Reading and ordained in 1981, David is married to Wendy and the father of 5 children, 3 of whom are still at home.

"I came to Sturminster 3 years after the closure of the cattle market. People were still grieving for the lost days of the past. They were nostalgic for the Monday market-days when the town was bustling and alive. There was a real sadness in the town. The old market area looked dilapidated and depressing. People spoke of a golden era that was ended. Sturminster was understandably feeling sorry for itself. What has happened now is that we have a new doctor's and dentist's surgery, The Exchange and a new supermarket. The town looks so much brighter and tidier. Even our population has increased. Now when I talk to people they will say, 'No, it's not like it used to be but it is so much better than it was just a few years ago.' Change is happening all the time. It's how we respond to change that is so important."

David believes passionately in an 'inclusive' society. He positively welcomes the new diversity but wants to see minority groups become a part of British society.

"The East Europeans who have come here – overwhelmingly they are hard-working and adding to this nation. We have Czech staff here at the dental surgery. At the Poet's Corner Cafe there is the splendid Yasar, who is a Turkish Muslim and married to an English girl Becky. Such people have enriched our community."

Does David see any particular social problems in Sturminster?

"I do welcome two councillors in particular from the Rixson estate, Clare Fallon and Michael Reid. There are problems of social deprivation there and Clare and Michael will, I am certain, seek to improve the facilities on the estate. It is good to have new blood on the council to make sure we do not become complacent. In general terms, we do all want to upgrade the town's facilities for everyone."

What I have not yet alluded to, though it was the subject of the first 10 minutes of our conversation, is the splendid collection of racing photographs that decorate the walls of David's study. It seems I have truly found a kindred spirit for David is a passionate follower of the Sport of Kings. Portraits of the legendary Irish mare Dawn Run and Oh So Risky generate an animated discussion of the relative merits of various Champion Hurdle winners. David is, I discover, even planning a part of his holiday to be taken during the Cheltenham Festival week. This clergyman is clearly a gentleman of the most refined and discriminating taste. He's also a life member of Hampshire CCC, thanks to the generosity of a certain Freddie Rowe, and a Reading FC supporter. We could easily talk sport for the next few hours but David is a busy man and it's time to let him resume his pastoral duties. His responsibilities also extend to St. Peter's at Hinton St. Mary and St. Thomas A' Becket at Lydlinch. Though he has a young American curate from Nashville, Rachel Green, to assist him his days are invariably full. We conclude on a suitably serious, ecclesiastical theme.

"I believe we are walking a tightrope between the old traditions of the Church, maintaining those precious Christian values, and embracing society as it is. Unless we are realistic in our dealings with the world around us, we will find ourselves talking to no one. I care passionately about the Gospels and what they mean. They can have huge relevance in peoples' lives but we must be able to communicate effectively."

And on the doorstep of The Vicarage just one last racing query – who's going to win the Champion Hurdle and the Cheltenham Gold Cup?

"The first horses past the winning post?"

We are still laughing as we shake hands.

While we are on the topic of matters equestrian William Fox-Pitt, from nearby Hinton St. Mary, secures a magnificent bronze medal in the Olympic Games in Beijing before claiming his fifth Burghley Horse Trials title with first and second places on 16 years old Tamarillo and Ballincoola, so equalling the performance in 1987 of Olympic champion Mark Todd, the only other rider to achieve five Burghley titles. William is, of course, married to Alice Plunket, the effervescent member of the Channel 4 racing team whose knowledgeable and unfailingly good-natured contributions this writer always enjoys.

While we are on the topic of horse-racing, there's a fairy tale ending for local amateur jockey Anthony Knott, or 'Knotty' as he is known in the town, when he rides Wise Men Say to victory at Wincanton to record his first success after 28 years of trying – then promptly retires. Described in the Racing Post as giving his mount 'an agricultural ride', it's a glorious finale to the 44 year-old Anthony's racing career and is widely recorded in national newspapers and on TV. Customarily up at 3.30am to milk a 300 strong herd of dairy cows, Anthony has been riding out at Colin Tizzard's stable and receiving instruction from Joe to improve his riding. He also receives a letter of congratulation from Sally and Robert Alner.

"Many years ago Robert rode a point-to-point winner for me in my colours – they were my dad's colours then – so that letter meant a lot to me."

In a year of so much media gloom, it's good to record such a happy event splashed across the pages of the newspapers.

At Sturminster Bakery I meet Karen and Stephen Blake.

"Apart from Gillingham we're the only independent baker in Dorset north of the A35."

That is an extraordinary and very sad statistic and reflects the near extinction of the small baker in vast swathes of the county. A hundred, even 50 years ago, no one would have believed it possible. But then who would have imagined that several Dorset towns would not have a butcher's or a greengrocer's? Long may Karen and Stephen thrive.

As I mentioned at the beginning of the chapter my intention was to visit Sturminster at the time of the 10th Cheese Festival. Having attended the previous year I was looking forward to the event. Unfortunately, all the initial preparatory work by the organisers, not least Jeremy Squire, the Chairman of the Cheese Committee, and Giles and Annie Henschel, of Dorset Business Award winning Olives Et Al, the sponsors of the event, was in vain when the heavens opened in the days preceding the event and the field was waterlogged. Last year, 2007, the Committee was able to distribute no less than £10,000 to various local organisations. Let us hope the weather is kinder to this most enjoyable festival next year.

One of the points picked up by the Revd. David Seymour was the remarkable growth in Sturminster's birth-rate in recent years – up some 68% since 2001, it seems. It is a source of some amused comment about the town. David Fox, with his tongue firmly in his cheek, asks: "Could Sturminster's towering literary reputation have attracted romantics to the town? On the other hand, perhaps there's been a series of power cuts with residents unable to pay their bills?"

Norman King, the amateur demographer who first noticed the trend, suggests that the rising birth rate could be a vote of confidence in the town. "People obviously think it's a good place to bring up children."

Karen Wheat, a local health visitor, points to the number of new houses in the area and the influx of young people into the town and unromantically quashes any possibility of a greater amorousness. "There's definitely nothing in the water!"

In my opening paragraph I made reference to the commemoration earlier in the year of the 100th anniversary of the death of the dialect poet Robert Young. Among those present at the cemetery was a distant relative of Young when a wreath of anemones and hellebores was placed beside the grave marker by the town council chairman, Charles Fraser. David Fox gave a reading of Young's 'Sturmi'ster Common in Zummer Time' and the Rev. Elford of the local Methodist Church led the ceremony and prayers. In the light of the changes in the past 100 years, it is interesting to reflect how Sturminster will look like when the bi-centenary of Young's death comes round? Hopefully, it will be little different in essentials.

'Cittaslow'. No, I'd not heard the word either until I came to Sturminster Newton but what a splendid vision lies behind a rather unappealing word.

"It's an Italian concept born of a love of good food and a different pace of life," explains Jane Williams."Many Italians revolted against the ideas of fast food and hamburger restaurants. Since then it's become all-encompassing and a kite mark for the quality of life in a town."

Alistair Wingate-Saul, who owns Sturminster butcher's Holebrooks Fine Food with his wife Nikki, adds that following a presentation from the Mayor of Ludlow he's all for it.

"Ludlow is a lovely place and the ethos of 'Cittaslow' is a very attractive one."

And my old chum, the town chairman, Victor Fox, concludes: "If we can get 'cittaslow' status we'll be the first town in the south of England to achieve it. It's all about staying local, whether that be eating, growing or producing – and getting the quality and pace of life right."

(Jane Williams and her supporters succeed in their aim. Sturminster Newton becomes the first town in the SW of England to be awarded Cittaslow status).

"My mother was actually a Fiddleford girl. Her parents and her grandparents before them ran

Fiddleford Post Office and the village shop. It was an association that dated back to 1895 and continued until 1965."

I've already mentioned Roger Guttridge earlier in the chapter. This morning we're sitting in his Wimborne home discussing his association with Sturminster and the surrounding area.

"I actually arrived in the town when I was 8 months old and duly attended Sturminster primary before following in my mother's footsteps to Blandford Grammar. Meanwhile she became the bursar at Sturminster High School. So my association with the town was a close one during the first 18 or so years of my life. Of course, when I went off to Loughborough University and later pursued a career in journalism I ceased to know it as intimately but, as a boy, I knew it very well. The Monday Market days were the highlight of the week and, during school holidays, my friends and I loved the bustle and excitement of those Mondays. There were rabbits and chicken and all the usual farm animals. The buses brought people in from the villages and, by the time we were teenagers, it provided an opportunity to meet the girls from all around. In those days there were 5 pubs in the town and they'd all be full – the old Rivers Arms was very popular, I remember. The market was the lifeblood of the town. I loved to watch the auctioneer in the cattle market taking bids. He would speak at an extraordinary speed, performing the most amazing verbal gymnastics, and I remember saying to my mother I was always frightened that if I so much as scratched my nose during the bidding, I'd finish up bringing a cow home with me! That was also the period when we still had a station and the railway was an important part of the life of the town. There was huge sadness when that was shut down along with so many others. What an asset it would be today!"

Roger's career as a journalist and author has proved to be both distinguished and varied. From the *Western Gazette* he graduated to the *Bournemouth Echo*, where he was appointed Chief Reporter in 1983. Today his major commitment is to the *Swimming Times* though he contributes extensively as a freelance to various Dorset journals specialising in local history stories. He also covers local swimming for the *Echo*. Extraordinarily he is soon to publish his 17th book.

"Though I am still some way behind Rodney Legg!"

I would guess Rodney is approaching the thousand mark by now, or have I underestimated his aggregate score? He could be described as the Barbara Cartland of Dorset publishing – but I'm not comparing literary styles, Rodney! Honestly! And what exactly is Roger's latest?

"It's called *Paranormal Dorset* in which I have investigated all sorts of unusual, inexplicable phenomena. I hope readers will find it interesting."

Back to the Sturminster of the 21st century and the most recent developments.

"I believe the town has succeeded in creating some fine new buildings like The Exchange and the Health Centre. Obviously it is impossible to recapture what has gone forever – the town of my youth. But everyone has worked very hard to rejuvenate the town after the terrible blows it suffered – and all credit to everyone involved."

Finally, since swimming is now Roger's specialist subject, is there a Dorset girl to look out for in the coming years?

"Amelia Maughan lives at Hinton St. Mary and she is quite outstanding. She's soon off to Talbot Heath from Port Regis School. Last year as a 12 year-old she was the fastest in the world in freestyle in her age group. She could, if she continues to progress, be a serious contender for Olympic honours in 2012."

I've known Roger for 20 years and he's still the same unassuming, kindly, sensitive individual I first met – and a highly professional writer. If not quite as prolific as our mutual friend, the wonderful Rodney Legg, he is 14 books ahead of me – and he's younger!

Inevitably my chapter on Sturminster Newton has focused on 2 aspects of the same theme- before and after the closure of the market. More than anywhere else in the county, save perhaps for Portland when the Royal Navy left the island, the town of Sturminster has been obliged to chart a new course. There is no doubt that adversity often brings the best out in individuals. It's very easy to ride along on the crest of a wave, but it requires strength of character and courage to respond to the sort of very real challenges with which Sturminster was confronted. That old cliché 'when the going gets tough, the tough get going' is a not inappropriate description of what has happened here in this quiet but stubbornly proud and dignified town. The townspeople, admirably guided and inspired by wise civic leadership, may feel justly proud of their recent achievements.

Marnhull

> 'Here under this stone
> Lie Ruth and old John
> Who smoked all his life
> And so did his wife:
> And now there's no doubt
> But their pipes are both out.'

An inscription upon the tomb of John Warren who did in 1752 at the age of 94 in Marnhull churchyard.

At the year's end villagers are shocked to learn that their Crown Inn has closed its door after the landlord finds himself in financial difficulties. The 16th century pub, renowned in Hardy circles for its role in *Tess of the D'Urbervilles* and its real ale, is often sought out by Hardy enthusiasts in their West Country itinerary of places to visit. Fortunately, our story has a happy ending when Philip Scott, who is also the landlord of The Martyrs Inn in Tolpuddle, rides to the rescue and promptly appoints Gemma Watts as the new manager of The Crown Inn. The good villagers of Marnhull sigh with relief and all Hardy lovers seeking out the actual model for The Pure Drop in the great man's celebrated work will be no less delighted.

One village success story is the 'Best Wessex village shop and PO' award for 2008 by the Countryside Alliance to Bob and Suzanne Young of the Robin Hill Stores & PO in Burton Street. Having also gained an accreditation from 'Direct from Dorset', a DCC initiative to promote local produce, it's a gratifying reward for lots of hard work by Bob and Suzanne.

Gillingham
Twinned with Le Neubourg (France)

'This is a beautiful place, full of little bridges, rivulets, mills and cottages – and the most beautiful trees and verdure I ever saw.'

John Constable RA , in a letter written to his wife Maria when he was in Gillingham as a guest of his friend, Archdeacon John Fisher (Vicar of Gillingham 1819-32) 5 September, 1823.

And nearly two centuries later? How does Gillingham compare?

"Unlovely Gillingham. Yes, I know that's what they say but the people are lovely inside!"

Julie Hansford, Mayor's secretary and planning clerk, is fiercely protective and proud of her town and its inhabitants.

"Julie is absolutely right. The people of Gillingham are resourceful, determined and very friendly."

At the Classic Vehicles Show, Gillingham Festival. *Picture: Julie Hansford*

That Ian Stewart, a former marketing man in telecommunications from Bootle, backs Julie's view is hardly surprising since he is, after all, the equally proud Mayor of his adopted town.

"Unfortunately I think our geography works against us. We're not on a hill, nor are we on the coast. Both locations do help a town to look aesthetically easy on the eye. Gillingham is essentially flat and divided by three rivers – the Stour, the Shreen and the Lodden – which has affected the natural growth of the town. The railway station was built not to serve the towns-people so much as the cattle market, and the ribbon development of the Thirties and immediate post-war years did not improve the appearance of the town. Furthermore, Gillingham has never been a prosperous town and there are few outstanding buildings. It's sprawled awkwardly outwards and much of the building, I would acknowledge, is rather plain and ordinary. Historically we had a gasometer, a glove works, and bacon and glue factories and those old sites have been developed piecemeal."

If many Gillingham residents are instinctively defensive and hurt by the criticism of their town it is entirely understandable. After all, how can a town renowned for its bacon and glue factories be expected to compete aesthetically with Poole and its magnificent harbour, Bournemouth and its gardens and sea-front, Sherborne and its Abbey, or Lyme and its Cobb? It simply isn't fair. There are additional difficulties for the town.

"Commercially the town cannot attract bigger shops because the roads are too narrow and the existing properties lack the depth for storage. We all concede that Gillingham isn't a pretty town in the traditional sense, but we are immensely proud of the nature of community life that exists here. There are, for example, scores of active societies and support groups here. I believe it's also true to say that in the past people felt that things happened TO them. They have had little say. What we need now is to take a greater grip on development, prepare a comprehensive plan for the future and the Gillingham Town Design Statement is a move in that direction."

Ian and his wife actually live in an attractive modern development off the main road which is unseen by motorists passing through. In fact, I discover similar pockets of new housing about the

Circus workshop skills, demonstrated by Flame. Gillingham Festival. *Picture: Julie Hansford*

town though, unfortunately, they cannot compensate for the dreary, unattractive approach to the town, not least along the Shaftesbury road, that inevitably catches the visitor's attention.

Janet Robson, a Freeman of the town, former Mayor and chairman of Gillingham School's Board of Governors, is a fifth generation local girl. Janet and her husband Philip run the art accessories and framing shop in the High Street, opposite the site of the old Free School founded in 1516, and they live in Chantry View, a property built in 1720. Janet has witnessed the remarkable growth of the local population from a mere 3,500 in her childhood to today's 11,000. She also retains vivid memories of the bacon and glue factories.

"Sometimes a pig would escape on its way to the slaughter house and run free through the streets causing absolute chaos. They used to make faggots at the factory which would be wheeled on trolleys through the town to the bakery which would bake them in the ovens after the day's bread-baking. I can still smell the lovely aroma of those faggots. I don't suppose it would be allowed today. I remember too when the lorries would wind through the town and, from our upstairs window, I would look down on the carcasses of the animals and their bones which were being transported to the glue factory to be boiled up. No one in the town hung up their washing on those days because the smell would impregnate all their clothes. The stench was appalling."

At this point I half expect Janet to exclaim, 'Ah, those were the days! I wish we could have them back!' But, for some inexplicable reason, she doesn't! Indeed, she seems almost relieved.

"But they're all gone now. Anyway, I love my Gillingham, whatever its blemishes."

As the chairman of governors, Janet is immensely proud of the town's comprehensive school.

"We have an outstanding school with an absolutely brilliant headmaster, Manil Lennarduzzi. Manil and his colleagues deserve so much praise for all they have done for our children."

One of the features of the past decade has been the influx of thousands of migrant workers from Eastern Europe ever since the barriers were removed on the free movement of workers between EU countries. Gillingham, I discover, has its own sizeable Polish population.

"They're mostly at Dextra Lighting Systems. At one time there were several hundred and the company bought a number of houses for them. I believe there was a very large group working on the night shift. They have an excellent reputation for hard work though I believe some are now returning

Civic Day, St Mary the Virgin. *Picture: Julie Hansford*

to Poland because of the recession here and the job opportunities back home. But I can only speak well of them. They're very friendly and smile at you in the street but it is strange when you pass a group of children and realise they are chattering away in Polish. Incidentally, one of the reasons so many people find Gillingham a convenient place to live is the fact that we still enjoy a main-line rail link. Quite a few people work in London and the platform in the morning for the 6.45 is absolutely full."

Described by Brian Nicholson, the chairman of the Chamber of Trade, as 'probably the last place in the county where you can go and ask for just one three eighths washer and be cheerfully served into the bargain', Crocker's is one of the most popular and long established Gillingham shops. Being one of the most useless DIY men in the county, I refrain from asking Brian what I should do with the afore-mentioned washer, lest he give me a rude answer. Instead, I concentrate my attention on its former proprietor and current chairman of Gillingham History Society, Brian Crocker. A quietly spoken, unassuming man, Peter has served the town diligently over the years as a councillor and Mayor. Just a few months ago the title of Freeman was bestowed upon him for fifty remarkable years of service to the Town Museum.

"My great grand-father opened the shop as an ironmonger's in 1882. Over the years the family sold bicycles, motor-cycles and farm implements."

As a historian Brian, like Janet Robson, sees the town in its historical perspective.

"We all acknowledge there is nothing dramatic or exciting about Gillingham. Few tourists ever visit us. In the post-war years the town became a bungalow heaven for people retiring from London. Now we are a dormitory town, principally for Yeovil and Salisbury. We're 24 miles to Salisbury and

20 to Yeovil. As far as the town's appearance is concerned I would very much like to see it smartened up. I'd love to see some riverside walks established. After all, we are very unusual in having three rivers. Let's make full use of them."

Another former councillor and twice Mayor, Brian Nicholson, who ran a printing business for some years, sees the town in a similar, realistic, no-nonsense way.

"We're not a picturesque town with lots of fine houses and landed wealth. It's an unprepossessing town and the entry is mostly through industrial estates and horrible polyglot buildings. We're also removed from decision-making and it's very much a case of looking after ourselves. For example, we have just one county councillor for 11-12,000 people. On the other hand, I also see Gillingham in a very positive light. We should congratulate ourselves on our successes, one of which is the Gillingham Show which is the best one-day show in the West. It's held every year on the third Wednesday in August and I would urge anyone who has never attended to come along to the next one. I guarantee they will be very impressed. Our chairman Mike Simpson and his volunteers do a brilliant job – they've even bought their own field. We also have a splendid Twinning Association with Nuremberg in France. Actually an interesting story is attached to that. It was in 1944 following D-Day that a tank driven by a Gillingham headmaster, John Webster, was apparently responsible for the bullet holes in the local church. But they seem to have forgiven us for that!"

One Gillingham resident of whom John Constable would undoubtedly warmly approve is Elizabeth Kendall who arrived in the town many years ago with her husband Jim and taught innumerable children of the locality. Elizabeth was the founder of Gillingham Action for Nature and the long-time Tree Warden, for which services she was created an Honorary Freeman. The morning I arrive at Elizabeth's cottage in Chantry Ford is one of the wettest days of an autumn full of wet days. I arrive resembling a drowned rat, late having met flooding on the journey, and dripping water everywhere. It's most fortunate the cottage has a stone floor and Elizabeth is a very understanding lady.

"We are susceptible to flooding here," she confides with a smile, "but I don't think we're under threat quite yet!"

That John Constable loved trees is beyond dispute and in the former teacher, Elizabeth Kendall, he would have found a true soul-mate. Her cottage is set amongst trees and she believes passionately in their therapeutic benefit to the human condition.

"Trees are so vital for the mental and physical health of a community. They soften the landscape, reveal the unfolding of the seasons and their colours are so beautiful."

If we added their significance for insect and bird life and their role in reducing the pollution of our atmosphere, and a dozen other benefits besides, we would still not complete the importance of trees in our world. And Elizabeth has planted hundreds of trees of all descriptions about Gillingham in recent years that generations as yet unborn are in her debt. Yet the lady is disarmingly modest. I try to tease from her some of her particular triumphs.

"Do remember many of the trees were planted as part of community garden projects and few are actually marked in any way. But there is an oak which is coming along nicely at the back of Focus and another in Orchard Park together with a number of flowering cherries about the town but, to tell you the truth, it's difficult to remember after the passage of time. It would be lovely to have some elms again and there are plans afoot for some disease resistant elms from Holland to be planted in due course. Actually we do now have a wonderful young Tree Warden – her name is Trudi Green. I describe Trudi as 'my legs' now that I do not quite have the energy of my youth. Besides the tree-planting, however, I do absolutely want to preserve Chantry Fields and its footpaths. Though I appreciate times have changed since my childhood, it does distress me that as soon as

Thorngrove celebrates its 40th birthday with the Mayor. *Picture: John Lockyer*

a daisy has raised its head someone wants to cut it off. And people are no longer simply used to brushing through cow parsley as we once were. So many people seem to want to sanitise and regulate everything. There's an obsession with tidiness but that is not nature's way!"

What a wonderful contribution Elizabeth has made to the Gillingham community and how richly she deserves her civic recognition.

It's still raining as I leave but, happily, there are no floods and I leave the town by car, not by boat.

When I began my journey I was pleased to report certain improvements in farming finances. However, as the year draws on, comes disquieting news that milk prices are falling back once more as supermarkets respond to the 'credit crunch' by squeezing margins. Among the protesting voices is that of Paul Gould, the chairman of Dorset NFU, who owns Townsend Farm at nearby West Stour. Paul also draws attention to new EU regulations regarding the spreading and storage of slurry which is going to cost many farmers dearly. The consequences of the crisis in banking and the incompetence of the regulators are certainly having far-reaching effects in so many areas of the economy.

In any town there are a host of worthies and 'characters' and it is impossible for me to meet any more than a mere handful of the individuals who deserve a place in these pages. Already several names have been mentioned to whom I must refer, albeit fleetingly. One is Colin Dann who has served as mayor of Gillingham on no fewer than 7 occasions. I don't know the record within the county but Colin must rank high in the list. Another 'character' who has received widespread praise is Nick Baker, the chairman of the Silver Band supporters, who also supplies barrel organs and steam engines for the local carnival and social events. A third is Mark Hebditch , a former deputy headmaster who has served the community admirably through his association with the Three Rivers Partnership, a body dedicated to establishing projects and securing funding in the locality. The fourth is distinguished local historian Sam Woodcock who lives at nearby Milton-on-Stour.

Another day

Strolling through Gillingham in the company of Julie Hansford has to rank as an especially pleasurable episode in my travels. It is also a most enlightening and informative experience. Plain Mayor's secretary and planning clerk may be her formal job description but Julie simply bubbles with an enthusiasm more fitting of the title of town ambassador. We call by first at the famous Crocker's emporium where I decide, notwithstanding Brian Nicholson's recommendation, to refrain from asking for a 'three-eighths washer'. Julie is immediately engaged in cheerful banter with staff members, David Flower and John Boarder. We depart with the sound of laughter in my ears.

"I never leave Crocker's without a smile on my face – all the staff are so much fun – and you didn't even meet Steve, Peter or Tanya. When they're all together it's like a comedy team!"

A few paces down the street and Julie pauses.

"This is one of my favourite shops in the town – Undercut's Clothing. There's a lovely lady called Hayley who runs it. You must come in!"

I simply do not feel comfortable when surrounded by lingerie, dresses, handbags and other feminine accessories. I am always conscious of the odd glances of lady customers. What are they thinking, I wonder? That I am sort of pervert, the kind of man who steals underwear from washing-lines perhaps? Being in the company of Julie does make it a little easier, and I will cheerfully acknowledge that of its kind Hayley's Undercut's Clothing is a perfectly admirable shop. However, I am still relieved when we are back out in the street. We've barely advanced a few paces before Julie stops again.

"You must meet Bruno. Come on in."

Bruno? A German watch-maker perhaps? Or a taxidermist though they are both rather thin on the ground these days? A tobacconist maybe? Didn't my grandfather smoke St. Bruno flake? As a little boy I used to watch with fascination as he packed the flake into the bowl of his pipe from a leather pouch, before lighting up in a cloud of white smoke. But if Bruno is a tobacconist why is Julie leading me into a Suite and Bed centre? I suppose Bruno must be the proprietor.

"Bruno's just gone out for a walk with Frank," says joint proprietor Rachael Pearce. "He'll be back in ten minutes."

We decide to return later. We're off again – but not for long.

"Look! There's Tamsin's gift shop. The shop is absolutely lovely. Do come in and meet Tamsin "

I meet Tamsin who smiles sweetly.

"I could stay in here for hours," whispers Julie.

To Tamsin's regret and my relief Julie doesn't linger for hours. Not on this occasion, at least. Back in the street and Julie is pointing across the road.

"It's a shame the Gillingham Tandoori isn't open at the moment but it's brilliant and Mohammed is wonderful."

It's becoming obvious to me that Gillingham possesses many of the finest shops in the county, possibly in the country, and there's little doubt in my mind that Mohammed's Tandoori is the finest this side of the Indian sub-continent.

We reach our destination – the Phoenix Inn – where I order the drinks and we take a seat.

"There are just so many good people around," Julie enthuses. "Do you know that Colin Westbrook and his team have raised £200,000 towards a new hut for the scouts and cubs? Lots of trades-people have offered their help too. 'Just give us a shout when you need a hand,' they say – and they will."

I'm sure they will. Julie has convinced me that Gillingham and its people are absolutely wonderful. They are possibly the finest, most socially responsible, good-natured folk to be found anywhere in the entire kingdom!

"And as for our youth centre, Trish Walker is a total bundle of energy. They even have their own recording studio there. It's situated near the cemetery, so guess what they've called it? Bones! It's great for all the boys and girls with musical talent."

For a couple of minutes our attention is focused on two figures dressed as Superman who have come through the door collecting for a cerebral palsy charity. Their names are Brendan Neill and Ken Cadwalladr and the very finest of fellows they clearly are, typical specimens of the locality.

"Have you heard of Mulberry Court? It's a marvellous residential home for adults run by Scope and the Thorngrove garden centre which works with people with cerebral palsy. It has recently celebrated its 40th birthday."

On our way back to Julie's office we drop by at the Suite & Bed Centre to make the acquaintance of Bruno. I look for a gentleman garbed in traditional lederhosenpossibly smoking a Meerschaum pipe – but in vain. However, I do see Rachael beckoning us over.

"Frank's gone to get a bite of lunch. Come and meet Bruno. He's going to school tonight to collect his bronze award."

So the mystery is solved. Bruno is the son of Frank and Rachael. And he's clearly excelled himself. Good old Bruno ! He clearly deserves our warmest congratulations. Rachael points.

"There he is, sitting in the window, chewing his toy caterpillar. The award is from the Kennel Club – it's the Good Citizen scheme."

And, sure enough, there is Bruno in the shop window chewing his toy caterpillar. Bruno is a black Labrador.

I really don't want to leave Gillingham. I've become oddly fond of it, not least its most splendid citizens. So what do I say to my readers? Everyone is familiar with the old cliché – 'Don't judge a book by its cover.' It is, of course, absolutely true and it certainly applies to Gillingham. Drive in, looking steadfastly ahead. Ignore, if you possibly can, the worst of the architectural horrors on either side of you. Anyway, even the drab bungalows are peoples' homes and many are doubtless little palaces inside. Discover Chantry Fields, seek out the vicarage where once John Constable stayed with his great friend, John Fisher. You will find some very pleasing buildings dotted about, as I did. Call in at the shops and pubs, talk to the people. They are among the finest people in the kingdom, if not the world. Ask the lovely Julie, she'll confirm my every word.

Shaftesbury
Twinned with Brionne (France) and Lindlar (Germany)

Writing from his address at No 6, Wimpole street, London in May, 1906, Dorchester born Sir Frederick Treves, the eminent surgeon who once counted 'The Elephant Man' among his patients, stated in the Preface to his masterpiece *The Highways & Byways in Dorset* that his itinerary began by entering the county at Shaftesbury.

'A bright, pleasant and healthy town where everyone walks in the road... each knows the other, so that scarcely a soul goes by without a word of greeting. The boys in the street are whistling a tune which was popular two years ago: many people stand at street corners, as if waiting for someone who never comes: most of the men carry sticks, and most of the women baskets.'

Today absolutely no one in Shaftesbury who values their life walks in the road. Yes, a few individuals

Gold Hill, the image that epitomises Shaftesbury. *Picture: Geoff Hill*

may greet one another but it is far more likely that they do not. With computer downloads on to their i-Pods few boys will be whistling tunes 2 years out of date. Besides, how often do you hear anyone whistling in the street at all in the modern world? As for hanging around at street corners, unless one wishes to be suspected of peddling drugs, it is generally an unwise course of action. And any man carrying a stick would quite likely be picked up for being in possession of an offensive weapon, assuming there was a policeman about which is, I suppose, highly improbable. Substitute a bag for a basket, as long as it is a 'bag for life' and therefore ecologically friendly, and that would remain a common enough sight though many of its contents would be unrecognisable to Sir Frederick.

Of course, the admirable Sir Frederick didn't deal in the stuff of local government. His primary interests on his travels were history and buildings. Perhaps he was wise since, were he now in my shoes, he would be asking himself how best to approach the vexed topic of Shaftesbury's Town Council. Having travelled the length and breadth of the county these past months, spoken with practically every mayor and chairman of all shapes, sizes, temperaments and political persuasions, nothing yet has prepared me for the vitriolic character of much of Shaftesbury's Town Council business in recent times.

My first encounter in the town is in the Bell Street bistro, run by Ben and Nicola Rutter. First impressions are distinctly favourable. For a start the mellow tones of an accomplished girl jazz artist are coming through the sound system. What a refreshing change from the hideous cacophony that so often assaults the senses in so many establishments. Ben tells me the singer is Sue Hawker and she's performing at the bistro later in the week. But it's my companion sipping his coffee across the table who intrigues me no less than the music. His name is Richard Thomas and he describes himself as a journalist and author. He's also served as a town councillor since 1999. Astonishingly in that period no fewer than 55 complaints, as at the time of writing, have been lodged against him for alleged breaches of conduct, almost without exception by fellow councillors. Yet the man seems reasonable enough in the flesh and I see only one head – and no horns.

"The schism on the Council is extremely debilitating. I know there is huge personal animosity towards me. I consider myself an out and out democrat. I feel passionately about transparency and mistakes should not be concealed but acknowledged."

Richard seeks to place the issue within a historical context.

"Historically speaking, Shaftesbury was a rebellious town with an unruly population. John Wesley couldn't get out fast enough."

And his commitment to the town in which he has lived for the past 15 years appears strong.

"I love this town. The Bell Cafe bistro reflects much of what makes the town tick for me. It presents great music and live performers. Next door is the Arts Centre where Myra Wood organises a brilliant programme of events. Though I love much about the town I do feel it could be so much better. Some of us are incomers and locals often seem to take the view that 'no one is going to tell us what to do.' Issues easily become personalised. Fanny Charles in the *Blackmore Vale magazine* wrote very perceptively on the subject recently."

So what exactly lies behind the bitterness so often displayed at Council meetings that has poisoned relationships between councillors and factions within the town's community? Is it even my business to poke and prod and enquire, or should I merely record the existence of this festering ulcer as a fact and move on to more agreeable themes? After all, Shaftesbury is a glorious outpost of this county with so many splendid features to admire. Yet I am not merely a stranger passing through, here only to gaze briefly at the antiquities before moving on to another town. Its people are my interest, they are the subject of my book. So what are the ingredients of this wretched divide, insofar as I understand anything of it? I hear of a huntsman and a hunt saboteur, a case of wrongful dismissal, of the culling or is it the non-culling of pigeons, of soiled wedding dresses, of spades being called spades, of a gardening column called Dirty Nails, of the Shaftesbury Mafia and its 'Godfathers'. It is, I fear, too much for a simple fellow like myself. I decide to visit Tourist Information to talk of more mundane matters.

I'm invited through to the inner sanctum where a lovely lady sets before me a large mug of steaming coffee, charmingly decorated with our smallest bird, a gold-crest. Suzanne May, from the village of Kingston Magna, tells me she is just one of 25 volunteers who help to keep the ship afloat. Suzanne has been a volunteer for 12 years.

"Keith Davies and Marion Purser preceded me and Rosemary Saxey actually started at the same time as I did."

Boxes and trays are stacked to the right of me, to the left of me, behind me and piled high above my head, all filled to the brim with selections of charity Christmas cards. I count the names of 36 different charities and idly wonder how many charities actually exist in the UK.

"We sold £20,000 worth last year. But if it wasn't for David, this place would have fallen apart a couple of years ago. We all work for David."

For the past 15 minutes I've overheard David in the shop, with infinite patience, guiding an elderly lady through the journey she's booked to London. Now, as if on cue, our hero appears. Devon born, Cockney raised, 25 years in the RAF attaining the rank of a Wing Commander followed by a spell of service with the police, David explains how his association with Tourist Information began.

"I arrived in Shaftesbury 10 years ago and became involved with the community, in the way one does. When North Dorset DC withdrew funding from the Centre because it was strapped for cash, I felt we had to act because it provided such a valuable service. I must add in fairness that we pay only a peppercorn rent. We are open 6 days a week, 52 weeks of the year. We have 25 brilliant volunteers – some of them work at the Abbey shop or the Arts Centre as well. I decided to make the Centre a permanent payment facility so people are able to pay their utility bills here, buy theatre tickets, book on National Express, besides offering the usual tourist information to visitors. For the Gillingham Festival we sold over £20,000 of tickets. Our annual turnover is £125,000."

David pulls down a file and thumbs through the pages.

"In the first nine months of this year we've had 23,313 British callers and 2,220 from overseas. Of course, many of the English are locals who have called in on a number of occasions but I like to think we are providing an invaluable service to the community and our visitors."

It's a modest claim by a singularly modest man. When he's out of earshot Suzanne whispers.

"David's brilliant at wheeling and dealing to obtain creature comforts on our behalf. We now have storage heaters and a microwave. Last winter we had to wear fleeces it was so cold. And I know for a fact that though he's paid for just 20 hours a week he often works for nearer 30!"

The John Peel Cafe

Derek Beer, a councillor for 20 years, a former Town Mayor, the chairman of the Chamber of Trade, the manager of the cafe, married to Angela, might reasonably be described as a stalwart of the Shaftesbury community. And, to judge by the good-natured banter between himself and his customers, he also clearly enjoys an excellent rapport with the young and the old.

"We have so many wonderful people living in the town and the young people here are so polite and helpful. One of my proudest duties as Mayor last year was to present 23 local people with their Hidden Heroes awards at the Town Hall. They were all ages, from a man in his 90's to a boy of 15. We recognised them for a whole host of reasons – from caring for their neighbours and patients in hospital, to their input into local organisations, fostering, helping with Shaftesbury in Bloom and the like."

Derek is one of those transparently good-hearted, socially responsible, dedicated individuals who are the very backbone of a thriving and healthy community.

"I am terribly upset by the acrimony on the Council. It's awful and unnecessary. Ray Humphries, for example, has devoted his life to the town. He and his wife Christina have done so much work on behalf of the carnival. There have been times recently when I wonder if my heart is still in it? I love this town and its people but I feel things have changed and I'm not sure if it's been for the best. People must learn to be tolerant and more patient – to work together in a spirit of co-operation and mutual respect."

The town's Historical Society is campaigning vigorously to secure funding for an upgrading of the Gold Hill Museum. As Anna McDowell, the society's chairman, Claire Riley, the education officer and Giles Harbottle explain, they are frustrated that they are unable to make full use of the artefacts the museum contains. It is hoped that Lottery funding may be made available so the project may move forward.

My next call is upon the Mayor, Win Harvey, a Shaftesbury resident for the past dozen years. Win spells out some of the difficulties running council business.

"Chairing is difficult at times."

I suspect that must be one of the understatements of the year.

"I think one of the difficulties of a small town is that there exist only a small number of people willing to participate in civic affairs. When there is a serious clash of personalities within that group life there are real problems. Fortunately, I have been used to working in a predominantly male environment so I don't feel intimidated by it but, clearly, it is very unfortunate. What we have to do as a council is to continue to try and serve the town as best we are able and make wise judgements."

Swan's Trust Office, Shaftesbury District Task Office

Lester Dibben is an authentic Shastonian.

"I was born in Castle Hill House which was then a maternity hospital. Now it's an old people's home. I'll probably die in the same place I was born," he laughs.

Now there's a chastening thought but, at least, Lester can laugh! Lester laments the disappearance of the outlying village communities he knew as a child.

"Besides the church and the pub, there'd be a school, a store, a Post Office, and probably a baker and a butcher. How many survive in that form today? It's such a shame. The character's gone out of so many of the villages. In some they've lost everything except the church and even that may hardly be used."

Born of a farming background, though a trained aircraft engineer at Westland, Lester has been a councillor for 10 years and was Mayor four years ago. This year he's the Deputy Mayor. He's articulate, manifestly honest and totally committed to the community in which he has spent his life.

"One interesting point about Shaftesbury is that although it's in Dorset the people from 15 parishes across the border in Wiltshire and 11 parishes in Dorset see the town as the centre of their world which adds up to about 22,000 people. We are particularly anxious, therefore, that the projected new hospital to replace the Westminster Memorial hospital should be located here. A site on the east side of the town has already been allocated. We also see the new Yeovil College as a part of the same development. It would be a rational economic use of resources to combine the two on the same site. Shaftesbury has a limited range of job opportunities. We do have two industrial estates at Longmead and Wincombe with a number of small businesses established there, and Wessex Electricals run by the local Morgan family, with father Tony and sons Alistair and Simon. Quite a large number of people daily commute out while others come in from many of the outlying villages."

I'm talking to Lester at the Swans Trust Office, Swans Yard, at the home of the Shaftesbury District Task Force which was set up as part of a community planning strategy for North Dorset, along with similar organisations in other towns in the area. Supported by the town council the Shaftesbury Area Community Partnership team comprises Lester, Rachel Caulwell, John Parker and Anne Kirkpatrick, supported by the administrator Louise Plumridge.

"We sit around a table and decide how we can best help a variety of community projects. Louise is absolutely brilliant in helping those who come to us with ideas to formulate them in the best way possible, to make each bid distinctive in character."

Louise identifies several projects the team has been able to help with critical financial backing.

"We've provided support for new windows at Motcombe School, a new mower to mow a ten acres site at Guys Marsh which is now used as a football field. for a number of teams. We've helped set up a Mental Health drop-in centre called Hope where a truly inspirational lady, Eileen Crew, helps people back into employment. And I could go on. Altogether a dozen projects are running with support from our Action Fund, the town council and other bodies. Often it's just a few hundred pounds that can make all the difference to the volunteers behind many of these schemes."

It sounds like something rather splendid, Louise. You are so right. So much can often be achieved with very little when it is appropriately targeted. Everyone associated deserves a pat on the back.

Gold Hill Parade, a part of the annual Gold Hill Fair staged every July – a joint Rotary/Task force event, 2008. *Picture: Dave Martin*

(Even as we go to print Lester is elected Mayor in succession to Ian Stewart with Tim Cook as his deputy)

One of the unqualified successes of the year is the taste of Dorset Awards which this year are staged in the Members Pavilion at the Dorset County Showground. Organised by the indefatigable Fanny Charles of the *Blackmore Vale Magazine*, Tamara Essex in the *Shaftesbury Contact* waxes lyrical about Roland Tucker and his team from Robinson's Florists who are responsible for the very imaginative table settings with a special feature from Michael Stoate's flour-mill at nearby Cann. As for Corinne Turnbull from Turnbull's Catering, Tamara heaps praise on her team which, catering for no fewer than 300 highly discriminating 'foodies' from across the county, succeeds triumphantly with a menu that leaves me wishing I had been invited. Perhaps next year some kind soul will remember lots of travel makes a man hungry!

The Shaftesbury School, to its immense credit, has for the second time won the International School Award. Links with schools from Spain to Botswana impressed the judges, as did a visit by Shaftesbury pupils to Rwanda and participation in the European Day of Languages.

"In our uncertain world, understanding and tolerance are paramount, and the range of activities undertaken by our students has helped to embed those qualities," observes head teacher David Booth. The Award was presented to deputy head Martin Williams by BBC news-reader, George Alagiah.

Widening the horizons of pupils and fostering international goodwill is of enormous importance and the school is to be warmly congratulated.

Bill Shreeves is a man whose life this past 30 years has embraced 2 communities. For many years the head of history at Gillingham School, he chose to live three miles to the south at Shaftesbury.

"I was actually born in Poole where my grand-father, Reginald Burt, who was later killed in action with Bomber Command, practised as a dentist. During my years of teaching in Gillingham my abiding memories are of the old industrial buildings that once stood there. I was always fascinated by industrial archaeology. There were, of course, the dairies and the glue and bacon factories. The best building of all, however, was the silk mill which was unfortunately burnt down by an arsonist. I do remember sending a couple of my girl students down to the town to photograph a particular building as a part of their coursework. They quickly returned to tell me it wasn't there. I didn't believe them but, when I checked, it too had been demolished when I wasn't looking. Like so many of the old industrial buildings, I still find the railway station a nostalgic place. I see the old photos with 30 or 40 staff at the beginning of the 20th century – now there are just 2 or 3. It's amazing too how different the two towns of Gillingham and Shaftesbury are in various ways. Even the weather is often very different though we are just 3 miles apart. And few people in Shaftesbury know anything about King's Court in Gillingham. Pevsner was rather damning of Gillingham when he referred to the unattractive pink buildings of the town. And, for many years, when visitors came to Gillingham to stand in the exact place where John Constable painted, they couldn't do so because a toilet block had been placed there! Yet there are some fine houses here, if you know where to look."

And Shaftesbury – what does our historian think of it? Bill loves the town.

"Of course, unlike Gillingham the town doesn't need to feel defensive with so many architectural gems and magnificent views."

These days, since his retirement, Bill has been able to devote more time to his greatest passion – butterfly conservation. He is, in fact, the official county butterfly recorder.

"What happened is really rather remarkable. Originally a small group of us used to meet here in my sitting-room back in the 1970s. We'd arrange butterfly walks on Fontmell Downs. We counted the species and kept simple records. We were checking conservation efficiency. From those beginnings it has grown to over 70 different walks across the county where we monitor very closely the various species and observe the impact of global warming. Nationwide there are over 1,000 such walks today collecting data. What is rather splendid is that something that is very enjoyable, namely walking in the countryside, is also serving an important scientific purpose."

And what is the state of Dorset's butterfly population today, remembering as I do in my childhood enormous numbers of butterflies in the fields and gardens and woodland?

"We have about 40 species in the county. The greatest loss has been the Pearl-bordered Fritillary that was common in May in Dorset woodland when I was a boy. It's a butterfly of woodland coppices but, with changing countryside practices, much of its old habitat has disappeared and it is now sadly extinct. On the other hand, some like the Speckled Wood and the Essex Skipper are expanding. The latter, incidentally, is rather difficult to identify. You have to peer at its antennae when it is roosting to be sure though I've never actually tried it."

Is Bill generally optimistic about the situation in the light of all the pressures of the modern world?

"I am more confident than I was because of the information now being collected. There is better organisation nationally with Natural England working on a number of projects, often in conjunction with farmers who are given grants for the purpose."

Bill has a theory about the dearth of cuckoos in the county.

"One of their major sources of food supply when they arrive has traditionally been hairy caterpillars. That food source seems to have been radically reduced. From the data collected from moth traps there has been, for instance, a collapse in the population of Garden Tiger Moths and, in general terms, we've lost one third of our common moth population in the county. Possibly warmer, wetter summers, even light pollution have been advanced as possible explanations for the decline. We are not really sure. But it may be that the cuckoos are arriving here but then moving through quickly to Wales and Scotland and the North of England in pursuit of food supplies. "

What Bill and his splendid team of volunteers are doing is collecting invaluable scientific evidence on behalf of us all. What would our gardens and parks and the countryside be without the sight of butterflies and moths? Just as the swallow and cuckoo are harbingers of spring, so too are those first sightings of the Brimstone and Small Tortoiseshell.

"And it's all done on the cheap, of course. We are enthusiastic amateurs. No Government could possibly afford to do what we are doing. But it's a hobby, something we all love and, if we can help the butterfly and moth population to flourish, it is all worthwhile."

This morning is my last in the town before I finally commit my thoughts to paper on all that I have seen and heard here. And what better spot to take a quiet, reflective stroll than along Park Walk with its incomparable views across the Blackmore Vale? Let me quote again from Sir Frederick Treves for the scene is little changed in the 100 years since the great surgeon set foot here.

'The view is across a vast, verdant, undulating valley of the richest pasture land – a plain without a level stretch in it. It ever rolls away into shallow valley and low hill, with now and then a wooded height or the glittering track of a stream. The land is broken up into a thousand fields, fringed by luxuriant hedges. In every hedge are many trees; trees follow every buff-coloured road, and gather round every hamlet or cluster of farm buildings. It is a country of dairies. Everywhere there are cows, for the smell of cows is the incense of North Dorset.'

Only in the detail of the dairy herds that Sir Frederick witnessed is there change for their numbers are far fewer than in his time and at least one field a mile or so across the Vale is full of grazing sheep. Such a change, we know, reflects wider altered practices in farming so it is not a surprise though we may regret it.

But what of this town called Shaftesbury, what should I make of it? I knew before I arrived of the bitter disputes dividing council members, for most of the published news of the town that reaches the wider world concerns the same wretched topic. But do such angry differences in the council chamber affect everyday life among the citizens of the town? Perhaps this morning I may discover deeper truths about the community. I continue my leisurely way along to Stoney Path, the track that descends steeply down to St. James. We meet half-way and pause for a chat. The lady's name, she tells me, is Jean Hardiman and she lives down the hill in Laundry Lane . Most days she likes to slip into town for an hour or so and to pick up a few groceries. Invariably she meets old friends. Jean lost her husband 18 months ago and she appreciates the comfort of conversation and a laugh or two.

"You know, there's not a door I couldn't knock on in the houses about me where I wouldn't be welcomed in."

Jean arrived 50 years ago from Corfe Mullen – she was a Burbidge in her early days – when she married a local man from Compton Abbas. We are joined by one of her friends, Jean Alford who lives in Tanyard Lane. She's just coming back down the hill. She was the early bird today.

"The council? Of course, we hear about all the nonsense but it's not a part of our lives, is it? Your life is what you make of it. We're lucky living in a wonderful town with so many friends."

I retrace my steps back up the hill with Jean Burbidge. She says she'll show me the view on the Castle Hill side.

"Some people say they think it's better but I don't agree."

Nor do I. The view is very fine but Park Walk wins by a couple of lengths. We meet postman Brian Dooley on his round. He's been delivering the mail around the town for 30 years.

"Brian's a lovely man," Jean whispers.

I ask Brian about the council and its trials and tribulations. He laughs.

"We don't let little things like that worry us, do we?"

We mustn't delay a man who's doing his job. I accompany Jean back to Park Walk.

"One person you must mention in your book is Pam Reynolds. She was the Mayor here – she kept the men in their place, so I've heard! But she died suddenly 18 months ago. She did a lot of good for the community, especially in respect of the swimming pool."

I promise to include Pam. She sounds like a big-hearted lady.

"Do you know, when my husband died I received over 200 cards? That's the sort of place that Shaftesbury is – full of good, kind people."

We shake hands and wish one another well. I know if I knocked on Jean's door in Laundry Lane a year from today she'd invite me in and offer me a cup of tea.

It's back down Stoney Path, past Jean's bungalow into St. James Street. I explored here once before. I liked it then and I like it even better today. It feels like a friendly, welcoming street. It's also customarily several degrees warmer down here than up in the town, so I've been told.

This morning I discover what I missed before – Rolt Millennium Green, an old allotment site, converted by volunteers into a public garden. Helen (Constancia) Rolt lived, it seems, at Number 81 St. James and administered the allotments for many years. Her nephew Ben Sladen arranged the sale of the land for its present purpose. Her friend, Vera (Ve) Twiss, who lived next door died in 2006, and now her son Brian and daughters Gill and Sarah have planted an apple tree and spring bulbs to add to all the other fine shrubs and flowers that fill the air with scent and the sound of bees. Paul Schilling and Caroline Lloyd help to organise the Sunday work parties. It was a project supported by Lottery money but, without the vision of volunteers, it would never have reached this glorious stage. I peer over the hedge at the end of the garden to discover a number of cows with their calves. I'm sure Sir Frederick would have been pleased. I walk on past the school and the cheerful sounds of children's laughter to the church of St. James. It's either locked or I'm too feeble to open the door. There's even a manor house here though it must be the smallest of its kind in the county, charming enough but scarcely the imposing building one usually associates with the local squire. I decide to retrace my steps, past the exquisite Pump Yard with its half a dozen cottages grouped around a garden, past Chapel and Quaker Cottages and the inviting open door of Ye Olde Two Brewers Inn where I vow to seek refreshment on my next visit – and on to Shaftesbury's own St. James's Park. No pelicans or exotic waterfowl, but a pleasant refuge for mums and dads with small children.

Gold Hill. Everything has surely already been written about one of the most famous streets in the length and breadth of the kingdom. I positively stride up it until I reach half-way, at which point I affect to examine more closely one or two of the cottages but, in reality, pause to get my breath. A lady descending the hill tells me she was invited in to one of the cottages last year by one of the householders to admire the view from the back of the property, but no one opens their door to me so I resume my ascent. I understand the famous Hovis scene will be shown no more on our screens. The advertisers have switched their attentions to Liverpool – it's difficult to follow their reasoning and a decision lamented by the Mayor Win Harvey. Sarah Jane, who runs the Little Red Hen gift shop in the High Street, and local resident Jane Hawthorn equally regret the company's choice and the move away from Gold Hill.

As Jane shrewdly observes: "A remake of the original would have shown that Gold Hill, like the Hovis loaf, was a constant in an ever-changing world."

In St. Peter's Church I meet an ex-army man, Chris Jones, formerly of the South Wales Borderers, who is kindly acting as a guide to visitors. Chris and his wife Jenny have not long moved down to the town from Alton – 'from the commuter belt to the tranquillity of Shaftesbury.'

"What has struck us both more than anything is the friendliness and warmth of everyone here.

Park Walk, Shaftesbury. *Picture: Geoff Hill*

We live in Park Walk and there was a problem with access. A meeting was held to discuss the matter with the Recreational and Environment Committee and I was very impressed by the manner in which we were listened to. The chairman was a gentleman named Kendall Carpenter and the whole affair was dealt with very sympathetically. As for activities in the town we are positively spoilt for choice."

My last call is at the old Benedictine abbey. The lady on duty, Patricia Ludovici, is very welcoming. She's moved down to be nearer her daughter from Cadogan Place.

"Just behind Harrods. And no, after a certain gentleman bought the business, I don't care for the place at all. It used to be so friendly."

We discuss the origin of our names. A number of Patricia's forebears were artists. I explain that as a Bennett my name derives from the old Benedictine monasteries though I know not which one. Was my distant ancestor a lay-worker on an abbey, or a monk who momentarily forgot/abandoned his vows of celibacy in the company of some buxom village maiden? I doubt I shall ever discover that particular secret but I know which one I prefer.

So, once more it's back to the car and I'm on my way again. Shaftesbury is a fine and handsome town and the overwhelming majority of its citizens are as Jean Burridge describes them 'good and kind people'. I trust the next traveller, who makes such as a journey as I have undertaken, will find a council in harmony with himself just as Shaftesbury's citizens clearly live in warm harmony with one another. Life is too short surely for festering bitterness and personal rivalries and animosities.

East Dorset

Verwood
Twinned with Champtoceaux (France) and
Liederbach-am-Taunus (Germany)

'The acidic nature of the locality's heathlands and poor agricultural soil......the village lying on the fringes of neighbouring great estates and of little importance to the major landowners.....these were the factors that led to it being designated as suitable for mass development and housing we see today.' Jill Coulthard *'Verwood – Village To Town'* (J & J.C publications 2007)

I'm sitting this morning with the author of those words in the small, book-lined, back-room of the Heritage Heathland Centre set aside for the use of the 100 strong Verwood Historical Society along with two of her friends, Pamela Reeks and Trevor Gilbert. Pamela, a former Parkstone Grammar girl, was for many years a primary school teacher at nearby Hillside and Trevor Gilbert, formerly a local coal merchant. Between them they share a century and a half of memories of Verwood life.

'Of children playing Pooh sticks in the stream near Station Road now covered over.'

'Of swimming at Doe's Hatches, a water meadow system, now a part of the golf course.'

'Of going into the local shoe shop to be told they didn't have a pair of the right size, but they'd get a pair sent down from their Salisbury branch by the next train.'

'Of catching a train to school in Wimborne or Parkstone.'

'Of travelling in the guard's wagon complete with pram and baby.'

As Trevor says "It was a spread out village with fields all around, a scattered community with lots of small-holdings. Everyone had a good-sized garden. Now people have bungalows in their gardens."

One of the curiosities of my journey has been to discover several new 'towns' in the county, a status Verwood officially achieved in 1987. Yet by what definition are they towns? Not for the first time do I return to my Shorter Oxford.

'Town' – 'An inhabited place larger and more regularly built and with more complete and local government than a village but not created a city.' There is no reference to a square or Town Hall, a High Street with a variety of shops, several churches of different denominations, a few (at least) grand houses, a public house or two, though most of these are, I suspect, implicit in most of our minds when it comes to defining a town? – Historically, of course, most towns grew up around sources of employment – coal mines, shipyards, cotton mills, steel-works – or else they were market towns serving areas of agricultural production, or ports of some substance. As some towns grew in size, especially during the Industrial Revolution, so other ancient boroughs declined in significance. Demographic change is a constant feature of man's existence. Population movement away from once thriving areas left us with 'rotten boroughs' such as Old Sarum near Salisbury, Bossiney in Cornwall and Dunwich which was largely eroded by the North Sea. Only with the Great Reform Act of 1832 were such decaying incongruities swept away together with the two MPs who represented each of the boroughs.But today is different from the past in one major respect. As Trevor Gilbert says: "Verwood is a classic example of late 20th century 'sprawl 'for, other than industrial estates like Ebblake which contains about 100 units and public service employment in the Health Centre, the council buildings and schools, most Verwood citizens of working age daily commute to neighbouring towns, or much further afield."

He adds: "At rush hour, morning and evening, there is either a mass exodus or a mass return of vehicles along the B3081 or B3082."

Not only do most of those who live in Verwood and Three Legged Cross generally work elsewhere, they also shop elsewhere and seek their entertainment elsewhere. Only at week-ends and night-time are most people physically in their homes and, even then, the focus point of their lives is likely to be the TV or the computer screen. Frequently they know no one in the immediate vicinity other than a next door neighbour or two. Does it matter? Not necessarily, of course. However, it is essential that the retired, young mothers and children do have access to the amenities vital for a civilised and fulfilling life.

"In those respects we are, I believe, reasonably well served. The Hub, which opened last year, includes a 300 seat theatre and provides a wide range of facilities. We also have the Leisure centre, the Memorial Hall and, of course, this building – the Heathland Centre," says Pamela. "We opened five years ago. It was the site of the old Crossroads Pottery, the last of the Verwood potteries, which closed in 1952. East Dorset DC acquired the adjacent land for the free car park and Robert Thorne, the timber merchant, generously gave the land to the village for the coffee shop and museum which was enlarged into the Centre."

"If there is one place which has proved an unqualified success it's here," adds Trevor. "And it's all run by volunteers."

"Not only is the pottery a museum but it is in regular use. Children come in at week-ends and learn the skills which were once so commonly used here in Verwood."

Pamela introduces me to some of the volunteers as they leave at the end of their morning's duty. They call themselves the 'Tuesday team' and what a riotous, unruly bunch they prove to be. One of them, I discover, is actually the sister of an old school friend, Edwin Ayteo.

"Sawn off, they called him," Anita Cox reminds me. "Because of his stumpy legs!"

Not that Edwin's 'stumpy legs', as I recall, diminished his prowess as a footballer for, in his pomp, he was a player with a terrier-like tackle both for the School XI and Verwood. Definitely a man you'd prefer to have on your side rather than in the opposition.

The trio of John Pym, Joan Clements and Joyce Jarvis treat me with a measure of respect but I'm having definite problems with a lady who admits she first saw the light of day in Shepherd's Bush four-score years ago for which, I suppose, I should make due allowance.

"Violet-Rose Strickland is her name," whispers Pamela in my ear. "Violet celebrated her birthday the other day."

If the lady is as cheeky as this at 80, whatever would she have been like as a child? A born trouble-maker, if ever I saw one. She would have been standing outside my class-room door in double-quick time!

Saying a fond farewell to the 'Tuesday team', though not before casting an admiring look at the watercolours of local scenes by Ray Reeks that line the walls, I join Jill on a drive through the village – sorry, I must correct myself, the town – to the former location of the railway station which closed its doors to passengers in 1964 and to goods the following year.

Jill points out one intriguing detail.

Verwood Concert Band at the national championships in Harrogate. *Picture: Paul Savage R&P photographics*

"The Albion pub you see before you was originally in the station yard and the road went over the railway at the back of The Albion. When they re-routed the road the Albion finished up on the other side of the road. Someone who came back here after some years away said in a state of shock. 'My God, they've moved the pub to the other side of the road!'"

Lucy Clarke spent her childhood days in Cavendish Road near Dean Park cricket ground. I suspect there were moments in Wilfrid Weld's childhood when he might have considered a swop with Lucy – her house for Lulworth Castle, that is. Though it is just possible Wilfrid's father might have had something to say about it. Certainly I would have loved to have lived there when at least 5 county cricket matches were regularly played there each summer. Lucy, married to John, is this year's proud Town Mayor of Verwood.

"Actually many of the mayors who visited us this year for our civic function confessed they'd never previously been to Verwood which, I suppose, tells its own story. We have grown very rapidly in the past forty-odd years. The population in the mid-Sixties was about 3,300, now it stands at 14,000, if you count Three Legged Cross. Though we are proud of what we have achieved, no one would claim there was a great deal for any visitor to see. But I did meet a lady recently, a newcomer, and I asked her if she had any criticisms of Verwood. She replied: 'Criticisms? My dear, we've just arrived from Slough and we think Verwood is paradise!'And despite its growth, I do feel Verwood has retained something of its village atmosphere. It exists on a positive 'sea of goodwill' with so many wonderful volunteers, clubs and societies and support groups. One recent achievement of which we are all very proud was the award last year of the Council of Europe Blue Flag of Honour to Verwood and Three Legged Cross. We are the only area in the UK to have one. It was given to the town's Twinning Society by way of our association with the town of Champtoceaux in Brittany and the German town of Liederbach am Taunus. By the way, one individual who deserves a very special mention is our splendid policeman, Sergeant Richard Partridge, who has earned so much respect within the community."

And how does Lucy see Verwood's future?

"We have come a long way in a very short time. I believe Verwood now needs to take a deep breath, take stock and see exactly where it wants to go." (Even as I complete my writing it is announced that Verwood's new Mayor to follow in Lucy's footsteps is Michael Dolan, who has been keenly involved in a number of community activities. His deputy will be Jean Hazel.)

It is, I believe, an appropriate moment to mention the passing of one of the most respected figures in Verwood life late last year, namely Mike Osmond Jones. A highly successful businessman, perhaps Mike's most significant act was the creation of the Heavy Horse Centre off Edmondsham Road. Not many of us leave behind more than a few memories amongst friends and acquaintances, but Mike achieved just that with his imaginative project and farm park which continues to provide much pleasure to all its visitors. Mike was also well-known for various charitable acts. He will be missed by many people in the local community, not least, of course, by his wife Alison and his numerous friends.

In the days of Wimborne Grammar School, its pupils journeyed from afar – from Holton Heath and Organford in the east, from Cranborne in the north, from Upton in the south, from Three Legged Cross and Verwood in the west. Curiously, we all knew where our friends and cronies lived but scarcely a soul knew anything of those places or could visualise them. Few of our parents owned a car, our horizons were limited, not by how far we could walk or ride a horse – it wasn't quite that long ago – but by the availability of public transport. Verwood, besides being a remote outpost of Christian civilisation, seemed to be overflowing with members of the same families like the Eyres brothers, Peter, John and Paul , the Hall brothers, Brian, Lawson and Geoffrey, the Ayteo brothers, Leon and Edwin, the Lake brothers, John, David and Richard and the Sims brothers,Harvey, Brian and Peter.Another train boy who lived there, also with a brother Roy, was Ken Nicklen. Ken later flew the nest only to return to the village in more recent times and it is to his house I am bound today.

"We've got a Manor Road – but no manor. A Vicarage Road – but no vicarage. And a Station Road – but no station!"

Ken Nicklen's eyes twinkle mischievously. He has known Verwood since he was a lad in short trousers. His father ran the local fish and chip-shop

"There were no street lights then – just a pool of light from Dad's shop."

And he remembers one of the British cinema's best-loved post-war character actors and directors, Lionel Jeffries who directed the flawless 'The Railway Children' and, like Ken, was a 'railway boy' travelling daily to Wimborne Grammar School.

"Lionel lived just 40 yards down Station Road where his father was the local garage proprietor."

Ken and his wife Faye, herself a lady with 300 years of Dorset ancestry coursing through her veins, share mixed feelings about Verwood's post-war growth.

"Of course, you can't live in the past but I'm not sure, in fact, I know that many of the older inhabitants have not welcomed the 'sprawl' of recent years. Too often the infra-structure has lagged behind the expansion. And we've had to fight hard to retain certain of the village's features. For instance, Job Brewer, gave the recreation ground to the village for all time. But the 'scheming rascals' on the district council tried to get their hands on it for development and it was only because of determined opposition from people like Brian Hall and his friends that we were able to retain it."

As the one-time deputy mayor of Weymouth Ken Nicklen knows all about the machinations of local government, though I suspect he does not necessarily regard all the members of the EDDC as 'scheming rascals'!

"We've lost so many of the old cottages and gardens – and much of the essential character of

Darren Kenny OBE, four gold medals in cycling in the Paralympics in China. *Picture: Pam Reeks*

the village. The development has been excessive and piecemeal and fragmented. Having said all of that...."

At this point Ken's amiable features break into his familiar grin.

"We still love it here. It's sentiment, I suppose, and the fact that we have so many friends here – and so much of our past."

The year 2008 will be remembered by too many of our citizens for the wrong reasons – above all, the 'credit crunch' and the economic recession which has cost many people their jobs, their security and their peace of mind. However, let me conclude my piece on Verwood with one story of personal triumph which cheered the whole local community – and the nation at large. I refer, of course, to the outstanding achievements of Darren Kenny at the Paralympics in China. Darren, who has cerebral palsy, gained no fewer than 4 gold medals and 1 silver in the cycling events to add to his 2 gold medals and 1silver in Athens 4 years ago. It is an astonishing record of success by 38 year-old Darren for he also suffered serious accidents as a young man that would have ended the sporting careers of lesser mortals. For his very proud mother Carol and grand-mother Olive, his wife Maria and his 10 year-old son Brandon, his achievements bring particular joy for they know how hard Darren has trained and his dedication to his sport. Darren put a smile on every face in Verwood – and that is something very special. (The ultimate reward for all Darren's extraordinary feats came a few weeks later with news that he was to receive an OBE at Buckingham Palace. What a year for our champion sportsman from Verwood.)

Had I more time I would have loved to stay and talk longer with the hospitable residents of Verwood and Three Legged Cross. But I am ever conscious of the passage of time and I still have many miles to travel. Once more then, I clamber into my car and move on – this time to another village of my childhood days that, like Verwood, has grown beyond recognition into a town in little more than a generation.

Ferndown
Twinned with Segre (France)

'Ferndown is a new district which belongs to the parishes of Hampreston and West Parley. It has a golf course and a large hotel famed for its cuisine and wine cellar. There are many new houses, pleasant with large gardens and well screened by trees, including the pine, birch and rhododendrons of the Dorset heathlands. This is an expanding residential area not far from the Stour valley.'

Monica Hutchings *'Inside Dorset'*1966 (Abbey Press)

Sir Frederick Treves in 1906 didn't mention it at all. Sixty years later Monica Hutchings devoted just one paragraph of 67 words to it. So how do I describe Ferndown today? For a start, it has expanded out of all recognition. It has a population of 20,196 at the last count, according to the most helpful Janet Cary of Ferndown Town Council, a comprehensive school with 1,048 students, a Town Council of 23 members including a Mayor, a chief executive, a large supermarket besides a wide array of other shops, a number of pubs, restaurants and takeaways, a Sports Centre and even – and this most clearly demonstrates its growth – its own by-pass.

It's true that a number of the older properties with their large gardens have disappeared, either to be converted into apartments or demolished and replaced by flats, especially along the Ringwood Road. Many of the large gardens have been sold off and filled with smart new houses. The Dormy Hotel to which Monica Hutchings was presumably referring has been razed to the ground and awaits development. I trust its fine cellar was carefully emptied prior to its demolition! There do remain pine and birch and rhododendrons, though not in the same numbers or density our lady writer described. The parade of shops in Victoria Road looks smart enough with an avenue of trees and flowers to brighten up the pavements. Tesco's Store, with its free parking, draws customers from far and wide into the town and, nearby on Penny's Walk, most conveniently situated in close proximity to one another, stand library, Day Centre and Social Services and, not far removed, the Medical Centre. Ferndown, like most of its residents, looks clean, tidy, well-groomed and comfortable.

The Barrington Theatre

Named after Jim Barrington, the inspirational figure behind its development, the Barrington Theatre was opened by HRH Princess Margaret in July 1986 and plays host to a wide range of community and theatrical activities. Brian Sutton is its affable general manager.

"The Centre is managed by Ferndown Community Association which elects a General Management Committee every year. My role is to engage performers and professional production companies and generally oversee the variety of activities that take place here. Besides the live performers and shows we also show a film once a month on a Tuesday afternoon. We have 4 paid employees here but we are very much dependent upon our splendid team of volunteers. Like so many similar theatres we couldn't function without their help. We try to keep on an even financial keel but it's always a delicate balancing act. There is a presumption that we are run by the Council but that is quite mistaken."

Who has been Brian's most successful commercial recent box-office attraction?

"Anne Widdecombe. Some people said to me beforehand – are you quite sure you know what you're doing? But she was splendid and she filled the hall!"

Enid Rothwell scrutinises the photograph on the wall beside the theatre office of the dozen or so individuals at the first committee meeting more than 20 years ago.

"Sadly a number of them have now passed away but half a dozen or so are still active, though not all are still on the committee – Derek Cooper, Len Hawker, Terry Holbert, Gerald Ridge, Martin Bell-

Chambers and Deirdre Challis. They all helped enormously to get the Barrington up and moving."

Enid was one of the first volunteers and loves what she is doing at the Barrington.

"There's a great feeling of teamwork here. We're doing something worthwhile for the community and that is very satisfying."

It is also appropriate that Ferndown's new Mayor, Queenie Comfort, a former volunteer, has chosen the theatre as her charity of the year.

It is splendid that, as at the Tivoli in Wimborne, the Marine in Lyme Regis and the Rex in Wareham, a core of willing helpers are on hand, quite literally, to keep the 'show on the road', individuals like Peter and Julie Geal, Margaret Bailey and Mary Tee, Frank Fortey and many others, too numerous to mention. As Frank observes:"We work very well together and we always have a laugh and a joke but a few philanthropists with long pockets would also help our cause."

Along the road at St. Mary's Kate Smith, assistant to the parish administrator, is busy at her computer. She's lived in Ferndown for many years and has witnessed considerable changes.

"On a Sunday we'll have a congregation of a couple of hundred. It's not quite full but a very good attendance. "

St. Mary's has acquired a new rector in recent times succeeding the popular Dick Luther. It's never easy to step into the shoes of a much-loved predecessor, but I understand the Rev Martin Howard is making a thoroughly good fist of it. With assistant clergy the Rev Ann Barber and the Rev Barry Lomax it's a well-liked team.

In the office behind her desk is a face I recognise. For a moment I seek to place it. Of course, it's Tracey Nicholls, a familiar figure in the cast of Wimborne Drama's excellent productions. This is Tracey's day-time role, the parish administrator at St. Mary's. She recognises my guide for the morning and Ferndown resident of many years, John Hill.

"Of course, Ann does all the donkey work here every morning – and a brilliant job she does!"

Tracey shows me the plans for an expansion of the church. "We want to create a proper community area here with the space for a number of activities. Nothing is decided yet – everything has to be approved. We'll just taking some of the car-parking space but it will enable us to provide so much more for our parishioners."

It looks to be an excellent scheme. The existing car-park is absolutely huge, the biggest I've seen anywhere in the county for a church and well able to accommodate the new building without difficulty. Besides, with such a charming advocate as Tracey, how could any planning officer refuse?

A hugely respected figure in Ferndown life is John Hanrahan, the manager of the Ferndown Jitsu Club. Local PC, Gary Elson, regards John with particular respect.

"The club is very important to the local community. It's not just the training he provides. It's all the other things John does, like his fundraising on behalf of the youngsters, so they can go away to events or abroad to meet other clubs."

Not one to blow his own trumpet, John's wife Christine says;" John has been a fantastic mentor for many children and young people on the Heatherlands estate. He's not only the manager of the Jitsu Cub, but the co-ordinator for Neighbourhood Watch, a Ferndown Carnival Committee member and a PTA helper. He's done all this in his own time in spite of having 8 heart operations in recent years."

It never ceases to amaze me what some people achieve on behalf of others – and their work is so often unknown and unsung unless someone mentions it.

Two figures from Ferndown who will be much missed in the coming years are the former twice Mayor of the town, Pat Young, who served the community in innumerable roles, including the British Legion, and the founder of the Wessex Youth Orchestra, Don Riddell. Don's daughter, Susanna, is assuming the mantle of her father with the Youth Orchestra. Often only when they are gone do we truly appreciate the enormous and unselfish contributions many individuals make to all our lives. Such was true of Pat Young and Don Riddell.

Ferndown, despite its busy roads and bustling shopping centre, is essentially a town of quiet and ordered respectability. Unflashy, unassuming, civilised, its citizens go about their everyday business and lives without hurting others and without great social tensions. It's a place its inhabitants are happy to call home. It's also a community that cares and when a family in its midst suffers heartbreak and loss, that community draws together to give it support. Most sadly, just such a tragedy befell a family in Ferndown this year.

The wars in Iraq and Afghanistan have created political divisions in the country at large. This is not the place to debate the rights and wrongs of the arguments for and against the wars.Besides, history will be the best judge. What no one questions, however, is the professionalism and courage of the British forces engaged in these conflicts. I have written elsewhere in these pages that, almost alone among the great institutions of British life, our armed forces still retain the respect, admiration and affection of the British public.

On March 30, while on patrol in Kajaki, in the Helmand Province of Afghanistan, two young Royal Marines were killed in an explosion when the vehicle in which they were travelling was hit by a roadside bomb. One was Marine David Marsh, 23, from Norton Fitzwarren near Taunton and the other was Lt John Thornton, 22, from Ferndown. Both soldiers were deployed to southern Afghanistan in September of last year and were 5 months into their tour of duty, with just 4 weeks remaining before they returned home. John Thornton had earlier attended Ferndown Upper School where he was an enthusiastic sportsman and played leading roles in drama productions. John's funeral was held at St. Mary's Church on April 17and attended by an estimated 1,500 people.

Lt. Col. Stuart Birrell RM, Commanding Officer 40 Commando Royal Marines, spoke at the service. "John's enthusiasm was infectious and his men responded magnificently to his leadership. JT, as John was affectionately known, was always to be found in the thick of the action, a courageous and brave commander. He never asked his men to do anything that he would not do himself. He led from the front and provided an outstanding example to his peers and men alike."

A guard of honour of the Royal Marines flanked the entrance to St. Mary's and a single Red Arrow was flown over the church piloted by Lt. Commander Matt Whitfield. As Geoffrey Beck, the managing director of De Havilland Aviation, explained:"I met John on several occasions and was always very impressed by his demeanour. John did, of course, fly with the Red Arrows after being named as top air cadet with the ATC." His former ATC commander, Philip Cubit, also from Ferndown, described John Thornton as "very simply, the best of the best and a major inspiration to us all."

John Thornton's parents, Peter and Linda, explained that their son had announced his determination to become a Royal Marine when he was 13 and wanted nothing else. Peter Thornton added: "John was a perfect son with a big heart and always had time for others which is why we have received so many letters of sympathy and cards of support."

His brothers Graham and Ian, the latter in officer training himself, commented:" John always said he would rather die early, having lived the dream, than grow old having worked in a bank all his life. Better a year as a lion than a decade as a donkey. Though his death is a terrible blow for us all, I do not believe he died in vain. His company was providing the security for the construction of the Kajaki dam to generate power to improve the quality of life of the people of Afghanistan."

John Spiers, a Ferndown resident and a former chairman of the Airborne Forces Association,

John Thornton with parents, Linda and Peter.

writing in the *Echo* beneath the headline *'Let the funeral be an inspiration'* caught the mood of many who attended St. Mary's that April day.

'I can only hope that the younger generation who may have witnessed this event, either first hand or through the news media, feel inspired by role models (such as John Thornton) to now enter a more meaningful lifestyle beyond the daily realms of alcohol, drugs and indiscriminate sex.'

As the weeks passed, deeply moved by the enormous public sympathy for their loss and aware of how the story of John's death had clearly touched the whole Ferndown community, Peter and Linda resolved to launch an appeal on behalf of the John Thornton's Young Achievers' Foundation 'to encourage and assist young people to climb as high as they can dream.' Peter and Linda have been thrilled and gratified by the response.

"The foundation works in association with Ferndown Upper School, Dorset & Wilts Wing Air Cadets and the Air Cadet Junior Leaders Course. There are a dozen trustees, mostly family and John's old friends and Simon Weston kindly agreed to become its patron."

I will quote directly Simon's words which appear on the Foundation's leaflet.

"Lt John Thornton RM laid down his life for our country and I am honoured and privileged to be invited to be the patron of the John Thornton Young Achiever's Foundation. I will do all I can to help this great charity promote the success and the achievement of true potential in young talented people."

John's brother Ian explains the procedures that lie behind the selection of those chosen to be recipients of financial support and the principles underlying the scheme.

"The organisations involved choose individuals who embody the values of the Royal Marines – determination and courage, cheerfulness in the face of adversity and unselfishness which were

The plaque to Lt. John Thornton RM is unveiled at the Royal British Legion at Ferndown. *Picture: Pat Timmons, Bournemouth Echo.*

all qualities exemplified by John. To give you an example of what I mean, one young man is now in India working as a volunteer in an orphanage helping to build a library. The foundation also supplied a laptop for the library. So our young volunteer is gaining valuable personal experience at the same time as he is helping others."

I'm sitting with Peter and Linda and Ian in the comfortable conservatory of their Ferndown home, surrounded by family photographs and mementoes of John and his brothers. Knowing the agonies each has suffered in the past 18 months since John's tragic death, to hear them quietly explaining their vision of how they wish to assist other young people as a way of honouring John's memory, is an experience I will never forget. Linda reports on the progress of the Foundation to date.

"So far we have raised about £50,000 for the Foundation and distributed about £10,000. In the next 12 months we would hope, as long as the money continues to come in, to distribute a further £30,000. I think John would be quite bemused by it all but very pleased. He touched so many people's lives. The people of Ferndown and Bournemouth have been so supportive, not just for the Foundation but for our family as well. We are very grateful."

Meanwhile, at his old school, his former friend, Edmund Rogers, arranged for a bench and some trees, kindly donated by Haskin's Garden Centre, to form a permanent memorial to John near the school's Sixth Form block. The informal ceremony was attended by headmaster Alex Wills, Capt. Ian Hurdle and Terry Head from Haskins. At the Royal British Legion building in the town a plaque in John's honour was unveiled in a service led by the Rev. Martin Howard and organised by the RBL branch club president, Denis Blanchard. The chairman Terry Burr read the exhortation and Sergeant Darren Joyce, his former troop leader, described John 'a as a great leader of men- and a great guy.'

Only a few weeks before my visit Linda and Peter climbed Mount Kilimanjaro, emulating both John and Ian, and in so doing raised a further £3,500 for the fund. Peter recalls their welcome on its summit.

"The boys arrived at the top in brilliant sunshine. We arrived in a blizzard!"

"All sorts of fund-raising events continue to be staged. A young local guy Chris Morgan is pushing a wheelbarrow across London in five days, starting at Twickenham, visiting every London football ground en route and finishing at Wembley on the day of the Charity Shield final. Crazy but brilliant. And Chris didn't even know John or the family. He was just moved by the whole story."

Ian, a keen footballer himself, laughs. "He's dividing the proceeds between the Foundation and Help the Heroes."

In just 2 weeks from the day of my visit Ian is marrying Vicky at the Haven Hotel in Sandbanks. After so much pain in the past 18 months it's wonderful that the Thornton family has an occasion to celebrate. That the whole family is immensely proud of John and all that he achieved is understandable. I am equally certain that John would be immensely proud of his brothers, Ian and Graham, and his mother Linda and his father Peter. I feel deeply privileged to have made their acquaintance.

(Every casualty in Iraq and Afghanistan has, of course, brought sadness to various families and communities. In 2006 Sgt. Paul Bartlett from the Poole-based SBS and Flt Lt Leigh Mitchelmore from Bournemouth were killed in action. Many servicemen have also been wounded in action, many seriously. Alas, it is impossible to meet every family but they should know that the people of this county – and the country at large – salute the courage of their sons and honour their memory.)

Christchurch
Twinned with Christchurch (NZ), St. Lo (France), Aalen (Germany), Tatabanya (Hungary) and Saint-Ghislain (Belgium)

'Where time is pleasant'. From the inscription on the clock outside the Mayor's Parlour in the High Street.

"I believe it was Eric Spreadbury who coined the expression and it sums up the town most aptly. You could describe it as the town's unofficial motto."

Most unfortunately, the splendid High Street clock came crashing down in April when a van reversed into the column outside the old Town Hall. The impact of the collision uprooted the pole-mounted clock and shattered the fluted iron-cast column. I hope it's not an omen and decide I will refrain from reminding my genial companion this otherwise cheerful winter's morning.

As the longest-serving county councillor with 34 years of service, including a spell as Leader of the DCC, two terms of office as Mayor of Christchurch, the former legal executive David Fox, OBE, has played a major role in Dorset local government for as long as most people can remember. Even David's wife Norma has played her part too by serving as Mayor of the borough. With its first recorded Mayor way back in 1297 – and there were probably others even before that – the importance of Christchurch retaining its identity is no small matter for many of its citizens.

"There are 4 proper chartered Mayors in the county, in Weymouth, Poole, Bournemouth and Christchurch. If I told you that Bournemouth's first Mayor wasn't chosen until 1900 you will understand why we wish to retain our identity. When reorganisation occurred and the county

Christchurch Priory. *Picture: Roger Holman*

boundaries were redrawn most Christchurch people were happy that the town should become a part of Dorset. As you may know the actual boundary shifted from County Gates to west of the Cat & Fiddle at Roeshot Hill. Within Hampshire we were a very small voice besides the likes of Southampton, Portsmouth, Basingstoke and Winchester. With a population in excess of 40,000 we could more easily be heard within Dorset. We were simply swopping masters from Winchester to Dorchester. Of course, if national Government should ever decide that Bournemouth, Christchurch and Poole should become one authority I doubt there would be much we could do to stop it."

David was deservedly awarded his OBE in 1993 for 'public and political services'.

"I suppose I am most proud of my work with the fire services, locally and nationally. I was for 20 years the chairman of the Fire Committee."

From one admirable local government servant of many summers to another, I am this morning in the company of Eric Spreadbury in Friar's Cliff. Eric is no less concerned with 'identity' than David Fox. .

"Bournemouth is a recent phenomenon. Until Victorian times it was heathland and dunes, yet there is a real danger that we will simply merge into Bournemouth. After all, Hurn Airport is actually in Christchurch, yet it's called Bournemouth International Airport. The university is situated in Poole, yet it's called Bournemouth University. Does it matter? I believe it does – civic pride is important and we have nearly 1,000 years of history behind us here. We are a proud and ancient borough and I am most anxious that Christchurch should retain its separate identity."

Eric Spreadbury MBE, Honorary Freeman, is a gentle, courteous man, married to Barbara, a town councillor for nearly 50 years and Mayor on no less than 6 occasions. It is a record of public service almost unparalleled in the county. Since arriving in Somerford in 1940 to serve his country as a draughtsman in the construction of Bailey bridges, "I was designated as a permanent temporary!", Christchurch has been Eric's home. He recalls with clarity the town in those early years of the war.

"There was a great variety of shops and almost no traffic!I especially recall Tucker's Provisions with its wonderful aroma of coffee lingering about the building until it became unobtainable, of course. Today, alas, we do not even have a baker, butcher or fruit & veg shop."

One of Eric's principal concerns is unfettered development.

"If we don't put up the sternest fight through strict planning controls we'll finish up with blocks of flats all along the coast. That would an unmitigated disaster."

What of Christchurch politics and its Council?

"I would describe us a very harmonious Council. We wear our robes. We like to keep the old traditions going."

And the town itself – are there any particular changes he would like to see?

"The renovation of Saxon Square would be foremost in my mind with a roof covering for the area, possibly another deck and more car-parking. There is so much that is good in Christchurch but we must remember we are in competition with our neighbours."

Bournemouth International Airport
(Just voted the third best airport in the world)

I may be treading on certain sensitive toes but I must be scrupulously accurate and include my piece on the airport where geographically, as Eric Spreadbury reminded me, it truly belongs – in Christchurch. Besides, as Ed Perkins of the Echo writes elsewhere, the people of Bournemouth are a generous bunch, so I am sure they won't mind sharing their award-winning airport with their neighbours, will they?

Whatever would the brave pilots of Fighter Command in 1941, flying up to intercept German bombers, have made of it all? A poll of 25,000 Daily Telegraph readers has just confirmed Bournemouth International Airport as inferior only to far-away, exotic Singapore-Changi and Hong Kong airports. It is a fairly amazing compliment whichever way you look at it.There is one little reservation, not about the airport itself, but rather its name. For years all the locals knew it as Hurn and quite a few of us still call it Hurn. Technically, it's actually situated in Christchurch – and not far from both Wimborne and Ferndown. Furthermore, Bournemouth and Dorset Councils sold it off to National Express in 1995. But that's progress for you. At such moments I recall R.H.Tawney's observation that 'Freedom for the pike is death for the minnow' for, without checks and balances, the big beasts invariably dominate. So Bournemouth has acquired an airport on the grounds that it's bigger and better-known and the great British public know where it is, even though it's not really in Bournemouth at all.

But, coming back to the verdict of those DT readers, as managing director, Rob Goldsmith says, "It's an incredible result and demonstrates the important role of regional airports in providing their communities with a fast and friendly service."

I'm at the airport today in the company of the charming Sally Windsor, the External Communications spokesperson.

"One of the key factors is getting home quickly after the holiday. After a long journey getting to the car-park speedily from the airport is something travellers really appreciate. We draw most of our passengers from a 90 minute driving range."

You're absolutely right, Sally. For myself and many of my friends the question I ask now when considering a holiday abroad is – can I fly from Bournemouth? If the answer is No, the chances are I will rethink the holiday destination. But Sally's also proud of the airport on a number of other counts.

"We're trying to be a good neighbour by building all sorts of energy efficiency into our latest expansion plans. We aim to be carbon neutral by 2015. Aircraft are also becoming quieter and more efficient. They can climb much faster so reducing noise. Economically the airport generates around 900 jobs, directly or indirectly, which puts an estimated £24 million into the local economy. About 3,000 are also employed on the adjacent business park with a diverse range of jobs which is very important to the whole community."

What really surprises me in this veritable hive of good-humoured efficiency all about me is the modesty of Sally's office. I use the word 'modesty' out of politeness. Actually it is a wretched little affair, at ground level with stark minimalist fittings, not one trapping of creature comfort let alone luxury, and looks out on a small staff car-park. Most of the inmates of HM prisons have better surroundings. If only I had known I would have brought some flowers for Sally to brighten up the room. And remember the lady is performing a very important job. She tells me there are no grand plans for improvement even in the brand new development. She even chides me good-naturedly when I raise the issue.

"But I love my room. We don't need to be sitting in expensive offices with water fountains outside. Our passengers are the ones who matter here. Keeping them happy and satisfied is our number one priority."

Judging by the activity all around us and with no less than £45 million allocated to the upgrading of facilities, there are going to be plenty of 'happy and satisfied' passengers passing through Bournemouth airport in the coming years. Rob Goldsmith anticipates no fewer than 3 million passengers a year. Operations director, Paul Knight, who began life at the airport nearly 30 years ago as a fire-fighter, expresses the general sentiments of the staff when he observes.

"When I started there was only one plane and it used to be the highlight of our day. Though things have changed so dramatically, we still want to preserve the same family atmosphere that's always existed".

So we've come full circle – from our heroes of WW2 who flew from here to the magnificent DT accolade of 2008. If the pilots of Fighter Command and the Telegraph voters could only hear Sally, Rob and Paul's admirable, selfless, public-spirited sentiments for themselves, they would all raise their glasses to them and the rest of the brilliant team at Bournemouth International Airport. Even if really it is Hurn near Christchurch!

Along my way I like to highlight, wherever it is possible, those splendid individuals performing invaluable voluntary services within the community. Such a body is the Red Cross Medical Equipment Service based in Christchurch. This team of 15 big-hearted volunteers provided assistance across the county last year to no fewer than 4,000 people who were returning from hospital, recovering from surgery after an accident or with mobility problems by providing vital medical equipment such as wheelchairs and walking frames. As Pat Mackinnon comments: "I enjoy helping people and the equipment can make so much difference to people's lives."

Another volunteer is 83 years-old Roy Coates from Verwood who says: "Doing people a service is a great joy. Some of our clients have serious, maybe even life-threatening conditions. If we are able to help them then that gives us all great satisfaction."

Each one of this admirable team deserves a pat on the back.

Grange School staff and pupils – The Railway Children – with the Mayor of Christchurch, Cllr. Josephine Spencer.
Picture: Bournemouth Echo

Wherever I have journeyed I have always endeavoured to write about the local theatre/cinema and Christchurch is no exception. Gary Theobald is the press officer for the Regent.

"The Regent Centre actually opened as a cinema on Boxing Day, 1931.Like many similar institutions up and down the country it has enjoyed its good times and its not so good times. There was a period 20-30 years ago when temporarily it became a Mecca bingo hall. Though you may think that was rather a come-down, in fact, bingo did actually save the Regent just as it saved similar buildings in many towns. Many would have been demolished but for the respite which bingo provided. There was also a period when the Regent was closed altogether. Happily a group of local enthusiasts were determined to restore it to its original use and, after a great deal of dedicated effort, you can see for yourself just what a fine job they have made of it."

With its wide High Street frontage, its cafe and gallery, a 450 seating capacity, backstage facilities and studio, the Regent Centre is now clearly in excellent order.

"The Borough Council maintains the fabric of the building which is obviously of great financial significance though there is no actual subsidy as such towards everyday running costs. We have 5 full-time staff and 4 part-timers and about 200 volunteers without whom nothing would be possible. Their contribution is absolutely critical to the success of the Regent Centre. It is impossible to praise their involvement sufficiently."

Since the full-time team is small, I will mention them by name. Aside from Gary, there's Keith

Lancing the manager – I missed Keith by just 10 minutes – the technical whizz-kid Shaun Luckly, stage manager Martin Short and marketing and IT expert Eliot Walker.

"Like the Tivoli in Wimborne we have a mix of cinema and live shows. Usually it's cinema on week-days with 2 or 3 matinees and live shows at weekends. We are drawing very pleasing audiences and, for some films and shows, we do attract full houses. One exciting development is that we are now able to show here at the Regent live stage performances beamed direct by high definition satellite from venues such as the Lincoln Centre in New York. To be able to see and hear the very best in international opera, for instance, is a major step forward for us."

What a vital role in so many communities these cinemas/theatres perform. If years ago, without the vision of dedicated enthusiasts, they had disappeared for all time, their loss would have been incalculable. As it is, the good citizens of Christchurch and areas around can drive in to the town, park without difficulty – in the evenings for free, of course – or simply walk into the town, enjoy a meal and a drink, see a film or a show for less than they would pay in Bournemouth and rejoice that the splendid Regent Centre gloriously survived all the vicissitudes of the past. And, because I know Gary was very anxious that I pay due tribute to the Regent's valiant 200 volunteers without whom this invaluable establishment simply could not function, I will repeat my praise of their contribution!

Plans are afoot for a new community centre in the town to replace the current dilapidated building. Christchurch Community Partnership recently launched a Buy a Brick campaign to raise funds for the new Druitt Hall to be built on the site of the existing centre. The Rev Sandra Prudom, the chairman of the Druitt Community Centre steering group, would like to see Christchurch residents get behind the scheme to provide a building which will ultimately be available for a variety of activities both during the day and in the evening. The target is to raise £1 million which, in these straitened times, will not be easy but it is an admirable goal. Having travelled extensively across the county, time and again I have observed what a critical role a modern, multi-purpose building can play in facilitating a wide range of activities and fostering community spirit.

Highcliffe Castle

One of the major success stories in the locality in recent times has been the restoration of Highcliffe Castle. It is a building with a distinctly chequered history. Constructed in the 1830s by Lord Stuart de Rothesay and his architect Williams Donthorne using materials salvaged from a number of French medieval buildings, it remained a family home until 1950.It was briefly occupied by a religious sect before 2 mysterious fires in the 1960s left the building derelict. Bought in 1977 by Christchurch Borough Council it was allowed to deteriorate further and certain individuals even advocated demolition. Thankfully, with the support of English Heritage and the Heritage Lottery Fund a major restoration project has transformed the house into one of Christchurch's jewels. Reopened to the public in 1995 further refurbishment work has continued and the recent completion of the great hall of the castle by Rob Hooker and the Poole based Greendale Construction Company is the latest step in restoring the building to its original grandeur. The Castle now plays host to a remarkable range of events, both indoor and outdoor, including concerts, exhibitions and weddings. Paying a recent visit I am full of admiration for all those associated with its splendid restoration. Although I cannot possibly compliment all the wonderfully skilled craftsmen whose individual talents have achieved so much I must, at least, congratulate the manager David Hopkins who has supervised much of the work and those on the council who never lost faith in the eventual success of the project. The whole of the Christchurch public as well as the many visitors to the Castle know that it is a valuable addition to the town's attractions and its aesthetic appeal.

Highcliffe Castle. *Picture: Roger Holman*

We all know that national surveys can sometimes produce puzzling results, but one which every Christchurch resident will savour is the finding that of 117 seaside towns in the UK it was voted number one when various factors relating to the quality of life such as the general environment, health facilities, weather, education, crime figures and so on were analysed. Among the clubs and societies in the town that undoubtedly enhance the quality of intellectual life among its residents is the flourishing Christchurch Local History society which traces its own history back to just before WW2 and boasts more than 300 members. The former mayor, Michael Hodges is rightly anxious that the townspeople in general should be aware of the rich legacy of Christchurch's past so that important features of its history are preserved for future generations to appreciate. As Michael points out, it is so very easy to lose important historic landmarks within a town through ignorance.

With among the highest property prices in the UK it is clear that Christchurch must accept some further infilling of available pockets of land and possible development at Roeshott Hill, especially for the provision of affordable housing, just as long as the infra-structure is in place. It is a situation recognised by local councillors like its leader, Cllr. Alan Griffiths.

"We do accept the need for growth but we must ensure that the high quality of Christchurch's environment is maintained."

It is imperative that planners consult with local communities and their representatives like Alan Griffiths with sensitivity. Of course, there are certain to be disagreements but these can be minimised with diplomacy and goodwill and a willingness to listen on both sides.

A recent addition to the many culinary delights of Christchurch – there exists a host number of fine eating paces about the town – is the arrival of the celebrated chef Gary Rhodes in the town. Though this is far from the easiest time for any restaurateur, if anyone can succeed then our personable Gary must have as good a chance as anyone. With the artfully named King's Rhodes brasserie in Castle Street and Rhodes South at the Christchurch Harbour Hotel (formerly the Avonmouth Hotel), it will be interesting to see if a famous name is sufficient recommendation in a crowded market-place in a period of economic recession.

In a previous chapter I described the tragic loss of Lt. John Thornton from Ferndown in the Helmand Province of Afghanistan. Hundreds of mourners also lined the streets and attended a service at Christchurch Priory to remember another brave young soldier, Marine Neil David Dunstan, who was killed by an explosive device while on patrol in November in South Helmand. Inside the Priory the Rev Canon Hugh Williams welcomed those attending the service while the address was read by the Rev. Peter Rickman of St. Mary's, Bransgore, where Neil was baptised. The coffin was borne by Royal Marine pall-bearers, the prayers were led by the Rev Simon Beveridge RN, the Royal Marine chaplain at Poole and a moving tribute paid to Marine Dunstan by Lt. Col Martin Taylor OBE. Ron Chapple, the branch secretary of Christchurch British Legion, announced a private reception at the BL club in Bargates after the service. Neil was soon to be married to his fiancée, Kate Miller, who read the poem *Remember Me*. For his family, his mother Sue Thwaites, his father Keith and brother Andrew, this was obviously a desperately sad occasion and a reminder to us all of the enormous sacrifices made by our armed forces in the service of their country.

In consecutive chapters I have made detailed reference to the deaths of 2 local soldiers in far-off Afghanistan. Had earlier writers made such a journey as I have undertaken, he or she might have described the heartbreaking news of casualties in war as it reached communities across the county from countries all over the world. Simply to glance at the memorials to the fallen from WW1 and WW2 is to appreciate the awful suffering endured by previous generations. For those families whose

The Redknapp family at the opening of Zoome. **(left to right)** Mark and Lucy Redknapp and son Harry, Louise Redknapp, Sandra and Harry, Jamie Redknapp and Frank Lampard. *Picture: Richard Crease, Bournemouth Echo*

sons who never came back from distant wars in centuries past, there was the added burden of often knowing nothing at all – save the grief of loss and loneliness. By making a conscious decision to include detailed pieces on both Lt John Thornton and Marine David Dunstan I hope they will serve to remind us all that, whatever our anxieties and problems, they pale into petty insignificance when set against the pain experienced by the families and friends of these 2 young men. We are the fortunate ones living in the material comfort of 21st century Dorset. We are each one of us in their debt. Let us never forget that simple truth.

News arrives that Cllr. David Flagg is asked to serve as the Mayor of this ancient borough for a second consecutive term of office, the first occasion in 48 years that such an event has occurred. Cllr. Josephine Spencer will again act as his deputy.

What I have shamefully failed to do so far is to acknowledge the sheer aesthetic delight to be experienced in exploring many different locations within the town -the historic Priory, the old castle, the quay, the Saxon water- mill, the riverside walks, many of the small streets with their handsome properties, both old and new, is unalloyed pleasure. Blessed by being a settlement enhanced by two fine rivers, the Avon and the Stour, the citizens of Christchurch have over many centuries contrived to fashion a town as handsome as any in the county. In the Priory I chat briefly with one of the 'welcomers', Don Mason. I mention that Canon Eric Davies insisted, unsurprisingly, that Sherborne Abbey was the finest building in the county.

"He would say that, wouldn't he?" laughs Don. "There may be those in Christchurch who would dispute his claim!"

It is tempting to pass many more hours in Christchurch but I know I must continue my journey. The town where 'time is pleasant'- it is a description most fittingly chosen. It is easy to understand why so many of our fellows have chosen to live in this exquisite corner of the county, just as communities settled here many centuries before when it was known as Twyneham. Most happily, thanks to the loving and skilled attention of M.C. Taylor in neighbouring Pokesdown, the town clock outside the Mayor's Parlour in the High Street is now restored to its rightful place and back in full working order. I know I will return many times in the future to Christchurch, but for now I must again place my scribbled notes in their folder and point the car eastwards.

Bournemouth
Twinned with Lucerne (Switzerland) and Netanya (Israel)

'Bournemouth....an interminable tract of sand and heather and pines and wild rhododendrons.' John Meade Falkner (1858-1932) Author of *Moonfleet*

'A place with a split personality, part faded Victorian resort, part corporate any-town and part mass-market holiday park...where wrinkly day-trippers and holidaying coach parties rub shoulders with stag parties, boozed up clubbers and conference delegates.' Lonely Planet's latest guide, *Bournemouth in 2008.*

'I'd be hard pushed to say where else I would prefer to be than here.' Ed Perkins, *Bournemouth Echo*

Once upon a time, not so many years ago, after the visit of J.M.Falkner and before the visit of *Lonely Planet*, everyone knew what Bournemouth was. Golden sands, the pleasure gardens, The Square, the Pavilion and Winter Gardens, the Pier, hotels, Dean Park in summer and Dean Court in winter, department stores, pine trees, Horseshoe Common, French students in August, the Russell Cotes and a few other things besides depending upon your age and interests. Today no one is quite sure what Bournemouth is.

However, for Mark Smith, Director of Tourism, Bournemouth remains one of the best places on earth.

"The high level of repeat visits gives the lie to such criticisms. Holiday-makers, day visitors and residents simply do not recognise the picture painted. Visitors to the town bring hundreds of millions of pounds into the local economy. Our business tourism income exceeds £100milion pa. The BIC holds 60 conferences every year. Our international education business continues to expand. None of these things would be happening unless people were satisfied with what the town offers. I would also add that I have never lived anywhere where I feel as safe as in Bournemouth."

Everywhere on my journey I have sought out local journalists to give their opinions on the communities in which they live. Day in, day out, they are tramping the streets, knocking on doors, talking to people from every segment of society. There is little that escapes their individual or collective notice. They know the good guys and the not-so-nice guys – and their feminine equivalents. Of course, they also have to be arch diplomats at times. Spill all the beans, break a confidence, betray a trust and a valuable contact can be lost. But they are walking repositories of knowledge and worldly wisdom and, from my standpoint, I'd be a discourteous idiot not to consult them.

The young woman covers many of the big news stories for the *Echo* and she's very good. In fact, she's excellent. She also smiles and laughs a lot – she's instantly likeable. We agree to 'somewhere quiet'. The Norfolk Royale is just across the road. With a journalist husband and a young daughter Maddie, she leads a hectic life. As a former Bournemouth School for Girls pupil Melanie Vass also knows the locality like the back of her hand.

"To be honest, I prefer Bournemouth in the winter – without the crowds. Yes, I know the local economy needs the visitors but, out of season, you can really appreciate the town with the unspoilt beaches, the gardens, lots of fine buildings."

She also loves the Cherries. "That's my dad's fault. I really am a big fan."

But these are desperate days. They've only just climbed out of minus points after the compulsory 17 point deduction. We decide to talk of matters more cheerful. To my horror she loves Castlepoint – but then most women do – and her parents live nearby so she can park there. That does make a difference, but only a marginal one as far as I am concerned. As a young married woman she no longer frequents the pubs and clubs. There was a time, of course, though only ever in a modest way – Bumbles, The Moon in the Square, The Opera House at Boscombe, The Venue at Tower Park. I'd quite forgotten about Tower Park. It was all the rage at one time. One of Richard Carr's early ventures, I believe. We decide to give Richard Carr a miss too.

"It's a children's play area now, I believe," she says.

But she does enjoy a night out in a restaurant in the Old Christchurch Road with Paul.

"I do enjoy the bustle. But for my parents and their generation, they'd never come into the town at night. It may be a mistaken perception, but it's real enough in their minds.She understands why the 'perception' exists.

"I suspect things did get a little out of hand. People trying to make easy money. Cheap drinks promotions. And the extended opening hours haven't helped."

And the Council? She is, after all, officially the local government correspondent. If it's possible to smile and grimace simultaneously the lady succeeds brilliantly.

"Whenever the Council is involved you do have your doubts. So many schemes come and go. Plans drag on forever or grind to a complete standstill. And if ever things do get finished, they're usually overdue and over-budget."

It's time for Melanie to hurry back to her desk and the next big story. I did pick up the local free paper in the Echo office while I was waiting for her. 'Dog fouling on the beach' was the headline above her name. She laughs.

"It's a topic that invariably generates passion."

I remember Adrianne Maslen in Lyme Regis. Wasn't she writing on exactly the same topic? Two pretty girls, one in the far west of the county, one in the far east of the county and just one subject on their minds – dog fouling!

(At the year's end I am delighted to discover that the lovely Melanie is rewarded for her consistently excellent reporting by being named Dorset Journalist of the Year, organised by the Dorset branch of the NUJ. At the same time Richard Crease is named Photographer of the Year. Both awards are richly deserved.)

This morning it's another 'news hound'. I've read Ed Perkins' Editorial comments on scores of occasions. Ed doesn't go in for verbal butchery in his column. There's usually a wry humour, a sense of mischief, an air of gentle questioning in his writing. If he was a cricketer he'd bat at Number 5 and it would be all subtle pushes and nudges and glances down to long leg.

"I do regularly pinch myself at my good fortune. I'd be hard pushed to say where else I would prefer to be than here."

Deputy Editor of the Echo, Ed Perkins, recognises though that Bournemouth is not yet settled on its 21st century identity.

"There are two different but overlapping Bournemouths – the day-time and the night-time. During the day it is still a resort that Bill Bryson recognised for its fine Victorian architecture, its parks and magnificent sea-front. The Russell-Cotes, for example, is a gem any resort would envy. The charm of Bournemouth has largely survived."

Does it still appeal to the family sufficiently?

"In fine weather, yes, it has everything. In bad weather, I'm not so sure. I suspect it does need more rainy day entertainments. It is such a competitive market-place."

And at night-time, what then?

"If I were 18 I would appreciate the night-time economy. What are you looking for at that age – clubs, dancing, pubs, the opposite sex, excitement? Bournemouth has all those in abundance"

Ed suddenly looks wistful. Is he wishing he was 18 again? So what is the future of the town? Can it combine the two very different cultures?

"Does it have to make up its mind? An identity will evolve. Meanwhile, Bournemouth is a very generous town with a community that gives. Whenever the *Echo* runs an appeal our readers are always remarkably warm-hearted and generous. It's a good place."

When the railways arrived in Bournemouth in the 1880s it was the beginning of a new era of development and expansion and prosperity for the locality. For 75 years that was how most holiday-makers found their way to the town, its hotels and guest-houses. After WW2 came coaches from every corner of the kingdom, filling the old coach station beside the Pleasure Gardens with the noise of their engines and their fumes. When I lived in London more often than not I travelled up and down by Royal Blue to and from Victoria. It was cheaper than the rail – though not by the same margin as today – and almost as quick. However, at the same time more and more visitors and local shoppers began arriving in the town by car competing for ever scarcer parking spaces which led, by an inexorable logic, to car-parking charges. As we all know, it's a trend that has continued, becoming ever more of a pain year on year. This preamble brings me to what is now a major bone of contention between town centre traders and the Council. The reality is that car-parking charges are now very expensive – prohibitive in the judgement of many. I will refrain from quoting figures for they soon become meaningless, suffice to say that the charges are deterring shoppers, if not tourists, from coming into the town. Every recent survey appears to confirm the same trend. The Town Council is responsible for some of the car-parks, but not all. At the same time, of course, we have Castlepoint off Castle Lane which offers free parking, even if the car-park itself has experienced some disturbing problems. When the old Hampshire Centre was flattened by the bulldozers and Castlepoint rose Phoenix-like from the rubble, there were critics who feared then the likely implications for the town centre. The Council leader at the time, Douglas Eyre, led the opposition claiming Castlepoint would be a disaster for the local economy, killing off many of its town competitors and reducing choice. He also argued that the infra-structure was not in place and certainly the queues at peak times have proved horrendous. Douglas Eyre has never visited the place since it opened its doors in 2003. On the other hand, other critics like Jim Courtney have changed their minds believing their original fears were misplaced and Castlepoint can now be counted a success. Unsurprisingly, Castlepoint manager, Peter Matthews, enthusiastically agrees and he also points to the worthy fundraising for the local War Memorial Homes and the Dorset and Somerset Air Ambulance. Cllr. Anne Rey was Mayor and actually opened the Castlepoint in a formal capacity during her term of office. She believes the way forward is for the Council to offer discounted parking in the town centre for residents to encourage them to return to former shopping habits. Jeff Bray, a senior lecturer in retail management at Bournemouth University, believes there can be co-existence between the two locations if the town centre plays to its strengths with initiatives that Castlepoint cannot offer.

Much thought is being given at present to the nature of The Square itself and the character of the shops. Nigel Hedges, the President of the Chamber of Trade, is quietly optimistic that once the present economic problems have passed, the range of shops will continue to attract visitors to the town centre. As Cllr. John Beesley pertinently observes: "Bournemouth has the character that out of town developments lack." That comment seems to me so obviously true. The Square is a very attractive location. Just to sit on a bench or enjoy a coffee at a cafe table and watch the world go by in such a location is pleasurable in a way that no out of town centre could possibly be. But perhaps I am not modern man and my personal preferences may sharply differ from the majority of my fellows. I must also confess that though I have tried hard to be dispassionate in discussing this whole theme, I am not someone who enjoys tramping around shops. While I am perfectly happy calling in to see the small shopkeepers in Wimborne, where I can enjoy good conversation and banter with people I regard as my friends, the mere thought of entering a large department store fills me with a sense of dread. With its artificial lighting, the piped cacophony of ghastly music, the hustling and bustling, the absence of fresh air and sunlight, allied to the illusion that the acquisition of material possessions equates with personal happiness, a big store represents my idea of hell. After all, what more do I need materially than my Racing Post and form-books, binoculars, my music and a pen and paper?

Palmair, Bath Travel and the legacy of a remarkable man
"What would Peter have done? It's still a question we ask ourselves whenever we have to make a major decision. We actually feel sometimes as if we are being watched over."

There are companies and businesses that earn our grudging respect even if we cannot bring ourselves to love them. There are others we actively dislike. They may tell lies or bully, they may be just plain incompetent. Then, of course, there are the banks and certain financial institutions. As the year draws to an uncertain conclusion most Britons feel a profound sense of outrage and anger at the sheer greed and utter uselessness of all too many in banking and finance who have betrayed us in so many ways. So it is, in this deepening economic and financial gloom, that we salute those companies and businesses, often small ones peopled by honest, dedicated staff, whose integrity and reliability

Peter Bath, an example to every other company director.
Palmair, the naming ceremony of 'The Spirit of Peter
Bath *Picture: Corin Messer, Bournemouth Echo*

stand out like shining lights in our midst.

David Skillicorn's words pay a remarkable and moving tribute to an extraordinary and much loved Bournemouth businessman. Though it was Peter Bath's father Reginald who founded Bath Travel in 1924, it was his son who elevated the company to an even higher level of public esteem after his father's death. It was also Peter who founded Palmair in 1958 with its flights to Palma in Majorca. And only days ago Palmair was named one of the best air-lines in the world – and won the short haul carrier title – at the *Which?* awards in London.

"Everything that moved was Peter's decision. He would leave the office here at 8pm, then have phone calls diverted directly to his home so he could attend to any problems. He always prided himself on seeing his passengers off and welcoming them on their return. He was the very visible face of the company and someone everyone trusted and liked. His philosophy was simple. When people spend their hard-earned money on a holiday, it is in all likelihood their sole holiday of the year. It is, therefore, our duty to do everything possible to ensure that holiday is a happy one. It is a policy we follow to this very day. Three of Peter's children work for Bath Travel and, though Peter is no longer with us, Teresia Rossello maintains the company's tradition. Teresia is at the check-in allocating seats and she stands in the departure lounge welcoming clients. And there is Carry Taylor, our executive manager of aviation service, who performs a brilliant job with our cabin crew."

It was Palmair's fiftieth birthday on October 25 and one can only guess at the huge sense of pride both Reginald and Peter would have taken in the light of the *Which?* award and the staff who have so honourably upheld the standards of both Bath Travel and Palmair. As for David Skillicorn, the managing director of the company personally chosen by Peter to work alongside him a dozen years ago, he too deserves much credit.

"Peter was 67 and wanted to take more of a back-seat when he appointed me, not that he ever retired completely. I spent an immense amount of time with him and his wife Elizabeth at their home in the early days. I do feel a great sense of responsibility. Bath Travel today has 70 branches from Devon to West Sussex. Then there is Palmair. Between them they employ 600 staff with probably a further 2,000 dependants. You cannot be careless or reckless when their futures are at stake. Their well-being depends on satisfying our customers, giving them value for money, making sure they come back to us again and that they speak well of us to their friends. Peter always used to say, "Treat your client as you would wish to be treated yourself." We have a very loyal and caring and compassionate staff. At a personal level I count myself the luckiest man on earth. I am doing a job I always wanted to do and no man could wish for more than that."

In March of this year Mrs.Elizabeth Bath, the widow of PJ as so many affectionately knew her husband, was made an Honorary Freeman of the borough of Christchurch where for many years she and Peter lived at Friars Cliff before moving to Avon farmhouse. Peter actually died in December, 2006, aged 79. Describing herself as immensely proud to accept the award on behalf of her late husband, Elizabeth was clearly moved by the warmth of the tributes to Peter. The occasion was a real family affair with their 4 children, Stephen, Andrew, Christine and Sallie all present at the special ceremony in Christchurch council chamber. Having travelled with the company on a number of occasions, I will simply add that Peter Bath was an extraordinary man and will long be remembered with great affection by very many people. He is an example to every other company director.

(An aircraft-naming party at Bournemouth Airport with 300 invited guests marked another exciting moment in the history of Bath Travel and Palmair in May, 2009. The £8million Boeing 737-500 was named *The Spirit of Bath* in honour of the great man and bears the most appropriate registration number of G-PJPJ. The ceremony was performed by his widow Elizabeth amidst a barrage of balloons, smoke and music. His son, Stephen, the joint managing director of the company, said: "This aircraft honours a very special person. Without him, there would have been no Palmair for the past 51 years – and no airport either- because for 6 years the only operator here was Palmair!)

I'm back with another journalist friend. This lady writes every week in the *Echo* on *'Faith Matters'*. She writes often on difficult and complex issues with great sensitivity and objectivity. For a change it's not the Norfolk Royale but the Olive Branch in Wimborne which seems a most aptly named location for our discussion.

"I must never misrepresent anyone I write about. To do so could cause the gravest offence. It is a responsibility I take very seriously, to represent the views and feelings of the different faiths in our community with a scrupulous respect for the truth."

Ruth Oliver is a practising Christian with a Baptist background. Ruth's is a column I always read because it is abundantly clear that its writer is a young woman of eminent good sense and judgement who is playing a constructive role in the religious and wider moral life of the local community by drawing together individuals from a variety of faith backgrounds

"Though I'm often invited to attend services in different churches, mostly I join the congregation at St. John's, Wimborne."

A generation ago Bournemouth and its neighbouring parishes would have been regarded as solidly Church of England with thriving pockets of Non-Conformism, Roman Catholicism and an active and influential Jewish community. In 2008 the total Jewish population in Bournemouth is an estimated 3,500 of whom 1,000 belong to the Hebrew Congregation which attracts an average synagogue attendance of 200. The newly arrived rabbi, Adrian Jesner, is a Scot and a passionate Glasgow Rangers supporter. The Reform Synagogue under Rabbi Neil Amswych enjoys a membership of 700 or so. In recent years the Catholic congregations at local churches have been dramatically swollen by the arrival of large numbers of Polish migrant workers. Most attend services at the Sacred Heart, Richmond Hill, where Father Krysztof Kosciolek reports that when he first arrived at the church in 2003 the congregation numbered 50-60. Since Poland joined the EU, however, it is more like 500-600 attending Mass with the majority aged between 20 and 35. Curiously the consequence nationally of East European migration has been to swell the number of practising Catholics in the UK to an

Snow on Richmond Hill. *Picture: Corin Messer,*
Bournemouth Echo

aggregate figure in excess of that of practising Anglicans. And, a development incomprehensible to an earlier generation, Bournemouth now hosts a growing and significant number of Muslims with their own mosque and Imam. Ruth meets regularly with the leaders of Bournemouth and Poole's religious communities.

"Against such a background I have been very impressed by our local religious leaders, their mutual respect and desire for harmony. Personally, I believe passionately in tolerance and inter-faith dialogue. The more we are able to promote activities in common, the more likely the prospect of long-term community harmony."

Indeed, such an example of inter-faith unity occurs at the year's end when members of the Faithlinks Council come together to respond to the fighting in Gaza between Arab and Jew. The Revd. Jonathan Martin, the acting chairman, calls on people of goodwill everywhere to pray for an end to the bloodshed. Only a few months earlier an interfaith meeting in Bournemouth took place involving Paul Williams, Rabbi Neil Amswych, Adam Thorn, Bob Vernon, Jack Horwood and Majid Yasin, representing different faith groups in the local community.

Another report of Ruth's that captured my particular attention relates to the work of Boscombe Salvation Army. Is there a more respected and loved group of Christians anywhere in our society than the Salvation Army? Even those who are atheists and agnostics will drop a few coins in the collecting box of the man selling *War Cry*. And why – because we know of all their good works. The splendid individuals of Boscombe SA, besides everything else, have been providing Sunday lunches once a month to members of the community who would otherwise be alone on a Sunday.

As Major Peter Mylechreest explains: "They find it really beneficial to have the company as well as receive the lovely hot food. The food is donated by Forerunner, a Southbourne based 'meals on wheels' company. Everyone makes an optional donation which we pass on, along with a contribution

Different faiths, a shared vision of love and justice . *Picture: Corin Messer, Bournemouth Echo*

from Forerunner, to Age Concern."

The managing director of Forerunner, Declan O'Toole, adds: "My ethos has always been to support the local community in addition to delivering daily hot meals to our customers. What better way to do that than providing our hot meals free of charge on a monthly basis to the Salvation Army?"

This is but a small story in the much bigger one of local voluntary work and I am delighted to be able to pay my own particular tribute to that splendid bunch of men and women and children who make up the Salvation Army.

It's a development few could have envisaged even 20 years ago – a Muslim community in Bournemouth with its own mosque. It's the most sensitive subject not just on my agenda in writing this book, but on the agenda of British society and Western society – our relationship with Islam. I might have steered away from it. After all, Dorset is not London or Bradford, Burnley or Luton. Dorset remains overwhelmingly white and Christian and is likely to do so for the foreseeable future. But there will be scarcely a person in the county who does not have a view on the subject. Many will have very strong opinions on the matter. I have heard them on my travels. Even the most liberal and tolerant in the community – and I count myself in that group – are anxious. I was privileged in the 1960s to attend the LSE, the most cosmopolitan university anywhere in the world. I counted individuals from every faith and no faith amongst my dearest friends. Curiously, we seldom talked of religion, none of us. I knew some attended mosques and synagogues and churches of every denomination, but it was a private matter. It would have been an intrusion to probe and unkind to challenge sincerely held beliefs. It also reflected the wonderful tolerance of the university community that we judged people only by their character, not by the colour of their skin or their religious beliefs. And, for heaven's sake, we were in Britain, as civilised and liberal a country as anywhere on earth. Yet, half a century on, we are all uneasy. When we turn up at Bournemouth International Airport, we will have very irritating safety procedures to negotiate. We know why though now we are usually too polite and fearful of being thought 'politically incorrect' to discuss it publicly. We are afraid of Islamic extremists and their bombs – with good reason. We do not worry about Sikh or Hindu terrorists, Catholic or Jewish suicide bombers, Baptists or Mormons carrying devices for maiming or killing in their luggage. But we do worry about Muslim extremists, not only on planes and trains and buses, but anywhere and everywhere. Yet I know, and every reader knows, our British Muslim community is overwhelmingly good, kind, decent and peace-loving. But 'overwhelmingly' is not the same as 'unanimously' and that is why we worry. Every time I now travel on the Underground I remember the horror of July 7. Today I am calling by at the spiritual home of Bournemouth and district's Muslim community to discuss some of these matters.

Bournemouth Islamic Centre

Majid Yasin is an impressive figure. Syrian born Majid arrived in this country 25 years ago and has lived in Charminster for the past 20 years. The father of 5 children, he is the Imam and Director of the Islamic Centre, formerly a Mormon school situated in St .Stephen's Road, and the spiritual leader of the local Muslim community. A man of moderate opinions, quietly spoken and good-natured, he is the very antithesis of Muslim extremism which he unequivocally condemns.

"For me the whole community is my family. Yes, I am a Muslim and for me that means I respect other faiths and also the laws of this country. I freely acknowledge that I and my family enjoy far greater freedom here in the UK than I would in many Muslim countries in the world. Freedom is very precious to me as it is to the great majority of Muslims who live in this country."

Several months before I made Majid's acquaintance, I read his observations in the Echo on the topic of the growing radicalism among a number of young Muslims in this country. He is happy to repeat those views and I am pleased to include them because I believe they are of great importance, not only to any Muslim readers of those pages, but to everyone in the wider community.

"Muslims who don't like British society should leave. If people don't like this society they should go back home to their own country – there are plenty of airports. Many Muslims bring their own traditions here from their home countries. But if people are living here they should respect this society and this country and not try to create a different society or culture. For British born Muslims I say the same thing – appreciate our free society and respect the views of others. Some people use the freedom here in the wrong way. By all means respect your traditions, but not by force."

I ask Majid how he feels about the media's attitude towards Muslims.

"First of all, I understand the anxieties of ordinary people but sometimes I feel the media is not helpful. When the question is posed, 'Are you more loyal to your religion than Britain?' it is, I believe, an unfair question. It is not a question that is put to Jews or Sikhs or Christians. Of course, we are loyal to this country. If this country was attacked by a foreign invader then I would fight for it. I am a Muslim and I have a duty to Allah but I also have a duty to everyone. I have no anger within me. I would be distressed if other people's actions contravened the laws of Allah but everyone has a duty to their faith. I find no fundamental conflict between Sharia law and the laws of this country."

Though acknowledging difficulties exist in reconciling different cultures Majid is quietly optimistic. He was pleased to welcome a local councillor to the mosque during Ramadan. He felt it was a positive and helpful move that will lead to a closer relationship between his community and the Council and its representatives.

"It is, of course, a transient population that we welcome through our doors. At the College, the University and the Language Schools there are many Muslim students, besides local residents, who attend our services. Friday is our congregational prayer day and there may be as many as 600 hundred attending. Sometimes we will have an overflow on the pavement because our mosque – or masjid, as we call it, a place of worship- is not large enough. The police are always very helpful in organising the extra numbers."

I ask Majid about the practice of some Muslim women who wear the burkha and the face veil? It is a practice that makes non-Muslims uncomfortable. It makes ME feel uncomfortable. It feels very un-British and a challenge to the openness of our society and its values.

"I would stress that there is no specific Muslim form of dress – simply that women should be modestly dressed."

Alongside Majid I meet Swanage born Tariq Palmer, a Muslim convert who works at the Islamic Centre as a volunteer assisting Majid with a number of his duties. Tariq grew up in Bournemouth and remembers 'a gentle, well-mannered, orderly town'.

"It was a very attractive shopping area for fashion conscious ladies with a number of high-class department stores like Harvey Nicholls, Plummer's, Bobby's, Bright's and Beale's. Now only the latter remains. The other day I was sitting on the bus and I counted the number of takeaways between Horseshoe Common and the Lansdowne. It was something like twenty. Unfortunately the streets are now littered not only with throw away cartons but vomit and what people have 'thrown up' after a night's bingeing and gorging. It's not the town I was once so fond of."

Tariq spent 20 years in the RAF before working in Saudi Arabia using his English to help businessmen and companies in their negotiations. It was in Djeddah, during a period of great personal difficulty in his life, emotionally and physically, when lying in a hospital bed that he picked up an introduction to Islam. As the months passed he realised he wished to convert to the Islamic faith.

"Today there about 3,000 indigenous Muslims living in Dorset.At other times of the year, especially in the summer months, there will be even greater numbers studying at the language schools. We also have a number of professionals – doctors, dentists, bankers and so on. Apart from assisting here at the Centre I also visit schools talking about Islam. I liaise with the police and the Social Services, putting my skills at the service of the community as best I can."

Of anti-Islamic feeling in the country, Tariq sees it in a historical context.

"Historically, there was a period when Jews were the scapegoats, then the Afro-Caribbeans were stigmatised, followed by the Irish during the IRA bombing. Now it is the Muslim community who are the whipping-boys. But it important to remember that the overwhelming majority of our community are peaceful, law-abiding citizens going about their daily lives like everyone else."

Both Majid and Tariq are distressed by what they see as the coarsening of British life – the swearing, excessive drinking, the drugs culture and the general decline in the standard of public behaviour. Majid articulates his particular concerns.

"It does not make it easy for parents bringing up their children when they see and hear so much that is offensive. I would urge Government and community leaders to condemn such conduct more strongly. Education can play a very important role in shaping society in terms of encouraging respect and tolerance and civilised standards but there must be a lead from the top."

There is no doubt the ordinary British public share many of the same anxieties expressed by my Muslim friends, Majid and Tariq. There are a number of very ugly features to contemporary society. I also believe that overwhelmingly the British public fervently hope that the multi-faith, internationally mixed society that we have become will, whatever the cultural divides that now exist, become one unified nation in the future. That some people wish we could rewind the past 50 years is undeniable, but we are where we are and most of us want to make a success of it. I would like to think that if there is one nation on earth that can make a success of such a challenge it is Britain with its long history of integrating many different nationalities, languages and cultures. But the Muslim community crucially must play its part in allaying the fears of non-Muslims by opposing the adherents of Islamic extremism by every means open to them. Its leaders have a great responsibility. Fortunately here in Dorset Majid Yasin, ably assisted by Tariq Palmer, is setting an example I, for one, warmly applaud and supported, I am sure, by all people of goodwill.

They make a formidable team and both have served the town as Mayor. Michael Filer was the Mayor of Bournemouth in 1984-5 and his wife Anne in 2007-8. This morning I am sitting in the lounge of the house built by Anne's grandparents in 1931, overlooking the site of the soon to be completed Boscombe surf reef. Anne talks enthusiastically of the town she's known since childhood.

"Obviously we all recall the Bournemouth of the past and much of its old appeal remains. To walk through the gardens during the day and see people in their deckchairs and children playing in the river, that's an unchanging image. But the town is constantly reinventing itself and adapting. The impact of the University has been enormous. At night it becomes a different town. Yes, it's become noisier, more exuberant, but the young people are just being what they naturally are – full of energy and vitality – but, for the most part, they are not rowdy. We have a greater variety of nationalities here than anywhere else outside London and a large and active gay community. I find the atmosphere of the town stimulating and exciting."

I remember reading of Anne's term of office and a letter in the *Echo* congratulating her beneath the heading '*Well done to our inclusive Mayor*'. The writer was referring to Anne's decision '*as a Jewish lady to invite a Muslim to read prayers in the Council chamber and to encourage a spirit of togetherness between people of different faiths.*' Another correspondent, Councillor Mike Carlile, warmly endorsed Anne's approach describing her as '*refreshingly different*'.

"Yes, that is something that is very important to me – reaching out to other communities and faiths. It is our future. A number of the people who come to study here enjoy the town so much that they want to stay. Some are starting small businesses and good luck to them!"

Michael Filer's term as Mayor embraced a significant period of inward investment into the town's economy.

"In years gone by there were too few career openings in the area for young people. As a Council we drew up a plan to encourage 'clean industry' into the area such as banking and insurance. In 1984 we were in negotiations with Chase Manhattan – now J.P. Morgan – which was looking to move out of London. They chartered trains on successive week-ends to bring down their wives and children to the town. I said to their executives that I could be on the tennis court within half an hour of leaving work, on the beach or in the country. After lunch we arranged for a fleet of estate agents to take them round looking at various properties. There was a vote within Chase Manhattan and Bournemouth was their choice. In the autumn of that year the Council sold them the land and they were on their way soon after. It was a hugely important moment for the town. Over the next 10-15 years many other companies decided to relocate to the area. After all, we are just 100 miles from London with a first-class rail and road service."

Anne sees both the positive side of recent housing development in and – and certain dangers.

"At the moment, of course, we are in a recession and the housing market is suffering problems but we all know it is likely to be a temporary blip. There has been some excellent, imaginative building with smart, elegant flats constructed as in the Keverstone Court and Green Park developments. On the other hand, there are planning issues. We must retain the essential character of the area. If there is no proper infrastructure to accompany development we are creating serious problems for the future. There is a danger of overbuilding with no gardens, insufficient open spaces, everything

'A pint – why, that's very nearly an armful.' (The Blood Donor). *Picture: Iconic Hancock, published by Harper Collins*

cramped together. It is difficult for the Council for, if we reject property developer applications, the chances are they will appeal and the Minister, because of the national pressure to provide more housing, is likely to grant permission."

Meanwhile Anne and Michael are looking forward to a trio of significant events.

"The year 2010 sees the celebration of the town's bicentenary and we are already making preparations for that. Next year 2009 will be the 25th anniversary of the BIC and the Pavilion will be 80 years old "

As the chairman of the 2010 Bournemouth Bicentenary Committee Anne will have plenty to occupy her in the coming year or two. For both Michael and Anne being busy is clearly a way of life. Before I leave Anne and I walk down to the foot of her garden and look across at the preparations for the reef. There have been problems and delays but Anne is confident it will ultimately prove a great success and play a critical role in the regeneration of the locality. We're all keeping our fingers tightly crossed.

He wasn't born in the town and he didn't die in the town, but he did live in Bournemouth for fifteen formative years and he did make his first stage appearance at the Avon Road Labour Hall. He also made his second stage appearance using 'blue jokes' at the Sacred Heart Roman Catholic Church Hall on Richmond Hill, a disastrous appearance that changed forever the character and content of his comedy routine. He also happens to be this writer's all-time favourite comedy actor. His name was, of course, Tony Hancock who committed suicide 40 years ago during a tour of Australia. In the light of Tony Hancock's close associations with the area – the family lived first in Strouden Road, then the Railway Hotel at 119 Holdenhurst Road and later at the Durlston Court Hotel – it seems entirely proper that a Hancock Museum of some sort should be created in the town. Malcolm Chapman, a Southbourne resident, recently addressed the Council on the subject of creating such a Museum, or even one devoted to the broader theme of British comedy. Archivist Keith Mason also believes such a venture would be both fitting and popular as a tourist attraction. As Neal Butterworth, the *Echo's* Editor, suggests the forthcoming bi-centenary of the town might provide an opportunity to celebrate Bournemouth's cultural, artistic and musical heritage. If this writer might chip in with his 'ha'porth', why not combine all these elements in a form which embraces all these excellent ideas to widen its appeal to the maximum? And I would ask that Wimborne's gift to the world of comedy in the form of the wonderful Billy Burden be included. There must be a space somewhere, even for a temporary collection before a permanent home is found. I'm sure 'local lad made-good' Tony Blackburn, with his musical background and his scrapbook of the worst jokes of the last 100 years, would be delighted to open such a museum.

It's undoubtedly the major social issue that confronts the town. It was back in 1997 that the *Muzik* magazine described Bournemouth as *'Britain's new clubbing capital.'* In the 10 years after that report many more clubs opened across the town, a number of them owned by local businessman Richard Carr. The figure of those coming into the town on Saturday nights for their entertainment was estimated, as recently as 2-3 years ago to be at least 50,000, possibly even at summer peak-times as many as 80,000. Of course, the great majority enjoyed a 'good night out' and behaved themselves. Inevitably, however, a minority didn't.Earlier this year in the same week that Adrianne Maslen in Lyme Regis was reporting to me that her police report for the week included 'a broken wing-mirror, one stolen handbag and a missing statue', the police in Bournemouth were investigating the violent killing of 2 young men in the Town Centre within 90 minutes of one another.' Six months earlier violent and intimidatory behaviour by gangs of youths on the seafront led to the cancellation of the popular Friday night fireworks displays. Large gangs of drunken youths have also been causing problems at Southbourne. As ever the root cause is the excessive consumption of alcohol.

At this point, it seems appropriate to congratulate Adrian Griffiths, Bournemouth's senior youth worker, Rob Jennings at Townsend Youth Centre, and youth-worker Tim Oliver of Bournemouth Youth Council, all of whom I know are greatly involved in projects to improve the prospects of young people in their communities. Without their efforts and those of their colleagues some of our local social problems would be much worse.

But back to the theme of alcohol consumption, Superintendent Stuart Katon of Bournemouth and Poole Police advised:" I would urge people coming into the town to drink responsibly."

Unfortunately, as we know, such wise words carry precious little weight with certain individuals. Father Tony Pennicott of the Sacred Heart Church on Richmond Hill, who has lived and worked in the town for the past 15 years, feels the atmosphere at night has become more threatening and is disturbed that so many young people are drinking to excess. Recently retired Canon Jim Richardson at St. Peter's believes there is a mistaken perception of danger. "When young people are noisy, the older generation can feel needlessly intimidated." But both the Father and the Canon are certain there are far too many pubs and clubs. (Incidentally, the excellent Canon Jim is now an Honorary Freeman of the Borough and an OBE for his splendid work within the community and his night-time ministry at St. Peter's).

Discussing the topic with one young woman who grew up in Wimborne and regularly returns to the town, lives and teaches history and politics in London, and has with her friends been into Bournemouth many times over the years on Friday and Saturday nights, she makes a number of interesting observations.

"I have personally never experienced or seen violence in Bournemouth although clearly it occurs. But that is true of everywhere in the UK. It is as true of small towns, as it is of bigger towns and cities and London. I have actually witnessed fights in 2 pubs in Wimborne on Friday nights. On a percentage scale, I doubt there is any more violence and drunkenness in Bournemouth than anywhere else. It is the sheer numbers coming into the town that makes it the more conspicuous. I also believe we need to have a sense of historical perspective. Throughout our history the English have had a reputation for drinking to excess. The Normans said the English drank too much to be able to fight effectively. In the 18th century it's said that in certain parts of London 1 in every 4 houses was a gin-house. Read what Dickens wrote about drink and violence in his day in Victorian England. In no sense am I condoning or defending such behaviour, but we are in danger of over-moralising, suggesting our society is going to rack and ruin when it isn't."

I suspect Mark Smith would agree with every word my daughter Fleur spoke to me. It is clearly a complex subject. We all wish young people did not drink as much. What is different about this generation, of course, is that it is the most affluent in our history, alcohol is relatively cheap, young women appear to be vying with young men to get drunk and many of the old social restraints have disappeared. What, by common consent, do not seem to be helping are the new relaxed drinking regulations. The intention may have been worthy but I do recall an old saying to the effect that 'The road to hell is paved with good intentions.' Clearly, if the experience of the next year or two confirms the trend to more drinking over an extended period with all the attendant knock-on effects, changes to the legislation will need to be made.

The general economic recession takes its toll in mid-summer of the biggest single player in Bournemouth's club scene when Richard Carr's business empire disintegrates about his ears, amidst ringing denunciations by Mr. Carr of the Bournemouth and Poole Town Council's failure to aggressively market the towns.

"Nobody wants to accept that bars and clubs are important and employing a lot of people."

Branding Bournemouth as 'tatty', he compares it unfavourably with Newquay. He also decries any suggestion that the club scene in general, and lap-dancing clubs in particular, are in any way responsible for 'any decline in the town's image'.

"Bournemouth's demise as a family resort is down to the fact that it is now cheaper to fly to Barcelona or Malaga than it is to drive from London to Bournemouth."

A different point of view on the part played by lap-dancing venues and the proliferation of bars and clubs is expressed by the chairman of the East Cliff and Town Centre Residents Association, David Clutterbuck, who has lived in Bournemouth for more than 50 years and observes:" I have seen Bournemouth go downhill. The town is acquiring a sleazy reputation."

Sgt. Richard Wilson, Dave Fish and Gary Briscoe from the Dorset police Alcohol Licensing Unit are, meanwhile, concentrating their energies on reducing the amount of alcohol readily available on the streets from off-licences and retailers in an effort to cut down on the public nuisance of 'street drinkers'. With problems not only in the town centre but at the Lansdowne and Boscombe precinct, Sgt Wilson comments:

"We're not talking about major crime but individuals making a nuisance of themselves. It impacts on people's quality of life, which is why it gets our attention."

That is very true. For families especially, not least those with small children, it is unpleasant to be accosted by drunken beggars and 'rough sleepers'. And, in a wider sense, there is undoubtedly a serious tension in the relationship at times between the traditional holiday-makers and the very different street life of Bournemouth of modern times. The pleasure boat-operator, Peter Lamb, remembers when the Pier Approach was a very different place with 'dancing waters music and light shows' and the popularity of evening cruises from the Pier. Numbers now enjoying such activities are significantly down, he reports.

An aerial view of the town. *Picture: Richard Crease, Bournemouth Echo, with assistance from Bournemouth Helicopters*

"It's the same with the theatre. People don't want to walk home. They don't want to be battling to get through the Gardens with lots of drunks. Old ladies feel especially intimidated."

Inspector Neil MacBean of the Dorset Police believes it is imperative that the town offers an alternative in the evening to noisy bars and clubs.

"We have a night-time economy reliant on alcohol. Nearly every premise now is a loud premise with a reliance on the supply of alcohol. There is little in the way of an evening economy. We want to encourage families and office workers to stay in the town centre, resulting in a more diverse mix of people."

Cllr. Ron Whittaker observes:" Hopefully things will change once the Winter Gardens and Pavilion schemes are completed. We must create an environment where all ages feel safe. There must be more family entertainment."

Ron is, of course, absolutely right. Unfortunately no one knows, especially at this time of economic difficulty, when the Winter Gardens and Pavilion schemes will be completed. Ron's words also remind me of the stark contrast with the years of my own youth, when my friends and I came into the town centre not to drink ourselves stupid, but to attend the 'big band' and pop concerts, the wrestling and boxing tournaments at those venues. The behaviour was impeccable and the idea that anyone might feel intimidated in the streets or The Square was unthinkable. Other than the odd individual 'the worse for wear', drunkenness was practically unknown. There was simply no youth culture of heavy drinking. We had better things to do with our very limited cash. And, of course, we had no credit cards.

I will let Tobias Ellwood MP sum up the picture as a whole.

The Red Arrows at Bournemouth Air Festival. *Picture: Richard Crease, Bournemouth Echo*

"Bournemouth is one of the most popular seaside resorts in the country and we must ensure it stays that way. We can't let the night-time economy change the character of our town and we must support the police and the Town Council who are endeavouring to make the Town Centre safe and attractive to visitors and our residents."

Inevitably any Council will be on the receiving end of brickbats when it makes mistakes, especially if they cost council tax payers money. Certainly, in recent years, there have been quite a number of such mistakes, of which the Imax (Waterfront) building was perhaps the most spectacular. It was approved by 35 councillors with just 7 against. It cost £20 million and has proved an unmitigated disaster. Today it stands idle and unloved and no one knows what to do with it. Then there have been some very costly job appointments – consultants with 'dodgy' backgrounds or questionable abilities appointed on huge salaries. One particular post that was advertised recently was for 'An executive director of transformation' with a salary of '£101,000, a £10,000 relocation package, a final salary scheme plus other benefits.' I will quote a few words of the 'job description'. *'He or she will strategically commission resources and activities to deliver agreed priorities and outcomes and lead, direct and performance manage specific services, building a valued, confident, developed, empowered and innovative workforce.'* There are a few additional sentences but I won't prolong the agony for those who appreciate the English language. It would be almost impossible to make it up, were it not true. Someone, somewhere, in one of Bournemouth's council offices, actually wrote those words. How long did it take him or her, I wonder? Was it a morning's work? He or she then, no doubt, sat down for several hours with various colleagues to discuss any fine tuning before it was sent off to the Guardian public advertisements section – and all of this at council tax-payer's expense. Then, of course, there's the matter of councillors' expenses and pension schemes which now often amount to more than the salaries of ordinary individuals in full-time employment. Political correctness also reared its silly, humourless, head just weeks ago when a number of council staff were suspended for an alleged breach of 'equality and diversity' regulations when a 'naughty' email was circulated. How much did that cost? There have been rumblings of discontent too about the Boscombe surf reef project because of the increased costs and delays in its construction. Already its budget has doubled. But, as I have written elsewhere, hopefully there will be a happy outcome to this venture.

But, if I have dwelt upon certain of its failings and absurdities, sometimes the Council does get things gloriously right and it's happened in 2008 with the triumphant August Bank Holiday Air Show drawing vast numbers into the town and being counted by everyone a spectacular success, in every sense of the word. It was so brilliant a triumph that another is intended in 2009 and another after that, if all goes according to plan. I will quote Andy Martin writing in the *Echo*. *'The small team at the Council, led by Tourism boss, Mark Smith, has done a fantastic job. Congratulations to all those involved.'* And so say all of us.

There is currently under way a public consultation exercise for a *'Town Centre Master Vision'* with *draft plans for the Bournemouth of 2035 – 'A garden town featuring al fresco dining, a treetop walkway, botanical gardens, outside performance areas, a range of all-weather attractions and a subtle mix of shopping facilities.'* On the subject of the recommended 'all weather attractions' I feel I should refer to a rather sad little letter published in the *Echo* several months ago which seems to me to contain certain important criticisms that really should be heeded. *'We've just had a miserable Bank Holiday in Bournemouth with our 2 grandchildren aged 8 and 5. Where are the facilities in wet weather – no swimming baths or playgrounds, no indoor play facilities, no bowling alley, no skating and no suitable films at the cinema either, and such expensive parking? Come on, Bournemouth. Stop concentrating on weekend stag nights and hen parties. Promote family life... along with proper indoor facilities for small children!'*

I fear I and many readers will not be around to see if 'The Master Vision (of 2035) ever comes to fruition', together with the provision of *'indoor facilities for smaller children'* but, there it is in black and white for another generation to pass judgement on its success or otherwise. Will 'Granny' Vass, sadly toothless, stooped and grey-haired by then, be writing in the *Echo* still of Council plans coming in 'overdue and over budget'? Or not coming in at all?

One man retiring this year is Stephen Godsall, the Council's executive for major projects. Stephen has clearly laboured hard over his 15 years of service. He makes a couple of interesting observations on the subject of projects like those involving the Winter Gardens, the Pavilion and the BIC.

"Councils change, political priorities change, the financial climate changes – the consequence is that particular schemes can be dropped, even if sometimes they are good ones."

Stephen also speaks well of local councillors.

"I have nothing but praise for the overwhelming majority. They are often unjustly maligned. They put in a huge amount of voluntary effort for very little reward and very little thanks."

I hope all those councillors put plenty in the hat when the collection for Stephen's retirement gift was being made!

One man who has earned the right over the years to be listened to in matters relating to the town is Honorary Alderman Keith Rawlings, former Mayor and chairman of Bournemouth Civic Society who, it is said, has resided in the borough since the days of Lewis Tregonwell himself, possibly even predating the great man. Keith believes a fitting memorial in 2010 to celebrate Bournemouth's bicentenary would be the creation of a Town Museum. Keith possesses his own considerable collection of memorabilia and has no doubt that a veritable treasure trove exists in and around the town of similar artefacts and items of historical interest. Sheila Levitt, the chairman of the Bicentenary Committee, does not rule out the prospect but is concerned at the funding aspects, not least at a time of economic belt-tightening. In a similar vein one of the town's younger councillors is eager to see Bournemouth become the 'culture capital' of the county. Cllr. Michael Griffiths believes the town is lagging behind other Dorset towns in promoting its cultural and artistic heritage and would like to see a greater fostering of contemporary interest in the arts. By liaising more closely with the Arts Institute and Bournemouth and Poole College, Michael believes it would help to transform the town's image. Cllr. Claire Smith agrees in principle and suggests that, in the longer term, a refurbished Winter Gardens could play an invaluable role in accommodating such a development.

For the past 50 years Bournemouth's language schools have played an important part both in the local economy and the community life of the area. Even as a small boy travelling by bus into the town en route to the County Cricket at Dean Park I was conscious of the impact of these summer migrants. To one small, shy country lad, these precocious, supremely self-confident, garrulous, fashionably dressed visitors both intrigued and intimidated me. They invariably spoke far too quickly for me to understand more than the odd phrase or two and seemed to belong to a world infinitely more sophisticated and chic than that of my own. In more recent times I did teach in a couple of the town's language schools for a couple of summers, with both young and adult students and found it a very stimulating experience. My daughter too taught several summers at the Anglo-Continental – one of her favourite nationalities being students from Kazakhstan. It wasn't so long ago few of us would even have known where it was! The importance of such international links between Bournemouth and abroad cannot be overstated, both in terms of income and the cultural value of such exchanges. The figure of £130 million has been suggested as the value of the town's 19 accredited language schools to the local economy with an aggregate total of 26,000 students coming each year. Charles Elder also highlights the number of overseas students at the Arts Institute and Bournemouth and Poole College. During this period of economic recession and the falling value of the pound, the appeal of the schools is even greater. One of the key figures who has played a hugely important role in promoting the local schools for many years is Mike Francis, the chairman of Bournemouth Tourism and the principal of Westbourne Academy Language School, who points out that the town is the largest provider of international education through its language schools outside London. The inspirational figure behind Bournemouth's twinning with the Swiss town of Lucerne and a variety of other excellent and imaginative initiatives, Mike deservedly receives an MBE in the New Year's Honours list. Sue Smith, the independent education representative on the Tourism Board, states the numbers coming to Bournemouth from overseas are holding up well, as does Clive Barrow of the Language Schools association, pinpointing grants from the Spanish and Saudi Arabian Governments to support their students.

Boscombe

By now a certain group of readers will be becoming understandably impatient. I refer to the good people of Boscombe, so often viewed as the poor relation of its more glamorous and affluent cousin along the Holdenhurst Road. Having followed the fortunes of local football clubs since I was 8 years old, I do clearly recall the days when it was Bournemouth & Boscombe Athletic. Indeed, because of the location of the ground, many of my friends always called the club Boscombe, not Bournemouth. Last year I read a splendid piece in the Echo by a young man named Oliver Benton, a resident since childhood of Boscombe in which he contrasted the popular image of the area with the reality he knows from his day to day experience of the locality. I will quote just a few of his observations.

'You can be sure that as soon as my home's location is disclosed in conversation (just off the ill-famed Crescent), eye contact drops, body language closes up and comments are invariably made like: 'Oh, do you get a lot of trouble?' Well, no actually, I don't. In almost a decade living here, I have

The 'Grim Reader' *Picture: Geoff Hill*

encountered no major problems whatsoever.'

Acknowledging there is a 'seedy side' to Boscombe with a proliferation of 'sex shops', the pushing of drugs and prostitution, Oliver says a major factor in the arrival of these problems has been *'the butchery of Boscombe's once grand houses into relatively cheap and often ludicrously small apartments......with the attendant side-effects.'* However, Oliver points to many positive aspects of the locality. *'There are fantastic aspects to life in Boscombe. Casting your eyes upwards reveals a rich concentration of beautiful Victorian architecture – such as the Royal Arcade and Opera House – which can be seen nowhere else in Bournemouth. An assortment of lively and unique cafes and restaurants. A diverse mix of nationalities.'* And Oliver sees the future though optimistic eyes with much evidence of regeneration with new housing developments, especially along the sea-front, the Boscombe Chine Gardens with many new facilities, the Honeycombe Chine development, a restored pier and, of course, the surf reef.

The Boscombe Forum reflects a cross-section of views on the locality. Gary Sherborne, a former Forum chairman and now project leader at the Tenant's Union observes: "The street life, deprivation and inequalities are as bad as ever they were. You can do as much as you like with the Opera House, but the image of Boscombe hasn't changed. There are two sides to the area. Unscrupulous business people are making a lot of money. We've got to look at ways to change the area which is still the drugs, sex and violence capital of the South Coast." Another who agrees with the analysis, Peter Castle, a local businessman, remarks:" I see people drinking on the streets at 8 am. We need a job centre – some symbol of motivation." On the other hand, Kathie Pearce seems more in tune with Oliver Benton describing Boscombe 'as a wonderful place with a real sense of community.' I suspect Pat Clark's judgement that' There are two parts to Boscombe, one with a lot of wealth, the other with severe deprivation' accurately sums up the general situation. Certainly it seems to accord with the findings of a recently published detailed statistical analysis in which it was revealed that 9 out of 10 of the most deprived areas in the South West region of the UK are located in Bournemouth and 4 of them fall in the Boscombe West ward – Boscombe Central, St. Clements, Drummond Road and

Boscombe South. The figures are based on factors such as income, benefits, employment, health and disability, education, housing and crime.

One group determined to fly the flag for the area is Boscombe Spa Resort Ltd, which embraces hoteliers, Alan Sibthorpe, Anne Eyles, Debbie Payne and Bryn Jones. Debbie Payne explains: "Our aim is to work together as a collective to promote Boscombe Spa resort as a tourist destination. We intend to advertise collectively which, we believe, will be a more economical and effective way of attracting visitors. With the new regeneration scheme there is every reason to be positive about the future."

All of which seems to be an intelligent, rational way forward. With two poor summers in a row and, against a backcloth of financial difficulties for many people, these are not easy times for hoteliers. The one advantage for them in the coming period is the poor value of the pound against the euro which should mean more Britons staying at home for their holidays.

A Boscombe resident who feels optimistic about the future of the area is Dorset Awards 'Entrepreneur of the Year', Mark Cribb, owner of the bistro Urban Beach and Urban Reef.

"Boscombe has had such a bad reputation for years. With the reef and the redevelopment it's a really exciting time for us."

As Alison Gandolfi, the chairman of the Bournemouth Area Hospitality Association comments: "At the moment the high tax levels in Britain do make it difficult in general to compete with other countries, but Bournemouth's own existing 'quality scheme' means we are doing our best to ensure the highest quality standards for our guests to ensure they thoroughly enjoy their holidays and feel they are getting value for money."

It is absolutely essential that when holidaymakers return home they do so, as Alison, Mark Smith and his counterpart in Poole Graham Richardson insist, they do so with smiles on their faces vowing to come back another day. That is a critical challenge for hoteliers and everyone engaged in the tourist trade. With 1 person in 4 in the Bournemouth area involved in some capacity in the tourist industry, no one can afford to be complacent or slipshod. While none of us can do anything about the weather, by providing good food and service with a smile, the goodwill thus engendered will fill beds and restaurants for many years to come. It is amazing how much can be achieved by simple acts of courtesy and kindness and a genuine desire to please.

AFC Bournemouth, the season of 2008-9, 'Up the Cherries'

No, there never has been such a season and every supporter will be hoping there never is such a season again.

One day perhaps the complex financial details will be unravelled and published explaining exactly how the club finished up in such a mess that it fell into the hands of the receivers. But, even without the detailed accounts, we all understand the fundamental reason. Like so many of the clubs in the kingdom, mighty footballing names and minnows, Bournemouth's financial affairs were conducted over a period of years with scant regard for the traditional principles of financial prudence. Elsewhere I have described Weymouth FC's catastrophic season. Forty miles to the east Southampton FC's footballing and financial fortunes are at their lowest ebb in the club's distinguished history. Inflated ambition everywhere has led to reckless boardroom gambles and mismanagement. As with ordinary individuals the books simply have to be balanced – expenditure must not exceed income. It may be possible to get away with foolish extravagance in the short-term but, sooner or later, the day of reckoning will dawn. For a number of years we'd read in the Echo of the monumental debts at Dean Court. There isn't space here to retell the tangled story of the ground itself, its sale and the uncompleted stand, and all the directorial manoeuvring. Suffice to say that the creditors,

The Bournemouth Squad 2009-10. *Picture: Michael Cunningham*

Eddie Howe being interviewed after a 'pre-season' with 'Spurs. *Picture: Michael Cunningham*

Jason Tindall, Eddie Mitchell and Eddie Howe. *Picture: Michael Cunningham*

most notably the Inland Revenue, decided mid-way through the season 2007-8 that 'Enough was enough'. The punishment imposed upon the club for its many financial irregularities was a 10 point deduction. Despite 6 consecutive victories and an away draw in the final game against Carlisle, the punishment proved just too much and Bournemouth suffered the ignominy of relegation to Division Two, the equivalent of the old Division Four. Without the deduction the club would have finished just below mid-table. It was a cruel blow to the players and especially to the manager Kevin Bond. This isn't the place to discuss the rights and wrongs of this form of penalty meted out by the

HOME						LEAGUE TWO	AWAY					
Pl	W	D	L	F	A		W	D	L	F	A	Pts
46	13	8	2	39	15	Brentford (C)	10	8	5	26	21	85
46	13	5	5	36	25	Exeter (P)	9	8	6	29	25	79
46	11	9	3	32	16	Wycombe (P)	9	9	5	22	17	78
46	14	4	5	36	19	Bury	7	11	5	27	24	78
46	12	7	4	38	21	Gillingham (P)	9	5	9	20	34	75
46	11	6	6	40	24	Rochdale	8	7	8	30	35	70
46	14	6	3	41	16	Shrewsbury	3	12	8	20	28	69
46	12	3	8	44	24	Dag & Red	7	8	8	33	29	68
46	11	10	2	39	18	Bradford	7	3	13	27	37	67
46	8	8	7	32	28	Chesterfield	8	7	8	30	29	63
46	9	9	5	29	24	Morecambe	6	9	8	24	32	63
46	11	6	6	36	23	Darlington	9	6	8	25	21	62
46	6	11	6	26	22	Lincoln	8	6	9	27	30	59
46	11	6	6	32	21	Rotherham	10	6	7	28	25	58
46	9	10	4	36	31	Aldershot	5	2	16	23	49	54
46	9	5	9	25	24	Accrington	4	6	13	17	35	50
46	7	7	9	30	35	Barnet	4	8	11	26	39	48
46	6	6	11	23	33	Port Vale	7	3	13	21	33	48
46	6	6	11	22	31	Notts Co	5	8	10	27	38	47
46	7	4	12	23	37	Macclesfield	6	4	13	22	40	47
46	11	6	6	28	15	Bournemouth	6	6	11	31	36	46
46	6	7	10	31	28	Grimsby	3	7	13	20	41	41
46	4	7	12	24	34	Chester (R)	4	6	13	19	47	37
46	7	8	8	34	34	Luton (R)	6	9	8	24	31	26

*deductions – Luton 30pts, B'mouth 17, R'ham 17, Darlington 10

Left: 'Fletch the lion-hearted' *Picture: Michael Cunningham.* **Above:** *The 2008-2009 League table*

football authorities. Many fans think it is very unfair but, there it is, rules are rules and life can be full of injustices at times. But, if relegation is bad enough, worse is to follow. The club is given a stark choice – begin the new season with a 17 point deduction or face a winding-up order and oblivion. Hobson's Choice, as Yorkshire folk used to say.

So the 2008-2009 season kicks off with Kevin Bond still in the manager's seat and surely secure for the time being. After all, it wasn't his fault the club was relegated. In fact, they'd finished on a high with headlines in the Echo referring to 'Bond's braves'. The son of John Bond, himself a fine player and successful manager in his time including a spell at AFC, Kevin's career actually began at Dean Court as a 16 year-old apprentice where I recall him as a skilful and cultivated defender, usually playing in the left-back position. I thought he'd made a thoroughly decent job of managing the club to date, especially in view of the financial restraints and the enforced departure of talented youngsters like Sam Vokes. Formerly the assistant to Harry Redknapp at Portsmouth, this was Kevin's first experience in the proverbial managerial 'hot-seat'. However, scarcely has the season got underway than Kevin is out on his ear and Jimmy Quinn is brought in by the directors. Quinn, an Irish international and free scoring forward, has already enjoyed a measure of success in non-league management. I saw him as a player at Dean Court but seldom recall him with a smile on his face. My immediate reaction is that he's seen as the hard man to bring some 'steel' into the side. Though Kevin Bond is widely regarded as a highly professional coach, there's a whisper he's just too 'nice' to be a manager. Certainly the haste with which Quinn is brought in so early in the season – it's still only September- suggests it's part of a pre-arranged plan. Had Kevin won the first 6 games, as he won 6 of the last 7- he might just have been safe. Even so, I suspect his face didn't quite fit with the directors. I feel an injustice has been done and actually sit down and write a letter to Kevin expressing my regret at the way he's been treated. Maybe Kevin will just throw my letter in the bin. On the other hand, people do appreciate a bit of support when they're down. Mind, he isn't unemployed for too long, quickly rejoining his old boss and good friend Harry Redknapp at Spurs. It is at this point that matters become all but impossible for anyone following the club's affairs from a distance to get a grasp of events. To make sense of the back-room shenanigans of the past year or two you would need to have been the proverbial fly on the wall in the director's box and boardroom. The *Echo's* admirable football reporters, Ian Wadley, Neil Perrett and Neil Meldrum do their very best to make sense of it all for their readers but I would guess even they are struggling. Just how genuine are some of the potential new investors in the club? After all, Weymouth has suffered the ridiculous antics of Stephen Beer. How many of the 'saviours' are merely playing games and wasting everyone's time, eager for a moment of glory on the back page of the local paper? Flashing their cash but running a hundred miles when it actually comes down to putting it on the table.

Not long before Christmas, I meet Cherries fan and *Echo* reporter, Melanie Vass, AFC having just scrambled out of the pit of 'minus' points. But they are still a long way from safety. Melanie and I – and no doubt her dad – are not very hopeful. Apart from Luton who started the season with an even bigger penalty deficit of 27 points and appeared doomed from the start, AFC's rivals are still well clear. It also begins to emerge that all is not that well on the training ground. Rumblings of discontent there and on the playing-field itself begin to surface. Quinn's tactics are being questioned. Is he getting the best out of certain players? Then, on New Year's Eve, another bombshell – Jimmy Quinn is out, Eddie Howe is in. The former Dean Court favourite is asked to take temporary charge of team affairs. I doubt there's a Cherries supporter who isn't delighted. The former Queen Elizabeth's School ,Wimborne, student from Verwood, the local lad who impressed everyone during a distinguished playing career prematurely cut short by injury, is now in charge of the club he supported as a boy. Clean-cut, courteous, possessed of a natural dignity, Eddie is someone everyone wants to see succeed. Three weeks later at the age of just 31 he's appointed the youngest League manager. I ring my daughter in London to tell her of the appointment. She was at QE, a couple of years behind Eddie. Naturally she thoroughly approves. The boys at the City of London School pause to discuss the news with her in the classroom and the corridor. She's the only AFC supporter in a school of 700 Arsenal, Spurs, Chelsea and Fulham fans. Eddie's the best face of football, a role model for the younger players and fans. Eddie chooses as his assistant his good friend and former Cherries player, Jason Tindall, who left Weymouth in the close season. Jason, it seems, is the talker. Eddie prefers to let the results do the talking. But it's going to be an uphill struggle to cut back the lead the other clubs in the table above them have built up and Eddie is under no illusions.

Everyone needs luck. A football manager not only needs it more than most mortals, he also needs inspiration. One week after his promotion into the managerial seat, Eddie turns in his hour of greatest need to a player who has never given anything less than 100% to his side's cause in his career? Not the fastest, nor the most nimble player who has graced the turf at Dean Court, and certainly not the most prolific goal-scorer, but a lion-hearted player and a huge favourite with the supporters – his name was on the match programme for a decade. It is, of course, that of Steve Fletcher. Released against the better judgement of many at the club 12 months earlier, 36 years-old Steve returns to the fold at Eddie's request. There are pivotal moments in every manager's career. It is doubtful, no matter how far Eddie is destined to journey in his managerial career, that he will ever make a wiser decision. Alas, there is not the space to record each and every detail of the rest of this extraordinary season in this volume. But I will give a brief outline.

By 3 March, following Steve Fletcher's first goal since his return, AFC move out of the bottom two for the first time in the season. But a series of indifferent results still leave them in desperate trouble. By mid-April it's still touch and go but a victory at relegation rivals Chester brings fresh hope of survival. On April 25, a dramatic 80th minute winning goal by – yes, you've guessed it, Steve Fletcher – against Grimsby at Dean Court, guarantees AFC's Division Two status for another season. Unbelievably, it is the big man's 100th League goal in his outstanding footballing career. But this has, unquestionably, been a team triumph in the widest sense. Every player deserves a pat on the back, every member of the back-room staff and every supporter, not least the travelling supporters, has earned a share of the praise. Without the encouragement, financial and vocal, of the fans the club would not have survived. As it is, the Cherries live to fight another day. Relegation to the Conference would have been a body blow and unmerited by the performances on the pitch.

If there is success on the football pitch, at last, in the close season, there is the news that every supporter has been anxiously waiting for – a resolution of the long-running ownership saga. Businessman Paul Baker departs, a sad figure with his business world another victim of the troubled economic times, to be replaced by a consortium headed by Eddie Mitchell, millionaire property developer and the former owner of Dorchester FC. The new team comprises Jeff Mostyn (vice chairman), Adam Murry (director of operations), Steve Sly (director) and, in charge of the day-to-day running of club affairs, Neill Blake, the son-in-law of chairman, Eddie Mitchell.

Dean Court – Thursday, 1 October, 2009

I'm greeted at reception by the bubbly Holly Maxwell. Holly's a Watford girl.

"I had no real interest in football until I arrived here but it sort of sucks you in. The players are lovely and there's always lots of banter. I'm really enjoying myself here. Mind, it wasn't so much fun last season when we were in administration but there's a great spirit about the club and everyone respects Eddie."

I've been invited over by media manager, Mick Cunningham. He's just taken the official team photograph. Mick's photographed the team for the past decade and travelled thousands of miles with the players. He's also kindly fixed it for me to see Eddie Howe in a few minutes.

It's an important day for the club. After a strict transfer embargo for the past 8 months, the FA has granted permission to the club to sign a non-contract player to ease its injury problems. A 19 year-old from West Ham, Anthony Edgar, has just signed on a month's loan. He's joining a side that is, at this moment, at the top of Division Three with 24 points. Yes, the Cherries are off to their best start in years. Heady days for every supporter.

The manager's office

> If you can meet with Triumph and Disaster
> And treat those two impostors just the same.'
> From 'If' by Rudyard Kipling

"Things can change so quickly. It's the nature of the game. You can be up one moment, down the next. But I know I am so privileged to be doing what I'm doing. It's something I often say to the players. Be grateful. Don't moan. Being a professional footballer is a wonderful job. We are all so fortunate."

You don't have to be in Eddie Howe's company for more than a few minutes to realise he's someone out of the ordinary. I am not going to burden him at this stage with flattering, fulsome adjectives but he is a deeply impressive young man. Articulate, highly intelligent, impeccably mannered, clean-cut, he's the Verwood schoolboy who attended QE, Wimborne, played football for Bournemouth and Portsmouth for a decade before injury effectively cut short his playing career.

"I dislocated my knee-cap. The last 3 years of playing I knew I was a shadow of my former self."

At 16 he'd chosen football rather than his A levels. At the end of his playing days he might have gone on to university, trained to be a games teacher - he's not quite sure what but the invitation to coach, to stay in the game he loved, was irresistible.

In a sense, we know the rest of the story. Sacked along with Kevin Bond, he was almost instantly reinstated to work with the youth squad before, at New Year, he received the offer to become the youngest manager in the football league at the age of 31.

"From one of the safest jobs in the game to one of the most precarious! I was told it was a matter of either keeping the ship afloat or presiding over the death of a football club - if we dropped into the Conference we were in deep trouble."

By any standards it was a daunting challenge, not least for someone without previous managerial experience. That football managers come and go with considerable regularity is one of the certainties of a very uncertain world. Some we admire for their professional skills even if we don't much care for them as human beings. Others are manifestly good men but deficient in their technical know-how and judgement. Some fall on their feet, others are just plain unlucky and retire licking their wounds. The Sir Bobby Robsons and Sir Matt Busbys of this world are uncommon. Respected and loved, their qualities transcend the game of football reaching out to a much wider audience. I ask Eddie about his footballing heroes.

"I've recently been reading Brian Clough's biography. I met him as a little boy with my grandad. He was very kind to me. Though I'm sure he had his faults I do admire him for all he achieved. He was amazingly successful with two unfashionable clubs, Derby County and Notts Forest. He was able to get the best out of the players in his charge. He also insisted his players conducted themselves as proper professionals at all times and not to argue with referees who are, after all, only trying to do a very difficult job with honesty."

The reference to his grandfather, Frank, is particularly significant and poignant.

"The two greatest influences on my life, the two people who really shaped me as a person, were my mother Ann and my grandfather. Ferrying me around all over the place as a boy to matches and training, getting my kit ready, looking after a football-mad kid, I owe so much to both of them. They supported me every step of the way. They gave me my values. They instilled in me the importance of good manners, of treating other people as I would wish to be treated myself. And I must mention my brothers, Steve, Daniel and Charlie and my sister Rowena. My family means a great deal to me and they've all played a big part in my life."

Sadly Frank died a couple of years ago and didn't live to see his grandson's appointment as manager.

"I also greatly admired Tony Cottee as a player. He never really got the credit for what he achieved. He was something of an underdog and I always have a soft spot for the underdog in life."

Of last season's heroics we talk of Steve Fletcher's contribution.

"There came a point after a couple of weeks as manager when I turned to Jason (Tindall) and I said 'We must get Fletch back' and Jason said 'What are you waiting for?' So I rang him and he was on his way back to Dean Court. I have a huge respect for Fletch because he played through injuries without complaining and he took quite a wage cut to return. He's just Bournemouth through and through. He's such a positive influence for good in the team. I must also pay a particular tribute to my friend Jason. He's been a huge support during the year. And Jon Dalzell has played a major role in our early success this season."

Does Eddie find it difficult to manage players who are sometimes his senior in years or scarcely his junior by many seasons?

"There has to be a certain distance when you sit in the manager's chair. It's a different relationship. But I have to say the players have responded superbly and I am impressed with the way they are conducting themselves."

Eddie's married to Vicky, lives in Merrick Park and now has little time for his many interests except for listening to his favourite band A'Ha, reading biographies and walking his beloved Boxer Eric.

"Win, lose or draw, he doesn't care. He's always just so pleased to see me at the end of the day!"

Eddie looks back across his career with immense gratitude.

"I wouldn't swap any of it, even the injuries. The experience makes you a better person. I've

Sunseeker – that there are individuals able to buy and crew them is a reminder of what constitutes real wealth.
Picture: David Baker.

always believed in trying to improve. It's a lesson I am constantly impressing upon the players. Never be satisfied. Listen, work and learn. There's always room for improvement."

As I leave we return to the subject that matters to both of us very profoundly.

"Playing the game in the right spirit is very important to me. You don't cheat and you don't argue. You play hard but fairly, you learn to lose graciously and you don't go over the top when you win."

Rudyard Kipling would have approved of Eddie Howe, as the Dorset public approve of one of their own who's carving out a new career with conspicuous success – allied to refreshing modesty and dignity. Long may he continue to do so.

I began the chapter quoting widely conflicting opinions and images of Bournemouth. It is inevitable that I leave the town with no resolution of the issue. Beyond doubt, we all know that the character of the town has changed irreversibly. The genteel, rather 'posh' picture conjured up by images of old postcard scenes of the pleasure gardens, the grand department stores and trolley buses, decorously attired ladies sitting in their deckchairs and elderly gentlemen playing bowls – that is Bournemouth past. The town's post-war prosperity relied heavily upon its appeal as a respectable family holiday resort and clearly that remains of critical importance for the town's future well-being. But we all recognise that the competition from overseas destinations and the resort's competitors has never been more acute. In more recent times the local economy has broadened to embrace insurance and banking and allied industries. It is now also a university town though most students are here for just 8 months of the year and tend to spend their money in specific areas of the town's economy. The success of the language schools has added an invaluable dimension to the breadth of employment and spending within the town. The burgeoning of the 'club scene' and the 'night-time economy' with its emphasis upon alcohol consumption and recreational activities has brought certain employment benefits to the town but also serious social problems in its wake. As Ed Perkins observed earlier, a new identity will gradually evolve that reflects all aspects of contemporary Bournemouth. What is of vital importance is that its new identity is consciously shaped, insofar as it is possible, by the town's wisest, most far-sighted leaders. And, by that, I mean a genuine cross-section of the community. What has happened in the past 25 years is that, to a considerable degree, Bournemouth's essential character has been determined by the pressure of events over which its leadership has been able to exercise only limited control. Wider social changes in respect of the 'drinking culture' and sexual mores have been exploited by individuals less interested in the general well-being of the town than in the health of their own bank balances. The truth is that Bournemouth is blessed with a host of natural advantages. With people of the right calibre in the critical areas of local government, business and the leisure industry, working together as a team, the future of the town is assured and bright. But narrow party political differences must be submerged and personal animosities abandoned. To be frank, party politics in local government in any form is unwelcome, unhelpful and unproductive. Of course, there are natural alliances of like-minded individuals but every issue should be judged on its intrinsic merits, not on ideological grounds. This is a crucial period in the history of Bournemouth. There are some splendid imaginative ideas in circulation and, though we all know finance is going to be in scarce supply for the foreseeable future, every one of Bournemouth's competitors is in the same cash-strapped boat. The town's former Mayor, Anne Filer, described the town as 'exciting and stimulating'. In many ways Anne is correct but, unfortunately, those are not the adjectives used by the people who presently stay away from the town in the evening because they are alienated and repelled by the excesses of the 'club scene' and the over-reliance on alcohol fuelled activities. Bridport is a very small town compared to Bournemouth but its status as a cultural centre stands alongside its reputation as a 'fun place' to live in and to visit. Let the natural leaders of the local community look around and learn from elsewhere every lesson that is there to be learned. Wouldn't it be splendid if the author of the next book on the county were to praise Bournemouth not only for the splendour of its physical beauty, its family appeal and the variety of its attractions, but also its stature as a nationally recognised centre of cultural excellence? And if the Cherries were also playing in the Premiership – now that would be something to celebrate!

Poole
Twinned with Cherbourg (France)

I do not recall precisely the first time I saw Poole though it would have been shortly after my eighth birthday. In the years that followed I came to know the town well and it was a very different place to the Poole of today. Of course, there remain a number of recognisable features, from the lifting-bridge to the Custom's House and the pubs along the quay, the High Street itself and the level crossing, the old library building and the George Hotel, but the changes in the past half-century have been numerous and dramatic. Standing across the road from the George Hotel and the huge Barclay's offices, watching the continuous stream of traffic navigate the confusion of roundabouts, lights and lanes, the bustle of people hurrying about their daily business, I find myself asking the question – do I prefer the new Poole to the old? It's an academic question, I know, for we are where we are, for good and for ill, but it is an interesting exercise for what is absolutely certain is that, fifty years hence, the scene will have changed again and another generation will be asking itself exactly the same question.

First of all, it is important not to romanticise the old Poole through the cosy glow of nostalgia.

I recall clearly a conversation a few years ago with Freddie Rowe, in his day a well-known local builder, race-horse owner and a former Mayor of Poole. We spoke of Poole in the immediate post-war years and the slum dwellings that existed just behind the pubs and the buildings along the quay.

"In those days whole families were sharing privies at the end of their back-yards in many of the properties. Conditions were quite shocking. I am proud of Poole's slum-clearance programme in that period. There was real poverty and deprivation in parts of the town."

Though I never saw that physical squalor at first hand, Freddie Rowe's words are a salutary reminder that the old Poole had a distinctly unsavoury side and, if we have reservations about some of the housing developments in and around the town in the last few decades, including the towering blocks of flats, we must remember the undoubted improvement in living conditions they represent for many of Poole's less well-off families.

That the quay in general is a far less interesting place than it was 50 years ago seems to me indisputable. In my childhood there were vessels of many nationalities berthing on both sides of the water, countless weather-beaten seamen speaking in a dozen languages strolling up and down, or sitting smoking their pipes or hand-rolled cigarettes, fishing-boats unloading their cargoes of sprats and mackerel, gulls wheeling noisily overhead or diving down on to the decks to seize whatever opportunity provided. It was a permanent, fascinating kaleidoscope of colour, bustle and noise. Today, by contrast, there will be a few charter-boats offering harbour cruises, luxury yachts of varying sizes and values, a marina at the Baiter end, a timber ship or two discharging its cargo across the water – and Robert Braithwaite's Sunseeker empire. Of course, Sunseeker is something both extraordinary and mind-boggling. That there are individuals in the world able to buy such craft – and crew them on a permanent basis – is a reminder of what constitutes real wealth. Fifty years ago Russia was still in the iron grip of Stalin's heirs. Today Russian oligarchs compete with Arab sheikhs and Texan billionaires to acquire the latest Sunseeker model. They are featured in the James Bond movies and Sunseeker provides many hundreds of jobs for highly skilled craftsmen in the local economy. No doubt, to the average visitor to the town, a quayside stroll remains an interesting experience and, on a fine day, it's never less than a pleasant way of passing a few minutes. But, if I had to choose between the quayside I knew as a child and now, I would choose Poole as it was. It was a proper, working port full of people doing their jobs and earning a living. Now it is almost sanitised, admirably clean and well-run, it is true, but peopled by those who have nothing to do but relax and spend their money on ice-creams and cartons of chips and burgers. I am delighted for them, of course, that they have the leisure to do nothing more strenuous, but they're deadly dull to watch compared with what I remember.

Walking up through the town brings back recollections of Valentine's antiques/junk emporium full of old settees and armchairs with the stuffing bursting out, ancient grandfather-clocks and mysterious curios from all over the world; Setchfields the newsagents where I would buy my weekly copies of *Champion, Hotspur, Wizard and Adventure*; the Amity cinema where I saw *Rock Around The Clock* in the company of an army of Teddy-Boys in their long jackets with velvet lapels and stove pipe trousers; Looker's, the stationers, where I bought my mother a fountain-pen for her birthday with the five shillings I had saved from walking to school instead of spending my bus-fare. At every step there are memories. Where once small, independent shop-keepers sold everything under the sun, now branches of the ubiquitous chains, innumerable restaurants and take-aways, charity shops and banks proliferate. The splendid Joey Bright's bread and cake shop is long since gone but, thankfully, there is a branch of the excellent Bennett's - Tony, Margaret, David and Mark Bennett – of Britannia Road, Parkstone, which was founded by Claude Bennett in 1951 when the family moved east from Paignton.

As a bookworm the old library was one of my favourite haunts in those childhood days. At the time I knew nothing of its history. Now, of course, it's a successful pub and restaurant, the Lord Wimborne – though there seems to be some uncertainty about the spelling – with some fascinating local history displayed on its walls. Its name is well-chosen since it was the Wimborne family, to be precise the first to bear that title, the Rt. Hon Ivor Bertie Baron Wimborne (1835-1914), who gave the land to the town for the building of a Free Library. The occasion was the celebration of Queen Victoria's Golden Jubilee in 1887 and a copy of the invitation to the ceremony at the Guildhall is among the documents displayed. The driving force behind the creation of the Free Library was an admirable John J Norton and one of the conditions of its existence was that there should be a Reading Room for Women. There is a certain irony that the old Free Library should have been converted into a pub since Lord Wimborne himself was a life-long abstainer!

The second of Poole's cinemas of my youth *The Regent* has also long ago been demolished. There it was, in the company of my friends, that I saw all the great – and some of the not so great – films of the Fifties and Sixties. Afterwards we would hurry across the road to wait for the No 33 to return us to Upton crossroads. It amuses me today, when I hear of the complaints about Poole Bus Station, legitimate though many of the grumbles may be – an issue raised by Ian Andrews of the Society of Poole Men – for in those days there were no shelters of any kind. We simply stood in the wind and rain and snow and waited. There was a 20 minute gap between the buses so we often got soaked to the skin or frozen through. Now, whatever its shortcomings, people do at least wait under cover at the bus station. Indeed, there are shelters at most bus-stops – and still people complain.

And so up the road to Poole Stadium and another host of memories – of the speedway and Poole Pirates and Poole Town FC. Poole is remarkable in that it has for 60 years been the home to one of the most successful speedway teams in the UK. Though the composition of the team is constantly changing Poole Pirates have not merely survived all the vicissitudes of the sport, they have flourished quite spectacularly. When famous tracks like Wembley and Haringay have closed Poole has gone from strength to strength, regularly drawing gates of 3,000 and attracting the biggest names in world speedway to the Stadium. (See page 358) Alas, the same cannot be said of Poole Town FC. Once the club was one of the leading sides in the old Western League and, though inevitably outshone by its more glamorous neighbour, Bournemouth & Boscombe Athletic, in a lower league than Southern League Weymouth FC, Poole FC still enjoyed its share of the glory days. I even travelled back from London on one occasion to see them narrowly defeated by Watford in the FA Cup. From Bill 'Chopper' Hatchard to England international, Wilf Mannion and the legendary Welshman, John Charles, Poole FC paraded a galaxy of local characters and stars, and drew good crowds to the Stadium. Then came the unfortunate expulsion from the ground where it had played for as long as most people could remember, so necessitating a nomadic existence as a club which only now may be coming to an end.

Poole Pottery

Of course, if there was one institution that was synonymous with the town it was Poole Pottery. Though lots of local families chose, through financial necessity, to buy and use on a daily basis the cheaper mass-produced pottery sold by Woolworth's and local hardware stores, the town was proud of its famous pottery and its nation-wide reputation. Visitors liked to take pieces back home with them as souvenirs or gifts. It was distinctive pottery, quite different from that which most of us saw on our tables at meal-times – more colourful, exotic even in some its designs. Collectors bought the more expensive, individually crafted pieces, its reputation and presence were surely secure forever. The pottery was also a valuable source of local employment. The idea that one day it might face hard times and close would have been unthinkable to an earlier generation. But the unthinkable did happen. Picking up the *Echo* we read first of job losses, then the dreaded words 'in administration' and bankruptcy, succeeded by complex negotiations and the search for new owners, followed by a move out of the town to a new site. It was, we all knew, the sad end of an era. A year ago even the re-constituted Sopers Lane factory, together with the quayside shop, were closed down, a hundred employees dismissed and we were told the sum of £1 million was owed to 300 creditors. Then, out of the financial ruins, emerged new owners, the Lifestyle Group, who decided to reopen premises on the quayside and appoint a new general manager, Alison Morgan. Alas, the company announced that manufacturing would not, however, be returning to Poole but re-located instead to Burslem, Stoke-on-Trent, the traditional home of the English pottery industry. The Lifestyle managing director, Peter Bello, also made it clear that no long-term guarantees were possible. The one consolation would be that a small studio of one potter, two painters and a sprayer would be employed at Poole.

This morning I am sitting in Alison Morgan's upstair's office on New Quay Road discussing the present situation of the pottery.

"I do remember my grandmother owning a Poole Pottery dolphin and my parents using a Poole dining-service when I was a child. This area was also a holiday haunt for us, so it's rather fitting I should find myself here so many years later. After all the problems of recent times I can confirm we are still in business, contrary to the perception that the pottery has closed. As you will have seen, the ground floor houses the pottery and china, including Royal Stafford ware which the company produces, and on this floor is our clothing range. You may have noticed the rather fine showcase display of examples of Poole pottery reflecting its entire history which our customers, especially collectors, find particularly interesting."

If the staff numbers today are down to single figures, one at least is a face familiar to an earlier generation. Master-potter and designer, Alan White, who joined the company at the age of 16, has worked at Poole for more than 40 years.

"I love making pots. I never tire of it. It helps to relax my mind. You must never take too long over a job. The longer it takes, the worse it's going to be."

Jane Brewer, who also sells watercolours and woodcarvings, is one of the two painters along with Nicki Massarella. She can paint a production line plate in just 2 minutes but loves the opportunity to paint more intricate one-off designs for a more select market.

In Sarah Morgan the Lifestyle/Poole Pottery shop certainly possesses an engaging and enthusiastic manager. What happened to the company we all grew up with is very sad, but it's a fact of economic life that every business has to be competitive to survive.It is to be hoped that, even in its much reduced form, Poole Pottery will still be in existence for many years yet and not merely a memory of a bygone age.

Tourism

"I grew up near the Pottery roundabout and as a boy I loved to scamper down to the beach at Branksome."

Fifteen years away from the locality working in the leisure industry, Graham Richardson returned to his native area to become the Head of Tourism for Poole, a post he has occupied for the past decade.

"While I was away Poole changed dramatically. The Power Station disappeared, Baiter and Whitecliff were extended, Tower Park was built and the Holes Bay dual-carriage-way was constructed. In the last few years the quay has been totally transformed."

How does Graham see the present employment scene?

"Today I suppose the public sector must be the biggest single employer. The hospital employs 2,000 or so, the Council 4,000 plus when you count the schools and Government offices. Second

The Society of Poole Men with (Poole's) Mayor, Joyce Lavender, at St James, Poole. *Picture: Ian Andrews*

would be banking and insurance with Barclay's, Liverpool & Victoria, the Bank of New York, Amex, Castle Cover and many others. Third would be manufacturing, mostly marine engineering, with fourth the tourism industry. I would guess there are 5,000 employed in that sector, hotels, restaurants, attractions and so on. Once Poole was regarded as 'cheap and cheerful' with no pretensions to being a serious holiday resort compared with Bournemouth. But today the town boasts a number of quality hotels catering for all kinds of tourism – short breaks, week-end breaks besides the usual extended holidays. We have half a million visitors a year with 2 million 'bed-nights'. Rockley Sands at Hamworthy is also a highly successful enterprise."

Does Graham feel the town is promoting itself as successfully as it might?

"We have the Poole Tourism Partnership which is financed by the Town Council. Businesses pay for advertising and they are then represented in the Poole Town Guide. We try to ensure that quality is guaranteed for those who come here by monitoring those who advertise."

How does Graham see the immediate and long-term future of tourism in the area?

"We have just endured two poor summers in terms of the weather, so we are surely due a few good ones to compensate! Besides which, with the exchange rate against the dollar and the euro, increased flight fares, we must be optimistic. There is, after all, so much to see and do in this area. Our main focus in Poole is on the quay, the harbour and Sandbanks. It is true that we must try to ensure that there are sufficient bad weather attractions. Of course, what most people do is to jump in the car and go off to Monkey World, the Tank Museum and similar places if the weather is unsuitable for the beach. We are fortunate in having such popular attractions not far away. We also benefit from special events like the Biker's Night on the quay on Tuesday evenings through the summer for 26 weeks, when we'll have a couple of thousand arrive on their machines. It is a very special affair, the behaviour is always exemplary and it's extremely well policed and controlled by the organisers. And then on Friday nights we have the older cars coming in which is a real family affair."

Graham spoke earlier of Poole's big, rather more glamorous neighbour, Bournemouth. Does he see the two towns being in competition, or do they complement one another?

"I think the latter would be nearer the mark. After all, we do between us share 10 miles of the best beaches in the UK. We both have our particular strengths. Success in either town has benefits for us both. I believe we should co-operate wherever it is possible, as in the area of transport, for example. At the same time, we should retain our separate identities. At the end of the day, both towns want their visitors to return home after their holidays here having thoroughly enjoyed themselves and wishing to return another day."

Panorama Road, Sandbanks – Sunday, 4 October 2009

"I've got two lovely sons, Jamie and Mark, two lovely daughters-in-law, Louise and Lucy, seven gorgeous grand-children – and a wonderful husband. I feel very privileged."

We're sitting this tranquil Sandbanks morning in the lounge of Sandra and Harry Redknapp's splendid house looking across Poole bay towards Studland. A variety of small craft drift leisurely past. Away in the distance the Purbeck hills are shrouded in the mist of early autumn. It's all a far cry from the East End of London where two 17 year-olds, both the children of dockers, first met at a dance at Stratford, fell in love and were duly married.

"We've been together for 44 years and married for 41 years."

It's easy to understand why Harry fell for the young hairdresser from Barking. Sandra's still a striking-looking lady and enviably slim.

"I enjoy reading and painting, I practise my yoga, I like to cook – especially when the family come round. I can't say Harry's what they call a 'new' man. If I wasn't here, he'd probably live on toast – though he can boil a decent egg. But I like it that way. I'm happy with what I'm doing."

Two years ago, however, great sadness engulfed the Redknapp family when Sandra's sister, Pat, died following complications after pneumonia.

"We were like twin sisters and it all came as a terrible shock."

Pat, of course, was England international star Frank Lampard's mother and married to Frank Lampard senior, a West Ham contemporary of Harry Redknapp. And what of the man himself, Sandra's partner for the last 44 years?

"I am very protective of Harry. I am also very proud of him and how he handles being a public person. He's so good with people. He can relate to them, especially some of the less fortunate. He always finds time and the right words."

And somehow, this first Sunday in October, 2009, with the book off to the printer in a few days, Harry's found time for me. He did phone me a few weeks earlier when he was on his way to the airport bound for China on a pre-season tour with Tottenham. I told him then I couldn't run fast

Harry Redknapp is interviewed at Dean Court.

Picture: Michael Cunningham

enough to catch him before he boarded the plane, but we've fitted our meeting in at the very last moment. He's the last piece of the jigsaw.

It's an extraordinary journey Harry's travelled – from Poplar to Sandbanks, from the obscurity of a humble working-class childhood in the East End to national, even international fame, as arguably England's most popular living football manager. A distinguished playing career alongside legends like Sir Bobby Moore, Sir Geoff Hurst and Martin Peters, followed by an even more successful managerial career with Bournemouth, West Ham, Portsmouth and now Tottenham Hotspurs. Promotion with Bournemouth and their highest standing in the club's history, FA Cup glory with Pompey, many memorable moments with the Hammers, Spurs hauled back from the brink last season, it's an enviable record. I ask him how he compares the game he knew as a young man with the game today.

"Don't romanticise the old days. They were hard, believe me. There were players who would kick you off the park. Tackling from behind was still legal."

Harry was, of course, an old-fashioned dribbling, bag of tricks winger. He often experienced the physical brutality meted out by certain defenders.

"Nowadays with TV and the new rules players can't get away with what they used to do. It's a much better game in that respect. On the other hand, I do regret the domination of the League by a small group of clubs though this season it does look more open than for some years."

How important is it for a team to play entertaining football?

"Of course, you like to entertain but, at the end of the day, supporters really care about only one thing – results. A manager lives or dies by results. It's the reality of football."

At intervals our conversation is punctuated by the antics of Harry's much loved British bulldog, Buster.

"He's 7 seven years-old and an old softie but he still hasn't really grown up."

And what if Harry's players misbehave themselves?

"I've got no time for it. They're very highly-paid. They have responsibilities. They must take care of themselves. Yes, I am a disciplinarian. I always treat players as adults but if they try to take liberties they know what to expect."

Is there room for hobbies in his life? Outside interests?

"As you know, I enjoy my round of golf – Jamie's inherited my love of the game. He plays in a lot of celebrity tournaments. Horse-racing, of course. I've got a couple in training, one with Brian

Smart, another with Walter Swinburn – 'Arry's 'Orse and Tuppeny Piece. But there's little time for anything else."

How does he sleep?

"Badly. The night after a game I sleep hardly at all. My mind's buzzing. There are always things going on in my head. But that's football. It's really all consuming. It's been my life. I owe everything to football – and my family."

The lounge is full of mementoes of both. Photos of ex-footballer son, Jamie, and his pop-star wife Louise with their son, little Charlie; Mark and his family; football books including one titled *The history of Tottenham Hotspurs from 1907*. What glories will be entered in the next edition marked 2008 onwards, I wonder? The lad from Poplar has already achieved so much, most recently in the company of his great friend, Kevin Bond, 'a lovely guy and someone I've known since he was a little boy.' A Premiership title, a European trophy?

"They're always possibles - but not probables. It's so competitive, you have to be realistic."

Retirement? After all, he's 62.

"Sometimes I say to Sandra, I think I'd be content just to slip away from it all -somewhere quiet down in Devon or Cornwall perhaps? I know how fortunate I am. Sandra's been the most brilliant wife. She's given me a wonderful family. I'm always so happy to get back home and spend time in her company."

And this morning I'm keeping Harry from his well-earned round of golf and, no doubt, Sandra's got plenty to do around the house. I can tell he's itching to be away on the ferry over to Studland to join his pals. It's been a long time coming and there are a thousand other questions I'd like to ask – but it's time to take my leave. Many thanks, Harry and Sandra. It's been a real pleasure.

Sandbanks

Thirty years ago I wrote a book called *The Extraordinary Mrs.D* (The Dorset Publishing Co.). My subject was Mrs.Louisa Eileen Dingwall, born 6 June, 1893, in Exeter of Irish parentage, better known to the world as Louie Dingwall, racehorse trainer extraordinary and certainly one of the most remarkable characters to have lived in the locality. This is not the place to retell her story, fascinating though it is. Suffice to say that, after various adventures, Louie arrived in Sandbanks in the early 1920s and lived in Panorama Road until her death 60 years later. In the mid-1970s as a history teacher at the Purbeck School, I had a horse-mad pupil named Wendy Corbin (later Towers). At that time, as a part of their CSE course, pupils had to submit a piece of original research on a subject of their own choosing. I suggested to Wendy that we make contact with Mrs.Dingwall to see if it would be possible for her to base her coursework on horses and racing and the lady's life. So began my friendship with the old lady and an invitation to write her biography, Wendy duly produced an admirable piece of research and even got to ride a race-horse or two. I tell this story merely to illustrate the fact that I got to know Sandbanks very well during that period, often standing on the beach – almost invariably when it was bitterly cold – as Mrs.D was exercising her horses, or boxing them up to take them on the ferry over to Studland for a 'breeze-up'. I reproduce just a few lines from my book as a preamble to the events of the past ten years or so.

'*Geologically recent, Sandbanks is in fact a bulb-ended peninsula a mile in length, connected to Canford Cliffs by an isthmus 60 yards wide, along which there runs today the motor road to the ferry and Swanage. At the tip of the Sandbanks peninsula is the mouth of Poole harbour, a mere 100 yards of sea from South Haven point, which is geographically part of the Isle of Purbeck. To the casual observer it might come as a great surprise to learn that below the sand which gives this area its name is clay. It is this solid foundation which has enabled builders to construct vast blocks of flats and hotels on it in recent years. On the seaward side there is a wide, flat belt of sand which affords the most splendid*

Louie Dingwall and friends. *Pictures: Keystone Press*

bathing, and on the opposite side is the vast expanse of Poole harbour. With its ten thousand acres of water and islands, Poole is the second largest natural harbour in the world, only Sydney harbour being more extensive.'

Those are the simple geographic and geological facts relating to Sandbanks. Before the Great War it was rumoured that the whole of Sandbanks was offered for sale for just £1,000. When Louie Dingwall arrived and fell in love with its largely unspoilt beauty, there were few dwellings on the peninsula, mainly an assorted collection of huts, corrugated iron shacks and old railway carriages. Her first habitation was indeed one of those old wooden huts measuring just 10 feet by 16 feet. What an extraordinary transformation has occurred in a little under 100 years when properties along Panorama Road are now selling for many millions of pounds.

Of course there were famous faces in Sandbanks before the more recent 'gold rush' began. The radio pioneer, Guglielmo Marconi, anchored his yacht the Electra in the harbour and took up residence for a time at the Haven Hotel, the band-leader, Billy Cotton, owned a house here, as did Max Bygraves and Mantovani. But it has really been in the last ten years or so that Sandbanks has been likened to Monte Carlo and its land prices set alongside those of Hong Kong, Tokyo and Belgravia as the most expensive in the world. I understand the price comparisons began in 2001 when the estate agent, Tom Doyle, sold a 1,200 square foot flat on the peninsula for £1million. His calculations made Sandbanks the fourth most expensive location in the world. Ever since there has been a queue of potential buyers and prices have continued their upward spiral. With most of the unpretentious and architecturally inconsequential Thirties properties being demolished as soon as they are purchased, grandiose new individually designed villas now occupy the waterfront.

When Piers Morgan and a team of TV cameramen descended on Sandbanks it was clear the presenter's agenda was to paint the locality in the most garish colours with a hedonistic life-style to boot. A newspaper featured an article headed 'Sandbanks, My Kind of Place – Brash, flash and vulgar beyond belief. Piers Morgan loves Sandbanks, Britain's costliest neighbourhood. But don't worry, it'll soon be under water...'

Featuring interviews with Tom Doyle, Tottenham Hotspurs manager Harry Redknapp, Ian

Poole lifeboat crew – the unsung heroes. *Picture: Sally Adams, Bournemouth Echo*

Davies, described as 'Britain's richest football hooligan, who now runs the local wine bar', club-owner Richard Carr and businessman/property developer, Eddie Mitchell, 'self-made millionaire Paul Mayden, who raked in £32 million in just nine months, owns 9 cars and could live anywhere but chose Sandbanks,' and references to Lamborghinis and Bentleys and Carr's yacht 'Agent provocateur', Piers Morgan painted a picture a number of locals simply did not recognise.

In estate agent's Tailormade, I'm chatting with Gill Emeny who grew up at nearby Lilliput, first entered her profession 30 years ago and has run the business in Sandbanks since 2001.

"I remember our first sale very clearly. Eddie Mitchell had built 9 'thin town-houses' priced at £275,000 each and we couldn't sell them at first. Today they're worth £2million."

Gill, who became the first lady chairman of the local branch of the Association of Estate Agents, contradicts the image portrayed to the world at large by Piers Morgan.

"Actually, for most of the year, Sandbanks is more of a quiet little village with lots of very pleasant, unassuming people. There's no brashness, flashiness, no airs and graces. People are very natural and very friendly. Yes, many will be very well-off financially and some of them will be at the top of their particular trees, but I see no evidence to support the picture painted by Piers Morgan."

It's a view reinforced by two of her team, Hilary Coleman and Anne-Marie Hall. Likewise her son, Robert, confirms his mother's assertion.

"Of course, there will be the odd individual but, in general, people who come to live in Sandbanks do not flaunt their wealth but rather to enjoy the beauty of the locality."

Gill adds this postscript.

"When I came here I thought I would be content to potter along, sell a few properties and wind down after so many years in the business. I never for a moment envisaged what was going to happen. As it is, we do try to maintain integrity in all our dealings – to work with Christian principles, no funny business, no cheating. no back-handers. That's not our style."

To prove that money cannot buy everything in life there are several long-time residents who obstinately refuse to be tempted by offers of fortunes from agents and developers for their properties. One property valued at £5 million belongs to Lalage Bailey.

Lalage and her late husband Frank, the son of Oswald Bailey who ran the chain of highly successful camping accessory shops, bought their property from Frank's father for £8,000 in 1949.

"No amount of money will change my mind about selling – I am staying here. On a nice day the views across to Brownsea are wonderful. Why should I move at my time of life?"

An identical opinion is voiced by an 86 year-old former RAF veteran by the name of Jack Holsgrove who bought his house in1972 for £60,000 and has absolutely no intention of budging.

"What would I do with millions of pounds at the age of 86? The agents can offer what they like but I am not moving. My family love coming down here to stay. I have a son, Stephen, who lives in Wimbledon and three granddaughters, Rachel, Rebekah and Alice. They'd kill me if I sold up!"

David Croft who, with Jimmy Perry, wrote this writer's favourite comedy series of all time 'Dad's Army', was actually born in Sandbanks 85 years ago and grew up in a house called Sharcroft, was not impressed by what he saw of Piers Morgan's Sandbanks. 'Awful people and ghastly houses too.'

As for Piers Morgan's observation that Sandbanks would 'soon be under water', this pessimistic forecast was based on the prediction by Dr. Edward Coombe, a consultant in coastal geomorphology, that rising sea-levels caused by global warming would be likely in 50 years or so to submerge many low-lying areas such as Sandbanks. This grim forecast is, however, what may be fashionably termed 'a worst-case scenario'. Besides, I do remember very vividly as a small boy, seeing men wandering up and down High Streets in London and elsewhere, bearing sandwich-boards with slogans such as 'The End Is Nigh' and several Jehovah's Witnesses predicting Armageddon in 1984. Well, they are now most of them certainly long since dead and gone and I am still here, so I do tend to be sceptical about the doom-mongers of our modern world – not least the 'climate change experts'.

When Louie Dingwall arrived in the 1920s and took up residence in a small wooden hut, whatever would she have made of these figures quoted by Juliette Astrup in the Echo in 2008?

'Panorama Road (where Mrs. D lived and housed her horses in some ancient and very ramshackle stables behind her garage) is the fifth most expensive street in the UK with an average property price of £4.15 million. Pearce Avenue, off Sandbanks Road, is at number 35 with an average of £2.6 million. Thirteen of the most expensive streets in the SW region of the UK are in Poole. They are all in the BH13 and BH14 postcode localities of Sandbanks, Canford Cliffs, Lilliput and Lower Parkstone.'

Let's leave Sandbanks and journey up Ashley Road, Parkstone, to meet a man engaged in an industry long associated with Poole – hundreds of years before tourism, insurance and banking played any role in the local economy.

The Fishing Industry

'If you are a Fisheries Minister you sit around the table arguing about fishermen – not about fish. You're there to represent your fishermen. You're there to ensure that if there are 10 fish you get your share and,

if possible, a bit more. The arguments aren't about conservation unless, of course, you are arguing about another country'.

John Gummer, one-time Fisheries Minister and Conservative politician.

Ian Carrier may not be the Fisheries Minister but his is no small responsibility. For 18 years Ian was in Fisheries protection, now from his small, unpretentious offices in Ashley Road, Parkstone, Ian and his deputy Neil Richardson administer 340 miles of coastline from Beer Head on the Devon border to Hayling Island in the Solent and 1,000 square miles of coastal waters.

"Within the county of Dorset, Simon Pengelly looks after the area from the Devon border to Lulworth, David Mayne is responsible for Lulworth to Mudeford and Rob Ayling operates east of Mudeford."

What exactly are the responsibilities of the fishing officers?

"We have to ensure fishing vessels are licensed and registered – that is obligatory if they are to operate commercially. Since Magna Carta in 1215 it is possible for anyone to take fish from the foreshore for their own use. However, if you wish to sell your catch, the vessel must be registered and licensed. My 5 officers will be engaged in patrolling, often acting on intelligence tip-offs. Each has his own van since a lot of travel between places is necessary. We also use 3 boats to assist our enquiries. When you reflect that we manage on a budget which includes salaries, running an office here with our office manager Debbie Vivian, and travel expenses – of around £400,000 per annum, I don't think anyone would consider us expensive!"

In general terms, what is a sea fisheries area?

"There a dozen of them around England and Wales. They were created in 1890 to manage fisheries."

What are the general rules around our coast?

"There's a 6 mile limit off the coast. Only UK vessels are allowed to fish within that area. Between 6 and 12 miles only the French besides ourselves because they have what are termed 'historic rights'. Outside the 12 mile limit any EU vessel may fish."

Just how important is fishing to the Dorset economy today?

"There are about 250 fishing boats operating. That's a reduction of 40% in the past 20 years. There are about 1,000 employed in the industry full-time. That would include skippers and their crews engaged in commercial fishing. There are probably another 5,000 involved in charter fishing, taking out anglers and so on, mackerel fishing and the like. Of course, some of that is seasonal but it is very important for the general economy. The anglers will often come down, stay in local hotels and b&bs, eat in the restaurants and pubs."

I understand, from my earlier conversation with Ken Lynham at Portland, that Monday nights at Poole ferry terminal presents a remarkable sight.

"Indeed it does. You must understand that 80% of the fish landed in the county is shellfish – crabs and lobsters together with oysters, cockles, mussels and clams – plus a few sea bass and other fin fish. The greatest demand for the shellfish comes from Southern Europe. And, yes, on a Monday there may be up to 80 Vivier lorries taking tanks of fish not only from Dorset, but as far north as Aberdeen and the Shetlands, down to Barcelona and other cities in Spain and Italy."

Recalling my time in Lyme Regis at the beginning of the year, has the scallops problem been resolved?

"Since July no dredging for shellfish or demersal fish is permitted. There was a voluntary agreement in place for several years that worked well. Unfortunately, as fuel costs rose, dredging the seabed became common practice and there was undoubted damage to the bio-diversity of the marine environment. John Worswick does dive out of West Bay for scallops and Darren Brown from

Broadmayne does the same out of Lulworth. They can be selective. The question that arises though is – will selectivity result in the biggest scallops being taken?"

What are the major problems facing the industry?

"In general, I'm afraid there are simply too many vessels chasing too few fish. DEFRA, the Department for the Environment, Food and Rural Affairs, is under pressure to reduce our fishing capacity to protect stocks. But, to be honest, we know more about the dark side of the moon than we do about actual fishing stocks. How can we possibly manage a resource in those circumstances? We need a thorough scientific survey. Peter Tinsley has been mapping the sea bed but it all costs money and we need more high-quality funded research."

We hear much of fish being thrown overboard dead because quotas have been exceeded.

"It is pure madness! Each country has a TAC, a Total Allowable Catch. One third of what is caught is commonly thrown away. To give you a couple of examples, someone may be fishing for whiting or haddock, but any cod must be discarded if the quota is overstepped. One fisherman said recently 'Could I donate 30 boxes of fish for charity – to Red Nose day?' The answer came back 'No.' It's not a conservation policy but I acknowledge there is no easy answer. Perhaps it would be possible to adjust the minimum size of the nets allowing the smaller fish to escape. Hundreds of minds have applied themselves to the problem without being able to come up with a satisfactory answer. At the moment we've got 27 countries arguing about it."

One fond memory of my childhood days was standing on the quayside at Poole watching the sprat boats coming in, buying sixpence worth wrapped up in newspaper and carrying them home for my mother to cook them for my tea with a plate of bread and butter.

"There are no longer the numbers of sprats about, I fear. And eating habits change. How many housewives would cook them today? It's more likely to be a convenience meal from the freezer, isn't it?"

Sadly Ian is absolutely right. And one last question – if he could be the Fisheries Minister for a day and allowed to pass one new law – what would it be?

"Very simply – that the 6 miles and 12 miles derogations be made permanent, or as near permanent as the politicians will concede, 60 years perhaps. No politicians like the word 'permanent' because conditions can always change. As it is, under Common Fisheries policy the sea is regarded as a common resource. Were we to lose our right to the 6 mile limit it would mean that any member nation of the EU could fish right up to our beaches. A new arrangement is due to come into place as from 1 January, 2012. I believe nation states must retain the right to fish their own waters. Even between 6 and 12 miles where France enjoys historic rights, we lack the power to do anything about French vessels. Negotiations in the next couple of years are, therefore, absolutely crucial. I really am profoundly uneasy about the outcome as I believe everyone else in the country will be when they realise the dangers."

The Harbourmaster's Office, West Quay Road

"I'd just qualified as a Class 2 pilot and it was my first assignment. It was 2 am, pitch black, blowing a gale, the rain was lashing down and I had to bring a Russian vessel into the harbour. I scrambled on board only to discover that the skipper couldn't speak a word of English, nor could any of the crew. It was disconcerting, to say the least. Happily the Russians usually let the pilot get on with it and, in fact, everything went smoothly. Afterwards, when I was describing the incident to a fellow pilot he just laughed and said, 'That was an easy one.'"

Poole's new Harbourmaster, Brian Murphy, is following in the considerable footsteps of Peter Booth who held the position for more than a decade.

"I worked alongside Peter for several years and I would describe him as the most meticulous of men. He's quite an act to follow."

Glaswegian Brian – he's a Celtic supporter – arrived in Poole following a distinguished career in the merchant navy where he served as a captain on container vessels. After a spell with Condor ferries and managing Poole's team of pilots he took over the 'hot seat' just weeks ago. The position of Harbourmaster at Poole must rank as one of the most coveted in the profession.

"Clearly it's not as big as Southampton or Liverpool but, in terms of location, that's certainly true. We haven't got any smelly oil tankers or terminals."

On the other hand, it also carries with it considerable responsibilities with Poole being the second largest natural harbour in the world after Sydney.

"Fortunately I have an outstanding team working with me. We have a staff of 26 and many of them are multi-tasking to attend to the variety of jobs we have to perform. Besides the administrative side, we have 1,200 piloted vessels entering the port every year and a further 4,000 movements of other craft which means there's always plenty to think about. One consideration is absolutely paramount – safety. With so much daily movement, especially in the summer months with the recreational activities, it's imperative that everyone obeys the rules. We do have clearly defined zones for yacht racing, water and jet skiing, kite and wind surfing and so on.I am most concerned with the 'pinch-points' where the likelihood of collisions and accidents are most likely to occur. If individuals do offend they will be prosecuted. It's simply not an area where one can tolerate rule-breaking. People's lives are at risk."

How is the harbour actually administered?

"We are a Trust port with a Board of Commissioners drawn from various walks of life – people with expertise. We derive our income from our commercial and passenger trade, moorings and so on. Though we do make a profit there is currently Government pressure to increase that profit. Whatever surplus we have is ploughed back into improved harbour facilities. I have actually been obliged to make a number of difficult decisions to reduce costs and maximise earnings. For instance, we were losing money on moorings fees and we have had to raise our charges."

Poole is of enormous importance as a wildlife area. To what extent is Brian involved in that sphere?

"Clearly with Brownsea Island, Arne, the mud-flats and the great diversity of wildlife in the harbour it is a subject constantly in our thoughts. We do employ a full-time specialist conservation adviser in Sally Porter who liaises with the other organisations such as the National Trust and the RSPB. And speaking of mud we also have a full-time hydro-graphic surveyor checking on the various problem areas within the harbour. We try to maintain a balance between the sand silt brought in by the tides and what is washed down in to the harbour by the rivers. Dredging to keep the channels open is obviously critical. What is dredged up is taken out of the harbour and dumped in the appropriate location off Swanage."

Another recent appointment of significance, alongside that of Brian, is that of Andy Ramsbottom as the new harbour engineer replacing Dick Appleton who retired after 36 years service in the position.

While it's been a fascinating discussion with Brian, I must confess to one major disappointment – the location of his office.Recalling other harbourmasters' offices along the coast with their picturesque views of the sea and passing craft, it comes as a sad disappointment that Brian looks out on nothing more appealing than an expanse of tarmac and the functionally drab buildings of the ferry terminal.

I've missed the centenary by a year for it was on August 1, 1907, that Major General Robert Baden-

Robert Stephenson Smyth Baden-Powell (1857-1941) –
English soldier and founder of the Boy Scouts.
Picture: David Baker.

Powell staged the first scout camp on Brownsea Island along with 20 local boys from a variety of social backgrounds and schools. The celebrations of that historic event took place last year. I suspect that, though it's a very different world, the hero of the Siege of Mafeking, would approve the choice of the new Chief Scout, Bear Grylls, a former SAS soldier and the son of the late Sir Michael Grylls and his wife Sally, who lived at Winterborne Zelston. Certainly Dorset Scouts county commissioner, Mike Parkes, is enthusiastic about the appointment.

"I believe Bear has exactly the right image for the modern scouting movement."

By way of contrast to last year's visitors to Brownsea, the island welcomes in 2008 Bill Oddie and Kate Humble for BBC's Autumn-watch live transmission. Bill Oddie describes Brownsea as 'one of my favourite places' which he first visited in 1957 and has returned to no fewer than 15 times. It's certainly an idyllic location with an intriguing history but that has been recorded by others and I have no intention of duplicating their work. As a bird-watcher since my childhood the island never ceases to fascinate with its population of 1,000 plus avocets and the UK's largest flock of spoonbills. With 200 of its 550 acres a nature reserve managed by the DWT, there is a wealth of wildlife to observe. Last year, after a number of barren visits, I even caught my first fleeting glimpse of a red squirrel. Thanks to a valiant team of 'rhododendron-bashers' from Barclays International, organised by David Bond, who often laboured through very wet and cold weather in recent years, a large area has now been cleared. As a result of the clearance and the consequent increased food supply of insects, Amanda Cooke of the DWT reports that 11 species of bat have now been identified on the island.

I am now confronted by a dilemma. The wonderful BSO has spent the greater part of its distinguished life in Bournemouth. However, with the sad demise of the Winter Gardens it now rehearses and performs in Poole. Am I now going to offend the good citizens of Bournemouth by including my piece on the BSO in my chapter on Poole? I fear I must but I would crave an understanding by the Bournemouth public of the delicacy of my position.

The Bournemouth Symphony Orchestra at the Lighthouse

"There are only seven comparable orchestras in the UK – the Halle in Manchester, the Birmingham Symphony, the London Philharmonic, the London Symphony, the Philharmonia, the Royal Philharmonic – and us!"

Anthony Brown laughs. "We shouldn't really exist! Obviously it's a long, complicated and fascinating story that began with the vision of Dan Godfrey."

Sir Dan Godfrey was a remarkable man who moved to Bournemouth in 1893 from London, originally to conduct the band music at the old Winter Gardens. He founded the Bournemouth Municipal Orchestra in 1894, then the BSO, attracting composers like Holst and Parry to conduct their work in the town. Sir Dan died on the eve of WW2 having established a legacy of musical excellence that still remains. His achievement was astonishing.

"The BSO was the first permanent symphony orchestra in the country. He helped to put the town on the map."

Anthony was for 15 years a professional violinist and tenor and now organises the day-to-day administration and marketing of the BSO along with a new chief executive Simon Taylor.

"Any orchestra of this size is always in a fragile financial state. Our annual turnover is of the order of £6 million. We do rely heavily on donations and membership. I am extremely proud of our very loyal and appreciative audiences and our 1,800 signed up membership. We also receive grants totalling £500,000 a year from the local councils and a grant of £2.3 million from the Arts Council. That means we need to take £3 million at the Box Office. We have 71 full-time musicians, 23 admin staff and a pool of free-lance musicians. From October to May it's a 40 hour week – about 25 hours of playing in concert and rehearsal, with15 hours of travel. We give 24 concerts in Poole, 6 in the Pavilion, 12 in Exeter and Portsmouth. We also play in Southampton, Bristol and Plymouth together with 8 outdoor concerts in the summer months. All in all, it adds up to about 120 concerts a year so you can see it's quite a workload of playing and travelling. Mainly we rehearse on Mondays and Tuesdays and when we travel we use a lorry and a coach. Of course, the orchestra also splits up into smaller units when we teach in local schools, play in old people's homes and so on. We also run a Rusty Musicians course which culminates in a public performance. In addition, we'll record 6 or more CDs every year with Naxos."

Anthony bubbles with enthusiasm for his work.

"I love to see people enjoying themselves. Coming to a concert can be a life-changing experience for people. Last night was a case in point – Shostakovich's Symphony No11, The Year is 1905. The orchestra was inspired. Our new conductor was brilliant!"

The new conductor is the young Ukrainian, Kirill Karabits.

"We're all excited by his appointment. He is replacing the splendid Marin Alsop who has been here since 2001. Kirill is virtually unknown in the UK although he has established a reputation in Europe. Everyone in the management team has to be happy when we make such an appointment. It takes 2-3 years to prepare for a new conductor and it's vital that we have a happy orchestra. Kirill is just 31 and quite a charismatic individual. He will be making several appearances in 2008-9 before taking up the position full-time in readiness for the 2009-2010 season of concerts."

Anthony most kindly promises to arrange for me to sit in at a rehearsal with Kirill in a few days time.

I seek out the review of the Shostakovich concert by Mike Marsh in the *Echo*. The superlatives are out in force – *'The sense of foreboding sent out icy tentacles among a rapt audience'*, *'Karabits kept a tense dynamic'*, *'He had the tension flowing'*, and *'The finale's incredible string march raised the flag of freedom sent waving in a heady blast of percussive jubilation.'* Mike Marsh's final words summed up his overall response. *'Welcome, Kirill, you've made my day.'*

Back at The Lighthouse, a Tuesday morning in mid-winter

Anthony confirms that Kirill is happy for me to sit in and observe. I quietly open the door and find myself a seat behind the orchestra. Other than the musicians and the conductor I am the only individual in the hall. Beneath me Kirill Karabits is seated on a stool, baton in hand, studying the score before him. He's a slim figure, dressed all in black, short greying hair fashionably cut, a slight beard, softly spoken.

"Thank you very much. May we try that again, please? Eight bars before…"

I fail to catch precisely 'before' what but the musicians rustle their sheets and prepare to play. I feel very privileged to be the only individual here. It's a little like looking over the shoulder of a celebrated painter as he moves his brush over the canvas. I am intrigued to see a conductor at work, not least with an orchestra still new to him as they are to him.

"Let's now do 185, please."

Once again there's a rustling of sheets as the musicians rearrange the scores on their stands.

The pattern is of two or three minutes of playing punctuated by pauses and conversations with soloists. Every exchange is courteous in the extreme with the occasional word of reassurance and a smile. The piece is Berlioz's *Symphonie Fantastique*, not a work with which I am especially familiar which, no doubt, reflects badly upon me but then there is so much music to listen to and there are only so many hours in the day. Now the musicians are standing up and stretching their arms and legs. The rehearsal is finished until after lunch.

Downstairs I meet Ian Bignall. Ian's been for the past 4 years the Orchestra Manager, I discover, but he's just taken a new appointment in London. He's having his leaving party at the Hall & Woodhouse Brewery in Blandford. 'Come dressed as a WAG or a Gent' is the instruction on the Orchestra's notice-board. 'Until closing.'

"The problem is we're rehearsing Tchaikovsky's Symphony Number 4 in the morning. Have I done the right thing?"

Ian laughs. "I suppose I'm 'the friendly face of management', someone any BSO member feels they can talk to, put their head on my shoulder, if necessary."

The former violinist enjoys enormously his role.

"Getting everyone together at the right place at the right time, putting on a good performance, seeing lots of happy faces afterwards. It's very satisfying. There are occasional problems. Someone goes sick. The other day our bass trombonist fell sick. I found a replacement – in Edinburgh! I got him on a plane for the concert, only to receive a text that he'd left his trombone behind in Edinburgh!"

Is there any chance of meeting Kirril, I ask?

"He may be having a quick sleep. I know he's been feeling tired."

But no sooner are the words from Ian's lips than the man himself arrives.

"Is there a piano I could possibly use, please?"

In fact, there's one right beside us, a Steinway beneath a cloth which Ian quickly removes.

"Thank you so much. I need to familiarise myself. I have not conducted the Violin Concerto for some months."

The Bournemouth Symphony Orchestra with its new principal conductor, Kirill Karabits. *Picture: Chris Zuidyk*

In a little over an hour the orchestra is rehearsing *Tchaikovsky's Violin Concerto* with the guest soloist, Ilya Gringolts.

For ten minutes his fingers play lightly across the keys, just a few bars of melody here, then other passages and critical musical junctures in the piece demanding particular attention. He clearly carries the whole piece in his head, every note, the rhythms, every nuance where he might influence the orchestra in his interpretation. He stands with a smile. He's quietly satisfied he's ready for the afternoon. He has a few minutes to spare.

"You know the musicians here in England are so quick to understand everything. I am so pleased to be here."

At close range his eyes are quite startlingly blue. Alert, inquisitive, friendly, I understand why Anthony enthused. The young man has presence. Confident but no hint of conceit or arrogance, as eager to learn as to impart, I also understand why the orchestra approves. Born a dozen years before the collapse of the old Soviet empire, he grew up in Kiev and has been conducting for 25 years – since the age of 6!

"It is what I always wanted to do. Most recently I was in France. This will be my first principal conducting position. Before I was a guest conductor in Strasbourg."

And the old Soviet Union – does he return often?

"You know it is now easier for me to conduct in the West than in Moscow."

He shrugs his shoulders and smiles. We both understand Russia's relations with some of the former Socialist Republics are not without tensions.

And his family, they must be proud of his achievements?

"My father is no longer alive, but my mother – I think she is proud. I hope she will come to see me here. I want to continue to explore musically, to understand myself, to share my emotions with my audiences."

I must not detain this charming and so courteous young man a moment longer.

"You are welcome to stay and listen this afternoon to Tchaikovsky and Ilya Gringolts."

Nothing would please me more but I have another appointment – this time in Bournemouth. Yet I have spent the morning with the Bournemouth Symphony Orchestra – in Poole.

(A replacement headstone has just been installed in St. Peter's churchyard in Hinton Road to mark the grave of the man whose musical contribution to the town is beyond measure – Sir Dan Godfrey (1868-1939), founder of the BSO and the BS Chorus and the president of the local branch of Unison. As Carolyn Date observed at the rededication: "Sir Dan was an amazing man, a great visionary who really put Bournemouth on the map." Sir Daniel Godfrey died in 1939 and so knew nothing of the outcome of the war or the collapse of the Soviet Union 50 years later. How delighted he would have been, I am sure, to learn that a young Ukrainian is now to assume the mantle of principal conductor with the orchestra he founded. Incidentally, Kirill Karabits will be taking up the role full-time for the season beginning 2009-2010.)

From the sublime of the BSO and Tchaikovsky to Turlin Moor, its problems and successes.

Turlin Moor, Hamworthy: The Poole Housing Partnership

For years the Turlin Moor housing estate has been synonymous with anti-social behaviour, problem families, criminal activity, burnt out cars, graffiti – Poole's own answer to some of the notorious, blighted council estates of our inner-cities. Fair or unfair, it's been the label. Exasperating, hurtful and demoralising for all the hard-working, law-abiding families that live there, but a fact of life nonetheless. Not that it should be like that. By any standards, it's a fine location. Decent enough housing when it was built, good-sized gardens and plenty of green, open spaces, a short walk to picturesque countryside and the water's edge of the harbour – other less privileged generations would have regarded themselves as princes to live half so well. Those who built the estate must have been proud and optimistic when they surveyed their handiwork. So what went wrong with the brave dream?

Let's be honest, shall we? I grew up next to a council estate 50 years ago. I might easily have lived there myself, if my parents hadn't managed to save up enough for a deposit on a small bungalow. A number of my friends lived on that estate. We went to the village school and later to the grammar school together. We played together. I delivered my father's cakes to many of the families who lived there. I recall only dignified families who took the most enormous pride in their houses and their gardens. There was friendly competition between the gardeners. Who would be the first to lift their new potatoes and pick their beans? There was no vandalism, no graffiti, no bad language, not in the streets, anyway. Everyone worked. There was a real community spirit and a spirit of neighbourliness. Of course, there must have been the odd tension and cross word but I was never aware of it. I am not romanticising. That was the old working-class of which I, my friends and their parents were a part. I said – let's be honest, shall we? The truth is we are not the society we once were. For a variety of reasons there now exists an 'underclass' which does not live by the rules of the rest of the community. Cushioned by the benefits system, contemptuous of the norms by which the rest of humanity abides, they can make a misery of the lives of those unfortunate enough to live side by side with them. So it has been on Turlin Moor for too many years. Good people have despaired. I taught boys from the estate who attended the local primary and, encouraged and supported by their headmaster and teachers progressed to Poole GS, boys who wanted to fulfil their potential by working hard, often in very difficult circumstances. I was especially proud and fond of those lads because of their achievement.

Mike Bailey, now the friendly, helpful face of car-parking at Poole Stadium: "I came for 6 weeks and I'm still here 16 years later," lived on Turlin Moor at one time.

"The kids knew they couldn't be touched so they got away with murder. There were some really bad families there. A great many people had just lost heart. They felt nothing would change or improve."

When Joe Logan arrived on the Poole scene toughened by the experience gained from working on the estates of North Peckham and Gloucester Grove, it must have been like a breath of fresh air for many of those weary householders on Turlin Moor who had been obliged to endure appalling neighbours and anti-social behaviour for years. Yet when Joe arrived he couldn't believe how good Turlin Moor appeared compared to what he had known in London.

"It didn't conform to my idea of a dysfunctional community. Even though there were burnt out cars, joy-riding, glass and litter all over the place, dog faeces, all symbols of neglect, the people themselves were fiercely defensive. If you'd spent time in Peckham, you'd know what I mean."

Joe was determined, however, to effect changes. In 2004 the Poole Housing Trust was created with Joe as the chief executive.

"We've built an excellent team – Bill Shaw, Carmeline Brown, Mike Harrison, Sue Phillips and Rob Ingleton. We've worked in close collaboration with the local police in a multi-faceted approach – carrot and stick. Zero tolerance of anti-social activity of any kind, similar to the New York police. Of the 800 homes on the estate about a half are privately owned. Some of the trouble-makers were in the private sector but, as a council, we recognised we had a responsibility beyond our boundaries. We needed to tackle the estate's problems irrespective of ownership. So, wherever possible, we began ejecting undesirables and insisting on changed tenancy agreements meaning people must maintain their gardens and property in good order. We got rid of all the evidence of social decay so the estate began to look better. If any graffiti appears it's immediately removed. If a car is just dumped we don't simply leave it sitting there for a month with a notice sitting on it. It's removed. Of course, there's a risk the owners will come back but we take that risk. It's a policy that pays dividends. You clean the streets immediately. An instant response – it's a building block that gives the community a sense of security."

And the carrot – what's on offer to encourage a sense of pride and social responsibility?

"We set up a mechanism to attract money into the town's housing fund. Over the past 4 years we've received £50 million from the Government. It's like a large mortgage with the Government paying off the loan charges. As a result we have been able to modernise many of the properties, installing secure doors, renewing kitchens and bathrooms, insulating roofs, re-pointing, removing asbestos and so on. We have given the tenants a feeling of security and they feel a greater sense of pride in their properties. It's a strategy that has reaped pleasing dividends."

The spokesman for the Government public sector watchdog, the Audit Commission, Kieran Colgan, described the Housing Partnership's performance as 'excellent, the best in the UK, and one from which other social housing providers could learn'. A Turlin Moor resident, Ali Khan, congratulates the Trust.

"The standard of service is fantastic and the people here are much happier."

Another resident, Helen Ross, remarks: "The investment is wonderful. The Trust actively seek our help, they are easy to contact and, best of all, promised action is always carried through."

Even as I take my leave Joe is preparing to welcome visitors from a London Council coming to have a look at Poole's achievements. From being an estate notorious in the locality, it's a pleasure to record the fact that it is now seen as a much more desirable place to live for the 5,000 people on the council's waiting list. Though, I have no doubt, problems do remain I see as I drive around no evidence of the old Turlin Moor. It's looking in better shape than it has in many years.

"Paul Chadwick, the headmaster at the local school, and his staff are doing a brilliant job with the children. It's there, of course, much of the groundwork for the future is being laid. What we would like to see now is a new community hall and youth centre."

Rome, as they say, wasn't built in a day. But it's a pleasure to be able to congratulate all those individuals, Joe and his team, the police, teachers, youth workers and those residents engaged in the exercise, on their hard work and the success they have already achieved.

(Alas, even as we go to press, it is evident that a hard-core of thuggish louts remain on the estate with reports of attacks on buses and their drivers by these individuals. One particular driver, Kevin Sanderson, has suffered serious injuries after being assaulted by a gang of youths late at night. There are even suggestions that late night bus runs to the estate might be discontinued as a consequence. It is intolerable that drivers fear for their own safety when carrying out their public duties.)

As boys my friends and I all knew Hamworthy tolerably well. The park provided the finest playing surface for football and cricket anywhere for miles around. As Upton youngsters we were obliged to play our ball games on traditional Dorset heathland amongst the heather and gorse, in farmers' fields, in the sandy lanes, or at the Rec behind Wyatt's the builders on the Dorchester Road. None of the surfaces were flat and though the Rec was the best by far, it often became rutted in very dry weather. Off-breaks became leg-breaks, fast-medium was as likely to arrive at the batsman as a slow googly, and the game became an amusing lottery of guesswork and chance. Occasionally we would make the excursion to Hamworthy Park for the extraordinary luxury of playing on a level surface. In those days the place would be swarming with boys – watched by a comparable number of girls – vainly trying to emulate their heroes Compton and Hutton, Trueman and Laker. Most of us possessed only a modicum of ability, of course, but we played every hour outside school we were allowed – cricket in the summer, football in the winter. We must have been unbelievably fit and, almost without exception, we were lean without an ounce of surplus flesh. We also ate ravenously what our mothers placed on the tables before us. It was good, honest food – a meat course and plates of vegetables, most of which our fathers had grown in their back gardens. The only boy I can remember amongst our circle of friends who was seriously fat suffered from an acute medical condition of some sort and died in his thirties. Today, however, whenever I visit Hamworthy Park or any similar green open space in the county, it is invariably almost empty. Just one dad with his son is the norm and a few people walking their dogs. Where are our boys and girls? Gazing at their computer screens, or lounging in their armchairs watching TV and videos, for the most part, I fear. Often twice the weight we were at their ages with backsides like prize oxes, thighs like Russian discus throwers and health problems of all kinds accumulating to blight their later years. Yes, I know a handful will be in gyms and pools and every bit as keen as once we were, but what is happening is no less than a national tragedy. Walk down any street and it is difficult to suppress a groan of horror at what is lumbering ahead of you or advancing upon you, a cigarette drooping from the lips, as often as not from the lips of a young woman – a sight virtually unknown in my childhood. Of course, we all know some individuals do suffer particular problems with their build and weight and that it is very difficult for them and we all sympathise. I also hate to appear needlessly unkind, but how can I write a truthful book of the county without mentioning such a startlingly obvious phenomenon of the modern age. I have waited until this moment for fear of causing offence and absolutely none is intended. But until relatively recent times, many of the good folk of Dorset were starving or subsisting on poor, inadequate diets. Families went to bed hungry and wretched. Is this latest monumental expansion of waistlines what the Tolpuddle Martyrs were campaigning for? I believe George Loveless and his friends would have been as horrified as I am to be a witness to this unrestrained orgy of self-indulgence. Of course, it is a free society and it is wonderful to know that our citizens no longer suffer from malnutrition and can fill their shopping trolleys until they overflow, but we know that what is happening is wrong and desperately sad. I am, as readers will already have deduced, an avid follower of the Sport of Kings and almost every jockey in the land is a living, breathing testament to what self-restraint in matters of eating can achieve. There, I've got it off my chest and I hope no reader is too angry with me but, throughout these pages, I have tried to face every issue squarely and honestly and this one has nagged at me for too long.

Many summers ago I spent my university vacations in Hamworthy, staying with my mother at her guest house Seacourt – still a guest house 40 years later – on the corner of Coles Avenue and Blandford Road. Each morning I set out on foot at 6.30am to walk the mile and a half to work as a cleaner at Rockley Sands. It was a job I combined with working an evening shift at Miller's pork pie factory at Sterte – just 3 men and 30 women! Rockley Sands is, of course, a major success story in the Hamworthy area. Beginning with just a few caravans it has expanded over the past 40 years to become a significant employer and a major tourist park. Splendidly located it deserves its reputation for providing good family facilities in an attractive environment. What is more, the whole area always looks neat, well cared-for and immaculately tidy.

Besides the phenomenal business acumen and technical skills that reside within Robert Braithwaite's Sunseeker empire, another locally-based success story is that of Lush, the purveyors of fresh hand-made cosmetics. The co-founder of the company is Mark Constantine who ultimately hopes to open 1,000 shops world-wide. With an emphasis on using fresh ingredients such as organic fruits and vegetables and operating a strict code of opposition to animal testing, allied to support for Fairtrade and Community Trade, its admirable ethical policies have succeeded in attracting a solid customer base, especially among the young. The chief executive, Andrew Gerrie, remains hopeful that expansion plans will continue, notwithstanding all the problems in the domestic and world economy. Of course, this particular period is a supreme test for companies dependent upon principled buyers, when there will be a particular temptation for shoppers to buy what is cheapest rather than what is ethically sounder. But good luck to the company, say its many supporters.

One of the sadder events of the year is the death at the age of 82 of Denys Lavender, the husband and official escort of this year's busy and diligent Town Mayor, Joyce Lavender. Joyce, who was Sheriff last year, has represented the Branksome West seat for some years.

It isn't often the activities of any town council becomes front-page news on the broadsheets, but it's happened this year and the town council whose activities have been under the closest scrutiny is that of the borough of Poole.

Fairly shameful and embarrassing headlines as well, accompanied by some damning comment in the Editorials. There must have been, indeed I would hope there were, a number of very red faces in the council chambers as a result. So what was it all about? Very briefly, a Poole couple, Tim Joyce and Jenny Paton and their 3 daughters were subjected to a round-the-clock surveillance operation in order to ascertain if they were living in the appropriate school catchment area. The couple had earlier made application for their 3 year-old daughter to be added to the list of children due to attend Lilliput First School where their older daughters had been educated. The problem arose because they wished to move to another house 2 miles away. Confirming their application was in order as long as they delayed their move until the end of January, 2008, Tim Joyce and Jenny Paton acted accordingly. However, using the Regulation of Investigatory Powers Act (RIPA), designed to protect society against criminal and terrorist activity, John Nash, the director of Poole's children's services, and his colleagues decided to put the family under surveillance for 2 weeks. Then the Echo found out, once again proving what a brilliant paper it is, and revealed the story for all the world to see.

"Why didn't someone simply knock on our door and ask a few questions?" asked Jenny Paton which does seem an eminently reasonable point to make. It would also be in order to ask just how much the whole wretched operation cost council-tax payers?

Unsurprisingly the national press and TV immediately latched on to the story and the storm of criticism began. Locally Cllr. Phil Eades observed: "Our Council has become a national laughing stock!"

Poole's own education cabinet portfolio holder, Cllr. Tony Woodcock, was unequivocal. "I don't agree with using terrorist laws for this kind of thing."

Cllr. Mike Brooke expressed similar views. "Is this sort of espionage the answer to tackling what is a recognised problem? It's really Big Brother in 1984 mode!"

My old friend, Margaret Morrissey, of the National Confederation of Parent Teacher Associations, said. "I can't really believe the Council could have gone this far. We are pointing the finger at China for its human rights record, but I am starting to ask if we are any better?"

The splendid Ed Perkins summed things up brilliantly in an *Echo* editorial. '*We have also discovered under the Freedom of Information Act the Council has used surveillance a total of 17 times in a variety of situations. We were told the Act (RIPA) was a weapon to be used against terrorism and cyber crime. I understand their decision to use these powers was taken behind closed doors. You can't help thinking that what needed spying on were those very meetings held in secret where the use of surveillance was being approved.*'

There really is no more to be said, is there?

The Property Scene

Poole's population statistics 1900 pop 19,000 1950 pop 80,000 2008 pop 138,00

Mention the name Dave Wells and chances are you'll get a reaction, especially if the person you are speaking to is local and has been around a few years.

Personally, I've no axe to grind. We've never met until this morning in Dave's office in Windham Road. There was a time, of course, when it was fast cars, living the high life, the club scene and more than a few brushes with the law. True, he's not yet been invited to sit on the Bench, but the gentleman across the table from me is now seen by many as a pillar of respectability in the local community, a doting grandad and often to be spotted walking his black, much-loved poodle Basil on the beach at Sandbanks. He's also building when most other developers are shutting up shop and mothballing half completed sites. Dave's actually got 270 units under construction on various sites, all for rent. He's also the landlord to 2,300 tenants, almost exclusively at the lower end of the market.

"I've got 250 bedsits, currently priced around the £65 a week mark. Shared facilities, of course, no council tax, pre-payment cards for gas and electricity. Mostly it will be single people on low incomes or housing benefit. There are different scenarios. Maybe a young trainee is sent down to Bournemouth, a bed-sit suits him fine, financially and socially. Or perhaps it's a relationship break-up. The feller finds himself out on his ear, nowhere to go. Or he loses his job. A bed-sit is the solution. Or it could be an ex-prisoner. It's so important for someone coming out of prison to have a roof over his head on that first night out. When he wakes up in the morning in his own room, at that moment he can begin to sort his life out. Hopefully I can hold his hand until he gets a job. In all these scenarios a bedsit is right. Let's suppose then our young trainee gets a salary rise, the divorcee gets lucky in a new relationship, our ex-con gets a decent break – then they'll come to see me and say: 'Dave, what have you got for me? Something a bit bigger and better this time?' And we can fix it for him or her, no problem."

For some in and around the Poole, hearing that Dave Wells is a reformed character or a 'big softie' will cut no ice. He admits in the past he's been no angel and, in his tearaway days of youth, he did some bad things. He made enemies. Many, he acknowledges, will never forgive him. The gangster image he was once proud to cultivate will probably live with him until he's nailed down in his box – Dave's own words, not mine. His experiences 'inside' years ago equip him better than most for his forays behind the walls nowadays to talk to serving prisoners. He liaises with NACRO, the body that deals with the care and resettlement of prisoners. He talks seriously of feeling a sense of responsibility to help those trying to get back on their feet. Inevitably Dave is a man full of contradictions. I ask him to describe his general philosophy of life.

"I don't hurt old ladies. I don't hurt children."

And what about those in between, Dave? He laughs. Of course, it's just a residual part of the old bravura, isn't it? He knows he'd lose street credibility with some of his old mates if he gave the appearance of going over to the other side completely. And business rivals? Again his words are delivered with a wry smile.

"If someone turns me over, I'll just bide my time."

Of course, long before he became a man of property, Dave was in the motor trade. Older generations will remember the ads in the intermission at local cinemas when Dave Wells Motors came up on the screen. There'd be a roar of recognition. Half the audience had bought a car from him at some time or the other, or been on to the forecourt. They also knew Dave had a 'reputation'.

"Actually the cinema gave me free tickets which I used, my family used and my friends used. I made more out of the tickets than the cost of the advertising!"

What was Dave's own first car?

"A Reliant. I even remember the registration number NJT 167. It was a van, not the 'Del Boy' type. It had a side valve engine, but the body was still plastic, commonly referred to, as I recall, as 'the plastic pig'!"

Today Dave's got a handsome property in Shore Road, two sons, 'a loyal and loving missus', three grandchildren and, of course, his great pal Basil the poodle.

"My wife Stella has been my inspiration – a wonderful woman. Long-suffering, you could say! Shane's my eldest lad. Steve, my second, will actually take over from me and I hope Shane will be a part of the business too. Steve's very calm, friendly, doesn't argue. People like him."

Dave's got a loyal team at Windham Road. Teresa Quehault is his PA, Sue Clarke, John Pottle and Geoff Stace all perform their roles in Dave's empire.

And I repeat, he's building when others aren't. He's filling a hole in the market-place for cheap accommodation, providing a service to the community and he says he genuinely wants to do his best for his tenants. Of course, he's after a profit on his investment. What businessman wouldn't be? But he likes to think of himself today as essentially a 'good guy' – someone who learnt some valuable

#	Team	Pl	Wo	Dr	Lo	Gf	Ga	Dif	Pts
1	Poole Town	42	38	2	2	144	34	110	116
2	VT FC	42	31	8	3	141	35	106	101
3	Moneyfields	42	29	4	9	99	44	55	91
4	Wimborne T	42	26	9	7	115	41	74	87
5	Brockenhurst	42	24	10	8	71	41	30	82
6	Newport IOW	42	24	5	13	87	64	23	77
7	Christchurch	42	22	8	12	77	48	29	74
8	Hamworthy U.	42	21	5	16	77	73	4	68
9	New Milton T	42	18	10	14	72	55	17	64
10	Fareham Town	42	16	13	13	64	53	11	61
11	Romsey Town	42	16	12	14	65	75	-10	60
12	Bemerton HH	42	16	5	21	56	67	-11	53
13	Cowes Sports	42	13	11	18	65	78	-13	50
14	Brading Town	42	13	8	21	62	70	-8	47
15	Bmth Poppies	42	12	8	22	60	89	-29	44
16	Hayling Utd	42	11	8	23	66	96	-30	41
17	Alresford T	42	11	7	24	53	88	-35	40
18	Lymington T.	42	10	8	24	58	104	-46	38
19	Alton Town	42	9	9	24	56	105	-49	36
20	Laverstock F	42	8	7	27	49	106	-57	31
21	Hamble Assc	42	5	6	31	30	121	-91	21
22	Horndean	42	5	5	32	45	125	-80	20

Left: Football – Wessex Premier League 2008/09

lessons in life years ago and would like to be seen doing his bit for society.

"I'm providing what housing associations do – but without a subsidy. And, by the way, before I forget to mention it, I'm a vegetarian, which seems to surprise a lot of people," Dave adds with a chuckle.

So what do we make of Dave in his vintage years? A lovable rogue or is he still a rascal? I have it on good authority from several sources that he's well-liked and respected in housing authority departments. When we discussed the wonderful Brooke charity that does so much brilliant work in various poor parts of the world on behalf of horses and donkeys and their owners, Dave told me he'd actually visited one of their clinics during a foreign holiday. There's clearly a lot more to this enigmatic figure than he generally lets on. The man I've met this morning is likeable and amusing and candid. He even agrees to find me somewhere half-decent should I fall on hard times! Finally, I ask him how he'd like to be remembered and what he'd like inscribed on his head-stone?

"I'd like to be remembered as a household name in Bournemouth and Poole – but for all the right reasons – for taking the politics out of housing and making it affordable and accessible to the man in the street. As for a headstone, I'd like to think my family will place me in a mausoleum!"

Poole Town FC

Though the Poole/Bournemouth area has never been a hotbed of soccer fervour, unlike some localities, it seems extraordinary that Poole Town has not even enjoyed the luxury of its own stadium for the past decade. Yet life has gone on and the club, its players and loyal supporters have sought to make the best of a bad job and the season 2008-9 proves to be an astonishing one in its history. As undefeated Wessex League champions boasting the best points per match tally in the country, the manager Tommy Killick and his players have achieved a magnificent result worthy of the highest praise. Remembering Tommy both at Purbeck School and then as an outstanding member of Wimborne FC's FA Vase Wembley winning side of 1991-2, this certainly ranks alongside those glory days as a personal achievement. Alongside Tommy at Poole Town, of course, is my old friend Taffy (Steve} Richardson still kicking the ball – and opponents – just as hard as in the halycon days at Cuthbury. (I don't mean the bit about 'kicking opponents', Taffy. Honest!) But what an example Taffy is to every other sportsman – still exhibiting that wonderful enthusiasm and passion at the age of 42. Getting married to the lovely Suzanne has clearly not diminished his powers. Poole Town's captain,

Simon Browne, also deserves a particular mention for his leadership qualities throughout a long and demanding season. I reproduce below an approximate squad list of the players who represented the club during the record-breaking season.

Squad: Harvell, Hogan, Poore, Whitley, Dibba, Browne, Taylor, T.Smith, Bailey-Pearce, Hubbard, S.Richardson, Middleton, Phillips, Austin, Swann, Sturgess, S.Smith, Skelton, Holmes, Gill, Cook, Brown, Culliford, Tong.

(Having played at the Tatnam ground throughout the season, there now is a real possibility of the club playing on a new home ground at Branksome Rec. The Council's intention is not merely to upgrade the football facilities but to construct a multi-use games area. Gary Knight of the Dorset FA, Chris Reeves, Poole FC's vice-Cairman and Andy Thompson, the secretary of Parkstone cricket club, all welcome the possibility of 'bringing new life into a tired facility' and expanding sporting opportunities for the wider community. Though a controversial decision, Cllr. John Rampton, chairman of Poole Council's environment panel, uses his casting vote to back the £1 million scheme. In spite of some local opposition from anxious residents living nearby, it's to be hoped difficulties and reservations can be satisfied and everyone is eventually happy with the outcome.)

Poole Pirates

If there is one name that runs like a thread through Poole speedway it is that of Middleditch. Has there ever been a more popular rider at Poole than Ken?

"Dad began riding during the war when he was in Italy serving with the RAF. He rode with the Pirates from 1951 to 1963."

Was it really that long ago? Like every other boy, and quite a few girls, I saw the Pirates many times in my youth. Speedway actually began at the Stadium in 1948 when nearly all the major cities and many smaller towns too had their own tracks and teams. More often than not I went along to the Stadium with my friend Brian Richmond who really was a serious fan of the sport. We'd buy our programmes, religiously fill in the details of each heat as it was run, be showered by the shale on the corners of the bend where we usually watched and join in the cheers for our heroes. My earliest recollections are of riders such as Terry Small, Roy Trigg, Charlie Hayden, Brian Crutcher and, of course, the fair-haired, modest hero who regularly clocked up maximums in spite of the fiercest opposition, Ken Middleditch. They called him 'the first gentleman of speedway' because he was the stuff of which real sporting heroes are fashioned. For a start, he was very, very good. He was also a scrupulously fair rider, tough but chivalrous. His opponents universally liked and respected him. He was also a local lad. In those far-off days most of our sporting heroes were local boys. Speedway riders, footballers, cricketers, they usually lived not far from where they turned out as sportsmen. Even the top football clubs like Manchester United and Liverpool were composed overwhelmingly of local boys made good. Our heroes were a part of the fabric of their local communities. That is an undoubted loss. It's impossible to feel quite the same about sporting mercenaries who may be here today and gone tomorrow.

"Mum used to take me to the stadium even when I was a baby so I've been close to the sport all my life. In those days, of course, Mum was always known as 'Ken's wife'. When I got involved she was known as 'Neil's Mum'. Poor Mum!"

I'm sitting in the workshop of Neil's business, founded by his father, at Bailie House, Sturminster Marshall. Like his father before him, Neil wheels and deals in almost everything under the sun – clothing, furniture, books, machinery, anything that can be traded at a profit. That's the intention anyway. But back to Neil's beginnings and his own very distinguished career.

"I was actually born above the fish and chip shop at the corner of St. John's Hill, Wimborne, where Mum and Dad ran a very successful business for a number of years."

Poole Pirates – We are the Champions! Congratulations to Matt Ford and Neil Middleditch. *Picture: Bournemouth Ech0*

Speedway – Elite League Table 2008

	P	W	D	L	F	A	Pts
Elite League 2008							
Pirates . . .	32	22	0	10	1600	1321	52
Lakeside . . .	32	22	1	9	1551	1375	52
Swindon . . .	32	17	2	13	1498	1434	41
Ipswich	32	16	3	13	1483	1439	40
Eastbourne .	32	15	0	17	1462	1472	34
Coventry . . .	32	12	3	17	1418	1506	29
Belle Vue. . .	32	13	2	17	1423	1491	28
Peterboro . .	32	13	1	18	1371	1528	28
Wolves	32	8	0	24	1341	1581	16

I remember it well, like most people in Wimborne. We all bought our fish and chips at Middleditch's and very good they were.

"I never thought of anything else but speedway as a career. I rode for Poole from 1973 to 1983. I retired from the sport and took over the family business when Dad suffered a heart attack."

Modestly Neil omits to mention that, like his father, he was the team captain for a spell and occupies an honoured spot in the list of the Top Ten points scorers for the Pirates during their 60 year history. In 1999 Neil was asked by promoters Matt Ford and Mike Golding to become the team manager in place of Neil Street who had held the position for 14 years. With two Elite League titles, two Knock-Out Cups, three Craven Shields and a British league Cup, Neil has proved an outstanding leader. In addition, for the past seven years Neil has also managed the England team resigning because, aside from the demands of his business commitments, he felt he had taken the side as far as he could. Earlier I wrote that years ago nearly all Poole's riders were local boys. Today there's not even a British rider in the Pirates line-up. It's a situation remarkably similar to that of Premiership football where clubs sometimes field only one or two players eligible to play for one of the home nations, exceptionally not even one. It's a source of frustration for Neil who admits, however, the remedy is not easy to find.

"It's impossible to put the clock back. The presence of foreign riders, though they are very gifted and exciting crowd-pleasers, is hindering the development of home talent."

One of Neil's proudest moments was receiving the BBC Sports Personality of the South Award for his achievements.

"You know, I never thought of anything but being a speedway rider as I grew up. I've been so fortunate. I have travelled all over the world, met so many wonderful people and been paid for doing something I love. That can't be bad, can it?"

The 2008 Speedway Season Poole Pirates celebrate their Diamond Jubilee as a club by winning the Elite League title

I will simply quote the excellent Ian Wadley writing in the Echo dated October 14.

'Pirate fans woke this morning with smiles on their faces after their team reinforced their position as the country's finest speedway outfit in forceful fashion last night. The verdict never looked in doubt in front of a packed (6,000) home crowd, who had queued in massive numbers outside the stadium in Wimborne Road.'

The result of the final home fixturePoole Pirates 60 Lakeside Hammers 33 (Poole win 108-75 on aggregate)

It's another great triumph for promoter Matt Ford and Neil Middleditch, as well as the riders. Another Echo journalist, Phil Chard, pays a particular tribute to Matt Ford for making the right decisions in the pre-season's team composition. Getting the team balance right and in line with the sport's existing regulations is never easy. Matt Ford and Neil clearly did a brilliant job.

(An interesting development for next season is Matt Ford's announcement that, not only will Poole Pirates be scorching up the straight at the Wimborne Road Stadium, but Bournemouth Buccaneers will be competing in the National League for the first time. It is a bold move at a time of economic recession but an exciting one for all speedway fans.)

It's time for me to leave behind the town which holds so many memories. I am, of course, acutely aware of how much I have missed and how many individuals deserving of a place in these pages are not included because of a lack of time and space. Just one final pause then before I leave at the admirable Deli on the Quay where Tony Chapman and Lesley provide hot soup and fresh crusty bread as tasty and warming as any I have savoured on my travels.

Parkstone Grammar School's 'Walk for Water' (Swanage to Poole, starting at 4 am) to raise money to provide an African village with water. *Picture: Hattie Miles, Bournmouth Echo*

There are two spots in the town, in particular, that encapsulate for me the extraordinary changes that have transformed the town in the past half century. One is the old graveyard which once belonged to St. James Parish Church at the junction of West Street and Dear Hay Lane. There you will still find 40 or so ancient headstones standing incongruously in a pleasant acre or two of grass and trees, while just yards away traffic thunders ceaselessly past on to the Hunger Hill roundabout. Only one or two of the headstones, presumably Victorian, bear more than a few decipherable words, their original inscriptions long since worn away by the passage of time and the elements. Several are clearly missing or broken. Whoever, I wonder, would have borne off with such weighty trophies? The Rising Sun pub stands hard by, along with a car-park and a couple of handsome old buildings. Before me in the distance towers the huge Barclays office block, in the foreground there's the fly-over and roundabout. The din from the cars and trucks is relentless and mind-numbing. It's just as well the dead cannot hear. Across the road sits the garish yellow and orange National Tyres & Motors and beyond, rising into the skyline, the RNLI HQ and various blocks of flats. I doubt there is anywhere else in the town where the old and the new stand in such close and uneasy juxtaposition.

The other place where sometimes I stand and stare and reflect lies on the fringe of Baiter near the Cherbourg roundabout. Pause there and you will observe a small terrace of unpretentious but pleasing houses, probably Victorian. Cross the road and not far removed, nearer the water's edge, is an unkempt area of tangled grasses and brambles with various boats in different stages of dereliction and decomposition. Some, I doubt, have put to sea in years. In the gardens of the adjoining houses, family garments of every colour, dimension and description billow in the breeze from the washing lines. The location of these very ordinary houses is one of the most prized on the harbour-side, their tenants or owners privileged folk indeed. Just yards away a Little egret probes the mud along with a dunlin or two and an oystercatcher. Throw a stone, though you'd be advised not to, and it would land among the luxury yachts berthed in the new marina. What would a developer offer, I wonder, for this incongruous, 'untidy' collection of dwellings and wasteland?

There is without doubt a tension between the old and the new in the town. See the designs for the huge blocks of harbour-side flats and the Twin Sails Bridge. The town is an ancient one with a proud history. It is very different from its neighbour Bournemouth which is little more than a hundred years old. It will be of great importance in the years ahead that Poole retains its differences and traditions. Not so long ago the towns were in different counties, of course, and strikingly dissimilar in character. But then they weren't physically joined up. While peaceful co-existence and co-operation is desirable in those areas where it is of genuine benefit to both parties, there do lurk serious dangers for the unwary. If Central Government discerns an opportunity to impose a unitary authority in the guise of greater efficiency, with all its underlying undemocratic and bureaucratic implications, it will be a black day for both communities. The good people of Poole need to be on their guard against those who affect to know what is best for them. But, as it is, though these are days of economic stringency, Poole is well placed to prosper when the good times return. There is a diversity of employment which is an underlying source of strength. My greatest concerns would relate to housing and transport. Already the roads in Bournemouth and Poole are often hideously congested at peak times and seldom less than busy. If we really are destined to have a national population of 70 millions in the not very distant future, the pressures on our roads and available building land will increase enormously. I hope that Dorset's next chronicler will be able to report that the county, especially in the most populated areas of Poole and Bournemouth, has contrived to confront successfully such problems. As it is, it is difficult to be optimistic. The long, slow, painful, depressing crawl to and from work or school for many motorists in the region looks set to continue and grow much worse before it gets better. Even now an accident and consequent road closure brings regular disruption to thousands of motorists and horrific delays. The days when in my old 1933 Singer Le Mans sports, the first ever car I owned, I could drive and park in the locality without difficulty, are sadly but a distant memory.

On the subject of cars, it's time to climb back into the driver's seat once more. So, farewell Poole past and present, for both are inextricably bound together in my thoughts. It's northwards I am bound – and the final lap of my journey.

Cranborne & Wimborne St. Giles

I visited Cranborne just once in my youth, travelling with the players and supporters of Lytchett & Upton United to the village football ground for a vital Dorset Division Three North & East fixture between our two evenly-matched sides. I stood on the touchline with my classmate, Ron Mansfield, who lives still in that wild northern outpost. The score, as I recall, was an inconclusive 0-0 draw. Over the years since I have sometimes called by at the Manor Gardens but that has been the sum total of my association with the village.

The next occasion of any significance when I visited the locality was 20 years ago to meet and talk with the 10th Earl of Shaftesbury at Wimborne St. Giles House in connection with my book on Wimborne. I found the Earl kind, charming and very helpful. When I learned of his mysterious disappearance in the South of France in the autumn of 2004 and then of his brutal murder I was, like

Daily Mail, Saturday, May 26, 2007   ¤ ¤ ¤   Page 7

Earl's call-girl wife gets 25 years for murder plot

By **Paul Bracchi** and
Ian Sparks in Nice

THE former call girl wife of the Earl of Shaftesbury was jailed for 25 years last night for plotting his murder.

Jamila M'Barak was found guilty of paying her brother Mohammed £100,000 to kill the peer for his £6million fortune.

Mohammed – described as a 'violent psychopath' in court – was also jailed for 25 years.

In dramatic courtroom scenes before the verdict, the 66-year-old earl's grieving sister said of the pair: 'I hope they rot in hell.'

The earl's son Nicholas, 27, the current Earl of Shaftesbury, stood up in court in Nice and told his stepmother she was 'manipulative, scheming and ultimately evil'.

The jury took two hours to convict the pair at the end of a four-day trial.

Jamila, 45, lured her estranged husband to her £1million Cannes apartment in November 2004 – their second wedding anniversary. Mohammed lay in wait.

The earl – full name Anthony Ashley Cooper – believed she had wanted to discuss details of a divorce settlement. He had left her for another Cote d'Azur prostitute.

Mohammed, 43, was said to have 'gloated and laughed' as he beat the ageing earl to the floor and strangled him.

His body was found six months later in woodland five miles away, still draped in the

The Earl: Beaten and then strangled

The 10th Earl of Shaftesbury with his third wife, Jamila M'Barek, who was sentenced to 25 years inmprisonment for the Earl's murder. *Picture: Daily Mail*

everyone else, deeply shocked and saddened. The Earl was a popular man on his estate, well-liked by his employees. As the grisly details of the murder emerged it became clear he was the victim of a particularly callous and scheming woman, his third wife Jamila M'Barek and her accomplice, her brother Mohammed. It was revealed at their trial that the Earl had been beaten and then strangled by Mohammed M'Barek. His body was later dumped in woodland in the foothills of the Alps 30 miles outside Nice. The skeletal remains of the Earl, still dressed in his Savile Road suit, were discovered in April, 2005. Jamila and Mohammed M'Barek were subsequently sentenced to 25 years imprisonment.

Two hundred mourners attended the funeral in September, 2005, in Wimborne St. Giles. Sadly, the Earl's elder son, Anthony (Atty), had died of a heart attack soon after the discovery of his father's body aged just 27. The earl's second son, Nicholas Ashley-Cooper, is now the 12th Earl of Shaftesbury.

It is an extraordinary and desperately sad story. In London's Piccadilly Square the finger of the statue of Eros, erected in honour of the great humanitarian and reformer, the 7th Earl of Shaftesbury, points directly towards the family's estate at Wimborne St. Giles. Every family has its share of triumphs and tragedies. The stories of neither the 7th nor the 10th Earl will ever be forgotten, but they will be remembered for very different reasons both by the wider world and the villagers of the locality.

Chettle

I missed it at the first attempt. Then I turned the car round and there it was. Would I have paused to explore but for a certain lady author? Probably not, because I cannot call by at every village on my travels or I would be on the road forever, no matter how inviting the local inn, how handsome

Joyce Prince.

the houses or scenic the countryside about. But now I'm here and I must give credit first to the lady who has written such a fascinating book. Her name is Joyce Prince and its title is *Enduring Village* (published by Prince Publishing). It's said that only a dozen villages in the kingdom are still wholly in private hands and Chettle is one of them. Is it one of the last vestiges of benevolent feudalism? In certain ways the answer would be Yes, though I haven't heard if they uphold the practice of 'droit de seigneur'?

John Sansom is a tenant farmer who works the same 300 acres dairy farm that once his father ran. He sums the relationship that exists within the village up with telling simplicity. "If it wasn't for the family here owning everything, none of us would still be here."

I've strolled past the Castleman hotel/restaurant, admired the pond, peeped at the great house through the trees, visited the shop/post office and said 'Hello' to post mistress, Rachel Hiscock. It's taken me all of ten minutes. The estate is owned by the Bourke family, Susan Favre, Patrick and Teddy Bourke, by common consent, all decidedly good sorts. Peter Bourke, Susan's nephew, and his wife Fiona look after the house, living in one part of it while the rest has been converted into 5 flats. Peter works as a solicitor in Salisbury. One day he will inherit the estate and the responsibilities. His family has owned all of the 42 farms, cottages and flats here on the 1,200 acres estate since the middle of the 18th century. The Revd. William Johnstone performs the service every Sunday in the church which is situated in the grounds of the house. The rents here are a fraction of what they would be in the commercial market-place with priority going to anyone who works in the timber-yard, the shop, the farms or the hotel. Teddy Bourke runs the Castleman Hotel where the chef is his wife Barbara, a most accomplished lady, I understand, from reports by those who have dined there. Chettle isn't overcrowded. The population is just below the 100 mark, including 22 children. The estate is even, most commendably, picking up the bill to pay the salary of the post mistress and so maintain a service for the community when other offices across the county are closing their doors.

As Juliet Ashworth says: "We're a thriving community. Everybody knows everybody and community life revolves around the shop and post office. If that were to close, we'd lose our focal point. People come from villages around and the shop is an important outlet for local growers to sell their produce."

In an age when all too often a selfish indifference to the needs of others prevails, the approach of the Bourke family is admirable. As another tenant, Netta Wase, observes: "This is a brilliant community. I really don't know what we'd do without Susan and her family."

I am indebted to Joyce Prince for acquainting me with Chettle.

Tarrant Monkton

It's Sunday lunch-time when I arrive. The garden tables are already fully occupied. While many public houses are struggling to keep afloat, the Langton Arms is bucking the trend. To achieve distinction in the annual Great British Pub Awards is a much coveted honour, besides being commercially a significant boost to turnover. The 17th century Langton Arms has long been regarded with favour by its clientele and there seems no doubt that it will be attracting even more customers after being judged the best Gastro-pub in the south-west. Its owner is Barbara Cossins, whose local farm provides much of the meat served in the restaurant. The key figure in the kitchen is head chef, Sion Harrison, who stresses the importance of local sourcing.

"Increasingly diners like to know where the food they are eating has come from. Buying locally wherever possible makes sense both for producers and our customers in terms of freshness and reducing 'food miles'."

It's true the Langton Arms is most pleasantly situated but it's the quality of the service and the management that ultimately decides commercial success. On that count it's evident that Barbara and her team have many satisfied customers.

Charlton Marshall

Alas, while I have reported many small triumphs, besides one or two bigger ones, on my travels, the good folk of Charlton Marshall have suffered a sad blow with the closure of their village post office and the departure of their popular sub-postmaster, Jonathan Whittle. In spite of a heroic campaign, including a march of 100 villagers led by local MP Rob Walter for 3 miles along the A354 into Blandford, the stern face of officialdom has said 'No' to any reprieve. Henceforth, local people will be obliged to use the main post office in Blandford's Tabernacle area. As Cllr. Ian Rodd, the chairman of the Parish Council, observes: "In the past decade we've lost 2 garages, our village shop and now the post office which had its counter in the church building and, therefore, cost the Post Office precisely nothing." Pam Higgins, the Parish Clerk, compliments all those who lent their support to the campaign.

It is desperately unfortunate that in so many communities across the county vital services are being lost. I can well imagine the deep sense of frustration being felt. First of all, it's not being able to pick up the morning paper, then the daily provisions, now the services provided by a post office counter. These are the small but so important pieces of a normal, everyday life for us all that it is very easy for us to take them for granted – until the day they are snatched away.

Blandford Forum
Twinned with Mortain (France) and Preetz (Germany)

'There are no suburbs, happily, to Blandford. Beyond the last line of houses is the untrampled country, so that a window on the fringe of the town will open over a corn field, and cows will rest under the shelter of orchard walls.' Sir Frederick Treves, *Highways & Byways in Dorset* 1906.

A hundred years on, Sir Frederick would, without difficulty, recognise the Georgian heart of the town, rebuilt by the Bastard brothers, William and John, after the catastrophic fire of 1731 which destroyed all but a handful of houses but, in all probability, did fortuitously bring to an end the smallpox epidemic then raging among its citizens. Sir Frederick could still stroll in the fine, open market place (Thursdays or Saturdays if he enjoyed the bustle of market days), sup or dine at The Greyhound or The Red Lion, call by at the Corn Exchange (if he wished to discuss some matter of council business) and cast another disapproving glance at the Church of St. Peter and St. Paul, 'ugly and tolerable only from a distance.' However, if he chanced to approach the town from the

Blandford Town Council with Cllr. Sara Loch, the Mayor. *Picture: Rachael Piper Harding*

direction of Wimborne or Salisbury, he would be shocked and, no doubt, dismayed to discover the extent of Blandford's 'suburbs'. For there are now several communities living close by the town whose postal addresses bear the name of Blandford, yet whose actual contact with the town are, in many instances, tenuous and fragile.

"The reality is that many residents on the Badbury Heights estate just across the road – and on a number of the other housing developments of the past 30-odd years – mainly drive off in the morning along the by-pass to their jobs in Bournemouth, Poole and Salisbury. In the evening they'll call in at the supermarket on their way home, taking advantage of the free parking, and return along the by-pass to their homes. We simply never see them in town. We delivered 400 leaflets a while back on the estate inviting people to join the Civic Society or get involved with the Council or the Town Museum and we received just 2 replies. I don't blame them but it is a great pity that so many people, though they live close to the town, actually have so little to do with it. I suppose it's a fact of modern living."

Chairman of the Town Museum and Civic Society, former Mayor and councillor, John Barnes, lives just off the roundabout on the Salisbury Road leading out of the town on to the A354.

"By the way, the Badbury Heights estate was built on the old air-field once used by the legendary Sir Alan Cobham and there should be some recognition of that association."

John, a retired builder and former proprietor of a DIY business in the town, regrets the manner in which Blandford's Town Council was itself by-passed by higher authority when it came to the expansion of the town's outer fringes.

"We couldn't even look at the plans. The River Stour is the parish boundary, Bryanston's a separate parish. Tesco's supermarket was built on the wrong side of the river at St. Mary's, so the town derived no benefit financially from the store. Blandford was once full of family shops but

I'm afraid the arrival of Tesco killed off many of them very quickly. It was the 500 square feet of non-perishable goods they were allowed to sell that did for many in the High Street – newspapers, medicines, clothing and so on. And, of course, Tesco's fuel station did for the small garages and filling stations. It's a lesson every other town council should take on board when considering proposals for supermarket development."

It was a very different Blandford in which John arrived as a 10 year-old refugee with his parents from St. Helier, Jersey, shortly after the Germans captured the Channel Islands in 1940.

"I spoke with a French accent, a sort of Jersey patois, and I felt very awkward and out of place. My parents were not very impressed either – it seemed very dull without ant life compared to Jersey."

However, the town certainly did liven up when the British Airborne Division stationed at Tarrant Rushton came into the town at weekends, determined to give the Americans stationed at Downe Camp a good hiding.

"There were 32 pubs in Blandford in those days and we would see some real fights in the streets. They'd pause to let an old lady pass by and then start up again!"

John does entertain one particular hope for Blandford in the coming years.

"Obviously I have a great affection for this town since it made my family so welcome when we were refugees in 1940. If I had one particular wish granted it would be that we really made full use of the area along the river to create an attractive riverside walk. It would not only be a permanent source of pleasure to our towns-people but an added attraction to bring in visitors."

The Old House, The Close

There remain two extant buildings of consequence in Blandford predating the Great Fire of 1731. One is Ryves Almhouses: '

A long, comely wrinkled building of brick in one storey bearing the date 1682. The other is an old, red-brick mansion, a solid, self-assertive house, with imperious chimneys, a very high roof and haughty windows. There is a rugged, un-English look about it, which some ascribe to the influence of a certain German doctor, Frederic Sagittary, who lived here before the fire.' Sir Frederick Treves, *Highways & Byways in Dorset*, 1906.

This afternoon I am sitting in the red-brick mansion with its imperious chimneys, set in one third of an acre, in the company of Sara Loch, its present owner and the Mayor of Blandford.

"I count my blessings every single day. One is that I bought this wonderful house, another is that I live in this town. Blandford has turned out to be everything I hoped for."

Sara arrived from Chelsea after a career in accountancy and IT systems in 1995 and was initially co-opted on to the Council 8 years ago.

"There's nothing that's 'life and death' in Blandford but, if you asked me for one particular wish, it would be that we were able to use the Corn Exchange as we would really like. It's a Grade One listed building with awkward stairs and no lift. They do hold yoga classes upstairs – but then you'd expect anyone doing yoga to be able to climb the stairs! Unlike you lucky people in Wimborne we have no cinema or theatre though, of course, we do have lots of wonderful societies and clubs. As for the future, I hope to continue to serve the people of Blandford as best I can for as long as I am able."

The old lady can't find a way into the clock to replace the exhausted battery. Cheerfully and courteously Tony Horrocks deftly solves the problem and replaces the battery. One grateful customer hands him a £10 note but there's a sting in the tail.

"Unfortunately, madam, you've come into the shop on the day we don't give change," he explains slipping the note into the till.

The old lady chuckles. She's clearly familiar with Tony's leg-pulling. Duly putting her change into her purse she exits with a smile on her face. She's enjoyed her visit and will call again. It's always a pleasure to witness the good shopkeeper at his or her craft. I've met many examples on my travels. Anthony Horrocks Esq, formerly of Swanage, is but the latest. His wife Trina's the president of the Chamber of Trade. Between them and their cheerful assistants, Pat Morgan and Stuart Ray, they constitute Horrocks & Webb, Jewellers of Salisbury Street.

"I thought I recognised you. You were once my history teacher," smiles Tony.

Is it an accusation or a mere statement of fact? I hesitate.

"I even recall a question you once asked the class. Which British Prime Minister's brother owned one of the finest collections of postage stamps in the kingdom – second only to the Queen? I've often chuckled at that one," he smiles. "We thought you were serious until you gave us the answer – Phil Attlee!"

It's just a few weeks before Christmas and Trina isn't unhappy about the level of trading though she recognises it's going to be an especially difficult post-Christmas period.

"The Blandford economy is quite buoyant and the opening of the new supermarket seems to have brought more people into the town. Fortunately we still possess a good number of small independent, specialist shops and there are very few empty premises. The Chamber seems to be on the up too and we've now got 50 members. We get together to organise events like late night shopping and last year we bought the Christmas lights – with the help of a contribution from the council. One man who deserves a lot of praise for all his brilliant efforts over the years is Trevor Roberts. He has been a really inspirational figure who's kept spirits up when everyone else was a bit down. And someone else who has earned the respect and gratitude of the local community, especially the shopkeepers, is PC Simon Evans. If we have ever encountered problems with anti-social behaviour Simon has proved brilliant at sorting things out. There's a great sense of belonging here and lots of warmth and kindness."

The Close

"Steve's setting up the Christmas lights in The Close. He'll see you there, if that's alright."

Steve Hitchens, taxi driver and retained fireman, did warn me he might be out on call, so it's not a complete surprise. Anyway, it's only a few paces down the road past Sara Loch's house so I know where to find him. When I do actually locate him he's peering up into the bare branches of a mature and historic oak. Behind him a fellow officer is shouting advice to a third member of the team struggling to wrap various trailing lengths of cable and fairy lights over the lower branches. The junior member of the party has, I learn, just been despatched to forage for essential victuals.

"This oak was planted in 1905 to commemorate the granting of the town's charter 300 years earlier in the reign of King James I."

Beneath his helmet Steve looks altogether too youthful to have been a district councillor for the past 20 years and the previous Town Mayor. He introduces me to his companions.

"Steve Garbutt's the retained station commander and a full-time officer. He's been on duty all night and came straight on here. He needs some sleep. James Plumley is the one up the tree."

It's clearly a fiddling, time consuming exercise with lots of cable, many branches and even more spindly lengths of growth and twigs. And the biting easterly blowing directly from the old Soviet empire is funnelling between the buildings straight at us as if it wishes to settle some personal vendetta. My companions are well insulated with many layers of warm, wind resistant clothing.

Blandford' police officers receive the Safer Neighbourhood Team of the Year award from Chief Constable, Martin Baker and High Sheriff, John Raymond.

They're also moving around, stretching limbs, keeping the circulation moving. As for me, stationary, poised with pen and paper, I am slowly losing all sense of feeling.

"They'll look brilliant when they're up and lit – if we get them lit". Steve Hitchens grins. "The lads all give their services voluntarily on these occasions. It's a small gesture but our way of giving something back to the community we all love."

There's constant banter and an obvious, deep-rooted camaraderie forged by a wealth of shared experiences, not infrequently dangerous and harrowing.Bob Smith, the scavenger, returns with trays of burgers and mugs of hot coffee. James drops easily down from the tree, the two Steves pause for a few minutes. Everyone agrees Blandford is a happy town with few problems.

"Of course, there have been drug issues like everywhere else and we do need to have more sports facilities. And some people who used to be involved are being deterred by Health and Safety. Yes, we need to protect the individual but it's all gone too far. Some of it is pure madness."

Steve Hitchens is a thoughtful, articulate man, as befits an ex-Mayor. Married to Lynn and the father of two, he cares passionately about the education of his children and the environment in which they're growing up.

"Fortunately this area of Dorset is the safest police division in the country. None of us would wish to live anywhere else."

His companions agree. Such men are the backbone of so many similar communities. Big-hearted, decent, and kindly, it has been a privilege to make their acquaintance here in the historic Close. As I take my leave I must silently confess to one trifling, sneaking regret. A shameful regret, I acknowledge.Much as I have admired their efforts to illuminate and cheer Blandford's Christmas, one part of me, one very small part of me, wishes they had been attending a fire instead.Only a very small, inconsequential fire, you must understand, a fire that was actually doing someone some good, if that were possible. At least then I might have been warm instead of feeling like one of Napoleon's army during the retreat from Moscow. In truth, I don't feel warm again until I clamber into my bed 10 hours later.

"Blandford is a unique example of a Georgian brick built town. It's what you'll see on the town sign as you enter. Sir Nikolaus Pevsner in his Buildings of England described it as the finest!"

Not actually a local lad, Peter Warrington, was born in Clacton though he has long since more than redeemed his dubious origins. Honoured as a Freeman of the borough in 1995 Peter is a man of many parts. At different times he's served as the chairman of the Chamber of Trade, councillor, Mayor and a school governor. He is a town guide, a role he shares with his good friend, Michael le Bas.

"Three walks, heritage, perimeter and church. We make a fine pair, he's a staunch Catholic and I'm a lapsed Methodist! By the way, Michael is one of the most brilliant geologists in the UK and he and his wife, Pamela, are experts on WW2 pillboxes. He's got one in his back garden! "

Peter also has close ties with the local Air Training Corps, the Civic Society and the Anglo-German Exchange group and the Scouts.

"I am delighted that here in Blandford we are one of the few groups nationwide which is actually increasing its numbers – cubs, beavers and scouts. And the scout hut has a further use every Friday when it serves as mosque for our local Muslim community who arrive with their prayer mats for their devotions."

But perhaps Peter's proudest achievement is his tree-planting.

"It began with 'Plant a tree in 1995' and so far we've planted a beech avenue of 40-50 trees near the Wimborne roundabout. Long after I've gone that avenue will be giving pleasure to other generations. That's a really satisfying feeling."

Blandford Army Camp

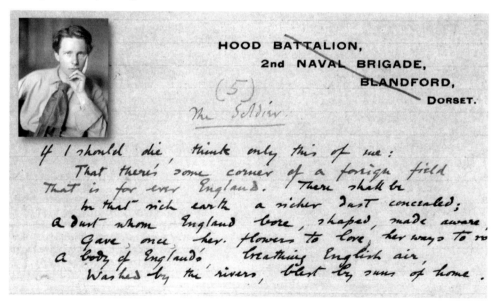

A copy of Rupert Brooke's immortal poem is pinned to the wall of Lt. Colonel Bob Brannigan's office wall. If it was at Canford Manor on 23 December, 1914, that Brooke actually scribbled the opening lines, it was certainly at Blandford Camp that Brooke laboured on the remainder of one of the best-loved poems in the English language.

Genial and approachable, Bob Brannigan is clearly a highly professional and knowledgeable man.Bob is also the public face of the military camp in the town. His official title is Garrison Staff Officer and he's responsible for liaising with the media and inquisitive intruders like me.

"Blandford actually became the home of the Royal Signals when they moved down from Catterick. Every member of the corps will have trained here at some time in their career.We have a through-put of 6,000 soldiers a year. Some may be here for merely a day's training. On the other hand, the stay may be as long as 15 months.In our very complex world electronic warfare plays a critical role. It may be that of relaying information or interrupting the flow of enemy information or confusing the enemy. By different means we have to keep the spider's web of communication functioning to keep people informed."

What is the Garrison's relationship with the town?

"Clearly it's a very important one.We do have the freedom of the town of Blandford which means that on ceremonial occasions we may march through with flags flying, bayonets fixed and drums beating. And, of course, our Gurkha soldiers enjoy an especially close relationship with the town. At any time we may have 1,100-1,500 plus soldiers training, together with their families and civilian employees and contractors – a total of 4,000 or so behind the wire.It's worth an estimated £14million to the local economy. I know there has been speculation about the future because of the Defence Training Review, but Blandford has been identified as a core site and its future is assured though there will perhaps be fewer single people here and more families. That may well be of benefit to the wider community in the locality."

(Even as we go to print there are celebrations among the Gurkha soldiers, past and present in the county, at the change in Government policy regarding their right to residency in the UK after their service in the Armed Forces. A former Gurkha soldier who is now the Chairman of the Blandford British Legion, Staff Sergeant Gayan Tamang, who served for 21 years, expressed his delight at the news. Asbahadur Gurung, a former Queen's Gurkha Signals captain with 28 years service, is equally thrilled. The owner of Sandford's popular Gurkha bar and restaurant, just outside Wareham, acknowledges the magnificent part played in the campaign by the actress, Joanna Lumley. In fact, I believe our entire nation owes Miss Lumley a huge debt for 'persuading' a most reluctant Government to honour its obligations to our Gurkha friends.)

In every respect Lynn Lindsay is a true child of Blandford. Her father was a serving soldier with the REME, her mother a local girl. Sadly her father died when he was just 45 and her mother became the breadwinner. Maintaining the family tradition Lynn herself duly married a soldier named Cliff from the nearby camp. Growing up on a council estate where she still lives, though most of the houses are now privately owned, Lynn feels passionately about family and community values. Just a few days before my visit the Prime Minister, Gordon Brown, announces plans for free nursery care for all 2 year-olds and Lynn, remembering her own experiences growing up in Blandford, is incensed.

"I think it's absolutely appalling. I was a young mother myself – my daughter is now 30 – and I believe strongly that a child needs a one to one relationship with its mother at least up school-days. With so many problem children I feel it's entirely the wrong direction for society to be heading."

For Lynn, now a town councillor who represents the same locality in which she grew up, she sees social policy in the context of the world around her including her home town.

"As children on this estate we played together, walked to school together and walked home together.Everyone knew who you were and looked out for you. There was a great feeling of unity and belonging and I feel we are in danger of losing that."

And the Blandford of today – how does Lindsay see the town?

"Of course there are the usual issues – drugs, petty crime, vandalism – but I find it almost impossible to find anything negative about Blandford. I love the town and it's a great place to live. But we must not lose that sense of togetherness and community."

I've been looking out for him in several locations and today I've cornered my prey. I pop into Oxford's for a loaf and he's just arrived with the day's deliveries from Alweston, a village outside Sherborne. Steve Oxford is a familiar face in many Dorset towns, not only as the personable public face of the family bakery business, but also in his capacity as chairman of Dorset Farmers' Markets Ltd. Descended from a long line of bakers dating back to 1911 when his great grandfather Frank Oxford established the business, Steve is deeply committed to the cause of the small producer.

"The original objective was to expand farm gate and retail sales for farmers who were often in the grip of the supermarkets. It was another retail outlet through which they could secure better prices for their products. We have a Board of 9 directors and about 100 members. We meet on a regular basis and we are actually responsible for setting up the markets. Each director keeps an eye on particular markets and constantly liaises with members."

Though Farmers Markets seem to have been with us for some years, they are a relatively recent phenomenon.

"The markets originated in Bath in 1995 and I actually became involved after attending the Dorchester Agricultural Show in 2002. The first markets in the county were staged at Bridport and Poundbury and much of the credit in those early days must go to Kevin and Amanda Crocker of Pampered Pigs at Bere Regis, Martin and Janet Pook from Melcombe Bingham, Clive Sage of Monkton Wyld with his lamb and Nick Ralph from Bishop's Caundle with his poultry. It actually began life as Dorset Food Links, a grant funded group of rural producers. In recent years the movement has expanded to sell fish, bread and preserves."

I put it to Steve that there has been criticism about sourcing. How closely are members monitored?

"If a new member wishes to join, two directors will go along – one of them a specialist in that field. We want to see invoices and receipts. We don't want them buying stuff down at the docks. They must be primary producers. We are anxious to preserve the absolute integrity of farmers' markets."

There's also been opposition from some existing traders who complain that they have to pay rents and council taxes and resent what they describe as unfair competition.

"We do, of course, pay a pitch fee and we are only in a town at intervals, not every day. It may be just once a month and we would argue that our presence does attract other shoppers into the town so everyone benefits."

Which towns currently stage the markets and are there plans for future expansion?

"The locations we presently attend are Blandford, Shaftesbury, Wimborne, Wareham, Sherborne, Christchurch, Bridport, Poundbury, Broadstone and Canford Cliffs. I think the focus at the moment is more on consolidating our present pitches, especially in the current economic climate."

It's a movement with which I have instinctive sympathy. Small businesses are the backbone of much of the rural economy. With the big beasts of the High Street wielding what many of us consider to be excessive power, it is vitally important for the small producers to preserve their financial independence. If farmers' markets are a part of that solution they need our support. No, there must not be unfair competition with local shopkeepers but, in truth, both groups share a common interest. Let's give them our custom whenever possible.

At Hall & Woodhouse Brewery

(Our conversation ranged far and wider. It was one of the most enjoyable of my interviews in the county. We laughed a lot, found interests in common but also talked seriously about a number of the issues relating to the pub trade and brewing in general. I drove away from Blandford that afternoon not only with a complimentary pack of bottled beers but with a warm image of an engaging personality and a caring man. When I heard the news of David Woodhouse's death early in the New Year I did at first find it difficult to believe that a man who had appeared so vigorously fit could so suddenly be struck down. Then I found myself grieving that such a manifestly kind and decent man should have passed away so cruelly young leaving a wife and family who would miss him terribly. There is no doubt that David's death will leave a major void in the life of the Blandford community for some years. He had far-reaching plans for the brewery itself and cared deeply about the well-being of the tenants and managers of the public houses owned by Hall & Woodhouse. As Fanny Charles, of the Blackmore Vale and Stour and Avon Magazines, commented: "We worked together as members of the Hall & Woodhouse Community Chest panel supporting a variety of projects and our relationship was both professional and cordial. David was always willing to listen and talk. He will be much missed." Rob Walter MP was equally appreciative of David's admirable qualities. "He carried out his duties as High Sheriff in a manner that served the whole community. He was a truly good and kind man." Now others will take up the challenge. I reproduce the following piece exactly as I would have written it were David still alive.)

"Have you read *Buddenbrooks* by Thomas Mann? It's about four generations of a business family and its decline – a magnificent book and full of lessons for family businesses."

Across the desk David Woodhouse laughs. We're surrounded by the family history of Hall & Woodhouse. Photographs, paintings, even a stuffed badger in a glass case. We talk racing. Of his uncle, the legendary Dick Woodhouse who won the Foxhunter's at Cheltenham on Woodside Terrace and Highworth. Of the Badger Chase at Wincanton, a race the company sponsors annually, though David confesses he's not really a racing man himself.

And so we progress to more serious topics.

"My greatest responsibility is running a viable business. We employ 1,400 people with a turnover of £90 million a year. I do have to make tough decisions. We had no choice but to shut down our soft drinks business and lay off 200 people. We'd have had to invest £20 million to make it work. It simply wasn't possible. When we made the decision the staff attitude was exemplary. Fantastic. They understood. It's the same with the pubs. We extend as far east as Kent, north up to Hertfordshire and west to Devon, about 267 pubs at the last count. A number will have to go. Nationally a fifth of pubs will close. When you look at the individual pub today it's got to take £250,000. Deduct VAT, beer tax, council tax, business rates, NI, income tax – the landlord and his wife are going to have to work 100 hours a week for less than the minimum wage. That makes no sense for them. It wouldn't be fair to put someone in a pub if they were going to struggle to make a living. It's a moral as well as an economic decision as far as I am concerned. There's been a massive change in the past 30 years with a huge swing away from pub sales. Though the pub sales have dropped from 36 million barrels to 18 million barrels, the 'take home' from supermarkets and off-licences has gone up from 4.6 million barrels to 14.6 million barrels. The smoking ban has further exacerbated the decline in pub drinking. Much of the atmosphere of the traditional local revolved around the bar. The landlord was a pivotal figure. The good landlord got embedded in the community. He might be the 'agony aunt', the raconteur, the man who made his customers laugh. At one time the father would be in the lounge bar, his son in the public. Any problems and the son could warn his father. Now, of course, young people are descending on town centres, often alcohol fuelled beforehand. There was seldom much trouble in well run pubs, certainly not in country pubs. And it was all over soon after closing, certainly by midnight. Now it goes on well into the wee small hours. We've invested £75million in our pub estate. As a reflection on modern times and the emphasis on food we actually employ, if you can believe it, no fewer than 47 Thai chefs!"

Inevitably we talk of the Greenridge Hotel, formerly the Upton Hotel, of which I have written elsewhere. David is frank about its problems.

"I'm afraid it was a classic case of a pub on a downward spiral. You can't get away from demographics. My grandfather built it. There were some serious problems relating to a minority of individuals who used it. It was a great shame. We would like to be able to do something with it that is good for the community. In order to get it de-rated we had to remove the tiles. Crazy but we had no choice. And, of course, we do have the St. Peter's Finger, which is a very successful pub and just a mile away."

David is immensely proud of the range, quality and flavours of the Hall & Woodhouse collection.

"We have won all sorts of awards in recent years and one man who deserves a lot of credit is Dr. Tim Morris, nicknamed 'The Doc'. Tim has been instrumental in many of our successes. He's retiring shortly and we'll miss his expertise."

It was at this point that David disappeared downstairs and returned with enough beer to sustain me for several months. Shortly afterwards, we shook hands and wished one another well. It proved, most sadly, to be the last time that I saw him. I am grateful, at least, to have this opportunity to honour a fine man. I understand that Anthony, David's brother, and Mark, David's cousin, have been appointed as joint managing directors. As Lord Rockley, the chairman of the company, said: "Anthony and Mark will be building upon David's legacy and taking Hall & Woodhouse forward as a successful, independent brewery."

To David's family and his successors every reader will, I know, convey their best wishes.

One final call – up the hill to the kennels of the Portman Hunt and an appointment with Charlie Frampton, Master of the Portman Hunt. Even as I arrive I hear the excited barking of the hounds, between 80 and 100 of them, together with 40 beagles. They're anticipating lunch.

Charlie, married to Issy and the father of 3 year-old twins, is possessed of a wonderfully languid quality – impeccably mannered, charming, friendly – he might be the youthful, powdered heir to an 18th century landed estate. Stowe educated, where he spent 4 years in the company of the school's beagle pack – and a few hours each week with his text books when time permitted – he migrated south to Exmoor and the legendary Ronnie Wallace in his gap year.

"Ronnie was just the greatest man in the fox-hunting world."

Charlie arrived at Bryanston 4 years ago to assume the mantle of responsibility. We discuss his duties and the structure of the Portman.

"My job is to manage the hunt, to liaise with farmers and keepers, to keep everyone happy. There's a lot of shooting today so it's vital to arrange the dates when we hunt to fit in with everyone else. The hunt year actually begins on 1 May and ends on 30 April. We hunt from September through to March – 7 months of the year in total. Last year we hunted on about 80 days. There are 2 joint masters besides myself, William Gronow Davis and James Gibson Fleming. A full subscription costs £1,300 a year and there are differing rates for farmers and students. Half our income derives from subscriptions and the rest from hunt balls and various fund-raising activities. We have 5 people employed here full-time and they all live in, looking after the horses and the kennels."

Of course, while we are all aware the Hunting Act was passed in 2005 banning the hunting of wild animals with dogs, except in certain circumstances, interpretation of the law has proved controversial.

"Legally we may hunt either by laying a scent for hounds to follow, or we may use 2 dogs to flush a fox or another mammal out for a bird of prey to kill – or it may be shot. If the hounds do kill a fox it

The Portman Hunt. *Picture: Hector Gibson Fleming*

must be an unintentional consequence. Whenever we begin a day's hunting I remind everyone that we must act within the law."

How does Charlie view the Hunting Act and the future?

"First of all, I believe the issue was not really about cruelty. It was a class issue. Certain politicians objected to hunting because they claimed it was only the upper classes who hunted whereas the reality is that our community is drawn from every section of society. And for them a day out with the hunt is all about the pleasure of jumping obstacles, enjoying the countryside and the camaraderie and banter of their companions. Of course, there are people who genuinely believe hunting is cruel. They talk of the poor fox being chased by a pack of hounds and they sentimentalise the issue. What would they prefer? Foxes to be shot, often to be wounded and crawl away to die in pain from their injuries or gangrene – or to be killed almost instantaneously by a hound? And often these are people who will eat battery hens who live no life at all and they will drink milk and forget that the cow has had her calf removed from her shortly after birth. If it's a bull calf the chances are that it will be killed immediately because it is worthless. Is that more or less humane than quickly despatching a fox with a hound? I will give another example. Let us suppose there are 4 foxes in a wood and one of them is sick and mangy. When foxes are controlled by shooting, it is indiscriminate. The 3 healthy foxes may well be shot and the sick one escapes. If they are hunted it will be the weakest that is taken by the hounds. Again, which is the most humane form of control? What we are all hoping for is that next year there will be a free vote in the House of Commons, which the Conservatives have promised if they form the next Government, and a repeal of the existing legislation. Do people realise that parliament spent 700 hours of its time debating hunting to produce an entirely unsatisfactory piece of legislation? Yet how many hours has it spent debating the Iraq war? We have passed the last few years under the shadow of anti-hunting legislation. I feel the countryside as a whole has united in that time. There's a feeling that our freedom is being needlessly and unjustifiably infringed. The Countryside Alliance march on London when nearly half a million of people arrived in the capital for the demonstration showed the strength of feeling that exists."

How does Charlie view the fox?

"I love the fox. He is a fantastic animal. The expressions as cunning or wily as a fox are not for nothing. I love to see a litter of young foxes in the spring."

For Charlie working a pack of hounds comes close to an art form.

"Remember hounds have been purpose bred for hundreds of years. We know each one by name and its lineage. We learn the character of each one and its individual talents. You've doubtless seen a great football team in action sweeping forward like a mighty army, or a flock of starlings in flight at dusk – the spectacle is amazing – it's the same with hounds. To see them moving in unison, sweeping forward as one single-minded unit, speaking to one another, following the line of the scent, it's immensely graceful and wonderful to watch. And, if the fox makes good his escape, fine."

Scott Garrett's official title is Countryman. He's about to allow 15 or so bitches through from a communal area into a separate area of the kennels to feed. It's intriguing to watch him at work. Calling each one of the bitches by name the hounds squeeze through between his legs one by one into the feeding area where a feast of raw meat awaits them. Scattered across the stone floor lie a number of carcasses of dead calves or sheep awaiting the hungry jaws of the hounds. To the unaccustomed nostrils the smell is distinctly pungent.

"They're fed every 48 hours. Canine stomachs are adapted to digest food this way. Actually they prefer the meat as it becomes smellier."

Where do the carcasses come from?

"The Hunt provides a collection service for farmers. They ring us before 9.30 am in the morning and we collect fallen stock for them on Tuesdays, Sundays and Fridays. If livestock is injured – a broken leg, for example – we'll despatch it and remove it for a small charge. Or they may be bull calves the farmer does not want and have no value. We bring the stock here, remove the skins which go to the tannery, then we butcher the carcasses for the hounds and what we cannot use goes for incineration. We are providing a valuable service to the local farmers and we benefit by having a regular supply of fresh meat for the kennels."

Outside the hunting season Scott and Charlie regularly exercise the hounds through the lanes accompanying them on their 'pushbikes' .

"We cover 12 miles or so. It is essential to keep them fit."

Scott arrived from at Bryanston from Wales where he regularly assisted the hill-farmers whose flocks were often attacked by foxes, especially during the lambing season.

As I leave Charlie reflects again on the hunting legislation of recent years.

"In some ways I believe, at the end of the day, providing we get the repeal, hunting will emerge the stronger. The air will have been cleared and the cruelty charges will be seen to have been unfounded and unwarranted. It may sound contradictory but the truth is that the hunt is the fox's best friend. With proper and thorough self-regulation, so that we eliminate any undesirables from the activity, I am hopeful that there is a good future for hunting – and the countryside will belong again to country people."

It seems a fitting moment to take my leave. I began by speculating upon the possible response to the town of Blandford were Sir Frederick Treves to return. So it's one final stroll through the market square and past the Corn Exchange. There's a notice posted on the Council notice-board that would have Sir Frederick shaking his head in puzzlement. It even leaves me bemused. It's the third paragraph.

'Members are reminded that the Council has a general duty to consider the following matters in the exercise of its functions: Equal Opportunities, (race, gender, sex orientation, marital status, religion, belief or disability), Crime & Disorder, Health& Safety and Human Rights.'

Brilliant surgeon that he was and possessed of the keenest intelligence, interpreting such a notice would, I suspect, prove beyond even Sir Frederick.

Over the bridge now in the direction of St. Mary's and Lower Bryanston and the great man would, for the moment, be still in familiar territory. Opposite the entrance to Bryanston School, in Sir Frederick's day the gates to the Portman estate, he would, no doubt, gaze upwards at the scores of rooks gathering in their raucous family groups in the tree-tops outside the Stour Inn beside the long since closed Ringrose Pottery. In all probability these birds are the descendants of those he would have seen in 1906. In Sir Frederick's day the nature books were full of the theories of 'rook parliaments' sitting in solemn judgement. Did he speculate then on the subject of their debate – the growing military might of Germany perhaps, or more prosaic concerns like the scarcity of leatherjackets and the disturbing accuracy of Lord Portman's gamekeeper's new shot gun? And today, what are our feathered friends high above our heads discussing – the likely effects of global warming on their food supplies, the appropriate response to the increasing population of buzzards – continued harassment or haughty indifference? Or simply, why is that silly man still staring up at us? I amble on towards Lower Bryanston, pausing at the junction where the road divides. Here Sir Frederick might pause, confused by the changes.

"The Winterborne Stickland road used to be the main road to Dorchester in the old days before they closed it off. You imagine, the buses would go up that narrow lane. There were a few near-misses, I can tell you! I was the dairyman for Mr. Woolway at Lower Bryanston Farm for many years and the fields over there, where you see the new houses, were full of cows once."

Bill Sherwood's just been into town. He's on his way back home. He looks wistful. So would I, in his shoes, a lifetime's memories buried beneath brick and timber and concrete.

Shall I ever find the time to return here? Perhaps, though more than likely not. A hundred years ago and Sir Frederick quite possibly stood hereabouts with similar thoughts. He enjoyed another 17 years after his visit. Would I settle for another 17 years? Yes, I'd hope for more but I'd settle for that. Seventeen more Cheltenhams with all those wonderful intellectual puzzles each March. Seventeen more years of Dad's Army repeats before I leave myself to join my already departed friends Sgt Wilson, Capt. Mainwaring and Private Godfrey. But I must not be melancholy. It's time to get back in the car and continue my journey which is now so close to its conclusion. It's almost Christmas and the year's end. The tree already stands in Wimborne Square. I've got presents to buy and cards to post. And, of course, there's the King George at Kempton on Boxing Day.

Farewell, Blandford. Thanks for the memories.

Sturminster Marshall

In which location shall I place our hero? For the past 7 years he's lived in reputedly the oldest cottage in Sturminster, but he's almost certainly an even more familiar face in Wimborne? In fact, for his vast admiring fan club, the lad is indelibly associated with only one spot on this planet, namely the car-park behind what was for as long as most of us can remember Tom and Malcolm Budden's emporium in Wimborne Square. However, since we are conducting our analysis of the many ills of contemporary society seated at a table in his Sturminster cottage, it seems most fitting to settle upon this most pleasant outpost of Christian civilisation and Western learning.

"From the deeds it dates back to 1502. Of course, there may be somewhere older in the village but parts of the building are certainly 500 years old."

Perhaps the lad's right-hand man, Tom Gurr, may remember it actually being built. Not that Kathy Ramsden, his right-hand lady, would recall. She's quite a bit younger.

"Both Tom and Kathy, in their different ways, are brilliant. Tom and I work so well together and Kathy keeps everyone in fits. And Luke (Willis), my step-son, who handles the catering side of the business is a great knifes-man."

John Bell of Bell's Famous Fisheries, is descended from a long and honourable line of fishmongers dating back to the time of his great grandmother in 1896.

"'Wet, dried and fried', on Lord Mayor's Walk, York, to be precise. Later grandfather Alfred prepared a meal for the French president, Raymond Poincare, in 1913 and that was when we were granted the title 'Bell's Famous Fisheries.'"

After various adventures John's own father Ernest migrated south to Dorset becoming in due course a manager with Macfisheries before the company was bought out by Unilever. Ernest duly acquired shops in Boscombe and Ferndown at which point his youthful and enthusiastic son joined the family business straight from school.

"My father was the finest fishmonger I ever saw. He knew all there was to know about fish and I learned so much from him. One of the most important lessons he taught me was to apply retail principles to a market stall."

With a shop in Kinson behind him John arrived with his van in Budden's car-park in Wimborne in September, 1993.

"The first day, I remember, I took just £50 and in that first week the princely total of £220. At that point I did ask myself 'What have I done?' But things did begin to pick up thereafter and here I am today."

Indeed, 'things' did soon begin to pick up and John Bell has, over recent years carved a niche for himself in the retail folk lore of Wimborne. His van has become the meeting ground for innumerable regulars and the location of the best conversation and repartee in the town. From where does he obtain his fish and what is a typical working day?

"My day usually begins at 4am and the fish is delivered to me in Wimborne between 4.30 and 5am. I use 5 regular suppliers and they know I will accept nothing but the best. I buy according to value for money. They phone or text me if anything special comes in to see if I would be interested. Just a few days ago, for example, I bought a 150 lbs por-beagle shark which was caught off Looe in Cornwall and I was able to dispose of it all. Often customers will ask me what I would recommend for the day. I've become acquainted with their buying habits over a period of time and I try to guide them. If I don't have exactly what they ask for, usually I can find a fish that I know they would enjoy. I also take a lot of pleasure and pride in suggesting ways of preparing the fish for the table. When you meet a new customer, maybe someone who is young and unsure what to buy, again I am delighted to help them. It is so important to make everyone feel comfortable, from the smallest customer to those who are spending a lot of money."

We are surrounded by memorabilia of John's hero, 'the greatest Englishman of them all', Winston Churchill.

"My grandfather was a huge admirer of the man – and my father too. I was 7 years old when he died and I can still remember the occasion. I've read his books and his speeches and I've collected various bits and pieces over the years, including cigar butts he's supposed to have smoked. I love his prose, his intellect, his courage, his genuine concern with ordinary people. I recognise that he was a deeply flawed man, a flawed genius, if you like, but what a contribution to British life he made."

It seems entirely appropriate that John lives in a village with a pub called The Churchill Arms, besides the Black Horse, the Red Lion and The Anchor at Shapwick. John is also a chess player, having won the Boardman Trophy some years ago as a member of Wimborne chess club. He even taught chess at Allenbourn School for 7 years. As I prepare to take my leave, John smiles.

"You know – I absolutely love my job and my customers. I really wouldn't want to be doing anything else."

The sentiment among your customers is mutual, John. We're all very fond of you and Bell's Famous Fisheries.

(Following the serious fire which gutted Martin's Post Office & Newsagents and 2 neighbouring properties, narrowly missing The Priest's House Museum, John has moved to adjacent premises in the car-park).

One splendid success story these past few years, just along the road, past the White Mill – is Chris and Wendy Pope's Barford farm. It's always a pleasure to record hard work rewarded. I've called by several times on fine summer days to sit in their garden and savour their wonderful ice cream. Over the years Chris and Wendy and their son William have built up a herd of 200 Holstein cows on their 600 acres farm and, after lots of careful consideration, decided in 2006 to take the plunge. They have been deservedly been rewarded with prizes at various regional shows.

I did conduct one other conversation in Sturminster Marshall, with Neil Middleditch at Baillie House, but this appears in the section headed Poole Pirates in the chapter on Poole.

WIMBORNE MINSTER
Twinned with Valognes (France) and Ochensfurt (Germany)

'Wimborne Minster is a commonplace town squatting soberly in the meadows about the Stour. It is a characterless place that, having set its face against any show of individuality, has become successfully mediocre. It looks best when seen from a distance.' Sir Frederick Treves, Highways and Byways in Dorset, 1906.

Our great surgeon and literary man painted a less than flattering portrait of the town. 'Commonplace', 'characterless' and 'mediocre', I wonder upon what day(s) and in what season Sir Frederick visited? Was he in ill humour upon arrival? Did he eat badly? Of course, he may well have been justified in his estimation of the town in 1906, but it is to be hoped that few visitors today reach the same depressing judgement.

I am presently sitting in the house of one man who would most certainly profoundly disagree with the eminent man. Despite its proximity to the traffic in Lewens Lane and Park Lane, within the walls of 'Wits End' it is surprisingly tranquil and quiet. It's a homely room with paintings of lifeboats in stormy seas, overflowing bookcases, greetings cards, comfortable chairs, family photographs and a wood-burning stove. It feels like a refuge from a busy life outside, a place to unwind without fuss.

"We arrived in the town, Christine and I, in 1984. We moved down when the RNLI moved its HQ to Poole. We actually met at a lifeboat film-show in 1962. Christine's own world was closely bound up with the Shoreham lifeboat, as her father assisted with the launching of the boat. We had a lifeboat wedding-cake and a lifeboat guard of honour and, of course, I spent much of my working life as a fund-raiser with the RNLI. After I came down I first joined the horticultural society, then from 1987 to 1991 I was the churchwarden at the Minster. I got on to the Town Council by the skin of

Anthony Oliver, MBE.

Sir Frederick Treves. *Picture: Rodney Legg*

my teeth – I was tenth of twelve in the election. Then I was invited to become Mayor. If I remember correctly, five members had already served as Mayor, two didn't want to do it, and so I was chosen."

I remember Anthony's term of office as Mayor with great clarity for it was the year I fortuitously chose to write a book about the town – and what a year that turned out to be with a General Election, restoration work going on apace at the Tivoli and, most gloriously, Wimborne FC winning the FA Vase at Wembley. Since those heady days Anthony has served as Mayor on four further occasions and, as chairman of Wimborne In Bloom, has been largely instrumental in the town winning a host of awards in the Small Town in Bloom competitions. Indeed, as George Willey is often referred to as Mr. Swanage, so Anthony has deservedly become known as Mr. Wimborne. If there is one lingering image I have of Anthony, it is of a tall, lean, straight-backed figure, barely after 8am on a summer's day, replacing flowers in one of the baskets or flowerbeds about the town, ripped out by some drunken idiot the night before.

It was just a few weeks ago that Anthony received his MBE from HRH Prince Charles at Buckingham Palace.

"It was the most wonderful surprise and honour when I received word of the award."

I warn him I will be watching most carefully for any evidence of megalomania and remind him again of Lord Acton's dictum about 'power corrupting'.

"What power?" he asks with a laugh.

The year 2008 has not been the happiest in Wimborne's recent history.

"In several respects it has been a very difficult year for the town with the Canford Bridge closure for major repairs, the general economic recession and of course, the Waitrose affair. As councillors we have been unable to comment on the scheme which many people have found difficult to understand and it has been very divisive. Families have been divided and people have agonised. Now it has been debated and a decision has been taken. Let us hope it proves to be a wise one."

As a councillor are there any other particular issues that concern him?

"I would particularly like to see much more attention being paid to the Leigh estate. It's out of sight and has tended to be overlooked too often. We need to do more for the people there. Then there are the plans for The Square itself. Obviously different individuals have their ideas of how best to enhance its appearance. If we can get that right it will, I believe, greatly add to the towns appeal."

Anthony's contribution to the town over the past 20 years has been immense. Had the RNLI relocated elsewhere than to Poole, Anthony and Christine would not have devoted their collective energies to Wimborne but some other fortunate community. Such is the role played by chance in human affairs. We are privileged to have them here and I am proud to count them as my friends.

It's been quite a year for him for my companion – the author of two books, published within a few months of one another, and the chairman of the Chamber of Trade in what must count as one of the most significant years in Wimborne's commercial history.

"Shall we take business before pleasure?" The ever amiable Malcolm Angel smiles. "As a Chamber we're not sitting on our hands, nor are we wringing them. It's a challenge. It's been difficult with the bridge closure and our members have suffered. In the months ahead we've got to build on our strengths and we need to stage more events through the year to bring people into the town. I believe the town needs to be more professionally and efficiently run – even to think in terms of a town manager to co-ordinate events and raise the profile. Instead of reacting to things that happen we need to plan strategically."

In that respect I believe Malcolm is working alongside Chris Slocock of Minster Press, and Martin Tidd, the former proprietor of the Community Magazine.

And the books? "It's something I've long wanted to do and what could be more appropriate than for me to research the county's most famous smuggler and Wimborne resident, Isaac Gulliver – a fascinating character who is, of course, interred in the Minster between the two churchwardens' seats – maybe so they could keep an eye on him. And my other book is based on one of the most

The 'Chain Gang' in Town. The Mayor, Cllr. Robin Cook, receives the quality town council award from John Raymond of Witchampton, the High Sheriff of Dorset. *Picture: Corin Messer, Bournemouth Echo*

remarkable and little known episodes of the Falklands war. It's the story of 22 Royal Marines, including my friend George Thomsen, stranded on the frozen island of South Georgia facing an Argentinian invasion force, during the Falklands conflict which actually changed the balance of the war."

Having counted Malcolm a good friend for nearly 20 years, I wonder what this remarkably energetic and talented fellow is going to come up with next. His contribution to Wimborne life in the past two decades has been huge and, like young Anthony Oliver, he remains such a likeable and easy-going individual.

The Tivoli

For every student who once attended Wimborne Grammar School in King Street, the Tivoli brings the memories flooding back. For stars of the silver screen like Lionel Jeffries and Richard Todd, for Robert Fripp of rock-band King Crimson, for golfing legend Peter Alliss, the Tivoli was a part of their school-days. Not only was it a cinema, it was the venue for our Speech Day prize-giving each autumn. Many illustrious scholars shook hands with distinguished guests on its stage – pimpled adolescents destined for distinction in science and medicine, the law and academia. Even this writer trod the boards of the Tivoli stage delivering lines as Hamlet and singing unaccompanied in French the theme song from La Ronde. Yet I am indebted to my friend, Tony Gould, for reminding me of the detail of my most entertaining moment. Having somehow contrived to gain a Sixth Form prize, I chose as my reward a copy of Karl Marx's Das Kapital (Volume One). Our headmaster, Dr.J.D. Neil, only discovered the nature of my choice on the morning of the presentation. Horrified that the guest of the afternoon, General Sir Dudley-Ward, a leading NATO general and a former old boy, would be obliged to present this wretched youth with a copy of Karl Marx, someone was despatched to the school library to find a large book in pristine condition to be presented in its stead. In consequence of which, I formally received that afternoon a copy of Songs from the Operas.

Of course, the Tivoli theatre's existence today owes a monumental debt to one individual in particular, Malcolm Angel. Under his inspirational leadership and a team of brilliant volunteers in the 1990s, a building that most Wimborne people feared would never open again was painstakingly restored not merely to its former grandeur but something even better. It now occupies a role in the life of thousands, not only in the town itself, but for miles around who see films as soon as they are released and who are treated to a range of theatrical and musical entertainment of the highest class. It also plays host to a number of local companies and groups. In short, it is a vital part of the very fabric of the town and the community.

There's more than a little wariness in our opening exchanges. I suspect he's placed me in the same league as some of the hard-nosed agents with whom he deals on a daily business.

"They'll trample all over you if you let them but it's my duty to protect this venue. At the end of the day, besides putting on first-class shows and films I have to make a profit. Despite public perception there's no outside funding though the council will finance capital projects like the seating."

Forres School and Milton Abbey in Dorset provided his education, 14 years in Canada, a spell in London, an ad in The Stage – it was a convoluted journey that finally brought Charlie North-Lewis to the Tivoli Theatre on July 1, 2002, to assume the mantle of responsibility.

"My mandate was to move the business forward. The entertainment industry has been my profession for nearly 30 years. To me it's never been a hobby. I believe the contacts I forged over the years have stood the Tivoli in good stead because we have been able to attract so many first-class acts. Our reputation in the world of theatre stands high. We take care of our performers. Look at the recent names who have performed here – Al Murray, Jack Dee, Joe Brown, Stacey Kent, Cleo Laine and the Dankworths among countless others."

There's a fine team around Charlie and he's proud of them all.

"Without our volunteers we simply wouldn't survive. It's as simple as that. It's difficult to pick out names but I must mention Wendy Frewer on the admin side and Andy Day who's done wonders with the building. Andy has painstakingly restored the original floor in the foyer – something he was told couldn't be done. As for Phil Wood, he's a brilliant technical manager. He's taken backstage to a new level of quality and he gets the best out of all those around him. I'm particularly pleased with what we've accomplished with our computerised box office. And, of course, our five Trustees provide their support and advice."

And ambitions for the Tivoli, what are his hopes?

"I wish we could be funded and so have more paid staff – but that's unlikely in the present climate. I'd like to open up the ground floor foyer and make the bar bigger and It would be exciting to create a little studio theatre for experimental productions with removable seats."

Is there one particular name on his wish list of stars he'd love to see perform at the Tivoli?

"The Rolling Stones – to lure them here to a warm-up gig before a major tour. After all, Charlie Watts has played here. It may be a crazy dream, but you never know!"

It seems a most appropriate opportunity to pay tribute to a much loved figure at the Tivoli, Ashley Thorne, who passed away recently. In the past decade Ashley, in his capacity as the resident stage manager, devoted so much of his time and energy to the theatre. Charlie North Lewis observed: "Ashley left an invaluable legacy of warmth and kindness to performers, regardless of their status. He was the same caring figure to amateurs as to household names." Roy Ward, the director of Wimborne Musical Theatre Society said: "Ashley was a friend to everyone. The Tiovoli and the theatre world will miss him". The knowledge of such love for Ashley is, at least, some consolation to his widow Linda, his daughters Sarah and Nikki and the rest of his family and friends.

Wimborne's farmers

"Fifteen years ago the four parts of our 1,200 acres farm shared equal importance. The pigs went in 1997. They were no longer an economic proposition – we were losing £8 on every pig. The 400 strong dairy herd went in 1998. The cows needed half of the farm – for grazing and silage. They became an economic liability. The last poultry will go next year when the new cage regulations come into force. Yes, it will be a sad moment but we have to be realistic. Today arable crops account for 80% of the farm of which two thirds is down to wheat. We'll probably try for more milling wheat – about 40% of our annual yield. The rest goes for animal feed. Prices were good last year though they've dropped a fraction this year."

Chilbridge Farm and the Richards family have been an integral part of the local landscape since 1869. My old friend, Jim Richards, reflects wistfully on the changed agricultural scene.

"Just after the war we employed about 40, now it's just my son Bill – the fifth generation of Richards here at Chilbridge, together with Pippa Burden who's responsible for our 150 beef cattle and our genus inseminator, Robert Burden and Kevin Boyt who's a 4th generation Chilbridge farmworker. Incidentally, our cattle numbers include 50 breeding cows which are either Aberdeen Angus or crossbreeds and, of course, we sell our beef through the shop".

Even the location of our conversation reflects the extraordinary transformation of the past 50 years in British farming. Seated on probably the most ancient settee in the county, we are looking out across a yard full of people and cars visiting Pamphill Dairy Farm Shop and restaurant.

"This barn was a farm-shed and the dairyman, David Cheater and his wife Joyce, lived in the cottage over there. In fact, Joyce would sell eggs, logs and vegetables at her door. Their garden was full of vegetables, just like everyone else's in the district. Now David's gone, the cows have gone, the cottage is let and this barn contains a mix of businesses at ground level. Mind you, 25 years on and Joyce still works with us in the shop. The shop, which has just celebrated its 25th anniversary, is now pivotal to our whole business. Simon Pritchard is the manager of the animal feed-store and Keith Ricketts, who was born here in Pamphill, is the resident butcher and sells the meat from local farms and, of course, our Aberdeen Angus beef from Chilbridge. His mother's the local churchwarden, by the way, so you see what I mean when I say it's very much of a community affair here. Altogether we employ 8-9 full-time in the shop and restaurant. Lulu, has been the restaurant manager here for the past 20 years."

It's an extraordinary statistic. There is twice the number of employees here at Pamphill Dairy than there are working a 1,200 acre farm. Even the cowman's old vegetable garden tells its own story. It comprises neatly manicured lawns and flower-beds. It really is the passing of an era. How many of us had heard of farm shops 30 years ago. Now they are a critical link between the farming community and the consumer, even though often only a part of the produce in the typical shop is grown or reared on that farm. But, as consumers, we like to feel we are retaining a precious link with the countryside and our farmers. It's not just about buying meat and vegetables for our tables. It's sentiment too for most of those who use farm shops. We are making a statement about our own values and re-connecting with our past. The story of Chilbridge Farm, the farm-shop and the Richards family is a parable of our times. Jim, of course, takes a backseat these days and his son, Bill, is now the managing director. That Jim may now be able to spend a few more hours each week with his lovely wife, Wendy, is only fitting after a lifetime of farming.

When I visited Angus Purchase and Janet in 1992 the 850 acres of New Barn Farm were just a year into set-aside. In 1996 Angus placed 270 of those acres, north of the Wimborne-Blandford A3082, into a habitat protection scheme lasting 20 years through to 2016.

"We have created mosaics of scrub and rough grasses and so on designed to encourage a variety of flora and fauna – with some success, I feel. Fifteen different kinds of butterflies have been identified there and also a nationally scarce species of bee – the shrill carder bee which needs a specific habitat to collect nectar and rough grassland for shelter."

With set-aside now officially ended, for the past couple of years a further 110 acres of New Barn is contract farmed by Chris and Will Pope of neighbouring Barford Farm with current crops of winter barley and oil seed rape.

"Of the remaining 450 acres, that's down to temporary grass. We slow mow it and leave what we cut. It's surprising how quickly it disappears. We receive the Single Farm payment for that which is being reduced year on year. The National Trust, our landlord, is quite happy with that arrangement. New Barn is an oasis within a huge area off arable and is, therefore, serving a useful purpose in that role."

How have the various conservation and breeding programmes fared in the past decade or so?

"We've had our successes and our failures. Our efforts to encourage the lapwing to breed here have largely failed though we're not quite sure why. The skylarks were doing well but not this year for some reason. We have, of course, allowed our hedges to grow a few feet taller and that has encouraged yellowhammers, linnets, whitethroats, goldfinches and greenfinches to nest and they have generally done well. Hares have unfortunately never really recovered from the 1960s when their numbers were severely reduced by the spraying of granoxone. They licked their paws and swallowed the poison. That's long been illegal but the numbers are still low. One beneficial side effect of the new hunting legislation is that coursing hares with dogs is now illegal and it appears to have stopped some of the gangs coming out with their animals. On the other hand certain unsavoury individuals are still 'lamping' – pulling down deer with their dogs."

Two generations of the Purchase family have now farmed at New Barn.

"My father Henry and my uncle Jesse came here in 1949 from Moreton, following 2 generations of Bartletts and 2 generations of Kents. Later my cousin George also played an active role on the farm. The farmhouse itself dates back to 1863.Like so many farms locally, it was until comparatively recently a typically mixed farm with 2 dairies, livestock, and a variety of vegetables. But, of course, things have changed beyond all recognition."

We walk out into the garden from which Angus, his family and predecessors at New Barn over the past 150 years, have been able to gaze across unbroken countryside to the Drax estate with Charborough Tower clearly visible on the skyline. Angus points out a handsome Monterey Cypress which stands in one corner of the garden where, to his delight, a pair of kestrels nested in the summer.

"You know, years ago we employed 25 on the farm. And, of course, because we had cows we also had lots of swallows. Their numbers are well down, like the house martins. Where once we had 15 pairs now there are none. Starling numbers have plummeted and I haven't seen a yellow wagtail in years. On the other hand, when the chap from the British Trust for Ornithology came out he spotted a short-eared owl and our local tawny owl population still keeps me awake at night!"

If there is one lesson to be learned at New Barn it is that farming is in a state of permanent and quite radical change. It would be a brave man to predict even a few years on from today.

The National Farmers Union with Rob Baxter

When this writer returned to Dorset in the late Sixties there were still dairy herds everywhere in the Wimborne locality. Regularly near the Horns Inn I remember meeting a dairy herd being walked through the lane to milking or back to the field after milking. Sometimes I must admit grumbling at the brief delay occasioned. Today I would welcome such a sight for cows are as scarce as the house-martins that once nested under innumerable eaves, as the cuckoos that told us that spring was arrived, as the moths that once fluttered against our window-panes every summer's evening, as the ladybirds that lived in every garden, as the hedgehogs that once ate our slugs.

"When I first came to Wimborne there were 20 dairy herds, now there are just four. It's not simply that there are fewer cows in total but the small men have retired or gone out of production because of falling returns or increased costs. The bigger herds have also increased in size and the yields have increased enormously. Today a dairy cow will yield 8,000-9,000 litres of milk a year which is double what it was a decade ago. Where once there were herds of Guernseys and Jerseys, then a period when Friesians predominated, today the majority are Holstein and Crossbreeds. Locally there is a herd of Red Devon at Kingston Lacy."

Rob Baxter, NFU local representative with his office off the Cornmarket, knows the local farming scene and its representatives as well as anyone.

"After WW2 farmers were held in high esteem. There was a national feeling of gratitude. There were farming voices in high places. MPs and ministers often had experience of agriculture. Today the Minister, Hilary Benn, grew up in leafy Holland Park and is a vegetarian. Margaret Beckett, a former Minister, enjoys the countryside on her caravanning holidays but was responsible for a department that made a catastrophic mess of the Single Farm payments which caused such hardship in the countryside for many months last year. Then there's the 'badger lobby' which will not scientifically address the issue of culling, in the interests of the badgers as well as cattle farmers .Much as we love him, Mr. Badger does present us with a serious problem. I fear that in general politicians are less and less interested in rural matters. There have been so many shifts of policy in recent years. We moved from subsidies to ensure food production and guaranteed incomes for farmers to subsidy removal, yet we continue to support many small European farmers, especially in France and Italy. Then it was into set-aside because of over-production, now it's out of set-aside because we need to grow more food. Benn now wants to take land out of conservation, yet there are grants for not removing a hedge, creating beetle banks and protecting lapwing sites and, to encourage wildlife, every arable field has to have a 2 metre strip round the edge of it."

What are land prices here in Dorset?

"The price of land in 2008 is, on average, £5,000 an acre which means that land has doubled in price in the past five years though the increase does not necessarily reflect the agricultural value of the land. Rather it is that the big hedge-funds and their like are investing in land because they see it as a good long-term investment."

I know that Jim Richards is abandoning battery egg production at Chilbridge, what about other local egg producers?

"There are a number of free range producers such as Nigel Batten at Pondhead, Rob Antell at Knowlton and Debbie Lovell (Tozers) at Sixpenny Handley. They have certainly responded to the public's call for more free-range production though the market can be more fickle in an economic downturn."

What is the NFU's approach to the GM debate?

"I would describe our attitude as neither for, nor against. What we do need are closely monitored scientific trials to determine the results. If we can grow disease resistant crops which need no artificial sprays, if we can produce drought resistant strains and grow crops where previously it has been impossible, then that has to be progress. The Government has called for a 50% increase in production in order to feed the ever expanding population. How are we to achieve this increase without the benefits that science can bring? I know GM is not exactly the same as applying scientific methods to livestock breeding but, without the advances over the past 200 years in that area, we would be in dire straits. Today we even refine the breeding techniques of cattle to adjusting the teat size of a dairy cow to fit the milking machine. We take the most enormous care over the selection of bulls to improve the quality of its offspring. Have you noticed that nearly all types of pig now look almost identical – the same size and conformation? Certain traits have been emphasised by selective breeding like reducing the amount of fat. Since pigs have a shorter gestation period and life span, we have been able to quicken the tempo of change within pig breeding to meet the customer's needs".

Is Rob confident about the future for Dorset's farmers?

"People do have to eat, that is a fundamental truth. But we must do everything within our power to ensure that farmers receive fair prices for their products. At the end of the year we've seen more anxieties for our dairy farmers. We need competence at the highest level of Government and a determination to protect the interests of our rural and farming communities."

One of the continuing success stories in Wimborne is Cobham plc, based both in Wimborne itself and at Bournemouth Airport. In the past year it has secured a series of lucrative contracts guaranteeing long-term employment prospects for its workforce. Julian Helebrand, group director of communications, announced most recently that the company, as a part of the consortium Air Tanker Ltd, had secured a 27 year contract with the MOD to supply advanced air to air refuelling and transport capability to the RAF. Cobham's Chief Executive, Allan Cook, explained that the contract, besides those secured in the past year with both the American Navy and the Royal Navy, was a result of sustained endeavour by the whole workforce to maintain the company's pre-eminence in a very competitive market-place.

"The contracts underpin our development plans for a new engineering centre of excellence in

The 40th anniversary of the Wimborne Minster twinning with Valognes – a visit to the Jubille Garden. *Picture: Fraser Bacon, Bournmouth Echo*

Wimborne."

It was half a century ago that Cobham's committed themselves – first the legendary aviator, Sir Alan, and later his son Sir Michael – to the Wimborne area. The encouragement the company received in the early days from the local council, not least through the efforts of Albert Maiden and his council colleagues, has reaped rich dividends for this area of south-east Dorset. Not only was Albert Maiden an outstanding English teacher, he was also a far-sighted councillor whose memory his many friends and former pupils still revere.

One of the happiest events during the year is the celebration of the 40th anniversary of the twinning between the town and Valognes in France. It was back in 1968 that Henry Purchase led the first official visit on behalf of the UDC and this year's guest of honour is his widow Gwen. Forty or so guests arrive in mid-May for their four day visit including the assistant mayor, Mme.Jocelyne Manceau, and the President of the Valognes Twinning association, Bernard Tardieu. There is a celebratory dinner at the church hall, St. Michael's, Colehill. Fraser Bacon, from the twinning association, describes the four days as 'an unqualified success'. Over the past 40 years I know there have been innumerable contacts between the two communities that have enriched the lives of both towns. When sometimes we despair of the modern world, it is salutary to reflect that the nations that warred at Crecy and Agincourt, at Trafalgar and Waterloo, are now bosom friends – well, almost!

At the year's end, another event to celebrate is the ceremonial re-opening of the Canford Bridge after so many months of traffic chaos that created exasperation for motorists and adversely affected

Sixth Form Forum, Canford School *Picture: Mike Laver*

trading in the town. A £3million refurbishment programme is commendably completed on time by the contractors. With flood arches dating back to 1675 the bridge was first opened to the public in 1813. The old Victorian structure which had served us all so well was closed for much of the year to traffic. It has now even acquired a new footway similar in design to the Millennium Bridge. With good fortune none of us alive today will be around to witness its next refurbishment. However, I fear Julian's Bridge is also in need of attention so that will be something for every motorist to look forward to in the future.

Sixth Form Forum at Canford School

(I would like to thank John Lever, the Headmaster of Canford School, for so readily agreeing to host this Forum on a Sunday. I would also like to express my thanks to Danny Meredith at Poole GS, Steve Tampling at QE, Wimborne, William Franklin at Parkstone GS and Hilary Laver at Canford for arranging for representatives from their Sixth Forms to participate in the debate.)

It's a grey, raw Sunday morning with a steady drizzle but a warm greeting from Canford's recently appointed Head of Sixth, Hilary Laver. The lovely lady has even arranged a splendid array of Danish pastries, assorted biscuits, fruit juice and coffee to nourish youthful minds and bodies.

Our young contributors are Ben Dymott and Dan Doherty from Poole GS, Ben Stuchbury, Florence 'Flossy' Wallis and Kate Rayner from Canford, Iona Wilmshurst and Karl Howard from QE, Lily Robinson, Rosie Hartman and Rosalyn 'Roz' Wikeley from Parkstone GS.

One topic is inevitably uppermost in everyone's mind – the 'credit crunch'. I don't know who coined the term and I don't much care for it, but there's no doubt that everyone present knows exactly what it means, not least its implications. Lily and Iona are of one mind. Lily leads the way.

"Whatever the Government is borrowing – or lending – it's our generation that is going to bear the greatest burden of paying for it all."

Iona is indignant at the injustice;"At the very moment we will begin repaying our student debt and tuition fees and looking to secure mortgages, we will also have to pay vast sums in taxation to the Government for their mistakes and those in the banking and financial services industries."

Roz also can barely conceal her contempt for the bankers.

"I'm so angry with the bankers. They even had the nerve to pay themselves huge bonuses when they didn't do well. And just how healthy is it for a society to borrow, borrow and borrow still more? We must inculcate healthier values, the merits of being financially responsible and thrifty."

Ben Dymott pours scorn on the so-called experts and whizz-kids of the City.

"The sub-prime mortgage business was a scandal. Surely they could see it would all end in tears and disaster. Or were they blinded by their own greed?"

Ben Stuchbury looks at the wider picture.

"The oil barons are making it even harder by raising prices or lowering production to preserve and maximise profits. The American economy is such a big player. Everyone seems to be out for themselves."

Karl points out the many contradictions and flawed values.

"There are so many conflicting messages. Six hundred million dollars was spent on the Obama election campaign, Manchester City FC has just spent £32million on one player Robinho and, at the same time, we have millions claiming benefits in our society, many of whom are exploiting the Welfare State."

Ben Dymott highlights similar contradictions. Ben is Oxford and Sandhurst bound with a career as an army officer in mind.

"I agree. I read recently that a lesbian soldier had been awarded a £250,000 settlement for 'hurt feelings'. That's more than a British soldier receives if he loses a limb."

Dan Doherty digs deeper.

"I believe it's a crisis for capitalism as an economic system. It's driven by the constant need to produce more and more."

Roz wonders whether we need a return to the past.

"Do we need a Maggie Thatcher to instil more discipline? "

On that count, however, Rosie is distinctly sceptical.

"But it was Mrs. Thatcher who created the impetus towards individualism and the pursuit of self-interest."

Inevitably immigration is a contentious issue. Lily pleads for cool heads to resolve a difficult subject.

"While I welcome diversity in our society there must obviously be limits. It's a balancing act, trying to find an equilibrium. On the one hand, it's flattering to think so many people want to come to the UK to build new lives, on the other their numbers must be controlled."

Rosie understands better than most the complexities of the issue.

"I have a Zambian father but my grandfather who, like many of the older generation lived in war-time London, does find it difficult to accept the great changes in our society in recent years."

Roz is also concerned to strike a civilised balance.

"Have the British people ever been properly consulted on immigration? Has the Government forced multiculturalism upon us without a proper debate? I accept unreservedly a society in which everyone is treated equally but it is ridiculous that, in some instances, our enemies are actually allowed to remain here – and even receive State benefits paid for by the ordinary tax-payer."

But Dan Doherty points out a danger.

"Can we though possibly send people back to countries where we know they may be tortured or shot? Doesn't that present us with a serious moral dilemma?"

At this point our young would-be parliamentarians take a break to demolish some of the mouth-watering Danish pastries and other refreshments so kindly provided by our hosts, scarcely pausing between mouthfuls to continue their debate.

Suitably revitalised Karl expresses concerns about the loopholes in our benefits system.

"People will always find a way to exploit the system but I believe we do need to much tougher on welfare cheats."

Roz is anxious about the long-term effects upon society.

"We do now have a dependency culture. Young woman have babies, often by different men, and they are constantly claiming more benefits. So begins a cycle of dependency. Lord Beveridge did not introduce the Welfare State at the end of WW2 for that to happen."

But Dan is anxious that the innocent are not penalised by any changes.

"We must protect the genuine single mother. It would be very wrong if we failed to do that."

We are meeting in the immediate aftermath of Barack Obama's victory in the US Presidential election. There seems to be unanimous agreement his election is a cause for hope.

Ben Dymott believes the US must change a number of its policies.

"Perhaps we can begin to get away from the notion that the USA has the right to police the world."

Flossie, Rosie and Iona are hopeful it is the beginning of a new era.

"We believe that Obama will reinvigorate American politics. He appears to possess the charisma to carry people along with him and he can inspire a new generation."

Roz expresses a few words of caution amidst the general euphoria.

"While I hope Obama will prove a successful leader, I don't think we should be carried away and invest unrealistic expectations in his election."

The recent broadcast by the BBC involving Jonathan Ross and Russell Brand in which they left lewd messages on the answer-phone of the highly respected actor, Andrew Sachs, does not find favour with Kate.

"The nature of the language in the broadcast is part of a culture of disrespect. It would be unthinkable in Hong Kong or Japan where I have grown up. The fact that it was allowed to be broadcast is to me deeply shocking. And, in general terms, it is quite unnecessary to swear or use foul language to get a point across."

Karl is disturbed by another aspect of modern society.

"In Bournemouth I understand that for every hour you spend in the town you are being surveyed by cameras for three quarters of that time."

Iona is equally concerned by the growth of the Big Brother culture.

"I am very anxious about the threat to our privacy – others knowing every detail of our lives."

Ben Dymott is no less troubled by the Human Rights legislation emanating from Europe and Westminster.

"In creating human rights they have actually removed other rights from us."

Karl is not greatly impressed by the quality of many of our members of parliament.

"MPs do not represent a cross-section of humanity. Too many politicians have little or no experience of the real world. And too many are destructive instead of being constructive."

We are fast running out of time. I ask our young friends to express one particular wish for the coming years but not of a personal character.

Karl: "I would simply want everyone to treat those around them as they would themselves wish to be treated."

Iona: "I echo that sentiment. It's a good principle by which to live."

Ben Dymott: "I would like to see the rebuilding of communities, for the family to be recognised for its crucial importance in maintaining social stability."

Roz: "It's so important that people learn their about their responsibilities before they learn their rights."

Dan Doherty: "I would like to see a return to economic stability. That underpins so much else."

Rosie: "To see true equal opportunities – raising a few 'glass ceilings' – that would be my wish."

Lily: "Economic order and an end to greed."

And so we shake hands, wish one another well and thank Hilary Laver for making us all so welcome and her husband for coming in to take the photograph. As a group we know we shall never meet again. Soon my young friends will be scattered about the kingdom on a variety of university campuses. They and thousands like them are the future of this country. I wish them every success and happiness.It was fortunate, perhaps, that we met before the subject of MP's expenses came to our attention. The language of our youthful speakers throughout our discussion was temperate and measured. I suspect, however, even the mildest-mannered of our contributors would have found it difficult to refrain from some strong language on that topic.

One modest but interesting event in the life of the town's religious community is this year's celebration of the bi-centenary of the arrival of Methodism in Wimborne.

As Geoffrey Baraclough of the local Methodist Church explains:"Though John Wesley visited the county much earlier, the first service in Wimborne was held on November 6, 1808, at a house in West Borough. The first chapel in the town was built in 1820. To mark the occasion a service takes place, led by the present minister of the church, the Revd. Marcia Hardy, in the church in King Street.

Wimborne in Bloom

After the heroic efforts of a team of 50 volunteers led by John Hare-Brown, the committee members receive a Silver Gilt trophy in the Small Town category at an awards ceremony in Crawley in early September. Having seen John on so many occasions with his volunteers about the town weeding and trimming, it is a fitting reward for so many hours of labour on behalf of the town. We all take pleasure in the displays which decorate the town for several months of each year and, while it's impossible to mention all the individuals who deserve our thanks, I will congratulate in particular Ron Currall and Jo Archer of the Rising Sun, Ken Short of Wimborne Engraving, Alison Board of Tilseds for their valued contributions.

John Hare-Brown is also the recipient this year of a special Civic Society Award for his services to the town. A retired police inspector with the Met, John and his wife, former deputy primary head-teacher Brenda, moved down from Tottenham 6 years ago and immediately involved themselves in voluntary work in and around the town.

"We chose to live in Wimborne because, very simply, it felt right from the moment we first visited the town. It's got everything we need and it is such a warm, welcoming community. Being a part of the voluntary team here is not only a way of making a useful contribution but a wonderful way of making friends."

But both John and Brenda are anxious about recent legal changes affecting sectors of voluntary work, not least the legislation relating to working with children. As a former police inspector and a teacher both have spent a lifetime in responsible positions dealing with people of all ages, not least young people.

"But today, for example, if we wanted to try and harness the enthusiasm and energy of scouts or brownies, or just young people in general, in projects about the town we have to undergo Criminal Records checks with lots of intrusive personal questions regarding bank details and so on that we feel are both unnecessary and unreasonable. What is even more ludicrous is that if you are cleared for one activity, the whole fun and games has to be repeated for another activity and it all costs organisations money. To tell you the truth, it feels rather like another stealth tax by Government. Then there are the host of procedures relating to health and safety – risk assessment and such – that have gone way beyond all reason. We both believe this is a serious problem that is already having an adverse effect and is deterring applicants from becoming involved in a range of voluntary work. What's happened to plain, old-fashioned common sense?"

Brenda and John, you are absolutely correct. Everywhere I have travelled individuals have complained of the bureaucratic, prying 'nanny' state we are fast becoming where common sense seems to have flown out of the window. But don't let it prevent you or your splendid friends from continuing all your admirable work on behalf of the community.

The Priest's House Museum

It is so easy to take for granted what we pass by every day on our way to the shops but, once again, this splendid attraction in the heart of the town provides so much information, learning and pleasure across the year for both the local community and visitors alike. For the 2,500 school-children alone who pay educational visits each year it is both intellectually stimulating and enormous fun. For visitors to the town it provides an opportunity to appreciate more keenly Wimborne's history. The achievements of the Priest's House team are recognised when it receives the highly regarded Sandford Award for a record third time for educational excellence. The assistant curator, James Webb, pays a special tribute to the work of the educational outreach officer, Anne Brown, Emma Ayling and the splendid team of volunteers at the museum.

One rather moving moment arrives in the naming of the latest building project in New Borough when our most honourable Mayor, Robin Cook, cuts the ribbons with developer, Dave Wells, at Perry Court named in honour of the much respected John Perry, a former Mayor and long-time councillor, who passed away last year. The twelve 'affordable' one and two bedroom flats will prove a valuable asset to the town's housing stock. As Dave observes: "John was a good friend and gave a great deal to the community. It seemed the natural thing to honour his memory in this way." Well said, Dave.

Another splendid Wimborne person, still happily very much with us, is Margery Ryan, who was recently awarded the Save the Children's highest honour for volunteers – the Lasting Achievement Award – which she received from Princess Anne in London. It's a much deserved acknowledgement of many years service to the charity for Margery. Another popular local figure whose services to the community are recognised at the year's end is former court clerk John Slow who receives an MBE. Once described as 'the Ken Dodd of the Justices' because of his humorous observations, it's a well merited honour.

Two faces from the glory days of British cinema may still be spotted about the town. One, of course, is the lovely lady, Margaret James, who appeared all of 60 years ago as Beryl, the tea-girl, in David Lean's classic Brief Encounter, one of the best-loved films of all times. Margaret actually abandoned acting when she became a mother and devoted herself to raising her son, Michael. As we know, tragically Margaret and Raymond lost their beloved organist son to cancer 20 years ago when they set up the Michael James Trust dedicated to helping young musicians through their training. One, I know, especially, who was fortunate enough to benefit, was my old Poole GS student and friend, Sam Hanson, now regarded as one of the finest young organists in the kingdom. The other actor you might glimpse is Michael Medwin, that splendid character actor who appeared in so many films in the years after the war and, until very recently, was still starring in panto in Bournemouth.

"We were first in the King's Head in 1979. It was a joint venture between the Civic Society and the Southern Tourist Board and the kiosk was manned by volunteers."

I'd long forgotten the origins of Wimborne's invaluable Tourist Information but I am reminded by a lady who has been virtually synonymous with it ever since. The ever cheerful Rosemary McDonald has been associated with TI for almost 30 years and has been the manager for the past 17 years. I remind Rosemary of Sir Frederick Treves's caustic observations in 1906 following his visit to the town. How incredulous the great man would be to return a century later and find that visitors now love to come here and tourism represents a valuable part of the economy.

"Tourism really received a major boost locally with the opening of Kingston Lacy and Moors Valley. Today, of course, besides the Minster we have the Model Town, Walford Mill and the market and lots of visitors come out from Bournemouth and Poole to look around what is a lovely, small market town. The response is overwhelmingly favourable. People love the small shops and the river and the general feeling about the town and there's so often something happening – like a wedding spilling out on to Minster Green, a craft fair at the Allendale, Chris Brown and his militia strutting their stuff, or the graduation ceremony at the Minster when the Arts Institute awards its degrees. And, of course, with Wimborne in Bloom, the town is full of flowers and looks so attractive. The words which sum up the town for me are its 'colour' and its 'warmth'. Finally, every attraction lies within walking distance and is on the level."

Rosemary and her splendid and unfailingly helpful team of Lindsey Hobson, Judy Wright, Debbie Wagstaff, Veronica Mills and Sharon Foster, also provide a range of other services at the counter – bookings with National Express, various events like the Steam Fair, theatrical productions, the Waverley and so on. Tourist Information is such a important feature of town life and it's difficult to imagine quite how we managed before its inception. On a statistical note, Rosemary tells me that 110,000 people came through the doors last year. One lady I must not forget, who was a greatly valued and popular member of Rosemary's team for many years, is Anthea Cross. Anthea retired just a year ago and lives out on the Cowgrove Road at Court House. One of Anthea's pet projects today is charity fund-raising through the sale of her jams and preserves at the door. This writer can personally vouch for the quality of her products.

Would Rosemary wish for any changes in the town?

"I have just one nagging concern – the next generation of volunteers. At the moment, we are reliant on a wonderful group of people but I'm looking for that next layer. I would like to see more people coming forward to replace the generation who have given such sterling service."

Fifty-odd years ago the secondary school at Pamphill was the most modern for miles around. Indeed, its facilities were the envy of the local grammar school in King Street, Queen Elizabeth's. As students at QEGS we trekked up to Pamphill to perform our annual school plays on the splendid new stage there. But that was half a century ago and the school at Pamphill, which metamorphosed into Queen Elizabeth's when the grammar school closed, has been in need of a major overhaul for at least a decade and now it's happening. Incorporating all the latest 'green' technological developments – solar panels, automatic lighting systems, woodchip burning boilers, rainwater recycling, recycled building materials, low energy usage – the only criticism I've heard so far of its transformation is the cost. Originally the projected figure was £4million. The final cost is now likely to reach £20million! How can anyone get their maths so wrong? Whoever – and I imagine it was an assortment of so-called expert economists, statisticians and computer whizz-kids at County Hall – was responsible for the forecast figure should be compelled to attend an intensive arithmetic course at QE when the work is completed, sitting at the front of the class with dunces' hats on their heads. Of course, that might adversely affect their 'self-esteem' and infringe their human rights, so perhaps we should just pat them on their heads and say 'Try harder next time.'

In the meanwhile, we all wish the headmaster, Andy Puttock, his staff and all QE students Good Luck when they move in to their new premises. I hope all the builders, engineers and construction workers who have laboured on the new buildings have a better grasp of mathematics than the 'experts' at County Hall or there might yet be a few further shocks in the pipeline.

My old friend, Rodney Legg, is very unhappy about the felling of more of the historic avenue of beeches on the Badbury Rings stretch of the Blandford Road and plans to cutback another substantial number.

"It's health and safety paranoia on the part of the National Trust. At the moment they're under constant pressure to err on the side of caution even when the risk is very small."

Planted by William John Bankes in 1835 I've not counted how many of the original 731 now remain but the number is diminishing year by year.

David Roberts, the manager of the Kingston Lacy estate, acknowledges the force of Rodney's criticism but responds:"We have to adhere to health and safety but I would stress we are not chopping down healthy trees – just the diseased and dying. It saddens us terribly to do it but we have no choice."

Nigel Chalk, NT gardens and countryside manager adds: "Beech trees in chalky soil are expected to live between 150 and 200 years. Age, disease, shallow roots and climate change are all contributing to the decline of the avenue. Sadly, we have to recognise it has little future."

It's a difficult one, isn't it? The fundamental problem is the litigious society in which we live and the readiness of many greedy individuals to rush to the courts if they sniff the opportunity to make compensation claims. It is affecting every part of our life. It's also to be hoped that the second avenue of trees planted back from the road 20 years ago begins to flourish when there is more light.

Incidentally, I wonder what our arithmetical experts at County Hall would discover if they were asked to count the trees as an academic exercise. I suggest the figures would vary between one fifth of 731 and a figure well in excess of the original. Shall we put them to the test – equipping them just with pencils and paper and a pair of stout shoes?

(Though the greater part of this chapter is collected at the year's end, in the closing stages of my journey, inevitably the narrative cannot be wholly in chronological order. The following is a prime example. The events of September 29, 2008, are of great significance in the town's recent past and are, therefore, described at length in the following piece I wrote shortly after the historic public meeting.)

Monday, 29 September, the Allendale Centre
Waitrose and Hanhams cricket ground, to build or not to build?

For 5 years we have waited as others have deliberated.Now the long wait is over and in we file, courteous, good-natured, earnest but divided Middle England to take our hard seats and listen.

Kingston Lacy's historic beeches. *Picture: Roger Holman*

Our worthy Planning Committee is precisely 9 minutes late. Mild barracking erupts from impatient Keep Wimborne Green supporters but our Committee members have been on a tour this golden September morning so they may be forgiven. One last inspection of Hanham's and adjacent points to ensure their picture is complete.

The hall is filled, every place taken, standing room only at the sides and back. Old friends and familiar faces are everywhere. I chat with two, Anthony Hannam and Bill Haskell, good democrats both, no rotten eggs or stinking fish evident about their persons. On the platform Mike Hirsh, chairman of the planning committee, warns us he is recovering from a cold and fears his voice may buckle under the strain. Just a few days ago he recommended rejection of the application. Now he begins to explain the reasons behind his decision. Unassuming, painstaking, gently humorous, possessed of a pleasant vocal delivery, Mike takes us through every stage of his reasoning – the protection of the conservation area, anxieties about traffic and drainage and the likely visual impact. On a large screen he presents a series of photographs taken from this angle and that angle. There's one of a gentleman named Neil Lancaster holding a stout pole on the cricket square. It's just as well there's not a game tomorrow. The abrasions made by the pole would make it a spinner's paradise. What is dear Jack Douch thinking at this moment, I wonder? Each twitch of that pole must be sending shudders down his spine. Mike's stamina is remarkable. Light of frame, he might have made a marathon runner in his prime. If he were a horse I'd back him each way for the National. And remember he's only just getting over a cold. What couldn't he achieve when fully fit? Then, as quietly as he began, he's finished. There's no rhetorical flourish, no bow to the audience, no knowing wink at the fairer sex, that's not the nature of the man. Mike has spoken for one and a half hours and he hasn't bored us. That is no mean achievement.

A 'comfort break', as it is euphemistically called now. A time to stretch legs, move various parts of the anatomy grown numb, exercise vocal chords. 'Well, what did YOU think?' is the question I hear on everyone's lips. In the foyer there's a long queue at the ladies'. Poor wretches, they always have to wait for ages on these occasions while we men are in and out like jack in the boxes. Aged, creaking, jack in the boxes, anyway. Then we're back on those hard chairs again and the protagonists prepare to lock horns in the final epic struggle for supremacy.

The anti's first. It's often more difficult to oppose. You can criticise until the cows come home but the neutrals are looking for more than mere opposition. With 7 speakers primed it's imperative any alternatives are presented as a coherent strategy. Andrew Kenyon does not care architecturally for what he sees on paper. 'Better suited to Slough or Basingstoke, but not Wimborne,' he declares. How would the good residents of Slough or Basingstoke respond to Andrew's slur, I wonder? Nicky Beaton from Streets Meadow not unreasonably doubts the 60 elderly residents in her care will appreciate staring at brick walls when they have been used to a pleasant expanse of greenery. John Pullen, the owner of nearby Stoneleigh's Rest Home, expresses similar sentiments. John Harper argues that the Council should buy the land and stage special events which would help to defray the cost of purchase. Brian Barraclough laments the passing of a scene from picture postcard England with a cricket ground at the very heart of a town. Engineer Keith Smart fears flooding and the dangers presented by man-hole covers, and the even greater dangers of missing man-hole covers? At least, I think that was what he implied but I am watching the faces on the platform at the same time. I must concentrate. Then it's Philip Atlay who has spearheaded the campaign for KWG. Just days ago he confessed to me how relieved he would be when it was all over and he could get on with the rest of his life. I think Philip's dear wife will be even more relieved. How many hours has Philip devoted to the cause? No campaigner could have fought a more valiant fight. Philip presents a well-argued, cogent case. No one in KWG objects to Waitrose the company as such, he says, rather it is the loss of a precious open space for all time. Philip doubts Waitrose shoppers will remain in the town. Will they even have time to wander over the new bridge? After all, Waitrose will want them in and out like greyhounds from the traps. Sentiment is one thing, but they want to hear those tills ringing, or whatever tills do these days. We'll have much more traffic Philip argues, without the benefits its supporters suggest. Like the other KWG speakers he deplores the proposed building on aesthetic grounds. It is the best speech by far and well received, but has he done enough to sway the EDDC?

It's time for the pro-Waitrose camp to explain their enthusiasm for their cause. Malcolm Angel, hero of the Relief of The Tivoli and Chairman of the Chamber of Trade, presents his case. By common consent, Malcolm is an admirable fellow. We all know what he has already achieved for the town. The Chamber of Trade, Malcolm declares, overwhelmingly backs the application. The town needs to be revitalised. A new anchor store could be the catalyst for an era of unbridled prosperity in the town's history. Everyone listens with respect because it's Malcolm. Then it's Gary Holman, of the long established family electrical household appliances store, who describes the traders of Wimborne as being in a state of deep financial depression. As a town we all approve of Holman's, not least dear old Roger, even though he's no longer the public face of the shop. Silver-tongued Chris Bulteel follows, while Peter Cooper and Christopher Undery represent two more units of Waitrose's citizen army.

Now it's the turn of the smooth Mr.Waitrose himself, Mark Price. Two hundred jobs will be created, he declares, and local property prices will go through the roof when Waitrose arrives. If he, Mr.Price, wishes to buy a house in the town he knows he will have to dig deeper in his pocket if his company wins the day. But that, he adds with a rueful smile, will be a small price to pay for such an eventuality. Is Mr.Price really going to become a Wimborne resident then? Will we soon see him in the queue at John Bell's fish van, or at Paul Keating's butchery? It couldn't be an ever so slightly cynical ploy, could it? It would be interesting to know if Mr.Price drops the same hint in other towns where Waitrose is seeking permission to build one of its food-stores? David Lawes from Wimborne cricket club pays a fulsome tribute to the Hanham's estate for its munificence in providing an alternative site on the Leaze. So I am mistaken in thinking Waitrose is paying the Hanham estate a large sum of money for the existing cricket ground, and footing the bill for the new pavilion and the preparation of the new ground on the Leaze? It must be the most extraordinarily altruistic gesture in Wimborne's long history? Clearly I've got it all wrong and muddled. This is philanthropy on the grand scale. Actually, while I do understand Mike's enthusiasm for the new pavilion and the club's security of tenure on the new ground for the next 25years, I fear there is an element of self-deception concerning the financial realities of the arrangement.

Suddenly, it's ended. It's nearly half-past one. We all need a break. Outside the sun is still shining but I sense the mood has changed among the protagonists. The green and white figures of KWG stand in subdued clusters. The pro-Waitrose lobbyists, in contrast, appear buoyant, more audible. Is it my imagination or are they not standing with straighter backs than the opposition?.The heavy guns of their artillery have been brought to bear with conspicuous effect on enemy lines.

The Olive Branch

"Two glasses of Merlot coming up. We do sell bags of nuts, but not crisps, sir."

Why don't they sell crisps, I mutter under my breath? Well, yes, I know the reason, of course, because they want me to spend more money on expensive food but there's also a certain snobbery about the whole business too. Two figures appear at my elbow, Malcolm and Mr. Mayor himself, the admirable Robin Cook. There's a part of me that wants to speak like Larry the lamb whenever I meet mayors but I always refrain out of good manners. Malcolm and Robin are drinking beer. We talk of Malcolm's forthcoming books. I compliment our Mayor on his exceedingly smart pinstripe. His son Russell is off for a job interview that afternoon, he confides. In that suit Robin should be at the interview. I have no doubt he'd get the job. What of the morning's events then, we ask one another? My companions appear quietly confident of success for their cause. We check our watches. We've barely arrived and already it's almost time to return. I open a book – what time will the vote be taken and the meeting declared closed? Whoever is furthest away buys the drinks next time. Malcolm suggests 3pm, Elaine opts for 3.30, Robin settles on 3.10. I always bet each way but with only 4 runners it must be win only. I decide it'll be a photo-finish with Mr. Angel. My money is down, a 2.59 conclusion. We return to the Allendale.

Our district councillors speak their minds first. Cllr. Don Wallace, having tried valiantly to gauge public opinion over recent months with a measure of accuracy, actually completed his reading of the 156 page report on the matter in bed, he confides. Don is the best of fellows, we all know, and a gentleman of unimpeachable integrity. He is the Robespierre of Wimborne – the incorruptible one.

He regularly helps old ladies across the road, even if they have no wish to do so. He expresses his frustration that he is not permitted to vote before leaving the platform. He also adds that his arms are still aching from holding that report. Or did I imagine that? Cllr. Pat Hymers, who has deliberated long and hard, gives her ultimate blessing to Waitrose before stepping down with her customary elegance. Cllr. Richardson offers qualified approval just so long as several hundred conditions are met. I cannot recall if he mentioned uncovered manholes but I suspect he may have done and, if he didn't, he should. So it continues and the minutes tick by – 2.59 has come and gone. So too Malcolm's estimated 3pm. Our predictions are out with the washing. At last, everyone has done and Mike Hirsh calls for the vote to be taken. Does the EDDC support the Waitrose application to build their store on Hanham's? Hands are raised – eight in favour, two against, one abstention. The time is 3.14pm. One half of the audience expresses its delight with exuberant and noisy applause, while the other half sits in stony silence.

Out we file, cock a' hoop, or our tails between our legs. Five years of campaigning has ended here on this sunlit afternoon at the Allendale. There is something to celebrate even if the cause is lost for this is England, a free society and a democratic decision has been taken. In other places, at different times, no mechanisms would have existed for such choices to be freely made. No one has lost their temper, not publicly at least, and no lives have been lost. The debate will be continued, of course, across dining-tables and bars but in civilised, measured tones for the most.

Philip Atlay resolves to continue the fight through all the remaining channels open to him and his team. But, for most of those present, there is no longer serious doubt that Waitrose will be built on Hanham's green and pleasant space. And for this writer, what does he feel? Throughout the 5 years of controversy I have been opposed to the development. A unique feature of Wimborne will disappear forever beneath concrete and asphalt. That is a terrible shame. Of course, I understand the cricket club's pleasure at acquiring a brand new ground and a fine pavilion and most shoppers recognise the existing supermarket is poor to indifferent. The argument has never been about Waitrose as a company. I think nearly everyone wishes they had bought the existing supermarket and converted it to meet their needs. Profound anxieties however, do remain. The traffic will undoubtedly increase considerably in the town and there is a serious possibility of acute problems in and around the entrance to the store. Certainly, while it is under construction, traffic will be severely dislocated at times. Will the hopes of the traders be fulfilled and their overall turnover markedly improved? There must be doubts, especially for those in direct competition with Waitrose. What is going to happen to the existing supermarket? I fear it will not long survive and suspect that in 2-3 years time the new Wimborne debate will be – what is to be done with Crown Mead? Finally, there will long remain a feeling that an opportunity has been missed. If Hanham's had to be lost as a cricket ground, there was an opportunity to create a splendid park for the community and visitors to enjoy in perpetuity. I hope, for the sake of the town that I love, my fears prove groundless and the best expectations of Malcolm and Roger and their friends are duly fulfilled. I presume too Mr. Waitrose, Mark Price, will soon be spotted peering in the window of Chris Batten or Alan Cosgrove.

Happily in and around Wimborne there survive many small independent businesses but there's often a thin dividing line between making a good living, just getting by and going under. As in every town in the county the number of small traders has diminished over the past fifty years, especially those in the food trade. But if we wish to ensure choice and variety in our towns this writer believes passionately that we must lend support to our small businesses – just so long as they are deserving of our custom, of course. For that reason, I have chosen to highlight several excellent examples in Wimborne and the locality of just such businesses. I might have selected a dozen others just as worthy but, alas, limitations of time and space preclude their inclusion. But I hope my advocacy of their merits will be seen as a vote of support for the small man, or woman, in business for their survival and prosperity is vital for the health of all our communities.

They make a good team, partners Phil Gough and Alan Danvers of Stanbridge Motors Ltd, and they need to be good to survive in a competitive world. With 57% of small filling stations/garages having disappeared from Dorset's villages in recent years, it's never been so difficult for the small man to survive. With undercutting competition from supermarket forecourts nearly all the independent filling stations have long since disappeared. With the pressures on new car owners from the main dealers to service their vehicles with them, invariably at far greater expense, together with the cost of investing in capital equipment, we have also witnessed the demise of many of the small garage repair proprietors.

"We estimate that if we were starting from scratch we would need to spend £40,000 to equip ourselves in order to be licensed to carry out MOTs. Then you can add another £3,000 annually to maintain that equipment."

Fortunately for Phil and Alan, their geographic location on the Cranborne road makes Stanbridge Motors, originally a petrol dump for service vehicles during WW2, the logical choice as the local MOT/servicing garage for many who live across a wide swathe of Dorset countryside.

"Witchampton to the west would be the nearest garage in that direction, Blandford to the north, Sixpenny Handley to the east and Wimborne to the south. With John Benns off to Ferndown and the site due to be redeveloped for building, that will leave only Tice's in the town itself. As for our business, we carry out about 2,500-3,000 MOTs annually. That's obviously the bread and butter, besides the routine servicing."

When I'd spoken to Phil a couple of years ago he was pessimistic about the long-term future for garages like Stanbridge. He is currently more up-beat, so too business partner Alan.

"As long as there are moving parts in vehicles, the usual skills will be required but I don't know how far we can look into the future. Ten, twenty years, who can tell? Cars are generally so much more reliable today. Many people now buy a second-hand car, ignore maintenance and drive them into the ground. Then they'll start all over again. As for new cars, I suspect they'll do as increasingly they do in the States and lease cars, rather than buy."

Michael Whitmarsh began his apprenticeship at Stanbridge way back in 1954 and remains an integral part of the team today. He's wryly amused by the changed vocabulary of the world he has inhabited for the past half century.

"These days we're no longer called mechanics but 'vehicle technicians'. We use diagnostic machines to trace electrical faults and we have almost ceased to repair cars as we did when I first came in to the trade as a 15 year-old. Rather we exchange units. It's certainly a different world."

Happily, Phil and Alan, Michael and Andrew Besant, Laurie Whyman and William 'Bob' Moorcraft who complete the team, have established an outstanding reputation in the locality.

In years past I was grateful for the skills of old friends Tony Hughes, Brian Hayter and Phil Manning. Today the team at Stanbridge continue to provide excellent service at fair prices. It is enormously reassuring in a world where it is easy to be 'ripped off' by unscrupulous individuals to know experts in their field you can trust 100%. Phil and Alan at Stanbridge Motors provide just that reassurance.

(With John Benns departing to Ferndown 2 popular and familiar faces will be leaving Wimborne simultaneously – John himself and Peter Pardy, for a number of years the unfailingly good-natured, so obliging pump-man who has assisted hundreds of old ladies uncomfortable with the mysteries of filling up their Jags and Porsches from self-service pumps. Peter was, of course, for many years one of the finest bakers and confectioners in the county based at Pardy's Hill, Corfe Mullen. Though I

Two of Wimborne's brightest musical talents – James Slocock (violin) and Sam Hanson (piano) rehearsing in the Minster. *Picture: Chris Slocock*

have met many fine bakers on my travels none has quite matched the quality of the crusts on Peter's sorely missed loaves. His loss to the bakery trade, however, was a gain for the old ladies of Wimborne and district – but whatever are they going to do now?)

"First it was my mother Rosemary and my sister Julia, then me – we've been here now since 1978, more than 30 years. Of course, the music scene has changed radically in that period. Radio has changed – what you used to hear blasting out on building sites. Top of the Pops has gone. The charts are now virtually meaningless and buying patterns have altered. I belonged to a generation for whom those things were of significance in their lives – buying singles and albums. The singles market has collapsed. Now people can download, legally or illegally, and they pick and choose what they buy – particular tracks from albums."

Paul Holman at Square Records, a talented musician himself who worked alongside Paul Chambers in the days of the Lemon Trees and missed chart success only by a whisker – he now plays with local band Loose Chippings – is the public face of Square Records along with popular, ever cheerful, modestly talented but wildly enthusiastic Sunday footballer, Rob Hoare. Paul's excellent team is completed by Julia Boughton and Kerrie Robinson. Paul is, of course, the son of Wimborne's brilliant photographer, Roger, and the younger brother of Steve and Gary (Gus) at Holmans in King Street. Just how difficult is it for the small record retailer in today's market-place? After all, it's a world where supermarkets will cheerfully use their muscle to undercut bookshops and record shops without compunction.

"In a shop like ours, we are catering for proper music lovers. We don't mind spending time looking for material for our customers. We try never to say 'No'. We'll look through the back catalogues and explore various avenues to obtain what our customers want. It's also terribly important to have the right staff with a sympathetic, helpful approach. An old lady may come in. In a big store she might feel silly asking for something unfashionable – let's say's for example, Glenn Miller. Here we take a pride in being helpful and accommodating our customers. That's the kind of service a small specialist store with the right staff can offer. I'm happy to spend 20 minutes with one customer trying to find what he or she wants because I know they'll come back another day, and they will recommend us to their friends. We can also compete in most areas pricewise. I am actually quite optimistic about the future. I feel we've built up a good reputation over the years and our customers appreciate the service we provide."

Paul is a season-ticket holder at Dean Court though he doesn't turn out with Rob's Sunday league team. I'll leave Square Records with this most revealing admission from Rob one day earlier in the year. I asked him which team was in opposition the following Sunday.

"They're bottom of the league. But I'm feeling quite hurt – I've been dropped!"

Paul Keating bought Wimborne's one surviving butcher's shop from Derek Burton 3 years ago and this personable young man has made a fine job of following in Derek's illustrious footsteps.

"I try to buy locally wherever possible. These days our customers like to feel they know where their meat is being produced. For instance, I buy lambs from Richard Harding at Canford Magna, Dorset horns from Mike Yeandle at Owermoigne, Red Devon beef from Mike and the Kingston Lacy estate, and venison from Mike Small, the deer manager on the Cranborne estate. Our poultry is all free range, of course. To tell you the truth, I believe TV programmes like those of Hugh Fearnley-Whittingstall, have done a lot of good and helped to educate the public who only want to buy free range from us these days. As for the turkeys you see around you in the shop, they are all from Graham Tory at Thornicombe near Blandford."

Paul has built a good team around him. Graham Montgomery admits to working in the shop for at least 30 years but it is the collective opinion of customers, colleagues and this writer, that he first arrived as an apprentice when Hitler's armies were marching into the Low Countries in 1940. Alex Webb, Rob Knowler and Wendy Mayne all provide service with a smile and a ready quip and even the legendary Derek Burton, when he isn't sitting by his treasure chest counting his money, occasionally provides a cheerful, helping hand.

Bookshops – only record shops can compare. Many individuals would cheerfully spend their entire lives in them. Supplied with endless cups of coffee, they would read their lives away.

"Many of our customers say they love the smell of a bookshop. We don't really notice, being so accustomed to the smell."

Anne Angel, Helen Webber and Gill Nixon have owned Gulliver's in partnership for 4 years now though Helen has actually worked there for the past 20 years.

"We wouldn't be doing it unless we really loved it. You don't come into bookselling to make a fortune but because you love books."

If I were one of the 3 ladies I would be furious that the supermarkets 'cream off' many of the 'best-sellers'. How outrageously unfair! For the most part supermarket staff know nothing of the world of books, they provide no service to customers who wish to buy anything else and yet they'll sell J.K.Rowling or Jordan's latest ghost-written autobiography at a discount which makes it impossible for the small, independent bookseller to make a profit. They even place them by the till appealing to the 'impulse buyer'. Yet, to a degree, the ladies are philosophical.

"Most of the people who buy books in supermarkets are not going to come into a bookshop anyway. And it may just encourage buyers to read more widely. We have to try and sell what the supermarkets don't sell."

I'd still be quietly seething if bookselling on the High Street were my business. Wimborne has also endured its fair share of problems in the past couple of years.

Left to right: Alex Webb, Rob Knowler, Graham Montgomery, Paul Keating. *Picture: Geoff Hill*

"What is so frustrating is that we've been powerless to do anything about the difficulties. Up to the Canford Bridge closure we were happy with our volume of business – but the closure for so long did reduce the numbers coming into the town. More recently, of course, it's been the recession and spending has declined. In a sense, it doesn't matter that any of us in the town run excellent shops – we just feel we have no control over our own destinies. And though the Government talks about helping small businesses, nothing tangible seems to emerge."

(In my piece on John Bell at Sturminster Marshall I referred to the serious fire in the town which has now added to the difficulties facing Wimborne's traders.)

Gulliver's Bookshop has now been serving the book-lovers of Wimborne and district for 40 years. It provides an absolutely invaluable service to so many people and it's now so amazingly fast in responding to demand.

"Generally we can obtain any book within 24 hours from our wholesaler in Norwich."

Like so many locals I place a very high value on Gulliver's existence in the town and hope that it is still here serving the public in another 40 years, even if Ann, Helen and Gill are browsing through the shelves in some other place. Incidentally, the 3 other faces seen behind the till are Mary Wallace, Ann's daughter Jane, and my old friend, former Poole GS scholar now at Durham University, one of the most appropriately named bookshop employees in the kingdom, 'Jamie' Joyce. (Did any of the great man's friends call him Jamie I wonder?). As I leave Ann reminds me of an important recommendation made by my illustrious namesake who possesses infinitely more talent – and money – than this impecunious scribbler, though I think I'm marginally better-looking!

"Alan Bennett always urges his readers to buy his books from an independent bookseller."

Ladies, I agree wholeheartedly with the great man and would urge every reader in the locality to use Gulliver's of Wimborne.

At Furzehill Post Office and Village Stores Ben Baxter has built what must be one of the finest small village stores in the county.

"I do try to source as locally as possible. I buy strawberries and various vegetables from Robin Hiscock up the road at Glen Farm, Holt, meat from Ian Butler at Oakley, Carol Sharp supplies me with 'bake off' bread, Margaret King from Stocks Farm supplies the plants and I buy a range of biscuits from Fudges and Moore's in the west of the county. One of my principal suppliers is D.W.Holley from Bristol. The company is owned and run by members of the Plymouth Brethren and I have to say they are quite superb. For much of our stock I buy through the local wholesaler's and we try to be competitive. However, my general pricing philosophy is a straight margin on everything. I really cannot be bothered with different price margins on a range of commodities. It's also much easier from a book-keeping perspective. What is absolutely critical about a shop like ours is the quality of the staff and the service they provide."

On that count, there is not the slightest doubt that Ben's team scores heavily. The staff at Furzehill must be second to none in the county. There may be comparable but there will be none better. That is not to say, of course, that their collective behaviour is always even-handed towards the sexes. The ladies, two in particular, clearly derive a particular pleasure from their baiting of many long-suffering male customers, not least this writer and my friend Roger Honess, and we are clearly regarded as fair game for their witticisms and barbed insults. But, if we are honest, we love it because at Furzehill we are treated as individuals in a world where so much shopping today is impersonal and deadly dull, if not downright rude. Notwithstanding the verbal crossfire we males heroically negotiate on a daily basis, not one of us would deny that the service is superbly efficient and unfailingly helpful.

Ben makes an interesting point with regard to the closure of many village stores across the county.

"Our turn-over here is sufficient for me to be able to employ staff right across the day from 7am to 7pm in order to meet the modern customer's demand for all day opening. If this were a smaller one-man or own-woman business, such long hours would soon become intolerable for one individual. No one could endure that kind of pressure for months, or even years on end. "

I am going to mention the names of all the staff here because, in spite of everything, I believe they do deserve their place in posterity – from history graduate 'Mr Reliable' Bob McConnell, Ben's right-hand man, to the most provocative members of the team Mary Glen and Lyn Maser and the mischievous trio of Sue Vaughan, Sarah Cook and Stella Goodman, not forgetting part-timers Kate Crumpler, Hannah King, Chris Vaughan and Ailsa Hearne.

There's no sign of Sid James or Kenneth Williams, Hattie Jacques or Liz Fraser, on the day I call by it at Wilksworth Caravan Park but I'm certain they'd have loved to 'carry on camping' here – even in the rain that's falling as I arrive and which is still falling as I leave.

"It's the sort of place that, if we were touring, we would like to stay at ourselves."

Wilksworth Farm Caravan Park is set in tranquil countryside just off the Cranborne road out of Wimborne. Though I've driven the road a thousand times I've never previously ventured within even though I've known Ray Lovell who, together with his wife Wendy, has run the enterprise for a number of years.

Ray's words reflect the civilised ethos of Wilksworth. The caravan park was originally the brainchild nearly 40 years ago of Wendy's mother, Shirley Purchase, who with her husband John farmed the 500 acres before passing it across to their son Ian and his wife Helen. Since 1995 the caravan centre, which is open for 8 months of the year, has been the responsibility of Ray and Wendy who have invested their energy and capital to such effect that Wilksworth Farm can now boast a 5

The Old Winburnians Association's Christmas lunch at Cobham's. Former students of Wimborne Grammar School in King Street toast 'Absent Friends'. The Association's oldest member is Wilfred Palmer aged 96. His brothers, Charles and Ken, are in their eighties. *Picture: Geoff Hill*

Star Tourist Board rating and a 5 Pennants AA rating. It is an unreservedly superb site with room for 85 touring caravans, 25 tents and 77 statics which can be occupied for 8 months of the year by their owners. At its peak the centre will be home to 500-600 visitors who will, of course, be spending their money in the locality. Wendy stresses the importance of the 'personal touch' she and Ray offer their visitors.

"We are always available and people know that if there's a problem we are here ready to respond. We have a very high percentage of repeat bookings each year which is proof enough of the popularity of the site."

The farmhouse, occupied by Ray and Wendy, is 500 years old and there may even be a resident ghost on site though it has been spotted only once.

"A visitor said she came upon a young girl covered in blood in what she said was an old stable.

In fact, it was the area we converted into the showers/WC area. She didn't, in fact, know it was once an old stables and Martin Rendell, who carried out the conversion for us, later confessed to us that he'd hated working in there. He said there was an uncomfortable atmosphere about the place. It's a strange story but there has been no repetition of the incident."

With an under cover games-room, a swimming-pool, a mini-football pitch and a host of other family friendly activities – and a safe environment for children to wander freely about the 11 acres site- its popularity is understandable. With 3 boys of their own, Luke, Clint and Josh, Ray and Wendy appreciate the importance that visiting families attach to such facilities.

"What we don't have is a club-house with a bar. It was a conscious decision. To be honest we're not trying to attract that market. This is beautiful countryside, it's peaceful and quiet, that's what our visitors enjoy and why they keep coming back."

And if Sid and Kenneth, Hattie and Liz, should turn up and fancy a night-cap before turning in, I'm sure Wendy and Ray will simply point them in the direction of The Stocks or The Barley Mow or, of course, our celebrated quartet might just prefer a cup of tea and a cuddle by the camp fire.

In the space of 18 months they are both gone. Sir Michael, the 12th baronet, and Lady Jane Hanham, the residents of Dean's Court for the past 35 years, have both died. Sir Michael inherited the baronetcy and the 200 acres estate from his cousin Maud in 1974 and he and his wife soon became engaged in a host of activities and organisations in the town. They were a genuinely popular couple, down to earth and kindly. Sir Michael flew with Bomber Command in the war, completing 55 missions over enemy territory. After the war he worked with BOAC and ran a garden furniture business. Reg Cunningham best summed up the town's feelings for Lady Hanham when he observed:"She was always first to ask how your family was if you bumped into her. That was the type of person she was – always thinking about others." Former secretary Susan Gibson described Sir Michael, a member of the Civic Society and chairman of planning for 22 years, very aptly as: 'A joy to know. Even in his electric chair or with 2 sticks he jolly well got there. You could count on him – he will be terribly missed." Sir Michael and Lady Hanham are survived by 2 children, William and Victoria.

As we go to print a new Mayor is announced, Wimborne born and bred John Burden who has lived on the Leigh estate for the past 30 years. John's wife Ann, another Wimborne girl, becomes the new Mayoress.

"Harry's coming over to do the draw sometime after 8pm. How many Premiership managers would do that, I wonder?"

There's a mood of expectancy in the clubhouse at Cuthbury. Although 17 years have passed since Wimborne's glorious expedition to Wembley and FA Vase glory against Guiseley in that thrilling, never-to-be forgotten final that ended 5-3, the club still boasts its loyal core of ever optimistic supporters. After all, next season it just might happen all over again.

Harry's coming over from Sandbanks to draw the lucky sponsor who will have his company's name on the club shirts next season. At £250 an entry 40 potential sponsors have already contributed an invaluable £10.000 into club funds.

There's also an underlying sadness about the evening for several of us. Ken Holloway, now 88, was the inspired, super-efficient club secretary in those heady days. Unflappable, unfailingly courteous – an old-fashioned gentleman, in short, and loved by all who know him – Ken is still a familiar figure about the town.Ken's son, Simon, no less a popular face in the town until earlier in the year, was a great supporter of the Magpies through the good and lean years. Tragically, after a courageous battle against serious illness, Simon passed away in October aged just 53. This evening preparations continue for the inaugural Wimborne FC v Wimborne U18s which will take place at Cuthbury for the Simon Holloway Cup. Generously the trophy has been provided by club chairman Ken Stewart and former manager Alex Pike.

"The club has been wonderful in the aftermath of Simon's death. I cannot praise them too highly."

It's to the credit of everyone involved that Simon is being recognised in this fitting way. There was no more enthusiastic supporter. Whenever we met he'd regale me with all the details of how the club was faring.

"Here he is – it's the man himself."

Harry Redknapp arrives with his wife Sandra to an appreciative round of applause. This is the authentic East-ender, the man who unfailingly provides pressmen with the most memorable quotes of any living manager. Of one player's disciplinary record he said:'He's got more previous than Jack the Ripper.' On another occasion he was quoted: 'I left a couple of my foreigners out last week and they started talking 'in foreign.' But I knew exactly what they were saying: "Blah, blah, blah, le b......manager, etc etc, useless b .....!"' And at the age of 62, like good wine, he still seems to be improving. Who would have guessed after he left his beloved Hammers that the best years were still to come? After guiding Portsmouth from the depths of the Championship to Premiership security and FA Cup glory, last season he picked Tottenham up by the scruff of the neck from the foot of the Premiership and led the club to the unlikely brink of European qualification. Tonight his first act is to spend several minutes chatting to a young man in a wheelchair. Any public relations agency could still learn lessons from the man. A few introductions about the room and it's time for an official welcome by vice-chairman Paul Miller – and the fateful draw. The successful businessman is Dave Scriven of Paramount Windows.

Harry remains 30 minutes or so, chatting politely and posing for photographs with a queue of fans. Tom Lockyer and I stay too, talking with Ken Holloway and Jamie Sturgess. Jamie scored twice at Wembley and there aren't many players, even the really famous ones with world reputations, who can claim such a feat. He's back at the club now in a coaching capacity. And he's a proud dad. We discuss that great side of '92 – and what a team it was! And how incredibly fortunate I was there to record it. Earlier in the evening, in the grand banqueting hall of the clubhouse with Ken and Paul Miller, I'd glanced down that list of names in the picture the brilliant Drew Snell produced.

'Shane Turner, Mark Allan, Trevor Ames, Phil Langdown,Kevin Leonard,Robbie Beacham,Andy Taplin,Brian Wilkins,Nicky Bridle,Dominc Barrett, Jason Lovell, Jamie Sturgess,Taffy Richardson (captain),Tommy Killick, Simon Lynn. With trainer Mick Sturgess, manager Alex Pike,officials, Brian Maidment, Phil Goulding, Ron Dinmore and, of course, Ken Holloway.' Not everyone played on that hallowed turf, but each played his part in that season no supporter will ever forget.

It's time to call it a day. Harry and Sandra are leaving too.

(Happily the Fun Day at Cuthbury and the inaugural Wimborne XI v U18s in memory of Simon Holloway is a great success. Dear Simon would have been thrilled.)

The Year's End, Topo Gigio's, Mill Lane – A couple of days earlier in the week)

"You are a great asset to the town, an old lady said to me the other day as she passed by the restaurant. That was as kind a comment as anyone could pay me."

He recently celebrated his 20th anniversary as a restaurateur in Wimborne and he still exhibits the same boyish enthusiasm as on the first day he opened the doors of Topo Gigio's all those years ago. Diminutive Nino Guaggenti arrived in England practically penniless as a 15 year-old from Palermo in Sicily but with a burning ambition to make a success of his life in his adopted homeland.

Topo Gigio's, New Year's Eve. **Left to right:** Gianfranco Poggi, proprietor Nino Guaggenti and young ladies.
Picture: Geoff Hill

"Within a square mile of us there are a dozen or more Indian, Chinese, Italian restaurants and take-aways, as well as 20 or so pubs. The competition keeps me on my toes! I cannot afford to be complacent. We make everything here on a daily basis – the bread, the pizza bases, our sauces. It does not come frozen or in boxes. Fortunately in the kitchen I have 2 splendid assets, Marisa Abieri who has been with me for many years and Andrea Latini from Florence. And, of course, my right-hand man, Gianfranco Poggi who comes from Milan. Franco has a wonderful work ethic and is invaluable, especially on days when I am not here."

What Nino does not add is that he is an AC Milan supporter while Franco is a Juventus man which is the equivalent of a Liverpool and a Manchester United fan working in tandem. In the circumstances it is a remarkable friendship! For both men, as for every Italian I have ever known, the family is of paramount importance in their lives. Franco loves a round of golf with his son while Nino's 3 children, Jessica, Alessandro and Kristina are a permanent source of pride and pleasure – the girls often assisting in the restaurant.

9pm New Year's Eve
Already every table is occupied, the conversation loud and animated, the laughter infectious. Though the year has scarcely been distinguished by acts of great statesmanship or wise fiscal leadership by our political and financial masters, everyone present is clearly determined to forget whatever anxieties have been troubling them in recent months and to let their hair down as the year draws to its unlamented close. While our lovely young waitresses scurry between tables bearing trays of

New Year, 2009, Wimborne Square. 'Should auld acquantance be forgot and never brought to mind? Should Auld acquantance be forgot Auld auld lang syne.' (Robert Burns) *Picture: Geoff Hill*

drinks and food, Nino and Franco exude a quiet air of relaxed confidence. When you've been doing this kind of thing for as long as they have, they know the truth of the old maxim 'More haste, less speed.' Geoff Hill, ace photographer and the locality's nearest equivalent to 'Arfur' Daley, and Yours Truly decide to take a quick look outside, leaving the ladies to their nibbles and their bottles.

In Mill Lane Robin Cook is leading the Mayor's procession into the Square and across the road into the King's Head. As yet there are no revellers to greet them, only a few youthful couples, oblivious to everything except their partners, are locked in lustful embraces in the shop doorways. Robin and his motley crew will no doubt be partaking of 'light' refreshments in the hotel before emerging just before midnight. I wonder if popular Alan Breakwell, the public face of the EDDC and only a year away from honourable retirement with a record of just one day off work since Neville Chamberlain declared it was 'peace in our time', is junketing with his Furzehill cronies. These councillors and mayors certainly know how to live life to the full. The court of Louis XVI scarcely knew such decadence.

Back in Topo's Exocet balloons are screaming across the room. Geoff proves to have more puff than anyone in the room but then he's a big lad. I couldn't blow up a bag, let alone one of these monsters. The whole world is wearing funny hats and we're all launching missiles at neighbouring tables. Everyone is joining in the madness. Nino's again the little boy he was in Palermo all those years ago before he set out for England seeking fame and riches. He crouches behind diners and fires his 'peashooter' at some unsuspecting customer. This is serious fun. The average age of the diners has dropped from fifty to five in as many minutes. Who cares about Northern Rock and Gordon Brown and Alistair Darling when you're reliving your childhood all over again? We're scrabbling about on the floor among diners' feet retrieving pellets for our peashooters. I definitely want to be here again in 12 months. I'll get that fellow with the bald head if I'm seated nearer next time round. The range of my peashooter means my missiles are falling short.

It's almost twelve, time to file out into the Square. Practically everyone is on their feet making their way to the door. We'll all be back – afterwards. Every face is flushed with the craziness of the past hour or two – and the odd glass of this or that. Everywhere it's smiles and laughter. The Square that was empty, apart from love's young dream, is heaving with exuberant humanity. Yes, of course, we know reality will return in an hour or so when we turn the keys in our front doors but, for the moment, we're living in the present. A year ago, at this precise moment, I'd barely arrived in Lyme. Have 12 months really passed since we stood on the Marine Parade outside the Harbour Inn with my travels ahead of me? Chris Brown's militia are gathering outside the King's Head, muskets at the ready. I love eccentrics. They put a smile on our faces. They make us all feel a little better with their harmless nonsense. The serious ones who think they know what is best for all of us, they are the dangerous ones.

It's here, the moment has arrived. The bells are ringing out, the mad musketmen are in their element, the piper's a'piping, The Square is overflowing with hugs and kisses and heartfelt good wishes for the New Year. Yes, we've done it all before and sometimes the next year is better than the last and sometimes it is worse but, at this moment, we're all hoping. Ian Willis, one of Wimborne's truly glorious eccentrics and a fellow we all treasure, shakes my hand and a passing posse of boys from Poole GS scuttle across to greet me. What brilliant lads I had the privilege of teaching. Back then to Topo Gigio's for a complimentary glass with Nino and Franco. I invite those seated at neighbouring tables to scribble their names on a piece of paper and express their hopes for the year ahead. All too soon it's time to depart. I wonder if we'll meet up again in 12 months? So we wend our various ways back to our beds. There's a big card of racing tomorrow and I need a good sleep and a clear head in the morning. The evening has been unreservedly brilliant, a fitting finale to an extraordinary year. Now all I have to do is the writing, to give it order and shape. Did I say – that's ALL I have to do?

Before me now, a crumpled sheet on the table, I have the names of all those who wrote their wishes. Most I can decipher, others are a problem but I will try – Toby & Denise Hunter, Lee Knight, Pat Young, Mary Ivett (?), Barbara Geldart, Jimmy Lee, Jess, Derek G, Tricia and Ray Humby, Kristina, Phil A ,Sarah Powell, Nino G and Franco.

One central theme underlines every wish – peace and harmony across the world. Amen to that.

Journey's End

So it's all over and my journey is done. Now I look back across the miles and the hundreds of pages and wonder if it was all a dream. Did I really meet so many people and ask so many questions? Did so many patient, tolerant, kindly individuals welcome me into their homes and their lives? At this moment, as I write these final paragraphs, there is only relief that soon I will be able to lay down my pen, switch off the computer and resume a normal life; relief that I will no longer wake in the early hours thinking of all the people I have missed and the places I still have to visit; relief that I may begin to sleep soundly again. For 18 months I have, of necessity, ceaselessly travelled the highways and byways in Dorset. My journey scarcely compares with those who have trekked across continents, up and down mountains and along the great rivers of the world. Besides those adventurers my efforts are puny and barely worthy of comment. But, in the time at my disposal, I know I could have achieved little more. I have done my best. Now my readers must judge my efforts.

When J.B.Priestley wrote his masterly *English Journey* in 1933 he described it as 'part travel book, part autobiography and part investigative journalism.' The great man began his travels at Southampton, journeyed westward to Bristol and the Cotswolds, before setting off across the Midlands, through the Potteries and Lancashire, before arriving in Durham in the north-east corner of England. It was the era of the Great Depression with stark and painful contrasts between the relative affluence and comfort of the southern counties and the appalling misery of the shipbuilding and mining areas in the north-east that were worst affected by mass unemployment. Priestley wrote with acute perception of the many contradictions and inadequacies of an economic system that generated great wealth for the few and wretchedness for so many others. As a Socialist he passionately denounced the failure of capitalism to produce a more equal and just world. The Thirties, other than the years of WW1 and WW2, were by common consent the worst of the century for the industrialised world. With the Bolshevik Revolution still fresh in peoples' minds and the most dreadful of Stalin's crimes against humanity largely unknown, many idealists believed Communism offered the solution to man's problems. However, J.B.Priestley was always a democratic Socialist and cared as deeply about freedom as social justice. The pages of English Journey are not only a testament to the brilliance of his prose and imagery, his innate wisdom and decency, but they also reflect vividly an extraordinary era of British social, political and economic history. In the Thirties, against the backcloth of the advance of Fascism and Communism, there was a polarisation of beliefs and ideologies. Today, as I write, we live in a very different political climate. In spite of the grave consequences of the 2008 banking and financial crises and their impact upon the daily lives of all Britons, not least here in Dorset, there is no profound questioning of the principles of our economic system and little serious political division. The debate is more about which party can best regulate and oversee the capitalist system. So my travels reflect little of the earnest discussion that characterised much of Priestley's journey. When I spoke of politics with various individuals along the way, the general mood was one of barely suppressed rage accompanied and tempered by expressions of resignation, impotence and cynicism. Whereas Priestley's literary brushstrokes were often painted in black and white, mine are more in dull shades of grey.

Though Priestley met and talked with many dozens of individuals on his travels he chose to mention no names in his narrative. This decision enabled him to paint word portraits of those he encountered knowing he would offend no one directly by his observations. It was a choice that enabled him to employ much more adventurous language and imagery than I dared to use. Had I described John X, the Mayor of Y, as 'a man with the political beliefs of Genghis Khan, a hairy wart at the end of his nose, bulging eyes, blackened teeth and rancid breath whose wife resembled a drunken harlot straight from a Cruikshank cartoon', it would doubtless have proved highly entertaining to readers. However, my description would have been not only deeply offensive to John X, his family and friends, but would certainly have rendered any further expeditions by this writer to Y hazardous in the extreme. In contrast, I decided at the beginning that I must mention by name the individuals I met unless, of course, they requested otherwise. It was, I believe, an entirely appropriate decision for I wished to record the authentic voices of the county and not composite, nameless figures which is the most serious weakness and danger of the alternative method.

In his magnificent work, published in 1934 to great critical acclaim which I unreservedly recommend to every reader – above all, the illustrated Folio edition of 1984 – John Boynton Priestley wrote these words.

'I had seen England. I had seen a lot of England. How many? At once, three disengaged themselves from the shifting mass. There was, first, Old England, the country of cathedrals and minsters and manor houses and inns, of parson and squire; guidebook and quaint highways and byways England.... Then, I decided, there is 19th century England, the industrial England of coal, iron, steel, cotton, wool, railways; of thousands of little rows of houses all alike... The third England belonged far more to the age itself than to this particular island. America was its real birthplace. This is the England of arterial and by-pass roads, of filling stations and factories that look like exhibition buildings, of giant cinemas and cafes...... There is almost every luxury in this world except the luxury of power or the luxury of power.'

If in 1933 Priestley identified 3 distinctive Englands, how many distinctive Dorsets 'disengaged themselves from the shifting mass' in 2008 for this traveller? Whilst the great landowners of Rider Haggard's day in 1902 no longer dominate the landscape of the county, vestiges do remain of that Old Dorset order, for there are still several individuals who possess 12,000 acres or more, together with a score or so of lesser landowners. Property and land rich though they may be – with some deriving vast incomes from outside the county (according to the Sunday Times Rich List of 2009 Charlotte Townsend of Melbury is worth £300 million) – today their political power and influence is inevitably much reduced, muted and circumscribed. Yet though their personal characters may, for the most part, be benign and enlightened, dare to tread on certain toes and you will still feel Old Dorset's displeasure and clout.

Not so long ago, outside its principal towns, Dorset was agriculture its length and breadth and even its towns held their regular market days when produce and livestock were seen every week in the streets. When Rider Haggard travelled across the county in the years 1901-02 it did not, of course, encompass Bournemouth and Christchurch. At that time it was 632,000 acres, 54 miles from east to west and 5 to 40 miles north to south. In practice the area of countryside is not greatly different today and still agriculture is carried on across most of the county. What is radically different, of course, are the numbers engaged in the business of farming for the workforce is enormously reduced thanks to mechanisation and ever greater efficiency, Rob Baxter of the NFU estimates 8,000-10,000 maximum. It is probabaly accurate to state that the agricultural workforce has shrunk ten-fold in the past 50 years. In Haggard's day much of the county was farmed by small tenant farmers, traditionally mixed farms with small dairy herds and other livestock. Today much of the land on the big estates is farmed 'in hand' as the older generation of tenants has retired and the next has decided to leave the land permanently. Haggard's words of 1902 ring true even today.

'They (the younger generation) leave the land for the greater variety of occupations in the towns, the recreational opportunities, the better pay and opportunities, the shorter hours of work, the opportunities for promotion. They leave because of the dullness of village life, the desire for fresh scenery and the inevitable restlessness of spirit among the young.'

Those smaller farmers who have survived all the problems of recent years are more likely to own their farms but they will, in most instances, have diversified in ways beyond belief to past generations. Farm shops, garden cafes, radio masts, caravan and camping parks, bed and breakfast, fishing lakes, musical concerts – anything that will turn an honest penny or two you will find somewhere in the county. Never has the old adage 'Don't put all your eggs in one basket' been more diligently practised. Few farmers rely simply on their incomes from agriculture. In innumerable instances wives will be employed in outside occupations to supplement the family budget.

As I have described elsewhere, the 2 largest towns of the county, Poole and Bournemouth, have diversified their economies radically over the years. While tourism remains of critical importance to both, the growth of banking and insurance in Bournemouth as companies relocated from the south-east, and the development of innumerable specialist engineering firms and companies such as Sunseeker in Poole, have provided thousands of job opportunities across the locality. No less important is the expansion of public service employment – in hospitals, health centres, education, social services and the like. Such a diversity of employment is the best guarantee, especially in times of economic recession, that the region remains relatively unscathed compared with many parts of the country.

What of the social structure of the county insofar as it is possible to identify specific changes? If the old landowning class has diminished both in numbers and influence and the agricultural workforce has largely disappeared, the growth of the middle classes is the most manifest change of the past half-century. If we are not quite all 'middle-class' today, it is true to say that Dorset contains a very high proportion of professional, relatively affluent residents and it is within this group that we see the most dramatic development of recent times. I am referring, of course, to the enormous expansion of that section of the population which is over 60 (for the most part), retired, comfortably off – many of them 'incomers' to their communities – energetic, socially responsible, imaginative and caring. These are the volunteers who run our charity shops, drive patients to and from hospital, show visitors around churches and NT properties, organise a host of fund-raising activities for deserving causes, keep our towns and villages attractive and inviting, support cinemas and theatres by working in box-offices and acting as usherettes and a host of other activities. In my youth, for the most part, no one retired before they were 65 and few pensioners had any energy left. Most sadly knew they were likely to die within a very short space of time. The importance of our new generation of 'volunteer labour' is of huge significance both economically and socially. If, as more than one individual on my travels wryly observed, this group went on strike or suddenly ceased to exist, our society would find itself in dire trouble.Many times I have been profoundly moved by the voluntary work performed by this wonderful group of people on behalf of their fellows. When we reflect on the unsavoury antics of too many of our politicians, bankers, financiers, media and sporting personalities, it is refreshing to remind ourselves that a vast swathe of our society remains kind-hearted, generous and unselfish.

What else? Another relatively new phenomenon, compared with the Dorset of my childhood, is the growth of female employment. Most of the mothers of my youth did not have employment outside the home, except perhaps the part-time job that enabled them still to be at home when their children returned after school and during much of the school holidays. The modern woman is more often than not juggling demands upon her time from her family and her employers. We know why this change has occurred and we understand why so many women, whatever their personal preferences, feel under financial pressure to work full-time. With property prices higher than the national average in Dorset, the financial demands upon families are often acute. Though, at a personal level, I believe it is highly desirable that mothers should always be there for the children in the early years of their lives, if it is practical and possible, I fully appreciate their dilemma. It is both sad and unfortunate when they feel they have no alternative. Yet, as a number of the young mothers I once knew as pupils in my classes have said to me, 'I wouldn't have missed those first years with my children for anything. No job can ever compare with the satisfaction and joy of being a mother.' I realise this is not a universal view but when we have an increasingly disruptive and undisciplined youth, I am not alone in entertaining grave reservations about present trends.

One last thought on the changing social structure of the county. Though not unique to Dorset – indeed, while it is less of a problem here than in many counties, it nevertheless constitutes a cause of serious social concern – we have witnessed in recent times a growth in numbers of what Karl Marx 150 years ago described as the 'lumpen proletariat'. Shorter Oxford Dict definition- 'the ignorantly contented lower orders of society.' Cushioned by the benefits system, housing allowances and whatever other 'scams' they are able to exploit, this group is content to be parasitic upon the working community. Many of the hard-working neighbours of such individuals are outraged that this segment of society is able to 'work the system' to its material advantage. I have encountered a number of such examples, particularly on certain estates, on my travels. Most of our social and criminal problem families are located within this group. How we tackle this issue is of importance for the presence in many of the county's schools of growing numbers of unruly children, conscious of their rights but not their responsibilities, is a source of anxiety to every parent.

There is, I am certain, no doubt but that the single most important issue in the county today is housing or, more accurately, the lack of housing for those on lower incomes. At the same time, for those already on the housing ladder, the most significant topic affecting their communities is the threat to their particular localities of more housing being built on their doorsteps. How to resolve this particular conundrum is going to test the imagination and political skills of a whole generation of local political leaders and planners. Not far behind housing must be the care of the elderly for we are an ageing population in the county. A number of small towns and villages, in particular, are going to face growing and very serious difficulties as the numbers of those in the 70 plus age group become more frail and vulnerable. The expanding need for health provision for this group will place acute pressure on county and local budgets. Another major cause for concern relates to transport. Not only am I referring to the dreadful congestion on many roads which already seriously affects people's everyday lives as they drive to and from work – and we all know that is going to get very much worse with the population set to grow significantly – but the absence of transport in isolated villages as residents grow older and are unable any longer to drive. With local shops, post offices and pubs having closed in innumerable communities, the problems for local residents are multiplying annually.

In his English Journey J.B. Priestley referred on several occasions to the German word 'leitmotif' to describe the gradual process by which his view of a particular location was shaped over several days. 'I have noticed this happening before, and every time it does happen one feels that a pattern has suddenly, momentarily, been imposed on the chaos of encounters and arguments and chatter.' It is a curious sensation but I know exactly what he meant. One arrives in a town or village for the first or perhaps only the second or third time. On an earlier casual visit, perhaps made years before, one had come merely to admire a particular building or participate in an event taking place in the locality. On such an occasion one left, in all likelihood, with a confusion of impressions. But engage residents in conversation, as I continually did, wander about or sit and reflect, be in no haste to move on, read the local press, eat and drink in the local pub and, after a time that collection of experiences coalesces into a coherent idea or image. 'Leitmotif', it is the perfect word to describe the process. At night, waking in the early hours, I found myself constantly retracing the events and exchanges of the day in a particular town or village. Often it was not even a conscious process. Rather, I would wake with an imperfectly formed but broadly accurate picture of the essential nature and character of that place.

It was impossible, at moments, not to be simultaneously astonished and dismayed at man's capacity for both extraordinary technical achievement and his talent for dissension, dispute and acrimony. Examine the extraordinary precision of the engineering skills possessed by those engaged in the manufacture of one of Robert Braithwaite's Sunseeker yachts , or the mechanical ingenuity of the machinery now carving out the Weymouth relief road, or the scientific knowledge required to create great storage gas caverns beneath the seabed in Portland, or the architectural principles that underlay the building of Sherborne Abbey or Christchurch Priory hundreds of years ago. Then cast an eye on a community or institution divided by hostile factions.

Priestley wrote with such perception. 'If we were half as clever in the matters that lie far outside machinery as we are about machinery itself, what people we should be and what a world we should leave our children! If life were only an internal combustion engine!'

My original intention was to complete my journey in just one year- beginning on January 1, 2008, in Lyme Regis and finishing on December 31 in my home town of Wimborne and, indeed, I did substantially accomplish my goal. The book begins on the Marine Parade in the Harbour Inn in Lyme Regis and I did celebrate the end of the year in Topo Gigio's in Wimborne with friends and family. However, as I then sat down to fashion all my notes and thoughts into a manageable, readable form I decided, where it was appropriate, to add certain additional facts as they presented themselves. The most obvious were in sporting matters for the extraordinary stories of Weymouth FC and AFC Bournemouth needed to be completed properly. Left in mid-season, they would have been tales half-told and unsatisfactory, not least for future generations of those who pick up the book. Readers will discover other similar examples but about 90% of the text is exactly as I originally assembled it from my jumble of assorted notes and jottings. The route I followed was, I believe, a logical one bearing in mind my starting and finishing points. As every reader will be aware, unless they have only just returned to these islands after a long spell abroad, the weather in the year 2008 was not greatly enjoyed by the natives, the summer being dismally wet and sunless for long periods. In fact, the economy matched the weather with a series of cataclysmic events within the banking system which, in turn, precipitated all manner of problems for the people not only of Dorset but the UK and the wider world. Falling property prices, a dramatic contraction of activity and employment in the housing industry, reduced demand for many other products, growing unemployment, further British and Allied casualties in the wars being fought in Iraq and Afghanistan – 2008 is unlikely to be remembered with great affection by many people.

Readers will not find many references to 'climate change' in these pages, nor do I dwell on many of the other gloomy prognostications on a range of topics which daily occupy the leader columns and feature pages of certain newspapers. I have lived too long to be greatly swayed by fashionable headlines or the current obsessions of so-called 'experts'. Never have we had so many 'experts' ready to step forth and pontificate on this or that with varying degrees of certainty, usually for a handsome fee. They seem to be proved wrong as often as they are proved right, so I have preferred to dwell on the realities of contemporary life in Dorset and the pre-occupations, activities and beliefs of its people. These pages reflect many shades of opinion and it is my hope that they will serve to generate lively discussion in the months and years ahead. I have tried to avoid being bland for that would have made for a much duller book though I realise that, here and there, the reader may feel disposed to rise from a comfortable chair, curse the author's name and aim a kick at the family cat – an ill-directed aim, I hope, for I am very fond of cats.

So I reach my final paragraph. Gazing back over my shoulder I see a kaleidoscope of images. The faces of friends and acquaintances mingle with a hundred scenes of places and events. Most of the faces are smiling though some I see are drawn with saddened eyes and the knowledge of grief and loss. Most of the places are bathed in sunlight but a few are enveloped in mist and melancholy. But that, I suppose, is life – the darkness and the light. I have met such warmth and generosity on my travels and I know I will never be able to thank enough all those who have helped me realise my dream. There has been the odd disappointment here and there, the rebuff, indifference, but rejection has been rare. And so many generous-hearted individuals have gone to remarkable lengths, not just to accommodate me, but positively to assist me. I am forever in their debt. I return weary but exultant that there are so many good people in our midst. I count myself profoundly privileged to have met so many of them during my Dorset Journey.